Sarah Halpin 2006

FORAGERS, FARMERS AND FISHERS IN A COASTAL LANDSCAPE

An intertidal archaeological survey of the Shannon estuary

Foragers, farmers and fishers in a coastal landscape

An intertidal archaeological survey of the Shannon estuary

Aidan O'Sullivan

with contributions by

James Lyttleton, Andrew J. Wheeler, Michael G. Healey,

Colin Breen, Claire Callaghan, Karl Brady, Mary B. Deevy, Stephen Mandal,

Emmet Byrnes, Chris Blythe, Vincent Butler, Maria Fitzgerald,

Elizabeth Anderson and Margaret MacCarthy

Discovery Programme Monograph No. 5

First published in 2001
by the Royal Irish Academy
19 Dawson St, Dublin 2.

Copyright © The Royal Irish Academy 2001.

All rights reserved. No part of this book may be reprinted or reproduced or utilised in any electronic, mechanical or other means, now known or hereafter invented, including photocopying and recording, or otherwise without either the prior written consent of the publishers or a licence permitting restricted copying in Ireland issued by the Irish Copyright Licensing Agency Ltd, The Writers' Centre, 19 Parnell Square, Dublin 1.

ISBN 1-874045-85-2

British Library Cataloguing-in-Publication Data.
A catalogue record for this book is available from the British Library.

Editor: Emer Condit
Cover design: Rachel Dunne

Typeset in Ireland by Wordwell Ltd
Origination by Wordwell Ltd
Printed by Colour Books Ltd

Cover image—Scenes from the Shannon estuary over Henry Pelham's (1787) map of Clare (the latter reproduced courtesy of the Neptune Gallery).

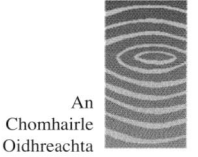

The Discovery Programme gratefully acknowledges the financial contribution of the Heritage Council towards the cost of publishing this book.

Discovery Programme/Royal Irish Academy, Dublin 2001

Contents

Acknowledgements	vii
List of figures	ix
List of plates	xii
Preface	xvii
Réamhrá	xix
Foreword	xxi

Chapter 1. Introduction — 1
Introduction
Archaeological, historical and placename evidence for settlement and coastal
    exploitation on the Shannon estuary — 3
Maps of the Shannon estuary since the late Middle Ages — 15
Origins and evolution of the Shannon estuary intertidal survey — 23
Summary of archaeological and palaeoenvironmental discoveries — 35

Chapter 2. Coastal landscapes and environmental change — 39
Introduction
The Shannon estuary and its environs — 40
Geological setting — 41
Glacial deposits and related features of the Shannon estuary — 44
Climate, soils and modern land use — 46
Fauna and flora — 47
Hydrography of the Shannon estuary: past and present — 48
Sea-level and climate change — 49
The palaeoenvironment of the Shannon estuary — 50
Reclamation history — 52
Conclusions — 54

Chapter 3. Neolithic submerged forests, red deer bone and coastal — 55
    wetland occupation site
Introduction
Mesolithic and Neolithic submerged forests — 56
Neolithic red deer bone deposits — 65
Mesolithic and Neolithic sites at Carrigdirty Rock — 69
Late Mesolithic wooden plank and brushwood — 71
Neolithic coastal wetland occupation site — 73
Interpreting Neolithic settlement, society and economy on the Shannon estuary — 87
Conclusions — 92

Chapter 4. Bronze Age house and trackway in coastal wetlands — 93
Introduction
Bronze Age settlement and environment at Carrigdirty Rock — 94
Middle Bronze Age worked wood, Coonagh Point 1, Co. Limerick — 106
Late Bronze Age post-and-wattle structure, Fergus estuary, Co. Clare — 107
Interpreting Bronze Age settlement, society and economy on the Shannon estuary — 121
Late Bronze Age and Iron Age houses and trackways on estuaries in Britain — 128
Conclusions — 134

Chapter 5. Early historic and medieval fishtraps — 135
Introduction
Early historic fishtrap, Fergus estuary, Co. Clare — 138
Medieval fishtraps, Deel estuary, Co. Limerick — 144
Medieval fishtraps, Bunratty, Shannon estuary — 151
Possible medieval fishtrap, Bush Island, Shannon estuary — 178
Interpreting early historic and medieval fishtraps on the Shannon estuary — 179
The archaeology of early historic and medieval fishtraps in Britain and Ireland — 186
Conclusions — 191

Chapter 6. Post-medieval and modern fishtraps — 193
Introduction
Post-medieval fishtrap, Inishbonane, Co. Clare (Inishbonane 1) — 195
Post-medieval fishtrap, Quay Island, Shannon estuary (Quay Island 2) — 197
Post-medieval creek traps, Bunratty, Co. Clare — 197
Post-medieval fishtrap, Green Island, Co. Clare (Green Island 1) — 198
Post-medieval fishtraps, Bush Island, Co. Clare — 200
Post-medieval fishtraps, Graigue Island, Co. Clare — 208
Post-medieval fishtraps, O'Brien's Point, Co. Clare — 208
Post-medieval fishtrap, Cratloe Creek, Co. Clare (Cratloe Creek 1) — 210
Post-medieval fishtraps and post-and-wattle trackways, Carrigdirty Rock, Co. Limerick — 212
Post-medieval fishtraps and post-and-wattle, Maiden Rock, Co. Limerick — 216
Post-medieval fishtraps and post-and-wattle, Fergus estuary, Co. Clare — 217
The ownership, use and abandonment of post-medieval fishtraps on the Shannon and Fergus estuaries — 220
Folklife and historical studies of some post-medieval fishtraps in Ireland — 229
Conclusions — 232

Chapter 7. Post-medieval shipwreck, harbours and lighthouses — 233
Introduction
Prehistoric, early historic and Viking Age boats — 234
Medieval boats and ships — 235
Late medieval and post-medieval ships on the estuary — 235
Eighteenth- and nineteenth-century ships and boats on the Shannon estuary — 238
The history and archaeology of shipwrecks on the Shannon estuary — 239
The history and archaeology of harbours and landing-places — 245
History and archaeology of lighthouses on the Shannon estuary — 250
Conclusions — 251

Chapter 8. People, place and time on the Shannon estuary — 253
Introduction
Archaeology and environment on the Shannon estuary — 253
The people of the estuary — 259
Landscape, space and place on the estuary — 262
Times, tides and traditions on the estuary — 267
The future of the past on the Shannon estuary — 270
Conclusions — 274

References — 275

Appendix 1: Radiocarbon dates — 295

Appendix 2: Summary inventory of intertidal archaeological sites recorded on the Shannon estuary and the Fergus estuary — 296

Appendix 3: Inventory of historic shipwrecks on the Shannon estuary — 314

Appendix 4: NMI reg. nos of artefacts found in the Shannon estuary survey — 331

Acknowledgements

First and foremost, I thank Eoin Grogan, director of the North Munster Project, for his support and encouragement. It was his recognition of the potential of this highly unusual project that allowed it to happen. I also thank him for his patience and forbearance in letting me go off to the mudflats when other equally pressing excavation and survey tasks were upon us. I would also like to thank Professor George Eogan, then chairman of the Discovery Programme, and the various members of the directorate and council (1992–2000). In particular, I am grateful to the programme managers, Ronan O'Flaherty, Brian Lacey and Anne Lynch, for their help and encouragement.

James Lyttleton played a major role in the successful completion of the Shannon estuary survey. His scholarship, hard work and good humour enabled the detailed appraisal of the rich historical sources and his skills in computer graphics will be seen in this monograph, while Karl Brady and Barry Masterson also helped to bring both text and figures to completion. I also owe a debt of gratitude to those unhappy few who worked with me out on the mudflats, particularly Mark Woods, Enda Malone, Barry Masterson, Sarah Cross, Donal Boland, Mary Deevy, Eoin Kiernan, James Lyttleton and Eoin Grogan, as well as my friends and colleagues in the North Munster Project, Tom Condit, Finola O'Carroll and Aoife Daly, for all the crack over those years.

This book has been greatly improved by the involvement of Andrew Wheeler and Michael Healey, who stepped in to write their overview of coastal and sea-level change on the Shannon estuary when it proved impossible to progress our previous palaeoenvironmental investigations. It should be seen as a significant baseline for future work. They would also like to thank Chris Blythe, Colin Hayes, Aileen O'Driscoll and Robert Devoy for their help. Colin Breen and Claire Callaghan's study of historic shipwrecks is also a major contribution to our understanding of life and times on the Shannon estuary. They would like to express their gratitude to David Sweetman, Fionnbarr Moore and Edward Bourke of *Dúchas* The Heritage Service for their support and permission to use material from the Maritime Archaeological Survey for this chapter.

I am also grateful to other specialists: Mary B. Deevy (wood studies), Chris Blythe (palaeoenvironmental studies), Vincent Butler and Margaret MacCarthy (faunal identifications), Stephen Mandal, Emmet Byrnes and Elizabeth Anderson (lithic studies), whose tragic early death took from us a wonderful person and a great scholar. I also thank Simon Dick for his marvellous reconstruction painting of the Bunratty medieval fishtrap. I am deeply grateful to Dr Jan Lanting, of Rijksuniversiteit Groningen, who facilitated at a crucial stage the production of up to twenty free radiocarbon dates, thereby opening the window of opportunity for further work. I am also grateful to the director and staff (particularly Ms Mary Cahill) of the National Museum of Ireland, the National Library of Ireland, Trinity College Library and the Neptune Gallery.

I also want to acknowledge the inspiration of Derek Upton, Gwent Coastal Warden, who introduced me in 1992 to the techniques of intertidal survey on the Severn estuary (if I had only known then . . . !). I would like to thank my friends and colleagues in Britain for their comments and advice. They include Martin Bell, Nigel Nayling, Richard Brunning, Rick Turner, Steve Godbold, Steve Rippon, John Allen, John Coles and Bryony Coles (Severn estuary/Somerset), Peter Murphy, Dave Strachan and Paul Gilman (Essex estuaries), Fiona Haughey (Thames estuary), Dave Tomalin (Isle of Wight), Robert van de Noort, William Fletcher and the late Ted Wright (Humber estuary).

I would like to warmly thank Brian Williams of the Environment and Heritage Service for giving me the opportunity to direct the Strangford Lough intertidal survey in 1996, as well as Colin Breen, Tom McErlean, Rosemary McConkey and Paul McCooey. I also thank those people who read this text for their helpful comments: Eoin Grogan, Barry Raftery, Martin Bell, Gabriel Cooney and John Bradley. I hope I have gone some way towards improving the book as they suggested.

I will always be grateful to many people in Clare and Limerick for their kind, if occasionally amused, welcome, especially the local farmers along the Shannon and Fergus estuaries who gave me permission to move through their lands. In particular, I would like to thank Deirdre O'Brien-Vaughan and Caoillfhionn Vaughaun (Newmarket on Fergus) and Paddy Connors (Islandmagrath), the members of the Shannon Archaeological and Historical Society, and Jim Elliott of the Shannon Rescue Team at Bunratty (for the use of their boat slip and facilities). I would also like to gratefully acknowledge the financial sponsorship provided by Shannon Heritage and Banquets (for the excavation of the Bunratty medieval fishtraps in February 1997) and Shannon Estuary Ports (for their general support, aerial photographs and the funding of surveys at the Carrigdirty Rock Mesolithic/Neolithic sites).

Under the National Monuments Acts 1930–1994, intertidal archaeological survey and excavation must now be carried out under licences issued by the National Monuments Service, *Dúchas* The Heritage Service. The Shannon estuary project was licensed from 1995 onwards under the following excavation licences: the Shannon estuary (95E0228, 96E0205, renewed for 1997), the Fergus estuary (95E0299, 96E0204) and the Cashen estuary, Co. Kerry (95E0230). In July 2000, a two-day visit to Bush Island, Shannon estuary, to record some post-medieval fishtraps was covered by an underwater survey licence (00D042). I thank Tom Condit and Edward Bourke for their help with these. This monograph provides the full and final publication for all of these licences. Finally, I thank Nick Maxwell, Emer Condit and Rachel Dunne for all their hard work and flair in the production of this monograph. On a personal note, I also thank Mary B. Deevy and my parents John and Kathleen O'Sullivan for their support and encouragement over these last ten years.

In conclusion, I should say that this book is aimed not only at local people and other archaeologists, but also at historians, geographers, folklorists and environmentalists, as well as everybody who is interested in the 'personality' of the Irish landscape. I hope that the results of the Shannon estuary intertidal survey have shown that there are many hidden places all the way around our coast, within which there are still many unwritten histories.

Aidan O'Sullivan
University College, Dublin
Autumn 2001

List of figures

Fig. 1— Map of Britain and Ireland, showing the location of the Shannon estuary and UK intertidal archaeological survey projects mentioned in the text (Barry Masterson, Discovery Programme).

Fig. 2— Viking sword found on a wooden causeway on upper Shannon estuary at Cooperhill, Co. Limerick (from *JRSAI* 1960).

Fig. 3— The Shannon estuary (*Senos*) on a reconstruction of Ptolemy's second-century AD description of Ireland (after Byrne 1984; Andrews 1997, fig. 2.1).

Fig. 4— The Shannon estuary depicted (at bottom right) on Giraldus Cambrensis's early thirteenth-century map of Ireland (National Library of Ireland, MS 700).

Fig. 5— The Shannon estuary and the medieval town of *Laymerich* as shown on an Italian portolan chart of *c.* 1339 (after Westropp 1913; Andrews 1997, fig. 2.2).

Fig. 6— The Shannon estuary as depicted on Baptista Boazio's map of Ireland, published *c.* 1609 (reproduced by courtesy of the Neptune Gallery).

Fig. 7— Murdoch MacKenzie's chart of the upper Shannon estuary and Fergus estuary, published in 1776 in *A maritim survey of Ireland and the west of Great Britain* (reproduced by courtesy of the Neptune Gallery).

Fig. 8— The upper Shannon estuary and Fergus estuary in Henry Pelham's map of Clare, 1787 (Phoenix Maps, reproduced by courtesy of the Neptune Gallery).

Fig. 9— The Shannon estuary landscape and intertidal archaeology: a schematic diagram illustrating intercalated peats and clays and the range of archaeological sites recorded.

Fig. 10—Map showing the Shannon River drainage basin and geographical context of the Shannon River system with respect to Ireland.

Fig. 11—General location map for the Shannon estuary, including all places mentioned in the text.

Fig. 12—Geological map of the Shannon estuary (after Synge 1969).

Fig. 13—Map of glacial features and deposits of the Shannon estuary (after Synge 1969).

Fig. 14—Generalised cross-section through the Quaternary deposits of the Shannon estuary.

Fig. 15—Soil map of the Shannon estuary.

Fig. 16—Proposed Natural Heritage Area and wildlife distributions.

Fig. 17—The 'family' of Irish sea-level curves, based on Taylor *et al.* (1986).

Fig. 18—Artist's impression of an estuarine palaeoenvironmental setting (after Silvester 1991).

Fig. 19—Map of Shannon estuary, showing location of Neolithic sites (Barry Masterson, Discovery Programme).

Fig. 20—Location map of Neolithic submerged forest at Poulnasharry Bay 1, Co. Clare, lower Shannon estuary.

Fig. 21—Section of Poulnasharry Bay 1 saltmarsh cliff, showing stratigraphical succession from fen peat to sphagnum peat to alluvial clays.

Fig. 22—Location of late Neolithic submerged forest and stone axe findspot at Meelick Rocks 1–2, Co. Limerick, on the upper Shannon estuary.

Fig. 23—Meelick Rocks stone axe (NMI 95E0228:3).

Fig. 24—Detailed location map of Neolithic red deer bone, Fergus estuary 3, Co. Clare.

Fig. 25—General location map of Mesolithic, Neolithic, Bronze Age and post-medieval intertidal sites at Carrigdirty Rock, Co. Limerick.

Fig. 26—Plan of Late Mesolithic wooden plank, Carrigdirty Rock 8.

Fig. 27—Carrigdirty Rock 5–8: contour plan of intertidal foreshore showing locations of Carrigdirty Rock 8 plank, Carrigdirty Rock 5 finds in minerogenic clays and Carrigdirty Rock 20–1 planks in peat (Barry Masterson, Discovery Programme).

Fig. 28—Digital terrain model of Carrigdirty Rock 5–8 foreshore, showing location of Mesolithic and Neolithic finds and their broad relationship with a sedimentary sequence identified by coring in the saltmarsh adjacent to the foreshore (Barry Masterson, Discovery Programme).

Fig. 29—Neolithic human skull fragment (drawing: Tom O'Sullivan).

Fig. 30—Worked and charred wood from clays at Carrigdirty Rock 5.

Fig. 31—Schematic drawing showing method of manufacture of coiled basket at Carrigdirty Rock 5 (Maria Fitzgerald).

Fig. 32—Slate axe (NMI 95E0228:15), possible hammerstone (pebble 1: NMI 95E0228:7) and chert flake 1 (NMI 95E0228:5) from Carrigdirty Rock 5.

Fig. 33—A deliberately ambivalent reconstruction drawing of early Neolithic activity at Carrigdirty Rock 5, in its potential original wetland environment. Was this an occupation site, a place for ritual, or both? (Aidan O'Sullivan.)

Fig. 34—Location of Carrigdirty Rock 5 Neolithic site in potential former estuarine wetlands (based on modern distribution of alluvium or gley soils in counties Limerick and Clare), with distribution of Neolithic stone axes and megalithic tombs along the upper Shannon estuary.

Fig. 35—Map of upper Shannon estuary, showing location of Bronze Age sites (Barry Masterson, Discovery Programme).

Fig. 36—Detailed map of Carrigdirty Rock foreshore, showing surveyed location of Mesolithic, Neolithic and Bronze Age sites.

Fig. 37—Plan of Carrigdirty Rock 1 Middle Bronze Age house.

Fig. 38—Schematic reconstruction drawings of Middle Bronze Age house at Carrigdirty Rock 1.

Fig. 39—Planks from Carrigdirty Rock 20 and Carrigdirty Rock 21.

Fig. 40—Location of Coonagh Point 1.

Fig. 41—Detailed location map of Late Bronze Age post-and-wattle structure at Fergus estuary west 1, Co. Clare.

Fig. 42—Plan of Late Bronze Age post-and-wattle structure, Fergus estuary west 1.

Fig. 43—Wood species and tree-ring ages of wood from Late Bronze Age structure at Fergus estuary west 1.

Fig. 44—Late Bronze Age worked wood from Fergus estuary west 1.

Fig. 45—Reconstruction drawing of Carrigdirty Rock 1 Middle Bronze Age house in fen-carr wetlands (Aidan O'Sullivan).

Fig. 46—Distribution of Middle and Late Bronze Age sites and artefacts on the upper Shannon estuary, indicating location of Carrigdirty Rock 1 Middle Bronze Age house site in the estuarine wetlands.

Fig. 47—Hypothetical model for Bronze Age landscape and settlement of the upper Shannon estuary wetlands.

Fig. 48—Map of upper Fergus estuary, Co. Clare, showing relationship between Late Bronze Age post-and-wattle structure at Fergus estuary west 1 and other possible Bronze Age sites on the neighbouring drylands.

Fig. 49—Reconstruction drawing of Iron Age rectangular house in estuarine wetlands at Goldcliff Building 1, Gwent, Severn estuary (drawing by S.J. Allen; after Bell *et al.* 2000).

Fig. 50—Late Bronze Age hurdle trackway excavated at Melton 25, Humber estuary, England (after Fletcher *et al.* 1999).

Fig. 51—Map of upper Shannon estuary, showing location of medieval fishtraps.

Fig. 52—Schematic reconstruction of a medieval fishtrap, showing principles and various structural features.

Fig. 53—Map of upper Fergus estuary, showing location of the early historic fishtrap at Fergus estuary east 2 and its relationship with the early historic ringforts at Drumoland and Ballyconneely on the ridge to the east.

Fig. 54—Plan of early historic fishtrap, Fergus estuary east 2, Co. Clare.

Fig. 55—Wood species identifications and tree-ring studies from Fergus estuary east 2, Co. Clare.

Fig. 56—Map of Deel estuary, Co. Limerick, showing spatial relationship between medieval fishtraps and the medieval hall-house and parish church at Tomdeely, as well as sites of castles and tower-houses at Ballynash, Courtbrown and Ballysteen.

Fig. 57—Plan of medieval fishtrap fence, Deel estuary 1.

Fig. 58—Plan of Deel estuary 2 medieval fishtrap fence.

Fig. 59—Map of Bunratty, Co. Clare, showing location of medieval fishtraps, Bunratty 1–6, in relation to the Anglo-Norman borough and other medieval settlement sites on the drylands.

Fig. 60—Detailed map of Bunratty foreshore at Little Quay Island, showing location of Bunratty 1–5 sites.

Fig. 61—Plan of Bunratty 1 post-and-wattle features.

Fig. 62—Plan of Bunratty 2.

Fig. 63—Plan of Bunratty 3, showing fences and baskets.

Fig. 64—Plan of medieval fishtrap at Bunratty 4.

Fig. 65—Schematic plan indicating possible phases of activity at medieval fishtrap at Bunratty 4.

Fig. 66—Plan of Bunratty 6 medieval fishtrap.

Fig 67—Plan and cross-sections of basket at Bunratty 6.

Fig. 68—Reconstruction of medieval fishtrap at Bunratty 6 in its original setting, with vertical post-and-wattle fences, a basket on a framework and local fishermen using and repairing the structure from boats (painting by Simon Dick).

Fig. 69—Wood species identifications from Bunratty 4.

Fig. 70—Wood species identifications from Bunratty 6.

Fig. 71—Woven portable eel-trap, 'kiddle' or 'weel' in use in an English mill-stream in an illustration in the fourteenth-century Luttrell Psalter (British Library: Luttrell Psalter, additional MS 42130: f. 181).

Fig. 72—Reconstruction of Anglo-Saxon fishtrap in use at Collins Creek, on the Blackwater estuary, Essex (painting by Nick Nethercoat, reproduced by permission of Essex County Council Planning Division).

Fig. 73—Map of upper Shannon estuary, showing location of post-medieval fishtraps and other structures.

Fig. 74—Location of Inishbonane 1 post-medieval fishtrap.

Fig. 75—Location of Quay Island 2 post-medieval fishtrap, on the south-west shore of Quay Island. There are also post-medieval wooden jetties off the south-east shore.

Fig. 76—Location of post-medieval fishtraps at Bush Island 1–17.

Fig. 77—Location of O'Brien's Point post-medieval fishtraps.

Fig. 78—Plan of Carrigdirty Rock 12 post-medieval post-and-wattle panel.

Fig. 79—Location of Fergus estuary east 9 post alignment, adjacent to Carrownanelly townland, Co. Clare.

Fig. 80—Schematic drawings showing types of post-medieval fishtraps used on the Shannon estuary.

Fig. 81—Distribution of shipwrecks on the Shannon estuary (Maritime SMR: *Dúchas*—The Heritage Service).

Fig. 82—The 'Cittie of Limerick' as depicted in *Pacata Hibernia c.* 1633, showing ocean-going ships docked at the Great Quay, constructed *c.* 1500. Other, smaller river craft and fishing-boats (with the fishermen using nets in the way they still do today) are also shown (National Library of Ireland: Ir 91405s2).

Fig. 83—The town of Askeaton on the River Deel, *c.* 1799, with large sailing-boats and other small craft at the quayside (National Library of Ireland: 1408 TA).

Fig. 84—Types of vessel, dates of loss, reasons for loss, ports of origin, and types of cargo (Colin Breen).

List of plates

Pl. 1— Aerial photograph of the upper Shannon estuary, looking north-westwards across the saltmarshes, mudflats, estuary channel and shoals, towards Graigue Island, Bush Island and Bunratty and the reclaimed corcass on the Clare bank (photo: Shannon Estuary Ports).

Pl. 2— Aerial photograph of the Late Bronze Age hillfort at Mooghaun, Co. Clare, situated on a hill overlooking the Fergus estuary (photo: Aoife Daly, North Munster Project).

Pl. 3— Aerial view of the early historic and medieval monastic site of Scattery Island, on the lower Shannon estuary (photo: *Dúchas* The Heritage Service).

Pl. 4— Medieval Limerick was a thriving port on the banks of the River Shannon. This early nineteenth-century depiction (*c.* 1827) shows the thirteenth-century Anglo-Norman fortress of King John's Castle within the medieval city, while Old Thomond Bridge and probably the timber-framed building to the right were also of medieval origin (National Library of Ireland: 1439 TA).

Pl. 5 —The late medieval Desmond tower-house at Carrigafoyle Castle, Co. Kerry, on the banks of the lower Shannon estuary (photo: *Dúchas*). Inset is a depiction from *Pacata Hibernia*, published in 1633, of the same castle under attack in 1580 (National Library of Ireland: Ir 9405s2).

Pl. 6— By the late seventeenth century the port of Limerick was exporting agricultural produce, textiles, timber and metal ores, while importing fruit and luxury goods from the West Indies. Thomas Phillip's prospect of Limerick (1685) shows the River Shannon's harbour and quays for the ocean-going ships that sailed up the estuary, as well as a rare view of a surviving late medieval townscape (National Library of Ireland: MS 3137 (25)).

Pl. 7— Aerial view of the upper Shannon estuary, looking towards the south-east and the location of the main intertidal archaeological sites at Bunratty, Quay Island, Bush Island and, on the far bank, Carrigdirty Rock (photo: Oscar Merne).

Pl. 8— Archaeologists waiting for the ebbing tide to expose a medieval (AD 1018–1159) fishtrap at Bunratty 4 so that it can be planned and sampled; the use of a boat in intertidal survey enables staff, drawing equipment and samples to be safely transported back and forth, and allows archaeologists to record sites up until the last minute on a flooding tide.

Pl. 9— Archaeologist photographing a Late Bronze Age (797–551 BC) post-and-wattle structure on the upper Fergus estuary (Fergus estuary west 1). Most archaeological sites on the estuary are located right at the low-water mark, meaning that they are only visible for brief periods.

Pl. 10—Archaeologist excavating a trench across a medieval (AD 1164–1279) basket at Bunratty 6, where the low elevation of the site on the mudflats meant that the features had to be excavated, planned, photographed and sampled inside 1–2 hours.

Pl. 11—Satellite image (Landsat MSS) of the Shannon estuary taken in 1976. Limerick City and Shannon Airport are clearly visible on the upper Shannon estuary.

Pl. 12—Aerial view of corcass at Carrigdirty Rock and Newtown townland, Co. Limerick, where there may be at least three ancient or relict sea-banks inland of the modern sea-bank. Cartographic sources and historical references suggest that reclamation may have begun here as early as the late sixteenth century.

Pl. 13—General view of Neolithic submerged forest at Rinevalla Bay 1, Co. Clare, on the lower Shannon estuary, with Scots pine and oak trunks exposed in the upper foreshore peats.

Pl. 14—Late Neolithic submerged forest roots and trunks on upper foreshore, Meelick Rocks 1. The early prehistoric stone axe at Meelick Rocks 2 was found on the lower foreshore, where the person is standing.

Pl. 15—Neolithic red deer bone at Fergus estuary east 3, Co. Clare.

Pl. 16—Possible Neolithic red deer bone at Fergus estuary east 7, Co. Clare.

Pl. 17—Aerial view of intertidal foreshore at Carrigdirty Rock 5–8 site. The Carrigdirty Rock 5 Neolithic basket, bone, worked wood and lithics were mostly found in the clays immediately in front of a low mud cliff, indicated by the dark line on the lower foreshore, while the Carrigdirty Rock 8 Mesolithic plank was found at the low-water mark (photo: Shannon Estuary Ports).

Pl. 18—Late Mesolithic wooden plank, Carrigdirty Rock 8, buried in clay at LWM; other fragments can be seen within the plank.

Pl. 19—Upper end of Late Mesolithic plank, Carrigdirty Rock 8.

Pl. 20—A fragment of carved wood from a small trough or vessel found in clays at Carrigdirty Rock 7 (*c.* 100m east of Carrigdirty Rock 8); possible tool-marks are visible on the thicker portion.

Pl. 21—General view looking to the north-east across Carrigdirty Rock 5 Neolithic site; the basket, chert flakes, skull fragment, worked wood and animal bone were found in reedy, organic-rich clays in front of the low clay cliff to the right.

Pl. 22—Neolithic human skull fragment found on clays at Carrigdirty Rock 5.

Pl. 23—Neolithic woven alder basket (NMI 95E0228:1) *in situ* in clays at Carrigdirty Rock 5.

Pl. 24—Schist axe from submerged forest at Meelick Rocks 2 (NMI 95E0228:3) and slate axe from Carrigdirty Rock 5 (NMI 95E0228:15) (photo: David Jennings, UCD).

Pl. 25—Intertidal zone to the east of Carrigdirty Rock, where a shelf of submerged peats is exposed all along the upper foreshore.

Pl. 26—Carrigdirty Rock 1 Middle Bronze Age house site. The site has not been excavated, but it was possible to identify the posts in the thin muds overlying the peat.

Pl. 27—Carrigdirty Rock 1: worked points, with tool-marks indicating use of a narrow metal axe.

Pl. 28—Carrigdirty Rock 3: pit with red deer bone and bird bone in grey clay fill.

Pl. 29—Carrigdirty Rock 4: worked and cleft wooden posts in peats (drawing: Tom O'Sullivan).

Pl. 30—Carrigdirty Rock 20: plank in peats.

Pl. 31—Late Bronze Age post-and-wattle structure at Fergus estuary west 1.

Pl. 32—Detail of horizontal post-and-wattle panels at Fergus estuary west 1, possibly pinned onto clays with vertical stakes driven through weave.

Pl. 33—Detail of post-and-wattle fences at west disappearing into the water at the low-water mark.

Pl. 34—View to east up the foreshore, illustrating the double row of vertical posts, Fergus estuary west 1.

Pl. 35—Withy or twisted wooden rope *in situ* in clays beside lower end of post-and-wattle structure, Fergus estuary west 1.

Pl. 36—Two Late Bronze Age worked ends at Fergus estuary west 1.

Pl. 37—Late Bronze Age gold dress-fastener found during marsh reclamation in the late nineteenth century on the upper Fergus estuary, Co. Clare, potentially close to the Fergus estuary west 1 site (reproduced by permission of the National Museum of Ireland).

Pl. 38—Reconstruction painting of Late Bronze Age hurdle trackway at Melton, on the Humber estuary, England. The site is interpreted as a creek bridge designed to enable cattle to be driven across the saltmarshes (painting by Les Turner, reproduced with permission of the Humber Wetlands Project, Wetlands Archaeology and Environments Research Centre, University of Hull).

Pl. 39—Post-and-wattle fence in modern fishtrap on the Severn estuary, leading towards ranks of baskets supported on frameworks (photo: Chris Salisbury).

Pl. 40—Woven basket in use in modern fishtrap on the Severn estuary. The basket is supported on a rectangular wooden framework, perhaps similar to that used on the Bunratty 6 medieval fishtrap (photo: Chris Salisbury).

Pl. 41—Early historic post-and-wattle fence, Fergus estuary east 2. A horizontal post-and-wattle panel lies to the right, exposed to a slightly greater degree in this photograph (taken in May 1995) than when the site was planned in July 1992.

Pl. 42—Medieval fishtrap at Deel estuary 1.

Pl. 43—Medieval fishtrap fence, Deel estuary 2.

Pl. 44—Detail of Bunratty 1.2 horizontal post-and-wattle panel from north-east.

Pl. 45—Bunratty 2 post-and-wattle fence, general view from north (the Bunratty 3 fence and woven baskets and then the Bunratty 4 medieval fishtrap with its multiphase fences are in the background).

Pl. 46—Detailed view of Bunratty 3A basket at low-water mark. This basket is only exposed to view for a few hours each year, during the lowest possible tides.

Pl. 47—Bunratty 4 medieval fishtrap from north, looking along post-and-wattle fence 4.2.

Pl. 48—Detail of upper fences at Bunratty 4 medieval fishtrap, showing evidence for several phases of repair and reconstruction.

Pl. 49—Aerial photograph of creek flowing through mudflats to the south of Bunratty. The medieval fishtrap at Bunratty 6 is located on the right of the large curve in the creek in the middle foreground, near the main Shannon estuary channel (photo: Shannon Estuary Ports).

Pl. 50—Medieval fishtrap at Bunratty 6, showing basket and posts of wooden supporting framework in foreground.

Pl. 51—Medieval fishtrap at Bunratty 6 from north-east, showing post-and-wattle fence.

Pl. 52—Detail of medieval fishtrap fence, showing repair in mid-length, the horizontal post-and-wattle panel in the clays, and the obliquely set supporting timber in the background.

Pl. 53—Detail of basket at Bunratty 6, from south-west, showing vertical posts along sides and at end.

Pl. 54—Detail of weave inside end of Bunratty 6 basket.

Pl. 55—Replica of Bunratty 6 basket on display at King John's Castle, Limerick, in summer 1999, illustrating its striking original size and appearance.

Pl. 56—Aerial photograph of the late medieval castle at Bunratty, probably located on the site of the Anglo-Norman borough (CUCAP AJW 03).

Pl. 57—Undated woven basket buried in dark grey clays by creek at Bush Island 3, possibly of medieval date.

Pl. 58—Aerial photograph of stone fishtrap at Chapel Island, Co. Down, Northern Ireland. Recent intertidal surveys on Strangford Lough by the EHS Coastal Research Unit have led to the identification of numerous intertidal archaeological sites there (photo: Gail Pollock, Environment and Heritage Service, Northern Ireland).

Pl. 59—Eleventh- to twelfth-century fish basket excavated at the former outfall of the River Nedern/Troggy, at Sudbrook, near Caldicot on the Welsh shore of the Severn estuary (photo: Steve Godbold and Rick Turner, Cadw, Wales).

Pl. 60—Modern wooden tidal head weir in Waterford Harbour, Co. Kilkenny, oriented to catch fish moving upstream or with the flooding tide. A long shore fence runs diagonally down from the shore to meet a shorter flood fence, with a raised platform situated at the eye of the trap. The Shannon estuary post-medieval and modern fishtraps were broadly similar (photo: Aidan O'Sullivan).

Pl. 61—Inishbonane 1 post-medieval fishtrap from east.

Pl. 62—Green Island 1 fishtrap fence, either a stake-net weir (with vertical poles holding nets) or a partly submerged head weir with the flood fence underwater.

Pl. 63—Bush Island 1 from south-east. This site is probably a nineteenth- or twentieth-century stake-net trap, with nets hung from straight poles running out into the channel.

Pl. 64—Bush Island 2B, a massive nineteenth- or twentieth-century (?) flood weir off the south-west shore of the island, with an upper shore fence measuring over 300m in length and a shorter flood fence 47m in length.

Pl. 65—Bush Island 4, a small undated fishtrap, perhaps constructed to hold a conical or tubular basket at the side of a creek. Although sited near some obvious post-medieval structures, it is similar in form and size to the radiocarbon-dated eleventh- to twelfth-century fishtrap at Bunratty 4, and perhaps is also of medieval date.

Pl. 66—Bush Island 5, a large, straight post alignment spanning the creek. These post-medieval creek traps may have simply used post-and-wattle to prevent the egress of fish from the mudflats.

Pl. 67—Bush Island 12, a post-medieval fishtrap in a creek to the east of the island, constructed of a C-shaped post-and-wattle fence, 36m in length.

Pl. 68—Bush Island 14, a large L-shaped fishtrap, with a long shore fence (104m in length) running across a creek to meet a short (26m) flood fence near the channel. Like other post-medieval fishtraps, its fence was secured against the rush of the ebbing tide by braces and hefty vertical posts.

Pl. 69—O'Brien's Point 3 post-medieval fishtrap fences. The parallel rows of posts clearly represent several phases of fishtrap construction in recent times, but the presence of late medieval castles and friaries on the nearby shore might suggest late medieval fishing activity here too.

Pl. 70—General view of Cratloe Creek 1 fishtrap, an eroded structure of late medieval or more probably post-medieval date.

Pl. 71—Carrigdirty Rock 12 post-and-wattle panel buried in clays, which could be interpreted as a trackway or as a wattle panel washed out from a fishtrap fence in the vicinity. It was radiocarbon-dated to the post-medieval period.

Pl. 72—Carrigdirty Rock 13 post-and-wattle panel at base of saltmarsh cliff leading towards creek, possibly a trackway.

Pl. 73—Carrigdirty Rock 14 post-medieval post-and-wattle fence. There are seventeenth-century references to fisheries in this location.

Pl. 74—Carrigdirty Rock 15 post-medieval fishtrap at LWM, possibly the remains of a small post-and-wattle fence leading towards a trap that is submerged underwater.

Pl. 75—Fergus estuary east 9 post alignment, possibly a post-medieval or modern fishtrap on the narrow Fergus estuary channel.

Pl. 76—Fergus estuary west 2 post-and-wattle trackway buried under clay on the lower foreshore, radiocarbon-dated to the post-medieval period.

Pl. 77—Fergus estuary west 3 and 4 (in background) structures, both probably post-medieval fishtraps.

Pl. 78—W.F. Wakeman's depiction in 1840 of the wooden head weir at Buttermilk Castle, Nook townland, Co. Wexford, downstream of Dunbrody on the east bank of Waterford Harbour. This site has been used as a fishtrap since at least the mid-sixteenth century (National Library of Ireland: 1975 TX Frazier Sketch Books).

Pl. 79—Stone fish-pounds on the Atlantic Ocean at Doonbeg Bay, Co. Clare, exposed during low tide. Although Went records this structure as being used in the early twentieth century, the siting of late medieval tower-houses overlooking the fishtraps raises the possibility that the pounds could be of late medieval date.

Pl. 80—Foynes Harbour, Co. Limerick, c. 1890–1910, with masted ships and small

Pl. 81—craft and gandalows in the harbour (National Library of Ireland: Laurence Collection R9707).

Pl. 81—Limerick City, with passenger steamboat pulling away from quay wall at the Wet Dock, *c.* 1900. These steamers conveyed people down the estuary to towns and villages and served to link the region together (National Library of Ireland: Laurence Collection R5297).

Pl. 82—Bunratty Castle, Co. Clare, with men sitting in Shannon estuary 'gandalow' in channel of River Owenagarney with a stone quay on the opposite shore, *c.* 1880. Bunratty was a significant outport for Limerick through the late Middle Ages, until siltation hampered its use (National Library of Ireland: Spec. Collection SP 1858).

Pl. 83—Kilrush Harbour, Co. Clare, in the late nineteenth century, with masted ships, steamboats and smaller craft at Cappagh Pier (National Library of Ireland: Laurence Collection R4252).

Pl. 84—Aerial view of site of Neolithic submerged forest stone axe findspot at Meelick Rocks, Co. Limerick. Neolithic communities probably settled the nearby hills, and hunted, fished and herded cattle along the estuary marshes (photo: Shannon Estuary Ports).

Pl. 85—View from Carrigogunnel hill, Co. Limerick, across the huge area of reclaimed corcass and estuarine alluvium out towards the Neolithic and Bronze Age occupation sites at Carrigdirty Rock. Bronze Age settlement sites, *fulachta fiadh*, standing stones and an important hoard of bronze horns are known from these hills.

Pl. 86—Medieval fishtrap at Bunratty 6. Other medieval fisheries must be located along the mudflats of the upper Shannon estuary.

Pl. 87—Probable post-medieval C-shaped fishtrap and post-and-wattle panel in clays at Bush Island 13. Further historical and folklife research could aim to establish the ownership and use of these fisheries.

Pl. 88—Early nineteenth-century fishing-boats and people on the foreshore below Wellesley Bridge (now Sarsfield Bridge), Limerick City, from Bartlett's *Scenery and antiquities of Ireland*, published in 1842 (National Library of Ireland: 1442 TA).

Pl. 89—Modern Shannon 'gandalow' drawn up on the bank at Clonmacken, Co. Limerick, with alder trees and reed-beds at the fringes of the saltmarshes of the upper Shannon estuary.

Pl. 90—Steamer loading cargo at the quay at Clarecastle, on the upper Fergus estuary, Co. Clare, *c.* 1900. The estuaries have long served as significant routeways and means of communication through the region (National Library of Ireland: Lawrence Collection NS 3032).

Pl. 91—Aerial view of Quay Island, looking westwards towards the Bunratty and Inishbonane mudflats. Archaeological and historical evidence suggests that there have been fisheries at this location since the Middle Ages (photo: Shannon Estuary Ports).

Pl. 92—The Fergus estuary saltmarshes, reed-beds and mudflats in December 1995. Although the coastal foreshore has previously been ignored by Irish archaeologists, the Shannon and Fergus estuary intertidal survey indicates the potential of coastal foreshore archaeology in Ireland.

Preface

Since it was established in 1991, the Discovery Programme has always aimed to be innovative; whether this is in terms of the application of landscape archaeological perspectives to later prehistory or the use of geophysics, survey technology and Geographical Information Systems. In many ways, having pioneered these approaches in Ireland, the Discovery Programme was then to witness them becoming standard practices within Irish archaeology as a whole. Similarly although maritime archaeology is now an accepted subject within the broader discipline, it is easy to forget how pioneering at the time was the North Munster Project's Shannon estuary intertidal archaeological survey.

In the 1990s the North Munster Project, directed by Dr Eoin Grogan, was engaged in a broad, integrated landscape study of later prehistoric societies in the region. As part of the Project's research, Aidan O'Sullivan devised and carried out a survey of the archaeological heritage of the intertidal zone of the upper Shannon estuary and the Fergus estuary. Although limited in terms of personnel, financial resources and time, this survey—carried out by a small team over a relatively restricted area—managed to introduce a new perspective to Irish archaeology, while also uncovering a wealth of new types of archaeological evidence.

This evidence is brought together here to provide us with an unparalleled view of past life and times on an Irish estuary. An introductory chapter uses historical, archaeological, folklife and placename evidence and early maps to trace the importance of the Shannon estuary for local communities across time. It also outlines the particular methodology and challenges of intertidal survey. The geology, soils, geomorphology, drainage and palaeoenvironmental deposits are described in a chapter which should form the basis for further work in the region. The archaeology of the upper Shannon estuary is then discussed in a series of chapters organised on a chronological basis. Neolithic submerged forests and red deer bone deposits are described, while an intriguing Neolithic occupation or mortuary site is presented and interpretations offered. Middle and Late Bronze Age houses, trackways and other potential features are also described and discussed in terms of contemporary settlement, society and economy in the region.

In the early Middle Ages, fishing on the Shannon estuary involved the use of complex wooden traps sited on creeks and channels. These remarkably well-preserved structures provide us with unique insights into fishing practices, woodland exploitation, crafts and the influence of tradition amongst local communities. Similarly, in the post-medieval period fish were clearly a valuable economic resource, and both the archaeology and historical sources hint at the scale of this industry, as well as at the possible conflict between social classes in the contesting of this resource. The estuary has always served as a busy route, so although few wrecks were identified in the survey, a chapter on the history of post-medieval shipwrecks hints at what may yet lie undiscovered. The concluding chapter, influenced by recent writing and interpretation in archaeology, reflects on the reality of past people's lives and practices and their experience of place and time in the estuary's coastal wetlands.

The Shannon estuary survey has undoubtedly changed the way that Irish archaeologists view coastal landscapes. No longer can we look out onto coastal marshes and mudflats and regard them as empty spaces. Given that the Shannon estuary is unlikely to be unique, we have to expect that our other estuaries, sea-loughs and inlets have a similar archaeological potential, albeit regionally and locally distinctive. Indeed, when we consider that we have on this island at least 7000km of coastline, we begin to see the enormous archaeological potential of that coastal fringe.

This is also an archaeological heritage situated within a uniquely dynamic environment. The Anglo-Saxon king Canute once tried to hold back the tide to show that some things are beyond our power to resist. Similarly, we have to accept that many coastal and intertidal archaeological sites—whether they are submerged settlements, shipwrecks or fishtraps—will inevitably be eroded away by the sea. What we need to do is to bear witness to their passing. We have to equip ourselves—commercial companies, state institutions and universities—to survey, excavate and understand such coastal archaeological sites before they disappear. Indeed, since the mid-1990s the Environment and Heritage Service, Northern Ireland, and *Dúchas* The Heritage Service have both made major advances in maritime archaeology.

In recent years the Heritage Council has been developing policy for the heritage management of Irish seascapes in the Republic, and their funding of the Discovery Programme here testifies to that commitment. The Shannon estuary intertidal survey duly confirms that we are now faced with the need to manage and protect a previously unknown coastal archaeological heritage. As we work as archaeologists in these coastal landscapes, we will also need to liaise closely with other users of the coastal zone, from port authorities and marine scientists to wildlife enthusiasts and local communities. It is only by so doing that we will move towards an understanding of ourselves as a people who live by the sea.

Michael Ryan,
Chairman
Discovery Programme

Réamhrá

Ón uair a bunaíodh é, sa bhliain 1991, ba é mian an *Discovery Programme* a bheith nuálaíoch i ngach réimse dá chuid oibre. Ba chuid de sin leas a bhaint as léargais a bhaineann leis an tseandálaíocht tírdhreacha agus iad a chur i bhfeidhm ar an tréimhse réamhstairiúil dhéanach. Ba chuid de freisin úsáid a bhaint as an gheofisic, as teicneolaíocht suirbhéireachta agus as Córais Gheografacha Faisnéise. Bhí an *Discovery Programme* ar thús cadhnaíochta maidir leis na cleachtais seo a úsáid in Éirinn, cleachtais atá anois ina ngnáthnósanna i measc lucht seandálaíochta na hÉireann trí chéile. Mar a chéile i gcás na seandálaíochta muirí, a nglactar léi go forleathan inniu mar ábhar de chuid na seandálaíochta féin. B'fhurasta dearmad a dhéanamh ar díreach cé chomh ceannródaíoch is a bhí an suirbhé seandálaíochta idirthaoideach a chuir Tionscadal Thuamhan i gcrích ar Inbhear na Sionainne.

Ba é an Dochtúir Eoin Grogan a bhí ina stiúrthóir ar Thionscadal Thuamhan agus ba é a bhí ar siúl acu sna 1990í ná staidéar tírdhreacha ar na sochaithe a bhí sa réigiún le linn na ré réamhstairiúla déanaí. Staidéar cuimsitheach comhtháite a bhí ann. Páirt de thaighde an Tionscadail ba ea an suirbhé a cheap Aidan O'Sullivan ar oidhreacht seandálaíochta an cheantair idirthaoidigh thart timpeall ar Inbhear uachtair na Sionainne agus ar Inbhear an Fhorgais. Ba é Aidan O'Sullivan a chuir an suirbhé i gcrích chomh maith. Cé go raibh srianta áirithe ann maidir le foireann, acmhainní airgid agus am, agus cé gur foireann réasúnta bheag a rinne an obair laistigh de limistéar réasúnta teoranta, cuireadh peirspictíocht nua ar fáil do lucht seandálaíochta na hÉireann de thairbhe an tsuirbhé, agus aimsíodh raidhse de chineálacha nua fianaise seandálaíochta.

Sa mhonagraf seo, féachtar leis an bhfianaise seandálaíochta seo a thabhairt le chéile ar shlí a thugann léargas ar leith dúinn ar an saol a bhí á chaitheamh ar an inbhear áirithe seo de chuid inbhir na hÉireann. Tá caibidil intreorach ann ina mbaintear feidhm as fianaise stairiúil agus seandálaíochta, as daonearraí, logainmneacha agus léarscáileanna luatha d'fhonn gaol na ndaoine le hInbhear na Sionainne a rianadh tríd na haoiseanna. Tá cuntas ann freisin ar an mhodheolaíocht ar leith agus ar na dúshláin ar leith a bhaineann le suirbhé idirthaoideach. Is é atá sa chéad chaibidil eile cur síos ar an ngeolaíocht, ar na hithreacha, ar an ngeomoirfeolaíocht, ar dhraenáil agus ar na sil-leaganacha pailé-ointeolaíocha ann. Is í an chaibidil seo an bhonnchloch ar a mbunófar aon obair atá le déanamh sa réigiún amach anseo. Pléitear seandálaíocht Inbhear uachtair na Sionainne i sraith de chaibidlí atá leagtha amach ar bhonn cróineolaíoch. Tugtar cuntas ar fhoraoiseacha báite Neoiliteacha agus ar iarsmaí chnámha na bhfianna rua. Cuirtear síos frisin ar láithreán Neoiliteach a d'fhéadfadh a bheith ina láithreán cónaithe nó ina láithreán adhlactha agus cuirtear léirmhínithe áirithe i láthair. Gheofar cuntas agus plé freisin ar thithe de chuid na Meánaoiseanna agus na Cré-Umhaoise Déanaí, ar chonairí agus ar ghnéithe eile. Déantar seo i gcomhthéacs an eolais atá ann i dtaobh lonnaíochtaí, sochaí agus geilleagar sa réigiún ó haois go haois.

Le linn na meánaoiseanna luatha ba nós le hiascairí ar feadh Inbhear na Sionainne feidhm a bhaint as gaistí ilchasta adhmaid. Ba ghnách na gaistí seo a shuíomh ar na caslaí agus na cainéil. Tháinig cuid de na struchtúir seo anuas chugainn agus iad i riocht maith i gcónaí. Is foinse eolais uathúil iad a thugann léargas dúinn ar chleachtais iascaireachta, ar an bhfeidhm a bhíothas ag baint as na coillte, ar cheirdeanna agus ar thionchar an traidisiúin i measc phobail na háite. Is léir gurb acmhainn eacnamaíoch an-tábhachtach a bhí san iascaireacht sa ré iar-mheánaoiseach freisin. Tá fianaise éigin curtha ar fáil ag seandálaithe agus ag staraithe a thugann le fios gur tionscal ríthábhachtach a bhí inti, agus gurbh fhéidir go raibh aicmí sóisialta in achrann le chéile i dtaobh sheilbh na n-acmhainní seo. Ba bhealach gnóthach mara riamh é bealach an Inbhir, agus cé nár aimsíodh mórán long báite sa suirbhé féin, tá caibidil anseo ar stair longbhristeacha sa ré iar-mheánaoiseach a chaitheann solas ar an méid a d'fhéadfadh a bheith ann is nár thángthas air fós. Maidir leis an gcaibidil dheireanach, a scríobhadh i bhfianaise cuid de na scríbhinní agus na léirmhínithe is úire sa tseandálaíocht, cuntas atá ann ar an saol a bhí á chaitheamh ag na glúnta a tháinig romhainn agus ar conas a chuaigh áit agus am i bhfeidhm orthu ar na bogaigh chósta seo thart timpeall an Inbhir.

Níl aon amhras ach go bhfuil dearcadh eile ar fad ag seandálaithe na hÉireann ar thírdhreacha cósta de thoradh ar shuirbhé Inbhear na Sionainne. Tá an lá imithe nuair a thiocfadh le duine breathnú ar riasca agus ar réileáin láibe an chósta agus a rá gur limistéir iad atá folamh. Ní dócha go bhfuil Inbhear na Sionainne eisceachtúil, ach go bhfuil an tábhacht seandálaíochta chéanna ag baint le hinbhir, le lochanna farraige agus le bearnaí eile sa chósta, bíodh is go mbeidh a cháilíocht réigiúnach agus áitiúil ag baint le gach ceann acu. Go deimhin, nuair a chuimhnítear go bhfuil ar an laghad 7000km slí ar feadh chósta na hÉireann, is léir cén saibhreas seandálaíochta is dócha atá ag baint le himeallbhord na farraige.

Chomh maith leis sin, is oidhreacht seandálaíochta í seo atá suite i dtimpeallacht a bhfuil suaiteacht thar na bearta inti. Bhí rí ar na hAngla-Shacsanaigh arbh ainm dó Canút a rinne iarracht cúl a choinneáil ar líonadh na taoide. Is amhlaidh a theastaigh uaidh a thaispeáint go bhfuil rudaí ar an saol seo nach mbíonn aon neart ag cine daonna orthu. Is mar a chéile dúinne é. Ní mór dúinn glacadh leis go ndéanfaidh an fharraige go leor leor láithreán seandálaíochta a chreimeadh, idir láithreáin chósta agus láithreáin idirthaoideacha. Ina measc sin tá seanlonnaíochtaí faoi uisce, longa báite agus gaistí iascaireachta. Is é án dualgas atá orainne ná taifead a choimeád ar an méid atá ag imeacht. Ní mór dúinn an trealamh agus na scileanna cuí a bheith againn—cuideachtaí tráchtála, institiúidí stáit agus ollscoileanna—chun gur féidir linn suirbhéanna a dhéanamh ar láithreáin seandálaíochta, iad a thochailt agus a thuiscint sula gcailltear ar fad iad. Go deimhin, ó lár na 1990í ar aghaidh tá dul chun cinn nach beag déanta i réimse na seandálaíochta muirí ag an tSeirbhís Chomhshaoil agus Oidhreachta do Thuaisceart Éireann agus ag Dúchas araon.

Le blianta beaga anuas tá polasaí á fhorbairt ag an gComhairle Oidhreachta maidir le muirdhreacha Phoblacht Éireann a bhainistiú agus is comhartha ar dhíograis na heagraíochta sin an Discovery Programme a bheith á mhaoiniú acu. Is léir ón suirbhé idirthaoideach a rinneadh ar Inbhear na Sionainne gur mithid dúinn an ghné aineoil seo dár n-oidhreacht seandálaíochta a bhainistiú agus a chosaint. Le linn dúinn a bheith ag saothrú i bpáirt le seandálaithe sna tírdhreacha cósta seo, beidh orainn freisin dlúth-theagmháil a choimeád le dreamanna eile a bhíonn ag plé le saol na gceantar cósta, idir údaráis phoirt, eolaithe muirí, díograiseoirí fiadhúlra agus pobail áitiúla. Teastaíonn sin chun gur féidir dul i dtreo comhthuisceana orainn féin, pobal daoine a chónaíonn cois farraige.

Michael Ryan,
Cathaoirleach,
The Discovery Programme

FOREWORD

Early in 1992, just after the commencement of the North Munster Project, Aidan O'Sullivan approached me with a research proposal to investigate the archaeology of the intertidal mudflats of the Shannon estuary. I had already developed my integrated landscape research strategy, but I was intrigued by his ideas. In his proposal, based on similar work in Wales and England, he reviewed the potential range and date of the archaeological evidence, showed how it could be used to develop a history of this estuarine landscape, and how that could be integrated into the overall North Munster Research Design. This type of work was only then emerging on the Severn estuary (where Aidan had been working with Nigel Nayling and other members of the Severn Estuary Levels Research Committee), and I had not realised the enormous archaeological potential that it represented. Aidan quickly put me straight: in the course of a thirty-minute conversation I was completely convinced that this was not only an essential component of our research portfolio, but also a highly innovative strategy that could greatly enhance the range and depth of the prehistoric landscape assessment that we were undertaking.

The Shannon estuary survey formed an integral part of the North Munster strategy, consisting of a compact module of the overall research under Aidan's direction. As part of the field programme we devised a training component that encouraged student members of the field survey and excavation teams to take part in the intertidal work. Some people got no further than their second step onto the mudflats, getting immediately rooted into the thick mud. Others clearly had mudlark genes (I might especially mention Mark Woods and Enda Malone) and became important contributors to the fieldwork. James Lyttleton, who made other important contributions to the post-fieldwork research, was also to make a major contribution to the discussion of the late medieval and post-medieval estuary landscape. None, however, could match Aidan's tireless commitment and enthusiasm. Anyone who has not experienced several hours of trudging, squelching, dragging or crawling across this remarkable and glutinous landscape will not appreciate the incredibly energy-sapping nature of this terrain. The sheer concentration of effort required to keep upright and moving made it difficult to comprehend the complexity and diversity of this special landscape. Working with Aidan completely removed that difficulty. His remarkable depth of vision enabled us to see the extraordinary character of the place and the long-term nature of human interaction with it. His interest in exploring and trying to understand the ebb and flow of history in the estuarine wetlands was also clear. That personal vision and empathy, together with a mastery of the archaeology, is one of the great strengths of the research and of this volume.

Of course the pace and timing of the work were dictated by the tides. This meant that Aidan also had responsibilities in the other aspects of the field programme, including archaeological survey in Clare, Limerick and Tipperary (especially with Tom Condit) and excavation (on Mooghaun hillfort). Again his commitment to the North Munster Project and his tremendous enthusiasm, interest and desire to learn had an infectious impact on the field teams. This involvement provided him with a broader landscape perspective and greatly enhanced the integration of the intertidal research with the archaeology along the wetland–dryland margins. This all accorded very well with the Project's overall strategy and greatly assisted in the integration of the intertidal study into the wider landscape study of North Munster.

The Shannon estuary survey revealed a new and unexpected landscape with a wealth of archaeological and environmental features ranging widely in date. As a result, although the North Munster Project had a very particular focus on later prehistory, it quickly became apparent that that particular narrow chronological window was no longer an appropriate view for us to adopt on the estuary. Accordingly, the strategy was restructured to properly record all archaeological deposits and material. This considerably widened and enhanced our view of the landscape. It also provided a very important diachronic background for our assessment of the later prehistory of the region. The Bronze Age marshland house, trackway and other potential features are unique and interesting contributions to our growing understanding of later prehistoric Ireland. However, some of the most spectacular and informative material discovered on the mudflats came from 'other' periods. It includes the intriguing Neolithic site at Carrigdirty Rock, the remarkable early historic and medieval fishtraps on the Fergus estuary, Deel estuary and at Bunratty, as well as all the post-medieval fishtraps, piers, jetties and sea defences. These have all provided significant insights into the use of the Shannon and Fergus waterways across time, and the increasing bustle of activity on the rivers themselves.

It is difficult to believe that this work started as recently as 1992, nor to credit just how innovative the Shannon estuary intertidal survey was at the time. It was truly a ground-breaking strategy and marked the introduction of intertidal archaeology to research in Ireland. This volume presents the detailed evidence retrieved during this field programme and assesses its place in the wider landscape of the prehistoric and historic development of the Shannon and Fergus estuaries. The changing nature of the estuary and the altering perceptions of this diverse landscape by those living in it are documented and discussed in a seamless narrative that brings to life this archaeologically and historically previously unexplored terrain.

Dr Eoin Grogan,
Project Director,
The North Munster Project

To Eoin Grogan, for his vision and generosity

1. INTRODUCTION

Introduction

Pl. 1—*Aerial photograph of the upper Shannon estuary, looking northwestwards across the saltmarshes, mudflats, estuary channel and shoals, towards Graigue Island, Bush Island and Bunratty and the reclaimed corcass on the Clare bank (photo: Shannon Estuary Ports).*

The Shannon estuary today is a waterlogged landscape of grey, muddy water, mudflats and marshes. On a darkening winter's evening, with squalls of rain and flocks of wading birds sweeping in over the mudflats, it can be a chill and desolate place. On a fine summer's day, as the sun glints off both mud and water, blending the two together under a humid white light, the estuary is a vastly different world of pastel greens, blues and grays, with low hills on the horizon barely visible in the heat haze (Pl. 1). This watery landscape is the place where the longest river in Britain and Ireland finally flows out into the Atlantic Ocean. It is also one of the biologically richest ecosystems on this island; the constant renewal of nutrients by the tides means that vast numbers of fish, shellfish and wildfowl are supported by a rich growth of algae. Although now largely tamed by hundreds of years of human toil, the Shannon estuary remains a dynamic frontier between the river and the ocean, one of our last wildernesses, lying between the opposing worlds of land and sea. In the past, before modern reclamation activities, the upper Shannon estuary especially would have flowed through a complex mosaic of estuarine and freshwater wetlands, with mudflats, saltmarshes, reed-swamps, fens and bogs giving way further inland to a scrubby, wet cover of carr woodland. The nearby rolling drumlin hills and upland terraces on both banks of the estuary would have been the main location for rural settlements, agriculture and woodlands.

Foragers, farmers and fishers

People have been living by the Shannon estuary since earliest times, fishing and wildfowling on its channels and creeks, herding livestock on its marshes, or travelling along its waters by boat and ship. Over the millennia, environments have shifted and changed on the estuary, and ancient landscapes have been submerged by sea-level rise. At low tide, these submerged landscapes are exposed to view again, allowing us to walk across them and to record structures and finds deposited there over the last few thousand years. In recent years, spectacular archaeological discoveries by the Discovery Programme's North Munster Project have transformed both our knowledge of the archaeology of the Shannon estuary and our perception of the archaeology of coastal wetlands in Ireland generally. They include prehistoric submerged forests, settlement sites, trackways and other features, early historic and medieval fishtraps in remarkable states of preservation, and numerous post-medieval and modern fishing structures. All of these archaeological sites were recorded by the project to be discussed in this book, the Shannon estuary intertidal survey (Fig. 1). In this introductory chapter, the aims, methodology and results of the survey will be outlined after a discussion of the previously known archaeology and history of the estuary which provides a useful background to our discoveries.

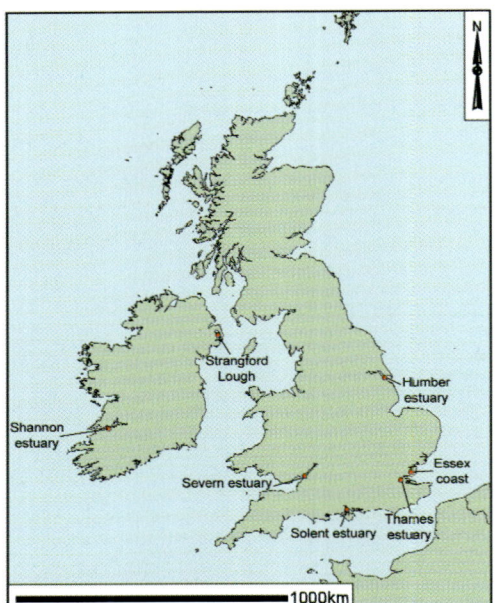
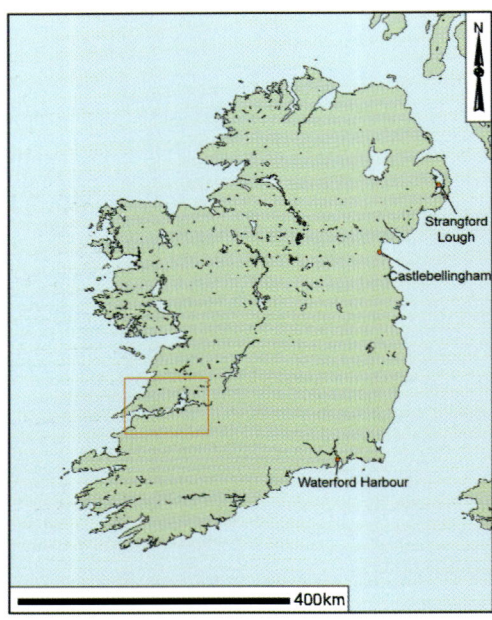
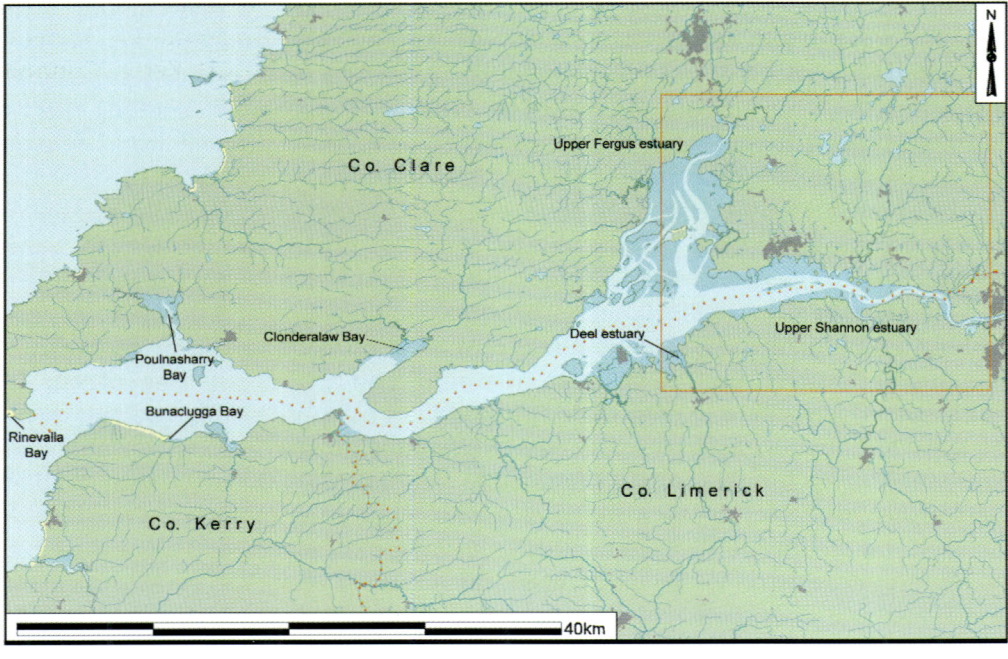

Fig. 1—*Map of Britain and Ireland, showing the location of the Shannon estuary and UK intertidal archaeological survey projects mentioned in the text (Barry Masterson, Discovery Programme).*

Introduction

Archaeological, historical and placename evidence for settlement and coastal exploitation on the Shannon estuary

AIDAN O'SULLIVAN AND JAMES LYTTLETON

Mesolithic hunter-gatherers in the Shannon estuary region

The earliest settlers in the Shannon estuary region were Mesolithic (7000–4000 BC) hunter-gatherers, who would have hunted, fished, and gathered plant foods along the estuary. A Late Mesolithic coastal occupation site has recently been excavated in the region, at Ferriter's Cove at the end of the Dingle Peninsula, Co. Kerry. This site was used over generations at about 4600–4300 BC by small parties who came to the bay during the late summer and autumn, fished for wrasse, whiting and cod in the inshore waters, gathered dogwhelks, periwinkles and limpets on the foreshore, and hunted wild pig, hare and birds in the neighbouring hazel–oak woodlands (Woodman *et al.* 1984; Woodman and O'Brien 1993; Woodman, Anderson *et al.* 1999). Early Mesolithic and Late Mesolithic sites have also been identified at several sites in Limerick. For example, a peat deposit beside a stream at Ballycahane Lower, Co. Limerick, produced a spread of burnt and heat-shattered stones and wild boar bones with a radiocarbon date of 6025 ± 45 BP (5036–4792 cal. BC; GrN-15405; Gowen 1988; Grogan 1989). Although little of the Late Mesolithic period has yet been found along the Shannon estuary itself, with its abundant wetlands and riverine resources it would have been an attractive location for coastal foragers, who could have based themselves along its hills, fished its creeks, gathered plant foods and hunted for pig, hare and wildfowl in its woodlands and wetlands. The estuary also provided access by boat to its own river, and on up that river deeper into the Irish midlands (Woodman, Anderson *et al.* 1999).

Neolithic farmers, their settlements and megalithic tombs

Neolithic communities (4000–2500 BC) would have been living in the Shannon estuary region by at least 4000 BC. Farming was probably initially introduced by small population groups moving into the region, although indigenous Mesolithic hunter-gatherer groups may themselves have made the social and economic changes towards a Neolithic lifestyle and society (Monk 1993; Woodman, Anderson *et al.* 1999). These earliest farmers may have combined cattle-herding, crop cultivation and the use of fixed dwellings with a measure of seasonal movement and hunting and gathering (O'Sullivan 1997b; see Chapter 3 below). However, it is also clear that at least some Neolithic farming communities in the region inhabited permanent dwellings all year round. Neolithic houses and settlements have been excavated at Lough Gur, Co. Limerick (Grogan and Eogan 1987; Grogan 1996), Tankardstown South, Co. Limerick (Gowen 1988), and more recently at Cloghers in the Lee Valley, Co. Kerry (Connolly 1999; Dunne and Kiely 1999). The distribution of Neolithic stone axes is another strong indicator of the widespread activities of early farmers in the region. About 1500 stone axes have been found throughout north Munster, with particularly interesting concentrations on the River Shannon itself at Killaloe, Co. Clare, upstream of the estuary's tidal headwaters (Stephen Mandal, pers. comm.; Grogan 1989; Cooney and Mandal 1998).

There is also increasing evidence for Neolithic funerary sites in the region. Neolithic farmers constructed and used both court tombs and portal tombs throughout east Clare, north Kerry and south-east Limerick (Grogan 1989; Grogan *et al.* 1996, 27–30, fig. 13). More recently, a possible passage tomb has been excavated at Ballycarty, Co. Kerry, lending support to the idea that there may have been a regionally distinctive 'Neolithic' in the Shannon estuary region, at least in north Kerry (Connolly 1999). Human burials were also placed in caves during the period, as can be seen from the intriguing early Neolithic skulls and pottery discovered at Annagh, Co. Limerick (Ó Floinn 1992). There is evidence for an expansion of settlement out from places like Lough Gur into the wider Shannon estuary region during the middle and later

Foragers, farmers and fishers

Neolithic, with the construction and use of Linkardstown-type burials, passage tombs and ultimately wedge tombs and embanked enclosures in south-east Clare, east Limerick and north Kerry (Grogan *et al.* 1996; Grogan and Condit 1994; Grogan 1989; see also B. O'Brien 1999 for a recent regional analysis of wedge tombs in the coastal south-west). Interestingly, most of this Neolithic settlement and funerary evidence is located well away from the Shannon estuary itself.

Bronze Age power, settlement and society in the Shannon estuary region

By the Early Bronze Age (2500–1600 BC) settlement was widespread throughout the Shannon estuary region, as is evident in the distribution of copper and bronze artefacts (e.g. Harbison 1969a; 1969b). The most significant copper-producing areas during the earliest phases of the Early Bronze Age were in south-west Munster, as indicated by recent excavations of copper mines at Mount Gabriel, Co. Cork, and Ross Island, Co. Kerry (B. O'Brien 1995). As the Early Bronze Age developed, there may have been a shift in power and control of metal resources northwards towards the Shannon estuary, as most bronze axes are found in the north of the province. There is evidence for Early Bronze Age settlement along the south bank of the estuary itself, particularly around Limerick City and at Shanid, in east Limerick (Grogan *et al.* 1996). The distribution of bronze tools, weaponry and gold suggests that the north Munster region was becoming more important by the Middle Bronze Age (1600–1200 BC), perhaps with the movement of peoples southwards from the Burren region and into south-east Clare, east Limerick and west Tipperary in particular (Grogan *et al.* 1996).

By the Late Bronze Age (1200–600 BC) the Shannon estuary was clearly the focus for a probably wealthy, hierarchically structured and powerful community (Eogan 1974). Population pressure, deteriorating climate and social and ideological change may have led to intensification in agriculture and land use. Recently, the North Munster Project's archaeological research has revealed evidence for a hierarchical, socially stratified settlement system, with the use of hillforts (Pl. 2), hilltop enclosures and smaller defended farmsteads (Grogan *et al.* 1996; Grogan 1999). Late Bronze Age communities were also involved in the ritual deposition of huge numbers of gold and bronze tools, weapons and ornaments in probable sacred places such as bogs, lakes and rivers (notably at Mooghaun Lough, Co. Clare, and the Bog of Cullen, Co. Tipperary; Eogan 1965; 1983; Grogan *et al.* 1996). The Cashen estuary and the north Kerry coast have also produced evidence for Late Bronze Age settlement and ritual activities, suggesting the increasing wealth of this western maritime region too. Indeed, it has been suggested that the Late Bronze Age communities of the Shannon estuary region maintained wider contacts with Atlantic Europe (Eogan 1993).

Iron Age maritime communities on the Shannon estuary

By at least the Iron Age (600 BC–AD 400), and probably before, it seems that the Shannon estuary was well known as a western port and routeway into the heart of Ireland. The mouth of the River Shannon (*Senos*) was known to the second-century AD Greek geographer Ptolemy of Alexandria. Significantly, the Shannon is one of the few rivers recorded on the western Irish coastline in Ptolemy's *Geographia*, while clearly important tribal groups such as the *Gangani* and *Auteini* tribes also lived in the vicinity of the estuary. Ptolemy's knowledge of the location and importance of the River Shannon would almost certainly have derived from contacts with the soldiers, sailors and merchants who would have plied the seas between Ireland and mainland Europe at this time (Raftery 1994, 204–6; Byrne 1984).

There is other archaeological evidence for ongoing contacts between the Iron Age peoples of the Shannon estuary and other regions of Atlantic Europe. A hoard of fourth- to fifth-century Roman military silver was found in the 1940s in a quarry at Balline, Co. Limerick. It included four silver ingots and three pieces of silver platter that had been hacked up. Some of the pieces were stamped with apparent Roman military inscriptions. This hoard may have been the wages of an Irish auxiliary who had

Introduction

Pl. 2—*Aerial photograph of the Late Bronze Age hillfort at Mooghaun, Co. Clare, situated on a hill overlooking the Fergus estuary (photo: Aoife Daly, North Munster Project).*

formerly served in Rome's armies in southern Britain, and who had then returned home. It is also possible that the hoard reflects the ongoing contacts between the people of the Shannon estuary and the Roman world of the early centuries AD (Raftery 1994, 216).

Early historic settlement and maritime communications on the Shannon estuary

There is a wide range of both archaeological and historical evidence for settlement along the Shannon estuary's shores in the early historic period (AD 400–800). The distribution of ringforts, church sites and monastic enclosures testifies to the intensive settlement of these landscapes. Ringforts, traditionally interpreted as the farmsteads of nobles, strong farmers and tenant farmers between the sixth and ninth centuries AD, are particularly concentrated along the north Limerick and north Kerry shores of the estuary, but are also widespread along the west Clare coast and on either side of the Fergus estuary (e.g. Stout 1997; Stout and Stout 1997, figs 41 and 51). Other significant indicators of early historic settlement are the early church sites and ecclesiastical enclosures found along the estuary (e.g. at places like Mungret, Co. Limerick, Coney Island on the lower Fergus estuary, and Scattery Island on the lower Shannon estuary). Historical sources also record the presence of various population groups. Perhaps the most significant group were the *Uí Fidgeinti*, whose control extended across much of the Shannon estuary region (Bhreathnach 1999). The *In Deis Tuaiscirt*, another significant tribal group, were located in the region around the upper estuary, in south-east Clare and north Limerick (Byrne 1973). On the lower Shannon estuary, the *Corcu Baiscinn* were located in south-west Clare, while the *Ciarraige Luachra* were located in north Kerry, in the region around the Cashen estuary.

In the early historic period the Shannon estuary was known in law-tracts, saints' lives and annalistic references not as the *Senos* but as *Inber Luimni* (the bay or river mouth of Limerick) or *Loch Luimni* (the sea of Limerick). For example, in AD 661, verses in the Annals of the Four Masters state that the body of St Cummine Foda, bishop of Clonfert, was conveyed from Munster to his burial-place by a boat that sailed on the waters of *Luimneach* (*AFM*, 273). Although it has traditionally been believed that the etymology of the word *Luimneach* derives from the Irish word for 'bare marsh', more recently it has been suggested that the name comes from the Irish adjective denoting 'cloaked or shielded'. This would certainly describe well the often narrow, enclosed landscape of the upper Shannon estuary in particular (Ó Maolfabhail 1990). Other historical sources include references to numerous local and regional kingdoms, to churches, boundaries, islands and other topographical features. For example, *Inis Da Droma* (Coney Island, on the lower Fergus estuary) is mentioned in the Irish Life of Brendan (Plummer 1922, 78) in relation to the saint residing there, cursing local fishermen and losing a boat to a storm. Coney Island, Canon Island and Deer Island all have early church sites and ecclesiastical enclosures. The important monastic island at *Inis Cathaigh* (Scattery Island; Pl. 3) on the lower estuary is also mentioned in the

Pl. 3—*Aerial view of the early historic and medieval monastic site of Scattery Island, on the lower Shannon estuary (photo: Dúchas The Heritage Service).*

Irish Life of Ciarán of Clonmacnoise (Plummer 1922), indicating the close links between it and that midland monastery and also the fact that the Shannon estuary was an important routeway into the midlands in the early Middle Ages.

Viking Age settlement and fleets on the estuary

By the ninth and tenth centuries AD the name *Luimneach* is also used in the historical sources to refer not to the estuary but to a Viking settlement on an island in the Shannon (*Inis Sibtonn*), probably King John's Island. Certainly this would have been an ideal location, being an easily defended site reached by a ford across the river. Indeed, situated at the estuary's headwaters, it was the first place where this huge body of water could be crossed (O'Rahilly 1995, 163; Wallace 1992, 39). Viking raiding parties were first using the estuary in the 830s, and fleets from Limerick sailed up the River Shannon to raid monastic islands on Lough Ree, deep in the heart of the Irish midlands, several times in the early tenth century (Edwards 1990, 174; Ó Danachair 1971, 55). There are various annalistic references to these fleets. For example, in 845, Forannán, abbot of Armagh, was taken prisoner by the Vikings at *Cluain Comarda* (possibly Colmanswell, Co. Limerick) and brought to the ships of *Luimnech* (AU, 345).

Apart from the historical evidence from Limerick, there is other evidence for Viking settlement along the banks of the River Shannon. Immediately upstream of Limerick is the townland of Athlunkard, Co. Clare, whose name (*Áth an Longphoirt*, 'the ford of the ship enclosure or encampment') indicates the possible presence of a temporary settlement there. A large D-shaped enclosure has recently been recorded on the riverbank in Fairyhill townland (immediately downstream of Athlunkard), from which tenth-century silver and iron metalwork was recovered in the 1980s. Although this site may well be the *longphort* of Limerick, it was probably quickly succeeded by the tenth-century settlement further downstream (Kelly and O'Donovan 1998). Placename evidence also indicates local Scandinavian influence, with a famous salmon weir on the River Shannon downstream bearing the name of the Lax Weir (Lax deriving from the Scandinavian word for salmon; Herbert 1946–7, 49).

The Shannon estuary would have served well both as a protected harbour for seagoing ships and as an *entrepôt* for traders and raiders intent on moving up into the Irish midlands. Indeed, the presence of local harbours and suitable places to draw up boats may be indicated by the townland name Coonagh East, Co. Limerick (from *An Cuanach*, meaning haven or place of shelter; Ó Maolfabhail 1990, 145), located where the Shannon estuary channel narrows as it nears Limerick City. Interestingly, a possible Viking Age wooden jetty or boat-hard was found across the channel from this townland. In 1958, during drain-digging for marsh reclamation at Cooperhill, Co. Limerick, an iron Viking sword (Fig. 2) was found at a 'depth of 16ft' in estuarine clays, apparently beside a creek flowing northwards into the main Shannon estuary channel. The sword was found lying on a substantial causeway of 'oak trunks all laid flat in one direction' (NMI files; Lucas 1960, 19, 32–3, fig. 10; Ó Floinn 1998, 149; Walsh 1998, 226–8). The site was off a former island (Muckinish or *muic inis*), which suggests that it was originally surrounded by wetlands (Ó Maolfabhail 1990, 223).

By 922 the town of Limerick or *Hylmrick* was well established at *Inis Sibtonn*. It was a centre of Norse power in the region and was almost as important as Dublin. The Norse kings of Limerick were also noted to have been occasionally resident at *Inis Cathaig* (Scattery Island), downriver in the Shannon estuary, in 974 and 977 *(AI)*. Annalistic sources and later texts suggest that Viking Age Limerick was a populous and wealthy urban settlement. According to the later *Cogadh Gaedhel re Gallaib* (a twelfth-century Ua Briain propaganda text which has to be used cautiously for earlier periods), in their attack on the Vikings of Limerick the Dál Cais 'carried off their jewels and their best property, and their saddles beautiful and foreign; their gold and their silver; their beautifully woven cloth of all colours and of all kinds; their satins and silken cloth, pleasing and variegated, both scarlet and green, and all sorts of cloth in like manner' from the town's settlers (CGG, 79).

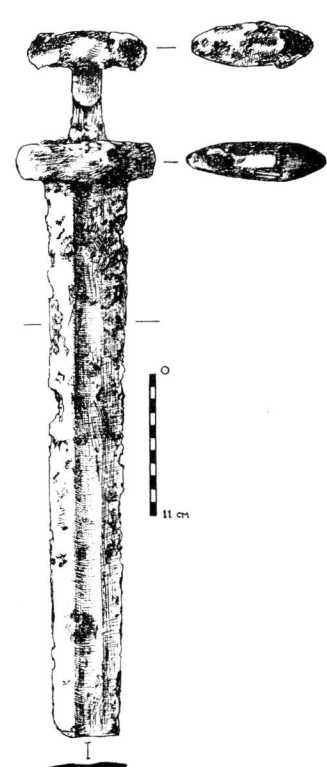

Fig. 2—*Viking sword found on a wooden causeway on upper Shannon estuary at Cooperhill, Co. Limerick (from JRSAI 1960).*

Foragers, farmers and fishers

By 977 Limerick and the wider Shannon estuary region had come under the dominance of the local Dál Cais dynasty, but the town continued to serve as a significant trading and fishing port during the eleventh and twelfth centuries (Byrne 1993, 28–9; O'Rahilly 1995, 165). In 1125 Toirdhealbach Mór Ua Conchubair brought a fleet down the Shannon, portaged his boats over the Doonass Falls upstream of Limerick, and sailed down the estuary to ravage the country around Foynes and capture the ships of local lords (*AFM*). Indeed, the twelfth-century text *Lebor na Cert* indicates that the kings of Munster themselves had fleets on the estuary (Dillon 1962, 140–3). Hiberno-Norse Limerick may also have been at the heart of an economic district and political territory that ran down both sides of the upper estuary. This territory, known in the later medieval period as the Cantred of the Ostmen, stretched from Cratloe Woods and the Owenagarney River in the west to Plassey in the east, and from the Slieve Barnagh foothills in the north to Ballyneety in the south. The territory of *Tradraige*, the later Cantred of Traderry, was also under Limerick's control, and this region probably stretched from the Owenagarney River to the Fergus estuary (J. Bradley 1988a, 62–4).

Anglo-Norman and Gaelic Irish settlement and maritime trade on the Shannon estuary

In the late twelfth and thirteenth centuries, Anglo-Norman invasion and colonisation had a major impact on the Shannon estuary's landscapes. Nucleated settlements were established and a manorial economy introduced which led to more intensive land use, an emphasis on arable agriculture and an increased importance of towns, markets and fairs. Limerick, already a prosperous urban settlement, was controlled by the O'Brien kings of Thomond during much of the twelfth century. In 1175 it was taken by the Anglo-Normans, at which time Giraldus Cambrensis described it as being a well-fortified place ringed by walls, a dyke and a fast-flowing river (*Expugnatio*, 151). In the early thirteenth century, with the agreement of the O'Briens, the Anglo-Normans settled Limerick county; most grants of land were given to various Norman nobles, while the city of Limerick and the forests of Cratloe on the north bank were reserved for the king (*CDI*, i, 580, 633, 881). The only Irish-held area to the south of the estuary was the barony of Iraghticonnor, north Kerry, where the O'Connors managed to hold out throughout the medieval period (MacCurtain 1988, 435).

On the north bank of the Shannon estuary, the districts of Traderry (in south-east Clare) and the cantreds of Corcovaskin (in west Clare) were also respectively granted to Anglo-Norman lords or retained in the hands of the Crown. Otherwise, the invaders made little initial attempt to settle Thomond, being content to let the O'Briens hold their land in return for rent and services. However, by the mid-thirteenth century Anglo-Norman castles were built at Bunratty and Clarecastle, and a substantial Anglo-Norman borough was established at Bunratty by the latter part of the thirteenth century. The Anglo-Norman overlordship of Traderry lasted until the battle of Dysert O'Dea in 1318, after which it declined, and by the middle of the fourteenth century the Irish had regained control there (J. Bradley 1988b, 19–20). Apart from the Anglo-Norman boroughs of Bunratty and Askeaton (O'Connor 1987; Westropp 1903a), other archaeological evidence for settlement along the estuary includes such sites as a possible twelfth-century motte-and-bailey at Clonmoney West, near Bunratty, a thirteenth-century hall-house with earthworks at Tomdeely North, Co. Limerick (Sweetman 1999, 89–91), and the well-known thirteenth- or early fourteenth-century O'Brien fortress on a prominence overlooking the estuary at Carrigogunnel, Co. Limerick (Westropp 1908; Sweetman 1999, 118). There are also several historical references to now-vanished castles along the upper estuary's banks (e.g. Westropp 1907, 31). Medieval monastic settlements are also situated along the upper estuary, such as the Franciscan friary in the town of Askeaton (Westropp 1903a) and the Augustinian abbey on Canon Island on the Fergus estuary, Co. Clare (MacMahon 1993), while medieval churches are found at places like Kilconry, Co. Clare (O'Carroll 1978, 32).

Limerick was an important maritime port in the thirteenth and fourteenth centuries

Introduction

Pl. 4—*Medieval Limerick was a thriving port on the banks of the River Shannon. This early nineteenth-century depiction (c. 1827) shows the thirteenth-century Anglo-Norman fortress of King John's Castle within the medieval city, while Old Thomond Bridge and probably the timber-framed building to the right were also of medieval origin (National Library of Ireland: 1439 TA).*

(Pl. 4). Horses, cattle, sheep, pigs, cheese, vegetables, wheat, oats, honey, wool, linen, timber, salmon and herrings were brought into the city's quays from the surrounding countryside and were exported to the western ports of England, France, Spain and the Netherlands, in return for salt, iron and lead (Hill 1997, 48). While piracy was quite common in medieval times, its dangers were not confined solely to the high seas, and crimes against merchants are also recorded on the estuary. In 1311 David Oketfagh and others were charged with stealing from Henry Troye 27 gallons of beer worth 40d. from a boat on the banks of the Shannon, and from William of Gloucester 40 gallons of wine worth one mark held in another boat on the same bank (*Cal. Justic. Rolls Ire.*, 205). The saltmarshes and corcass (a local term for the reclaimed estuarine levels, derived from the Irish word *corcaigh* or 'marsh') would also have been important as grazing for cattle, sheep and horses, as indicated by a court case in 1313, when Walter, son of John, and William Ó Mynok were charged with stealing cattle from the king's marsh (Corkanree, immediately downstream of Limerick City) and slaughtering them in a cellar in Limerick (*Cal. Justic. Rolls Ire.*, 311).

Limerick gradually declined in importance relative to Galway from the mid-thirteenth century onwards (Hill 1997, 50). But during the course of the fifteenth century its fortunes improved as its merchants became involved with the developing economies under the local Anglo-Irish and Gaelic Irish magnates, rather than with the traditional manorial farm system which had been seriously disturbed since the late thirteenth century (T. O'Neill 1987, 130–1). Fishtraps were also being constructed on the river. On 26 February 1430, one Nicholas Thomas Arthur, a wealthy Limerick merchant, 'was given a license by Henry VI to construct a fishery, suitable for the taking of salmon and other fish on the bank of his farm at Castle Blath to the mid-channel of the River Shannon (but in such a way that free passage was left for all vessels sailing to and from the port of Limerick)' (Lenihan 1866, 367).

Late medieval and post-medieval settlement and exploitation of the Shannon estuary's resources

By the fifteenth century, the Fitzgeralds of Desmond on the south side and the MacNamaras of Thomond on the north side had built various fortified residences or tower-houses along the estuary. Churches were also being reconstructed or built at

Foragers, farmers and fishers

Pl. 5 —*The late medieval Desmond tower-house at Carrigafoyle Castle, Co. Kerry, on the banks of the lower Shannon estuary (photo:* Dúchas*). Inset is a depiction from* Pacata Hibernia, *published in 1633, of the same castle under attack in 1580 (National Library of Ireland: Ir 9405s2).*

some of these locations in the late sixteenth/early seventeenth century, for example at Cratloemoyle (beside the MacNamara tower-house), Bunratty and Kilconry, Co. Clare (Ryan 1985). Some of the tower-houses were situated right at the edge of the Shannon estuary mudflats (J. O'Brien 1977). Those at Beagh, Co. Limerick (Westropp 1907), and Cratloemoyle, Cratloekeel, Castledonnell and Bunratty, Co. Clare (Westropp 1913–15; McInerney 1978), would have been highly visible from boats moving along the upper estuary channel, and no doubt they were constructed as visual symbols of power and status, as well as to control access to the navigation and fisheries in the channel. The tower-house at Carrigafoyle (on the lower estuary), Co. Kerry, operated as a customs station, processing incoming ships before they could proceed to Tarbert or Limerick (Pl. 5). Indeed, the earls of Desmond had the rights to treasure trove and shipwrecks, a right that was exploited by the placing of misleading beacons along treacherous stretches of coastline at Beal Point and the cliffs of Doon (MacCurtain 1988, 442).

By the turn of the sixteenth century the people of the Shannon estuary were enjoying a period of relative peace, with an active fisheries and mercantile trade being sustained. Limerick itself was also thriving. William Body wrote in 1536 that Limerick was 'a wonderous prosperous city' (Brewer and Bullen 1867, 105), and in 1574 David Wolfe noted that Limerick was 'the mightiest and most beautiful of all the cities of Ireland' (Bradshaw 1975). Merchants' Quay, which was originally named the Quay or Great Quay and was constructed about 1500, could handle ships carrying loads of 200 tons or more (Spellissy 1998, 119). In 1575 Queen Elizabeth I granted the corporation of Limerick certain privileges on the estuary in 'that no ship coming within the river there do sell or discharge any munitions, shot, powder, wines or other wares to any other than to the said corporation' (Brewer and Bullen 1868, 26).

The granting of the Shannon estuary's fisheries, which had previously belonged to the monasteries, to secular interests followed a common trend in the aftermath of the Tudor dissolution of the religious houses (Went 1960b, 141; 1981, 107). At Ennis, Co. Clare, in 1570 the Franciscan friary was granted to James Naylane, along with 'a water mill, salmon weir and eel weir upon the river Fergus and other appurtences in Inch' (*Fiants* 1569, 190). In 1587 Queen Elizabeth granted to the mayor and citizens of Limerick the island of Iniscathy (now Scattery Island), with fishing dues to the effect

Introduction

that for every boat of oysters which came to Limerick, 1000 oysters per year were to be given to the city, and 500 herrings per year for every herring boat (Frost 1893, 85). The fisheries at Limerick City were also important sources of revenue for certain individuals. In 1576 Queen Elizabeth granted to Edward Molyneaux 'The weirs, commonly called the fisher's stent, near the city of Limerick, which do lie from the Lax Weir, or Common Weir, in the east part, until the river nigh to Castle Donell . . .'. This grant of riverine and estuarine fisheries was made despite earlier charters of Henry V and Henry VI which gave the Lax Weir to the city of Limerick (Herbert 1946–7, 53–4). In 1609 King James I granted a charter to the city of Limerick, conferring exclusive jurisdiction over the whole of the Shannon estuary, with the mayor holding the rank of admiral. This charter was later interpreted as giving the corporation complete rights over the fishing of the Shannon from a point nearly 5km above the city to the sea (Herbert 1946–7, 55; Lenihan 1866, 134).

The Desmond rebellion of 1579 raised concern amongst English officials about the threat from insurgent and foreign shipping on the exposed west coast of Ireland, and Scattery Island became a base from which to carry out naval operations (Brewer and Bullen 1868, 199–200). Carrigafoyle Castle, a rebel stronghold on the north Kerry coastline, was subjected to a two-pronged artillery bombardment from both the mainland and the river (MacCurtain 1988, 429). In the aftermath of the rebellion in the early 1580s the Elizabethan administration granted confiscated lands to more loyal Protestant settlers in the Shannon region. This wave of settlement brought more villages and towns, with a focus on the development of an expansionist mercantile trade in such areas as forestry and iron-smelting (D. Power 1991). Rebellion by the Sugán Earl of Desmond and the major Gaelic Irish families of Ulster in the 1590s led to war in the Shannon estuary region again. The north side of the estuary was plundered on one occasion by Red Hugh O'Donnell (Frost 1893, 79, 259). Piracy by the Gaelic Irish was a problem for shipping on the estuary during these unsettled times (*ibid.*, 79, 255). Royal vessels patrolled the river in an attempt to counteract this (Atkinson 1974, 245). Indeed, the Dublin government used the Shannon estuary as a means to supply its garrisons and to attack insurgent strongholds (Atkinson 1899, 202, 480, 321, 385).

Political differences between King Charles I and the English parliament created conditions in Ireland which resulted in a rebellion in 1641 led by an uneasy alliance between the Catholic Old English and Gaelic Irish lords. One of the main parliamentarian strongholds on the Shannon estuary was the earl of Thomond's residence at Bunratty Castle, and it was kept under siege by the Confederation (Share 1995, 48; J. O'Brien 1978). The value of the corcass for local farming can be seen by the fact that the besieged parliamentarians kept their animals on these marshlands. On 4 June 1646, 80 of their mares and colts were seized by the enemy (Penn 1833, I, 159–211). The rest of the decade saw strife between the various factions representing the confederate, royalist and parliamentarian interests, eventually resulting in victory for the parliamentarians. As a result there were forced property confiscations, and Catholics were forbidden to settle in a security band one mile wide along the Shannon estuary that was cleared for the planting of new Protestant settlers (Ó Murchadha 1984, 33).

Various historical accounts testify to the importance of the fisheries of the Shannon estuary in the seventeenth century. The Civil Survey of the 1650s indicates that tidal head weirs or fishtraps were being used on the River Shannon and on its tributaries such as the River Deel, the River Maigue, Co. Limerick, and the River Feale, Co. Kerry (Went 1964; 1981). With the restoration of Charles II, a number of fisheries on the Shannon, including the 'great Salmon Weir called the Lax Weir', were granted to one Sir George Preston (Herbert 1946–7, 55). A Franciscan priest, Father Anthony MacBrody, in 1669 described the rivers Fergus and Shannon as places abounding in good stocks of salmon, eels and trout (Ó Dálaigh 1998, 41). Indeed, in 1684, as part of Limerick's attempt to prove jurisdiction over the whole length of the Shannon estuary, the city's mayor, William Gribble, sailed as far west as Scattery Island and levied a tax

Foragers, farmers and fishers

Pl. 6—*By the late seventeenth century the port of Limerick was exporting agricultural produce, textiles, timber and metal ores, while importing fruit and luxury goods from the West Indies. Thomas Phillip's prospect of Limerick (1685) shows the River Shannon's harbour and quays for the ocean-going ships that sailed up the estuary, as well as a rare view of a surviving late medieval townscape (National Library of Ireland: MS 3137 (25)).*

of 1000 herrings and 1000 oysters on each fishing boat. This tax was eventually halved, but it illustrates the richness of the region's fisheries (Lee 1997, 121).

Thousands of acres of rich corcass grasslands in south-east Clare were protected by flood banks (Ó Dálaigh 1998, 68), suggesting an expansionist agricultural economy by this time. Cole seed, a commodity first brought in by the new mid-seventeenth-century immigrant Dutch merchantmen of Limerick, was a crop grown on the marshlands (*ibid.*, 69). However, these banks were an insufficient defence against the power of nature; in 1667 and 1698 violent storms accompanied by high tides resulted in massive floods which wrecked ships, carried away buildings, levelled the banks and destroyed the crops of the surrounding fields (Kemmy 1997, xiii; Spellissy 1998, 187).

Ennis, the county town of Clare, attracted a number of merchants who were involved in the transport of hides, tallow and butter via the River Fergus to Limerick (Dinan 1987, 84; Ó Murchadha 1991, 33). In the reign of James II, the port of Limerick (Pl. 6) was exporting meat, crops, textiles, timber and ore (silver and lead from the mines of the nearby county of Tipperary). In turn, the town's merchants imported luxury goods such as oranges, lemons, West Indian sugar, coffee and tobacco (Spellissy 1998, 119–20).

The Shannon estuary in the eighteenth century

The early 1700s saw the new Protestant Ascendancy, confident of their place in Irish society, building proper country mansions with an emphasis on comfort and style rather than on security, surrounded by landscaped wooded demesnes. These grand houses can be seen around the Shannon estuary, and some (e.g. Cratloewoods, Co. Clare, Mellon House and Shannongrove House, Co. Limerick) were built to command excellent vistas across the estuary's waters. A few older residences, such as Bunratty Castle, were to be replaced by these estate houses. A surveyor in the employ of the Thomond estate, Thomas Moland, described Bunratty in 1703 as being 'the model for strength more than pleasure', and it was in a derelict state (Ó Dálaigh 1998, 80). The character of the local countryside was gradually changed with the enclosing of fields under various parliamentary acts. Thomas Moland in his survey refers to the Shannon estuary's corcass as having good agricultural value (*ibid.*, 80). Arthur Young, agriculturalist and travel writer, also noted in 1776 that there were 20,000 acres of rich corcass along the Shannon and Fergus estuaries, all suitable for both pasture and tillage

(Hutton 1970, 285, 287, 291–2).

While it took a number of decades for the Shannon region to recover from the instabilities of the seventeenth century, by the mid-eighteenth century Limerick played a part in exporting the agricultural surplus from its hinterland to other parts of the British Empire (Spellissy 1998, 199). Lloyd's *Tour of Clare*, published in 1780, mentions that there were a number of vessels from overseas daily transporting goods through the Shannon, while local cargo boats brought agricultural produce to neighbouring markets such as Ennis and Tralee. Cities and towns such as Limerick were transformed with the building of new streets based on the principles of Georgian planning and architecture. There was an active turf trade, with 70 large turf-boats transporting turf to Limerick and various other villages along the estuary (Henry 1996, 174–6). The corporation of Limerick leased the Lax Weir, while all kinds of shellfish and flat-fish stocks were being exploited further down the estuary by fishermen. About 1790, along the sides of the estuary during the month of May poorer people built temporary causeways several yards out into the water, fishing with nets for eel fry (Spellissy 1998, 186).

The Shannon estuary in the nineteenth century

During the Napoleonic Wars, the military and economic importance of the Shannon estuary was reflected by the construction of a number of forts or batteries at Kilbaha, Kilkerin, Scattery Island, Dunaha, Foynes Island, Carrig Island, Tarbert Island and Kilcredaun to prevent an invasion and to keep trade open (Henry 1996, 145; Lewis 1837, 14; Ó Danachair 1971, 63). However, unable to compete with the mass-production factories of England, indigenous industries in Ireland went into decline. During the 'Terry Alt' disturbances of 1831, caused by a fall in cereal prices and a poor potato harvest in the preceding months, three ships on the Fergus were actually boarded and arms were taken (Power 1986, 16). However, local strong farmers and landlords continued to make profits, and it was recognised by Samuel Lewis in the late 1830s that the corcass lands along the Shannon and Fergus estuary were very fertile and could produce 18–20 crops successively without any fertiliser being applied. The corcass also supported the fattening of huge numbers of cattle for export through Limerick and Cork (Lewis 1837, 16–17). An interesting social aspect of this was the fact that landless herdsmen and labourers were employed by local farmers to herd cattle on the islands and marshes; they were expected to transport the livestock there by means of their own boats, and they were also expected to save the farmer's hay and maintain his field boundaries in return for grass for their own cattle, sheep and pigs. Again, social unrest and antipathy between farmers and herdsmen was to lead to violence and death in the 'Terry Alt' disturbances of the 1830s (Enright 1981).

In the 1830s there was an active trade in turf between Poulnasharry and Limerick. This valuable fuel was transported in boats, the same vessels sometimes returning laden with limestone from Aughinish and Askeaton (Lewis 1837, 20). Passengers were also carried by boat. As early as 1817, an entrepreneur, James Patterson, owned one of the first steamboats to ply the estuary between Limerick and Kilrush. The site of the early seventeenth-century ferry point at Beagh also witnessed passenger steamers calling in, while just to the west of Beagh Castle a private pier was built to serve a nearby silver mine operated by Edward Odell-Westropp (Feheney 1998, 151). To further develop the region economically, the Commissioners for the Improvement of the River Shannon in 1837 recommended the construction of a shipping wharf at Foynes, which, along with new road links, would dispel disaffection and unrest in the area (O'Farrell 1983, 116–17). River pilots and other necessary personnel were established on Scattery Island with their families in the 1840s to facilitate a growing trade (Henry 1996, 173).

Although the sea-fishing industry of the first half of the nineteenth century was moribund, herring were still taken by boats using nets off Scattery Island. Oyster beds were also important along the narrow inlets and sandy shores of the estuary's mouth, and were harvested at Scattery Island, Querin and Poulnasharry (Lewis 1837, 23). The head weirs of the seventeenth century had mostly disappeared by 1836 when the

Foragers, farmers and fishers

Second Report of the Commissioners of Inquiry into the State of the Irish Fisheries was published (Went 1960b, 140; 1981, 109). However, salmon and eel fisheries were still thriving; stake-net weirs and bag nets were utilised on the Shannon estuary from the beginning of the 1800s (Went 1981, 109, 113). Indeed, the value of the Limerick Lax Weir is demonstrated by the series of legal cases between the leasees of the weir and the local fishermen between 1816 and 1845 (Herbert 1946–7, 57–8).

The Great Famine of the 1840s struck the people of the Shannon estuary as hard as anywhere else, wiping out the poorer rural classes by death and immigration. It also reinforced trends that were already in train, such as the growing emphasis on pastoralism and the flight from the land, resulting in an economic and social transformation of the Irish population. Transportation links (roads and railways) were improved and shops were established in every town and village to facilitate the workings of a modern market economy. A new act of parliament renamed the Limerick Bridge Commissioners as the Limerick Harbour Commissioners, allowing them to borrow £50,000 to develop the port's infrastructure. The Wet Dock, with a handling capacity of 6000–8000 tons of shipping, was built in 1857 by the Harbour Commissioners (Spellissy 1998, 236). Along the estuary, projects to increase land capacity were undertaken, such as the rebuilding of a reclamation bank in 1872 to replace an 1828 structure near Castletown by Rev. John Thomas Waller on the south side of the river (Feheney 1998, 117).

Foynes, Glin, Tarbert and Kilrush saw both local and overseas trade from the Continent and North America. The Deel estuary was a trade route; grain, fish and seaweed were landed at Askeaton, while farm produce and timber were exported (Henry 1996, 141). Foynes successfully developed as a port (Lenihan 1866, 731). Killadysert, Clarecastle and Barrington piers (near Limerick City) were utilised for the unloading of supplies for their localities, such as provisions, medicines and coal (Henry 1996, 176). However, well-settled modes of exploiting the surrounding environment were being undermined by technological advances, such as the railways and, later, road freight, which sounded the death-knell for much of this water-borne trade. Another industry phased out by progress was the extraction of sand from the riverbed for construction purposes. In one area between the Lax Weir and Island Point outside Limerick City several generations of 'sandmen' exploited this resource until the 1950s, when dryland pit sand completely superseded it (Hannan 1981).

Local farmers, labourers and other people of course continued to live and work along the estuary through the late nineteenth century and into the early twentieth century. Several islands in the Fergus estuary and the Shannon estuary (e.g. Quay Island and Saint's Island) were inhabited until the 1950s, with their lands given over to tillage and pasture (Rowe 1988). Seaweed was also gathered around these islands for fertiliser ('sea-manure'), while the sally woods and reed-beds at Rineanna were harvested for basketry and thatch (O'Carroll 1980). Small specialist fishing villages, such as that at Beagh Castle, Co. Limerick, still existed until earlier this century (Feheney 1998, 91, 155; Wilkins 1989, 304–7). Shellfish farming, carried out in the late nineteenth century, is still practised at Carrig Island, Poulnasharry and Killimer (Wilkins 1989, 184–8), and the Shannon estuary boat fishermen continue to draft-net for salmon on the tides of the upper estuary, using techniques that (judging by cartographic depictions of Limerick) go back to the late Middle Ages.

Placename evidence for landscape and economy through the historic period

Archaeological and historical sources clearly indicate, then, the long-term role of the Shannon estuary for travel and coastal wetland exploitation. Local placenames provide another interesting perspective on landscape and settlement along the Shannon estuary. Of particular importance are local townland names, which probably derive from several different periods from the early historic to the early modern period. P.W. Joyce's (1913) *Irish names of places* provides some interesting comments on the derivation of some of these names, although his etymologies are unreliable. More recent commentaries have been offered by Barry (1977) and O'Carroll (1978). The recently published and much more authoritative placename survey of County Limerick also illustrates several interesting features of the estuary wetlands (Ó Maolfabhail 1990). A number of townland names reflect the importance of the upper Shannon estuary as a harbour. For example, Coonagh East (*An Cuanach*, meaning 'haven, place of shelter') near Limerick City may refer to landing-places or creeks where smaller boats were laid up. Routeways are indicated in the name Ballinvoher ('the settlement of the road'), a townland name on the Limerick shore which may refer to a routeway leading to the seventeenth-century ferry point across the river at Beagh Castle. Various physical features are also referred to in townland names along the Clare shore, such as headlands (Rineanna—*Rinn Eanaigh*, 'wet headland' or 'bird swamp') and drumlin hills (Tullyglass—*An Tulach Ghlas*, 'green hill'; Tullyvarraga—either *Tulach Uí Mheardha*, 'O'Meara's hill', or *Tulach na Fairrge*, 'hill of the sea') (O'Carroll 1978, 32).

Certain placenames on the upper Shannon estuary may indicate ownership of the saltmarshes and reed-beds. Corkanree, near Limerick, may derive from *Corcach an Rí*, ('the marsh of the king'), possibly referring to the reservation of grazing rights on the marshes immediately downstream of the town. Clonmacken (*Cluain Maicín*, 'the meadow of Maicín'), Co. Limerick, straight across the estuary, may also indicate former water-meadow grazing rights. Clonmoney (*Cluain Muine*, 'meadow of the thicket or overgrown plain'), on the Clare bank, also indicates the use of marshy meadows along the estuary. The placename Muckinish Point on the south bank of the upper Shannon estuary derives from *Muic Inis*, 'the island of the pigs', a slightly elevated hillock of dry land within the south bank's marshes which could have been used for both protecting and grazing pigs. Other townland names on the upper Shannon estuary (although also common elsewhere throughout the country), such as Aughinish (*Each Inis*, 'horse island'), Conigar (*An Coinícéar*, 'rabbit warren'), Co. Limerick, and Garrynamona (*Garraí na móna*, 'garden by the bog'), Co. Clare, similarly suggest former economic activities. Several placenames attest to the people associated with settlement: for example, Ballymorris and Ballycasey (*Baile Uí Cathaisaigh*), Co. Clare, refer to the settlements (*baile*) of Morris and Casey (Barry 1977), while Courtbrown (the court of *An Brúnach* or *de Brún*) and Ballynash (the *baile* of *An Naiseach* or *de Nais*), Co. Limerick, similarly preserve evidence. There are also several placenames that testify to the altered landscapes of the modern estuary. Islandmagrath ('the island of MacGrath') and Islandavanna ('the island of the river') on the upper Fergus estuary, Co. Clare, are both former islands that are now enclosed within the reclaimed corcass.

Maps of the Shannon estuary since the late Middle Ages

KARL BRADY AND AIDAN O'SULLIVAN

Introduction

The Shannon estuary has been a focus for the attention of historians, travellers, writers, artists and poets for several centuries (e.g. Kemmy 1996; 1997; Spellissy 1998). Another useful perspective is provided through the work of the cartographic surveyor and mapmaker. The Shannon estuary, as a significant topographical, political and economic feature of the Irish coastline, has been depicted on a wide range of maps of Ireland since the late Middle Ages. Mapping the topography of this complex landscape has always been a difficult task, its numerous inlets, bays, headlands, smaller estuaries and expansive intertidal zones often confusing or deterring the early mapmaker from surveying the estuary with any great conviction. In the following study, the depictions of the Shannon estuary on a small selection of maps held in the National Library of Ireland and by the Neptune Gallery are discussed, with a view to tracing this gradual charting of the estuary across time; other significant published maps of the Shannon estuary can be seen in Andrews 1997 and Swift 1999.

Foragers, farmers and fishers

The Shannon estuary in late medieval maps

Ptolemy's description of Ireland, second century AD

The earliest account of the Shannon estuary is in Ptolemy's second-century AD *Guide to geography*, which provides map projections, tables of latitude and longitude and brief descriptions of places for different parts of the world. Ptolemy's accounts of Ireland were first published as a map in AD 1477. According to Petrus de Turre's *Ptolomaei Geographia*, dating from 1490, the *Auteini* and perhaps also the *Gangani* tribes were located in the general vicinity of the upper Shannon estuary (Andrews 1997; Orpen 1894). The Shannon estuary is one of the few river mouths shown on the western coastline of Ireland, signifying that Iron Age Continental traders were aware of its importance (Fig. 3).

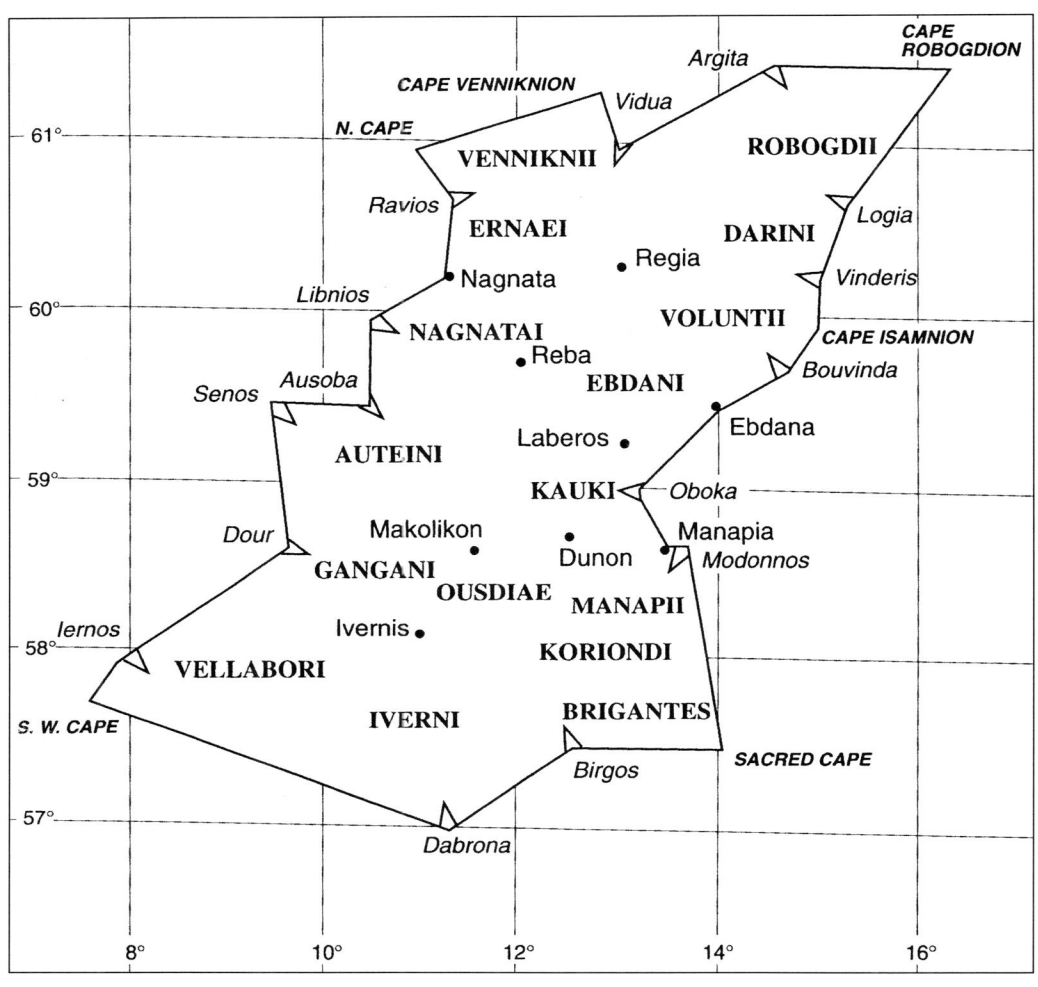

Fig. 3—*The Shannon estuary* (Senos) *on a reconstruction of Ptolemy's second-century AD description of Ireland (after Byrne 1984; Andrews 1997, fig. 2.1).*

Giraldus Cambrensis's map of Europe, c. 1200

The Shannon estuary is marked as the *Sinnenus* on Giraldus Cambrensis's depiction of Ireland in his map of Europe (drawn *c.* 1200). Limerick City (*Limericum*) is shown near the mouth of the estuary, which is undifferentiated from the rest of the River Shannon. The River Shannon itself is shown as having two outlets, a confusion arising from the belief that the River Erne and the River Shannon were one river (O'Loughlin 2000). The Shannon estuary was probably included because of its reputation as a sheltered harbour, a landmark for sailors, a fishing-ground and, most importantly, as a navigation route to Limerick City (Fig. 4). Indeed, Giraldus Cambrensis saw the Shannon as Ireland's principal river, stating that

'The Shannon rightly holds the chief place among all the rivers of Ireland
. . . on account of the magnificence of its size, its long meanderings, and

Introduction

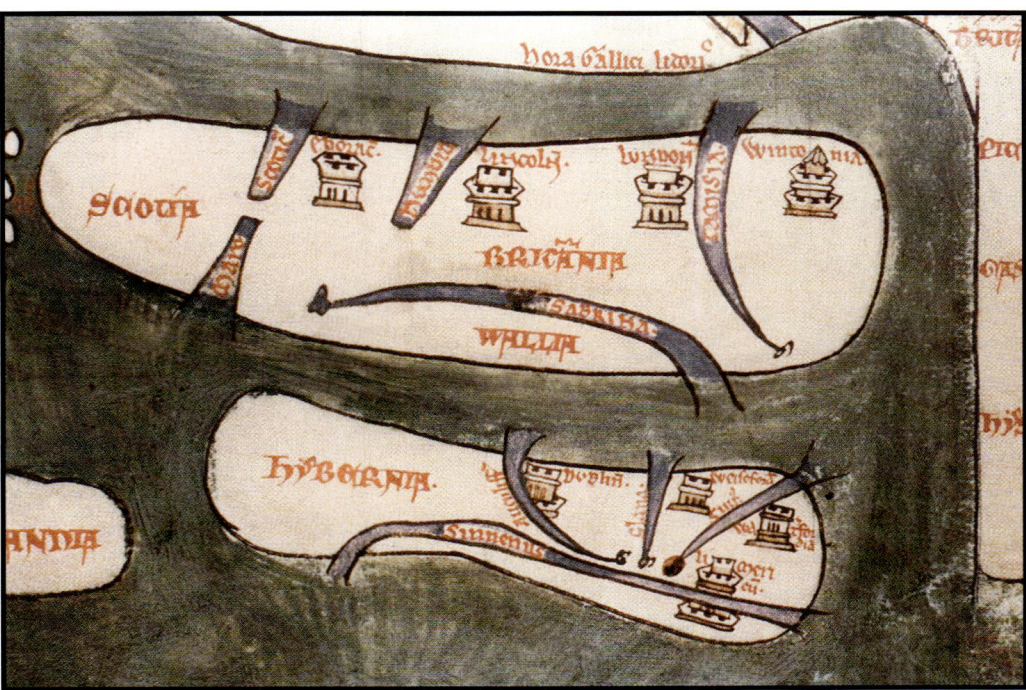

Fig. 4—*The Shannon estuary depicted (at bottom right) on Giraldus Cambrensis's early thirteenth-century map of Ireland (National Library of Ireland, MS 700).*

the abundance of fish . . . [it] takes in Limerick, and separating the two Munsters from one another for a distance of one hundred miles and more, pours itself into the Brendanican sea' (*Topographia Hiberniae*).

Italian and Catalan portolan charts of the late Middle Ages
In the fourteenth and fifteenth centuries, Italian and Catalan sea charts, commonly called portolans, were intended to facilitate economic contact and trade around Atlantic Europe. In his study of the Italian maps of the Irish coast Westropp (1913) notes that they recorded over 150 names of ports, safe harbours, inlets and towns suitable for seagoing vessels. The Shannon estuary is shown as a small, featureless inlet on most of the portolans. For example, in the portolan chart of Angelino Dulcert, drawn *c.* 1339, it is depicted as a funnel-shaped embayment, with an island near its mouth (Fig. 5). This may be one of the earliest depictions of Scattery Island, reflecting its significance for mariners. The medieval town of Limerick or *Laymerich* is shown in its correct location at the head of the estuary (Andrews 1997).

The Shannon estuary in sixteenth-century maps

Gerard Mercator's maps, 1564/1595
By the middle of the sixteenth century a new era of mapmaking emerged, as cartographers such as John Goghes, Gerard Mercator and Baptista Boazio became interested not only in coastal ports and towns but also in mapping the interior of Ireland. These mapmakers were usually politically motivated, as they followed the armies involved in the Tudor reconquest of Ireland. Gerard Mercator is one of the most famous of all, born in Flanders in 1512 and responsible for the most original maps of the island since Ptolemy (Andrews 1997, 26). Mercator's map of 1564 (entitled *Angliae Scotiae et Hiberniae nova descriptio*) is reckoned as a milestone in the cartography of Ireland. In this map (see Andrews 1997, fig. 2.8) the Shannon estuary (*Shenyn fluvius*) is shown as a long straight channel, only narrowing and curving at the River Maigue before continuing to Limerick. The Fergus estuary and its many islands are presented only as a smaller river. Scattery Island (*Ines catty*) is shown in the outer estuary, and an unnamed island, most likely Foynes, is in the middle of the estuary. Early mapmakers had a tendency to populate blank spaces with islands and consequently the islands are

Fig. 5—*The Shannon estuary and the medieval town of* Laymerich *as shown on an Italian portolan chart of c. 1339 (after Westropp 1913; Andrews 1997, fig. 2.2).*

shown as over-prominent landmarks (Andrews 1997, 1). However, Scattery Island figures prominently in many of these early maps, presumably because of its beacons, anchorage and pilots. The importance of several ports on the upper estuary is also indicated by their inclusion, with both Askeaton (prominently depicted) and Bunratty (wrongly located) shown, while Limerick (*Lymhrich*) itself is accurately shown as being on an island.

Baptista Boazio's maps of Ireland, 1599–1609

In 1599 the Italian artist and cartographer Baptista Boazio produced an attractive and highly influential map of Ireland (Andrews 1997, 59; Moroney 1998, 21). In Boazio's *Irlandiae accurata descriptio*, published *c.* 1609, the upper Shannon estuary is still portrayed as even in width along its entire length (Fig. 6). Otherwise, rivers, islands, headlands, towns and castles are all faithfully recorded. *Enis Catu* (Scattery Island), Carrig Island (off Ballylongford, Co. Kerry) and probably Foynes Island are shown. Smaller islands are also located in the upper Shannon estuary, indicating by now the presence of the various shoals and rock outcrops that are exposed at low tide. The Fergus estuary is depicted in a manner close to its true shape, with six unnamed islands more or less evenly spread throughout its length, and the River Maigue (*Flu. May*) is prominently depicted. Most striking of all are the numerous towns and castles shown along both shores, including, merely for example, *Cargonia* and *Newton* (possibly Creggaun and Newtown, Co. Limerick), *Pallace* (Pallaskenry, Co. Limerick) and *Donratte* (Bunratty, Co. Clare). Castles depicted include *C. Nash* (Ballynash) on the River Deel, *C. Cratelough* (Cratloe, Co. Clare) and *C. Donel* (Castle Donnell, Co. Clare). The depiction of these castles reflects their visibility and continuing importance as settlements in the early seventeenth century. Indeed, Limerick City (*Limmerick*) itself is almost lost amongst all the names of places and people shown along the estuary's banks.

Introduction

Fig. 6—*The Shannon estuary as depicted on Baptista Boazio's map of Ireland, published c. 1609 (reproduced by courtesy of the Neptune Gallery).*

John Speed's 'The kingdome of Irland', 1612

By the time of John Speed's map of Ireland, published in his *Theatre of the empire of Great Britaine* in 1612, recent Irish rebellions had been subdued and the way was clear for the English government to continue to properly map and survey the island. In Speed's map of Ireland and his provincial map of Munster there is a big improvement on Boazio's depiction of the Shannon estuary. However, the size of the upper Shannon estuary and the Fergus estuary is exaggerated, and the resulting open spaces are populated with overly enlarged islands. Speed's map also includes many placenames and most of the larger towns and villages along the estuary, including Tarbet, Co. Kerry, Glin, Co. Limerick, and Bunratty, Co. Clare.

Maps and surveys of the Shannon estuary in the seventeenth century

Dutch maps

In the seventeenth century Dutch maps continued to have a strong influence, although in Ireland they were often more or less based on the work of Mercator, Boazio and Speed. This can be clearly seen in a number of Dutch maps, including Janson's

Foragers, farmers and fishers

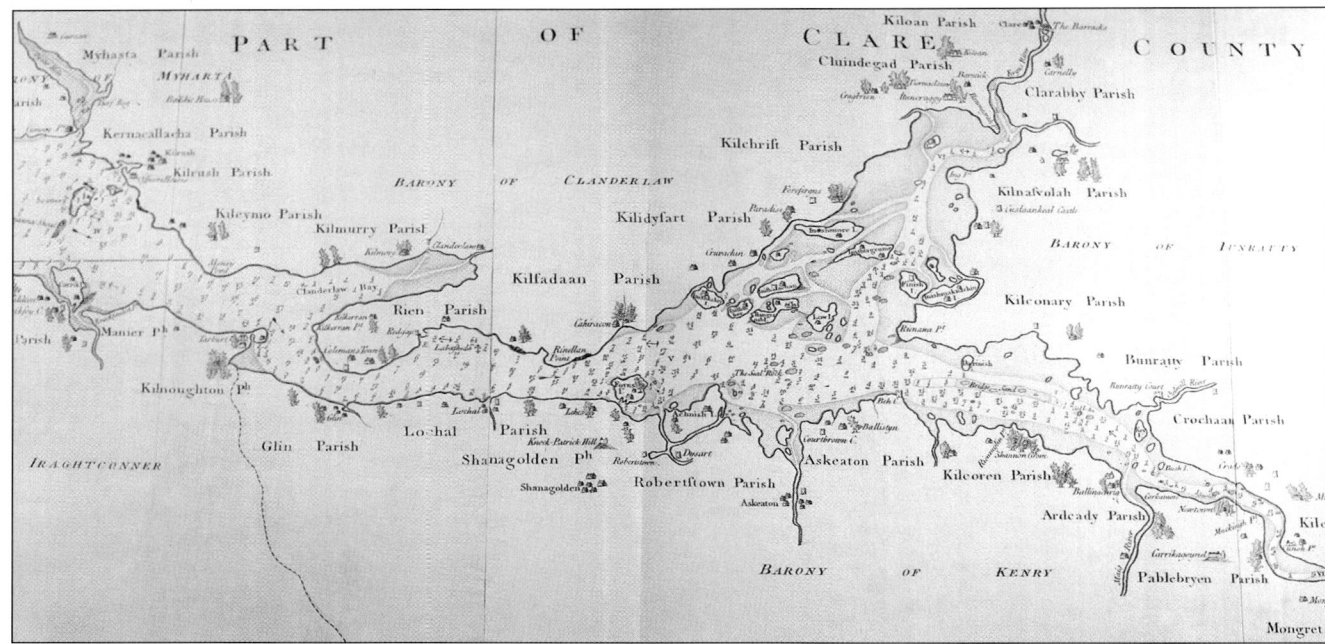

Fig. 7—*Murdoch MacKenzie's chart of the upper Shannon estuary and Fergus estuary published in 1776 in* A maritim survey of Ireland and the west of Great Britain *(reproduced by courtesy of the Neptune Gallery).*

(1636), Sanson's (1665) and F. de Wit's (1680) maps of Ireland. They all depict the Shannon estuary in a similar way, showing a curving entrance into the too-wide estuary. Although attractive to modern eyes, the Dutch maps are not remembered for transforming Irish cartography. Interestingly, however, one sixteenth-century Dutch cartographer, Blaeu, was among the first to carry out pioneering work with the mapping of the intertidal zone around Ireland. This type of survey mainly dealt with the harbours and focused purely on the shape of the coastline and the intertidal zone, leaving the interior of the country blank.

The 'Down Survey', 1654–6

Throughout the mid-seventeenth century, surveys and mapping continued with a view to accelerating land confiscations. William Petty, responsible for some of the greatest advances in the cartography of Ireland, is mainly remembered for his work on the Down Survey (1654–6), which aimed to map and record all the land in Ireland held by Catholic proprietors at the outbreak of the confederate rebellion in 1641. These lands would then be handed over to Cromwellian soldiers and other adventurers. On the Shannon estuary, Clare was not surveyed as this had already been done during the earlier Strafford Survey, carried out in 1640. Limerick was mapped, the upper Shannon estuary was shown in some detail and territorial boundaries were included, although Petty did not utilise the earlier maritime surveys by Blaeu, thus leaving out various details of the coastline, islands and intertidal zone. Nevertheless, the Down Survey maps do provide some hints as to coastal change along the estuary, particularly the process of land reclamation in the seventeenth century. For example, indentations on the coastline east of the River Maigue at Carrigdirty Rock, on the Limerick shore of the upper estuary, can be compared with ancient banks in the corcass, suggesting that they originated in the sixteenth or seventeenth century.

Maps and maritime surveys in the eighteenth century

Maritime surveys

By the late eighteenth century, accurate coastal maps had become necessary owing to increased shipping in harbours and shipping channels. Without good knowledge of the location of rock outcrops and anchorage points, or of safe shipping channels, a simple journey along the Shannon estuary could end in disaster (and often did, as can be seen in Chapter 7). Murdoch MacKenzie in 1776 published *A maritim survey of Ireland and the west of Great Britain*, printed as an atlas; the single chart devoted to the Shannon estuary showed it at low tide (Fig. 7). This was the first accurate map of the Shannon estuary, with soundings and anchorages depicted throughout. Many of the upper estuary's islands (e.g. Foyns I, Dorinish, Key I, Bush I) were positioned correctly, and intertidal rock outcrops and shoals (Bridge sand, Scarlets) were no longer confused with permanent islands. Prominent settlements are also shown to aid mariners, such as Beh C. (Beagh Castle) and Bunratty Court, on the 'Oylmill River' (the Owenagarney River, which led to Oil Mills upstream at Sixmilebridge). Although the reclamation of corcass on the upper Fergus estuary and at Bunratty had been accomplished by this time, at other places—for example between Ringmoylan and Beh C., on the south bank—some islands were still isolated out on the mudflats. MacKenzie's work was so good that when L. Whittle published *A new and exact hydrographic survey of the River Shannon from Limerick to the sea* in 1794 there was little scope for further improvement. The coastline had to be defined with slightly more accuracy and some of the channels had since shifted slightly on the mudflats, but essentially little new had to be added.

Henry Pelham, 1787

Most of the maps discussed here are national or regional maps, but obviously local county and estate maps depict the estuary in closer detail. In particular, the Shannon and Fergus estuaries were mapped in Henry Pelham's 1787 map of County Clare, produced for the 'Grand Jury of the County' (Harbison 1999). It was published in twelve sheets at a scale of 0.9 miles to an inch, a scale that was not to be surpassed until the production of the Ordnance Survey maps in the 1840s. Pelham's map is extremely detailed, showing an accurate Shannon estuary coastline even by today's standards. Its portrayal of the Shannon estuary intertidal zone and mudflats is excellent, and even extremely localised changes in creeks, mudflats and marshes can be traced today (Fig. 8). Islandavanna, Co. Clare, on the Fergus estuary, for example, is still shown as an island, prior to its enclosure within corcass sea-banks in the 1880s (Connors 1999).

The Ordnance Survey of Ireland in the nineteenth century

Many maps, too numerous to mention, were produced in Ireland by various individuals and bodies in the early nineteenth century, including government estate maps, private estate maps, and regional and county maps. However, the most significant development was the establishment of the Ordnance Survey of Ireland in 1824, whose main aim was to survey and measure the townlands of Ireland for taxation purposes (Reeves-Smyth 1983). The Ordnance Survey's first and second edition six-inch maps have traditionally been the main series used by Irish archaeologists in archaeological surveys, landscape projects, and monument management and protection schemes. The Shannon estuary is depicted in these six-inch maps in a highly accurate and detailed fashion, showing settlements, antiquities, townlands, parish and barony boundaries, roads and fields, as well as the essential elements of drainage, vegetation and topography. The low-water mark of estuary channels is shown, as are coastal marshes, sea walls, fish-weirs, harbours, jetties, piers and causeways. Rock outcrops are also defined on the intertidal zone, as well as different areas of sand, mud and silt. Indeed, comparison of the various editions of the maps can aid study of local changes in the estuary landscape.

Conclusion

The cartographic depiction of the Shannon estuary evolved slowly according to the political and economic demands of the times. Prior to the nineteenth century, most (if not all) Irish maps were produced by Continental surveyors such as the Dutch and French, or on behalf of the English administration. People who knew well the

Foragers, farmers and fishers

Fig. 8—*The upper Shannon estuary and Fergus estuary in Henry Pelham's map of Clare, 1787 (Phoenix Maps, reproduced by courtesy of the Neptune Gallery).*

intricacies of the Shannon estuary or who lived in that watery landscape were not involved. However, the maps do provide interesting information on both the perception of and, to a slightly lesser extent, the character of the Shannon estuary at the time of their making. The late medieval Italian and Catalan portolan charts represented the Shannon estuary from a maritime perspective, indicating its importance as a seaway and port. In the sixteenth century, national and regional maps show a rough outline of the estuary and some of its key topographical details. By the seventeenth century, major surveys by William Petty and the Down Survey maps offer more detailed clues to changes in the estuary landscape. In the eighteenth century, with concerns over shipping losses around the island, the Shannon estuary was mapped by maritime surveys, with channels, shoals and anchorages shown in greater detail, so that by the mid-nineteenth century the Shannon estuary emerges cartographically as a dynamic wetland landscape.

Introduction

Origins and evolution of the Shannon estuary intertidal survey

AIDAN O'SULLIVAN

Introduction

A wide range of archaeological, historical, placename and cartographic evidence indicates that the Shannon estuary has served as a defining political, social and economic feature of the region since earliest times. However, until recently there was no archaeological evidence for the social and economic activities of local people on the estuary itself, its marshes, creeks and mudflats. Indeed, this lack of knowledge about the archaeology of past estuarine and coastal landscapes has been typical of Irish archaeology generally before 1992.

In spring 1992, the Shannon estuary region became the focus of a major archaeological research project, when the North Munster Project was established in the Discovery Programme with a brief to investigate the societies of this part of south-west Ireland during the Late Bronze Age and Iron Age. The project was to be a regional landscape study, within which it was intended that a wide range of integrated archaeological, historical and palaeoenvironmental data would be used. Archaeological excavation, survey, aerial photography, archive research and artefactual research were all to be employed to tease out aspects of the periods.

It was also proposed that smaller-scale thematic studies would be carried out, preferably using innovative and unique archaeological techniques to study little-known aspects of the past landscape. Thus between 1992 and 1997 the North Munster Project embarked on an intertidal archaeological survey of the Shannon estuary, the first to be carried out on the Irish coast. In contrast, the archaeological potential of estuarine and coastal wetlands has long been known in some regions of Britain, and the history of these developments provides the academic and methodological background to the Shannon estuary surveys.

History of intertidal archaeology in Britain

Arguably, intertidal survey as an archaeological technique began on the Essex coast, in south-east England. In the 1930s, Hazzeldine Warren, Stuart Piggott and others investigated the submerged 'Lyonesse' or old ground surface of the Essex coastal intertidal zone. Their work indicated that Late Neolithic Grooved Ware and 'pit dwellings' and Early Bronze Age wooden structures were actually preserved *in situ* on the ancient land surface that was exposed to view at low tide (Warren *et al.* 1936). At about the same time, Edward V. Wright and his brother were investigating exposed Holocene peats on the intertidal zone at North Ferriby, on the south bank of the Humber estuary, leading to a sequence of discoveries of Middle Bronze Age boats of European archaeological significance (Wright 1976; 1990; Buckland *et al.* 1990; Ellis and Crowther 1990). More recently, Middle Bronze Age trackways have also been excavated on the Humber estuary at Melton (Van de Noort and Ellis 1999). After the early Humber estuary and Essex coast investigations, large-scale intertidal surveys and excavations were not really carried out again in England until the Hullbridge Basin survey (on the Essex coast) in the 1980s around the Crouch, Stour and Blackwater estuaries. Neolithic occupation sites on submerged soils, Bronze Age and Iron Age trackways in estuarine clays (Wilkinson 1986; 1989; Wilkinson and Murphy 1986; 1988; 1995), and recent discoveries of Anglo-Saxon fishtraps on the mudflats of the Blackwater estuary (Gilman 1998; Strachan 1997; 1998a; 1988b) all indicate the continuous importance of these harsh but bountiful landscapes to local communities.

However, there is little doubt that the Severn estuary, especially the Welsh shore, has been the most significant focus of intertidal archaeological survey and excavation in recent years, following on from the remarkable discoveries made on the Gwent foreshore during the 1970s and 1980s by Derek Upton, the local Gwent coastal warden. This work has also been pioneered by the various individuals and institutions involved

Foragers, farmers and fishers

in the Severn Estuary Levels Research Committee (e.g. Green 1989; Whittle 1989; Bell and Neumann 1998; Nayling 1993). Mesolithic human and animal footprints preserved in ancient submerged alluvial clays have been recorded at Uskmouth (Aldhouse-Green *et al.* 1993). Bronze Age post alignments, wattle structures and the remains of a plank-built boat have been recovered from former tidal creeks at Caldicot on the Gwent levels (Nayling and Caseldine 1997; Nayling 1993), and Bronze Age settlements have been recorded on the foreshore at Chapeltump, Magor Pill and Rumney Great Wharf (Whittle 1989; Allen 1996; Bell and Neumann 1998). Remarkable Iron Age rectangular houses spectacularly preserved in an intertidal peat shelf at Goldcliff have been the subject of particularly detailed archaeological and palaeoenvironmental investigations (Bell 1992a; 1992b; 1992c; 1993a; 1993b; 1995; Bell and Neumann 1996; 1997; 1998). Roman and medieval ships have been located at Barlands Farm and Magor Pill (Nayling 1996; 1997; 1998), and Anglo-Saxon and Norman fishtraps have been excavated on the mudflats at Sudbrook (Godbold and Turner 1993; 1994). The Gwent Levels have also been the location for probably the most detailed investigation in the UK of coastal wetland reclamation in the historic period (Rippon 1995a; 1995b; 1996; 1997). In brief, the Severn estuary remains one of the most exciting locations for intertidal archaeological research in these islands.

Coastal and intertidal archaeology is now a subject of increasing interest in Britain (Fulford *et al.* 1997), following on from intertidal survey projects carried out at various locations around the English, Scottish and Welsh coasts. The intertidal surveys of the Isles of Scilly pioneered by Thomas (1985) were more recently followed up by more intensive archaeological and palaeoenvironmental investigations there (e.g. Ratcliffe and Straker 1996). There have also been intertidal surveys of Chichester Harbour in Sussex (Cartwright 1984; Darvill 1987, 58) and Portsmouth Harbour in Hampshire (R. Bradley and Hooper 1973; Darvill 1987, 58), as well as some work on Hartlepool Bay, Cleveland, in north-east England (Tooley 1978; 1980; Innes *et al.* 1991). At Wootton-Quarr, on the north shore of the Isle of Wight, a major intertidal survey project funded by English Heritage and the Isle of Wight Council was carried out over a five-year period along a 4km stretch of coast. The Wootton-Quarr survey and excavations revealed possible Neolithic fishtraps and trackways, Late Bronze Age and Anglo-Saxon post alignments, and Anglo-Saxon fishtraps. Palaeoenvironmental investigations were also carefully integrated into the project, including studies of sea-level change, pollen analysis, and diatom and beetle studies (Loader *et al.* 1997). Significant intertidal survey has also been carried out recently on the Thames estuary by a combination of student, academic and local volunteer labour, investigating the alluvium and intertidal foreshore upstream of, within and downstream of the city of London (Allen *et al.* 1997; Milne *et al.* 1997; Haughey 1999).

History of intertidal archaeology in Ireland

In contrast, there is virtually no tradition of intertidal archaeological survey in Ireland, although it is possible to trace some brief early interest amongst Irish antiquarians in intertidal archaeological material. In 1800 a Late Bronze Age gold dress-fastener was found on the strand at Youghal, Co. Cork. A local antiquarian noted at the time that 'the strand at Youghal is generally covered with sand or sea silt but frequently the violence of the sea and waves, wash away the sand when underneath is discovered a bog, thick set with stumps of fallen trees which extend a considerable way under the sea. When this happens a number of curious remains of antiquity are washed on shore, such as arms [*sic*], rings, bracelets, etc.' (Cahill 1998, 43–4). Archaeological finds were also recorded by W.H. Patterson in the intertidal zone of the County Down coast in 1891. These archaeological deposits were exposed when the sea removed the fine, silty sand from the muddy foreshore. The finds included at least 200 unrolled, black-stained flints, including cores, chips and possible hammerstones. There was also a possible hearth and three pieces of split bone, of ox, deer and wild boar (Patterson 1892).

In 1879 a possible crannog or lake-dwelling was recorded on the coastal foreshore

Introduction

at Ardmore Harbour, Co. Waterford, after erosion of a sandy beach exposed a wooden structure in a bed of peat beside a small stream that ran down the foreshore (Ussher 1903; Ussher and Kinahan 1879; Wood-Martin 1886). The structure consisted of a large circular wooden palisade, measuring '100ft' in diameter, constructed of a double row of oak piles, pointed at their lower ends, which were driven to depths of between '1 and 4ft' into the peat. The peat inside the palisade was studded with stakes, upright split oak planks and post-and-wattle fences. Finds included animal bone, a carved wooden handle, a wooden disc with a central perforation, and a cradle of green twigs with leaves in it. The description of the site indicates that it was most probably a wetland settlement constructed in coastal fens or saltmarshes that were protected from the sea by coastal dunes or some other natural barrier. Unfortunately there is no trace of these deposits today, and marine erosion appears to have completely destroyed the last vestiges of both the structure and the peat in which it was found.

In the twentieth century Irish archaeologists displayed little interest in intertidal archaeology. Ironically, the best work was done by a non-archaeologist, Arthur E.J. Went, who as an officer with the Irish Fisheries Board carried out extensive historical research and fieldwork on Irish fisheries in rivers, estuaries and coastal waters. Indeed, Went's work has proven to be an immeasurably important contribution to the maritime and coastal archaeology of north-west Europe. In recording the dying tradition of Irish fishing techniques, he preserved the gradually fading knowledge of the methods of constructing, repairing and using fishtraps. He recorded several coastal fishtraps during his fieldwork, notably the stone fishtraps at Doonbeg Bay, Co. Clare (Went 1946, 190; 1964), the wooden traps at Castlebellingham, Co. Louth (Went 1946), and the tidal fish-weirs in Waterford Harbour (Went 1946; 1959). Despite the scarcely believable flood of publications produced in academic journals by Arthur Went during his career (e.g. Went 1945; 1946; 1948; 1950; 1953; 1956; 1958; 1959; 1960a; 1960b; 1961; 1964; 1966; 1969a; 1969b; 1976; 1981), it does not appear to have occurred to any Irish archaeologists of his time that the physical remains of these historically confirmed medieval fishtraps might be worth looking for.

In contrast, Irish historical geographers have occasionally noted the presence of ancient structures on the coastal foreshore. Estyn Evans (1951; 1957) described two stone fishtraps at Newcastle, Co. Down, and also discussed the use of stone 'field-systems' on the intertidal zone at Millin Bay for the harvesting of kelp and wrack for fertiliser and industry. Irish geographers have also shown interest in intertidal peat deposits, especially as they pertain to studies of sea-level rise and environmental change. Frank Mitchell (1989, 100) described field walls submerged in *Phragmites* peat dated to the early Iron Age on the foreshore at Reenroe, Ballinskelligs, Co. Kerry. Ancient field walls exposed on the foreshore at low tide are also known from An Trá Mór on Inis Mór, the largest of the Aran Islands, although these may be more related to coastal erosion of dunes. Recently, cultivation ridges in peats have also been recorded during the Iveragh archaeological survey on the foreshore at Fahamore, Co. Kerry (O'Sullivan and Sheehan 1997).

The Shannon estuary intertidal survey, initiated in 1992, was therefore the first attempt by Irish archaeologists to systematically explore the archaeology of the coastal foreshore. Since then, however, other projects have also taken up the challenge. In the Republic of Ireland, intertidal survey projects have now been carried out on Baltimore Harbour, Co. Cork (Kelleher 1998), Waterford Harbour, the Boyne estuary, Lough Mahon in Cork Harbour (Donal Boland, pers. comm.), and Killala Bay, Co. Mayo (Karl Brady and Eoin Kiernan, pers. comm.). In Northern Ireland, certainly the most sustained intertidal surveys carried out on the island have explored the archaeology of Strangford Lough (Williams 1996; O'Sullivan *et al*. 1996; 1997), while intertidal surveys have also been undertaken at Ardglass (Colin Breen, pers. comm.) and Dundrum Bay, Co. Down (Deirdre O'Hara, pers. comm.). Further intertidal surveys are planned for elsewhere in Northern Ireland (McErlean *et al*. 1998). At the time of writing, environmental impact assessments of intertidal archaeology are now being routinely carried out as part of the planning process in coastal developments, and several commercial archaeological companies routinely advertise intertidal survey as one of the services they offer.

Origins of the Shannon estuary intertidal survey

The origins of the Shannon estuary intertidal survey lie in my own involvement in coastal wetland archaeological projects on the Severn estuary in the early 1990s. At this time, the local community of academic and contract archaeologists working in south Wales were beginning to recognise the unique and significant archaeological and palaeoenvironmental deposits (particularly of Late Bronze Age and Iron Age date) that were being exposed on the coastal foreshore of the Welsh shore of the Severn. Almost as importantly, it was also realised that this archaeological resource was under threat from both natural coastal erosion and development projects (particularly the construction of new bridges and industrial sites). This was an exciting time to be an archaeologist in south Wales, and wetland conferences regularly hummed with news of the latest discoveries. While I was working as a wood specialist on the Caldicot Bronze Age wetland excavations and for the Cadw intertidal archaeological project on the medieval fishtraps at Sudbrook, it gradually dawned on me that this was a type of landscape entirely unexplored by Irish archaeology. I returned home at Christmas 1991, a time also of some excitement and optimism in Irish archaeology. However, of particular interest to me was the news that the newly established Discovery Programme was initiating a major archaeological project directed by Dr Eoin Grogan on the north Munster region in later prehistory.

Obviously, given the fact that the north Munster region contained Ireland's largest estuary, there was now a chance to do an intertidal survey. I approached Eoin with a suggestion to include such a survey in his project design; he promptly agreed, and we prepared a preliminary outline of how the work might begin. In spring 1992 I returned to Wales to work again as a wood specialist on the Caldicot excavations. At weekends I was lucky enough to get Derek Upton to bring me out onto the Severn mudflats at Magor Pill and Cold Harbour Pill, where he introduced me to the techniques of how to recognise ancient structures and how to move around this potentially treacherous and life-threatening landscape. In June 1992, back home on the Shannon estuary, I took my first nervous steps onto the mudflats and began, slowly at first and with little real understanding, a survey of the archaeology of the Shannon estuary mudflats.

Aims, objectives and evolution of the Shannon estuary intertidal survey

The survey gradually evolved within the North Munster Project as a thematic study, aimed at widening the scope of our understanding of the use of later prehistoric landscapes in the region. Its main aims were:

(1) to confirm the potential of the intertidal zone for archaeological research in Ireland;

(2) to investigate the character, date, contexts and condition of prehistoric and historic archaeological sites in the chosen intertidal survey areas on the Shannon estuary, concentrating on any later prehistoric sites in particular;

(3) to integrate these intertidal sites with the archaeology of the surrounding drylands, to achieve an understanding of the social and economic role of the Shannon estuary's coastal wetlands in the later prehistoric period.

We soon realised that unique archaeological sites of all periods, from early prehistory to the post-medieval period, were to be seen on the Shannon estuary foreshore. The research emphasis shifted at an early stage towards the investigation of sites of all periods (early prehistoric to post-medieval). A preliminary literature and

Introduction

cartographic review was undertaken out to establish a basic methodology. Intertidal surveys were first carried out by a team of three in June 1992 along the east side of the upper Fergus estuary, Co. Clare, in Clonderalaw Bay, Co. Clare, and in Rinevalla Bay, Co. Clare. In all these areas, much of our time was spent hauling ourselves through deep, soft muds that we now know completely bury and hide any potential archaeological sites. However, the initial results of that season were promising enough. They included a post-and-wattle fishtrap fence on the Fergus estuary (which was to be radiocarbon-dated to the early historic period in spring 1993) (O'Sullivan 1993–4; 1994) and Neolithic submerged forests in Poulnasharry Bay and Rinevalla Bay (O'Sullivan 1996a), as well as a number of post-medieval fishtraps in Clonderalaw Bay (O'Sullivan 1993).

In spring 1993 I carried out a brief two-week season of work on the Deel estuary, Co. Limerick (with a few days on the lower Shannon estuary), by myself (not to be recommended), leading to the recording of what later proved to be a complex of medieval fishtraps (O'Sullivan 1995b). Over a three-week season in summer 1994, two of us walked the south bank of the upper Shannon estuary, from Cooperhill to the Maigue estuary, as well as a limited area on the west side of the upper Fergus estuary. This season revealed the first hints of the extraordinary Neolithic and Bronze Age occupation material from Carrigdirty Rock (although our initial interpretation of the chronology of these sites was in error), as well as a Late Bronze Age structure on the Fergus estuary (O'Sullivan 1995a; 1996b) and the numerous post-medieval fishtraps around Bush Island and Graigue Island. In autumn 1995 we carried out surveys over about three weeks in August and September, concentrating on the north shore of the upper Shannon estuary, from Bunratty eastwards to Meelick Rocks, with discoveries of remarkable medieval fishtraps on the great expanse of mudflats south of Bunratty (O'Sullivan 1997a) and the Neolithic submerged forest and stone axe at Meelick Rocks. In 1996, owing to my involvement with the Strangford Lough survey in Northern Ireland, the Shannon estuary survey was limited to a couple of weeks' work based around site visits (typically to Carrigdirty Rock) for archaeological sampling, initial palaeoenvironmental coring and instrument surveying, in May and July 1996. Our final main phase of fieldwork was in February 1997, when, thanks to financial support from Shannon Heritage and Banquets, it was possible to carry out archaeological excavations of the medieval fishtraps at Bunratty, Co. Clare (O'Sullivan 1997a; O'Sullivan and Daly 1999). This was the first time that a team of archaeologists was assembled to target a specific task, and the quality of the information was consequently greatly enhanced. Finally, in July 2000 a two-day visit to photograph some previously identified fishtraps at Bush Island for this monograph led to the discovery of eighteen new sites, some potentially of medieval date.

In summary, the Shannon estuary survey was typically carried out over a three-week period each summer or autumn between 1992 and 1997, generally in August or September, usually at the same time as the North Munster Project's archaeological excavations at Mooghaun hillfort (when accommodation, equipment and staff were available). It has to be admitted that this was not a lot of time for an archaeological survey; by the end it hardly amounted to more than a total of about fourteen weeks' survey and excavation, carried out by a small survey team of two, and very occasionally three, archaeologists. Yet even during each brief season's fieldwork, each day's survey on the mudflats typically produced at least one new prehistoric or medieval site. Although in hindsight we can see clearly that the intertidal surveys were producing astonishing archaeology and would have repaid a greater investment of time and resources, it has to be remembered that these resources were simply not available as the Discovery Programme was then carrying out several large-scale landscape and excavation research projects (the Tara Project, the Western Stone Forts Project, the North Munster Project and the Ballyhoura Hills Project). Each of these projects required substantial levels of funding and human resources, while the Discovery Programme was also committed to carrying out several other small-scale projects and educational tasks.

Pl. 7—*Aerial view of the upper Shannon estuary, looking towards the south-east and the location of the main intertidal archaeological sites at Bunratty, Quay Island, Bush Island and, on the far bank, Carrigdirty Rock (photo: Oscar Merne).*

A more significant, and indeed critical, flaw was our failure to establish an integrated palaeoenvironmental research programme in tandem with the intertidal survey. In 1995, stratigraphical coring and palaeoenvironmental sampling were begun at the Neolithic/Bronze Age sites at Carrigdirty Rock and the Bronze Age site at Islandmagrath. Indeed, a student dissertation was written on pollen and lithological studies on peats in the saltmarsh cliff at Islandmagrath (Malone 1996). Unfortunately, for various reasons, it was not possible to carry this palaeoenvironmental work on to full completion, leaving us largely in the dark about many aspects of the environmental contexts of the archaeology found on the Shannon estuary. However, these archaeological and palaeoenvironmental sites are still there and could certainly now be the subject of more detailed multidisciplinary investigations.

The study areas—the upper Shannon estuary and the Fergus estuary

The Shannon estuary is the largest inlet on the Irish coast, with several hundred kilometres of intertidal zone exposed along the indented coastlines, bays and islands of counties Clare, Limerick and Kerry. The obvious constraints of time, resources and personnel outlined above meant that it would never have been possible to carry out a total survey. The Shannon estuary intertidal survey therefore concentrated on two main study areas: the upper Shannon estuary and the upper Fergus estuary.

On the upper Shannon estuary (Pl. 7) the study area comprised the south bank from below Limerick to the Maigue estuary, and a short stretch from Beagh Castle to the Deel estuary (the area between the Maigue estuary and Beagh Castle was only briefly surveyed and is largely a vast, featureless mudflat of deep silt, with modern reclamation having removed previous creeks and inlets). On the north bank, intertidal survey was carried out from below Limerick to about Saint's Island, with a rapid survey onwards to Rineanna (i.e. Shannon Airport). On the Fergus estuary, the study area was

Introduction

concentrated mostly on the narrow upper part of the estuary, from Inch to Clarecastle on the east shore and from Islandavanna to Clarecastle on the west shore. There was also some intertidal survey on the vast, soft mudflats to the north of Clenagh on the east bank and in the area of Crininis on the west bank (although nothing of archaeological significance was found in either zone). No surveys were carried out amongst the myriad channels and flats around the lower Fergus estuary's many islands, although these would certainly be worth exploring in future. A few weeks of intertidal survey were also carried out in 1992 and 1993 on the lower Shannon estuary, at Clonderalaw Bay, Poulnasharry Bay and Rinevalla Bay, Co. Clare, and Bunaclugga Bay, Co. Kerry, mostly leading to the identification of submerged forests.

Within the upper Shannon estuary and the Fergus estuary study areas, the project also focused on specific places. These included the Carrigdirty Rock foreshore, Co. Limerick, the mudflats immediately south of Bunratty, Co. Clare, and the north bank from Bush Island to Meelick Rocks. This focus on particular places resulted from a need to maximise the archaeological record from sites of known significance. Obviously, detailed archaeological survey at one place against a more general approach to the wider space of the estuary foreshore has led to a spatial bias. However, the Shannon estuary foreshore is not a blank, abstract space on which a survey grid can be imposed rigidly. For example, there were spaces within the study areas where survey was not carried out simply because of the dangers of walking across deep, soft muds. In addition, there are islands and isolated mudbanks on the lower Fergus estuary and on the upper Shannon estuary that can only be reached by boat, a means of transport that was not available to us during the early stages.

Perhaps the most significant location identified was Carrigdirty Rock, on the south shore of the upper Shannon estuary, Co. Limerick. Here the Shannon estuary channel swings to the south, thus eroding a narrow ribbon of mudflats between the marshes and the channel. At the west end of this foreshore lies Carrigdirty Rock itself, an outcrop of limestone bedrock which is almost entirely submerged at high water. Along the foreshore to the east of the island lie a complex intercalated series of Holocene environmental deposits, comprising sandy silts, silts, saltmarsh deposits, peats and fenwood, and estuarine clays. Within these environmental deposits, archaeological and palaeoenvironmental evidence of Mesolithic, Neolithic, Bronze Age and post-medieval date was found. However, this evidence only emerged slowly, the result of repeated visits between 1994 and 1998. Oddly enough, while every visit would lead to one or two new discoveries, it was rare that more than that was found in the soft muds. In other words, repeated visits to the intertidal zone at Carrigdirty Rock almost served as a slow-motion excavation.

Methodology of Shannon estuary intertidal survey

Identifying archaeological and environmental deposits in submerged landscapes

The environmental bases of intertidal archaeology are complex and derive from the various fluctuations in land level brought about by isostatic readjustment after the melting of ice-sheets and the continual change in sea levels by eustatic recovery. Holocene drowning of old land surfaces is known from various parts of Britain and Ireland, where on low-lying coasts a change in relative sea level of only a few metres can mean the drowning of large areas of land.

Where the Shannon estuary channel is today eroding the foreshore, different types of exposure of palaeoenvironmental sedimentary sequences and archaeological deposits are visible. Along the edge of saltmarshes, vertical cliffs are cut near the mean high-water mark, exposing the clay and peat sediments in section, whereas lower down the shore truncation of deposits is less clear and often obscured under mobile sediments. On the lower foreshore it is possible to walk across a Holocene stratigraphy as bands of different types of clays and peats in plan. The Shannon estuary intertidal sites typically consisted of well-preserved wooden structures in estuarine clays or

Foragers, farmers and fishers

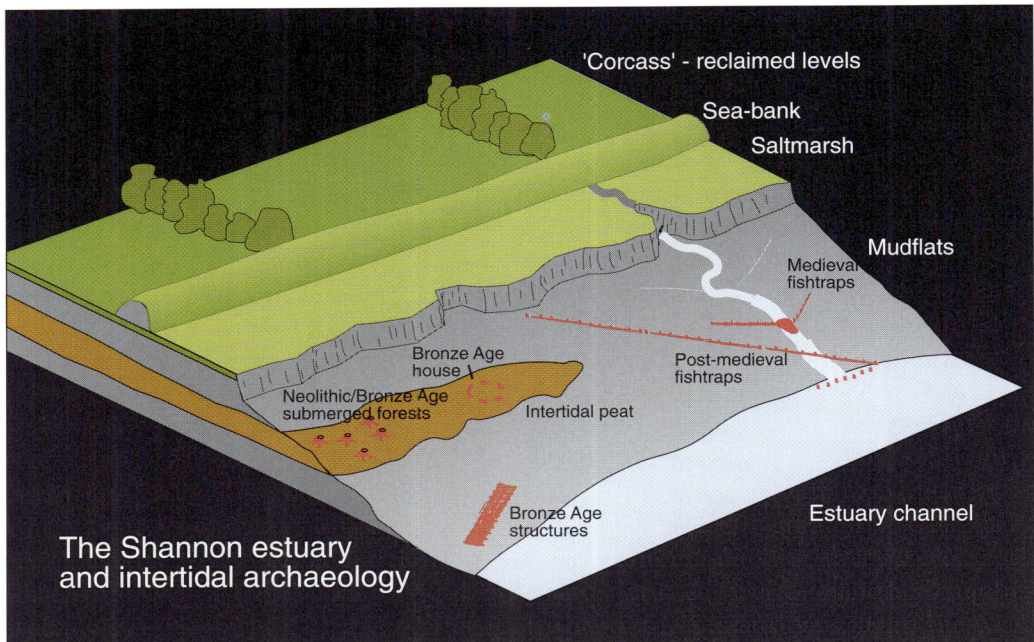

Fig. 9—*The Shannon estuary landscape and intertidal archaeology: a schematic diagram illustrating intercalated peats and clays and the range of archaeological sites recorded.*

wooden structures and scatters of finds in peats. Wooden structures were typically exposed in plan on the foreshore, although occasionally wooden features could be traced running in to the saltmarsh cliffs (Fig. 9).

The Shannon estuary intertidal survey was typically carried out by a small team of archaeologists (two or three individuals) walking the foreshore and identifying sites for more detailed recording. Parts of the Shannon estuary are relatively remote from roads and access routes, so that on some days the intertidal foreshore itself could only be reached by walking 2–3km across the reclaimed corcass fields and along the summit of the sea walls. A particular stretch of foreshore was then walked and marked off on a copy of the relevant section of the six-inch map. On the following day, the survey would usually carry on from the last area examined.

The intertidal survey thus moved slowly along the estuary coastline. At the beginning, the field-walking techniques used were highly rigorous, taking a 'terrain-oblivious' approach to the foreshore. Both soft and firm muds were walked as straight transects, separated by 20–30m intervals. However, after the first season in 1992 it was patently obvious that imposing an abstract field-walking grid on the Shannon estuary was exhausting, pointless and even dangerous. Frequently, we would have to walk through very soft muds to keep this grid system going, often sinking up to our thighs in deep, muddy silts. Therefore in subsequent years we concentrated our efforts only on the firm, eroding clays found along some creek banks and the muds at the low-water mark (LWM). These mudflats could be recognised from a distance by virtue of their dark colour, while with experience it became possible to predict more or less accurately the location of eroding foreshores in relation to the curve and orientation of the channel (eroding clays were usually to be found on the outer curve of a meander in the channel).

Time and tides in intertidal survey

Intertidal archaeological survey is a peculiar technique, bound by the strictures of time and tides. Published guidelines on the methodology of investigating the archaeology of the intertidal zone (Wilkinson 1989; Fulford *et al.* 1997; Milne and Goodburn 1993) all outline the particular constraints of time and safety in this dynamic environment. Intertidal archaeology has been described as both 'a guerrilla technique' and 'snatch and grab archaeology', such is the need to work within the shifting time-frame of tidal exposures. The intertidal archaeologist advances down the shore with the retreating tide, recording, cleaning and sampling relevant cultural or

Introduction

Pl. 8—*Archaeologists waiting for the ebbing tide to expose a medieval (AD 1018–1159) fishtrap at Bunratty 4 so that it can be planned and sampled; the use of a boat in intertidal survey enables staff, drawing equipment and samples to be safely transported back and forth, and allows archaeologists to record sites up until the last minute on a flooding tide.*

natural exposures before retreating before the flooding or advancing tide. It is considered absolutely vital to work within a precise knowledge of the local tidal conditions. Tidetables are consulted to check the times of low and high water, and the hours of fieldwork are built around them. As tidal times vary through the month from springs to neaps, potential working hours can be very erratic, perhaps stretching from early morning to late evening, with a six-hour break in the middle of the day. In contrast, later in the month or later in the year there may only be one low tide in daylight hours (often in early morning or late afternoon). Summertime is therefore considered the best season for fieldwork, as daylight and low tides coincide most often then, although autumn and winter have their own advantages in that tides are lower and storms and waves can produce a cleaner foreshore.

The methodology of the Shannon estuary intertidal survey was dominated by these time constraints, but the particular character of its archaeology often meant that structures and deposits were only exposed for very short periods of time. On the Shannon estuary, virtually all of the sites are situated right at the LWM, so that their lower ends are usually invisible at any time other than full ebb tide. This can lead to surprises, as in the case of the medieval fishtrap at Bunratty 4, first discovered in autumn 1995. On the late September morning when it was recorded (a neap tide), about 2–3m of post-and-wattle fence were exposed on the mudflats. In early February 1997, we returned during the lowest astronomical spring tides of the year, when large areas of the previously unseen foreshore were stripped clear for the first time. We could see that most of the site was actually typically submerged in the grey, muddy waters of the River Owenagarney channel (Pl. 8). Does this suggest that intertidal survey on the Shannon estuary should only be undertaken during particularly low spring tides, to enable full recording of all features? Perhaps so, but it would mean that we could only carry out fieldwork for 2–3 hours over 10–15 days a *year*!

Another example is the early historic post-and-wattle fence on the upper Fergus estuary (Fergus estuary east 2). It is typically only exposed for about 40 minutes on a low spring tide, and less at other times of the month. The Early Neolithic coastal wetland occupation site at Carrigdirty Rock 5 was rarely exposed for more than 1.5 hours at any one tide. Clearly, a strategy of repeated visits is necessary to fully examine and record archaeological sites on such narrow foreshores. Even so, work often has to be focused on a small, localised intertidal area. A team arrives on site, waits patiently until the full ebb tide, and records the sites inside the 1–2 hours before the rapidly flooding tide prevents further work. By this stage (i.e. 2–3 hours into the flood tide) most other sites on the estuary are also being submerged. It is now far too late to attempt to get to them. Although some projects can work a second tide, on the Shannon estuary the depth of the muds and the difficulty of walking through them can make a second visit daunting for an exhausted team. So, a day's fieldwork on the intertidal zone can sometimes be limited to 3–4 hours' effective recording. This, I suppose, was part of the challenge!

Safety in intertidal surveys

Safety is a vital element for consideration in intertidal archaeological survey. The Shannon estuary and the Fergus estuary have vast expanses of soft, muddy intertidal clays and silts (particularly beside the saltmarsh cliff and in creek beds) that are difficult to walk across. The pace of the incoming tide on the Shannon estuary is not spectacularly fast (in contrast to the famously rapid tides of the Severn estuary), but it is swift enough to be dangerous, with hundreds of metres of soft mudflats to be crossed before you can reach the safety of the saltmarshes again. Over the years people have been drowned on these mudflats, cut off from safety by a returning tide.

The intertidal zone is a potentially dangerous place to work, and precautions are needed. There are some basic principles to be followed. It is generally considered inadvisable to visit unfamiliar foreshores alone because of the risk of sinking in treacherous creeks or in deep, soft, semi-mobile muds. Tight wellingtons are better than waders for the inexperienced, as they are easier to slip out of if your foot becomes stuck, so that you can crawl to firmer mudflats. Divers' drysuits are definitely not suitable either, for similar reasons. Indeed, I would emphasise that no reader should visit any of the archaeological sites described in this book without contacting either me or experienced local port authorities, fishermen or rescue crews along the Shannon estuary.

Using a boat in intertidal survey

Readers have probably reached their own conclusions about how we might have avoided our sweaty struggles through the muds of the estuary. Unfortunately, it was not until towards the end of the project that we had access to a boat, not only for transport to sites but also for actual survey and prospection. In February 1997 a team was assembled for the excavation of medieval fishtraps at Bunratty, Co. Clare. The full team (four archaeologists, a surveyor and a palaeoenvironmental team of three) and their equipment (cameras, planning frames, ranging rods, excavation tools, sample bags and crates) were transported to the isolated sites on the intertidal zone by means of a 5m RIB (rigid inflatable boat) with an outboard engine (Pl. 8).

It was possible to arrive on site well before the low tide, wait patiently for that particular structure to appear out of the gloomy water, and then carry out the detailed recording and excavation. However, we could also use the boat to survey the intertidal zone, by speeding up and down estuary and creek channels and using binoculars to inspect the exposed banks of muds. Indeed, a number of post-medieval fishtrap structures (e.g. Green Island 1, Inishbonane 1) were discovered and recorded in this way. Separated as they were by huge areas of mudflats, it would have taken days to identify them on foot. The only potential drawback to the use of a boat is that it is only really possible to see structures immediately adjacent to the channel; structures located in creek beds back in the main mudflats are hidden behind the banks of mud.

More recently, I have carried out intertidal archaeological surveys for environmental impact assessments of dredging developments on the estuary of the River Barrow (Waterford Harbour) and on the Boyne estuary. Travelling slowly up the channel on a pilot boat, using binoculars to identify individual sites that were then marked on six-inch maps, we were able to survey 14km of intertidal foreshore in a day, leading to the discovery of 48 new archaeological sites. In March 1999 I also had the opportunity to travel down the Shannon estuary from Limerick to Rineanna on one of Shannon Estuary Ports' pilot boats. The experience was perhaps a little chastening.

Introduction

Pl. 9—*Archaeologist photographing a Late Bronze Age (797–551 BC) post-and-wattle structure on the upper Fergus estuary (Fergus estuary west 1). Most archaeological sites on the estuary are located right at the low-water mark, meaning that they are only visible for brief periods.*

Firstly, it was obvious that huge areas of mudflats could be inspected using binoculars, and several new fishtraps (at Bush Island) were exposed. Secondly, my perception of the upper Shannon estuary shifted: seen from a boat it suddenly seemed smaller and more intimate, with the various places I had struggled across on foot now easily accessible.

Site recording

Sites and features discovered on the Shannon estuary mudflats were recorded by photography, written descriptions and a selection of 1:10 and 1:20 plans (Pl. 9). The insertion of bamboos into the sediments enabled sites to be relocated at a later date. Some sites were sampled for radiocarbon dating, wood technology and palaeoenvironmental studies. A few significant sites were chosen for small-scale excavation (see below). Most sites were located on six-inch maps by means of triangulation or dead reckoning, using paced measurements of distances to creeks, saltmarshes, rock outcrops and dryland features, and by later reference to aerial photographs. A few sites, such as those at Carrigdirty Rock 1–4 and 5–21 and Fergus estuary west 1, were surveyed in more detail using a Total Station, and in some of these cases it was possible to tie the features into benchmarks on the drylands and to provide precise Ordance Datum heights.

Sites were named after topographical features rather than townland names. This is because archaeological structures and finds on the intertidal zone are not actually located within any townland, as these boundaries halt at the high-water mark and run parallel to the channel along the edge of the saltmarsh cliff. Instead, sites were named after islands (e.g. Quay Island, Bush Island), rocky outcrops (e.g. Carrigdirty Rock, Meelick Rocks), river and creek channels (Cratloe Creek) or headlands (Inishbonane, Coonagh Point). In a few cases, particularly well-known local names (other than townlands) were used (e.g. Bunratty). The Shannon estuary's own topography therefore emerges nicely in the survey record. Unfortunately, there are some fascinating names along the estuary that could not be used (e.g. Dead Woman's Hand Rock, Battle Island, Kippen Rock). Individual features (i.e. baskets, etc.) in structures were numbered on plans accordingly (e.g. Bunratty 4.3).

Site excavation

Most of the investigations carried out were restricted to sampling for radiocarbon dating, for wood species studies or to assess immediately the character, condition and

Pl. 10—*Archaeologist excavating a trench across a medieval (AD 1164–1279) basket at Bunratty 6, where the low elevation of the site on the mudflats meant that the features had to be excavated, planned, photographed and sampled inside 1–2 hours.*

likely date of a structure. Owing to the damaging effect of tidal action on any exposed material, such work is usually only embarked upon if it can be completed before the next high tide. However, archaeological excavations were carried out at Bunratty, Co. Clare. In February 1997, four days of archaeological excavation were carried out on six medieval fishtraps. The sites were exposed by rapidly cleaning back the mobile sediments and planning the structures in the 2–3 hours available between tides (Pl. 10). Although there were practical and logistical difficulties, it was possible to carry out limited archaeological excavations across features too. Incidentally, it should be pointed out that more ambitious excavations of the intertidal zone can certainly be done (mostly on sites exposed for 3–4 hours at least), using, for example, small sleds to haul tools to the site and to drag soil or wood samples out (Murphy and Wilkinson 1991). In recent years there have been major excavations of Iron Age houses at Goldcliff (Bell and Neumann 1997; 1998) and of a medieval boat at Magor Pill (Nayling 1998), both on the Severn estuary. In the latter case, a barge, a JCB and heavy lifting equipment were all used to remove the boat timbers from the clays.

Designing future intertidal projects

One of the benefits of doing a project is that you learn how *not* to do them. Looking back, I realise that the survey, even with its small resources, could have been carried out to a higher standard by focusing on a smaller study area (although it is only now that I know where this study area should be located!), by assembling a full-time team of four archaeologists and palaeoenvironmentalists for a defined period of time, and by following a series of stages laid out in a carefully plotted project design. In the hope

Introduction

that my rueful reflections may be of benefit to other Irish archaeologists, I would now suggest that an intertidal project on an estuary could proceed by way of the following phases.

Project design: relatively comprehensive cartographic, aerial photographic, historical and archival background research, and the establishment of contacts with archaeologists, palaeoenvironmentalists and other specialists at an early stage, leading to a project design with financial estimates as to resources, personnel and timing for fieldwork in a carefully chosen study area.

Phase 1: rapid boat survey of the entire study area by cruising up and down the river, preferably on a decked pilot boat, inspecting the shore with binoculars and getting a 'feel' for the landscape and an insight into its potential zones of archaeological significance. Initially identified sites or deposits could be rapidly marked on maps.

Phase 2: walk-over surveys of zones of high potential and detailed individual site recording (written descriptions on laminated feature sheets or waterproof notebooks, scale planning, photography, definitely the use of GPS in site survey) in smaller areas by a team of four archaeologists and palaeoenvironmentalists, using a small RIB with outboard engine to reach foreshores inaccessible on foot. Other zones should also be walked (some sites will only be found by standing on them).

Phase 3: detailed survey and excavation of particular sites, including instrument survey (using a stop–go GPS) of large structures and foreshores. A sustained programme of palaeoenvironmental studies (palynology, stratigraphical coring, beetles, diatoms, etc.) and extensive site sampling (radiocarbon dating, wood studies), followed by total excavation of chosen sites.

Post-excavation and publication: review of data, leading to preparation of site catalogue, post-excavation analysis, archaeological and palaeoenvironmental synthesis and interpretation, both based on integrated landscape analysis.

Summary of archaeological and palaeoenvironmental discoveries

Archaeological structures and finds

Despite its limitations, it is worth saying that the Shannon estuary intertidal survey has significantly increased our understanding of a previously unexplored type of Irish landscape and that it pioneered the techniques of intertidal archaeological survey in Ireland. It led to the discovery of the Neolithic and Bronze Age submerged forests at Poulnasharry Bay, Rinevalla Bay, Co. Clare, and Bunaclugga Bay, Co. Kerry, the possible early Neolithic occupation site at Carrigdirty Rock 5, and two discrete spreads of Neolithic red deer bone on the upper Fergus estuary, Co. Clare. A Middle Bronze Age occupation site at Carrigdirty Rock, with its wooden structures and cattle bone, and a Late Bronze Age trackway structure on the Fergus estuary are also useful contributions to our knowledge of Irish later prehistoric settlement. For the early historic and medieval periods, the first identified and earliest known fishtraps in Ireland were identified on the upper Fergus estuary, Co. Clare, the Deel estuary, Co. Limerick, and at Bunratty, Co. Clare, while many other undated sites were probably used in the Middle Ages too. However, easily the most numerous sites recorded were post-medieval fishtraps, with various types identified on the upper Shannon estuary especially.

Oddly, we were largely blind to the potential of the post-medieval maritime archaeological record (this is something which is only now changing in Irish archaeology generally). Indeed, it is embarrassing to recall how easily we walked past massive stone-built lighthouses (e.g. the tower on The Scarlets) while scrutinising the muds carefully for the smallest wooden feature. However, while there is some evidence on the upper Shannon estuary for post-medieval landing-places and quays, there is definitely much less than is typically seen on other Irish estuaries and sea loughs (e.g. Strangford Lough or Waterford Harbour), presumably because the mudflats and creeks were themselves used as landing-places. There was virtually no evidence for boats or shipwrecks in the two study areas (only a single boat timber was seen at Bush Island 19), although they are undoubtedly out there somewhere in the muds and channel. Thankfully, in 1995 the Maritime Archaeological Survey was established within *Dúchas* The Heritage Service, with a brief to establish an inventory of shipwrecks, harbours, piers, landing-places and lighthouses in Irish waters. In Chapter 7 of this book, Colin Breen and Claire Callaghan draw from this research and provide a much-needed maritime perspective on the Shannon estuary.

Palaeoenvironmental investigations

Palaeoenvironmental investigations begun during the Shannon estuary intertidal survey included coring for stratigraphical analysis, pollen analysis, diatom studies, Foraminifera studies, wood species identifications and tree-ring studies. The stratigraphies of peats, clays and silts were examined both in exposed sections in saltmarsh cliffs and from cores taken by a narrow-gauge auger and a monolith tin. The results of these initial palaeoenvironmental investigations were presented in the form of brief archive reports (e.g. Blythe 1996; Blythe *et al.* 1996a; 1996b). Unfortunately, it has proven impossible to bring these studies to a detailed level, so we still have only a very basic understanding of sea-level change, environmental change and human impact on the Shannon estuary's landscapes. Indeed, it is surprising how under-studied this landscape is in comparison to other Irish coastal wetlands.

The discovery of some deposits may be of use in the future. Important indicators of coastal and sea-level change in the Shannon estuary are the intercalated estuarine/marine clays and organic peats and muds found on the foreshore and in section in the saltmarsh cliffs. For example, at Rinevalla Bay, Co. Clare, a Neolithic submerged forest is located in peats on the upper foreshore. The earliest deposits there appear to be the valley gravels found on the lower foreshore. An inorganic estuarine/marine clay is found at the base of the peats on the upper foreshore, suggesting an early post-glacial marine transgression. Neolithic Scots pine stumps, root systems and fallen trunks seem to be based on this clay. Thereafter, a marine regression allowed deep deposits of peat to form over the trunks. Substantial oak stumps are found within this organic peat, suggesting occasional phases of drier, terrestrialised peats. Finally, continued marine transgression has now located these deposits in the intertidal zone of the estuary.

The sequence of relative sea-level changes on the upper Shannon estuary also appears to be one of phases of marine regression and transgression, against a background of gradually rising sea levels. Submerged carr woodlands in peat of probable Late Neolithic or Bronze Age date have been found at Meelick Rocks 1, Co. Limerick, and probably also at Carrigdirty Rock 16, Co. Limerick. The woody peats in particular could only have formed at some height above contemporary mean sea levels, possibly caused by a marine transgression owing to sea-level changes or alterations in local coastal geomorphology. In Chapter 2, Andrew Wheeler and Michael Healey present a significant overview of the coastal landscapes of the estuary, and provide a baseline study on which future research can now build.

Wood studies

Wood studies were carried out on samples from five wooden structures of different periods: the Early Neolithic occupation site at Carrigdirty Rock, the Late Bronze Age post-and-wattle trackway and early historic fishtrap on the upper Fergus estuary, the

Introduction

medieval fishtraps at Bunratty 6, Bunratty 4 and Bunratty 2, and the post-medieval fishtrap at Cratloe Creek 1. Wood species identifications and tree-ring counts were carried out according to standard scientific techniques (Schweingruber 1990). Identification of wood has been taken either to species level (because of anatomical properties or the known range of species native to Ireland) or to the broader genus level (where the evidence of cell structure alone is insufficient to identify a piece to species level). Some wood species identifications have to be taken to a multi-genus level (e.g. the Pomoideae). Tree-ring counts were simultaneously made under the microscope. At least nine native Irish tree species were identified from the various wooden structures sampled, including hazel (*Corylus*), alder (*Alnus*), ash (*Fraxinus*), oak (*Quercus*), birch (*Betula*), holly (*Ilex*), *Prunus* sp., probably cherry (*Prunus avium*), and willow (*Salix*)/poplar (*Populus*). A number of Pomoideae species were also identified: these could be apple (*Pirus malus*), pear (*Pirus communis*), hawthorn (*Crataegus* sp.), or mountain ash (*Sorbus* sp.).

Woodworking samples were taken from some structures during the surveys. Indeed, the rapid inspection of woodworking evidence on site was often used to quickly assess the date of structures, as stone, bronze and iron tools all leave characteristic types of tool-marks. Wood technology studies followed guidelines previously established in wetland archaeology projects on prehistoric wooden trackways in the Somerset Levels (e.g. Orme 1982; Orme and Coles 1983; 1985), on Neolithic, Bronze Age and Iron Age wooden trackways in the midland bogs of Ireland (O'Sullivan 1996c), and on Bronze Age riverside settlements in Wales (Brunning and O'Sullivan 1997).

Chronology and radiocarbon dating

The chronological periods used in this study are defined as follows: Mesolithic (7000–4000 BC), Neolithic (4000–2500 BC), Bronze Age (2500–600 BC), Iron Age (600 BC–AD 400), early historic (AD 400–800), Viking Age (AD 800–1100), medieval (AD 1100–1350), late medieval (AD 1350–1534), post-medieval (AD 1534–1700) and modern (AD 1700–1900). In the absence of any previous archaeological or palaeoenvironmental investigations on the Shannon estuary, there is as yet no established chronology of the Holocene environmental stratigraphy. However, preliminary dates can be suggested for some sites on the basis of their state of preservation, the degree of waterlogging of structural wood, tool-marks and general environmental context. For example, it is believed that most of the sites recorded in the intertidal peats at Carrigdirty Rock (see Chapter 4) are of Late Neolithic or Bronze Age date. Furthermore, the excellent condition and the density of the wood in many of the large fishtraps discussed in Chapter 6 suggest that they are indeed post-medieval in date. The chronology of some sites was established by radiocarbon dating of samples submitted to Rijksuniversiteit Groningen (prefix GrN-) and Beta Analytic Laboratories (prefix Beta-). These dates are presented in this study (see Appendix 1), calibrated at two-sigma deviations, at a 95% statistical level of probability, using the computer programme CALIB 4.2 (Stuiver and Reimer 1993; Stuiver *et al.* 1998; available on the internet at http://radiocarbon.pa.qub.ac.uk/calib/calib.html).

2. Coastal landscapes and environmental change in the Shannon estuary

Andrew J. Wheeler and Michael G. Healy

Introduction

Pl. 11—*Satellite image (Landsat MSS) of the Shannon estuary taken in 1976. Limerick City and Shannon Airport are clearly visible on the upper Shannon estuary.*

The Shannon estuary environment is surprisingly under-studied relative to other parts of the west of Ireland or to comparable European estuarine systems. This chapter provides an introduction to the physical landscapes of the Shannon estuary (with an emphasis on the upper Shannon and Fergus estuaries), including an overview of environmental processes and the palaeoenvironmental setting, as well as a summary of environmental research in the area. The data presented here are of a preliminary nature, derived from current research work, rather than a definitive statement on the present and former environments of the Shannon estuary. However, significant field research is currently in progress on land reclamation, relative sea-level history, stratigraphic (sedimentary sequence) studies, environmental change, the flood embankments and the settlement history of the estuary. Substantial advances are being made in our understanding of the functioning of the estuary through time, and the role of human activities in its evolution. Up to now there has been little published work on the palaeoenvironment of the Shannon estuary. A comprehensive understanding of the palaeoenvironmental history of the area requires substantial additional and expanded research, which will offer the potential for an exciting insight into the undiscovered wetland environmental record of the Irish mid-west.

The Shannon estuary and its environs

The Shannon estuary, situated on the Atlantic coast of Ireland, is the largest estuary in this island (Pl. 11). It is fed by the rivers Shannon, Fergus, Suck, Inny, Maigue and Brosna, which together drain an area of *c.* 15,700km^2, or about one third of Ireland. The drainage basin associated with these rivers includes most of the Irish central lowlands and some major inland lakes, including Lough Derg and Lough Ree (Fig. 10).

The greater Shannon estuary area comprises the lower reaches of the River Shannon (*c.* 96km between Limerick City and the sea) and incorporates the Fergus estuary south of Clarecastle (Fig. 11). It includes parts of north County Kerry, north County Limerick and west County Clare. The lower estuary comprises the area to the west of Pallaskenry, Co. Limerick, on the south bank, and west of Kildysart, Co. Clare, on the north bank. The upper estuary comprises the remainder as far as Limerick City. Water depths vary from *c.* 37m at the estuary mouth to *c.* 19m at its confluence with the Fergus, shallowing eastward to less than 5m in the channel at Limerick City. The land adjacent to the upper Shannon and Fergus estuaries is generally low-lying and level, with surface elevations seldom exceeding 60m OD. The majority lies between the tidal high-water mark (HWM) and 30m OD (Ordnance Survey of Ireland 1974). Exceptions to this may be found on the southern shore of the lower Shannon estuary between Tarbert and

Fig. 10—*Map showing the Shannon River drainage basin and geographical context of the Shannon River system with respect to Ireland.*

Fig. 11—*General location map for the Shannon estuary, including all places mentioned in the text.*

Foynes and on the northern shore between Labasheeda and Clarecastle, where the relatively narrow coastal lowlands rapidly give way to higher ground. In this area the estuary is at its most constricted, being typically *c.* 1.25km wide; its widest dimension can be found at the confluence with the Fergus estuary, where it measures *c.* 14.5km across. Much of the lowland area is subject to intermittent flooding in periods of high rainfall and is dependent on flood embankments for protection from marine flooding. The lowlands are drained by a dense network of rivers, streams, creeks, artificial drainage channels and sluices.

Geological setting

The regional geology of the Shannon estuary has a strong influence on local topography and physiography. The area is underlain by Ordovician to Carboniferous deposits (Anon. 1860; Anon. 1862; Lamplugh *et al.* 1907; Sleeman and Pracht 1999) which were laid down between 450 and 280 million years ago (mya). The rocks form a conformable succession (Table 1; Fig. 12), with the oldest (Ordovician and Silurian) being overlain by the upper Old Red Sandstone. These are overlain in turn by Carboniferous rocks. The oldest rocks outcrop in the east, with progressively younger rocks becoming exposed to the west (Lamplugh *et al.* 1907).

The oldest rock series, outcropping near Limerick City, was deposited during the Silurian and consists of marine fossiliferous muds. These are faulted against Silurian laminated siltstones, coarse-grained sandstones, conglomerates and graded greywackes (Baily 1859; Harper 1939; Weir 1962; 1975; Holland *et al.* 1988). These are overlain by the upper Old Red Sandstone Series (Harper 1939; Khan 1955; Bridge *et al.* 1980), which consists of coarse-grained yellow quartzites (quartz-rich sandstones) that are occasionally conglomeratic (consisting of well-rounded pebbles), calcareous and often interbedded with thin, sandy shale (mudrock) partings. These beds were deposited on land, as is evident from occasional fossil plant remains found in the area (Anon. 1862; Sleeman and Pracht 1999), and appear to have formed as a result of the erosion of nearby highlands (Walsh 1968) and deposition by meandering rivers (Sleeman and Pracht 1999).

The overlying Carboniferous Limestone can be divided into three: the Lower Carboniferous Limestone Shales, Carboniferous Limestone and the Upper Carboniferous (Namurian) sediments. These rocks underlie most of the upper Shannon estuary and the Fergus estuary and are easily eroded both chemically and physically, resulting in estuary widening and low relief. The 'Lower Limestone Shales' are

Age	Geological rock unit	Rock type	Environmental conditions
Quaternary	Glacial drift and alluvium	Glacial drift and alluvium	Erosion followed by terrestrial sedimentation
Namurian	Feale Sandstone Formation, Tullig Sandstone, Gull Island Formation, Ross Sandstone Formation and Clare Shale Formation	Sandstone, siltstone, shale and mudstone	Near-shore and coastal wetland environments
Visean	Magowna Formation, Parsonage and Corgrig Formations, Slievenaglasha Formation, Burren Formation, Tubber Formation, Shanagolden Formation, Durnish Formation, Rathkeale Formation, Herbertstown Formation, Knockroe Formation, Lough Gur Formation, Athassel Formation, Finlough Formation, Ballycar Formation, Visean Limestones (undiff.), Waulsortian Limestones, Ballysteen Formation and Ballymartin Formation	Limestone, shale, basaltic tuff and lava	Shallow warm seas with localised volcanism
Tournaisian	Ballyvergin Formation, Ringmoylan Formation and Mellon House Formation	Mudstone, siltstone, sandstone, crinoidal limestone and calcareous shale	Shallow warm seas rich in life
Devonian	Old Red Sandstone Series: Kilmore Formation, Inshaboy Formation and Glandahalin Formation	Mudstone, siltstone, sandstone and conglomerate	Terrestrial floodplains and alluvial fans
Silurian	Cratloe Formation, Slieve Bernagh Formation, Broadford Formation and Cornagnoe Formation	Laminated siltstone and sandstone, conglomeratic sandstone, fine to conglomeratic graded greywacke	Marine sediments with near-shore influences
Ordovician	Ballymalone Formation	Black graptolitic shale and chert	Marine

Table 1—*Schematic geological succession for the Shannon and Fergus estuaries.*

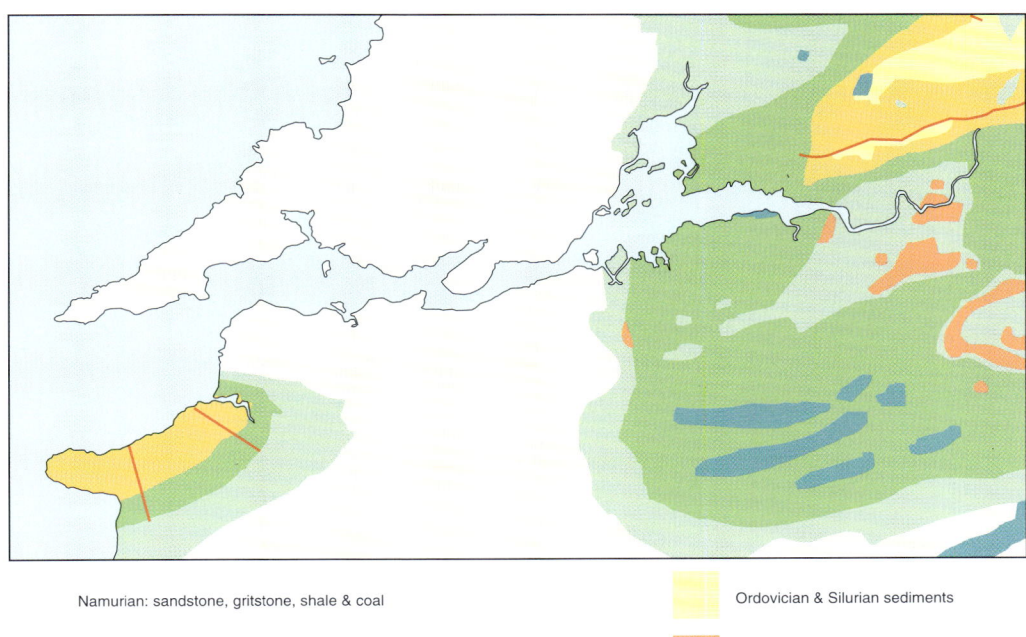

Fig. 12—Geological map of the Shannon estuary (after Synge 1969).

composed of coarse-grained grits, blue/grey shales and dark blue argillaceous (clay-rich) limestones that become increasingly influenced by grey, massive (structureless) magnesium limestones through progressively younger beds (Anon. 1862; Lamplugh *et al.* 1907; Shepard-Thorn 1963; Hudson and Sevastopulo 1966; Clayton *et al.* 1980; Sevastopulo 1981; Somerville and Jones 1985; Diemer *et al.* 1987). This decrease in shales and grits suggests that the sea level was probably rising and terrestrial sources of sediment were becoming more distant. The rocks are rich in fossils, especially bivalves (shellfish) and corals, having accumulated in shallow tropical seas (Lamplugh *et al.* 1907). The majority of the upper part of this sequence is composed of fossil-rich limestone.

The initiation of volcanism and associated processes caused dramatic changes in the environment and resulted in the formation of the fossiliferous Carboniferous Limestone, which formed in warm shallow seas but contains interbedded volcanic deposits and clastic (sedimentary) material (Hodson and Lewarne 1961; Shepard-Thorn 1963; Schultz and Sevastopulo 1965; Clayton *et al.* 1980; Sevastopulo 1981; Dolan 1984; Somerville and Jones 1985; Somerville and Strogen 1992; Somerville *et al.* 1992; Gallagher 1996; Sleeman and Pracht 1999). The Carboniferous Limestone consists of chert (microcrystalline silica) beds and massive magnesium limestone beds with shale partings. These rocks also include large biogenic carbonate banks or reefs (Waulsortian Limestone), which form the largest accumulations of their type in the world (Lees 1964; Strogen 1988; Lee and Miller 1995). In parts of the Limerick City area some of the limestones are oolitic, formed by calcium carbonate precipitation in warm, high-energy waters under the influence of wave activity. Intercalated with the chert and limestone beds are volcanic deposits that often outcrop as hills or ridges. These consist of blue, green or purple volcanic ash beds composed of coarse-grained breccias (composed of angular volcanic fragments), conglomerates or fine grits. They often contain inclusions of country rock (sedimentary rock) as well as pumice, porphyry and amygdales (Anon. 1860; Lamplugh *et al.* 1907). Most of these ash beds represent volcanic debris reworked by wave and current action. Also present are basaltic and dioritic intrusive formations (solidified intruded magma) occasionally containing

Foragers, farmers and fishers

xenoliths (inclusions) of limestone (Lamplugh *et al.* 1907).

During the Upper Carboniferous, olive/black shales were deposited, overlain by sandstones and grits. These deposits were also laid down in relatively shallow marine conditions, although the lower biological productivity did not result in limestone formation. The deposits are predominantly overlain by sandstone beds (Anon. 1860; Anon. 1862; Hind 1905; Lamplugh *et al.* 1907; Hodson 1954a; 1954b; Hodson and Lewarne 1961; Rider 1974; Gill 1979; Sleeman and Pracht 1999) forming part of a submarine fan. During the Upper Carboniferous a relative sea-level fall resulted in coal formation in shallow near-shore waters and coastal wetlands on an emergent delta. These rocks consist of olive grits, shales, clays and thin beds (*c.* 20cm) of anthracite which have been economically exploited in the area (Anon. 1862). The Upper Carboniferous rocks are resistant to erosion, producing a narrowing of the lower Shannon estuary.

All of the rock series described above were gently folded during the Variscon orogeny in the Late Carboniferous. The northern limit of intense folding associated with this mountain-building event occurs just south of the Shannon estuary. More recent glacial and alluvial (riverine) Quaternary deposits overlie the folded rocks in this area.

Glacial deposits and related features of the Shannon estuary

There appears to be general agreement that Midlandian ice occupied the upper estuary at the last glacial maximum and for some time subsequently (Edwards and Warren 1985). The ice limits (Fig. 13), while tentative in their detail, are generally discernible from frontal and 'push' moraine features, including the reconstructed 'Southern Irish End-Moraine' (McCabe 1985). Ice flow was from the north-west to the south-east. Evidence for this flow direction is preserved as striations on some outcrops

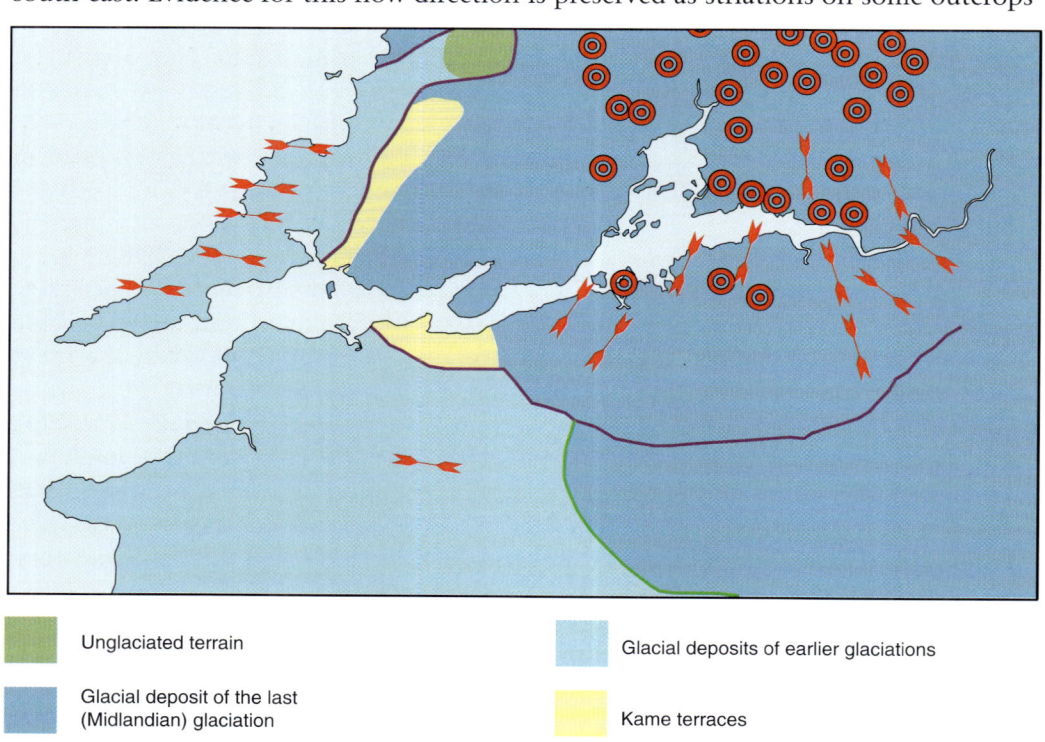

Fig. 13—*Map of glacial features and deposits of the Shannon estuary (after Synge 1969).*

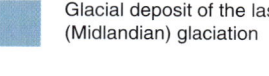

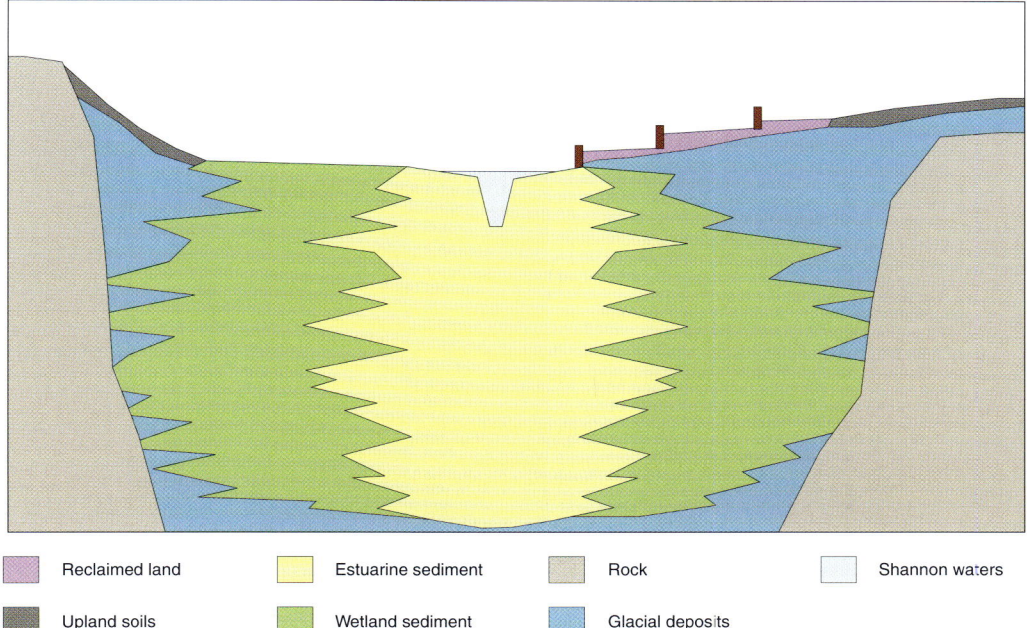

Fig. 14—*Generalised cross-section through the Quaternary deposits of the Shannon estuary.*

of Old Red Sandstone in locations north and south of the upper Shannon estuary (Lamplugh *et al.* 1907).

During meltwater phases associated with retreat of the ice-sheets, subglacial processes resulted in the formation of drumlins in County Clare, which extend onto the northern shores of the Shannon and Fergus estuaries. Drumlins occur in lowland areas (less than 150m OD) and in general are concentrated within major ice limits collectively known as the 'Drumlin Readvance Moraine'. The well-defined moraine complex limiting the drumlin fields around the Shannon estuary has been interpreted as an ice re-advance feature related to a deterioration in climate about 17,000 BP (Synge 1969).

Glacial till (previously commonly referred to as boulder clay) is extensive in the area and covers much of the underlying geology. The till, consisting mainly of clay-rich deposits, contains clasts of local rocks as well as chalk in some instances. Synge's (1966) Glacial Drift Map of County Limerick distinguishes a number of till fabrics on the basis of lithology, including tills containing Carboniferous sandstone and shale, Carboniferous limestone, Devonian Old Red Sandstone and Silurian shale and slate. End moraines are widespread south of the Shannon, with glacio-fluvial sand and gravel also commonly found. Drumlins and drumlinoid features are concentrated in an area between the River Deel and the River Maigue in County Limerick, with the main cluster occurring close to the south bank of the Shannon.

It is difficult to ascertain how significant a role ice may have played in modifying the estuary's morphology. Glacial striations have been noted on rock outcrops within the Shannon area, indicating that glaciers and ice-sheets physically ground down exposed rocks. The relatively soft limestone formations in the area would have been more susceptible to this process than the more resistant sandstone beds. However, the degree of glacial abrasion and the volume of material moved are not known. Similarly, although meltwater discharges in advance of an ablating ice-sheet were considerably higher than contemporary river discharges, it is not possible to say definitively what effects these had on the current estuarine morphology. It is possible that the contemporary Shannon estuary exists in a valley cut by previous rivers during former interglacials or earlier. It is likely that large-scale sedimentary fluxes were associated with ice advance and retreat. As no significant subsurface profiling has been carried out to date, the volume of unconsolidated sediment deposited around the estuary remains unquantified. However, stratigraphic evidence from sites within and adjacent to the estuary shows sedimentary sequences in excess of 30m (e.g. at Aughinish), while

Foragers, farmers and fishers

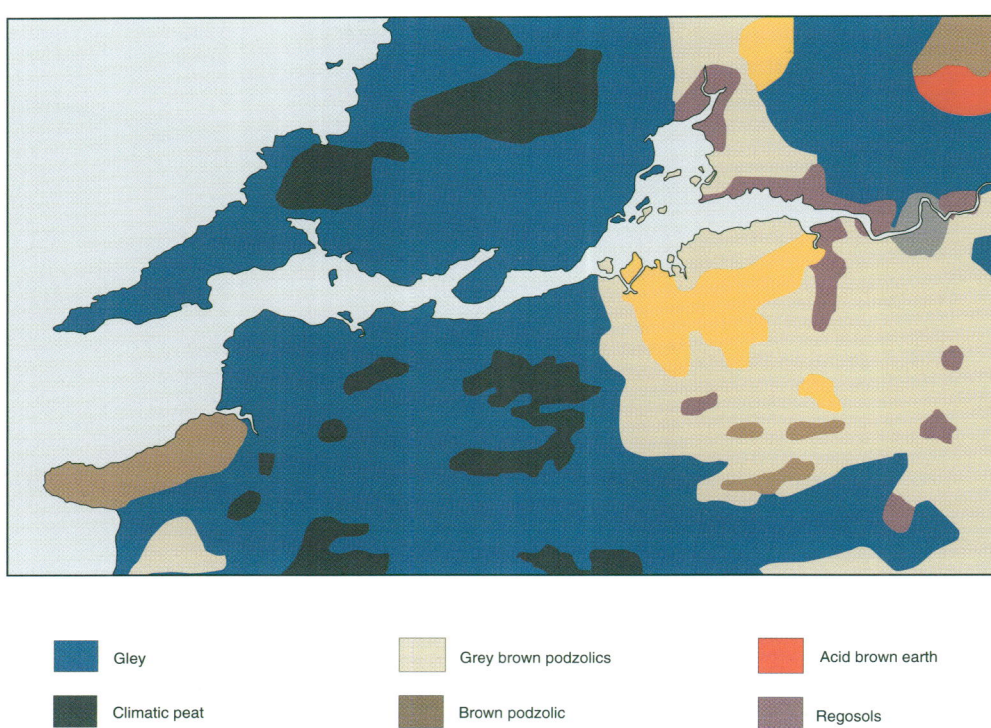

Fig. 15—*Soil map of the Shannon estuary.*

sequences of more than 5m have commonly been encountered in the course of recent stratigraphic work at Carrigdirty, Cooperhill, Islandmagrath and Islandavanna. It is likely that these sequences consist, at least in part, of reworked glacigenic materials. A generalised Quaternary sedimentary succession is presented in Fig. 14.

Climate, soils and modern land use

Ireland has a typical western maritime climate, with cool cloudy summers and mild damp winters. The Shannon estuary region, compared with the country as a whole, has higher annual average humidity and rainfall, lower mean annual temperature, and shorter frost-free and sunshine periods. Annual average rainfall (1951–80) for the upper Shannon estuary is between 800mm and 1000mm, and for the lower estuary is between 1000mm and 1200mm (Rohan 1986). Mean daily temperatures (1951–80) vary from 5.0–5.5°C (January) to 15.0–15.5°C (July) (Rohan 1986), with relative humidity readings within a range of 69–92% (An Foras Talúntais 1966). The dates for 50% probability of first and last frosts (1951–80) are 15 November and 1 April respectively (Rohan 1986), and average wind speed (1951–80 at Shannon Airport) is 5.6m s^{-1}, mainly from westerly and southerly directions (Rohan 1986).

Soils within the lowlands immediately adjacent to the Shannon estuary (Fig. 15) have been classified as gley (waterlogged)/brown earth/peaty gley (Association 43) by An Foras Talúntais (Gardiner and Radford 1980). These soils have a poor drainage capability, with a clay/loam texture and a sticky consistency when wet. An organic-rich surface horizon over a grey and mottled sub-horizon of massive structure is a primary characteristic. The silt content of these soil profiles is high (*c.* 50%), and the clay content decreases from *c.* 28% near the surface to less than 10% near the soil base. Soils in this area are frequently waterlogged, with the water-table rarely occurring more than 0.4m below the ground surface. These soils typify what has been termed the 'wet mineral lowland' (Culleton and Gardiner 1985); in the absence of drainage and nitrogen enhancement, they are only suitable for grazing or forestry.

Much of the lowland consists of alluvial deposits on flat relief at or below sea level.

The flats comprise a mixture of partially drained pasture and marsh/saltmarsh. Some of the lowland has been reclaimed. The primary land use is agricultural, with rough, seasonally grazed pasture predominant. Reclaimed areas are drained by a system of channels leading to flap sluices and other outlets, while the marshland is poorly served by a combination of artificial drainage channels and dense meandering creeks and their tributaries.

Outside of the lowlands, soils around the Shannon estuary catchment vary considerably according to the pattern of geological and glacigenic parent materials, as well as the influence of soil-forming factors (climate, living organisms, topography, time). Soil survey data from County Limerick and County Clare (An Foras Talúntais 1966) demonstrate the presence of soils of the Brown Earth Group (good, arable soils), Brown Podzolic Group (good, arable soils with management), Grey-Brown Podzolic Group (good grassland soils, also cultivable), Gley Group (suitable for pasture), Podzol Group (rough grazing, forestry), Regosol Group (lowland, immature, variable productivity), Lithosol Group (rough grazing, forestry) and Organic Soil (Peats) Group. These main groups are subdivided into local Soil Series according to site-specific criteria.

Modern settlement along the lowlands adjacent to the upper Shannon estuary is generally sparse, though several small villages occur on or near the alluvial flats (e.g. at Pallaskenry, Clarina, Bunratty and Hurler's Cross). Larger towns such as Foynes, Newmarket-on-Fergus, Ennis and Clarecastle support substantial populations. In addition, there is important industrial and transport infrastructure adjacent to the estuary, including the Shannon Industrial Complex and Shannon Airport. Limerick City, the largest urban centre in the region, lies at the head of the Shannon estuary and acts as the main industrial, commercial and transport hub for the Irish mid-west region.

Fauna and flora

The Shannon estuary offers a diversity of habitats, from open water to mudflat (G. O'Sullivan 1983; Merne 1985), saltmarsh to freshwater wetland, and pasture to upland. This diversity of habitats within a confined area, coupled with its high wetland biological productivity (Chapman 1977), provides a sustainable and diverse food

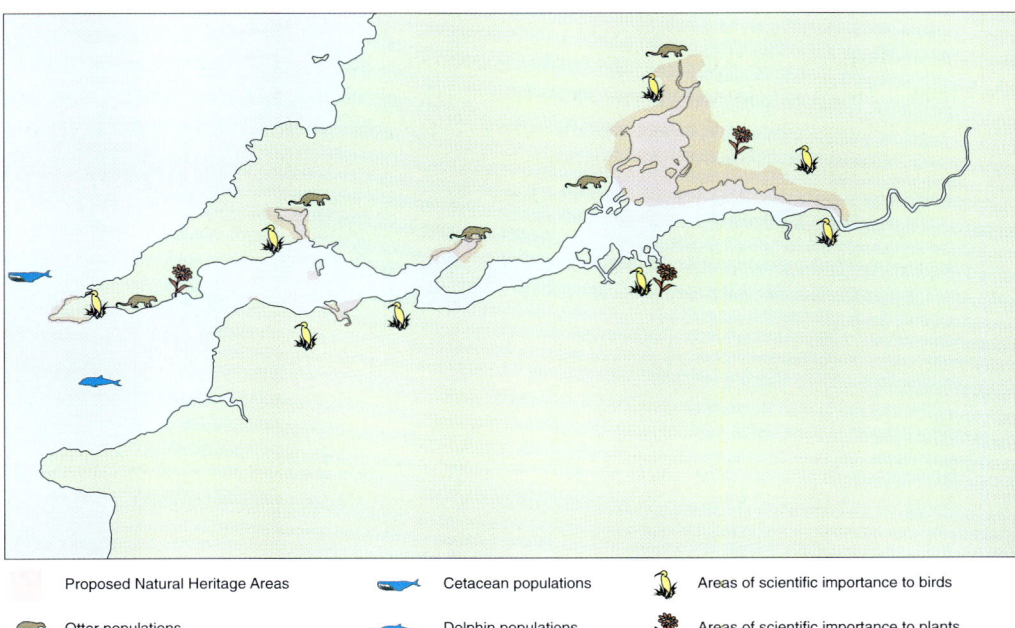

Fig. 16—*Proposed Natural Heritage Area and wildlife distributions.*

resource for fauna and flora. The Shannon estuary is of critical ecological importance today, as is evidenced by its status as a cSAC (candidate Special Area of Conservation) under the terms of the EU Habitats Directive (92/43/EEC) and Natura 2000. It also contains an SPA (Special Protection Area) under the EU Birds Directive (79/409/EEC) (La Tène Maps 1999), and the National Parks and Wildlife Service propose nine NHAs (Natural Heritage Areas) on the estuary (Fig. 16).

The wetlands and waters of the Shannon estuary form a large estuarine complex containing many habitats and species listed in Annexes I and II of the EU Habitats Directive (*Dúchas*, pers. comm.). Included are the priority habitat lagoon (Cloonconeen Pool and Shannon Airport Lagoon), the only known resident population of bottle-nosed dolphins in Ireland and all three Irish lamprey species (*Lampetra planeri*, *L. fluviatilis* and *Petromyzon marinus*). A number of Red Data Book species are present, perhaps most notably the thriving populations of triangular club-rush (*Scirpus triqueter*), opposite-leafed pondweed (*Groenlandia densa*), meadow barley (*Hordeum secalinum*), hairy violet (*Viola hirta*), golden dock (*Rumex maritimus*), bearded stonewort (*Chara canescens*) and convergent stonewort (*Chara connivens*). Several species listed in Annex I of the EU Birds Directive use the estuary for wintering or breeding (e.g. peregrine falcon, sandwich tern, common tern, chough, kingfisher, kittiwake and guillemot). In general, the estuary supports more wintering wildfowl (51,423 counted in 1995–6) and waders than any other site in the country (Wood *et al.* 1996; Berrow *et al.* 1996; *Dúchas*, pers. comm.). It has had internationally important numbers of black-tailed godwit and redshank, with nationally important numbers of cormorant, greylag goose, shelduck, wigeon, teal, mallard, scaup, golden plover, grey plover, lapwing, knot, dunlin, bar-tailed godwit and curlew. Other local wildfowl include mute swan, white-fronted goose, brent goose, tufted duck and oyster-catcher. It is likely that the quantity and diversity of flora and fauna now found around the estuary were at least as great prior to the arrival of a significant human population in the area (Sheppard 1993).

Hydrography of the Shannon estuary: past and present

The tidal limit of the Shannon estuary is above Limerick City, which is 96km from the open ocean. The deepest part of the estuary is at its mouth, although relatively deep water also exists in the constricted Tarbert Race, where the tidal flows are greatest. The upper estuary, east of the Tarbert Race, is generally shallower, with extensive tidal flats (especially on the lower Fergus estuary and the upper Shannon estuary east of Rineanna). Tidal range within the estuary varies, increasing with distance from the estuary mouth. Mean tidal range within the estuary is between 3.6m and 4m at spring tides and between 1.5m and 1.8m at neap tides. Maximum tidal velocities occur in the narrowest part of the estuary at Tarbert Race, reaching 2.5m s^{-1} north-east of Tarbert Island (Nairn *et al.* 1997). Freshwater flow into the estuary is relatively low in the context of its overall size, and tidal waters account for 70% of the volume of the upper estuary. A turbidity (suspended sediment) maximum (5%) is located approximately halfway between Shannon Airport and Limerick City (Wilson *et al.* 1993). Overall pollution in the estuary is low, according to Jeffrey *et al.* (1985).

The extensive modification of the estuary through historical reclamation works has probably had a significant impact on palaeohydrography. The present estuary is considerably narrower than it was in former times, especially the upper estuary. Before reclamation, it is probable that the maximum area that was subjected to tidal inundation was substantially greater. The reduction in the extent of the intertidal area has inevitably produced modifications in tidal conditions and current strengths. Wider, shallower estuaries have a greater capacity to dissipate tidal energies through frictional drag on the bed. Prior to reclamation, tidal flows were probably slower and

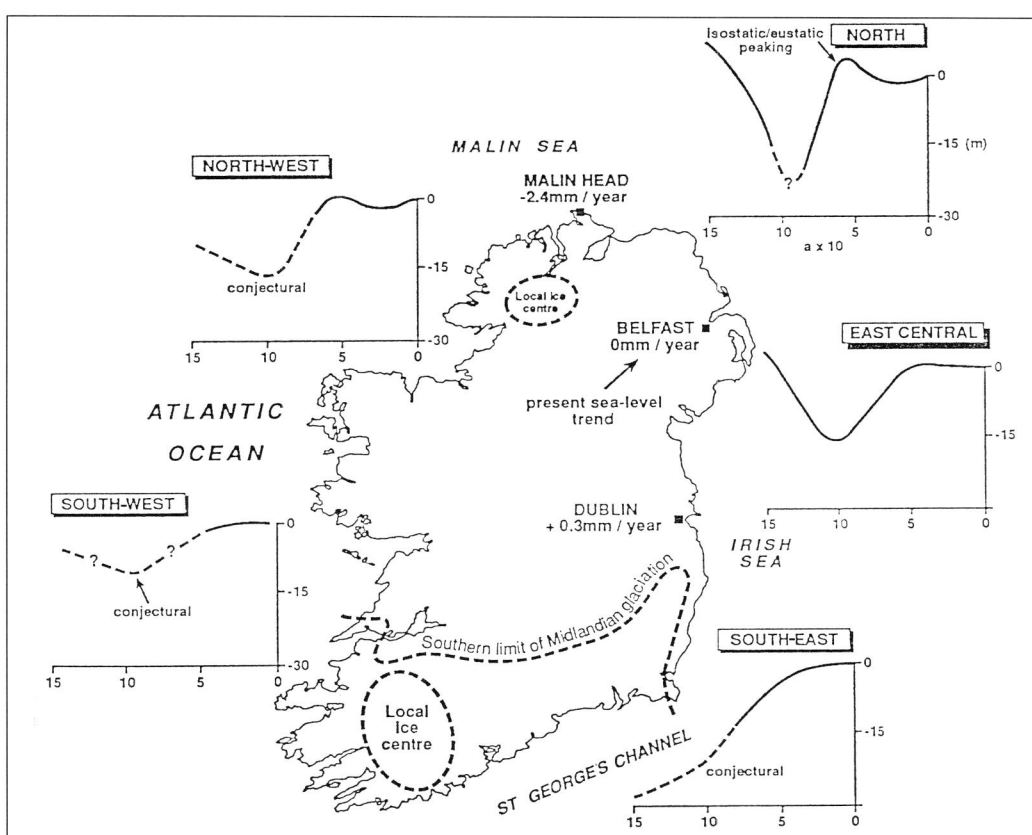

Fig. 17—*The 'family' of Irish sea-level curves, based on Taylor et al. (1986).*

less competent in carrying coarse-grained sediments. This appears to have resulted in a process of slow infill of the estuary with fine-grained sediment. The continuity of this process depended on the balance between sea-level movements and sediment supply. It is therefore possible that the intertidal area of the Shannon estuary may have expanded and contracted through time, depending on the balance of these two variables. The post-reclamation confinement of the estuary has resulted in increased flow strengths with very low net deposition at present.

Sea-level and climate change

One of the major controls on the environmental evolution of the Shannon estuary has been the effect of relative sea-level change during the Holocene (the last 10,000 years). Sea-level change and associated processes offer the most likely mechanism for the formation of intertidal deposits that bury and preserve archaeological sites. Appreciation of the nature of relative sea-level change is therefore vital to understanding coastal environmental conditions affecting the Shannon wetlands in post-glacial times.

Reconstruction of past relative sea-level and related environmental change involves the study of stratigraphic sequences, including the documentation of the elevation of individual sediment strata and the materials of which they are composed. Preserved pollen, diatoms, ostracods, Foraminifera and other microscopic fossils within sediments are commonly used as environmental indicators, along with macrofossils where appropriate. Radiocarbon (^{14}C) dating, used to establish the age of organic- or carbon-rich sediments within stratigraphies, remains the most commonly used dating mechanism in the reconstruction of Holocene relative sea-level histories. Time (chronological) and elevation (altitudinal) data are used to produce relative sea-level curves (e.g. Fig. 17), while micro- and macrofossil data indicate the condition of the environment in the time-span which the curves represent.

Relative sea-level movements are such that shoreline position is constantly migrating, frequently over large distances, in relatively short time-periods (Healy 1995a). This is particularly likely in low-elevation coastal environments such as the Shannon wetlands, where low-magnitude relative sea-level change could have initiated widespread environmental alterations of the local landscape.

Past patterns of relative sea-level movements around the Irish coastline may be portrayed in a 'family' of five sea-level curves which reflect regional patterns around the Irish coast (Fig. 17). The influence of glacial loading and associated isostatic factors (the rebound of the crust owing to the lifting of the weight of the ice-sheets following their melting) can be seen from the differences between the curves from the northern and southern areas of the country. The southern part of Ireland reflects a general absence of ice loading, with a rising relative sea-level trend during the post-glacial period. Data from the south-east and south-west coasts (Carter et al. 1989; CEC 1995) show that this rise was initially rapid between around 6000 and 3000 years before present (BP), with a deceleration in the rate of rise in the period between 3000 BP and the present day. Over the last 2000 years, this rise has been at a rate of between 0.8mm and 1.1mm per year (Carter et al. 1989). A more complex pattern is evident for the north coast of Ireland, with sea level showing a falling trend, followed by a rise, a fall, and then a rise again to the present day. Data from Malin Head (Carter 1982) show that, at present, sea level is falling in the far north of Ireland, although recent unpublished data show that a positive trend is probably more realistic for the last few decades (B. Scott, pers. comm.).

While relative sea-level data from Irish coastal sites continue to accumulate, the history of sea-level movements around the coast in the course of the post-glacial period remains patchy (Carter 1991). This is particularly so in relation to the Atlantic coast, and perhaps most significant is the complete paucity of data for the Shannon estuary. This is reflected in the sea-level curve for the south-west (Fig. 17), which is conjectural prior to 5000 BP. While a start has recently been made, sea-level research in south-western Ireland and the Shannon estuary area requires concentrated work in the short term to elucidate the coastal environmental history of the Irish mid-west region.

The palaeoenvironment of the Shannon estuary

The archaeology and settlement patterns of coastal wetland environments are inextricably linked to the physical and ecological regimes governing coastal evolution. The position of the coastline changes over time and space, controlled by factors which include relative sea level as well as sediment supply, coastal morphodynamics, ecological processes and human activity (Healy 1995b; Carter and Woodroffe 1994). These factors also play an important part in determining the character of the environment available for human habitation and utilisation in coastal lowlands. The coastal zone is a valuable resource for humans today, as it has been in various ways for much of the Holocene period. For this reason, coastal palaeoenvironmental change is critical when considering the archaeological record found within the Shannon estuary.

The concept of vegetation succession and change in coastal environments is long established (Godwin and Turner 1933; Godwin et al. 1935; Walker 1970; Long and Shennan 1994) and describes how palaeoenvironments develop through time. Accurate reconstruction of prehistoric wetland succession patterns is difficult, since possible modern analogues are affected by the impact of human activity (e.g. agriculture, coastal defence works, land reclamation). Shennan (1986) proposes a number of zones representing palaeoenvironments and succession stages within the broader coastal wetland environment, which are defined below. Figure 18 shows a reconstruction of the possible palaeoenvironmental setting that might be found in places like the upper Shannon and Fergus estuaries and illustrates the relative spatial relationships between these stages or zones.

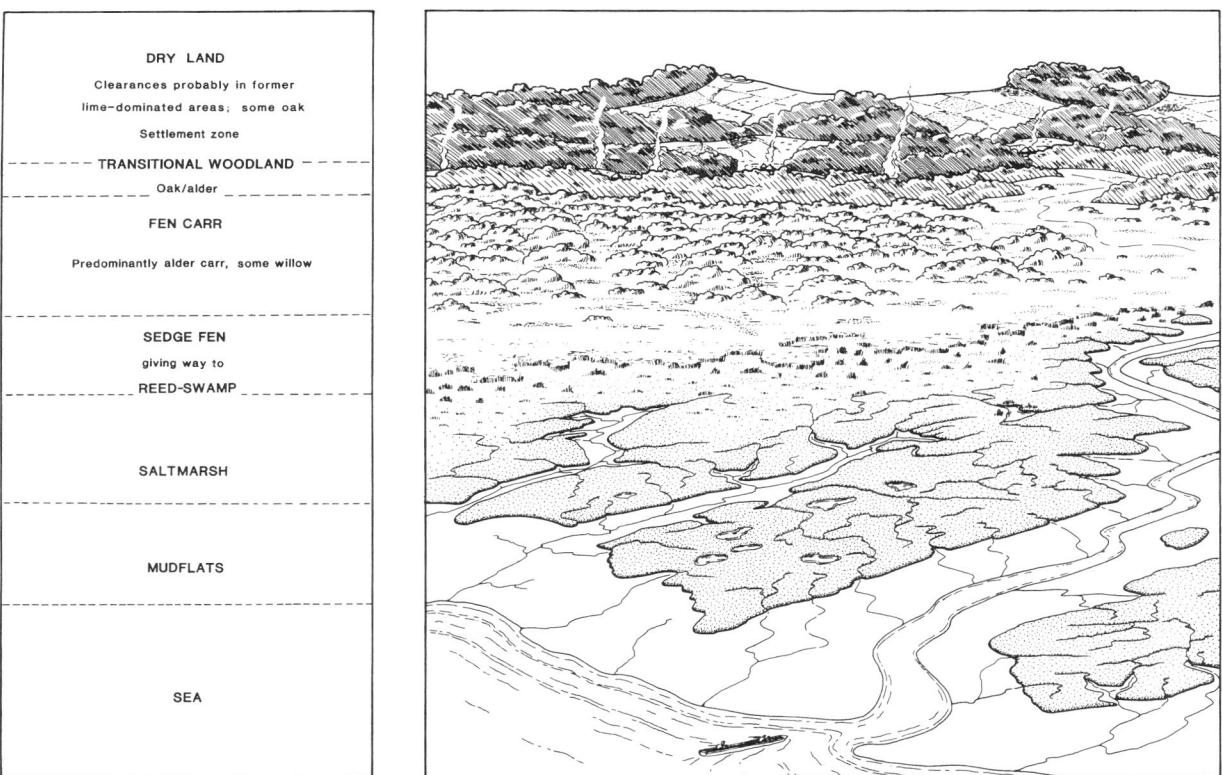

Fig. 18—*Artist's impression of an estuarine palaeoenvironmental setting (after Silvester 1991).*

The most seaward zone identified by Shennan (1986) is Zone 11, consisting of intertidal sandflats of fine to medium sand and less than 5% clay content. Zone 10 is a pioneering mudflat environment, where sediments consist mainly of silt (50–90%) and roughly equal proportions of sand and clay. This zone is transitional to Zone 9 (upper mudflat), which occurs between mean high-water mark of neap tides (MHWNT) and mean high-water mark of spring tides (MHWST). Sediments are generally finer than in Zone 10, with fine sand (up to 10%) in the lower part of the zone and clay content at *c.* 30–40% at higher levels; some organic material is also present. Zone 8 relates to creeks and creek levees, which in some estuaries are relatively common (e.g. the Wash, UK, on which Shennan's model was largely based). This is probably not a significant zone in the Shannon estuary, despite some aerial photographic evidence suggesting that they once occurred around Carrigdirty and Muckinish. Zone 7 consists of 'intercreek' areas, representing a gradual merging of the predominantly marine-influenced Zone 9 and the more freshwater-influenced Zone 6. This zone may be characterised by brackish standing water (Wheeler 1995).

In Zone 6, which consists of coastal reed-swamp, a fully vegetated environment prevails, representing a transition between the fully marine or brackish systems and freshwater wetland. The seaward boundary of Zones 6/7 lies between MHWST and midway between MHWST and highest astronomical tide (HAT). Here, *Phragmites australis* is the characteristic vegetation, and sedimentation is principally organic, leading to peat development. Inland of Zone 6, a transition to freshwater wetlands occurs through sedge fen, alder carr and oak fen woodland.

Whilst this and other schemes are useful for the interpretation of palaeoenvironmental data, they do not imply a direct succession from one environment to another. However, the model described has been used successfully in some archaeological investigations in UK wetlands (e.g. Waller 1994; Van de Noort and Ellis 1995), providing a basis for interpreting the subsurface palaeoenvironmental record. However, in the Irish context higher precipitation levels and the greater maritime influence on the climate may produce vegetation associations other than those found in the UK, leading to divergences from the UK model in the Irish sedimentary record from which palaeoenvironmental changes are inferred.

Coastal wetlands represent an interface between marine and terrestrial systems (Carter 1988). These environments change through time, either as part of a succession process or because of external forcing processes (e.g. relative sea-level movements) or events (e.g. storms). For instance, mudflats are environments of net deposition and therefore the elevation of the mudflat surface may rise through time, eventually resulting in reduced tidal inundation and colonisation by vegetation. This process may facilitate increased stability of the substrate, allowing the coastline to prograde seaward and resulting in the 'terrestrialisation' of the former mudflat. Such processes may be halted, retarded or reversed by changing external influences. As climate varies, the influence of components of the atmosphere (e.g. wind) and the hydrosphere (e.g. wave regime) also varies through time. These changes in environmental conditions have occurred continually throughout the history of the Shannon estuary, inextricably linking its evolution to processes of environmental change. In addition, the influence of human activities (e.g. land clearance, land reclamation, flood protection), operating in tandem with 'natural' environmental change, has introduced alterations in the development and functioning of the Shannon estuary wetlands on a wider scale than might otherwise have proved possible.

Reclamation history

James Lyttleton, Aidan O'Sullivan, Andrew Wheeler and Michael Healy

The morphology of the Shannon estuary has been significantly affected by the reclamation of its wetlands and marshes. Reclamation has had consequences for sedimentary and morphodynamic processes within the estuary, probably including changes in water and sediment transport patterns and changes in the tidal prism. These may in turn have led to localised changes in hydrology and relative sea level. Reclamation reduces the area over which wave energy can be dissipated, producing higher-energy environments (Brampton 1992). Drainage and reclamation can also lead to subsidence and compaction of sedimentary sequences, affecting the preservation of archaeological material (Van de Noort and Ellis 1995) as well as the value of sedimentary sequences for environmental reconstruction (Tooley 1978; Shennan 1994).

In contrast to elsewhere in northern Europe, there has been little historical research on coastal reclamation in Ireland (but see Rowe and Wilson 1996 for studies on Wexford Harbour). There are extensive tracts of reclaimed estuarine alluvium (locally known as corcass) along the Shannon and Fergus estuaries. In County Clare (Shannon estuary and Fergus estuary) there are c. 5900ha of estuarine alluvium (Finch 1971), while around the Shannon, Maigue and Deel in County Limerick there are about 5601ha of estuarine alluvium (Finch and Ryan 1966). This land is below spring tide levels and has been reclaimed using a system of dykes, sluices and sea walls.

The earliest reclamation efforts on the estuary possibly date from the late medieval period, although local tradition ascribes them to the Vikings (O'Carroll 1978, 32). Earthworks, low banks and substantial walls visible today inland in the corcass may be former reclamation banks. The earthworks around Bunratty Castle, traditionally interpreted as fortified ramparts for either tenth-century Viking or thirteenth-century Anglo-Norman settlements (e.g. Westropp 1913–15, 314–15; J. Bradley 1988b), have recently been shown to be seventeenth-century in date (J. Bradley and King 1991). Although these earthworks may be related to sieges of the castle at this time, it is possible that they were actually built to protect the low-lying lands around Bunratty from high spring tide flooding. Historical and cartographic sources certainly suggest that some reclamation banks were in place by the mid-seventeenth century. For example, the Civil Survey's description of the landscape along the south bank of the upper Shannon

Coastal landscapes in the Shannon estuary

Pl. 12—*Aerial view of corcass at Carrigdirty Rock and Newtown townland, Co. Limerick, where there may be at least three ancient or relict sea-banks inland of the modern sea-bank. Cartographic sources and historical references suggest that reclamation may have begun here as early as the late sixteenth century.*

estuary at the River Maigue (Simington 1938, 388–9, 392) includes references to lands that were 'embanked' and meadows that were 'overflowing' at spring tides. These earlier sea-banks can now be seen in the corcass at Newtown, Co. Limerick, set hundreds of metres inland from the bank of the estuary (Pl. 12). Another early reference to reclamation is found in a lease of land made by the earl of Thomond's agent to Colonel Henry Ingoldesby, on the Fergus estuary near Clarecastle, dated 2 October 1656, where a directive is issued to 'make up the seabanks and sluices' (Ainsworth 1961, 353–4).

Extensive reclamation had taken place by the seventeenth century. In a description of Clare in 1682, Hugh Brigdall, an attorney living in Ennis, stated that 'towards the brink of the Shannon the south east bounds of this county lieth a rich vain of land with many thousand acres of marsh defended with banks from the fury of that river' (Ó Dálaigh 1998, 68). The sea-banks had to be maintained to safeguard the agricultural value of the lands. For example, during the Williamite wars, in 1690, Terlagh O'Brien promised to supply King James's administration with 300 tonnes of hay or corn from his land at Latoon (beside the Fergus estuary). However, by 1691 it was reported that he had allowed his farmland to go derelict and 'had suffered the seabankes, draines and sluces thereon to goe to decay . . .' (Ainsworth 1961, 469). Incidentally, immigrant Dutch settlers introduced the growing of coleseed on the marshlands in the seventeenth century, and it may not be a coincidence that these settlers came from the nation with the most expertise in land reclamation (Ó Dálaigh 1998, 69).

In Thomas Moland's survey of the earl of Thomond's estates in Clare for the year 1703 there are references to corcass banks, sea-banks and sluices along the Fergus estuary in the parishes of Kilfentinane and Kilnasullagh. Those corcass lands in the vicinity of Islandmagrath were exposed to damage by the river (Ó Dálaigh 1998, 80–1, 90). Maintenance of these sea-banks was a capital-intensive exercise. One bank running between Islandmagrath and Clarecastle was repaired in 1763 with several hundred men being employed (Ainsworth 1961, 496–7; Connors 1999). However, investment in reclamation could be amply rewarded, as illustrated by the observations made by Arthur Young, the noted agriculturalist and travel writer, in 1776 that 'there are 20,000 acres called the carcasses' and that 'when in tillage, they sometimes yield extraordinary crops; 50 stat barrel an acre of bere have been known, sixteen of barley, and from 20 to 24 of oats are common crops . . .' (Hutton 1970, 285, 291–2).

Travellers in Ireland, such as the architect and botanist Joseph Woods in 1809 and the celebrated Victorian author William Thackeray in 1842, admired the fertile quality of the corcass bordering the Shannon and Fergus (Ó Dálaigh 1998, 144, 198). Immediately after the Famine, a Scottish agricultural expert, James Caird, carried out a survey on farming in the south and west of the country on behalf of the British government in the autumn of 1849. He alluded to the tracts of rich alluvial land, the 'corcases', which had provided very high rents before the onslaught of the Famine (Ó Dálaigh 1998, 240). On the western side of the Fergus estuary, around Islandmagrath and Islandavanna, substantial areas of land were reclaimed from tidal marshes in a series of works in the nineteenth century. In 1864, plans for the drainage of more than 7000 acres were proposed, including substantial areas of embankment at a cost of around £26,000 (Anon. 1864). Most of the embankments were built and maintained by the local landed gentry until the passage of the Land Purchase Acts, when responsibility passed to local trustees set up by the Land Commission. However, these embankments were never maintained properly and breaches occurred from time to time (Anon. 1979).

The care of embankments was transferred to the Commissioners of Public Works under the terms of the Arterial Drainage Act, 1945. During the 1950s a number of important schemes were carried out by the Commissioners to enhance the flood protection along the Owenagarney River near Bunratty, from Bunratty to Rineanna on the north side of the Shannon, and at the mouth of the Fergus. In 1961 a severe storm resulted in the breaching of embankments along the Shannon estuary. In the worst-affected areas farmland was flooded to a depth of 5m, and at Coonagh houses were flooded to the eaves. This prompted further schemes at Coonagh, the Ballinclough embankment, the Mellon–Ringmoylan embankment, the Ringmoylan–Foynes embankment and along the River Maigue, north of Kildine. The development of well-constructed embankments in the second half of the twentieth century allowed the protection and drainage of existing agricultural land with some reclamation, and aided the industrial development of the region with a focus on Shannon Airport (Anon. 1979).

Conclusions

During the last 14,000–15,000 years the Shannon estuary has witnessed relatively rapid environmental change as the last of the Pleistocene ice-sheets waned, climatic amelioration ensued and ecosystems became re-established in areas that had been glaciated or in proximity to ice-sheets. The adjustment to more congenial climatic conditions involved considerable changes in floral and faunal assemblages, as well as changes in soil genesis. On the basis of available evidence relating to geology, soils, climate and modern-day conditions, as well as environmental analogues elsewhere, this chapter characterises our present knowledge of the Holocene environment which formed the context for human activity around the Shannon estuary. A detailed history of how the Shannon estuary evolved cannot yet be reconstructed, and many of the opinions on the nature of the Shannon palaeoenvironment presented here remain conjectural. Future research will go much further in establishing a better understanding of environmental change around the Shannon estuary.

3. NEOLITHIC SUBMERGED FORESTS, RED DEER BONE AND WETLAND OCCUPATION SITE

Introduction

The earliest archaeological and palaeoenvironmental sites recorded during the survey include Neolithic submerged forests in peats at Rinevalla Bay and Poulnasharry Bay, Co. Clare, and Bunaclugga Bay, Co. Kerry, on the lower Shannon estuary (for locations see Fig. 1) and at Meelick Rocks, Co. Limerick, on the upper Shannon estuary (Fig. 19). Neolithic deposits of red deer bone were also identified at two locations on the upper Fergus estuary, Co. Clare (Fig. 19). Early prehistoric sites identified at Carrigdirty Rock, Co. Limerick, on the upper Shannon estuary, include a Late Mesolithic wooden plank (Carrigdirty Rock 8) and a possible Early Neolithic wetland occupation site (Carrigdirty Rock 5) in minerogenic or estuarine clays on a narrow sloping foreshore (Fig. 19).

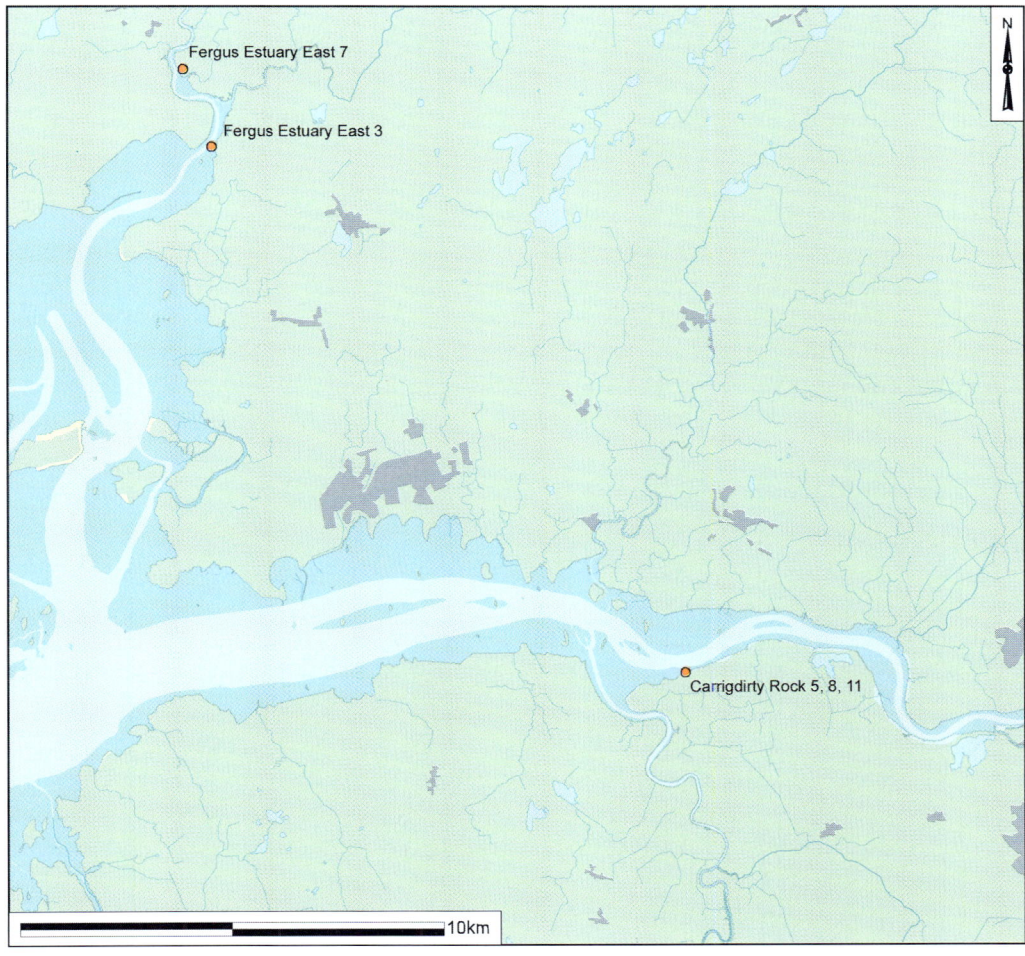

Fig. 19—*Map of Shannon estuary, showing location of Neolithic sites (Barry Masterson, Discovery Programme).*

Foragers, farmers and fishers

These early prehistoric sites were probably all originally set in quite different environments, such as riverine woodlands, marshy carr woodland and possibly saltmarsh or reed-swamp. In the Mesolithic and Neolithic it is possible that the upper Shannon estuary and Fergus estuary had several broad, shallow channels flowing through huge expanses of mudflats and saltmarshes, with a surrounding marshy landscape of reed-swamps, fens and carr woodlands of alder and willow. The surrounding hills and terraces were probably densely covered by oak, Scots pine and elm forests, with impenetrable stands of hazel and ash growing by the wetland margins. Sea-level rise and coastal geomorphological change have led to the submergence of these landscapes under subsequent layers of organic peat or estuarine silts. Our knowledge of these early prehistoric environments can only be conjectural for the moment in the absence of the palaeoenvironmental studies necessary to establish their true character. However, we can draw some preliminary conclusions from the soils, geology and drainage and from the evidence that sea levels were somewhat lower in early prehistory (see Chapter 2; Carter *et al.* 1989; Woodman, Anderson *et al.* 1999).

Mesolithic and Neolithic submerged forests

Introduction

Mesolithic, Neolithic and Bronze Age submerged forests are common features of intertidal peat deposits around the British and Irish coastlines. At the mouth of the Shannon estuary, at Rinevalla Bay, Co. Clare (Pl. 13), a Neolithic submerged forest of Scots pine and oak survives embedded in peats exposed near the top of the foreshore (Mitchell 1990, 143). At Poulnasharry Bay 1 and Poulnasharry 3, Co. Clare, Neolithic submerged Scots pine trunks and root buttresses are emerging from peats on the intertidal zone and in the saltmarsh cliffs at the east and north-west sides of the bay. At Meelick Rocks 1, Co. Limerick, immediately downstream of Limerick, a Neolithic submerged forest (possibly of oak and alder) is exposed in peats on the upper foreshore, while the peats of the lower foreshore have produced a stone axe as well as cattle, pig and dog bone. Probable Late Neolithic or Bronze Age submerged forests in peats can also be seen at Carrigdirty Rock 16, Co. Limerick, at Bunaclugga Bay 1, Co.

Pl. 13—*General view of Neolithic submerged forest at Rinevalla Bay 1, Co. Clare, on the lower Shannon estuary, with Scots pine and oak trunks exposed in the upper foreshore peats.*

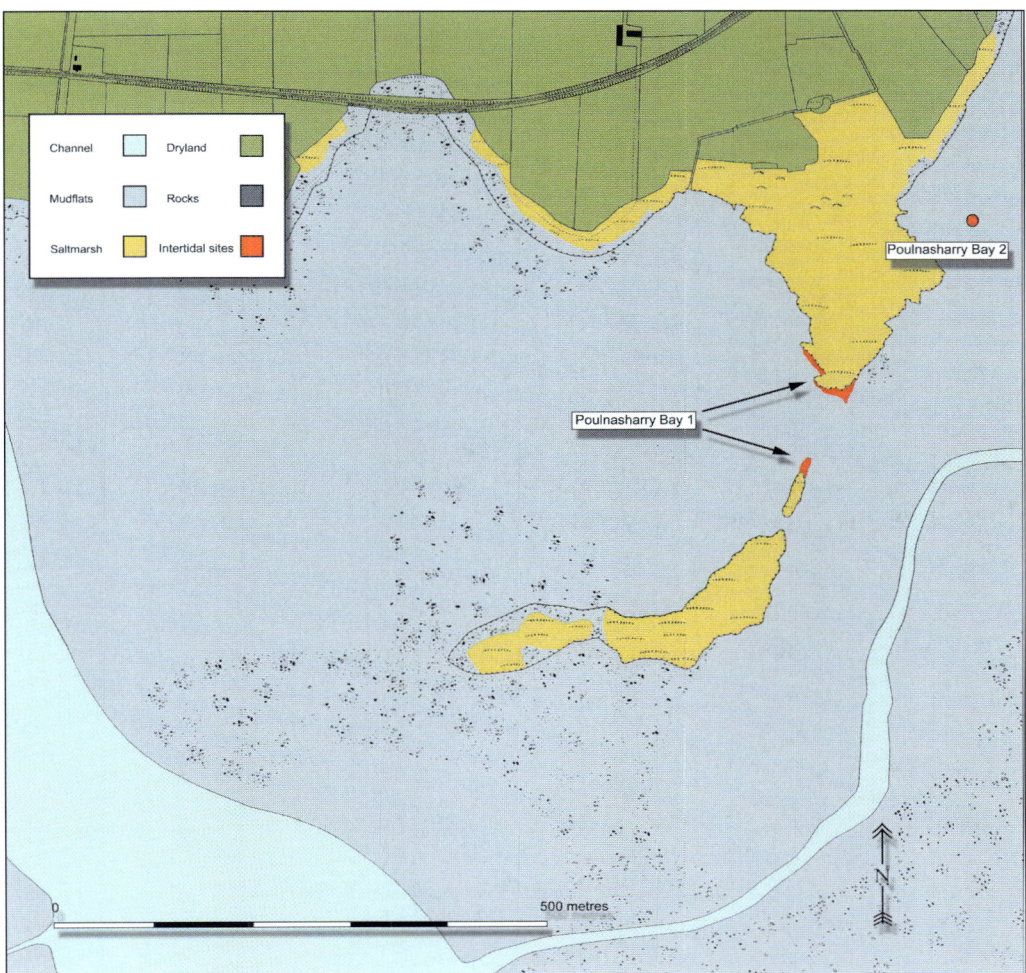

Fig. 20—*Location map of Neolithic submerged forest at Poulnasharry Bay 1, Co. Clare, lower Shannon estuary.*

Kerry, and possibly at Bunratty 5, Co. Clare (see Appendix 2). Palaeoenvironmental investigations have been carried out on similar submerged peats in the intertidal zone at several locations in south-west Ireland. At Ballycotton, Co. Cork, and at Knockaunaglanshy and Fahamore, Co. Kerry, palynological and macrofossil studies and radiocarbon dating of peat and saltmarsh sediments all provide evidence for the prehistoric growth of extensive oak–alder woodlands and fen in areas now long submerged (Carter *et al.* 1989; Devoy 1991). The early prehistoric submerged forests from the Shannon estuary are described here mainly to enable other researchers to undertake such palaeoenvironmental studies.

Poulnasharry Bay 1—Neolithic submerged forest

Site location

The Poulnasharry Bay 1 submerged forest is located in a bay on the north shore of the lower Shannon estuary, adjacent to the townland of Moyasta, Co. Clare (Figs 1 and 20). It can most clearly be identified at two locations: in the sides of the deep creeks that dissect the saltmarshes throughout the north-west end of the bay, and at the substantial trunks and root buttresses exposed on the foreshore between the saltmarsh and a small island at the eastern side of the bay (Fig. 20). At this latter location, the submerged forest trunks are eroding out of peats under the saltmarsh cliff and are also exposed over an area of intertidal shoreline some 200m in length. The Poulnasharry Bay submerged forest site was first discovered in summer 1992, and was recorded in 1992 and 1995 by means of a vertical section cut into the saltmarsh cliff. Samples for radiocarbon dating were taken from the peat/clay contact towards the top of the section and from a submerged forest root bedded in the basal peats.

Foragers, farmers and fishers

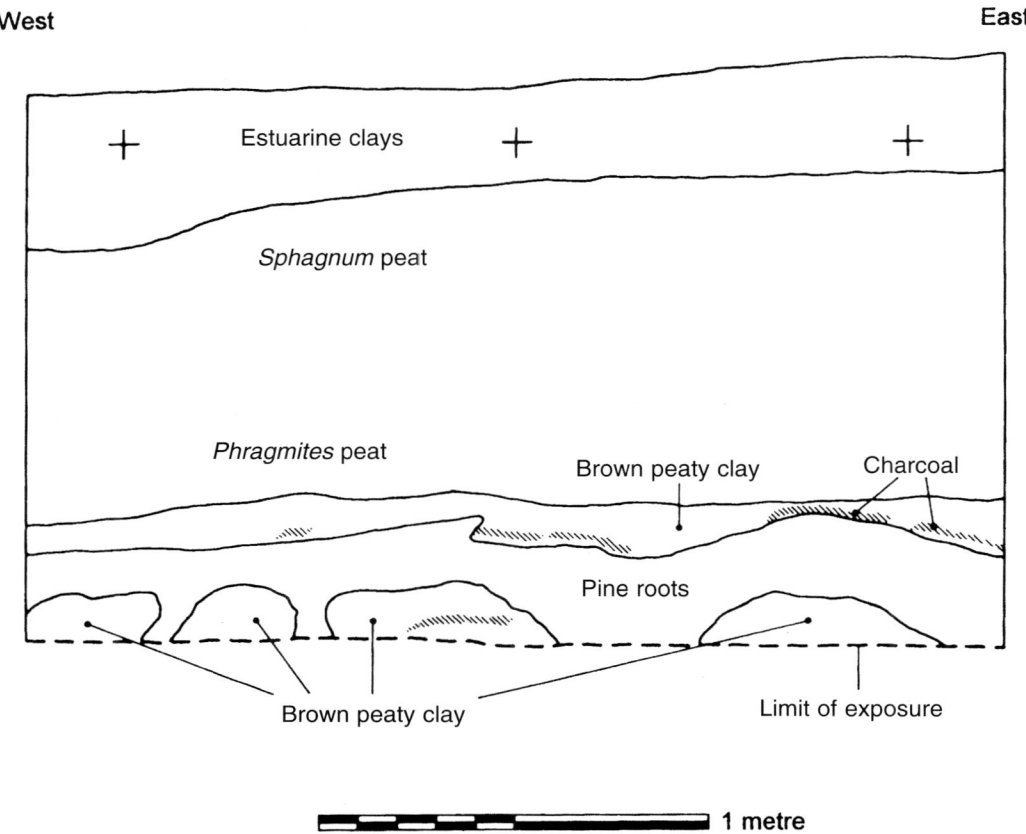

Fig. 21—*Section of Poulnasharry Bay 1 saltmarsh cliff, showing stratigraphical succession from fen peat to sphagnum peat to alluvial clays.*

Site description

The submerged forest trunks were identified as Scots pine (*Pinus sylvestris* L.). They survive to heights of up to 1.5m and range in diameter from 0.35m to 0.8m (see Table 2). The root bases or buttresses of these trunks are quite large, up to 6m wide. Tree-ring estimates made in the field (which typically underestimate true ages) indicate that the trunks were more than 80 years old. A section of the saltmarsh cliff was cleaned and recorded (Fig. 21). This revealed that the root systems lie at a depth of 1.5m below the saltmarsh, and are based on peaty clays which are overlain by a thick, discontinuous band of charcoal. A single sample from a submerged forest root produced an Early Neolithic radiocarbon date of 4960±35 BP (3892–3655 BC; GrN-20145). The submerged forest trunks are set in brown peaty clay with a high organic content, with vegetal matter and charcoal scattered through it in bands. The layers of charcoal are tightly packed, measuring 0.05–0.06m in thickness. The charcoal is found both below and above the pine root systems.

The Scots pine trunks and the thick charcoal layer are overlain by up to 1m of peat. The lower part of the peat is rich in *Phragmites* and other fen plants. The upper layers are of *Sphagnum* peat, with some rhizomes of *Phragmites* and some *Eriophorum* present. These *Sphagnum* peats are then capped by a 30cm depth of estuarine clays laid down by spring high-water levels. The peat/clay contact is quite sharp, possibly indicating rapid erosion of these peats and a deposition of modern estuarine clays. A sample from the peat/clay contact produced a Late Iron Age radiocarbon date of 1640 ± 40 BP (cal. AD 262–534; GrN-21928).

Table 2—*Neolithic pine trunks from Poulnasharry Bay 1 submerged forest.*

Trunk no.	Species	Diameter	Height	Tree-rings	Context
1	Scots pine	51cm	65cm	60+	Saltmarsh cliff
2	Scots pine	35cm	50cm	—	Mudflats
3	Scots pine	60cm	1.5m	—	Peats on foreshore
4	Scots pine	50cm	60cm	75+	Mudflats
5	Scots pine	40cm	70cm	80+	Mudflats
6	Scots pine	80cm	1.2m	—	Mudflats

Discussion

Scots pine (*Pinus sylvestris* L.) is a native Irish tree species, colonising the landscape from the Early Mesolithic onwards. It grows to heights of 35–50m, with a straight, tapering trunk from which rises a flat crown. The submerged Scots pine forest at Poulnasharry Bay 1 is a coastal example of a common feature of Irish raised bogs, blanket bogs and intertidal peats on the west and south-west coast (e.g. O'Connell 1988). Although Scots pine may have survived in Ireland in isolated locations into the early medieval period, subfossil pines have largely proven to date from *c.* 2000–1500 uncal. BC (e.g. McNally 1990). The submerged trunks at Poulnasharry Bay seem to be based on peats, and this could represent in west Clare the stable sub-boreal climatic conditions and terrestrialisation of peat which allowed pine woodland to spread on to bogs elsewhere (Moore and Bellamy 1974). Subsequent peat accrual under wetter oceanic conditions may have led to the submergence in peat of the pine woodlands, and thereafter rising sea levels in the estuary region caused the peats to be capped by estuarine clays. It is probable, then, that the Poulnasharry Bay submerged forest testifies to both climatic fluctuations and rising sea levels in the Shannon estuary since the Early Neolithic.

Meelick Rocks—Mesolithic/Neolithic submerged forest

Site location

The Meelick Rocks submerged forest is located on the north bank of the upper Shannon estuary, adjacent to the townland of Coonagh East, Co. Limerick, where intertidal peats and forest trunks are being exposed to the south-east of a natural rock outcrop (Meelick Rocks) that lies on the east bank of the outlet of the Crompaun River (Fig. 22). Erosion on this foreshore is exposing complex environmental deposits of peat, estuarine clays, gravels and an area of outcropping bedrock.

Site description

The Meelick Rocks submerged peats lie on both the upper and lower foreshore and are spread over an area measuring approximately 150m in length (north-west/south-east) by about 50m in width (north-east/south-west). The peats are sealed under estuarine clays in the saltmarsh cliff at the top of the foreshore. The peat contains substantial recumbent tree trunks, extensive root systems and branches, especially at the eastern extent of the site (Pl. 14). Preliminary species identifications suggest the presence of oak and alder carr woodland. A radiocarbon date of 4160 ± 20 BP (2875–2634 cal. BC; GrN-21930) was obtained from a narrow root from a large group of buttresses on the upper foreshore. This indicates that the submerged trunks and peats of the upper section of the foreshore date from at least the Late Neolithic.

A low ridge of stone and gravel runs along the low-water mark, south and south-west of the Meelick Rocks outcrop. The ridge is generally oriented north-east/south-west and also rises towards the natural bedrock outcrop. A deposit of peat and clay lies along the north-east side of this gravel and stone ridge. This peat itself overlies a white,

Foragers, farmers and fishers

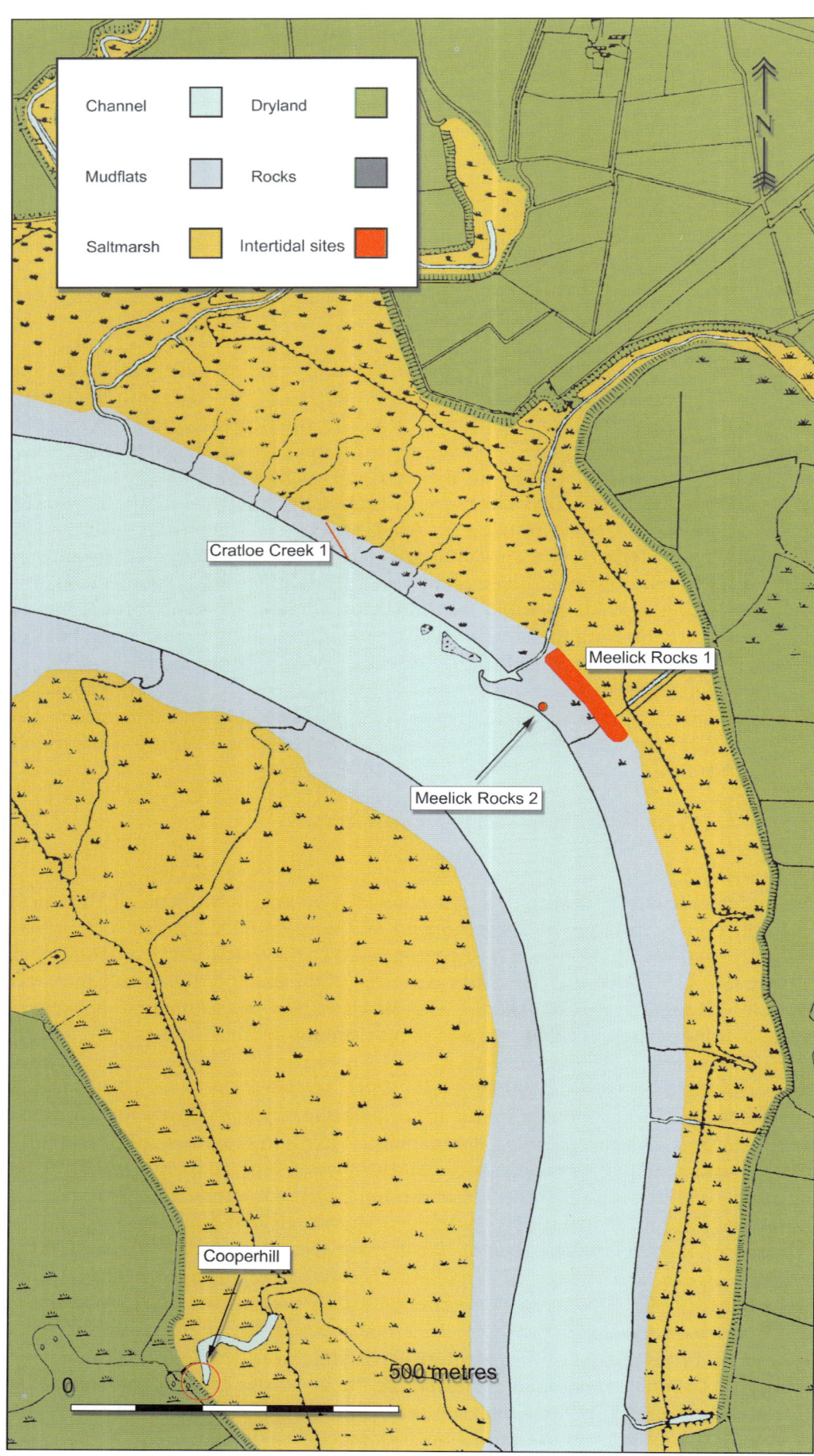

Fig. 22—*Location of late Neolithic submerged forest and stone axe findspot at Meelick Rocks 1–2, Co. Limerick, on the upper Shannon estuary.*

Neolithic submerged forests, red deer bone and wetland occupation

Pl. 14—*Late Neolithic submerged forest roots and trunks on upper foreshore, Meelick Rocks 1. The early prehistoric stone axe (right) at Meelick Rocks 2 was found on the lower foreshore, where the person is standing.*

marly clay (exposed on the foreshore to the south-west, and possibly of freshwater lacustrine origin). There are also some tree roots and trunks in this area. A stone axe was found at Meelick Rocks 2 (Fig. 22), in gravels overlying the surface of the exposed peat. Its location suggests that it is a fluviatile deposit, washed into this place from somewhere upstream. A sample was taken from roots in the peat directly beside the findspot of the stone axe and radiocarbon-dated to 6240 ± 25 BP (5299–5078 cal. BC; GrN-21929), possibly indicating peat formation against the rock outcrop in the Later Mesolithic period. There were also animal bones lying in this peat. Their date and origin are unclear, and they may also be fluviatile deposits.

The stone axe
EMMET BYRNES AND STEPHEN MANDAL

The Meelick Rocks stone axe (NMI 95E0228:3; Fig. 23) was manufactured by pecking or hammering and was then ground to smooth out any surface irregularities. Its sides are broad and rounded. The junctions of the sides with the cutting edge are clear on the left but damaged on the right. There are also clear junctions of the sides with the butt. The original shape of the cutting edge (i.e. in plan) is indeterminable owing to a few large post-manufacture chips in the centre and a very large post-manufacture flake scar on the right side. The cutting edge is straight in profile. The blade area is damaged on the right side of face 2 by the large post-manufacture flake

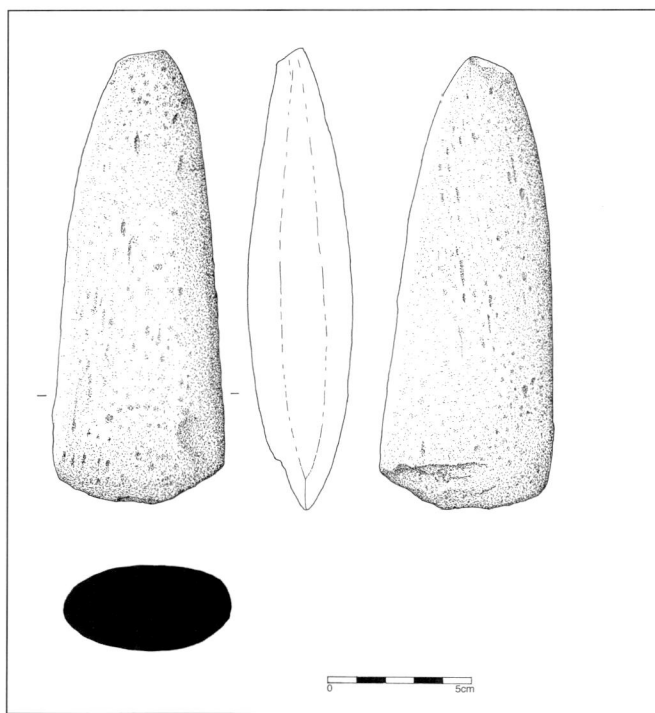

Fig. 23—*Meelick Rocks stone axe (NMI 95E0228:3).*

scar which extends from the cutting edge. A small, shallow and well-ground remnant flake scar adjacent to the junction with the right side on the face 1 blade area suggests that this portion of the cutting edge may have been resharpened on at least one occasion. Both the blade area and the faces are very well ground and very regular. The butt has only been partly ground. The axe is slightly asymmetrical in profile and oval in cross-section. The entire surface of the axe is covered with fine remnant peck-marks, many elongated owing to the schistose nature of the rock. The axe measures 16cm in length, 5.6cm in maximum width (at the junctions of the sides with the cutting edge) and 3.3cm in maximum thickness, and it weighs 445g.

Petrography

The Meelick Rocks stone axe was macroscopically identified as a coarse- to medium-grained dark grey/brown iron-rich schist, of doleritic origin. Schist is the only clearly metamorphic rock type (other than porcellanite) that was commonly used for stone axes in Ireland. It accounts for 525 (3.3%) of the total recorded to date (Mandal 1997). Of the schist axes recorded, 20% form a distinct petrographical subgroup, found mainly in Ulster (particularly in County Antrim). Small numbers have also been found in the south of Ireland. These are coarse-grained and green to green-grey in colour, and exhibit a strong schistocity which is parallel to the length and thickness of the axe (a feature also seen on the Meelick Rocks axe) (Cooney and Mandal 1998). Woodman and Johnston (1991–2) have described chlorite schists similar to these from the Mesolithic sites at Mount Sandel (Early Mesolithic) and Newferry (Later Mesolithic). A second, smaller, distinct petrographical subgroup of schist axes are dark grey to black in colour and medium- to coarse-grained. Again the schistocity is parallel to the length and thickness of the axe. The Meelick Rocks stone axe does not fall into either of these subgroups. Indeed, it is different from Irish schist axes in general in that it is relatively dense, probably owing to a high concentration of iron minerals.

Potential sources

The largest extent of metamorphic rocks in Ireland is centred in County Donegal and west County Derry, and extends to the east in north-east County Antrim and to the west in west Mayo and Galway. The distribution of schist axes in Ireland generally follows this pattern. Woodman (1977, 189), in discussing the occurrence of schist axes (similar to the chlorite schist axes discussed above), particularly in the lower zones of the Later Mesolithic site at Newferry, Co. Antrim, suggested that they were derived from local glacial erratics. The crude nature of many of these schist axes, particularly the chlorite schists, supports this observation, as does the overall distribution pattern.

It is possible that the schist axes in counties Galway and Clare are derived from the metamorphic rocks of west Connemara. These are also the closest outcrop sources for axes from counties Limerick and Cork. It is therefore possible that the Meelick Rocks axe was made from a schist source within these outcrops in west Connemara, or from a more local glacial erratic derived from them (see Mandal 1996; Cooney and Mandal 1998). To date, more than 1500 stone axes have been recorded from the north Munster area. Of these, more than 65% are made of shale or mudstone, and only seventeen are schists. Of these schist axes, sixteen were found in the vicinities of either Lough Gur, Co. Limerick, or Killaloe, Co. Clare, where Neolithic activity is well documented (e.g. Mahr 1937; Condit and O'Sullivan 1999). The Meelick Rocks axe is particularly interesting as it is the only schist axe in the north Munster area recorded outside of Lough Gur and Killaloe, and it is of unusual petrography.

The animal bone
VINCENT BUTLER

Seven bones were recovered from the immediate vicinity of the stone axe findspot (from an area measuring 5m in radius around it), one of which was unidentifiable to species level. Cattle were represented by two rib fragments and a complete ulna. The olcranon of the latter was unfused, indicating that this particular animal was under three and a half years of age at the time of death. A humerus (L) from an immature pig and a complete humerus (L) from a dog (*Canis familiaris* L.) were identified. As the proximal epiphysis of the latter bone was fused, the animal must have been at least fifteen months old at time of death. A single sawn fragment of bone found near the site was not identified.

Table 3—*Meelick Rocks animal bone.*

Bone no.	Species	Bone type	Details	Metrical data (mm)
MR 1	Cattle	Rib	Blade fragment	—
MR 2	Cattle	Rib	Blade fragment	—
MR 3	Cattle	Ulna (R)	Complete, proximal epiphysis unfused	—
MR 4	Pig	Humerus (L)	Immature, missing proximal end and distal epiphyses	—
MR 5	Dog	Humerus (L)	Complete, proximal and distal epiphyses fused	Greatest breadth distal end (Bd) 36.4; greatest length (Gl) 197.0

Discussion

The Meelick Rocks stone axe, and perhaps the undated animal bone as well, may indicate Neolithic settlement activity in the vicinity of the upper Shannon estuary. It is, of course, possible that the stone axe is of Mesolithic date, contemporary with the peat on which it was found, as Mesolithic schist axes are known (Woodman, Anderson *et al.* 1999). However, given its location in fluviatile gravels and its form, it seems more likely to be Neolithic in date (Gabriel Cooney, pers. comm.). Other early prehistoric stone axes are known from along the upper Shannon estuary—from Gallowshill, Bunratty East and Tullyglass Point, Co. Clare, to the north and west and also from Carrigdirty Rock 5, Co. Limerick (see below). There is little other good evidence for

Neolithic settlement, although Late Neolithic wedge tombs are located at Brickhill and Ballinaphunta on the western slopes of the Cratloe hills, Co. Clare, while a Late Neolithic stone macehead was also found at Ballycar South, to the north-east (Condit and O'Sullivan 1999).

Obviously a stone axe found near an early prehistoric carr woodland would seem to be particularly tangible evidence for Neolithic forest clearance and other woodland activities. Indeed, pollen studies from the neighbouring peats might well support such an assertion. However, the chronological relationship between the stone axe and the submerged forest of the upper foreshore cannot be clearly established. The axe may originally have been deposited upstream in the river channel and washed down to this location. It is also possible that the stone axe was originally deposited in coastal wetlands (carr woodlands, marshes, saltmarsh) rather than the open water of a river channel. Stone axes have commonly been found unhafted and deliberately deposited in springs, bogs and rivers throughout Ireland. Indeed, river dredgings in the River Shannon further upstream from Meelick Rocks, at Killaloe, Co. Clare, produced huge numbers of stone axes that were probably deliberately deposited there (Cooney *et al.* 1990; Grogan *et al.* 1996; Condit and O'Sullivan 1999).

Interpreting the use and perception of Neolithic woodlands on the Shannon estuary

The Neolithic submerged forests on the Shannon estuary should certainly be the subject of further archaeological and palaeoenvironmental investigations. These would allow us to reconstruct the ecology of prehistoric woodlands on the Shannon estuary, prior to the transformations brought about by millennia of human intervention and climatic and ecological change. These submerged forests could be investigated in a number of ways. The distribution of different tree species, the density of tree growth, the age structure of the woodland, the longevity of individual trees, the understorey and woodland floor vegetation, and the associated beetles and molluscs could all be studied in detail.

The submerged trunks, roots and branches also highlight the fact that our knowledge of the character, extent and ecology of Neolithic woodland in Ireland typically comes quite literally from the tiniest of evidence. Pollen grains, charcoal and occasionally well-preserved pieces of wood are used to reconstruct the character and varying extent of woodlands in the early prehistoric landscape. Traditionally, archaeologists have interpreted the fluctuations of these palaeoenvironmental indicators as representing direct evidence for the waxing and waning of human populations as well (i.e. increased woodland cover is usually taken to denote a hiatus in human activity). In other words, prehistoric woodlands are interpreted only as a blank space to be cleared for agricultural purposes or as a resource to be felled for timber. Obviously, this hinders us from thinking of woodlands as significant places in the Neolithic landscape.

The Shannon estuary submerged forests also offer an opportunity to reflect on the physical reality of woodlands and how Neolithic communities experienced them. The Rinevalla Bay and Poulnasharry Bay woodlands may have been growing along stream banks and river valleys and were later covered by fens and raised bogs. The Meelick Rocks and Carrigdirty Rock (see below) woodlands were probably wet carr woodlands of oak, alder, birch and willow growing near fens and saltmarshes. These could have been the location for a range of Neolithic economic activities. However, it is important to remember that the Shannon estuary coastal woodlands would have been recognised as important places in the local cultural landscape. Certainly, they might have been economically exploited (hunting, wildfowling, cattle-grazing, etc.), but they could also have influenced the organisation of local territorial boundaries, routeways, settlements and sacred landscapes.

Neolithic red deer bone deposits

AIDAN O'SULLIVAN AND VINCENT BUTLER

Introduction

Neolithic and Bronze Age animal bones were relatively common finds on the Shannon estuary mudflats. Red deer, pig, cattle, swan, pink-footed goose, sheep/goat and dog bones were discovered in the submerged forest at Meelick Rocks, at the Early Neolithic occupation site at Carrigdirty Rock 5, and at the Middle Bronze Age house, posts and pit at Carrigdirty Rock 1–3 (see Chapter 4). However, discrete deposits of Neolithic red deer bone were also recorded at two specific locations, both of them on the east bank of the upper Fergus estuary, Co. Clare (Fergus estuary east 3 and 7). These deposits were localised spreads of partly articulated bone buried in grey estuarine or minerogenic clays. In neither case is there any indication of human activity (i.e. no evidence for the presence of wooden traps, tools, butchering, etc.). It is likely that both spreads of bone are natural in origin.

Fergus estuary east 3—red deer bone

Site location

This compact spread of red deer bone was found on the east bank of the upper Fergus estuary, adjacent to the townland of Ballygirreen, Co. Clare. It was first recorded in July 1992, and again in May 1994 (by which time most of the bone had been removed by erosion). The site was located where the channel broadens as it swings past Crow Island and turns down towards Islandavanna (Fig. 24). The animal bone was set in inorganic, blue-grey estuarine clays, 3m east of the LWM. The single femur bone produced a Late Neolithic radiocarbon date of 4245 ± 40 BP (2919–2689 BC; GrN-20140).

Site description

The bones were spread over an area measuring at least 1m by 0.5m and were firmly embedded in the clays, some positioned at vertical or acute angles (Pl. 15). They were articulated, the vertebrae in particular being still attached together. Seven bones were retained and were all identified as being of red deer (*Cervus elaphus* L.); they comprised a single example each of the left mandible, femur, tibia and metatarsal, as well as three articulated vertebrae. The bones were well preserved, although those exposed were somewhat weathered. The femur, tibia and metatarsal were all left side elements, confirming that this was a single individual. Based on the erupted permanent dentition and its wear pattern and the degree of fusion of the epiphyses of the longbone elements, the evidence suggests that this was a mature animal. In the absence of cranial material sexing was impossible.

Table 4—*Neolithic red deer bone, Fergus estuary east 3.*

Bone no.	Bone type	Metrical data (mm)
BRD1	Thoracic vertebra	—
BRD2	Thoracic vertebra	—
BRD3	Thoracic vertebra	—
BRD 4	Mandible (L)	Length of M3 28.3; breadth of M3 13.2
BRD 5	Femur (L)	—
BRD 6	Tibia (L)	Greatest length 349
BRD 7	Metatarsal (L)	Greatest length 278; greatest breadth 36.9

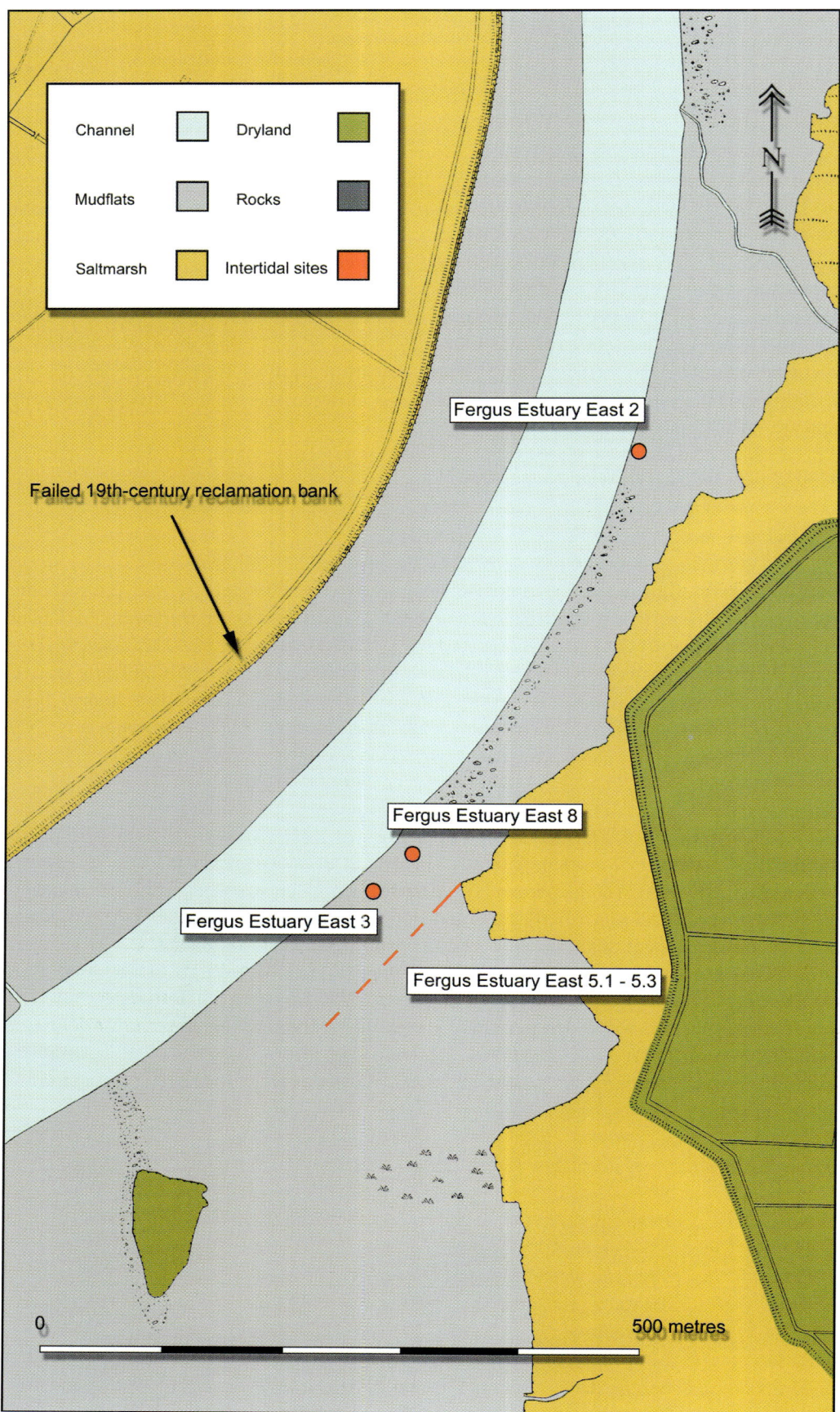

Fig. 24—*Detailed location map of Neolithic red deer bone, Fergus estuary 3, Co. Clare.*

Pl. 15—*Neolithic red deer bone at Fergus estuary east 3, Co. Clare.*

Fergus estuary east 7—red deer bone

Site location

This compact spread of red deer bone was located on the east bank of the upper Fergus estuary, adjacent to the townland of Carrownanelly, Co. Clare (Fig. 1). The bones were set in inorganic, grey estuarine clays, on a very steeply sloping foreshore near the LWM (Pl. 16). They were recorded in August 1995, when six bones were retained for faunal analysis. It is likely that the site has since been removed by erosion. While the bones are undated, the general similarity in elevation and context to Fergus estuary east 3 suggests that these bones are also Neolithic in date.

Site description

The bones were spread over an area measuring 1m by 0.2m. Some were articulated and all of these were identified as belonging to red deer (*Cervus elaphus* L.). They consisted of an atlas, axis and cervical vertebrae, and a humerus, radius and ulna. Both sets of bones presumably belong to the same animal. The vertebrae represent the upper neck, while the longbones are from the right upper front leg. All of the epiphyses of these latter specimens were fused, showing that the animal was mature at time of death. Each fragment was complete. There were no indications as to cause of death.

Table 5—*Red deer bone, Fergus estuary east 7.*

Bone no.	Bone type	Metrical data (mm)
CN 1	Atlas vertebra	—
CN2	Axis vertebra	—
CN3	Cervical vertebra	—
CN4	Humerus (R)	Greatest breadth, proximal end (Bp) 74.5; greatest breadth, distal end (Bd) 56.5; greatest length (GL) 275.0
CN5	Radius (R)	Greatest breadth, proximal end (Bp) 55.8; greatest breadth, distal end (Bd) 49.1; greatest length (GL) 286.0
CN6	Ulna (R)	Greatest breadth across the coronoid process (Bpc) 32.5

Pl. 16—*Possible Neolithic red deer bone at Fergus estuary east 7, Co. Clare.*

Discussion

Red deer (*Cervus elaphus*) is a species indigenous to Ireland, although it appears to have been absent from the Early Mesolithic period and may have been a late immigrant (van Wijngaarden-Bakker 1989). It is known from Late Neolithic and Beaker levels from around the passage tomb at Newgrange, Co. Meath (Mount 1994). A possible ritual deposit of red deer bone was found with wood ash and Early Bronze Age axes at Carhan, Cahersiveen, Co. Kerry (Waddell 1998, 128). Otherwise, red deer is a consistent, although relatively uncommon, find on Neolithic, Bronze Age and Iron Age settlement and sacred sites (McCarthy 2000, table 1, 109). Deer meat, skin, antler and bone were used occasionally by prehistoric communities, but evidence for hunting is scanty. Indeed, it is possible that red deer may only have been present in very small numbers in the country throughout prehistory.

How did Neolithic red deer bone come to be on the Fergus estuary mudflats? Some insights can be gleaned by a study of the habits of red deer populations in south-west Ireland (Ryan 1998). In the Killarney region, large red deer populations inhabit the wet alder woodlands, between the reed-beds and the grassland pastures, around the lakes. In summer, most of the day is spent grazing and chewing the cud, while lying up in the long grasses. Troubled by flies, both the stags and the hinds wallow in deliberately excavated pools and muddy hollows in the bogs and marshes. Indeed, some of these watery wallows are used year after year as deer return to them. In midsummer, the stags, hinds and young calves gather into large herds in the mountains and in the lowlands, typically in open areas where predators can easily be seen, to graze on the grasses, sedges and rushes, and also to browse on the leaves of birch, oak, holly, alder and whitethorn.

As the autumn moves on, and certainly by October, the rutting season is well under way. After the rut, the deer generally come down from the mountains and hills and into the lowland woods. During winter, bark is stripped from willow, birch, holly and hazel, or whatever trees are available. Mortality rates peak amongst the deer herds in April, when fat reserves are lowest. During the frosts and rain of these months, most of the deer carcasses are to be found in the valley bottoms and near streams, amongst the rushes, furze and heather where the animals seek shelter. Mortality is highest amongst the calves (as many as a third of the summer calves die), the sick and the aged. Causes of death include drowning, liver fluke, pneumonia and hypothermia.

The deer whose bones were found in the Fergus estuary mudflats probably died of hunger and exposure, although accidents or disease are also possible causes. The deer may have drowned while attempting to cross the river and its tributaries, or they may have become stuck in the soft, muddy silts and were drowned at high tide or starved to death. Carcasses are typically torn apart within a few days of death by predatory ravens, grey crows and foxes. Usually only the large leg bones and some of the vertebrae are left. The Fergus estuary deer may have expired in some isolated location in the estuarine marshes or mudflats, away from the eyes of most bird or animal scavengers, and were slowly buried under the muds.

Mesolithic and Neolithic sites at Carrigdirty Rock

Introduction

Carrigdirty Rock is a low, natural bedrock outcrop presently exposed on the intertidal zone on the south bank of the Shannon estuary, 2km east of the outlet of the River Maigue, adjacent to the townland of Newtown, Co. Limerick (Fig. 25). Similar rocky islands can be seen out in the estuary channel itself and also further inland, where they appear as large grassy mounds in the reclaimed corcass. A range of multiperiod archaeological and palaeoenvironmental deposits have been found to the

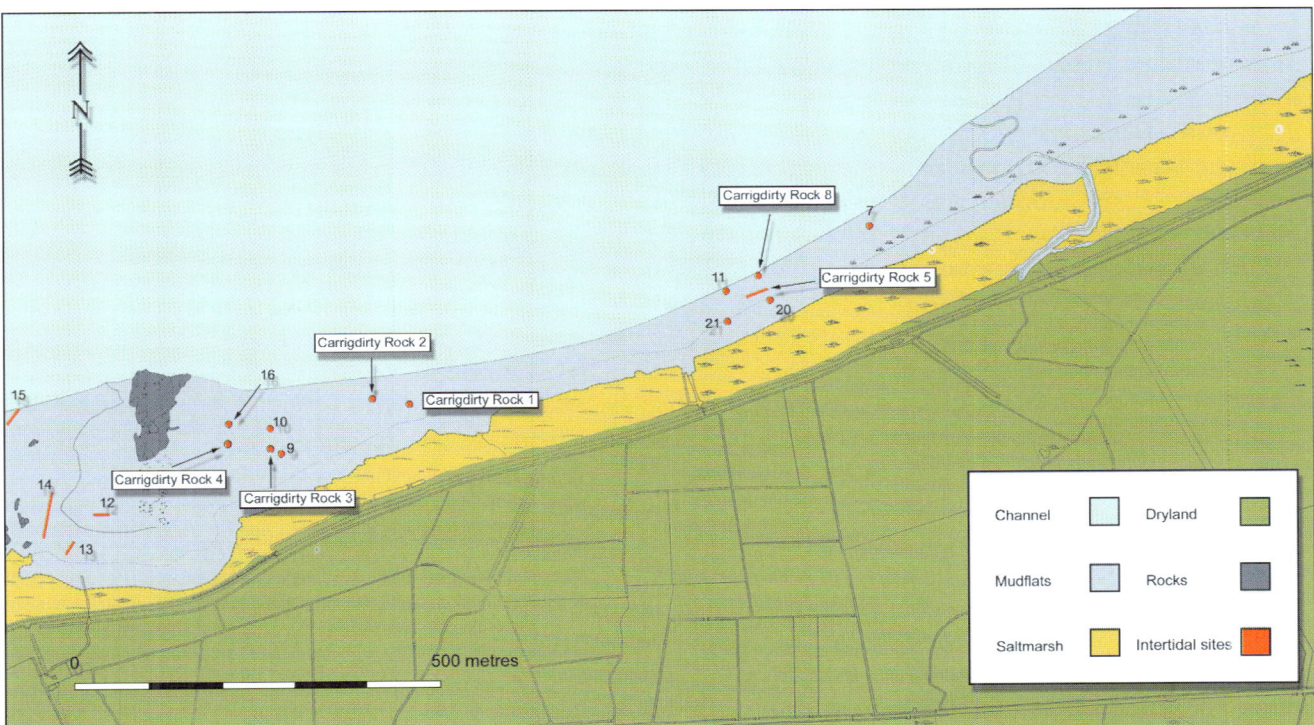

Fig. 25—*General location map of Mesolithic, Neolithic, Bronze Age and post-medieval intertidal sites at Carrigdirty Rock, Co. Limerick.*

Pl. 17—*Aerial view of intertidal foreshore at Carrigdirty Rock 5–8 site. The Carrigdirty Rock 5 Neolithic basket, bone, worked wood and lithics were mostly found in the clays immediately in front of a low mud cliff, indicated by the dark line on the lower foreshore, while the Carrigdirty Rock 8 Mesolithic plank was found at the low-water mark (photo: Shannon Estuary Ports).*

east of Carrigdirty Rock, over an area measuring 820m (east-north-east/west-south-west) by 50m (north/south), both in a shelf of organic peats on the upper foreshore and in minerogenic or estuarine clays on the lower foreshore. The overall sediment sequence at Carrigdirty Rock appears to represent a record of a series of marine transgressions and regressions or other events resulting in fluctuations in marine activity in the area. Stratigraphic evidence for such a pattern of events is reflected in the presence of the intercalated minerogenic-dominated strata (clays and silts) with organic-rich layers (i.e. peats).

The archaeological sites identified include the Mesolithic/Neolithic finds to be discussed here, as well as possible Bronze Age wooden house or hut structures (Carrigdirty Rock 1–2), planks (Carrigdirty Rock 20–1), a post feature (Carrigdirty Rock 4), a pit (Carrigdirty Rock 3), and stray finds of animal bone (Carrigdirty Rock 9–10) from the organic peats on the upper foreshore (see Chapter 4).

The Mesolithic and Neolithic sites were exposed in minerogenic or estuarine clays on the lower foreshore, c. 820m east of Carrigdirty Rock itself (Fig. 25; Pl. 17). They include a Late Mesolithic wooden plank (Carrigdirty Rock 8), a spread of brushwood (Carrigdirty Rock 11) and a possible Early Neolithic wetland occupation site (Carrigdirty Rock 5). The original environmental context of these early prehistoric sites is unclear. Preliminary studies on the minerogenic-dominated strata of the lower foreshore (where the Mesolithic and Neolithic material has been recovered) indicate a palaeoenvironment with a strong marine influence. The deeper stratigraphic sequence, exposed to view on the lower foreshore at Carrigdirty Rock 5–8, shows a sequence of calcium carbonate-rich detrital silts and clays with some fine sand. Preliminary diatom studies suggest an environment strongly influenced by marine or saline conditions (Blythe *et al.* 1996b).

The radiocarbon date derived from the wooden plank (Carrigdirty Rock 8) found in the sediments at the LWM has revealed that these deposits accumulated sometime before and after 5820 ± 40 BP (4779–4551 cal. BC; GrN-21936). The basketry found in the reedy, minerogenic clays at Carrigdirty Rock 5 has been radiocarbon-dated to 4820 ± 50 BP (3702–3386 cal. BC; GrN-6520) and 4820 ± 50 BP (3702–3386 cal. BC; Beta-102087), suggesting continued estuarine conditions at c. 3400 BC.

Late Mesolithic wooden plank and brushwood

Carrigdirty Rock 8—wooden plank

Site location

Carrigdirty Rock 8 is a single wooden plank situated in dark grey estuarine clays, on a gently sloping foreshore just above the extreme LWM (at NGR 147830, 157699; OD –2.375m). The plank was exposed at its western end, along a clay shelf eroded by tide and wave action, while to the east most of the plank lay buried under *c.* 8–10cm of firm, grey estuarine clays. The site was visible for about 10–20 minutes at MLW.

Site description

The plank is a long, narrow fragment of poplar wood (*Populus* L. — aspen, white poplar or black poplar), measuring 4.3m in length, 37cm in maximum width and 7cm in depth (Pls 18 and 19; Fig. 26). The side edges and base are quite thin, measuring 0.9–1.4cm in thickness. The fragment was slightly U-shaped in cross-section towards its eastern end, being nearly flat at the western end. The buried end of the plank was investigated by excavating a small area, 1m (east/west) by 40cm (north/south). This revealed that the plank curves at the end, from which a small fragment was broken away. The upper surface of the plank varies, with a knotty, corrugated, rough appearance in some parts, while in others it was smooth and even. There was no

Pl. 18—*Late Mesolithic wooden plank, Carrigdirty Rock 8, buried in clay at LWM; other fragments can be seen within the plank.*

Pl. 19—*Upper end of Late Mesolithic plank, Carrigdirty Rock 8.*

evidence for tool-marks on the surface. Examination of the undersurface of the plank at the exposed end near the LWM indicated that sapwood and bark may be adhering to it. The tree-ring or growth patterns of the trunk were also examined at the exposed end of the plank and were concentric with the curve of the plank in cross-section. A thin, narrow fragment or strip of wood was also recorded in the clays inside the plank, at its lower end. A sample from the edge of the main plank has been radiocarbon-dated to 5820 ± 40 BP (4779–4551 cal. BC; GrN-21936).

Site interpretation

This plank, with its slightly U-shaped cross-section and curved upper end, has previously been interpreted as the base of a dug-out boat (e.g. O'Sullivan 1997b) on the basis of comparisons with similar plank fragments found elsewhere in northern Europe (especially Denmark), where such an interpretation would probably be readily accepted. Late Mesolithic dug-out boat fragments from Denmark, such as those found at Lystrup, Aero and Tybrind Vig, were all long, narrow, curved planks of lime, alder or poplar, surviving from light, thin-sided vessels with a long, narrow, lanceolate shape, ideal for navigating coastal creeks and channels (Christensen 1990; Andersen 1987; 1994). However, the interpretation of the Carrigdirty Rock 8 plank as a dug-out boat fragment can be questioned. A dug-out boat of this form would certainly be quite different from the few known early prehistoric Irish canoes, which are mostly large, heavy oak craft (Brindley and Lanting 1996; Fry 2000, 116–17). The Carrigdirty Rock fragment is fairly uniform in thickness, and nowhere measures over 1–1.5cm in thickness. In contrast, the Danish dug-out boats, although typically 2–3cm thick at the side edges, generally thickened to 5–6cm at the base and at the bow end.

It is possible that the Carrigdirty Rock 8 plank instead derives from a natural tree trunk that exfoliated a thin, U-shaped plank away from the heartwood. The lack of clear evidence for woodworking, the fragility and thinness of the plank, its corrugated appearance in parts, the possible presence of bark and sapwood on its undersurface, and the presence of another, very similar thin strip or fragment of wood within it may suggest such natural cleavage or splitting of a strip of bark and wood from a fallen trunk. A similar, naturally curved or concave plank (4.14m in length, 35cm in width, 8–10cm in thickness) was found in an Early Bronze Age trackway at Annaghbeg, Co. Longford. This also had sapwood and bark adhering to it (Raftery 1996, 168, fig. 227).

However, an undated carved wooden fragment (Carrigdirty Rock 7) of similar appearance and species was found in clays *c.* 100m to the east of the Carrigdirty Rock 8 plank, slightly higher up the foreshore (Fig. 25; Pl. 20). Although this fragment was found at quite some distance from the Carrigdirty Rock 8 site, it might indicate at least some woodworking activities or the cleaving of wood in the vicinity.

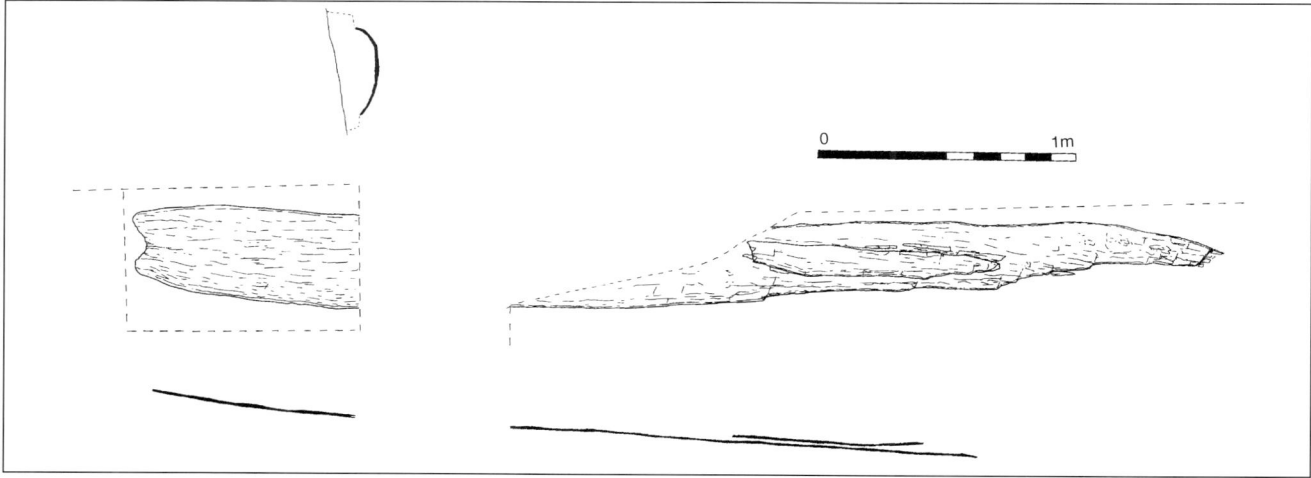

Fig. 26—*Plan of Late Mesolithic wooden plank, Carrigdirty Rock 8.*

Pl. 20—*A fragment of carved wood from a small trough or vessel found in clays at Carrigdirty Rock 7 (c. 100m east of Carrigdirty Rock 8); possible tool-marks are visible on the thicker portion.*

Carrigdirty Rock 11—brushwood feature

Site location

Carrigdirty Rock 11 is a scatter of brushwood or woody stems exposed along a low clay shelf, just above the LWM, approximately 15m to the west of Carrigdirty Rock 8.

Site description

The site consists of brushwood, typically oriented north/south, spread along an area 2m in length, exposed into the clays for a distance of 30–40cm. The individual rods were quite narrow, measuring 1–2cm in diameter. A single piece, 3cm in diameter, lay diagonally across the brushwood. The site was briefly investigated in 1994, when a narrow cutting, measuring 1m (east/west) by 10cm in width (north/south) by 10cm in depth, was excavated 50cm further up the shore. This indicated that brushwood rods and branches also lay buried at a depth of 5–10cm under the clays. There was no evidence for tool-marks.

Site interpretation

This brushwood feature is probably natural in origin, being the result of natural twigs and branches lying together in the clays. However, the regular alignment and tightly packed nature of the brushwood could suggest a platform or trackway laid down to consolidate or firm up some marshy or reedy ground. Its date is unknown, but its similar elevation to Carrigdirty Rock 8 suggests a Late Mesolithic origin.

Neolithic coastal wetland occupation site

Carrigdirty Rock 5 — organic and lithic artefacts and bone

Site location

Carrigdirty Rock 5 was a scatter of lithic and organic artefacts and animal bone located on a narrow, sloping foreshore on the south bank of the Shannon estuary, adjacent to the townland of Newtown, Co. Limerick (a precise location for one definitely stratified piece of worked hazel wood is NGR 147814, 157690; OD –1.591m). This site is located *c.* 6–7m to the south of and 0.78m higher up the foreshore than the Mesolithic plank at Carrigdirty Rock 8 (Pl. 21).

Foragers, farmers and fishers

Pl. 21—*General view looking to the north-east across Carrigdirty Rock 5 Neolithic site; the basket, chert flakes, skull fragment, worked wood and animal bone were found in reedy, organic-rich clays in front of the low clay cliff to the right.*

The site was recorded by means of repeated visits (on about eight occasions) between summer 1994 and summer 1997. During each visit, the foreshore was carefully inspected by pacing up and down at intervals of 5–10m. Finds were collected and labelled. The topography of the foreshore was surveyed using a Total Station set up on the nearby saltmarsh cliff (where a temporary survey station was established using a grid peg), thus enabling a contour map and digital terrain model (DTM) of the foreshore to be created. The precise spatial location and elevation of some finds was recorded by means of this Total Station; the location of other finds was recorded by reference to the topography, the sediments and earlier findspots. Preliminary palaeoenvironmental investigations involving a series of stratigraphical cores were also carried out on the saltmarsh to the south (Blythe *et al.* 1996b). The vertical stratigraphy of the peats and clays can therefore be linked in a general way with the detailed topographical survey and the location of finds (Figs 27 and 28).

Site description

The site is located over a narrow stretch of intertidal foreshore measuring about 30m (east/west) by 2–3m (north/south), and is defined by a small scatter of worked and charred wood, charcoal, hazelnuts and burnt bone, a stone axe, two chert chips, a possible hammerstone, woven basketry, two pieces of human bone, and several bones from swan and young cattle. The finds are being exposed by erosion from a narrow (*c.* 2m wide, *c.* 10–15cm deep) band of grey, reedy and woody minerogenic clays directly beneath and north of an eroding clay 'cliff' on the lower foreshore. This 'cliff' is *c.* 15–20cm high and runs parallel to the low-water mark, *c.* 10m to the south of the MLWM. Some of the finds (e.g. the basket fragment, the worked and charred wood, and the human clavicle and cattle bone) were stratified in this organic-rich clay. Other finds (e.g. the stone axe, the possible hammerstone and pebbles, other cattle and bird bone, and the human skull fragment) were recovered as unstratified surface finds lying on this band of clays or at locations 2–3m lower down the foreshore.

The environmental context

The stratified finds emerged from a particularly organic-rich band of dark grey minerogenic clays containing well-preserved narrow reed stems, woody fragments and other plant materials. The reed stems are bedded horizontally and are tightly packed, suggesting that a former marshy area of reed-beds had been pushed down and

Neolithic submerged forests, red deer bone and wetland occupation

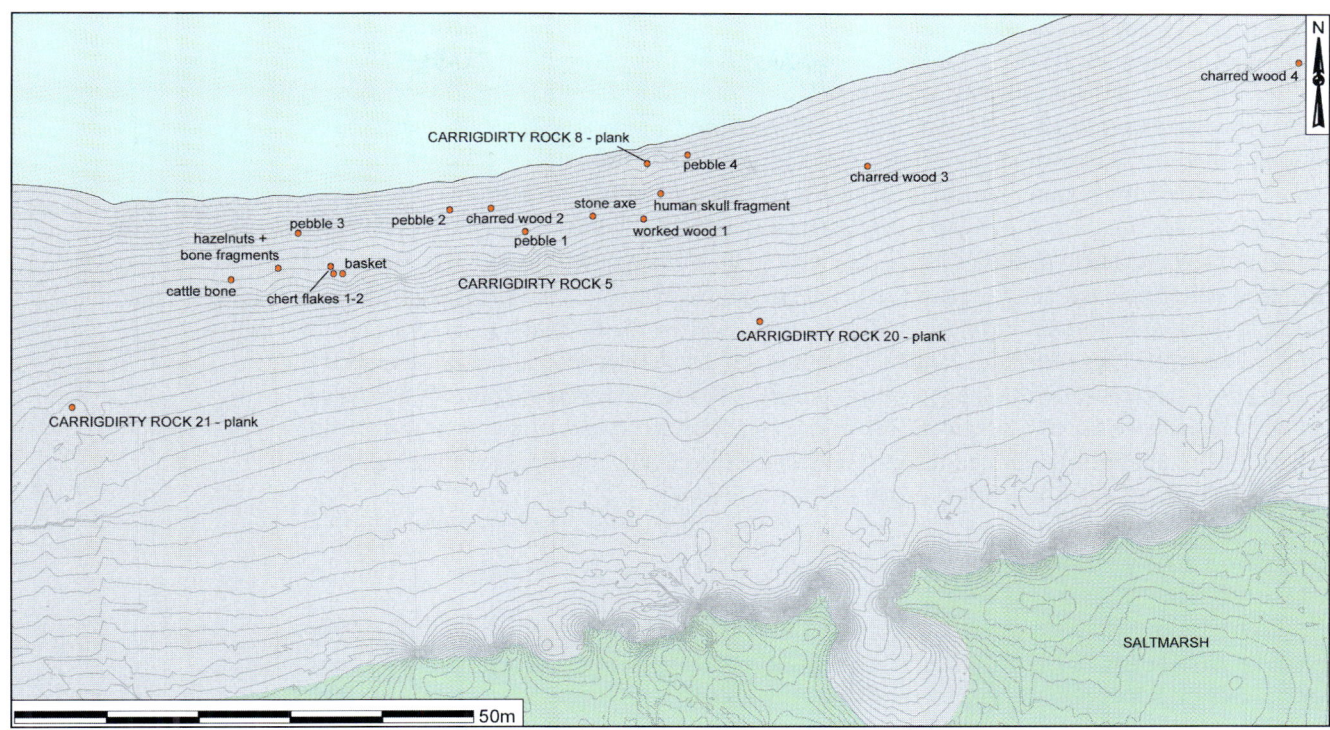

Fig. 27—*Carrigdirty Rock 5–8: contour plan of intertidal foreshore showing locations of Carrigdirty Rock 8 plank, Carrigdirty Rock 5 finds in minerogenic clays and Carrigdirty Rock 20–1 planks in peat (Barry Masterson, Discovery Programme).*

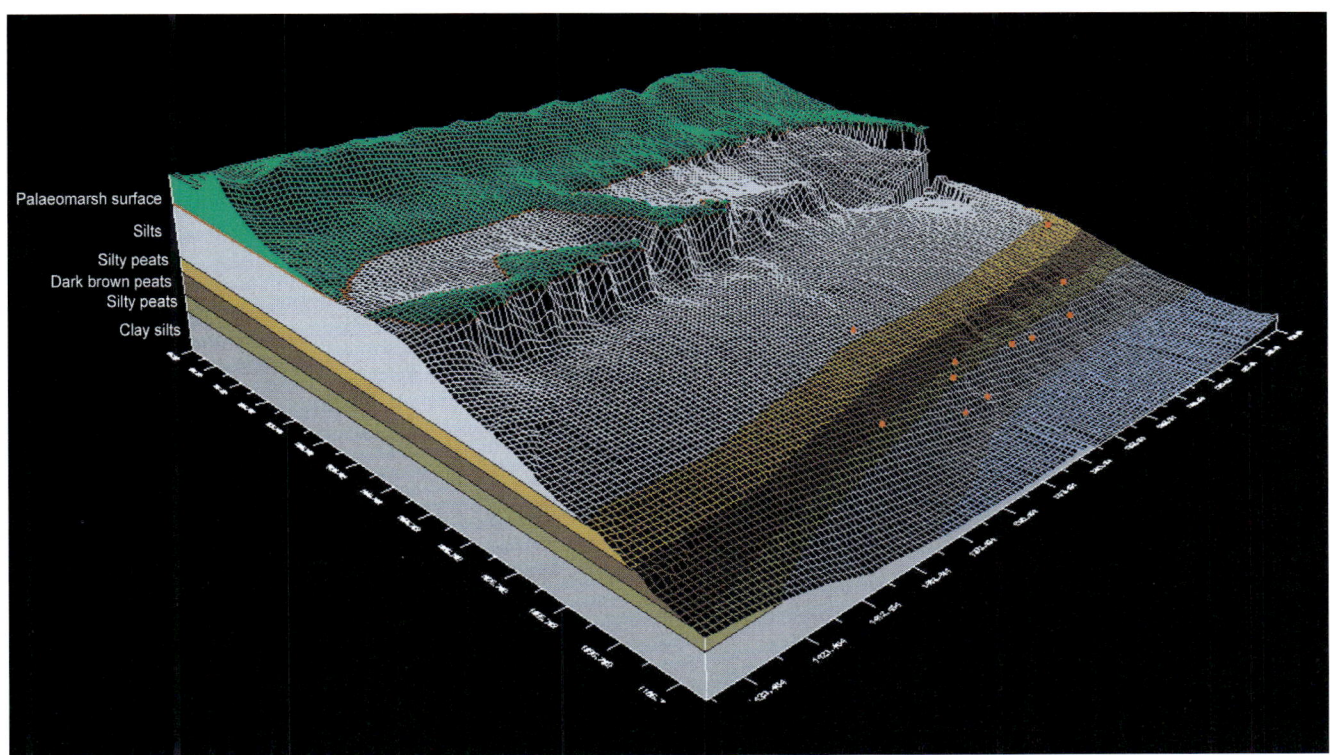

Fig. 28—*Digital terrain model of Carrigdirty Rock 5–8 foreshore, showing location of Mesolithic and Neolithic finds and their broad relationship with a sedimentary sequence identified by coring in the saltmarsh adjacent to the foreshore (Barry Masterson, Discovery Programme).*

flattened, probably through water action. Several fragments of roots and roundwood were also embedded in these clays. The wood was well preserved, retaining bark and twigs, and was typically knotty and branch-like, probably deriving from the topwood of small trees and bushes. The roundwood measured up to 20–30cm in length and about 2–3cm in diameter and, although also found at this elevation further to the east, was typically concentrated in the area north of the clay 'cliff'.

These minerogenic clays were subsequently overlain by a bed of organic peats, rich in woody fragments and root systems, which is exposed further up the foreshore beyond the cliff to the south at a slightly higher elevation. These peats clearly post-date the minerogenic clays and are probably contemporary with the main shelf of peat that is to be found all along the Carrigdirty Rock foreshore to the west (over an area 820m in length (east/west) by 50–60m in width (north/south)). Another local topographical feature is a rock outcrop in the estuary channel, visible at extreme low water, 5–6m north of the LWM. This rock outcrop (and the swirl of water it produces) may be partly responsible for the erosion 'cliff' on the lower foreshore.

Human, cattle and bird bone
Margaret McCarthy

Eight bones were recovered from the Carrigdirty Rock 5 site. These have been identified as animal (3), bird (3) and human (2) remains. Bone survival was extremely good but the sample size is too small for valid analysis and interpretation. The following account summarises the general points, such as species present, age and butchery. No measurements could be taken as all of the bones were fragmented.

Human bone

A large fragment of a human skull, broken from the frontal-parietal part of the cranium, probably derived from an individual aged over 25–35 years (identified by Barra Ó Donnabháin). This was an unstratified find from the eastern end of the site (in July 1994) (Pl. 22; Fig. 29). The skull fragment produced an AMS radiocarbon date of 4710 ± 60 BP (3634–3370 cal. BC; Beta-102086). A right clavicle from an adult human was also found on the clays, and displays some marks suggesting that it may have been chewed by a dog.

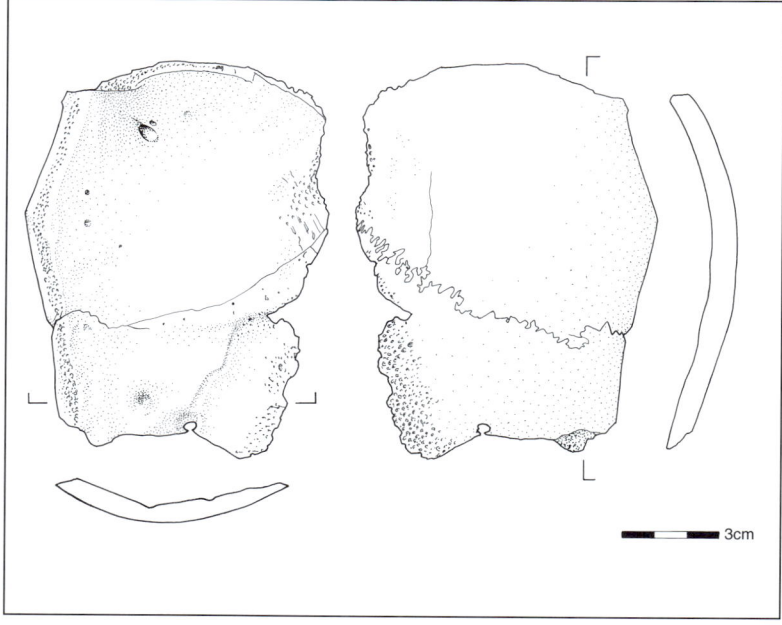

Pl. 22 *(left)—Neolithic human skull fragment found on clays at Carrigdirty Rock 5.*
Fig. 29 *(above)—Neolithic human skull fragment (drawing: Tom O'Sullivan).*

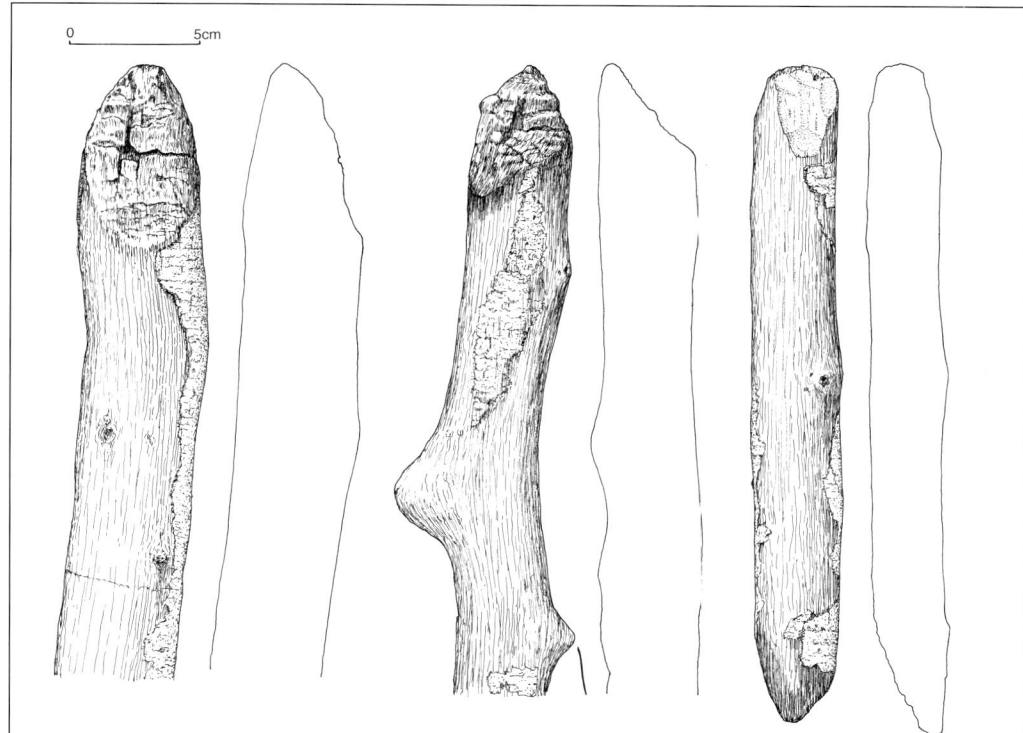

Fig. 30—*Worked and charred wood from clays at Carrigdirty Rock 5.*

Cattle bone

At least one juvenile is represented. A proximal portion of a metacarpus was recovered from the clays at the west end of the site. This is small and porous and suggests an animal aged around ten months. Two cattle lumbar vertebrae were also recovered. The lateral processes were broken off and, except in one instance, the vertebral plates are not fused to the centrum. The metacarpus and the vertebrae probably belong to the same individual.

Bird bone

The three bird bones have been identified as the remains of an adult swan. They come from the peripheral, non-meat-bearing areas of the wing and leg, and again probably derive from a single individual. The midshaft portion of a left tibiotarsus (lower leg bone) was recovered from near the basket. Two wing bones (radius and ulna) were found in the reedy clays. The dorsal ends of the bones were removed in antiquity, although no clear cut-marks can be observed. The bones make a perfect match with a modern mute swan, *Cygnus olor,* skeleton. This is the only resident species of swan and is commonly found on lakes and rivers throughout Ireland.

Hazelnut fragments
AIDAN O'SULLIVAN

Hazelnut fragments were relatively common in the clays, scattered across the site, and some may have been charred. There were also small, discrete deposits of a gritty shell-rich clay (near the basket findspot), containing tiny fragments of unidentified broken and charred bone, pieces of wood, and broken and whole hazelnut shells. A single unstratified pine nut was also picked up from the foreshore near this deposit.

Worked and charred wood
AIDAN O'SULLIVAN AND MARY B. DEEVY

The worked and charred wood in the band of organic-rich estuarine clays was widely scattered across the site, although it was particularly common towards the eastern end. Six pieces of worked and charred wood were sampled for analysis (Fig. 30). Two pieces of oak were identified on site. The other pieces were identified as the rods or branches of hazel (*Corylus* sp.) and pomaceous fruitwood (Pomoideae sp.). The roundwood was aged 6–11 years and measured 3.5–4.5cm in diameter. There was a single piece of definitely worked hazel roundwood, with stone axe tool-marks visible on the sharpened end and charring at the opposite end. It was chopped to a wedge-shaped point with a stone axe wielded at shallow cutting angles of 10–15 degrees to reduce the diameter, and it had then been torn or snapped away from the trunk. The tool-marks on the worked end were narrow and short (facet length 1cm, facet width 1cm), with facets that were slightly dished in profile and cross-section. The individual tool-marks were rough and abraded, with rough facet junctions. This type of tool-mark evidence suggests the use of small ground stone axes or flaked flint axes. The edges of the stone axes used were clearly not sharp, the main action of the tool being a tearing or splitting action (see O'Sullivan 1996c for discussion of stone axe tool-marks). Two other pieces of possibly worked wood had been burnt and charred in a fire, as indicated by their blackened and fragmentary pointed ends, while a large chunk of totally charred wood was also recovered.

There were also several fragments of split and charred oak (*Quercus* sp.) lying horizontally in the clays. These measured up to 25–40cm in length and were derived from oak roundwood trunks that were originally 10–15cm in diameter. The charring was typically found only at one end, as might be expected from roundwood left lying in a fire that had burnt out or had been extinguished. The evidence for woodworking on these pieces was generally limited to cleaving and tearing techniques. Small pieces of wood charcoal, typically measuring 2–3cm in width by 5cm in length, also lay scattered across the site.

Table 6—*Carrigdirty Rock 5 Neolithic site: wood species identifications.*

Sample no.	Species	Tree-ring age	Diameter	Length	Woodworking?
1	Hazel	6–7	3cm	24cm	Tool-marks, charred opposite end
2	Hazel	—	4.5cm	10cm	Charcoal block
3	Pomoideae	6	4.3cm	25cm	Pointed, charred
4	Hazel	11	3.5cm	20cm	Pointed, charred
5	Oak	—	15cm (orig.)	20cm	Cleft
6	Oak	—	10cm (orig.)	40cm	Cleft

The species identifications, tree-ring ages and dimensions of the small sample of charred and worked wood suggest the presence of a relatively dry oak, fruitwood and hazel woodland, possibly transitional between the neighbouring drylands and the wetlands, somewhere in the vicinity of the Carrigdirty Rock 5 site. This woodland could have been growing on one of the rocky islands in the marshes (e.g. Carrigdirty Rock itself), or at the edge of the marshes. However, it seems more likely that this woodland was growing in close proximity to the site and was being used as a source of fuel, with whole charred branches and charcoal being subsequently deposited in the muds of a nearby creek.

Basket

MARIA FITZGERALD

A woven basket fragment (NMI 95E0228:1) was found embedded in the reedy minerogenic clays, 3m north of the clay 'cliff' at the extreme western end of the site in July 1994 (Pl. 23). This large fragment was recovered in two parts (A and B) from the clays. A third, small fragment was recovered as an unstratified find from the eastern

Pl. 23—*Neolithic woven alder basket (NMI 95E0228:1) in situ in clays at Carrigdirty Rock 5.*

end of the site at the same time, but probably derived from the main fragment. The basket therefore survives in the form of three fragments (A, B and C) which are all in a very fragile condition and which are twisted upon themselves in several places. Prior to conservation, this basket is too fragile to move, so these comments should be considered preliminary to a more detailed study. Two samples were sent for radiocarbon dating and produced identical dates of 4820 ± 50 BP (3702–3386 cal. BC; GrA-6520) and 4820 ± 50 BP (3702–3386 cal. BC; Beta-102087).

Fragments of the vegetal material used were microscopically identified by Ingelise Stuijts. The basket was woven from thin shoots of alder (*Alnus glutinosa* (L.) Gaertn.). These were aged less than one year and were used whole (rather than split). Alder grows well in wet, marshy conditions and was probably growing in the vicinity of the site. It is probable that deliberately coppiced alder was used for the basket, as this would have been the best source of the narrow but regular shoots needed.

The fragments are derived from the wall or rim portion of a basket constructed using the coiling technique, in which two elements—a coil or core (passive element) and a wrapping or sewing strip (active element)—are utilised. The foundation coil, consisting of a bundle of shoots, is wound spirally from the base of the basket and fastened together with a sewing strip. In the absence of a surviving base we cannot identify the type of centre from which work began.

In the Carrigdirty Rock basket the coils were fastened closely together, and it is therefore described as 'close coil'. The structure of this basket conforms to Crowfoot's Type 1 (Crowfoot 1954, 416, fig. 258A), where the sewing strip passes around the latest coil and pierces the edge of the one already in place below. A simple non-interlocking stitch is used, passing around a coil and through a portion of the underlying foundation coil without engaging the underlying stitch (Fig. 31). This produces a basket wall where the stitch chains lie at right angles to the coil. The individual slant of the stitches is /, indicating that the work was carried out from right to left, and the working surface of the basket can be identified by the numerous small holes left by an awl. The non-working surface has a neater, more regular appearance. The rim, identified as the terminal circuit on a close-coiled basket (Adovasio 1977, 87), is classified where preserved as a 'self-rim', in which the rim is sewn with the same stitch as the wall of the chamber. No modification in the make-up of the rim coil is apparent.

This basket was semi-rigid in form, with an average thickness of *c.* 6.5mm. The coils, composed of a bundle of shoots, range from 5.1mm to 6.6mm in diameter, with an

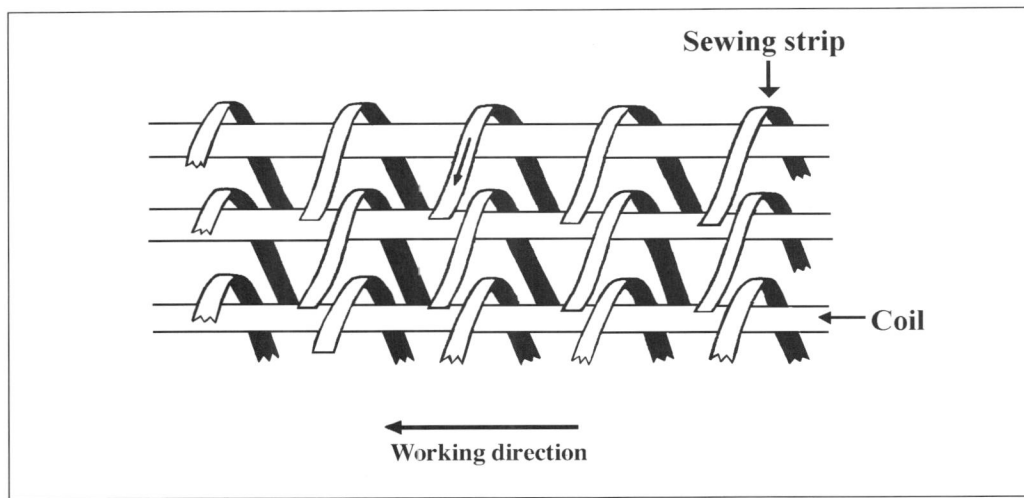

Fig. 31—*Schematic drawing showing method of manufacture of coiled basket at Carrigdirty Rock 5 (Maria Fitzgerald).*

average width of *c.* 5.7mm. The sewing strip ranges in width from 2.1mm to 3.8mm, with *c.* 2–3 stitches per centimetre. The gap between individual stitches along the coil ranges from 2.2mm to 5.1mm, and averages 3.35mm. Fragment A consists of a flat, rectangular (171mm long by 56mm wide) piece of basketry which remains attached to a confused region of the basket (*c.* six coils) with a short length of twisted rim measuring 71mm in length. Fragment B is the largest piece of the basket and is preserved in a twisted position. It measures *c.* 496mm in length and from 50mm to 80mm in height. The rim coil of this fragment is *c.* 350mm long and appears to be slightly larger, with a diameter of *c.* 7.5mm, and may incorporate a larger bundle of shoots. Fragment C represents a small portion of the side of the basket (eight coils), and measures a maximum of 50.3mm in length by a maximum of 108.2mm in width. It is difficult to estimate the original size of the basket: the rim fragments collectively measure more than *c.* 420mm in length, which would suggest that the basket was more than *c.* 134mm in diameter.

The materials used in basketry, in contrast to weaving, are generally unspun and are therefore limited in length. As a result, it is imperative during the course of basket construction to execute a splice, the point along the coil where one stitch ends and a new one is introduced. On the working surface (the surface facing the basket-maker) the beginning of a new stitch is called the *fag end*, and on the non-working surface the end of a stitch is called the *moving end*. Adovasio (1977, 90) refers to splices as the 'fingerprints of long-dead basket makers' because their execution is so individual, but they can be difficult to detect as the basket-maker strives to make them inconspicuous. Tracing the movements of ends usually requires either partial or total disarticulation (*ibid.*), but the antiquity and fragility of this basket fragment make extensive probing inadvisable. The ends may be either clipped short or bound under one or more successive stitches: numerous splices are evident on these fragments of basket, and there are examples of each method on both the working and non-working surfaces.

The basket from Carrigdirty Rock is comparable to other examples of prehistoric basketry found in bog contexts in Ireland (J. Raftery 1970). At a depth of 13ft in Mill Bog, Aghintemple td, Co. Longford, a triangular fragment of basket with a maximum length of 2ft was found folded over a small polished stone axehead and was interpreted as a woven bag; its association with the axehead dates it to the Neolithic period (*ibid.*). At Timoney td, Co. Tipperary, 'eight circular mats', made by binding together thin alder rods arranged in a close spiral, sat inside a round-bottomed wooden bowl discovered at a depth of *c.* 9ft in the bog. Two coiled discs of basketry about 40cm in diameter were found 11ft deep in a raised bog site at Twyford, Co. Westmeath. The coils were made from thin rods or slivers of wood with a spiral centre, and were stitched together using a woody plant around the coils. The two discs were bound together along their edges, and on each side there was a double handle made of thin twisted rods. This was interpreted as a bag or circular purse-like container. These examples of basketry from Timoney and Twyford, found at such considerable depths in the bog, are interpreted as prehistoric in date (*ibid*.).

The earliest finds of basketry occur in pre-ceramic Neolithic contexts in the Near East, such as Jarmo (dating from 7000 BC) and Çatal Hüyük (*c*. 6000 BC) (Barber 1992, 132). Coiled basketry is recorded at a slightly later date at pre-dynastic Egyptian sites such as Fayum and Badari. Pottery impressions of coiled basketry from Palestine (Jericho, Ghassul and Wadi Ghazzeh) probably date from the fourth millennium BC. In Europe, the submerged settlement of the Ertebølle culture at Tybrind Vig on the west coast of Funen in southern Scandinavia, occupied in the Late Mesolithic period from about 5500 to about 4000 BC, produced evidence for fine baskets (Coles and Coles 1989, 67). Other early fragments of coiled basketry come from the Swiss Neolithic lake-dwellings, such as Lake Morat (Forbes 1964, 180), and are generally dated to the fourth millennium BC. From Mohenjo-Daro, in the Indus Basin, a site dating from about 3000 BC, there comes a pottery impression of a coarse coiled mat. At a slightly later date, from the Cueva de los Murciélagos, Andalusia, Spain, where more than 60 burials were discovered, coiled baskets made from esparto (a type of grass native to Spain) date from the Late Neolithic period (late third millennium BC) (Barber 1992, 144). The habitation levels at the French site of Les Matignons, Charente, dated to 2515 BC, also produced evidence for coiled baskets (J. Raftery 1970, 168). In Britain, pottery impressions of coiled baskets are recorded on a pot from Rinyo in Orkney dating from the Early Bronze Age, and on the bases of Late Bronze Age urns recovered from a megalithic tomb at Knackyboy on the Scilly Isles.

The coiled basketry from Carrigdirty Rock 5 represents the earliest surviving evidence in Ireland for basketry; together with the previously discussed Neolithic and prehistoric finds, it highlights the important role that organic materials played in society, particularly for use as containers and matting. All of the early extant fragments of basketry from Ireland have been identified as close-coiled basketry. While this group of finds obviously represents only a tiny sample, and future finds may reveal other basketry techniques, at this point the coiling technique seems to predominate. Coiled basketry is considered to be the earliest and most important form of basketry (Forbes 1964, 180). Its structure, unlike other forms of basketry such as twining and plaiting, has little affinity with weaving (Crowfoot 1954, 415), as the coils are sewn together rather than interlaced with the sewing strip. The gap of several millennia between this basket and the first primary evidence from Ireland for woven fabric (found at Armoy, Co. Antrim, and dated to the Late Bronze Age (750–600 BC)) suggests that coiling was the earliest technique adopted, and that experimentation with interlacing systems considerably post-dates this phenomenon.

Basketry products are typically stiff and self-shaped (Barber 1992, 5), and as a result can perform a variety of functions. While they were primarily used as containers for carrying or storing, their use as items of personal dress, such as hats or caps, has also been recorded: such items have been found on Neolithic wetland sites such as Bodensee in central Europe (Coles and Coles 1989, 112, ill. 77). According to Adovasio (1977, 54), mats were seldom made from coiled basketry and it was more commonly used for producing containers, hats and, very rarely, bags. The other Irish examples, from Aghintemple, Timoney and Twyford, were identified as bags and mats, suggesting that the technique was applied to a wide range of objects in Ireland. The incomplete nature of the fragment from Carrigdirty Rock means that its form can tell us little about its original function. The context of this find—on what is interpreted as an Early Neolithic settlement site of short duration, possibly for the purposes of cattle-grazing, foraging or hunting—makes it most likely that the basket was used as a container. It may have been made on the site, as raw materials such as alder shoots, reeds and rushes were plentiful in the immediate marshy environment, and then subsequently abandoned after it was damaged. Presumably it could have been used to transport plant foods, nuts and berries: the hazelnuts and chert flakes found close to the basket and

Foragers, farmers and fishers

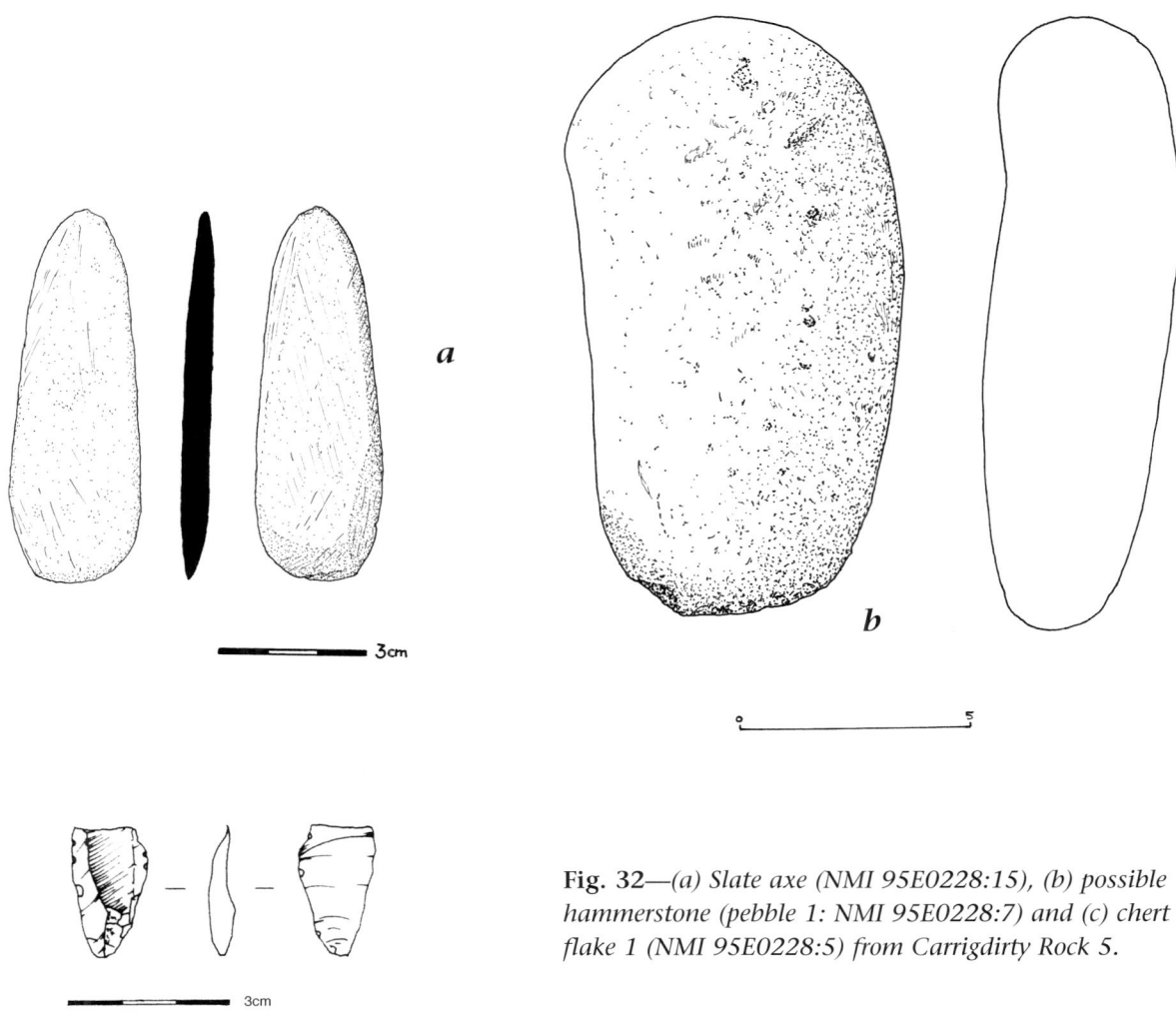

Fig. 32—*(a) Slate axe (NMI 95E0228:15), (b) possible hammerstone (pebble 1: NMI 95E0228:7) and (c) chert flake 1 (NMI 95E0228:5) from Carrigdirty Rock 5.*

the rigid nature of the basket itself lend support to this hypothesis. Alternatively, were the site to be interpreted as a burial site, the basket could represent the incomplete remains of a hat or other item of clothing associated with the deceased, or may have been used to store food for the afterlife.

Stone axe
STEPHEN MANDAL AND AIDAN O'SULLIVAN

The stone axe (NMI 95E0228:15) was recovered as an unstratified find in 1998 from the surface of the clays at the eastern end of the site, immediately to the north of the original findspot of the human skull fragment. It was made of a small, water-rolled pebble of fine-grained micaceous slate. It measures 7.6cm in length, 2.5cm in maximum width (1.5cm from the cutting edge) and 0.6cm in maximum thickness. The faces, sides and butt were ground, but no surfaces were polished (Pl. 24; Fig. 32).

The axe is ovate symmetrical in shape, with a narrow oval cross-section, flattened faces and pointed sides. In profile it is thin and symmetrical. Its edge is curved and asymmetrical. The blade profile is asymmetrical with a junction with the lower face. The butt shape is bluntly pointed in plan and profile. The end and the sides near the end are chipped and damaged, possibly deliberately for hafting. The sides have been ground and are pointed in profile. The edge has been worn but is relatively straight in profile. Both faces of the axe are natural cleaving faces, but they exhibit grinding

Pl. 24—*Schist axe from submerged forest at Meelick Rocks 2 (NMI 95E0228:3) and slate axe from Carrigdirty Rock 5 (NMI 95E0228:15) (photo: David Jennings, UCD).*

marks. The butt is well finished and ground to a blunt point. The surfaces of both the faces and sides of the axe are covered with fine, remnant striae from the grinding process; indeed, some of these grooves are quite pronounced.

The axe is unusual, both in terms of its size and petrography. Slate is quite uncommon amongst the 20,000 or so known Irish axes: less than 100 slate axes have been identified. The use of slate would have made it relatively easy to grind, but the object would have been light and easily broken. Indeed, it should be emphasised that the object is interpreted here as a stone axe, despite its small size, because it has the typical face shape and appearance of the most common form of Irish stone axes, and it also has a definite sharpened blade. However, its small size, light weight and the difficulty of hafting it effectively pose problems for this interpretation. If it was a stone axe, it is possible that it was primarily a symbolic object, resembling a stone axe but not serving as a functional item. On the other hand, it is interesting that the tool-marks on the worked wood (see above) indicate that a small, light stone axe was used in tree-felling and branch-cutting (it is possible to trace differences between different types of stone axe tool-marks; O'Sullivan 1996c). It is conceivable that this stone axe was used on site for woodworking or carving.

There are, of course, possible alternative interpretations. The object could have been a stone chisel (Cooney and Mandal 1998), and it is also somewhat similar in size and general shape to several ground stone points recently recovered from the Late Mesolithic site at Moynagh Lough, Co. Meath (e.g. J. Bradley 1999), and from other wetland sites, such as on the River Bann (Woodman, Anderson *et al.* 1999, 81–3, pl. 5.8). These objects were probably arrows or spearheads used for fishing, fowling or hunting. However, the Carrigdirty Rock 5 object's point is rather blunt and its edge is convincingly sharp, so on balance it seems most likely that this was a small stone axe.

Pebbles
STEPHEN MANDAL AND AIDAN O'SULLIVAN

Four pebbles, of limestone, quartz, green dolerite and granite, were recovered as unstratified finds from the clays. Pebble no. 1 may have been used as a hammerstone and was found near the clay cliff (Fig. 32). It is a water-rolled fossiliferous limestone pebble with some slight evidence for crushing and abrading of the butt end (although this could have been the result of natural weathering processes). The pebble fits well in the hand, and its narrow butt would have provided a focus for its weight. The broken hazelnut shells and fragments of bone identified on site may well have been crushed by a similar implement. Other pebbles found nearer the low-water mark were simply water-rolled cobbles of quartz clasts, green dolerite and granite, derived from local glacial till or outcrops such as the subtidal rock outcrop at Battle Island and the intertidal rocky island at Carrigdirty Rock. It is possible that they were carried onto the site by human hand, but it is just as likely that they were washed onto the site from a small rock outcrop in the channel visible below the low-water mark.

Table 7—*Carrigdirty Rock 5 Neolithic site: pebbles from foreshore.*

Pebble no.	Length	Width	Thickness	Petrology	Potential evidence for use
Pebble 1	13.2cm	7.5cm	5cm	Limestone	Possibly crushed end
Pebble 2	8.5cm	5.6cm	4.4cm	Quartz clasts	None
Pebble 3	10.1cm	7.7cm	5m	Green dolerite	None
Pebble 4	9.5cm	5.6cm	9.47cm	Granite	None

Chert flakes
ELIZABETH ANDERSON

Two small struck chert flakes were found stratified in the clays beside the basket findspot at the western end of the site. They probably indicate some limited repair or retouch of chert implements on site. Chert flake 1 is a complete unretouched tertiary flake made of relatively good-quality, fine-grained chert (Fig. 32). It exhibits a small, flat, plain striking platform and terminates in a hinge fracture. It is undiagnostic and is slightly abraded. Irregular and intermittent damage is visible along both lateral edges. Chert flake 2 is an unretouched flake of similar chert.

Table 8—*Carrigdirty Rock 5 Neolithic site: chert flakes.*

NMI no.	Chert no.	Length	Width	Thickness	Comments
95E0228:5	Chert 1	2.4cm	1.4cm	0.5cm	Tertiary flake
95E0228:6	Chert 2	1.9cm	1.8cm	0.4cm	Flake

Reconstructing and interpreting the Carrigdirty Rock 5 site

Site formation

The Carrigdirty Rock 5 site is essentially a small scatter of lithic and organic finds and faunal remains potentially deposited there in antiquity by water action in a creek, reed-bed or on a saltmarsh surface. The site is clearly derived from a period of human occupation or other activity in the wetlands, with finds including a stone axe, chert flakes, woven basketry, two pieces of human bone, swan and young cattle bone, worked wood (with evidence for use of a stone axe), charred blocks of wood and large chunks of charcoal, fragments of bone, broken hazelnuts and one possible hammerstone. The human skull and basketry have been clearly dated to the Early to Middle Neolithic, with radiocarbon dates of between *c.* 3700 and 3400 cal. BC.

Clearly this is an unusual site, and it is instructive to recall that in a dryland context (e.g. a ploughed field) only the stone axe and chert chips would have been recovered; little of the organic material would have survived. Indeed, this also raises the point that even small scatters of lithics in ploughsoil have to be regarded as potentially significant indicators of human activity. However, before interpreting Carrigdirty Rock 5 we need to consider how the site was formed and to pose questions about the chronology and contemporaneity of the finds recovered from the site and the potential behaviour of the finds as localised fluviatile deposits (see Schofield 1989; Shackley 1978).

It is possible that these finds accumulated at this place over weeks, months or years, being lost or deposited in a tidal creek at some other location further upstream and, through gradual build-up, finally coming to rest in a backwater or channel meander. However, it is more likely that the finds were deposited during a single event or phase of activity at a location close to the present site. The definitely stratified finds, such as the basket, worked wood and animal bone, all derive from the same reedy, organic-rich clays situated 2–3m to the north of the clay 'cliff'. The stone axe, hammerstone and chert chips were also recovered as surface finds from these reedy clays, but it is unlikely that these heavier objects moved very far in the sluggish waters of a silty water-channel. The animal bone and the human bone were all recovered from this same general level of the foreshore. It seems most likely that the finds are being exposed by erosion from the clays north of the clay 'cliff', potentially from beneath it. Although planks are set in the peat on the upper foreshore, at no stage of the project was this peat exposed or eroded, suggesting that the main ongoing erosion is of the clays on the foreshore and in the clay cliff.

It is also true that the finds were recovered from a concentrated area. This was established by systematic search of the wider foreshore, 100m to both the east and west of Carrigdirty Rock 5, in an attempt to define its extent. Although roundwood is certainly occasionally found further along the foreshore to the east in particular (to a distance of 50–60m), the basketry, worked wood, charcoal, and human and animal bone were only located within a short, 30m stretch of foreshore north of the clay 'cliff'. In conclusion, it appears that the finds represent a single phase of early prehistoric human activity in a coastal wetland environment.

The site in its original wetland environment

The local environmental context of the Neolithic site at Carrigdirty Rock 5 remains unclear. The context of the finds in organic-rich minerogenic clays, with well-preserved reed fragments and woody debris, suggests that the lithics, bone and organic artefacts were deposited in an estuarine wetland environment, possibly of reed-beds and mudflats, with mixed hazel, oak and fruitwood (i.e. apple, pear, quince or hawthorn) woodland somewhere in the vicinity. At a broader scale, it is also very likely that the site was located in an entirely wetland landscape with several creeks and channels flowing through extensive fens, reed-swamps and woodlands. The siting of Carrigdirty Rock 5 in terms of the modern distribution of estuarine alluvium suggests that this wetland could have measured at least 3.6km (north/south) by 4.8km (east/west). The nearest dryland to Carrigdirty Rock 5 would have been about 3km to the west (at Ballynacarriga, at the mouth of the River Maigue) or 1.7km to the east (on a headland at Newtown). This wetland landscape would also have had several small dryland islands protruding above the marshes. These islands are now limestone rock outcrops or low grassy islands on the mudflats (e.g. at Carrigdirty Rock and Bush Island to the west and Graigue Island to the north-east). They may have been covered in a hazel–oak scrub woodland.

Interpreting the site's function

The Carrigdirty Rock 5 site could be evidence for a brief phase of activity perhaps associated with cattle-grazing (calf bone was identified), hunting, fishing or wildfowling (swan bone), although human burial or some other symbolic activity is also suggested by the presence of human bone (see discussion below). The lack of large shelters and the presence of broken hazelnuts might suggest a temporary occupation in the warm weeks of autumn. The burnt wood and charcoal suggest that fires were lit, using hazel, oak and fruitwood (hawthorn, apple, pear or quince). The tool-marks on the chopped hazel roundwood suggest that stone axes were being used to fell bushes and shrubby trees for use as fuel. Indeed, the tool-marks indicate the use of small stone axes, perhaps similar in size and weight to the stone axe recovered. The basket

Foragers, farmers and fishers

fragment might suggest that there was some basket-making on site, using the nearby alder wood, although it is more likely that the basket was brought to the site and abandoned there when damaged or torn. Although a stone axe and chert flakes were found on site, there was hardly any lithic production, probably no more than the sharpening of already existing blades. Pebbles found on the foreshore might have been used for smashing hazelnuts for food or for breaking up bone (tiny fragments of bone have been found). The site could therefore be interpreted as evidence for a temporary Early Neolithic occupation site in the marshes and islands during summer or autumn, when the coastal wetlands would have been rich in wildfowl, red deer (see above), wild pig and fish. If this was an occupation site, it was probably used for no more than a few days by a small group of people, perhaps only two or three individuals (Fig. 33).

Fig. 33—*A deliberately ambivalent reconstruction drawing of early Neolithic activity at Carrigdirty Rock 5, in its potential original wetland environment. Was this an occupation site, a place for ritual, or both? (Aidan O'Sullivan.)*

Interpreting Neolithic settlement, society and economy on the Shannon estuary

Introduction

Traditionally, the Shannon estuary and the south-west region have been seen as an 'empty space' in terms of early prehistory, but in recent years increasing evidence has emerged for Neolithic settlement and burial traditions throughout the region. It is likely that Neolithic farmers were present by at least 4000 BC, probably as the result of small migrant farming groups moving into the region, bringing with them an economy based on livestock and arable crops (Grogan 1989; Grogan *et al.* 1996; Monk 1993; B. O'Brien 1999). It is also possible that the region's Mesolithic hunter-gatherers were responsible for this shift to a Neolithic economy, as significantly early cattle bone (radiocarbon-dated to 4495–4165 cal. BC) has been found on the Late Mesolithic coastal foraging site of Ferriter's Cove, Co. Kerry. This suggests that the region's hunter-gatherers were in contact with farming communities, perhaps obtaining cattle as a 'prestige gift' through social contacts with farmers living outside Ireland, somewhere along the Atlantic coast (Woodman, Anderson *et al.* 1999; B. O'Brien 1999, 267). These social contacts might have led to an acculturation of indigenous hunter-gatherer groups and their adoption of a Neolithic lifestyle.

There is also emerging evidence for Early and Middle Neolithic settlements and houses. It is possible that the Neolithic settlement at Lough Gur, Co. Limerick (Grogan and Eogan 1987; Grogan 1996), was occupied in the earlier Neolithic (Eoin Grogan, pers. comm.). Early Neolithic houses have been excavated at Tankardstown South, Co. Limerick (Gowen 1988), where there were at least two rectangular structures on a site overlooking a stream valley, and more recently a substantial rectangular Neolithic house has been excavated at Cloghers, in the Lee Valley, near Tralee, Co. Kerry (Connolly 1999; Dunne and Kiely 1999). Otherwise the evidence for Neolithic settlement is still largely based on the distribution of stone axes, whose far-flung findspots could be interpreted as indicating widespread but isolated single farmsteads of extended family groups. There are particularly interesting concentrations of Mesolithic or Neolithic stone axes from the River Shannon at Killaloe, Co. Clare, but it is likely that these were deliberately deposited at a river fording-point rather than being evidence for large-scale settlement activity (Grogan 1989; Cooney and Mandal 1998). Otherwise evidence for Neolithic settlement remains relatively scarce, especially along the estuary itself and in the west of the region. It is uncertain how truly this archaeological record reflects the nature of Early Neolithic settlement, as lithic scatters in ploughsoil (which usually give a broader indication of settlement evidence) have rarely been investigated in the region.

However, there is increasing evidence for the use of megalithic tombs and other burial forms in the wider Shannon estuary region during the Early to Middle Neolithic (Grogan 1989; Grogan *et al.* 1996, 27–30, fig. 13). In recent years, a possible passage tomb of unusual design has been excavated at Ballycarty, Co. Kerry, and this adds to the idea that there was a regionally distinctive 'Neolithic' in the south-west (Connolly 1999; Cooney 2000b). Other evidence for a regional 'style' of burial is perhaps provided by the intriguing Early Neolithic skulls and pottery discovered in a cave at Annagh, in east County Limerick (Ó Floinn 1992). Possible Early–Middle Neolithic court tombs and portal tombs are also known from Clare and Cork. At Poulnabrone, Co. Clare, there is evidence that burial activity in the portal tomb dated from the Early to Middle Neolithic (Lynch and Ó Donnabháin 1994), roughly contemporary with the Carrigdirty Rock 5 site (*c.* 3700–3400 BC). There is evidence for an expansion of settlement throughout the Shannon estuary region during the Middle and Later Neolithic and into the Early Bronze Age, with the construction and use of Linkardstown-type burials, wedge tombs and embanked enclosures in south-east Clare, east Limerick and north Kerry (Grogan *et al.* 1996; Grogan and Condit 1994; Grogan 1989; B. O'Brien 1999; Condit and Connolly 1998).

Foragers, farmers and fishers

Neolithic farmers and foragers in Ireland

Although there is in a sense a regionally distinctive Neolithic in south-west Ireland, the evidence for settlement could still be broadly interpreted in similar ways to elsewhere on the island. In particular, in recent years Neolithic landscape, settlement and society in Ireland have been discussed in terms of a largely sedentary lifestyle and economy (Cooney and Grogan 1994; Mallory and McNeill 1991; Cooney 1997), with the use of large, permanently occupied houses and settlements (e.g. Grogan 1996), and extensive, well-organised field systems (Caulfield 1978; 1983; O'Sullivan and Sheehan 1997). It is believed that cattle were the most important domesticated animals, followed by pig and sheep, but it seems likely that cereal-growing (using emmer wheat and barley) was at least as important as stock-raising (Cooney and Grogan 1994, 37; Grogan 1996; Harbison 1988; O'Kelly 1989).

Neolithic houses, including both large rectangular and circular structures, are interpreted as the permanent domestic residences of extended families (Grogan 1996, 54), and variations in their form and size are taken to indicate emerging social ranking by the Late Neolithic. These houses occur singly, in small groups (e.g. as at Tankardstown, Co. Limerick) and as large-scale agglomerated settlements, such as at Lough Gur, Co. Limerick (Grogan and Eogan 1987), and possibly at Mullaghfarna, Co. Sligo (Grogan 1996). Neolithic houses and settlement enclosures are also interpreted as domestic residences within wider bounded and territorial landscapes. For example, at Céide in north Mayo settlement enclosures and megalithic tombs were set amongst extensive field systems by the Early to Middle Neolithic. The scale and layout of these fields are again interpreted as evidence for both a sedentary society and cattle-grazing on a grand scale (Caulfield 1978; 1983; 1988). This interpretation of an Early Neolithic sedentary society in Ireland contrasts with most recent archaeological interpretations in Britain, where it is believed that Early Neolithic societies continued to be largely mobile, with cattle-herding and occasional farmed clearances in an otherwise wooded landscape (Thomas 1991; Whittle 1996), although recently this view has been increasingly criticised on both archaeological (e.g. Cooney 1997; 2000a) and palaeobotanical grounds (Monk 2000).

However, it is also important to remember that there must have been regional variation in settlement practices in Ireland, and in particular some localities may have witnessed a degree of settlement mobility, seasonal or otherwise, and perhaps also broad-spectrum forager–farmer economies (e.g. Cooney 2000a; Waddell 1998, 39–42). It is certainly the case that foraged, wild resources are found on permanent settlements. At Tankardstown, Co. Limerick, hazelnuts and crab-apples were found along with emmer wheat grain inside the rectangular house, indicating the continued importance of gathered foods alongside arable crops (Gowen 1988; Cooney 2000a). Secondly, there is also clear evidence for movement through the wider Neolithic landscape, in terms of both local activities around dwellings and transitory, seasonal or specialised occupation sites at more remote locations in the landscape (uplands, woodlands, low-lying lakeshores and rivers). It is probable that Neolithic communities made use of coastal and maritime resources in ways that were both socially and economically complex. For example, at Glencloy, Co. Antrim, and around Knocknarea, Co. Sligo, there is evidence that local communities ranged across the entire coastal landscape, from the uplands down to the foreshore. Neolithic settlements were situated back from the coast in strategic, low-lying locations in the valleys, while the beaches were visited for the exploitation of flint, and specialised hunting or lithic production sites and megalithic tombs were situated in the uplands behind the settlements. Cooney (2000a, 77) suggests that different social groups, in terms of age, rank or gender, within the community might have been responsible for these various economic activities.

At numerous locations around the Irish coast, Early Neolithic shell middens have produced flint tools, pottery and an array of evidence for the seasonal exploitation of shellfish during the fourth millennium BC. At Culleenamore, Co. Sligo, coastal shell middens, dated to *c.* 3800–3100 cal. BC, may have been seasonally exploited by the same Neolithic communities that constructed the passage tombs of Knocknarea (Waddell 1998, 55). Seasonal or temporary occupation sites such as Townleyhall, Co. Meath (Grogan 1996), or Knocknarea, Co. Sligo (Bengsston and Bergh 1984; Bergh 2000), also occasionally produce small huts, perhaps associated with specialised crafts, the movement of cattle to upland or lowland summer pastures, or hunting, fowling and fishing. At Rathjordan, Co. Limerick, Island MacHugh, Co. Tyrone, and Lough Enagh, Co. Derry (and on several crannog sites), lakeshore settlements may also have been used for seasonal habitation at optimal wetland locations, for lithic production, wildfowling and fishing the migratory eel runs (O'Sullivan 1998, 59–69). Occasional deposition of flint hoards or human remains in bogs suggests that wetlands were being used as places for ritual offerings to the spirits or ancestors. Interestingly, too, the Early and Late Neolithic trackways at Corlea, structures that evoke ideas of movement and pathways through the landscape, tend to be fairly well made and were probably designed for the repeated passage of both people and animals (Raftery 1996). Although the lack of evidence for permanent Neolithic settlements in proximity to some of these lakeland, riverine and coastal sites may indeed be due to the history of archaeological research and site invisibility in areas of pasture, it is also possible that it truly represents a more mobile settlement strategy (albeit largely localised) adopted by some members of the community.

Neolithic 'forager-farmers' at Carrigdirty Rock?

It is interesting, then, that archaeological evidence for Early Neolithic settlement along the upper Shannon estuary is very scanty (Fig. 34). There are only eight stone axes from the hills overlooking the estuary, with two from Ballinacarriga, Co. Limerick, at the outlet of the River Maigue (found while ploughing a field), single examples from Tullyglass Point and Bunratty, Co. Clare, to the north-west, and to the north three from Gallowshill, Co. Clare. To the east there is of course the stone axe found on the foreshore at Meelick Rocks, Co. Limerick (see above), and a stone axe from Coonagh East on the north bank of the upper estuary. There are also at least four stone axes from further eastwards around Limerick City (just off the eastern edge of Fig. 34), perhaps reflecting the regional importance of the river's fording-points at this location. In south-east Clare, to the north of the estuary, there are a few hollow-based arrowheads of possible Early Neolithic date, and the hill at Mooghaun may have been the location for a small hunting camp (Grogan *et al*. 1995; Grogan and Condit 1994). Interestingly, the archaeological evidence from south-east Clare suggests that it was not until the Late Neolithic that substantial farming groups moved into the locality, and similarly that it was not until the Late Neolithic that probable wedge tombs were being used along the Shannon estuary, with megalithic structures (wedge tombs) known from Ballinaphunta and Brickhill, on the west slope of the Cratloe Hills, Co. Clare, while a megalithic structure (a possible wedge tomb) is also located at Corcamore, *c*. 4km to the south of Carrigdirty Rock. Grogan (1996) has suggested that the south-east Clare and east Limerick wedge tombs represent Late Neolithic–Early Bronze Age population expansions out of Early Neolithic settlement core areas in the Burren, Co. Clare, and at Lough Gur, Co. Limerick.

These various strands of evidence can be drawn together to present a potential social and economic context for the Carrigdirty Rock 5 site. It may well be that in the Early Neolithic the local population around the upper Shannon estuary was relatively small, a community who combined foraging and farming in a largely wooded landscape. It is interesting, then, that recent detailed pollen studies at Mooghaun Lough in south-east Clare (*c*. 10km to the north of Carrigdirty Rock) indicate that there was only limited woodland clearance and little evidence for farming in this landscape prior to the Late Neolithic (*c*. 2850–2250 cal. BC). Indeed, the first clear pollen evidence for a *landnam*, or a major phase of woodland clearance, does not occur there until the later Bronze Age (*c*. 1100–650 cal. BC; Molloy 1997; forthcoming). The combined archaeological and palaeoenvironmental evidence may support the assertion that the

Foragers, farmers and fishers

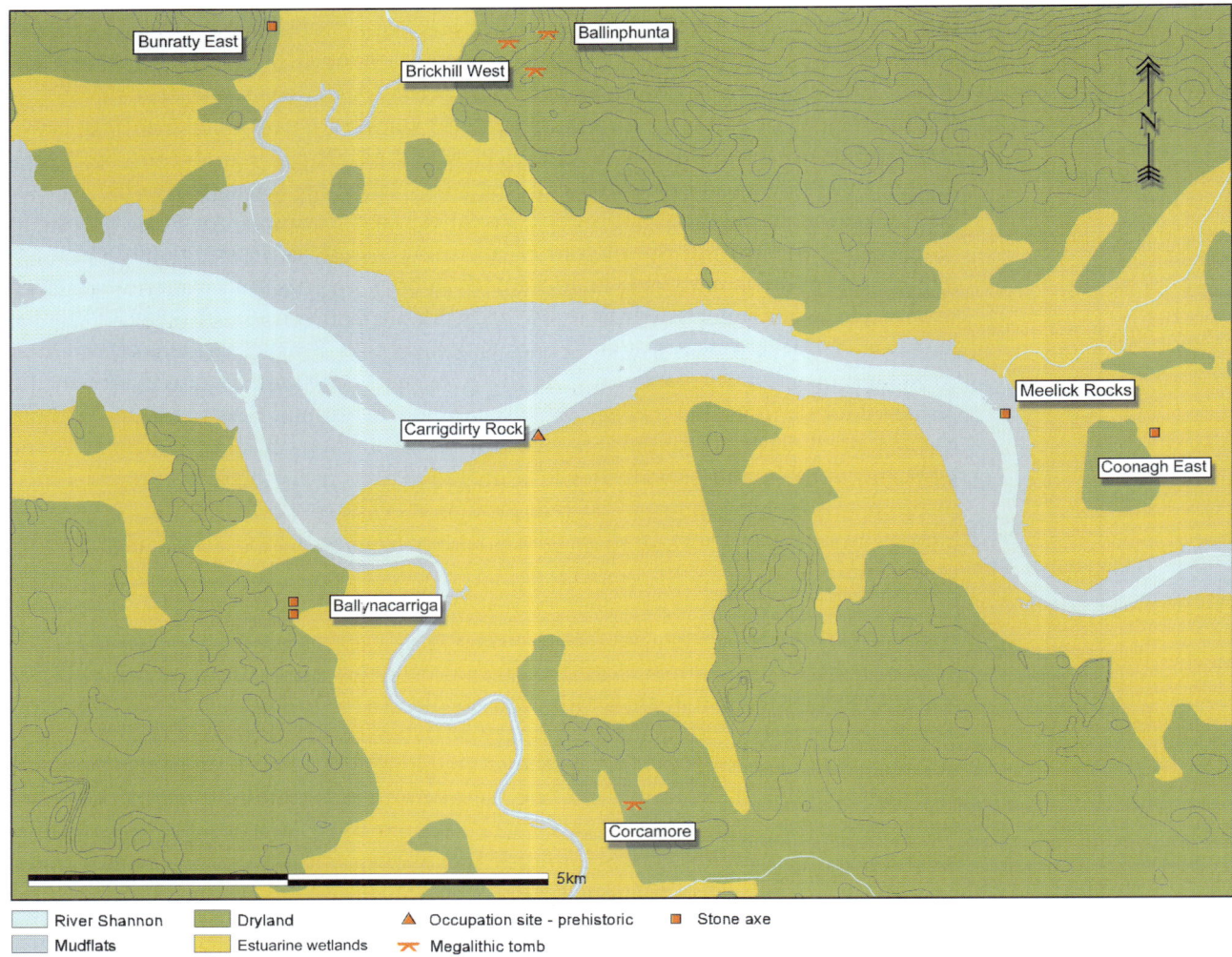

Fig. 34—*Location of Carrigdirty Rock 5 Neolithic site in potential former estuarine wetlands (based on modern distribution of alluvium or gley soils in counties Limerick and Clare), with distribution of Neolithic stone axes and megalithic tombs along the upper Shannon estuary.*

people of the Shannon estuary in the early to middle fourth millennium BC lived an essentially 'forager-farmer' lifestyle.

In the Late Mesolithic the Shannon estuary may already have been a focus for settlement, given its rich wetland resources and the access the river provided for hunter-gatherers moving into the heartlands of the island (Woodman, Anderson *et al.* 1999). By the Early to Middle Neolithic, local communities may have modified their settlement strategy and economy somewhat, as they came into contact with farming groups located on the Burren to the north or around Lough Gur, Co. Limerick. In particular, the introduction of cattle and agriculture would have diversified and expanded the local wetland resource base and would have made the Shannon estuary margins an ideal location for settlement. Neolithic houses, field systems and other activity areas could have been located on the dryland terraces and low hills to the south of Carrigdirty Rock, where light, well-drained grey-brown podzolic soils over a limestone bedrock provided excellent agricultural land. Local Neolithic forager-farmers could have herded their cattle down to the marshlands during the summer and autumn, while the abundant resources of fish, fowl and plant foods could have been exploited through most of the year.

The evidence for early prehistoric settlement of coastal wetlands elsewhere in northern Europe, such as the Rhine–Meuse estuaries and delta, can be explored for possible analogies for a forager/farmer transition economy on the Shannon estuary (Louwe Kooijmans 1993a). It has been argued for this admittedly entirely coastal wetland region that wetland settlement was a deliberate choice made by early prehistoric communities. In Phase 3, the Early/Middle Neolithic semi-agrarian settlers of the wetlands are seen as having a 'broad-spectrum economy', with classic Mesolithic subsistence activities (hunting, fowling, fishing, foraging) extended by the raising of livestock and the consumption of cereals, but neither the wild nor the domestic resources dominated. It can be seen that the Carrigdirty Rock site, although set in a dryland/wetland landscape, would seem to fit well with this model, with its bird bone, hazelnuts and cattle bone perhaps also suggesting the finely balanced use of both wild and domestic resources. The site could even be seen as fitting within a 'substitution' phase of early farming, having an element of localised seasonal mobility around permanent residences, with summer and winter activities along the course of the estuary or elsewhere in the wetlands.

Neolithic burial activities in 'sacred wetlands'?

However, the presence of human bone at Carrigdirty Rock 5 is highly intriguing, and raises the possibility that the site needs to be understood in a quite different light altogether. It is possible that Carrigdirty Rock 5 was some type of Neolithic mortuary site, involving the deposition of human bone and 'grave-goods' at a natural wetland setting, such as a riverbank, an estuary channel or a marsh pool. Other Neolithic finds of pottery, lithics and stone axes in bogs and lakes have also been regarded as votive offerings (Cooney 2000a, 130). The stone axe may then be seen as a symbolic rather than a functional object for the deceased, and the basket could have been a container for ritual food. Neolithic human remains are known from wetland sites elsewhere in Ireland—at Stoneyisland Bog, Co. Galway, for example, where a body may originally have been placed in open water before it settled to the bottom of a lake. The bone was radiocarbon-dated to 4200–3800 BC (Ó Floinn 1992). Neolithic human burials are known from natural settings elsewhere in south-west Ireland, such as the human skulls associated with Western Neolithic pottery from a cave at Annagh, Co. Limerick (Ó Floinn 1992). It could be pointed out, though, that the Annagh burial may have been a deliberate attempt to recreate the image of a Neolithic passage tomb, rather than being a burial 'in nature'.

It is also important to point out that the treatment of human remains is not uniform, and that after death the body may not be immediately disposed of in a ritual fashion. For example, the human skull fragment from Carrigdirty Rock 5 could even have been a practical object, albeit respectfully treated, used for certain symbolic or important tasks. The human skull and shoulder bone at Carrigdirty Rock 5 could also have been carried onto the site by somebody within the community, for some reason other than burial (as an heirloom, a war trophy, or even as a symbolic but practical item). On the other hand, it is possible that the bone was actually treated with great disrespect, as McCarthy (see above) has suggested that the human clavicle was actually gnawed by a dog. Clearly, then, the presence of fragments of human bone indicates the potentially complex perception and handling of human remains in the Neolithic. Local communities may have had complex ideas about the use of natural places for symbolic activities, which did not exclude simultaneous practical or profane activities. It is therefore possible that the Carrigdirty Rock site was at one and the same time a 'sacred place' and an environmentally 'bountiful place' in the Neolithic wetlands.

Conclusions

The Neolithic submerged forest recorded at Meelick Rocks offers a useful future opportunity to explore ancient woodland on the upper Shannon estuary and to calibrate coastal and sea-level change in the region. Neolithic deposits of red deer bone also offer some insights into local estuarine environments and fauna. At Carrigdirty Rock 5, a unique site emerging from eroding estuarine clays produced both stratified and unstratified human bone, cattle and bird bone, basketry, a stone axe and other lithic and organic artefacts. This has been interpreted as a Neolithic seasonal, short-stay occupation site, possibly used for hunting, fishing, wildfowling and cattle pasture in summer or late autumn, although the presence of a human skull fragment suggests the possibility of burial and other sacred activities in wetlands. It is considered a useful and intriguing addition to our understanding of Neolithic settlement and society in the Shannon estuary region.

4. BRONZE AGE HOUSES AND TRACKWAY IN COASTAL WETLANDS

Introduction

Fig. 35—*Map of upper Shannon estuary, showing location of Bronze Age sites (Barry Masterson, Discovery Programme).*

By the Late Neolithic and Bronze Age, the upper Shannon estuary may have had a range of estuarine landscapes, with some parts perhaps dominated by saltmarshes, mudflats and tidal creeks, while in other locations (such as at Carrigdirty Rock) carr woodlands, sedge fens and even raised bogs may have been forming inland of the estuary channel. At Carrigdirty Rock 1, Co. Limerick, and Coonagh Point 1, Co. Limerick, archaeological sites recorded in extensive palaeoenvironmental deposits of such fen and carr woodland peats, buried in the saltmarsh cliffs or exposed to view on the foreshore suggest Middle Bronze Age activities in the wetlands (Fig. 35). By the Late Bronze Age, rising sea levels or changing local coastal environments also led to structures being built in mudflats. A Late Bronze Age post-and-wattle structure (Fergus estuary west 1) in estuarine clays on the upper Fergus estuary suggests travel and communication across the wetlands. There is a range of evidence for Late Bronze Age activity in the neighbouring wetlands and drylands: tools, weapons and gold

93

Foragers, farmers and fishers

ornaments have all been found along the Shannon estuary and Fergus estuary. Recent archaeological research by the North Munster Project has also revealed extensive evidence for Middle Bronze Age and Late Bronze Age settlement and society in the wider Shannon estuary region, and the Bronze Age sites to be discussed here can be understood against this wider context.

Bronze Age settlement and environment at Carrigdirty Rock

Introduction

A range of possible Bronze Age sites were recorded at Carrigdirty Rock, on the south bank of the upper Shannon estuary, adjacent to the townland of Newtown, Co. Limerick (Fig. 36). Carrigdirty Rock 1 is a Middle Bronze Age house site. Other, as yet undated but probable later prehistoric features found nearby on this foreshore include Carrigdirty Rock 2 (a possible hut site), Carrigdirty Rock 3 (a pit with animal bone) and Carrigdirty Rock 4 (a post feature), while two cleft oak planks were also recorded in peats further eastwards at Carrigdirty Rock 20 and 21.

Submerged peats at Carrigdirty Rock
AIDAN O'SULLIVAN AND CHRIS BLYTHE

The submerged peat shelf at Carrigdirty Rock is located on the upper foreshore, to the east of the island (Pl. 25), and is exposed for at least 820m (east/west) across the upper to mid-foreshore. It is typically exposed over an area 40–50m in width (from the saltmarsh cliff to 10–15m above the LWM). The peat overlies minerogenic clays and is itself buried under later estuarine silts in the saltmarsh cliff. Palaeoenvironmental and stratigraphical coring in the saltmarsh opposite the Carrigdirty Rock 1 site indicates

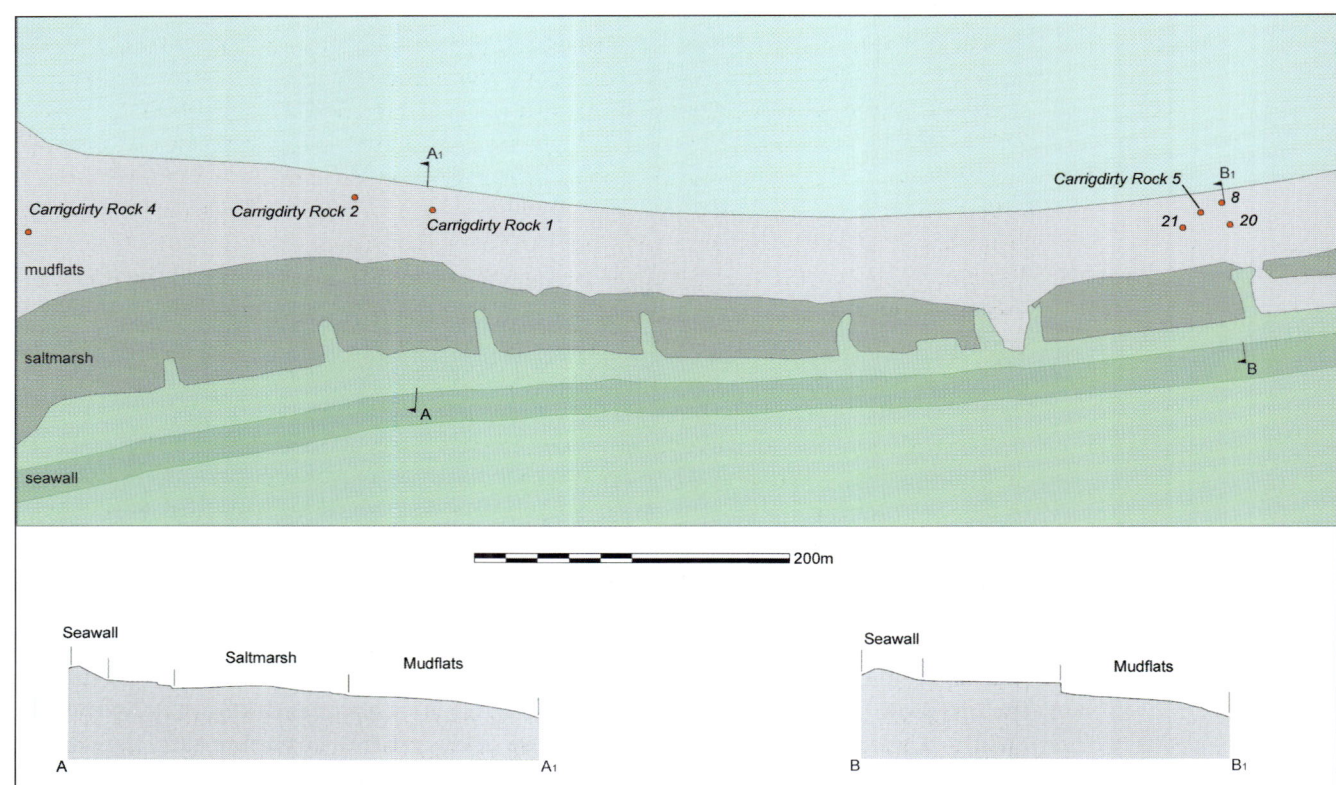

Fig. 36—*Detailed map of Carrigdirty Rock foreshore, showing surveyed location of Mesolithic, Neolithic and Bronze Age sites.*

Pl. 25—*Intertidal zone to the east of Carrigdirty Rock, where a shelf of submerged peats is exposed all along the upper foreshore.*

that the upper surface of the peat lies at *c.* 1.85m below the saltmarsh surface (at 0.957m OD). The base of the peat is *c.* 4.8m below the saltmarsh surface (–2.193m OD). However, it varies in depth along the foreshore, measuring between 1.8m and 2.25m in thickness. The peat shelf is best exposed at the west end of the foreshore, where a submerged forest of densely clustered fen-wood roots and narrow trunks is visible. Since 1994 this foreshore has been steadily buried under a deepening mantle of silts being deposited there by the channel, and the surface of these peats has never been fully exposed to view. This deposit of peats can also be seen in the modern field drains behind the sea wall.

The date of the formation of this peat deposit and its later submergence under minerogenic clays is unknown, but there are some hints from the dated archaeological finds below and within the peat. A Neolithic basket (at Carrigdirty Rock 5) dated to *c.* 3702–3386 BC was deposited in minerogenic or estuarine clays (at about –1.6m OD) below the organic peats. A Middle Bronze Age wooden structure (Carrigdirty Rock 1) *within* the peat (at –0.465m OD) was dated to *c.* 1681–1529 BC. This suggests that the peats began forming in the Late Neolithic or Early Bronze Age (*c.* 2800–1800 BC). Certainly Late Neolithic and Middle Bronze Age peats are known from Meelick Rocks 1 (see Chapter 3) and from Coonagh Point 1 (see below) on the north bank of the estuary, further upstream. A subsequent marine transgressive phase, possibly of Late Bronze Age (1200–600 BC) or Iron Age date (600 BC–AD 400), may have led to the Carrigdirty Rock peats being sealed under estuarine clays.

The preliminary palaeoenvironmental investigations at Carrigdirty Rock included a programme of stratigraphical coring and preliminary diatom and pollen studies. However, the data available are limited, and any interpretations provided here should be treated as, at best, a preliminary approximation of the Carrigdirty Rock environment during these phases of organic-rich sediment accumulation. The peats vary in appearance according to depth, ranging from a dark brown, poorly humified silty peat (between 0.957m and 0.417m OD) to a dark brown, well-humified crumbly peat, with frequent vertical and horizontal reed fragments (at –2.193m OD). There are also occasional layers of dark grey organic silts with reed fragments, perhaps indicating saltmarsh formation or episodes of marine flooding. The peat is often quite woody, and in the exposed submerged forest at the west end of the foreshore (Carrigdirty Rock 16) there are hundreds of exposed small root stumps, branches and a few recumbent trunks of small shrubby trees, *c.* 8–10cm in diameter, over an area measuring *c.* 150m (north/south) by 100m (east/west).

Foragers, farmers and fishers

Pl. 26—*Carrigdirty Rock 1 Middle Bronze Age house site. The site has not been excavated, but it was possible to identify the posts in the thin muds overlying the peat.*

Preliminary pollen analysis of the organic-rich sediments at Carrigdirty Rock indicates that arboreal pollen is plentiful, with pine (*Pinus*), oak (*Quercus* sp.), hazel (*Corylus* sp.) and alder (*Alnus* sp.) pollen prevalent. Pollen of *Betula*, *Ulmus* and *Fraxinus* is also found, along with a variety of herbaceous pollen derived mainly from Gramineae and Cyperaceae. Caryophyllaceae and Chenopodiaceae pollen is also present in substantial quantities. Aquatic pollen occurs only occasionally. Spores of *Equisetum*, *Polypodium*, *Isoetes* and *Sphagnum* are common. This suggests that the organic sediments are derived mainly from a herb-dominated, wetland environment. Relatively large proportions of *Quercus* pollen suggest that oak scrub woodland, including birch, hazel and some ash, occurred on or adjacent to the wetland, within which water-loving/tolerant plants predominated. The presence of Chenopodiaceae and Caryophyllaceae pollen may suggest a saline influence near the site, and the large component of grass pollen may include *Phragmites* pollen. This initial pollen record suggests the existence of a wet, fen–carr–marsh environment, possibly prone to episodic flooding, perhaps during very high spring tides.

Carrigdirty Rock 1—Middle Bronze Age house site

Site location

Carrigdirty Rock 1 (Pl. 26) is located in the intertidal peat on the mid-foreshore (at NGR 147343, 157573; OD –0.465m). Covered by semi-mobile silts, the site was only identified when our feet encountered a post while walking across the muddy foreshore. Careful searching around this first post revealed that others lay hidden under the silts. The site was then investigated by clearing back some of the shallow silts by hand and carefully searching the remaining sediments for vertical posts. These were marked with bamboos and planned. It is likely that other unrecorded posts remained hidden, and this structure should certainly now be investigated by a programme of archaeological excavation. A single sharpened alder post from the north-west side of the structure produced a Middle Bronze Age date of 3330 ± 25 BP (1681–1529 cal. BC; GrN-20976).

Site description

The Carrigdirty Rock 1 site consists of at least 23 vertical roundwood posts, spaced over an area measuring 6.2m (north/south) by 6m (east/west) (Fig. 37). They were all driven vertically (not at an angle or obliquely) into a dark brown peat, rich in reed

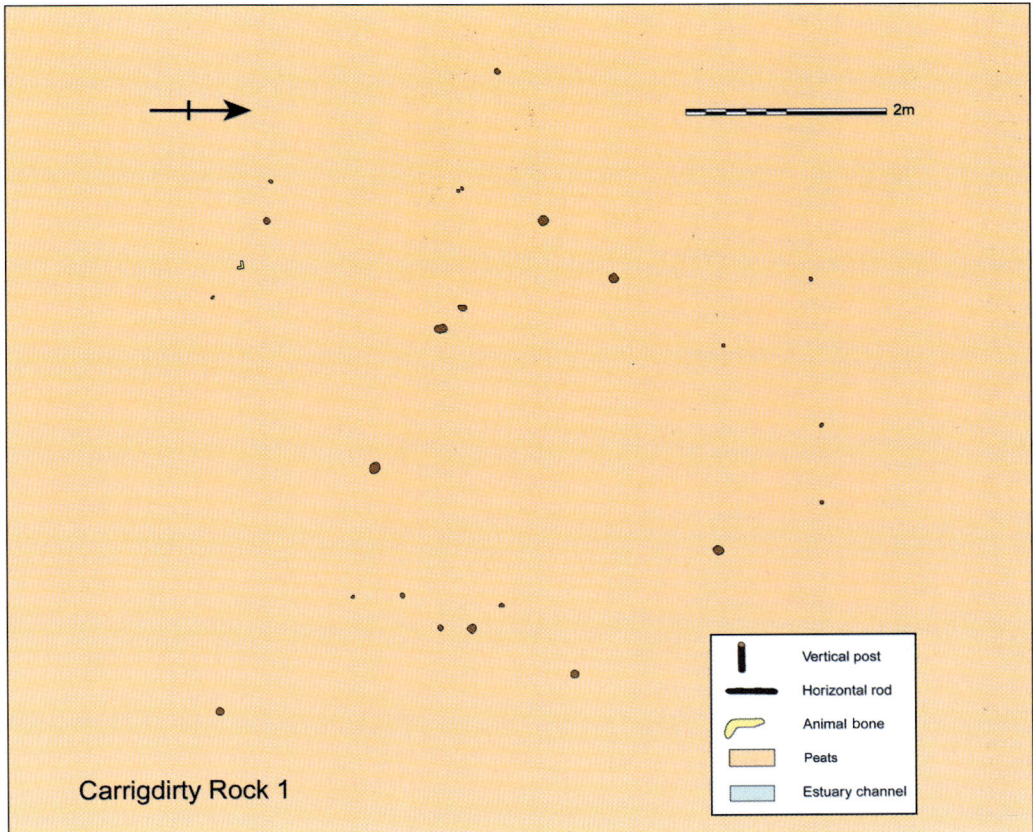

Fig. 37—*Plan of Carrigdirty Rock 1 Middle Bronze Age house.*

stems and fen-wood tree roots. There were at least seven larger posts, 8–12cm in diameter. The others were smaller, typically measuring only 4–5cm in diameter. The posts survived to lengths of only 15–30cm, in most cases only the sharpened tips remaining in the peats. There were four small limestone slabs on the mudflats immediately to the east of the structure.

There were also two concentrations of dense fen-wood tree roots in the peat, at the southern side of the ring of posts and outside it to the north-east. These roots probably pre-date the structure. It is likely that the floor level of the house has been eroded away and its posts survive only as the sharpened tips.

The larger posts, spaced at intervals of 1.5–2m, form an inner ring measuring approximately 4.8m (east/west) by 4.6cm (north/south). The narrower rods or stakes set around this inner ring may represent a wattle or brushwood 'fence'. The posts survived only as the sharpened tips, and tool-marks were visible on the sides of the unexcavated posts (indicating erosion down to this level). Four individual posts were excavated, lifted from the peat, photographed and recorded on site (and then replaced). These were all of narrow roundwood (no cleft wood was used), with bark and sapwood still attached. The evidence for woodworking was recorded on site (Pl. 27). The posts were all worked at shallow cutting angles (15–20°), producing pencil points and variant wedge ends. The individual tool-marks measured 2–3cm in width and 4–5cm in length, and were slightly concave in cross-section and flat in profile, as is typical of Bronze Age tool-marks. A single post had a jam curve near its sharpened end, indicating the use of a narrow metal axe with a tightly curved cutting edge (see O'Sullivan 1996c for analysis of Bronze Age tool-marks).

Cattle bone
VINCENT BUTLER

A single piece of animal bone was recovered from a stratified position in the peat, between two vertical stakes at the south-west edge of the structure. This was the mandible of a calf under six months old.

Foragers, farmers and fishers

Pl. 27—*Carrigdirty Rock 1: worked points, with tool-marks indicating use of a narrow metal axe.*

Table 9—*Carrigdirty Rock 1: calf bone at house site.*

Sample	Species	Bone type	Details
M7:1	Cattle	Mandible (R)	Premolars 2/3/4 erupted. Molar and vertical ramus section missing.

Site interpretation

Carrigdirty Rock 1 is interpreted as a Middle Bronze Age house of fairly substantial construction, using roundwood posts (*c.* 8–10cm in diameter) either as the main features in a small 'bender' hut (*c.* 4.6m in diameter) or as internal roof supports in a larger oval or circular structure (*c.* 6m in diameter) with outer walls and roof supports angled down to the ground (Fig. 38). On balance, given the wide spacing of the main ring of large posts and the fact that they are vertical and not angled into the ground, the latter interpretation seems more likely. In this larger structure, the inner posts may have held tie-beams which would have supported diagonal roof timbers. The smaller narrow stakes scattered around the larger posts could then have been the post-and-wattle walls of the structure. The cluster of vertical posts and stakes at the north side may have been associated with an entrance feature. The limestone slabs found to the north-east of the structure may originally have been used as hearthstones or as post-pads for larger roof timbers.

The inner ring of posts at Carrigdirty Rock 1 are certainly similar in size and spatial arrangement to the proposed inner roof supports of a 6m circular house at Lough Gur, Co. Limerick (Cleary 1995), and also to the inner roof supports of Middle Bronze Age houses from Meadowlands, Co. Down (Pollock and Waterman 1964), and Cullyhanna, Co. Armagh (Hodges 1958). Indeed, circular and oval wooden houses of similar size and appearance are known from several other Irish Middle and Late Bronze Age settlements, such as Ballyvourney, Co. Cork (O'Kelly 1954), and Hut 1 and Hut 3 at Curraghatoor, Co. Tipperary (Doody 1987; 1997), while Chancellorsland, Co.

Bronze Age houses and trackway

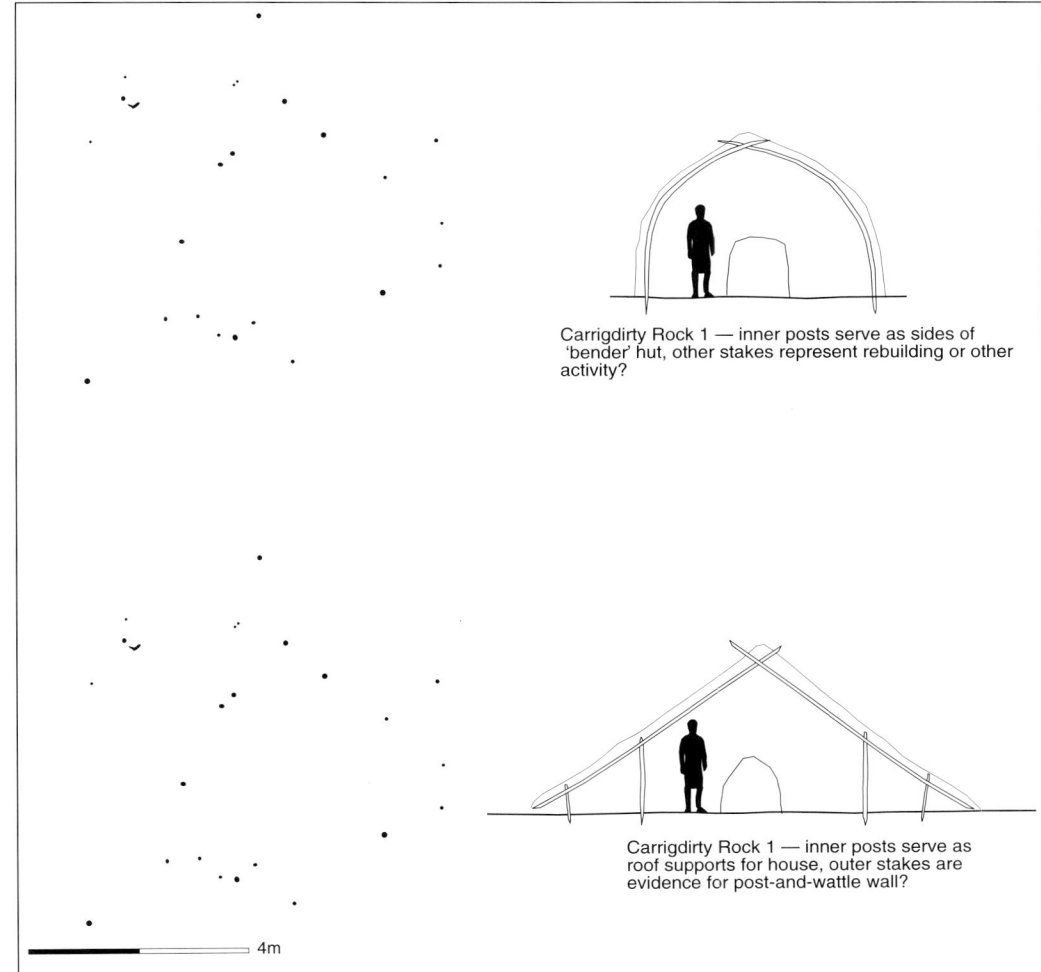

Fig. 38—*Schematic reconstruction drawings of Middle Bronze Age house at Carrigdirty Rock 1.*

Tipperary (Doody 1997), and Moynagh Lough, Co. Meath (J. Bradley 1997; 1999), have also produced medium-sized houses of Middle Bronze Age date. These structures were built of vertical wooden posts and stakes, with walls of post-and-wattle or turf blocks; the roofing was presumably of rushes, heather or turf. Interestingly, Bronze Age wooden houses in the same environmental context have been recorded in intertidal peats at Chapeltump and Cold Harbour, Gwent (Whittle 1989), and at Collister Pill (Bell *et al.* 2000) on the Severn estuary, while the larger Bronze Age rectangular houses at Redwick and the Iron Age houses on the intertidal shore at Goldcliff, Gwent, on the Severn estuary may be similar in function, if not in appearance (Bell 1993a; 1993b; Bell *et al.* 2000; see below for discussion of UK parallels for the Shannon estuary Bronze Age sites).

Carrigdirty Rock 2—wooden posts, stone slabs and cattle bone

Site location

Carrigdirty Rock 2 was located in dark brown peats on the mid-foreshore, *c.* 45m to the west-north-west of Carrigdirty Rock 1 (at NGR 147294, 157577; OD –0.622m) but slightly lower down the foreshore, nearer the LWM. The site was recorded only by written descriptions, so excavations would now be needed to clarify this structure.

Site description

Carrigdirty Rock 2 consisted of a cluster of vertical wooden posts, limestone slabs and a spread of animal bone in the peat. The posts were of narrow alder and oak roundwood, 8–10cm in diameter, surviving to lengths of up to 30cm. They were sharpened with a narrow metal axe, similar to that used at Carrigdirty Rock 1. The stone slabs typically measured 40cm long by 30cm wide by 20cm thick. The posts and stones were spread over an area measuring 8m (north/south) by 5m (east/west). The posts appeared to be arranged in an arc, 5m in length. There are also other isolated, vertical roundwood posts in peats 25m to the west-north-west.

Cattle bone
VINCENT BUTLER

There were several animal bones in the peats, immediately to the south of the vertical posts. Three bones were sampled and were identified as the mandible, tibia and femur of cattle (*Bos taurus* L.). Based on the tooth eruption/wear data and the state of fusion of the epiphyses of the femur and tibia, a single animal may be represented, aged between two and four years.

Table 10—*Carrigdirty Rock 2: cattle bone at posts.*

Sample	Species	Bone type	Details	Metrical data
M8:1	Cattle	Mandible (L)	Tooth row fully erupted, premolar 2 missing. Slight damage to angle	Length of M3 35.8mm Breadth of M3 14.7mm
M8:2	Cattle	Femur (L)	Almost complete. Damage to trochanter major. Proximal, distal epiphyses fused	Breadth of distal end 86.0mm
M8:3	Cattle	Tibia (R)	Proximal end missing. Distal epiphysis fused	Breadth of distal end 55.5mm

Carrigdirty Rock 3—pit with animal bone

Site location

Carrigdirty Rock 3 was located on the upper foreshore to the south-west of Carrigdirty Rock island, *c*. 225m to the west of Carrigdirty Rock 1. The pit was first identified when bone was seen protruding above the mobile sediments. The bone was exposed and was seen to be within a pit feature. This was fully excavated, described and photographed in December 1995, and all bones were retained.

Site description

The site consists of a shallow pit cut into a dark brown, woody peat with reed fragments lying both horizontally and vertically in the peat (Pl. 28). The pit was oval in plan, measuring 90cm in length (north-west/south-east) by 50cm in width. It survives to a depth of 15cm. It may be the remains of a deeper pit originally dug into a peat or saltmarsh surface at a higher level. It contained a gritty, shell-rich grey clay deposit and the disarticulated bone and antler of red deer and pink-footed goose. There was no evidence for butchering or working of deer antler.

The animal bone
VINCENT BUTLER

Eight bone fragments were recovered from the pit. Six bones were identified as antler, mandibles and ribs of a mature red deer (*Cervus elaphus* L.). A fragmented humerus of goose (possibly pink-footed goose) was also identified. A single fragment

Bronze Age houses and trackway

Pl. 28—*Carrigdirty Rock 3: pit with red deer bone and bird bone in grey clay fill.*

was unidentifiable to species level. There were also some animal bones from the peat surface in the vicinity of the pit. A single deer antler from a mature animal (Carrigdirty Rock 9), apparently broken away from the skull rather than shed, was found 10m to the south-east of the pit and may originally have derived from it. There were also two unstratified fragments of animal bone from the surface of the peats 10–15m north of the pit (Carrigdirty Rock 10; bone sample nos CRS2:1, CRS 2:2). These were identified as a lower jaw from a red deer (*Cervus elaphus* L.) and a possible rib from a pig (*Sus domesticus erxl.*). The pig bone had been hacked through its articulation using a metal blade.

Table 11—*Carrigdirty Rock 3: animal bone stratified in pit.*

Sample no.	Species	Bone type	Details
CRS1:1	Red deer	Antler	Portion of main beam and two tines
CRS1:2	Red deer	Mandible (l)	Complete, all permanent teeth erupted
CRS1:3	Red deer	Atlas	Body intact, wings damaged
CRS1:4	Red deer	Rib	Almost complete
CRS1:5	Red deer	Rib	Damaged blade and articulation
CRS1:6	Red deer	Rib	Damaged blade, missing articulation
CRS1:7	Goose	Humerus (L)	Distal end missing

Site interpretation

The site could be interpreted as a pit for food storage or for the disposal of discarded food remains. It may also have been a ritual deposit of animal bone in the wetlands. It may be contemporary with the house at Carrigdirty Rock 1, although its higher elevation on the foreshore might suggest a slightly later date, perhaps in the Late Bronze Age or Iron Age.

Carrigdirty Rock 4—post feature in peats

Site location

Carrigdirty Rock 4 was located in peats on the upper foreshore (at NGR 147096, 157519; OD –1.141m), exposed at the sloping east bank of a modern creek to the

Foragers, farmers and fishers

Pl. 29—*Carrigdirty Rock 4: worked and cleft wooden posts in peats.*

south-east of Carrigdirty Rock itself. This feature was first noted in December 1995, when a sharpened roundwood post was observed, excavated and replaced (but later eroded out by tides). On a return visit in July 1996 a second roundwood post, driven at an oblique angle into the peats, and a cleft ash post lying horizontally in the peats were excavated and recorded. Despite a careful search, no other features of this enigmatic site could be traced in the surrounding peats.

Site description

The site consists of two roundwood posts and one cleft post set at varying angles in the peats. The stratigraphy of the peats and clays at the site were as follows. The upper layers (0–34cm below the peat surface) comprised a red-brown woody peat with *Phragmites* stems. This overlay a grey-brown silty peat (34–50cm), which itself overlay a firm, dark grey minerogenic clay (50–55cm). Post 1 was a roundwood post (1m in length and 8cm in diameter) lying horizontally on the upper peat surface. It was sharpened to a pencil point, with tool-marks similar to those left by a sharp stone axe or a narrow bronze axe. Post 2 was situated 30cm to the west. It was a roundwood post (50cm in length and 9cm in diameter) driven at an oblique angle (40°) into the peats, with its upper end pointing towards the south (Pl. 29). It was sharpened using cleaving techniques, with 3–4 strips of bark and sapwood torn from around the trunk, reducing its diameter to a blunt point. This sharpened end was crushed by its impaction on the firm, dark grey minerogenic clays beneath the peat. Post 3 was situated 40cm to the south-west of Post 1. It was a cleft ash fragment (28cm in length and 6cm in width) and lay at a slight angle in the peat.

Bronze Age houses and trackway

Site interpretation

This post feature may be the remains of a small structure built with stout roundwood posts, sharpened using both an axe and cleaving techniques. The date of the site is unknown, although it is interesting that similar sharpening techniques have been observed on wood from Neolithic trackways. In particular, Post 2 is similar to the cleft points from the Neolithic trackways at Clonbony and Corlea 9, Co. Longford (Raftery 1996; O'Sullivan 1996c). Cleaving techniques to sharpen posts are also known from Neolithic trackways on the Somerset Levels, England, and at a Mesolithic/Neolithic transition site at Swifterbank in the Netherlands (Casparie *et al*. 1977). This may have been a Late Neolithic or Bronze Age wildfowling structure, or the remains of a small shelter or windbreak.

Carrigdirty Rock 20 and 21—wooden planks

Site location

The Carrigdirty Rock 20 and 21 oak planks were located in the peats on the mid-foreshore, at the eastern end of the peat shelf, *c.* 820m east of the island, 4–5m to the south of the Carrigdirty Rock 5 Neolithic site (see Fig. 27). However, these planks were set 1.3m higher in elevation than that site and were embedded in a grey-brown silty peat, rich in woody fragments and reed stems. These planks and peats were also buried under *c.* 10cm of a dark grey peaty silt, and thereafter under *c.* 5cm of modern mobile estuarine silts. The planks were in poor condition, suggesting that they had originally been exposed to rot on a saltmarsh.

Site description

Carrigdirty Rock 20 lay on its horizontal surface and was oriented north/south (precisely located at NGR 147844, 157683; OD –0.405m). It was tangentially cleft from a large oak trunk, and measured 3.4m in length, 46–54cm in width and 5cm in thickness. The northern 1.8m section of the plank was excavated. This revealed that its side edges were irregular, with opposing notches at the northern end. The eastern edge was relatively straight, but the western edge had two notches in its side. The plank widens to 54cm at its southern end. The irregular side edges of the plank, with their notches and protrusions, appear to be due mainly to the knotty character of the original trunk, or to rot in antiquity, rather than being deliberately worked features (Pl. 30; Fig. 39). The side edges of the plank were quite thin or feather-edged, probably as a result of the cleaving process.

Pl. 30—*Carrigdirty Rock 20: plank in peats.*

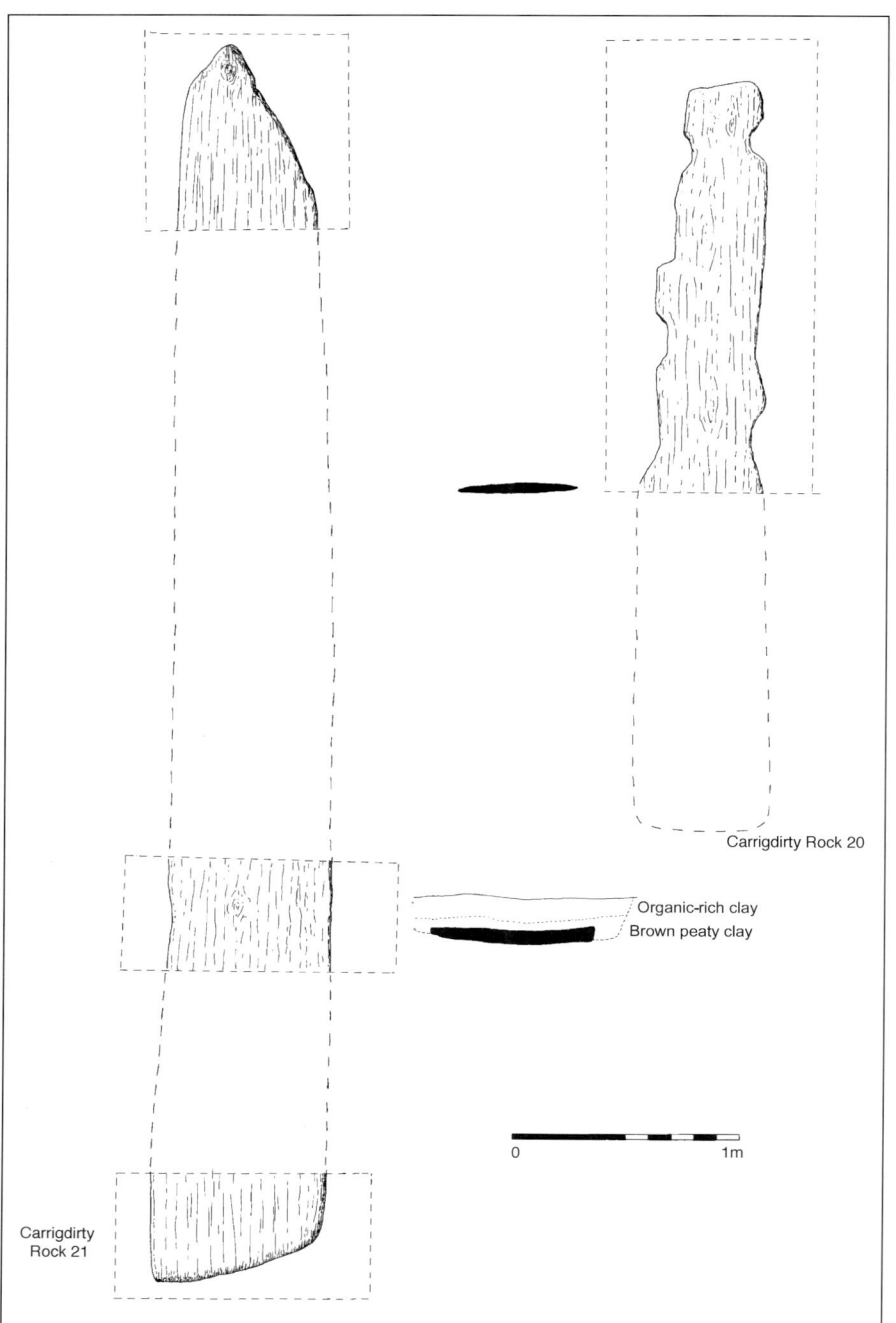

Fig. 39—*Planks from Carrigdirty Rock 20 and Carrigdirty Rock 21.*

Carrigdirty Rock 21 was situated *c.* 30m to the west along the foreshore, 2m south of the northern edge of the intertidal peat shelf (precisely located at NGR 147777, 157660; OD –0.425m). It lay on its horizontal surface and was oriented east/west. It measured 5.6m in length and 76cm in maximum width. It was 5.5cm thick at its northern edge, and 2cm at its southern edge. It was tangentially cleft from an oak trunk; some knots on the surface indicated that this was a fairly knotty trunk. A narrow cutting, measuring 1m (north/south) by 50cm (east/west), was excavated across the width of the plank, 1.45m from its E end. This cross-section revealed its flat surface and its burial under the peaty silt layer. The plank was also examined at its eastern end. It had straight sides, was worked to an oblique point at its western end (sloping in from the northern edge), and was cut directly across at its eastern end. It was possibly charred at the western end. Although the plank was clearly deliberately cleft and worked at either end, there were no worked features on the surface (Fig. 39).

Site interpretation

The date and function of these planks are unknown, although their location at this elevation (at –0.425m OD) in the peats may suggest a broadly similar Middle Bronze Age date to Carrigdirty Rock 1 (–0.465m OD). They may have been used in a prehistoric plank trackway constructed in a saltmarsh to provide access across the wetlands to the intertidal zone. Oak planks were commonly used for narrow pedestrian raised bog trackways in the Irish midlands (Raftery 1996). However, the planks are unusually large (e.g. Carrigdirty Rock 21 was a massive 5.6m in length by 76cm in width). Recently discovered large oak planks in estuarine contexts at Caldicot and Goldcliff, Wales, at North Ferriby on the Humber estuary and at Dover have all proven to derive from Bronze Age sewn plank boats (Wright 1990; Nayling and Caseldine 1997; Bell *et al.* 2000; Parfitt and Fenwick 1993). However, there are no obvious woodworking features (raised features known as 'cleats', stitch-holes or mortises) on the Carrigdirty Rock planks that could be used to support this assertion. It is possible that planks or features lie buried in the surrounding peats, making this site a significant focus for further investigations.

Discussion of the Carrigdirty Rock sites

The sites in their original environment

The Carrigdirty Rock house structure, post features, pit and planks were all firmly embedded in organic-rich peats, with the well-preserved remains of reeds and sedges as well as the roots, narrow trunks and branches of shrubby trees. This suggests an environment dominated by freshwater, perhaps fen, carr woodland or a high saltmarsh. However, it is possible that some of these features were originally constructed on saltmarshes at a higher level, leaving only the lower ends of the posts to survive in the modern exposure of the foreshore. It is also just as likely that the different Carrigdirty Rock features in the peats are not contemporaneous and were variously located in a range of different estuarine wetlands, saltmarsh, fens or carr woodland, all of which may have been prone to spring tide flooding.

The Middle Bronze Age house at Carrigdirty Rock 1 would have been set in a predominantly wetland environment, possibly a sedge fen or carr woodland that was occasionally subjected to flooding episodes at periods of very high spring tides or during particular climatic conditions. The local environment may have been dominated by sedges and reeds growing in a waterlogged, peaty locality. Small copses or woodlands of alder, willow and birch might have grown on drier ground in the vicinity, while stands of oak, hazel and ash may have grown on the small dryland islands protruding above the marshes. These islands (e.g. at Carrigdirty Rock, Bush Island to the west and Graigue Island to the north-east) would have been the only truly dry ground in the immediate vicinity. As with the Neolithic site at Carrigdirty Rock 5 above, local geology, soils and drainage may suggest that this broad area of Bronze Age estuarine wetland measured at least 3.6km (north/south) by 4.8km (east/west). The nearest dryland would have been the low uplands, rolling hills and limestone terraces or rockland at the edge of the marshes.

In terms of function, the size of this house and the general environmental context and location of the Carrigdirty Rock sites suggest fairly long-term, although seasonal, activities in the marshlands. Seasonal occupation might be suggested by the difficulty of undertaking any activities in such winter-flooded wetlands and by the presence of an immature calf jawbone (under six months old). Historically, calves were usually born in spring or early summer, so the presence of the bone suggests activity six months later, in late summer or early autumn. A possible ethnological parallel for the Carrigdirty Rock house may be the local transhumance activity described in early medieval Irish historical texts, the *buaile* or *áirge* (booleying), which continued to be a social and economic feature of Irish agriculture until recent times. Cattle herds were driven to nearby summer pastures from May to November (Lucas 1989; Ó Danachair 1983–4); these were typically found on mountain slopes, but in lowland regions wet or scrubby land (*díthrub*) was used (Fergus Kelly, pers. comm.). The Carrigdirty Rock structures could be the huts or houses constructed for several weeks' habitation on the marshes. In contrast to historical booleying, this would not have involved long-term residence, the travelling of large distances or the wholesale movement of the local community. The Carrigdirty Rock house was probably no more than a few hours' difficult walk across the marshes or a shorter boat-trip away from the main settlement sites on the drylands to the south-west or south (see discussion below). It is also possible that the site was associated with hunting or fishing in the wetlands, as perhaps suggested by its location and by the red deer bone and pink-footed goose bone from the undated pit at Carrigdirty Rock 3.

Middle Bronze Age worked wood, Coonagh Point 1, Co. Limerick

Site location
Coonagh Point 1 consists of worked wood buried in submerged peats exposed in the saltmarsh cliff on the north bank of the upper Shannon estuary, adjacent to the townland of Coonagh West, Co. Limerick (OS 5:13:2; NGR 154226, 156545). There are also large, eroded-out and isolated tufts of peat out on the mudflats of the upper foreshore. A large drainage sluice is situated immediately to the east of the site, and a modern navigation beacon is set on the saltmarsh immediately north of the cliff (Fig. 40).

Site description
Coonagh Point 1 consists of several recumbent oak trunks, roots and branches, within which there was also a cleft oak stake and two sharpened roundwood posts. The trunks may largely derive from a submerged forest, and can be traced along at least 30–40m of the exposed saltmarsh cliff in a peat layer 1.2–1.5m thick. The peat is buried under a thin (30cm) layer of saltmarsh clays. The oak trunks appear to lie at slightly varying levels in the cliff, but they are typically situated at a depth of *c.* 1–1.5m below the top of the saltmarsh. They typically measure 20–25cm in diameter and can be traced for lengths of up to 1m in the saltmarsh. Two large oak timbers protrude horizontally from the cliff face of a small tuft of saltmarsh further down the foreshore. These were oriented south-west/north-east, and both had rectilinear cross-sections measuring 20–25cm in width.

A section of the saltmarsh cliff, due south of the beacon, was briefly cleaned and inspected in 1995. Two narrow worked posts, 50cm apart, were recorded at the base of the saltmarsh cliff (1.5m below the top of the saltmarsh), set in peats contemporary with the submerged forest trunks. These posts were of immature roundwood with bark still attached. They measured 5–8cm in diameter and survived to lengths of 15cm. They were both cut to wedge-shaped points, using narrow, tightly curved axes, producing tool-marks of classic Bronze Age form. A radially cleft oak stake (4–5cm in width and 40cm in length) lay horizontally in the peat 2m to the east of the vertical roundwood posts. This provided a Middle Bronze Age date of 3240 ± 20 BP (1598–1441 cal. BC; GrN-21926).

Site interpretation
It is impossible to interpret this site without further investigations. It is possible that the peats are Bronze Age in date, although their relationship with the sharpened wooden posts and cleft stake is unclear. It is possible that the site represents some form of utilisation of a natural spread of timbers for use as a platform or trackway in the Middle Bronze Age.

Late Bronze Age post-and-wattle structure, Fergus estuary, Co. Clare

Fergus estuary west 1—post-and-wattle features

Site location

The Fergus estuary west 1 site (previously referred to in publications as 'Islandmagrath') is located on the west bank of the upper Fergus estuary, adjacent to the townland of Islandmagrath, Co. Clare (Figs 35 and 41). It lies on the eroding southern side of a gently curving meander in the channel and is being exposed on a narrow foreshore (which measures no more than 30m in width from the saltmarsh cliff to the LWM) that slopes steeply down towards the channel to the north-east. A modern mudflat creek runs out from behind a spur of saltmarsh and flows directly across the lower part of the post-and-wattle structure. This creek seems to be entirely a product of the modern sea wall, and with every low tide it drains the huge expanse of saltmarshes and corcass located off to the south-west. A Late Bronze Age radiocarbon date of 2540 ± 20 BP (797–551 cal. BC; GrN-20974) was obtained from a single narrow hazel rod woven around one of the vertical posts on the mid-foreshore.

The structure was set in firm, finely laid, dark grey minerogenic clays. Palaeoenvironmental studies of the structure itself consisted mainly of sampling for wood species identifications (see below). The adjacent saltmarsh cliff was also the focus of preliminary palaeoenvironmental investigations in 1995, including analyses of pollen (Malone 1996), foraminiferans, ostracods and diatoms (Blythe 1996; Blythe *et al.* 1996a), although these studies mostly relate to later Iron Age and early historic environmental developments. The Fergus estuary post-and-wattle structure itself was also sampled for preliminary diatom analyses, which suggest that it was built in periodically inundated estuarine silts, with reed-swamp vegetation in the vicinity (Blythe 1996).

Site description

The post-and-wattle fences and woven panels

The structure consists of two parallel post-and-wattle fences, between which are several horizontal post-and-wattle panels as well as numerous pieces of brushwood (Pl. 31; Fig. 42). The structure is generally oriented west-north-west/east-south-east, and runs diagonally down the foreshore at an oblique angle to the low-water mark. It measures at least 35m in length and typically about 2m in width. It drops in elevation as much as 1.5m down the steeply sloping foreshore, from where it first appears near the saltmarsh cliff down to well below the LWM. It is

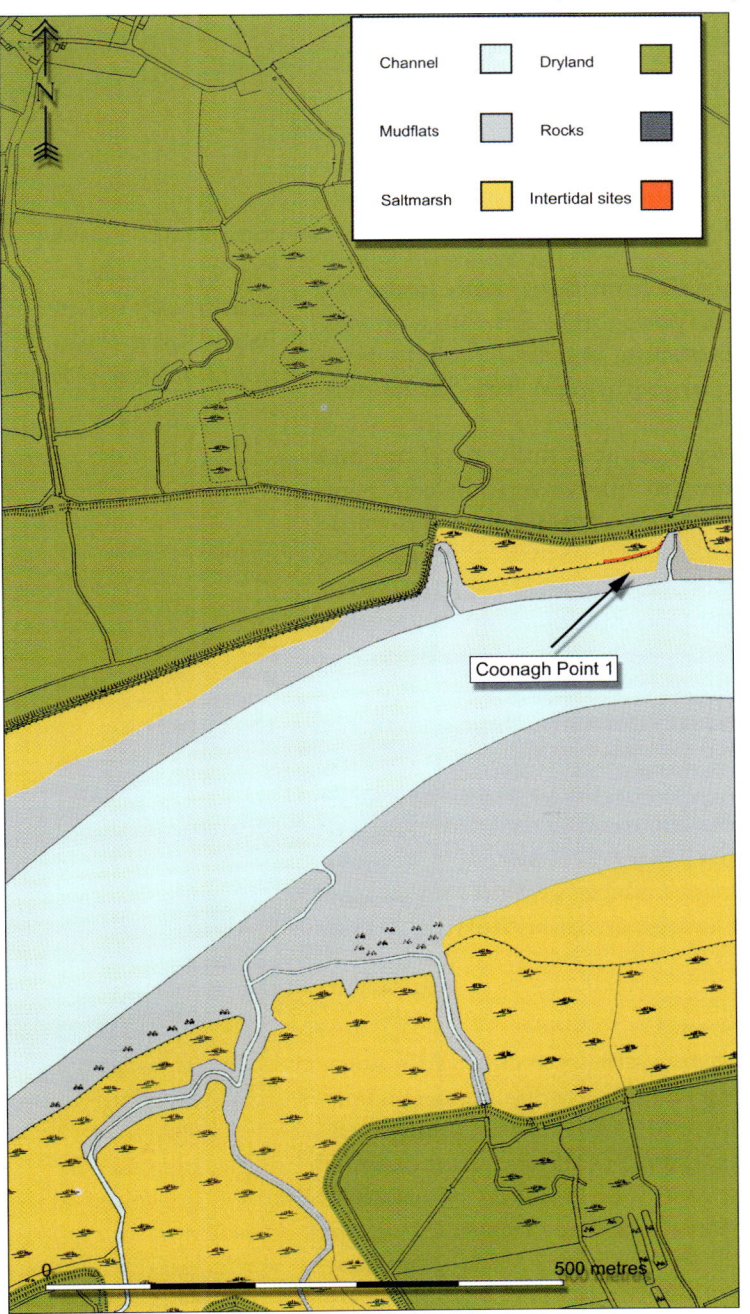

Fig. 40—*Location of Coonagh Point 1.*

Foragers, farmers and fishers

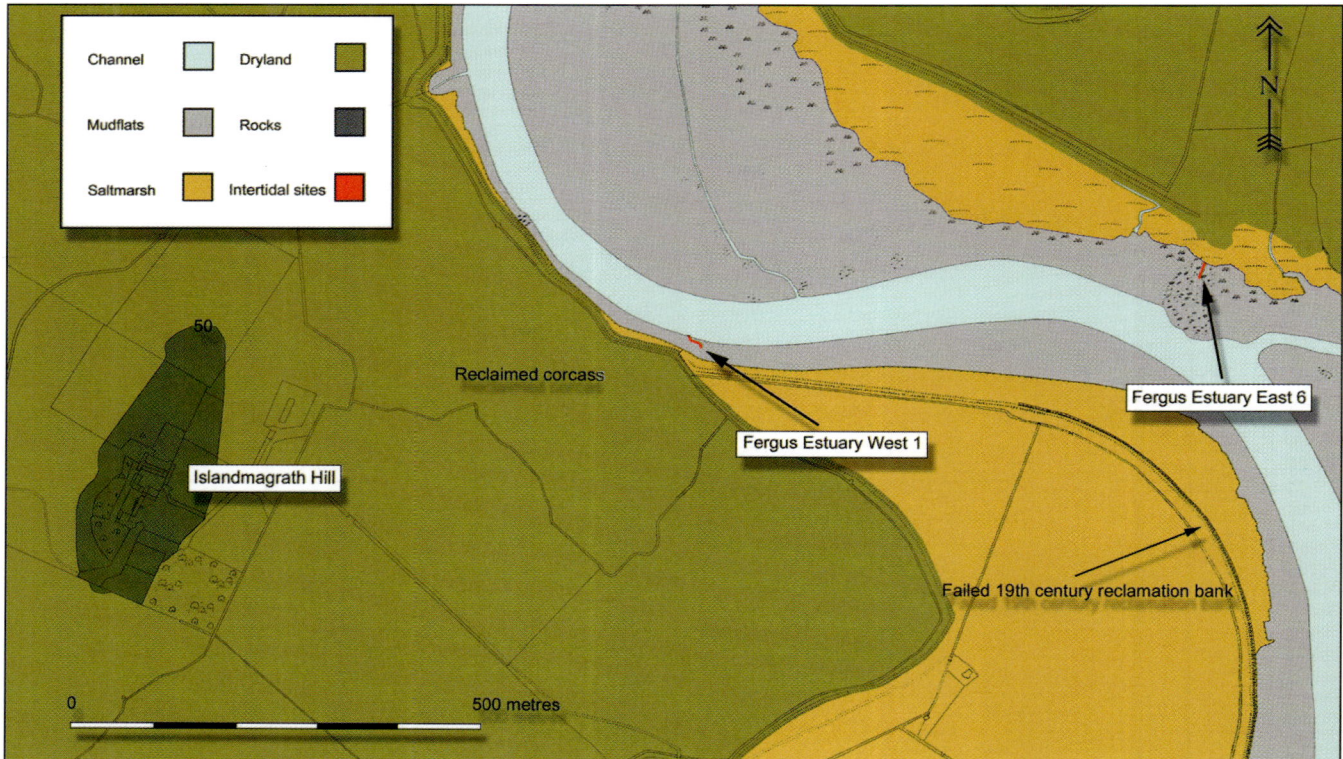

Fig. 41—*Detailed location map of Late Bronze Age post-and-wattle structure at Fergus estuary west 1, Co. Clare.*

likely that much more of this structure remains buried from sight, both under the upper foreshore clays and underwater (vertical wooden posts can be felt with a ranging rod out in the channel). The entire post-and-wattle structure weaves irregularly down the foreshore, presenting an irregular or S-shaped plan with slight 'bays' at its midpoint.

The posts of the vertical post-and-wattle fences were set at either vertical or quite oblique angles in the estuarine clays, and rods were roughly interwoven between them. In the space between these two post-and-wattle fences, horizontal post-and-wattle panels appear to have been laid on the mudflat surface and pinned in place using vertical posts driven through the weave of the horizontal panels (Pl. 32). Other roundwood branches, twigs and rods are also present on the foreshore, lying both beside and along the length of the post-and-wattle fences. This roundwood is particularly apparent at the northern end.

The structure will be described here in terms of its main elements. These include the upper foreshore posts at the south-eastern end of the site, the double post-and-wattle fences and horizontal wattle panels on the mid-foreshore, and finally the vertical post-and-wattle fences at the north-western end of the site. The site is described in terms of these various elements because there is a possibility that they reflect discrete or separate features within the overall structure. Indeed, wood species analyses would seem to bear this out, with certain species being used for different elements within the overall structure.

The vertical post-and-wattle fence on the upper foreshore

On the upper foreshore, only the northern or channel-side post-and-wattle fence was exposed to view (Pl. 31). This stretch of the vertical fence measures approximately 10m in length. It curves gently down the foreshore, generally oriented west-north-west, running firstly down the foreshore, then running parallel with the water-channel before turning slightly down the foreshore again. The posts were set at an oblique angle in the clays, each tilting at an angle of 45° to the north-east. They typically measure 6–7cm in diameter and are spaced at intervals of 20–40cm. These vertical posts have 2–3 rows of heavy branches woven horizontally between them. The branches were

Pl. 31—*Late Bronze Age post-and-wattle structure at Fergus estuary west 1.*

taken from the topwood of immature trees and are knotty, with side branches and twigs. A second row of vertical posts, 2–3m in length and oriented north-west/south-east, runs down the foreshore towards the main fence.

The double post-and-wattle fences on the mid-foreshore

By the mid-foreshore, a second vertical post-and-wattle fence appears on the southern or saltmarsh side of the structure (Pl. 32). The two vertical fences thereby create a double post-and-wattle structure running diagonally down the foreshore for 4.6m, oriented north-west/south-east. The two fences were generally 0.8–1m apart, running parallel with each other. The roundwood posts, which are set vertically or

Foragers, farmers and fishers

Fig. 42—*Plan of Late Bronze Age post-and-wattle structure, Fergus estuary west 1.*

Pl. 32—*Detail of horizontal post-and-wattle panels at Fergus estuary west 1, possibly pinned onto clays with vertical stakes driven through weave.*

angled obliquely (to the north) in the clays, measure 4–5cm in diameter and are closely spaced at intervals of 25–30cm. Stout rods, 3–4cm in diameter, were interwoven between the posts.

The horizontal post-and-wattle panels on the mid-foreshore

Two horizontal post-and-wattle panels were found between the vertical fences on the mid-foreshore, with the same orientation as the fences. They were partly buried in the clay (Pl. 32). The south-eastern panel was 1.2m long and 70cm wide. It was woven of at least six sails, 4–5cm in diameter, and 12–14 interwoven rods, 2–3cm in diameter. The sails were generally spaced at 30cm intervals. The rods were fairly tightly woven together, separated by no more than 2–3cm. Double sails were occasionally used in the weave. The second panel, situated *c*. 40m to the north-west, was 1m long and 60cm wide. It was woven of four sails and fifteen rods, the former at intervals of 30cm, the latter at intervals of 2–3cm.

The entire structure then changes course again and runs west-north-west/east-south-east for its remaining length of 12.8m (Fig. 42). To the north-west of the horizontal wattle panels, it becomes increasingly difficult to ascertain its precise nature. There appears to be another horizontal post-and-wattle panel (2m long and 80cm wide) adjacent to the upper post row, immediately to the south-east of the modern creek. However, the structure, as before, generally takes the form of two

Pl. 33—*Detail of post-and-wattle fences at west disappearing into the water at the low-water mark.*

Pl. 34—*View to east up the foreshore, illustrating the double row of vertical posts, Fergus estuary west 1.*

Bronze Age houses and trackway

parallel post-and-wattle fences.

There is also a quantity of narrow branches, roundwood and twigs on the lower foreshore, to the north side of the structure. This wood appears to have been deliberately dumped on the clays and was not woven into the vertical fences.

The post-and-wattle fences on the lower foreshore

The structure is crossed by the narrow, shallow channel of a small mudflat creek. This is a modern feature and has no chronological or functional relationship with the Bronze Age structure. The banks and sections of this mudflat creek could be closely inspected, showing that there are no other features buried deeper underneath the structure. On the lower foreshore there are at least two parallel post-and-wattle fences, oriented north-west/south-east (Pl. 33). The posts are typically separated by intervals of 40–60cm, with stout interwoven rods between them. They tip in a pronounced manner towards the north and the channel (possibly owing to slippage of the estuarine clays from the south). However, there are also numerous other vertical posts and stakes off the alignment of the main fences, suggesting repair or reconstruction, and the structure is quite complex on these steeply sloping clays just above the low-water mark (Pl. 34).

Withy or twisted wooden rope

A length of withy tie or twisted wooden rope was found in the clays beside the posts at the north-western end of the structure (Pl. 35), but was removed by tidal erosion before it could be recovered. It was a single, roundwood branch, with bark and bast still attached, twisted around in a loop as a simple knot. It measured 32cm in length and 2cm in diameter. Twisted wood fibres make strong ties, often with a high load-bearing capacity. The twisted withy tie may have been used to bind a collection of rods for dumping onto the foreshore at the site. Bronze Age ropes or twisted withies are known from other later prehistoric sites, such as the Late Bronze Age boat site at North Ferriby, Humberside (Wright 1990, 156), a Late Bronze Age riverine site at Caldicot, Gwent (Nayling and Caseldine 1997), and a Late Bronze Age ritual shaft or well at Wilsford, Wiltshire (Ashbee *et al.* 1989).

Pl. 35—*Withy or twisted wooden rope* in situ *in clays beside lower end of post-and-wattle structure, Fergus estuary west 1.*

Foragers, farmers and fishers

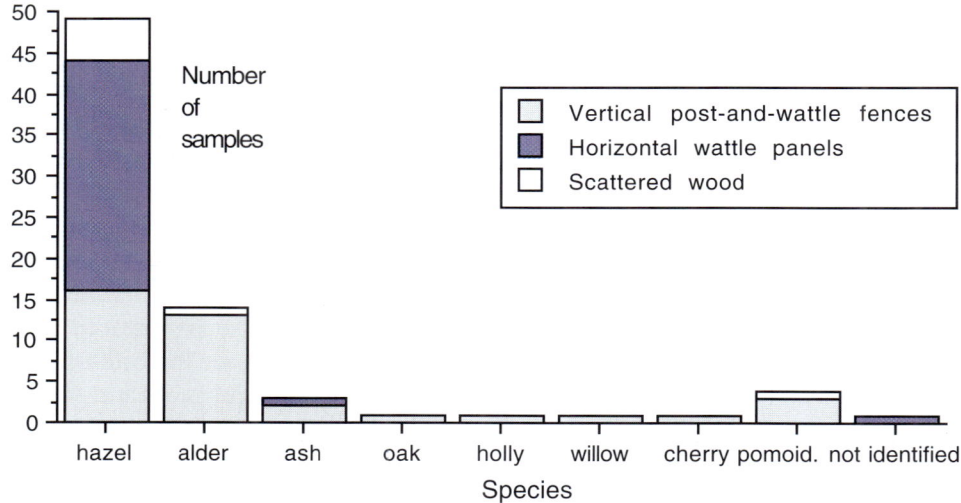

Late Bronze Age structure: Fergus estuary west 1
Species of vertical fences, wattle panels and scattered wood.

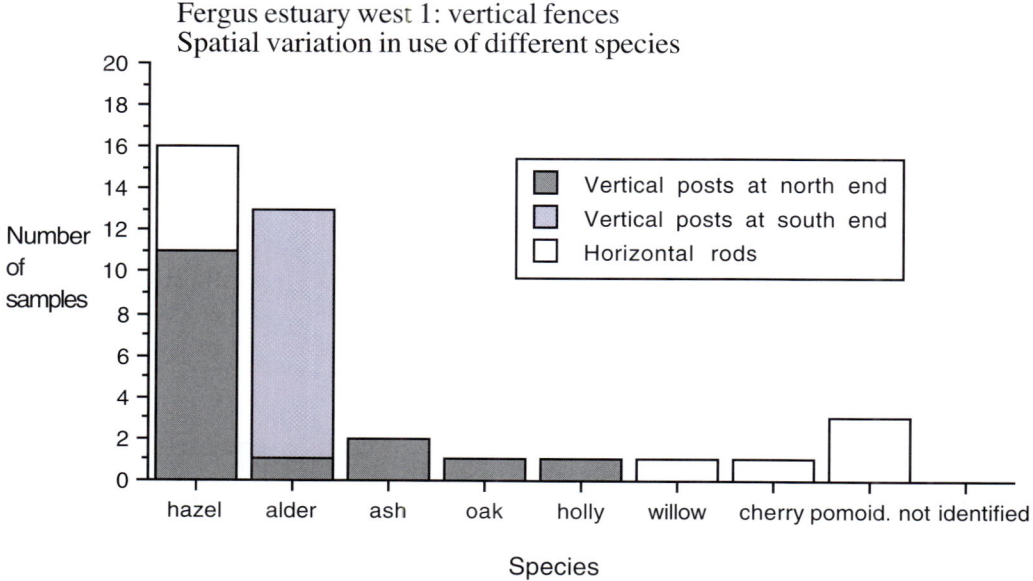

Fergus estuary west 1: vertical fences
Spatial variation in use of different species

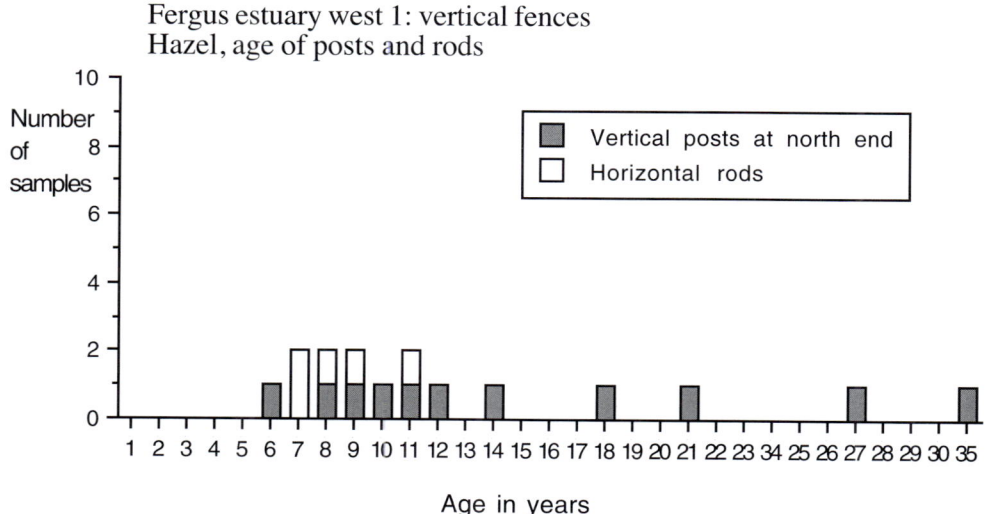

Fergus estuary west 1: vertical fences
Hazel, age of posts and rods

Bronze Age houses and trackway

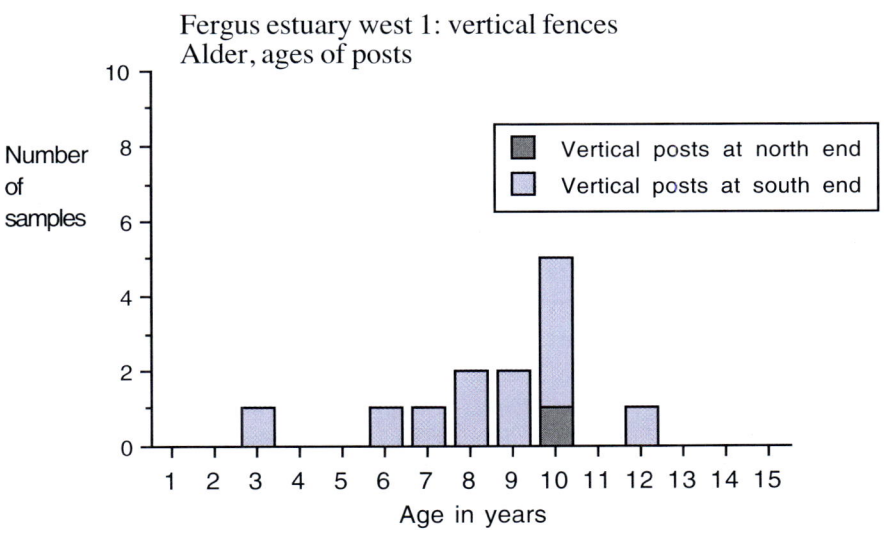
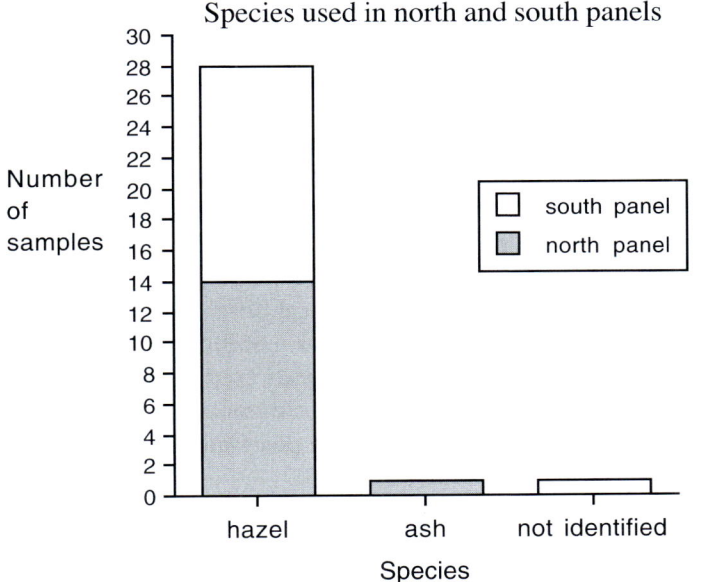
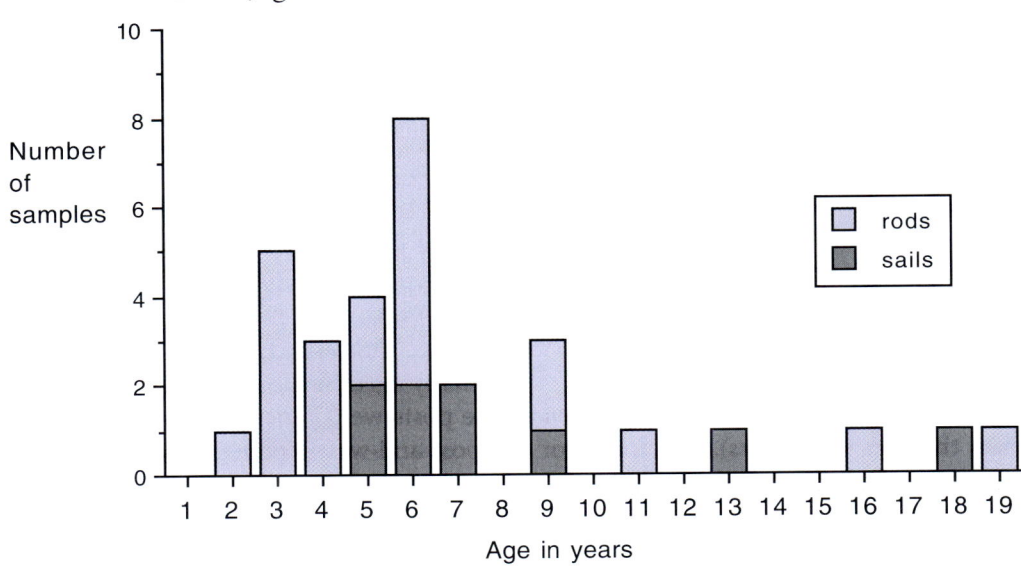

Fig. 43—*Wood species and tree-ring ages of wood from Late Bronze Age structure at Fergus estuary west 1.*

115

Foragers, farmers and fishers

Wood studies
AIDAN O'SULLIVAN AND MARY B. DEEVY

Introduction
Wood species identifications and tree-ring counts were carried out on 75 pieces of wood sampled for study (Fig. 43). These samples were taken from several different features within the overall structure, including the vertical posts on the upper foreshore, the two horizontal post-and-wattle panels on the mid-foreshore, and the scatter of roundwood on the lower foreshore. A surprisingly wide range of Irish native tree species was identified. Hazel (*Corylus* sp.) dominated the assemblage with 49 (65%) pieces of roundwood, while alder (*Alnus* sp.) was also common with fourteen (19%) pieces of wood. Other tree species included three pieces of ash (*Fraxinus excelsior*), four of pomaceous fruitwood (Pomoideae sp., either apple, pear, quince or hawthorn), one of oak (*Quercus* sp.), one of holly (*Ilex aquifolium*), one of willow (*Salix* sp.), and one of cherry (*Prunus avium*). The roundwood used in the entire structure ranged widely in age from two to 35 years, with an average of ten years of age. The samples ranged in diameter from 1.1cm to 8cm, with an overall average diameter of 2.9cm.

Species selection in the vertical post-and-wattle fences
There were some spatial patterns in the use of wood across the structure. The widest range of species was found in the vertical post-and-wattle fences, which were constructed mostly of hazel and alder, with roughly equal amounts of ash, oak, holly, willow, cherry and fruitwood. However, towards the south-eastern or upper foreshore end of the structure the posts were typically of alder, while towards the north-eastern end hazel predominated, with lesser amounts of alder, ash, oak and holly. The rods woven between the vertical fences were mostly of hazel, but willow, cherry and fruitwood were also occasionally used. In general terms, the wood for the vertical fence seems to have been cut at about 9–10 years old. The vertical posts were generally aged between 8 and 12 years, although towards the north-east end of the structure they were older, with some samples being up to 35 years of age. The rods used in the vertical fence were generally aged 7–9 years. The posts tended to be stouter, typically measuring between 3.1cm and 5.5cm in diameter, with the thickest posts measuring up to 7cm. The rods typically measured 1.1–4.5cm in diameter.

There was little evidence for woodland management in the hazel and alder wood. The hazel used in the vertical fences (for both posts and rods) was typically 2.1–4cm in diameter and 7–12 years in age, although some of the posts at the north-east end of the site were aged up to 35 years. The evidence suggests that the posts and rods for the vertical fence were being cropped from relatively even-aged hazel woodland, but there is little other evidence to suggest that this was coppiced or deliberately managed woodland. The alder wood was typically aged 6–10 years, with a peak at the latter age, and measured between 3.1cm and 6.5cm in diameter. It is likely that the alder wood was also being cropped from rough woodland, growing perhaps in hedgerows or in the coastal marshes.

Species selection in the horizontal post-and-wattle panels
In contrast to the vertical fences, the horizontal post-and-wattle panels were made almost entirely of hazel. Thirty samples were analysed: virtually all of it was of hazel, and only a single piece of ash was found (in the north-west panel). The hazel wood used in these panels was relatively restricted in age. Although there was a wide range of ages (2–19 years), most of the wood was actually aged between 3 and 6 years, with only a few pieces aged 9, 11 and 13 years. The posts were generally older (5–7 years) than the rods (2–6 years). The hazel for the post-and-wattle panels might well have been taken from managed woodland.

Bronze Age houses and trackway

Pl. 36—*Two Late Bronze Age worked ends at Fergus estuary west 1.*

The evidence for wood technology

Wood technology studies were carried out on several worked ends, according to techniques established in previous wetland projects in the Somerset Levels (e.g. Orme 1982; Orme and Coles 1983; 1985), on Neolithic, Bronze Age and Iron Age wooden trackways in the midland bogs of Ireland (O'Sullivan 1996c), and on Bronze Age riverside settlements in Wales (Brunning and O'Sullivan 1997). The worked wood studied included hazel, alder and fruitwood posts and rods 3–8cm in diameter, and the woodworking sample can therefore be considered to be fairly representative of the entire wood assemblage (Pl. 36; Fig. 44)..

The woodworking evidence suggests both tree-felling and sharpening. The posts and rods were cut at shallow angles (15-25°), typically to chisel points or wedge points. A single chisel end was chopped at a steep angle (50°), indicating that rods and poles were being cut up into lengths. The smaller rods, 3.2–4.5cm in diameter, were quickly slashed through on one surface only, producing chisel points with only one worked surface. A single narrow rod was cut to a wedge point, being chopped from both sides. The larger poles were generally cut on opposing surfaces to make pencil points. In the production of these pencil points, however, most of the chopping was carried out on one surface only, the post being then turned around at the end so that the final axe-blow detached it from the trunk. The tool-marks were often in poor condition, suggesting that many of the worked ends were exposed to water action and rot. The tool-marks were usually quite small, on average 2.5cm in length by 3cm in width. They were generally flat, or only slightly concave, in cross-section and concave in profile. Jam curves on some points indicated the use of narrow cutting edges with curved blades. The edges were quite sharp, although two axes had nicks or grooves in the blade, leaving blade signatures on the tool-marks. One axe was quite damaged, with a large nick missing from the axe edge.

Foragers, farmers and fishers

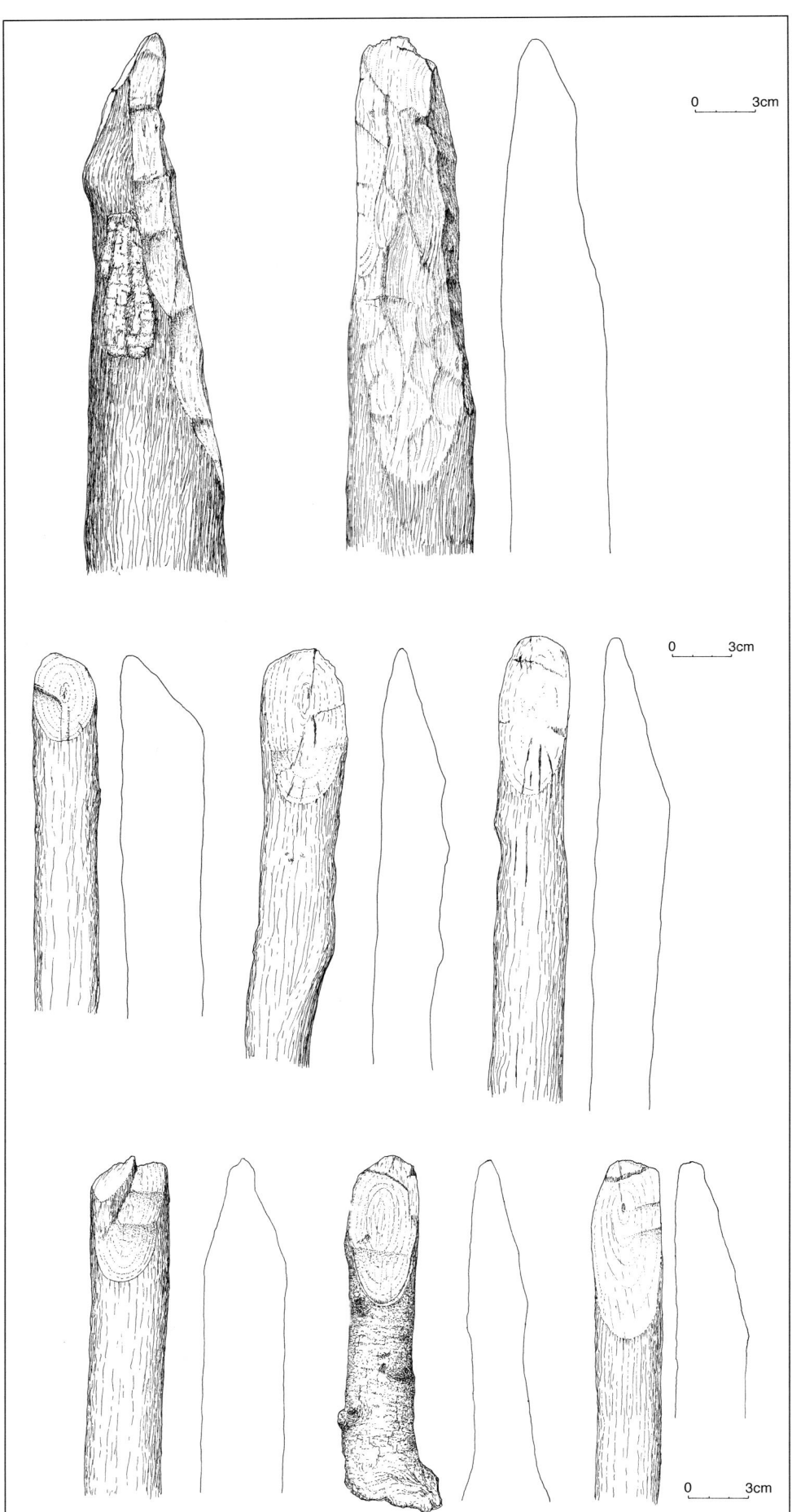

Fig. 44—*Late Bronze Age worked wood from Fergus estuary west 1.*

The worked wood was similar in size, character and tool-mark attributes to Late Bronze Age woodworking from Corlea and Derryoghil trackways, Co. Longford (Raftery 1996; O'Sullivan 1996c), and to the Late Bronze Age worked wood from Haughey's Fort, Co. Armagh. The evidence from the Fergus estuary structure indicates that hazel, alder and fruitwood brushwood was being cut with a number of small, flat and narrow axes (at least 4cm in width at the cutting edge), with slightly convex cutting edges. It is likely that these were bronze socketed, looped axes of a fairly flat or rectangular cross-section (e.g. Eogan 2000), although the slightly flat nature of the tool-marks is reminiscent of iron axes. The potentially late date of the structure suggests that iron axes could have been used, as O'Neill (2000) has also identified a shift from bronze to iron axe tool-marks at *c*. 600 BC.

Reconstructing Late Bronze Age trees and woodland on the Fergus estuary
In summary, wood species identifications and tree-ring counts indicate that a range of woodland habitats were being exploited for the construction of the Late Bronze Age trackway. The evidence for woodworking suggests that this wood was both felled and sharpened using narrow, flattish axes with curved cutting edges—possibly socketed, looped axes. The structure was mostly built of hazel (*Corylus* sp.) and alder (*Alnus* sp.), with much smaller amounts of ash (*Fraxinus excelsior*), oak (*Quercus* spp), willow (*Salix* sp.), cherry (*Prunus avium*) and holly (*Ilex* sp.). This species range indicates that most of the woodland being cropped was growing on well-drained dryland soils. Although hazel will grow in a range of habitats, it prefers the marginal environments between wetlands and drylands, where it has less competition. Hazel–ash woodlands are often found at the base of dryland slopes over wetland marshes. There were also some species used which may have been growing on the neighbouring wetlands, such as alder and willow. It is likely, then, that the hazel, ash and blackthorn were growing on the dryland margins, while the willow and alder probably grew on or immediately adjacent to the estuarine marshes. This woodland may have been growing fairly close to the site, possibly on the hillslopes a few hundred metres to the north.

Discussion
AIDAN O'SULLIVAN

Introduction
The Late Bronze Age post-and-wattle structure at Fergus estuary west 1 was probably originally constructed on an intertidal foreshore of estuarine clays and silts that sloped down towards the north-west. Preliminary palaeoenvironmental studies suggest that this was an intertidal foreshore in proximity to reed-swamp vegetation, so it is likely that the post-and-wattle structure was constructed down the sloping sides of a large saltmarsh creek or channel. Wood studies suggest that a range of both local wetland and dryland trees and bushes were used in its construction. This wood could have been cut in the wetlands and on the drylands in the immediate vicinity of the estuary and dragged down onto the saltmarshes.

Building the structure
The trackway could have been built in a relatively short period by a small group of people. The roundwood posts were probably sharpened with axes at the edge of the saltmarsh and the two lines of posts driven down into the clays of the mudflats. These vertical posts may have stood to some height. Rough rods and branches were woven around them to construct heavy post-and-wattle fences. Brushwood could then have been thrown down onto the mudflats, and post-and-wattle panels carried out onto the muds and laid between the two vertical fences, pinned in position by driving sharpened posts between the weave of the panels.

Foragers, farmers and fishers

A boat-hard or fishtrap?

It is possible that the structure was intended for use by boats. Bronze Age post-and-wattle structures previously recorded in coastal wetlands in Britain (see discussion below) have on occasion been associated with wooden boats and so have been interpreted as hards for beaching craft on, or as structures to provide easier access to the channel where a large plank-boat may have been drawn up. At North Ferriby, on the Humber Estuary, a smaller, simple wooden structure was dated to *c.* 1590–1200 cal. BC, contemporary with the well-known plank-built boats (McGrail 1983; Wright 1990). Recent excavations in a former tidal creek at Caldicot, south Wales, have revealed similar Later Bronze Age pile and post-and-wattle structures, associated with such finds as a plank-built boat, wooden artefacts, pottery, metalwork and animal bone (Nayling 1993; Nayling and Caseldine 1997). In the context of boats, it is interesting that willow ties similar to the single example found at the Fergus estuary structure were used to stitch together the planks of the Brigg 'raft', a flat-bottomed vessel from the River Ancholme dated to *c.* 800 BC (McGrail 1981). However, it has to be said that a boat-hard would have been unnecessary on the Fergus estuary, as both large and small craft could easily have been beached along the mudflats. More importantly, the structure is much too narrow for any large craft; even a dug-out boat could only with difficulty be dragged along it. Another possibility worth considering is that the structure served as a fishtrap. However, this would not explain several features, such as the pair of closely parallel fences and the use of dumped brushwood and horizontal wattle panels between the fences.

An estuary marshland trackway?

It is more likely that this structure was a trackway constructed to cross the mudflats. The parallel line of the two fences, the dump of brushwood and branches on the foreshore, and the placing of horizontal post-and-wattle panels on the muds suggest that it was intended to provide a walking surface on the mudflats. The horizontal post-and-wattle panels would have been prevented from slipping sideways by the vertical posts to either side. The slope of the structure may reflect the original foreshore topography directly, or, if the mudflats were very steep, it may have been constructed at an angle to the channel, thus providing a relatively gently sloping routeway down a steeply sloping shore. Similar Bronze Age and Iron Age trackways, causeways and creek bridges are known from the Thames estuary, the Essex coast and from the Humber estuary (see below). In this sense, the Fergus estuary west 1 structure may also be comparable to the Bronze Age hurdle trackways that have been found in large numbers in the midland raised bogs, particularly at Corlea and Derryoghil, Co. Longford. These trackways were mostly constructed of brushwood and hurdles and frequently indicate repair and replacement over long periods (Raftery 1990; 1996).

The Fergus estuary structure can be seen to be on a narrow part of the estuary and also the shortest distance between the drylands (i.e. the drumlin ridges at Carrownanelly and the isolated marsh island at Islandmagrath). A routeway following the topography at this location would run along the dryland ridges and hills, down onto the saltmarshes, cross the tidal creeks, and lead out towards the islands of Islandmagrath and Islandavanna, which in late prehistory (and indeed in more recent times) were isolated out in the marshes. This trackway may also be seen as a shorter pedestrian routeway, designed to provide access for people to the marshes for hunting and wildfowling. It is also possible that cattle and sheep were herded through the marshes, and that post-and-wattle structures were laid down to provide easier crossing-points of particularly intractable creeks.

Interpreting Bronze Age settlement, society and economy on the Shannon estuary

Introduction
In recent years the Shannon estuary region has been the location for landscape archaeological research, survey and excavation by the North Munster Project, which is investigating later prehistoric settlement and society in the region (Grogan *et al.* 1995; 1996; Grogan and Condit 1994; Grogan 1999). The project has shown that by the Middle Bronze Age (1600–1200 BC) the upper Shannon estuary was becoming an area of increased social and economic importance. The distribution of settlement sites, *fulachta fiadh*, standing stones, barrows, bronze tools and weaponry suggests the movement of peoples southwards from the Burren region into south-east Clare, and the expansion of settlement throughout east Limerick and west Tipperary in particular (Grogan 1995). By the Late Bronze Age (1200–600 BC) the upper Shannon estuary emerges clearly as the geographical focus for a wealthy, hierarchically structured and influential community, with the votive deposition of huge quantities of gold and bronze tools, weapons and ornaments in probable sacred places such as bogs, lakes and rivers (notably at Mooghaun Lough, Co. Clare, and the Bog of Cullen, Co. Tipperary) (Eogan 1965; 1983; Grogan *et al.* 1996). The range and types of Late Bronze Age gold ornaments (in particular) found in the region have traditionally been taken as indicators of this community's wealth and control of agricultural and mineral resources, as well as its trading and other contacts with the later prehistoric peoples of Atlantic Europe (Eogan 1974; 1993; Grogan 1999).

The North Munster Project's archaeological survey and excavation and its regional landscape analysis of a wide range of artefactual evidence have demonstrated the hierarchical and socially stratified nature of Middle and Late Bronze Age society along the upper Shannon estuary (particularly in south-east Clare). Grogan (1999) has proposed a model for the social, economic and ideological structuring of this landscape, and he envisages a three-tiered hierarchical system of both social and settlement organisation. Hillforts (Pl. 2) were used as central places for subregional chiefdoms, places of community power and status, albeit controlled by a few individuals. Other locally powerful individuals may have occupied and used hilltop enclosures and enclosed lakeshore settlements such as Knocknalappa, Co. Clare (Grogan *et al.* 1999). At the base of this settlement hierarchy were small enclosed farmsteads, with low stone walls (50cm in height) of double kerb and rubble fill enclosing areas 18–20m in diameter. These stone enclosures were not heavily defended and are associated with small field systems; they are typically located on rocky ridges and limestone terraces. Similar stone enclosures have been excavated at Lough Gur and Aughinish, Co. Limerick, where they produced Bronze Age circular houses, working areas, quernstones, pits and coarseware pottery. It is likely that these small stone enclosures were the farmsteads of well-off, but not powerful, farming families. It is also likely that unenclosed settlements were a feature of this landscape, with perhaps small clusters of houses representing the extended family habitations of the poorer members of society, but there is no evidence for 'villages' or nucleated settlements (Grogan *et al.* 1996; Grogan 1999).

The Middle Bronze Age house site at Carrigdirty Rock 1 and the Late Bronze Age trackway on the upper Fergus estuary, although situated at some distance from the core of this settlement landscape, can be usefully interpreted in terms of these wider local and subregional developments.

Middle and Late Bronze Age settlement and economy in Ireland
Indeed, in recent years it has become clear that later prehistoric communities settled the Irish landscape in a complex, intensive way, with settlements ranging in location from mountains and hilltops down to low-lying wetlands. Middle and Late Bronze Age

settlements and domestic habitations vary in form, and include single houses enclosed within stone walls, as at Carrigillihy, Co. Cork (O'Kelly 1951), or wooden palisades, as at Cullyhanna Lough (Hodges 1958), or clusters of houses enclosed within ditches and palisades, as at Chancellorsland, Co. Tipperary (Doody 1997). The Middle Bronze Age roundhouse with field systems excavated at Belderrig, Co. Mayo (Caulfield 1988), also confirms the use of unenclosed settlements. The inhabitants of these Bronze Age farmsteads and dwellings were typically engaged in intensive mixed farming on light, well-drained soils, herding cattle, pigs, sheep and goats in the locality, and probably cultivating wheat, barley and other arable crops within field systems.

However, it is also clear that settlement activities extended down into low-lying or wetland areas. Middle and Late Bronze Age wetland settlements or metalworking sites are known from the edges of lakes (O'Sullivan 1998), such as at Cullyhanna, Co. Armagh (Hodges 1958), Lough Eskragh, Co. Tyrone (Collins and Seaby 1960; Williams 1978), and Moynagh Lough, Co. Meath (J. Bradley 1997). At the Middle Bronze Age lakeshore settlement at Cullyhanna Lough, Co. Armagh, a circular house with a hearth and a number of smaller wooden structures were enclosed within an irregular post palisade. Meagre finds from the site included coarse pottery, flint scrapers and a flint core. The site could be interpreted either as a low-status permanent settlement or as a seasonal dwelling associated with hunting, fishing and livestock-grazing (Hodges 1958; Hillam 1976). A Middle Bronze Age coastal fen-edge occupation excavated at Meadowlands, Co. Down, produced two circular houses with hearths and possible cooking-pits with burnt stone; finds included cordoned urn pottery, a stone axe and several flint scrapers (Pollock and Waterman 1964; O'Kelly 1989, 350). The Meadowlands occupation was situated at the edge of the former estuarine marshes of the River Quoile, possibly indicating that its inhabitants were engaged in similar coastal wetland activities to those residing at the Carrigdirty Rock 1 site (Pollock and Waterman 1964). Other common indicators of Middle Bronze Age activity in wetlands are *fulachta fiadh* (burnt mounds of fire-cracked stone, clay and ash, associated with troughs for boiling water and typically dated to *c.* 1600–900 BC), probably the most numerous type of archaeological site that has been identified in the Irish landscape. They may indicate short-term or seasonal activities in river valleys, lakeshores and boggy ground, and may have been used repeatedly as cooking-places, saunas and baths, or places for treating leather or human remains (Brindley *et al.* 1989–90; Buckley 1990; Antonia Doolan, pers. comm.).

This Middle and Late Bronze Age settlement activity in wetland landscapes could be taken as evidence for population pressure, social instability, increasing growth of blanket bog, and perhaps even climatic deterioration caused by deforestation and volcanic eruptions. Certainly, these various factors, allied to increased social stratification and competition for land, may have led to the inclusion of wetlands in a wider social and economic use of the landscape. However, it is more likely that Later Bronze Age communities were making use of various localities in the landscape simply as part of a flexible economic strategy established since early prehistory. In other words, while permanently occupied, dispersed farmsteads were of key importance in society, there may also have been at least some members of the community involved in wetland habitation, settlement mobility and the seasonal movement of cattle or sheep herds.

Middle Bronze Age landscape and settlement on the upper Shannon estuary

The Carrigdirty Rock house and other features have been interpreted here as wetland occupation sites associated with otherwise sedentary pastoralists (Fig. 45). Interestingly, there is some evidence for Middle and Late Bronze Age dryland settlement in the vicinity, particularly in the low hills about 4.3km to the south-east (Fig. 46). Further inland from Carrigdirty Rock, the estuarine alluvium (and former wetlands) extends for at least 2.4km up to the dryland edge. The land then rises steeply to low, rolling hills, 100ft in height, with rock outcrops and protruding limestone

Fig. 45—*Reconstruction drawing of Carrigdirty Rock 1 Middle Bronze Age house in fen-carr wetlands (Aidan O'Sullivan).*

terraces around Carrigogunnel. The Middle Bronze Age settlement evidence on these hills includes at least two *fulachta fiadh* at Ballymacashel, and possible standing stones at Conigar, Castlemungret and Moneteen. These sites are also located around a cluster of small settlement enclosures at Tervoe, Duane and Loughanleagh, whose size and topographical location might suggest that they are later prehistoric in date. Although there are no known Middle Bronze Age artefacts from this location, the evidence might suggest relatively intensive settlement activity along the south bank of the estuary, c. 1600–1200 BC. There is also some evidence for Late Bronze Age activity near Carrigdirty Rock. A hoard of three Late Bronze Age bronze horns was found in a bog at Carrigogunnel, Co. Limerick, in 1787 (Eogan 1983, 103). Although the precise findspot is unknown, our recent inspection of the Down Survey maps of the 1650s has led to the identification of a place depicted as 'Carrigogunnel bog' at a location about 2.5km south-south-east of Carrigdirty Rock. This was probably the findspot of the hoard. Interestingly, a large hilltop enclosure stands at the edge of a terrace overlooking the bog (immediately west of Carrigogunnel Castle). This may be of late prehistoric date, contemporary with the Late Bronze Age hoard (Eoin Grogan, pers. comm.).

There is also some evidence for Middle or Late Bronze Age settlement 3.2km to the south-west of Carrigdirty Rock, on the far bank of the River Maigue. There are two small settlement enclosures and possible ancient field systems in Ballynacarriga townland, situated on the low (50ft) sloping terraces overlooking the corcass and wetlands of the River Maigue and with good views beyond to the Shannon estuary. It is possible that these enclosures are Middle or Late Bronze Age in date. Certainly, there is artefactual evidence for later prehistoric activity here. A Late Bronze Age socketed bronze axe was found 'at some depth' in a sandpit in Ballynacarriga townland (Eogan 2000, 95). There are other Late Bronze Age finds from the upper Shannon estuary, such as the gold gorget found in a bog at Shannongrove, near Pallaskenry, about 4km to the west of Carrigdirty Rock (Powell 1974). This site, also on the south bank of the upper estuary, was no more than c. 400m from the estuary mudflats.

This range of evidence is comparable with that from the south-east Clare region, situated to the north of the Carrigdirty Rock site on the far side of the estuary, where

Foragers, farmers and fishers

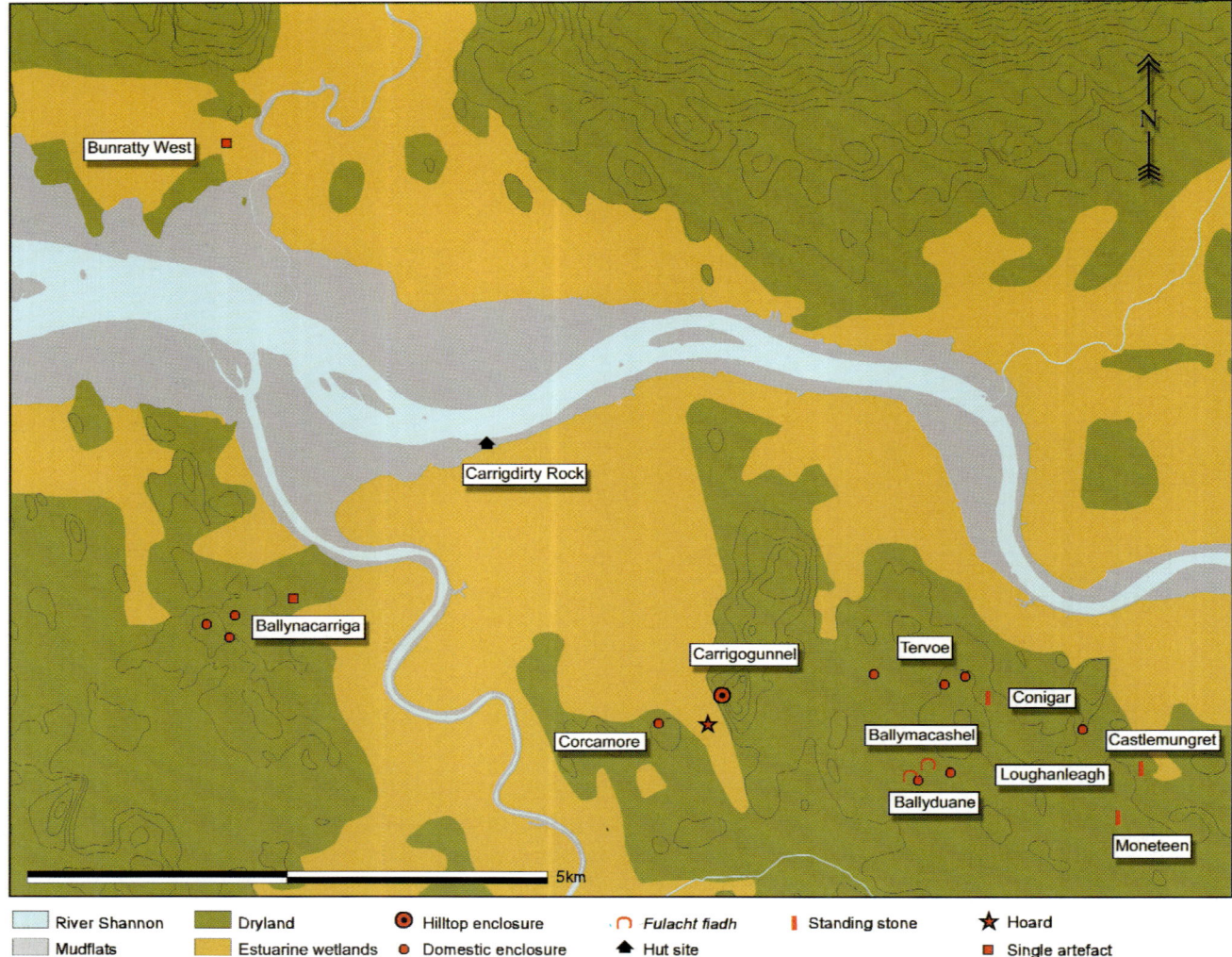

Fig. 46—*Distribution of Middle and Late Bronze Age sites and artefacts on the upper Shannon estuary, indicating location of Carrigdirty Rock 1 Middle Bronze Age house site in the estuarine wetlands.*

detailed archaeological studies have revealed that this low-lying landscape of drumlin hills, bogs and lakes first became the focus for intensive settlement in the Middle Bronze Age (Grogan 1999; Grogan *et al.* 1995; 1996). If, as seems likely, there were Middle Bronze Age settlements on the neighbouring hills in the vicinity of Carrigdirty Rock, these local communities may not have been particularly wealthy or did not have access to metalwork. By the Late Bronze Age, however, local families or individuals on the south bank of the Shannon estuary had achieved an impressive level of power and wealth (e.g. the Carrigogunnel hoard and the Shannongrove gorget), in common with their neighbours in south-east Clare.

A hypothetical model for landscape and settlement organisation can be proposed for the upper Shannon estuary sites (Fig. 47). The possible stone enclosures, field systems, standing stones and *fulachta fiadh* on the hills around Carrigogunnel and Ballynacarriga may represent permanent farmsteads, with livestock maintained on the hills through the winter and arable crops grown in fields. In the spring or summer, cattle may have been driven down across the marshes and turned out onto summer grazing areas. Cattle and sheep on the marshes would have been subject to various dangers, such as deep muddy creeks, water-channels, tides, wolves and perhaps raiding neighbours. It is likely, then, that livestock would have been accompanied by herders. The difficulty of actually moving on a daily basis through these marshes (creeks, mudflats and marshes provide a formidable and exhausting obstacle to movement) may have led these herders to choose to stay out with the livestock for weeks or months, living in relatively substantial wooden roundhouses in the wetlands.

While there, these human occupants may have exploited the estuary's wetlands for their other rich natural resources. The Carrigdirty Rock 3 pit, although as yet undated, produced red deer bone, antler and pink-footed goose, while pig bone was also found on the peat surface in the vicinity. Although there is relatively little evidence for hunting, fowling and fishing in later prehistoric Ireland, in particular wetland locations (such as the upper Shannon estuary) farming may have been combined with the hunting of red deer, wild pig, otter and hare, while salmon, eels and trout could have been caught and geese, duck and waders trapped in early autumn (McCarthy 2000). It is certainly the case that coastal shell middens were being used in the Bronze Age. Interestingly, the Late Bronze Age stone enclosures at Aughinish, Co. Limerick, sited on a low island in the upper Shannon estuary (to the west of Carrigdirty Rock), produced evidence for a domestic settlement with circular house sites, coarseware pottery, saddle querns and bronze artefacts. Significantly there were also apparently some rock-cut pits that had been filled with seashells, evidently the refuse from food-gathering in the nearby intertidal zone (Kelly 1974; Raftery 1990).

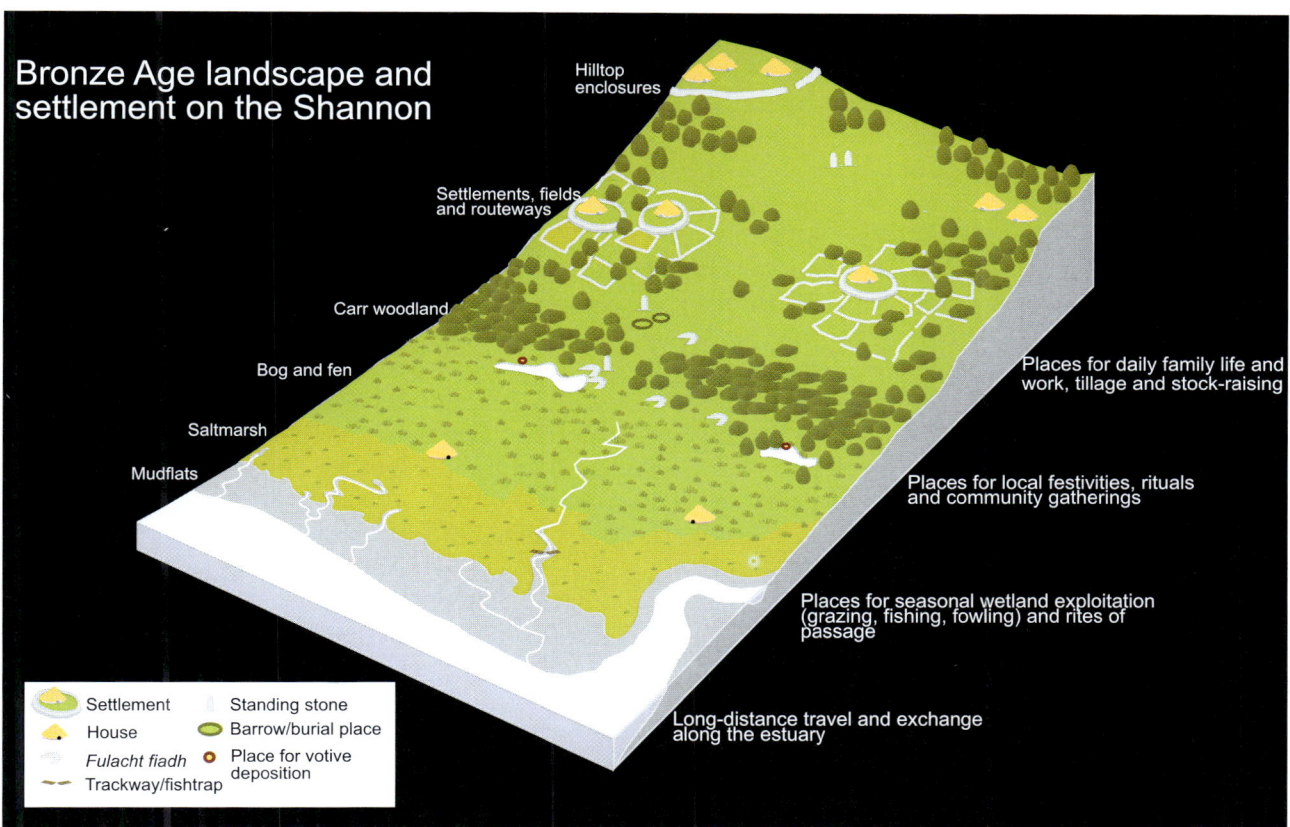

Fig. 47—*Hypothetical model for Bronze Age landscape and settlement of the upper Shannon estuary wetlands.*

Late Bronze Age landscape and settlement on the upper Fergus estuary

The Late Bronze Age structure at Fergus estuary west 1, if used as a trackway, may also show that local communities were interested in keeping communications open to isolated islands. People, cattle and sheep crossing channels and creeks could have used such a structure to bridge particularly difficult areas along a longer pathway running across the marshes. By the Middle and Late Bronze Age, there is increased evidence for trackway construction in bogs in the midlands of Ireland, possibly signifying wetter bog surfaces, increased local populations and an ongoing concern with maintaining access out to isolated areas ('bog islands') of agricultural land (Raftery 1996). Similar

Foragers, farmers and fishers

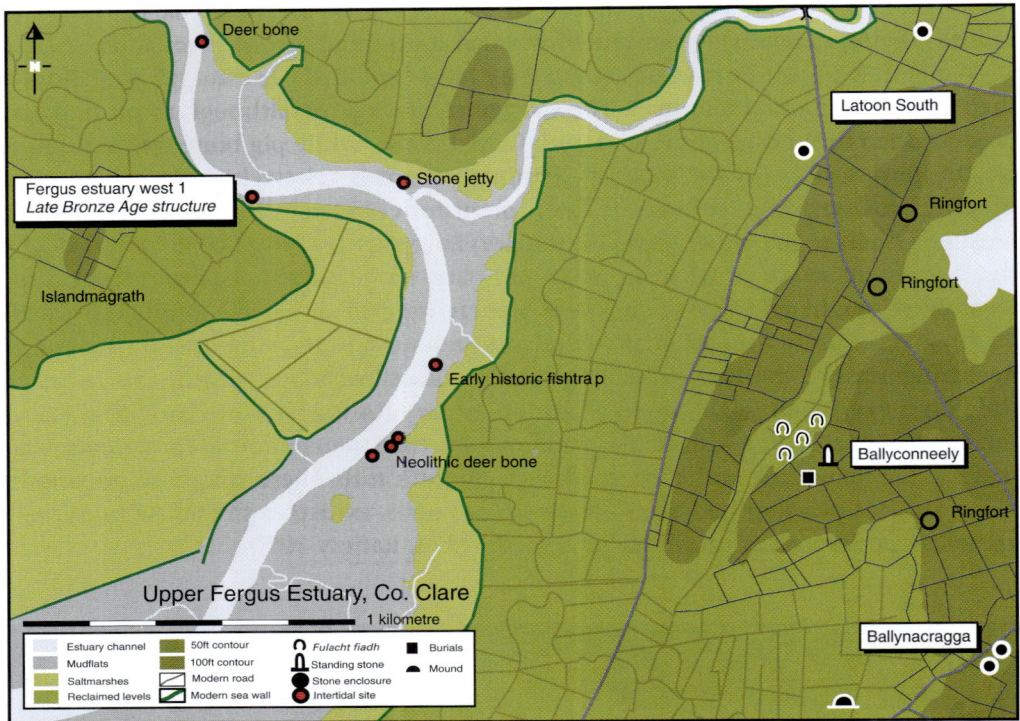

Fig. 48—*Map of upper Fergus estuary, Co. Clare, showing relationship between Late Bronze Age post-and-wattle structure at Fergus estuary west 1 and other possible Bronze Age sites on the neighbouring drylands.*

causeways, hurdle and timber trackways and platforms have been recorded at Lisheen, Co. Tipperary, where there appear to have been significant peaks of trackway-building activity on the bog between *c.* 1600–1000 BC and *c.* 600–200 BC (O'Neill 2000). Many of the Lisheen trackways merely provide access out into the bog (or across fens or local wet patches) rather than cross it entirely. Similarly, the Fergus estuary trackway may have been designed not to cross the marshes to the islands of Islandmagrath and Islandavanna, but simply to enable movement out into the saltmarshes and estuarine wetlands themselves, for purposes of cattle-herding, hunting, fishing and fowling. Indeed, the use of saltmarshes for animal pasture and wildfowling in late prehistory is known from several other coastal regions in north-west Europe, particularly the Netherlands (Louwe Kooijmans 1985; 1993b), the East Anglian fenlands (Pryor 1999) and the Humber estuary (Van de Noort and Ellis 1999) of England (see discussion below).

It is clear, too, that the trackway on the Fergus estuary, dated to the end of the Late Bronze Age at *c.* 797–551 BC, was located at the western edge of a territory or landscape that had already been intensively settled for hundreds of years (Fig. 48). The North Munster Project's research of the archaeological evidence of metalwork hoards, single finds, settlement sites and pollen studies indicates that the south-east Clare region was only first intensively settled in the Middle Bronze Age (Grogan *et al.* 1995; 1996; Grogan and Condit 1994) and it was not until the Late Bronze Age that local woodlands were being cleared (Molloy 1997; Grogan 1999), suggesting that only then was the landscape opened up for settlement and farming. By the Late Bronze Age (*c.* 950 BC), hillforts, hilltop enclosures and small domestic enclosures served as the major fortifications and dwellings of this landscape. By the Late Bronze Age, too, substantial hoards of gold and bronze metalwork were being deposited in Mooghaun Lough and Lahardaun bog, while there are numerous stray finds of Late Bronze Age socketed bronze axes, spearheads and swords in the area.

The political and symbolic centre of this Late Bronze Age territory was Mooghaun hillfort (Pl. 2), a massive trivallate fortification situated on the only local hill, *c.* 5km to the east of the Fergus estuary trackway. The hillfort had substantial defences and entrances, house sites, and domestic and industrial working areas. In social terms, it has been interpreted as a communal construction but reserved as the residence of a chieftain and his followers (Grogan and Condit 1994; Grogan 1999). Hilltop enclosures at sites like Cahercalla, Langough and Ballykilty and lakeshore settlements such as Knocknalappa may have served as the dwellings or defended residences of locally powerful individuals or groups (Grogan *et al.* 1999). There are also numerous small stone enclosures or domestic habitations in the Mooghaun landscape, frequently found on terraces overlooking lakes, bogs and coastal marshes.

There is some evidence for Late Bronze Age settlement on the hills overlooking the Fergus estuary marshes and the site of the trackway around Islandmagrath (Fig. 48). At Ballynacragga, Co. Clare, 2.5km to the south-east of the estuarine structure, stone enclosures with associated field systems may well represent the agricultural settlements of small family groupings. These enclosures have extensive views of the Fergus estuary and look north-west towards the site of the trackway (O'Sullivan and Condit 1995). There is also some evidence for Middle or Late Bronze Age ritual or funerary activity on the drumlin hills at the north-east side of the estuary. At Carrownanelly, 2.6km to the north-north-east of the trackway, there is a substantial barrow and standing stone site located on level ground. In recent years, rescue archaeological excavations in advance of the Newmarket bypass have identified evidence for Late Neolithic and Bronze Age settlement, burial and other activities along the eastern edge of the estuary (Chris Reid, pers. comm.).

Interestingly, the possible Bronze Age stone enclosures and other sites (at Ballynacragga, Latoon, and possibly at Ballyconneely) at the edge of the Fergus estuary seem to be placed at fairly regular intervals (between 0.7km and 1.2km apart) along the edge of the marshes. These may be the farmsteads of family groups who were controlling strips of coastal wetlands adjacent to dryland territories. In a similar way, Late Bronze Age wooden trackways have been identified as concentrations spaced at 1.2km intervals at Sharpham, Skinner's Wood, Meare Heath and Shapwick Heath in the wetlands of the Brue Valley in the Somerset Levels. These concentrations have been taken to represent just such separate, but contemporary, communities exploiting the resources of both the marshes and the dryland slopes of the Polden Hills (Coles and Coles 1986, 131). It is also worth remembering that, while the trackway was a local feature, it may have been part of a wider communications system, situated on an important crossing-point of the Fergus River. It is possible, therefore, to view the trackway both in its local context and in terms of wider Late Bronze Age landscape and settlement in south-east Clare. In broad terms, a similar landscape model to that suggested for the Carrigdirty Rock Middle Bronze Age site (Fig. 47) may also apply to the Fergus estuary site at the end of the Bronze Age, with cattle and sheep driven down to the estuarine pastures during the summer by communities who normally resided within enclosed or unenclosed settlements on the ridges and hills.

Late Bronze Age 'sacred places' at the edge

However, there may be other explanations, unrelated to resource exploitation, for Bronze Age activities in the Shannon and Fergus estuary wetlands. Although most of the region's Late Bronze Age metalwork has been recovered from lakes and bogs, there is also some evidence for the deposition of objects in the estuarine marshes. A Late Bronze Age gold dress-fastener (Pl. 37) was recovered during late nineteenth-century saltmarsh reclamation operations on the Fergus estuary (Scott 1906, 29; Eogan 1994, 143). Its precise findspot was unknown, but it is interesting that the major reclamations on the upper Fergus estuary during the late nineteenth century were those carried out around Islandavanna and Islandmagrath. In other words, it is possible that this object was found in the general vicinity of the Fergus estuary west 1 trackway. There are other metalwork finds from the Fergus estuary, including a Late Bronze Age gold bracelet with unexpanded terminals found on the mudflats at Crininish on the west bank (NMI files).

There are also several significant Late Bronze Age metalwork hoards from bogs along the margins of the upper Shannon estuary, often found at locations that are only a

Foragers, farmers and fishers

Pl. 37—*Late Bronze Age gold dress-fastener found during marsh reclamation in the late nineteenth century on the upper Fergus estuary, Co. Clare, potentially close to the Fergus estuary west 1 site (reproduced by permission of the National Museum of Ireland).*

short walk today from the estuary channel. For example, as stated above, a hoard of Later Bronze Age bronze horns was found in a bog at Carrigogunnel, Co. Limerick, in 1787 (Eogan 1983, 103), to the south of Carrigdirty Rock itself. Further westwards, at Shannongrove, Co. Limerick, a gold gorget was found perhaps only 10–20 minutes' walk from the Shannon estuary mudflats (Eogan 1994, 83). It is possible that gold dress-fasteners, bracelets and gorgets and bronze horns were being deliberately placed in coastal fens and marshes. The Shannon estuary wetlands may have been seen as liminal spaces along the margins of the settled landscape, and as places where spirits, deities or ancestors could be contacted or negotiated with. Indeed, it is likely that both secular economic and sacred activities were always ongoing in these marshes, as the sacred and the profane are rarely separate activities amongst small-scale societies.

Late Bronze Age and Iron Age houses and trackways on estuaries in Britain

Introduction

The Middle Bronze Age house site at Carrigdirty Rock and the Late Bronze Age trackway from the Fergus estuary can also be usefully compared with similar structures in coastal wetland environments in Britain. In recent years, Bronze Age and Iron Age houses and trackways have been found on both organic peats and minerogenic clays on the Severn estuary, the Humber estuary, the Essex coast and the Thames estuary. Many of these sites appear to have had a similar function to the Shannon estuary sites, although it is also clear that there are differences in dating, size and local context.

Late Bronze Age and Iron Age houses and trackways, Severn estuary, Wales

The Carrigdirty Rock house site is most similar to the Middle Bronze Age roundhouses in peats from the Welsh shore of the Severn estuary. At Chapeltump I, a circular roundhouse with a central post and hearth enclosed within a circle of stakes 6m in diameter has been radiocarbon-dated to 1320–920 cal. BC (2910 ± 70 BP; Car-405; Whittle 1989; Bell and Neumann 1997; 1998). Circular wooden huts and hearths have also been recorded at Rumney 3, where one structure produced a radiocarbon date of 1460–1210 cal. BC (3080 ± 50 BP; Beta-46951; Allen 1996). At Collister Pill a substantial roundhouse had an inner post-ring measuring 3.6m in diameter, with an outer circle of stakes measuring 6m in diameter (Bell *et al.* 2000, 302). These circular house sites have also been interpreted as seasonal, coastal wetland occupation sites.

If the Carrigdirty Rock 1 main structural posts were to be interpreted as an inner ring of roof supports, then it would be similar in size to the Collister Pill structure. However, unlike these sites, Carrigdirty Rock 1 has not, as yet, produced pottery, hearths or charcoal, suggesting that it was a more temporary (or summer-based?) occupation site (see discussion of Iron Age houses below). Other Middle Bronze Age houses from the Severn estuary foreshore are quite different to the Carrigdirty Rock 1 house. For example, at Redwick four substantial rectangular, round-cornered structures, dated to *c.* 1510–930 cal. BC, were constructed on a raised bog on which estuarine silts were occasionally deposited during very high tides (Bell and Neumann 1998). These structures were defined by narrow gullies in the peat, with large internal posts. Charcoal, fire-cracked stone and animal hoofprints were found in the vicinity of the buildings.

Iron Age houses are also known from intertidal peats at Goldcliff West (Bell 1992a; 1992b; 1992c; 1993a; 1993b; 1995; Bell *et al.* 2000), where rectangular structures were constructed on raised hummocks in a raised bog or on fen peats (Fig. 49). Dendrochronological and radiocarbon dates suggest construction and use in the fourth and early third centuries BC. Evidence for repair, beetle analysis and the presence of lenses of clay between occupation horizons suggest episodic use, interspersed by periods of flooding under brackish water. The buildings were quite substantial, measuring 4.8–8.4m in length by 4.2–6m in width. The walls were constructed of alder roundwood and oak planking, entrances were situated at the ends, and internal or axial posts suggest that the structures were roofed. Where evidence survived, there were indications of flooring of rough roundwood, reeds or straw. Finds recovered from the entrances or the palaeochannels around the buildings included wooden withy ties and bucket fragments, while cattle hoofprints could also be identified in the clays of the channels around the structures.

Beetle studies indicated the presence of decaying vegetation, dung and reeds. Lice in the palaeochannels indicated the presence of cattle, and human fleas suggested that people and cattle shared the same structure (Bell 1999; Bell and Neumann 1997). This scenario is similar to that postulated for Site Q in the Assendelver Polders of the Netherlands, where Iron Age rectangular buildings with internal divisions have been

Fig. 49—*Reconstruction drawing of Iron Age rectangular house in estuarine wetlands at Goldcliff Building 1, Gwent, Severn estuary (drawing by S.J. Allen; after Bell* et al. *2000).*

interpreted as dwelling-places for both people and cattle (Therkorn *et al.* 1984). Interestingly, in nineteenth-century Ireland the peasant byre-dwellings of the west were occupied by both people and animals, the latter being kept in one end of the house. Danaher (1985, 20) stated that cattle raised on grass do not produce malodorous dung, meaning that people would benefit from the warmth of animals within the dwelling without having to put up with bad smells.

The Middle Bronze Age Redwick and Iron Age Goldcliff house sites may relate to periods of increased marine transgression, when marine flooding may have altered local vegetation in ways that made the raised bogs good places for grazing animals. The lack of hearths, charcoal and ash from the Goldcliff houses suggests that these were specialist sites and not domestic habitations in the conventional sense, and that there may have been episodic activity 'extending over periods of years' (Bell 1999). The presence of cattle hoofprints also strongly suggests activity relating to cattle-grazing during the summer, when people could live comfortably on the marshes without domestic fires. Bell (1999, 23) concludes from the presence of neonatal calf bone (typically born in the spring months) that occupation was in May and June, when tides were lowest and the bogs would not have been so regularly inundated by the monthly high spring tides. The inhabitants of these houses need not only have practised cattle-grazing. It is possible that other coastal activities were carried out in the vicinity, such as fishing for salmon (on their way upstream in spring) and eels (on their way downstream in autumn) or fowling for wildbirds.

Late Bronze Age trackways somewhat similar to the Fergus estuary structure have also been found on the Severn Estuary. A Late Bronze Age or Early Iron Age hurdle structure from Cold Harbour Pill was dated to 790–530 cal. BC (Bell and Neumann

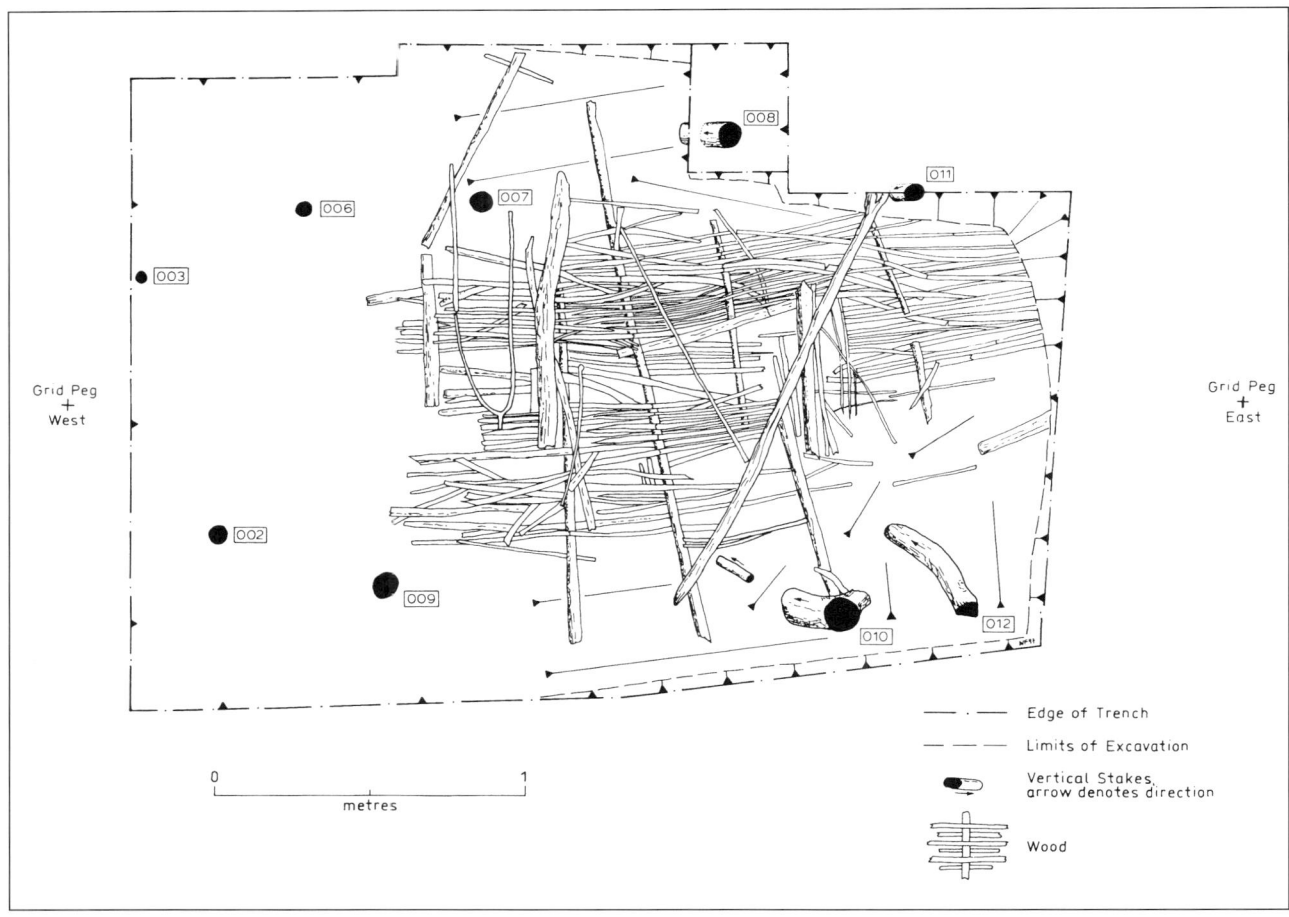

Fig. 50—*Late Bronze Age hurdle trackway excavated at Melton 25, Humber estuary, England (after Fletcher* et al. *1999).*

1997, fig. 2) but has been interpreted as some form of fishing structure. Oak planks associated with the construction (and destruction) of prehistoric boats have been investigated on the Severn estuary, at Caldicot, on the Gwent Levels (Nayling and Caseldine 1997; Parry and McGrail 1991), and at Goldcliff, where they had been reused in a Late Bronze Age trackway (Bell 1993b). However, these planks differ from the Carrigdirty Rock 20–1 planks in that clear features associated with boat-building were identified.

Late Bronze Age trackways, Humber estuary, England

The Fergus estuary trackway is also comparable with hurdle trackways recently excavated on the Humber estuary in north-east England. Bronze Age hurdle or brushwood trackways were recorded in the 1930s at North Ferriby (Wright 1990), where they were interpreted as structures relating to the North Ferriby Bronze Age boats and to movement by people across the mudflats (Wright 1990; Crowther 1987). More recently, at Melton, to the west of the North Ferriby site, a number of Middle to Late Bronze Age trackways have been excavated by the Humber Wetlands Survey (Fletcher *et al.* 1999; Van de Noort and Ellis 1999).

The Melton-25 (Fig. 50) and Melton-26 hurdle trackways were laid in estuarine clays and, like the Fergus estuary structure, sloped down a former creek bed at angles of 10°. They were constructed of short lengths of hurdle panel laid on the muds, with brushwood dumps and vertical posts driven into the clays at the sides of the hurdles. The individual hurdle panels were only 2–3m long, but other posts on the same alignment suggest that the total structure measured at least 30m in length. The use of long vertical stakes beside the hurdle panels is reminiscent of the Fergus estuary west 1 structure, and may also have been intended to prevent the trackway from sliding sideways across the muds, especially when cattle were walking across it. Both trackways were dated to the Middle to Late Bronze Age. Melton-25 was radiocarbon-dated to 1440–1310 cal. BC (3105 ± 35 BP; GU-5708) and Melton-26 to 1100–840 cal. BC (2810 ± 50 BP; GU-5711). Palaeoenvironmental studies indicate that the Melton trackways were laid down across tidal creeks that were cutting through the saltmarshes, and they are interpreted as creek bridges for the use of sheep or cattle on the saltmarshes (Pl. 38).

Late Bronze Age and Iron Age trackways, Essex coast, England

The Fergus estuary structure can also be usefully compared with Bronze Age and Iron Age structures in minerogenic or estuarine clays on the estuaries of the Essex coast, where structures associated with specialised coastal activity, such as wooden trackways, platforms, hurdle structures and salt-processing mounds, have all been recorded. On occasion, these wooden structures were associated with oyster-beds and may have been constructed to enable exploitation of such marine resources (Wilkinson *et al.* 1988, 227–8; Murphy and Wilkinson 1991). In contrast to the Fergus estuary structure, the Essex Bronze Age and Iron Age trackways were usually quite small, rarely measuring over 4m in length.

Short trackways or bundles of brushwood were thrown down to bridge creeks or areas of soft muds on saltmarsh or mudflats. There were also short wooden structures used as landing-stages at the edge of the saltmarshes to gain access to the channels. Small hurdle bridges were found in palaeochannels, where they had originally been laid across the small creeks that divided mudflats during low tides. It is thought that the trackways were intended to facilitate access to and from saltmarshes for people and animals. In the Middle Ages, similar hurdle 'sheep-bridges' were used on the Essex saltmarshes to allow sheep to escape across creeks during high tides, and literally thousands of sheep were maintained out on the valuable coastal pastures.

However, as with the Shannon estuary, the Essex foreshore has also produced Bronze Age structures and finds that hint at more than the simple economic exploitation of coastal resources. A Late Bronze Age wooden platform at Crouch Site 1,

Foragers, farmers and fishers

Pl. 38—*Reconstruction painting of Late Bronze Age hurdle trackway at Melton, on the Humber estuary, England. The site is interpreted as a creek bridge designed to enable cattle to be driven across the saltmarshes (painting by Les Turner, reproduced with permission of the Humber Wetlands Project, Wetlands Archaeology and Environments Research Centre, University of Hull).*

at Fenn Creek on the Crouch estuary of the Essex coast, was associated with spreads of brushwood and gravel. Two human skulls had previously been recovered from the platform, which was constructed of horizontal rods secured by vertical poles. The Fenn Creek skulls may have been intentionally deposited on the platform, in a ritual act associated with burial or the afterlife (Wilkinson and Murphy 1995).

Late Bronze Age trackways and post alignments, Thames estuary and Solent estuary

Middle Bronze Age hurdle trackways, brushwood structures, waterfronts, enigmatic post alignments, wooden platforms and other structures have been recorded on the Thames estuary in south-east England (Meddens 1996; Needham and Longley 1980) during intertidal surveys, riverbank excavations and developer-led rescue excavations in the alluvial soils further back from the river. A large number of finds of late prehistoric metalwork and human skulls have also been recovered from the River Thames itself (R. Bradley 1990; R. Bradley and Gordon 1988). Most recently, it has been suggested that Bronze Age bridges and hurdle trackways may be associated with both economic and symbolic activities on the estuary. In particular, the Thames estuary archaeology indicates how widespread and intensive was the exploitation of the estuary wetlands during the Middle and Late Bronze Age. An intriguing wooden structure has recently been recorded on the Thames foreshore at Vauxhall. This is a double row of posts, 4m in width and *c.* 18m in length, constructed of massive roundwood trunks up to 60cm in diameter, set inclining inwards. The structure has been dated to 1605–1285 cal. BC and is interpreted as a Middle Bronze Age 'bridge' leading out to a former island in the Thames estuary. It is like several other post structures of similar scale and date from elsewhere in Britain, and may have served a range of functions—as a routeway, a territorial boundary-marker and a ritual causeway (Haughey 1999, 18–19). At Wootton-Quarr, on the north side of the Isle of Wight, Late Bronze Age post alignments and rectangular structures were recorded on the foreshore, often associated with palaeochannels. Unlike the Fergus estuary west 1 structure, these appear to have been used as fishtraps or as hides for trapping waterfowl (Loader *et al.* 1997).

Bronze Age and Iron Age estuarine archaeology in Britain and Ireland— emerging regional patterns

The Shannon estuary sites, although still few in number, thus provide interesting comparisons and contrasts with Bronze Age and Iron Age houses, platforms and hurdle structures from the Severn estuary, the Humber foreshore and the Essex and Thames estuaries. It appears that for the later prehistoric period we can trace evidence throughout Britain and Ireland for the emergence of intensive activities in coastal wetlands, implying seasonal habitation, travel and resource exploitation (see Evans 1987; Hall and Coles 1994). Interestingly, although some fishtraps have been recorded, hunting, fowling and fishing do not appear to have been of great importance, suggesting again that wetland pastoralism was the main activity. There are also regional contrasts. On the Essex coast, most wooden structures are associated with minerogenic clays and imply specialised, temporary coastal wetland activity. In contrast, on the Severn estuary there is good evidence for settlement on raised bogs, fen peats and saltmarshes in the Middle Bronze Age and the Iron Age. Indeed, at places like Goldcliff West, and perhaps at Magor Pill, these houses have to be seen as substantial buildings potentially occupied for reasonably long periods. Other structures, such as the houses at Collister Pill or Carrigdirty Rock 1, while also relatively large buildings, may have been more short-term dwellings. It is interesting that, despite the small number of sites recorded, the Shannon estuary survey has produced evidence for both travel and habitation in the Middle and Late Bronze Age coastal wetlands. It must be the case that other Irish estuaries preserve similar later prehistoric sites.

Conclusions

In summary, the Middle Bronze Age house site at Carrigdirty Rock 1 (and the potential later prehistoric hut, post features and pits at Carrigdirty Rock 2–4 and planks at Carrigdirty Rock 20–1) provides evidence for occupation in a wet fen or carr woodland environment, perhaps associated with seasonal grazing, hunting or wildfowling and travel across the estuary. A Late Bronze Age post-and-wattle structure at Fergus estuary west 1 (Islandmagrath) may have been a jetty or fishtrap, or a trackway constructed to enable travel across the wetlands, either to gain access to the islands or to the saltmarsh itself. The evidence for Bronze Age landscape and settlement along the estuary also shows the interest that contemporary communities had in such wetland environments, and similar patterns of coastal wetland exploitation in the later Bronze Age and Iron Age have been identified on other estuaries around Britain and Ireland.

5. EARLY HISTORIC AND MEDIEVAL FISHTRAPS

Introduction

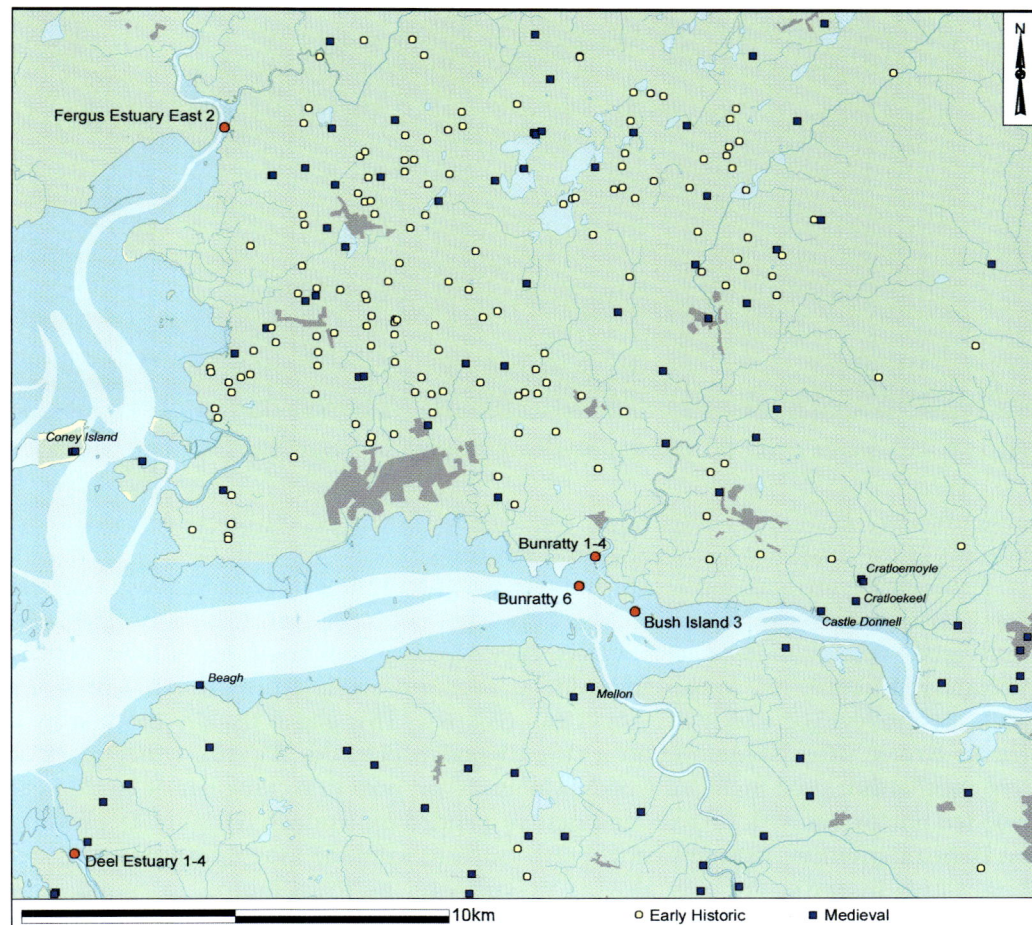

Fig. 51—*Map of upper Shannon estuary, showing location of medieval fishtraps.*

The early historic (AD 400–800) and medieval (AD 1100–1350) sites recorded on the Shannon and Fergus estuary mudflats are all wooden fishtraps dated to between the fifth and fourteenth centuries (Fig. 51). An early historic fishtrap post-and-wattle fence (Fergus estuary east 2) was recorded on the upper Fergus estuary, adjacent to the townland of Ballygirreen (O'Sullivan 1993–4; 1994). Medieval fishtraps were recorded on the Deel estuary, Co. Limerick, dating from between the eleventh and fourteenth centuries (O'Sullivan 1995c; 1995d), and spectacularly well-preserved medieval fishtraps were also investigated on the north bank of the Shannon estuary, at Bunratty, Co. Clare. These latter fishtraps, with their complex post-and-wattle fences and their intricately woven baskets, have been dated to between the eleventh and thirteenth centuries (O'Sullivan 1997a). It is possible that many of the other, as yet undated, wooden fishtraps found elsewhere on the Shannon estuary are also of medieval date (e.g. the basket at Bush Island 3 and the U-shaped post-and-wattle structure at Bush Island 4). The presence of medieval fishtraps on the mudflats suggests that, in general environmental terms, sea levels were broadly similar to today's, although there have

Foragers, farmers and fishers

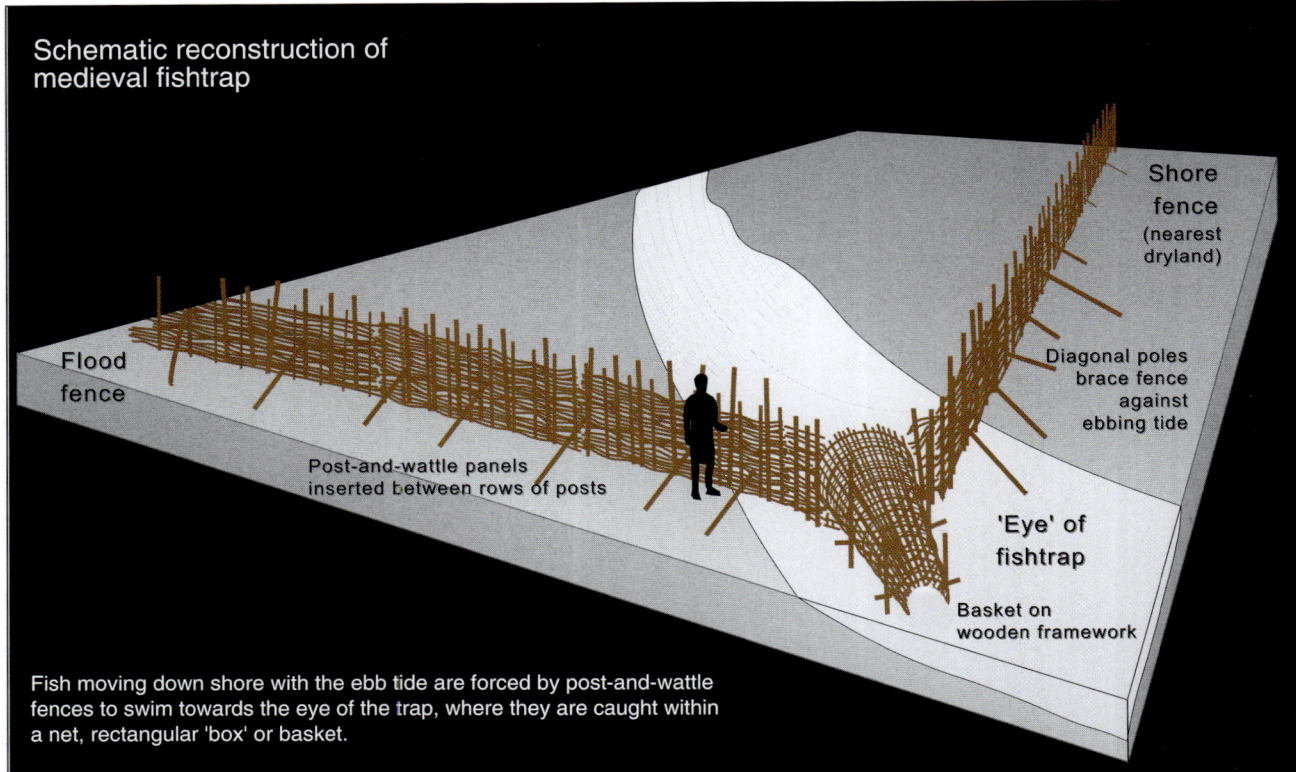

Fig. 52—*Schematic reconstruction of a medieval fishtrap, showing principles and various structural features.*

undoubtedly been many significant changes in terms of the local topographical features of the mudflats, saltmarshes and channels.

Fishtraps are artificial barriers of stone or wood built in rivers or estuaries to deflect fish into an opening where they can be trapped in nets or baskets (Salisbury 1991, 76). In riverine, coastal and estuarine waters, they typically took the form of head weirs— V-shaped structures of converging vertical post-and-wattle fences (Pl. 39) or stone walls, at the 'eye' of which is a small gap (Fig. 52). This gap is usually blocked by a wicker basket, often supported on a raised wooden platform (Pl. 40). Other types of trap mechanism used included wooden 'pounds' or 'boxes', rectangular or curvilinear wooden enclosures with no exit, and nets suspended on wooden uprights. Depending on their orientation, fishtraps caught fish (such as salmon) moving upstream to the headwaters in spring, or eels moving downstream in the autumn. In coastal and estuarine waters, fish tend to move up the shore with the flooding tide and drift back down with the ebbing tide, being attracted by feeding in the shallow water and by the nutrients in freshwater streams and rivers moving into the estuary. Therefore coastal fishtrap structures can also be built to catch fish either moving down with the ebbing tide (ebb weirs) or up with the flooding tide (flood weirs). The fence nearest the drylands, running up the foreshore, is known as the 'shore fence', while the lowermost or in-water fence is known as the 'flood fence'.

Recent years have seen an explosion of interest worldwide in the archaeology of ancient fishtraps. Fishtraps have been the subject of recent archaeological investigations on the north-west coast of Canada (Moss and Erlandson 1998; Stewart 1977), on the north-west and east coasts of North America (Bryam 1998; Betts 1998; Decima and Dincauze 1998; Dincauze 1988; Chaney 1998), Australia (Dortch 1997; Flood 1995, 241) and New Zealand (Barr 1998). In Europe, Mesolithic and Neolithic fishtraps have been recorded in the Netherlands (Louwe Kooijmans 1987), Denmark (Pedersen 1995; 1997) and France (Mordant and Mordant 1992). Although such early traps have not yet been found in Britain or Ireland, Neolithic wooden structures potentially associated with fishtraps have been recorded at Wootton-Quarr, on the Isle

Early historic and medieval fishtraps

Pl. 39—*Post-and-wattle fence in modern fishtrap on the Severn estuary, leading towards ranks of baskets supported on frameworks (photo: Chris Salisbury).*

Pl. 40—*Woven basket in use in modern fishtrap on the Severn estuary. The basket is supported on a rectangular wooden framework, perhaps similar to that used on the Bunratty 6 medieval fishtrap (photo: Chris Salisbury).*

of Wight in the Solent estuary (Loader *et al.* 1997).

However, in recent years, intertidal archaeological surveys around Britain and Ireland have led to the survey, excavation and detailed analysis of fishtraps dating from Anglo-Saxon, Norman, late medieval and post-medieval times (Fulford *et al.* 1997, 143–5). Anglo-Saxon and Norman fishtraps have now been recorded at various locations in Britain, such as on the River Trent, Nottinghamshire (Salisbury 1991; 1996), on the Essex coast (Strachan 1997; Gilman 1998; Clarke 1993; Crump and Wallis 1992), on the Thames estuary (Milne *et al.* 1997), on the Isle of Wight in the Solent estuary (Loader *et al.* 1997), and on both the Welsh and English coasts of the Severn estuary (e.g. Godbold and Turner 1993; 1994; Nayling 1997; McDonnell 1993). Stone-built fishtraps or 'yairs' are known from the coast of Scotland (Bathgate 1949; M. Cressey, pers. comm.). In recent years, impressive early historic and medieval fishtraps

Foragers, farmers and fishers

have been recorded on Strangford Lough, Co. Down (e.g. O'Sullivan *et al.* 1997). Indeed, it has long been known that fishtraps were used in medieval Ireland, owing to the exhaustive and detailed historical research carried out by Arthur J. Went (1946; 1960b; 1964; 1981). However, prior to the Shannon estuary survey, there was little archaeological evidence for fishing techniques in medieval Ireland, despite the importance of fisheries to an island people and its economy.

In this chapter, the Shannon estuary early historic and medieval fishtraps will be described and analysed as individual sites and interpreted in relation to early historic and medieval period settlement evidence on the adjacent drylands. The sites will then be discussed as a whole in terms of local maritime economies, siting, method of construction, use, repair and abandonment. Finally, the Shannon estuary fishtraps will be compared with early historic and medieval fishtraps from elsewhere on the British and Irish coastlines, to illustrate how regional patterns and styles of medieval fishing practices can be identified in these islands.

Early historic fishtrap, Fergus estuary, Co. Clare

Fergus estuary east 2—post-and-wattle fence

Site location

A post-and-wattle fence found on the mudflats of the upper Fergus estuary probably represents the earliest-dated fishtrap recorded. This site is located on the east bank of the estuary, adjacent to the townland of Ballygirreen, Co. Clare (Figs 24 and 53). A radiocarbon sample provided a date of 1495 ± 35 BP (cal. AD 442–644; GrN-20139).

The Fergus estuary channel is relatively narrow in this area, flowing through a gently curving meander that is presently causing erosion on the eastern side. The foreshore is narrow (*c.* 50m) and slopes gently down to the west from the reed-beds and saltmarshes. The foreshore is entirely composed of fine estuarine clays and silts. At the lowest part of this foreshore, along the mean low-water mark, the channel is eroding a low shelf in the blue-grey clays *c.* 0.1–0.15m high, and is gently revealing the structure there in plan and section.

The recorded stratigraphy of the clays at this shelf was as follows. The clays, to the depth of at least 1m beneath the structure, were composed of fine-grained blue-grey clays with occasional shell inclusions. The wooden structure was set in this clay and was covered by a thin (*c.* 5cm) lens of reddish-grey clays rich in shell remains (possibly suggesting a slightly different water regime at the time they were laid down). These are then succeeded by further grey clays; otherwise the upper foreshore is covered with modern, mobile sediments. It seems likely that the fence was erected on the upper foreshore of a narrow estuarine channel.

Site description

The structure comprises at least 25 roundwood posts driven vertically to a depth of at least 70cm into blue-grey estuarine clays and arranged in a straight line (Fig. 54; Pl. 41) at intervals of 25–35cm. They measure 2–3cm in diameter and are sharpened to simple chisel and wedge points at their lower ends. Between these vertical uprights are at least three bands of horizontal interwoven rods. The rods are slightly narrower, measuring 1.7–1.9cm in diameter. The structure thus forms a post-and-wattle fence oriented in an east-north-east/west-south-west direction, measuring at least 8.2m in length (*c.* 5.6m is exposed on the clays, and a further 2.6m can be traced underwater).

It is clear that what survives is the base of this fence, as the rows of horizontal rods are not found any deeper in the clays. However, the fence can also be seen in plan at the north-east end, where a portion of it fell in antiquity before being covered by clay sediments. At this point the clays are also being slowly washed away, gently exposing

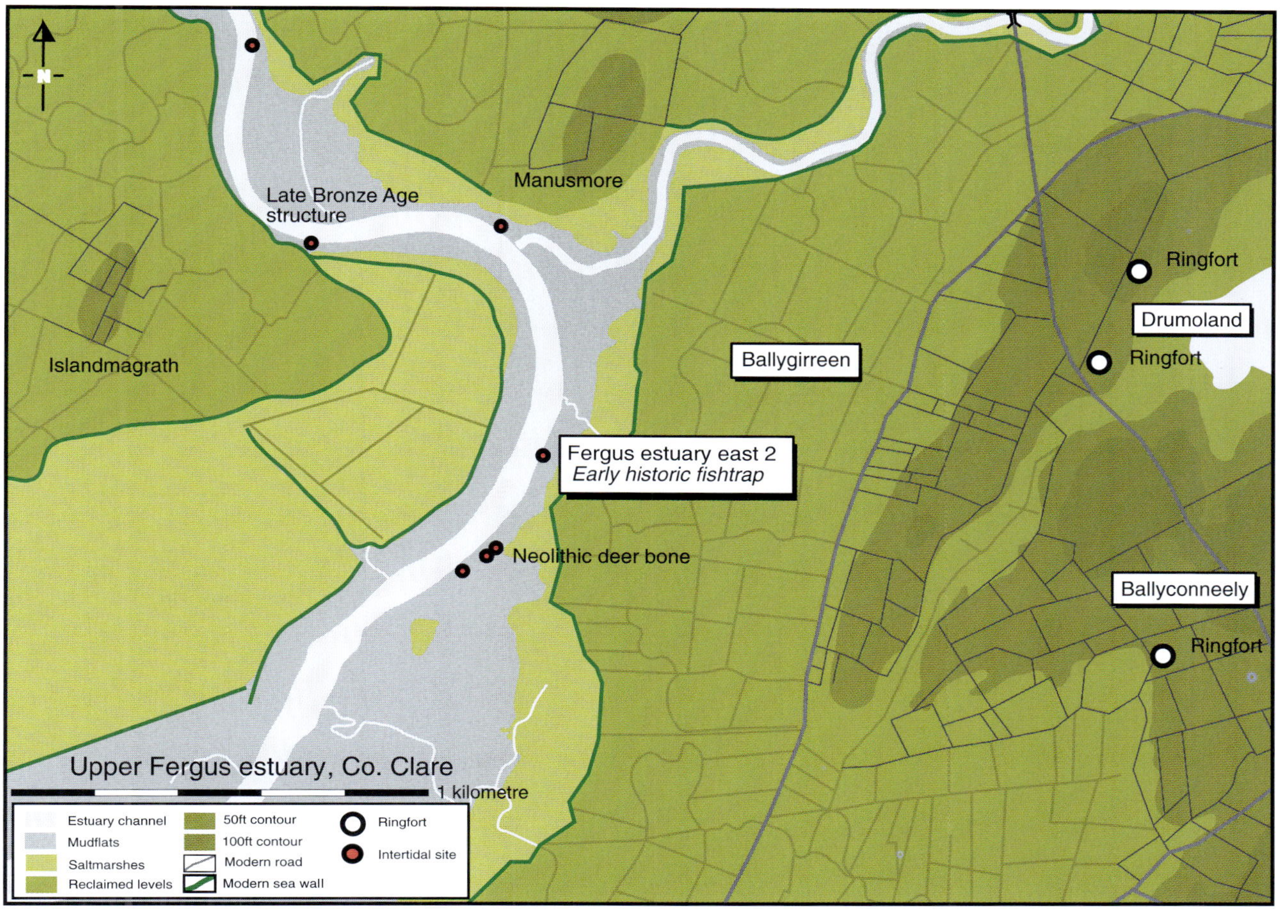

Early historic and medieval fishtraps

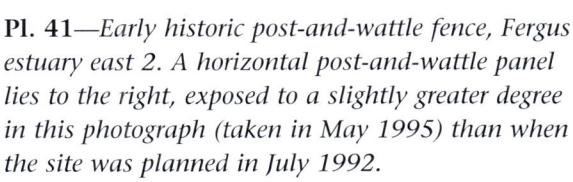

Fig. 53—*Map of upper Fergus estuary, showing location of the early historic fishtrap at Fergus estuary east 2 and its relationship with the early historic ringforts at Drumoland and Ballyconneely on the ridge to the east.*

Pl. 41—*Early historic post-and-wattle fence, Fergus estuary east 2. A horizontal post-and-wattle panel lies to the right, exposed to a slightly greater degree in this photograph (taken in May 1995) than when the site was planned in July 1992.*

Foragers, farmers and fishers

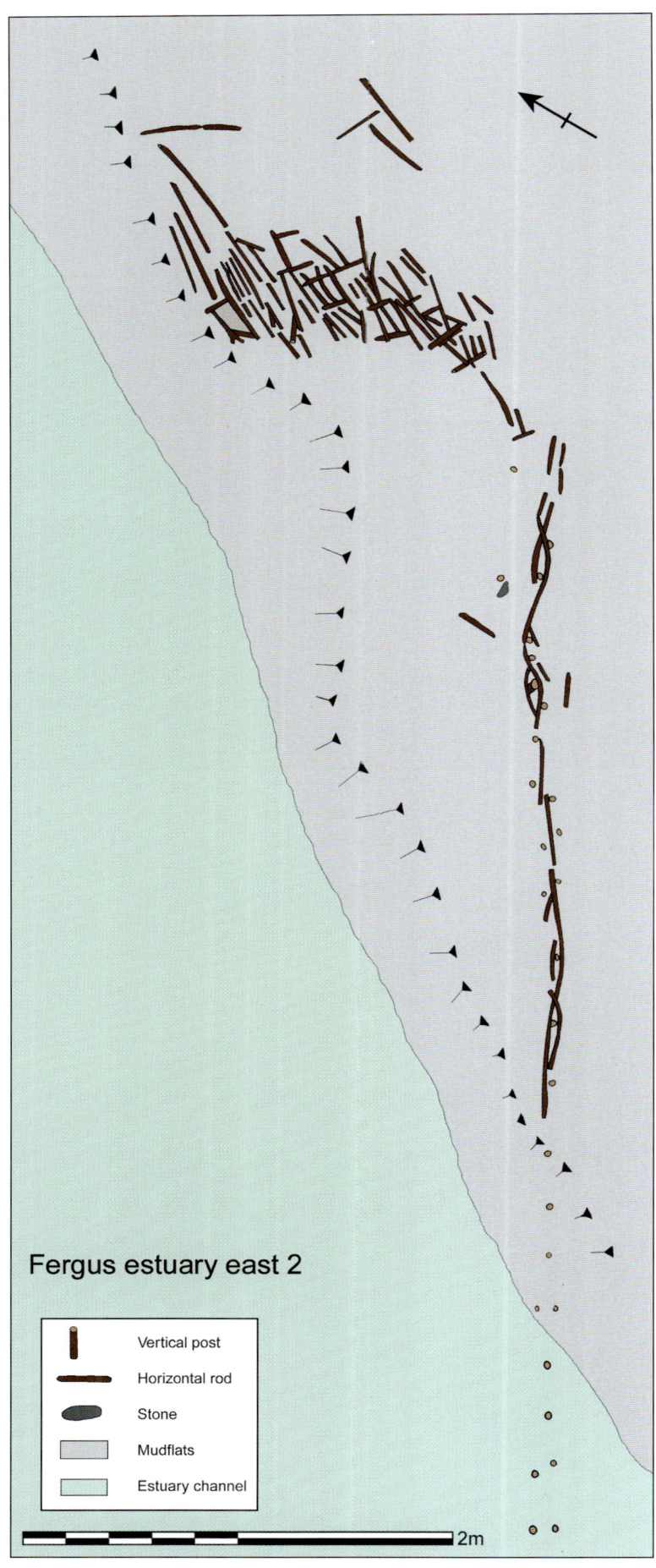

Fig. 54—*Plan of early historic fishtrap, Fergus estuary east 2, Co. Clare.*

an intact portion of the panel of posts and rods that is now oriented north-north-east/south-south-west. This panel is a useful survival as it suggests that the original fence stood to a height of at least.1.5m. The fence disappears into the sloping clays of the foreshore to the north-north-east. At a distance of 6.5m further to the south-west, downstream of the fence, two closely spaced small roundwood posts were driven vertically into the clays. These were probably of similar date and possibly had a related function. The post-and-wattle fence is oriented diagonally to the modern river channel, pointing downstream.

Site interpretation

The structure, situated at low water in estuarine clays and running diagonally down the foreshore to the river current, can best be interpreted as the remains of the leading fence of a small fish-weir designed to trap fish on an ebbing tide. The fence is unusually lightly built, but would have been usable for several years. It is likely that further remains of this structure lie submerged underwater and buried under the clays of the upper foreshore. Return visits in May 1995 revealed the presence of more horizontal post-and-wattle at the north-east end of the site.

Wood studies
AIDAN O'SULLIVAN AND MARY DEEVY

Forty-seven wood samples, each piece 4cm in length, were taken from the post-and-wattle fence (Fig. 55). Although occasionally weathered on the surface, the wooden posts and rods were found to be in good condition. In terms of woodworking, the posts and rods had been left as unmodified roundwood; the bark was still attached. The posts were sharpened by simply chopping on one side of the branch with a flat-bladed iron axe or billhook. A number of worked ends could also be seen on the rods, evidence that each of them was cut to the required length.

Twenty samples were identified as willow (*Salix* spp), ten were alder (*Alnus glutinosa*), fifteen were hazel (*Corylus avellana*) and two were birch (*Betula* spp). The willow rods were typically aged between three and six years; the alder was rather older, aged between seven and eleven years. The hazel displayed no particular tree-ring pattern, ranging from three to nine years of age. The species, size and age of the wood used in the Fergus estuary structure provide evidence for local woodland character and its exploitation. The predominance of willow and alder reflects, unsurprisingly, the surrounding marshland landscape. Willow was used for posts, but narrow willow rods seem to have been especially preferred for the interwoven rods. Alder was used equally for posts and rods. Hazel was also used for both posts and rods.

Hazel–ash woodland is especially common on the thin, lime-rich soils found in this part of south-east Clare. The posts for the structure were typically taken from immature branches. The tree-ring evidence suggests the selective cutting of rods and posts for their appropriate size. Woodland was an important economic resource in early historic Ireland and there is historical evidence that it could be owned and carefully managed. The alder and willow rods used in the post-and-wattle fence are fairly tightly clustered in age, possibly indicating their origins in deliberately coppiced woodlands, but it is just as likely that they were cropped from the plentiful supply of underwood that would have been growing in the wetlands.

Discussion

There is a range of archaeological evidence for early historic settlement along the upper Fergus estuary. In particular, three ringforts are situated on the dryland ridge to the east (Fig. 41): two univallate ringforts 2km to the east-north-east in Dromoland, and a substantial banked ringfort 2.1km to the east-south-east at Ballyconneely. There are also two small univallate ringforts in Knockanimana, on the east bank of the estuary, 3.2km to the north. Indeed, these latter forts, although more distant, may have been more accessible to the estuary site, through the use of coracles or dug-out boats.

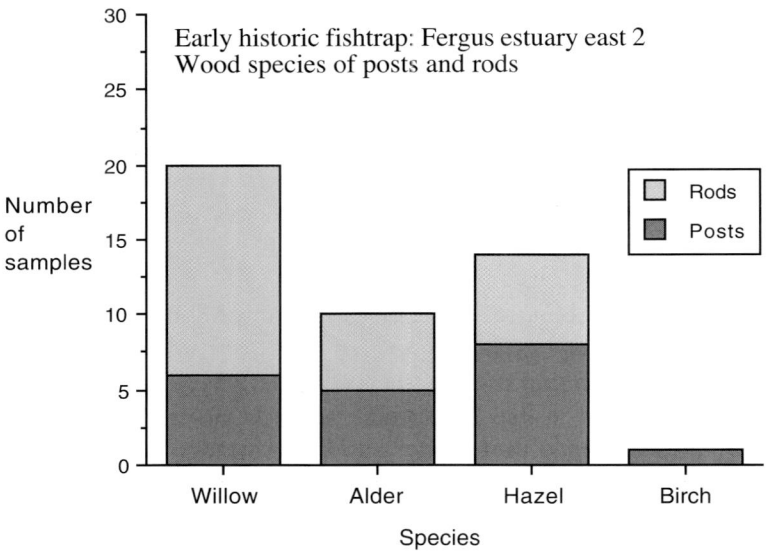

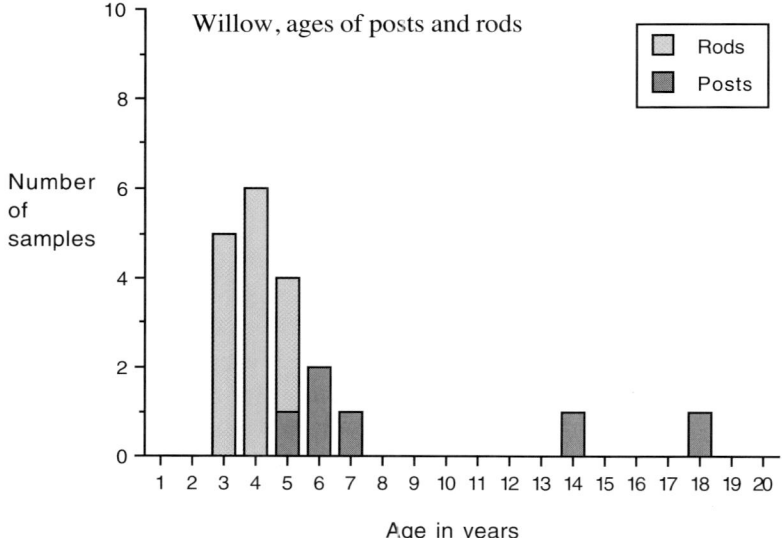

Fig. 55 *(left and opposite)—Wood species identifications and tree-ring studies from Fergus estuary east 2, Co. Clare.*

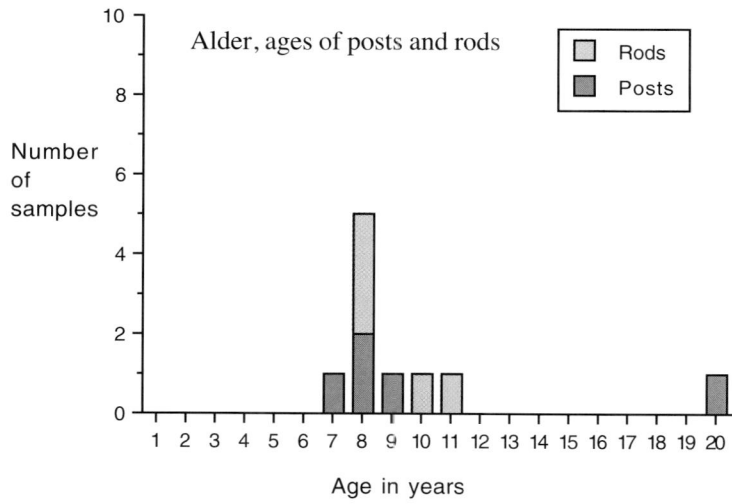

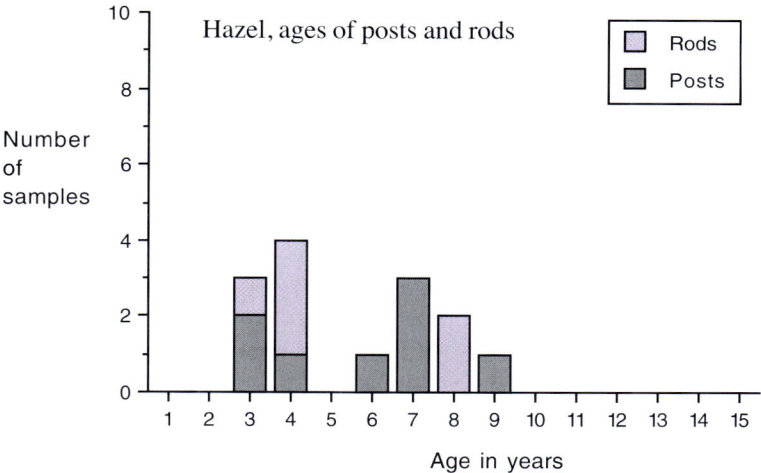

These ringforts were probably the farmsteads of local *boaire*- and *ocaire*-grade tenant farmers and their families, the circular earthen enclosures containing domestic houses, other buildings and places for livestock, food and equipment (M. Stout 1997). The ringforts are sited on south-facing, well-drained slopes with good views to the south and west over the Fergus estuary. It is interesting that the Ballyconneelly ringfort in particular is located at the edge of the estuarine levels. This might suggest that its inhabitants were actively exploiting the coastal wetlands for raw materials, cattle-grazing, some fowling and possibly the use of fishtraps along the estuary. It is also worth pointing out that the siting of these ringforts along the dryland ridge may be influenced by its use as a north–south routeway along the estuary in the early historic period.

Fish may have been an important element in the diet of some early historic coastal communities, while literary sources point to the high status of salmon and trout, at least for the upper classes of society. Bones of eel, cod, haddock, plaice and salmon/sea trout have all been found in an early historic coastal shell midden at Oughtymore, Co. Derry. An early historic coastal promontory fort at Larrybane, Co. Antrim, produced evidence for cod, saithe, pollack, whiting and wrasse, which were most probably caught with nets. Fish bone found at the Viking Age settlement at Beginish Island, Co. Kerry, included wrasse, which—judging by the net- and line-sinkers—were probably caught by angling and netting techniques. Iron multipronged eel and salmon spears have been found on early historic crannog sites at Strokestown and Lagore. Fish bones are now being increasingly found on well-sieved archaeological sites (O'Sullivan 1993–4; Edwards 1990; McCarthy 1998, 61–2).

The use of fishtraps is well attested in the early Irish historical sources, particularly in texts dating from about the seventh and eighth centuries. Early Irish annals, law-tracts and hagiographies all mention the construction, use and ownership of the *cora éisc* (*cora* denoting a stone wall, *éisc* denoting fish). Fishtraps were also referred to by the word *aire*, which simply means 'woven fence'. The early Irish laws are particularly tantalising. One seventh-century law-tract dealing with the valuation of types of land has a sentence stating '*Di ba ar inber eisg nanta*' ('two cows for an estuary of permanent fish'), indicating that proximity to an estuary increased the value of land by this amount (F. Kelly 1997). The obvious benefit of such a location would be access to water, salt and the fish stocks themselves. There is also an implication in another law-text, *Coibnes Uisci Thairidne* ('kinship of conducted water'), that a fish-weir could be erected in water adjacent to a neighbour's land. It seems likely that early Irish law contained more detailed legal guidelines on the ownership and use of estuarine waters, perhaps outlined in the now-lost *Cáin Inbir* ('the law of the estuary'), which was apparently part of a law-tract called *Muirbretha* ('sea-judgements').

Foragers, farmers and fishers

Several texts emphasise the importance of fish in the early historic Irish economy and there seems to have been an awareness that fish stocks needed to be protected. This protection appears to be defined in a fragment of eighth-century law-text preserved in O'Davoren's Glossary, which states: *'Ní téchta ní bes (mó) n trian inn uisce do aire .i. do ime'* ('It is not proper to (build) a weir, i.e. a fence, more than one third of the water'). This seems to indicate the legal enforcement of a gap in the fish-weir, allowing at least a certain percentage of the fish stocks to move upstream unimpeded. This opening would have been intended to conserve fish stocks or, more importantly perhaps, to allow weir-owners upstream to catch fish. Fishtraps could also be publicly owned; the glossator of one text stated his opinion that *Cáin Inbir* was used to regulate public weirs. It is possible that legal issues mostly arose in relation to estuarine weirs. One text described the problems encountered if a weir-owner constructed his trap too far out into the river, and the length of the fences could be increased if a landowner held lands on both sides of a river or estuary (F. Kelly 1997, 286). It appears that fish were occasionally stolen from traps, as legal commentaries laid down heavy fines for stealing fish from a weir (*ibid.*, 289).

Some fishtraps would have been the property of nobles or wealthy farmers, as one Old Irish legal fragment refers to the 'fish-weir of a lord' (*aire éisc flatha*) (*ibid.*, 288). However, it is likely that most fishing was carried out by other members of the community, including specialist or full-time fishermen. The seventh-century wisdom-text *Audacht Morainn* states that amongst the attributes of a just king must be the abundance of fish swimming in his streams. Another wisdom-text opined that it was the justice of a ruler that brought fish into estuaries (*ibid.*, 286). According to one law-tract, *Di Astud Dligid ocus Chirt*, a law-abiding freeman was permitted a single swift dip of a fishing-net in a stream, and was also entitled to a single salmon from a river near his own house (*ibid.*, 286). In contrast, the professional fisherman (*íascaire*) was a person of low legal status, being accorded only the honour-price of one yearling heifer in the *Uraicecht Becc* (the law-tract on status) (*ibid.*, 286). Fishermen would have tended the trap on a daily basis during the season, repairing its fences and removing newly caught fish. The law-tracts refer to the *seiche corad*, 'weir hide', meaning a small, coracle-like craft which was used for taking fish from the traps (*ibid.*, 290). The Fergus estuary fishtrap, distant as it was from the ringforts on the drylands, may therefore have been tended from a small boat.

Medieval fishtraps, Deel estuary, Co. Limerick

Introduction

The Deel estuary medieval fishtraps are on the east bank of the upper part of the estuary, adjacent to the townland of Ballynash, Co. Limerick (Fig. 56). The fishtraps (Deel estuary sites 1–4) are located at the low-water mark, along the stretch of foreshore north of Goleen Creek and south of a smaller mudflat creek which flows in from the east. They were discovered in May 1993 and were planned and photographed in July 1994.

The Deel estuary flows northwards out of hilly country around the town of Askeaton, out into the middle of the south bank of the Shannon estuary. On the east side of the Deel estuary the drylands rise to low-lying, rolling, hilly ground, while to the west, beyond Tomdeely Point, lies a wide expanse of mudflats between Greenish Island, Moreena Point and Aughinish. Although the River Deel is narrow, rocky and shallow as it flows out of the town of Askeaton, its estuary broadens out and exposes large areas of mudflats between Tomdeely Point and Ballynash, at about 3km north of Askeaton town. To the north of the mouth of Goleen creek, the channel of the Deel estuary swings around to the north-west in a broad, sweeping meander. The fishtraps

Early historic and medieval fishtraps

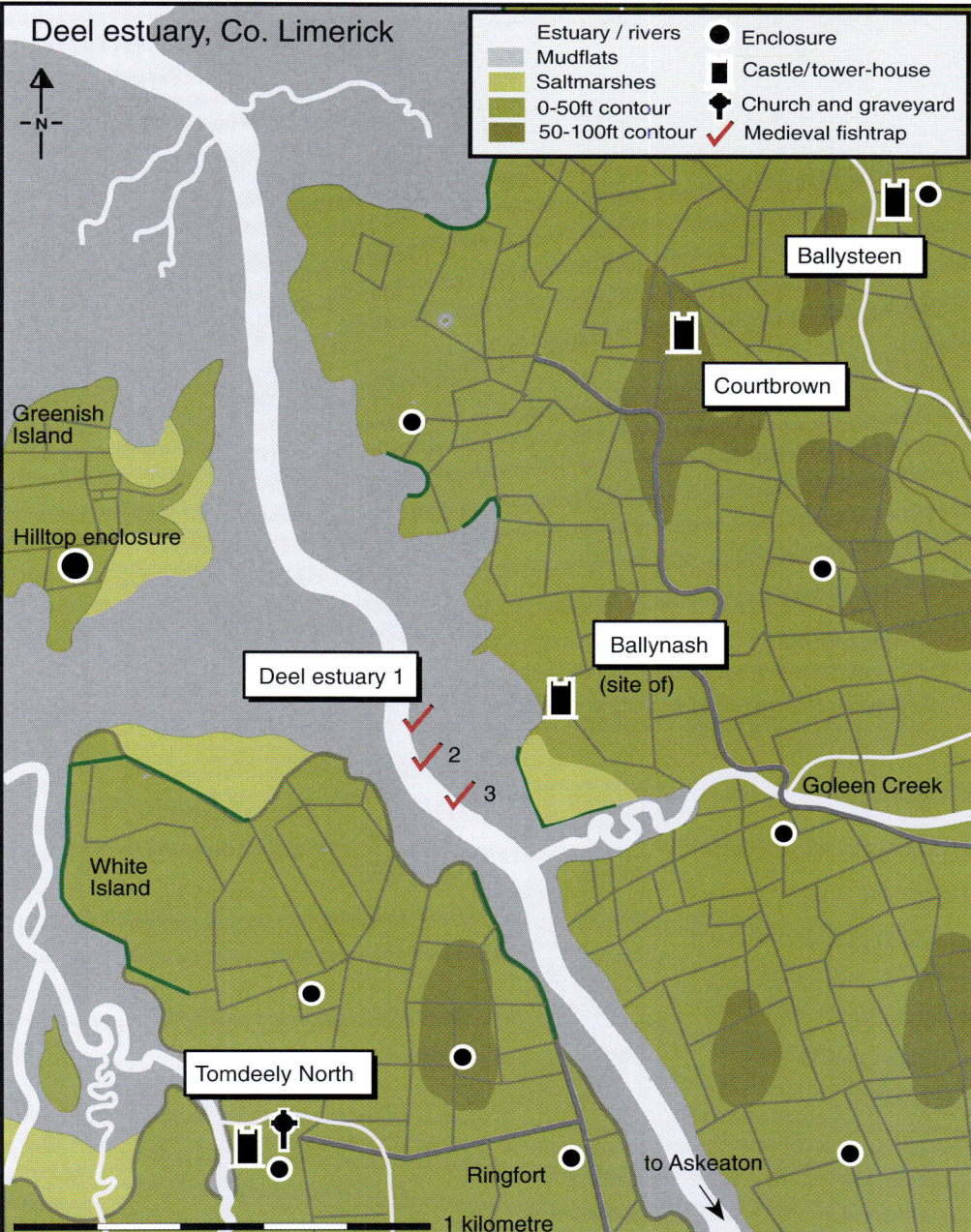

Fig. 56—*Map of Deel estuary, Co. Limerick, showing spatial relationship between medieval fishtraps and the medieval hall-house and parish church at Tomdeely, as well as sites of castles and tower-houses at Ballynash, Courtbrown and Ballysteen.*

were found on the east side of this meander. On either side of this channel, the foreshore just above the low-water level slopes steeply, but thereafter levels off into a broad, open foreshore of soft silts and clays across which are strewn rocks and seaweed.

Deel estuary 1—fishtrap

Site location

Deel estuary 1 is situated on a gently sloping foreshore of firm, blue-grey estuarine clays on the east bank of the channel, approximately 550m north of Goleen Creek and about 20m south of the mouth of a smaller mudflat creek. The site consists of two converging rows of post-and-wattle fences, with a cluster of posts at the apex of the fences. It was recorded during relatively low summer tides, but the post-and-wattle fence definitely continues down underwater, and it is very likely that there are other submerged, unrecorded features. The post-and-wattle fence also disappears into a rising mud-bank to the north-east.

145

Pl. 42—*Medieval fishtrap at Deel estuary 1.*

Site description

Deel estuary 1 is a V-shaped fishtrap constructed of two converging post-and-wattle fences, at the apex of which lies a cluster of roundwood posts (Pl. 42; Fig. 57). A single vertical post from the largest fence provided a radiocarbon date of 900 ± 20 BP (AD 1041–1208; GrN-21932). The fences were of vertical roundwood posts, 2–10cm in diameter, spaced at intervals of 20–30cm and driven to a depth of at least 35cm into the clays. The posts now protrude to a height of about 5–10cm above the mudflat surface. Horizontal wattle rods are visible, particularly towards the south-west of the main fence, where it has been most exposed by erosion. These horizontal rods measure 2–3cm in diameter and are interwoven around the posts to a depth of at least 5cm.

The main post-and-wattle fence, the 'shore' fence, runs north-eastwards up the foreshore from the low-water mark. It measures at least 11m in length and is oriented north-north-east/south-south-west. It is partly buried under clay and may in fact measure over 26m in length (similar posts on the same alignment are being exposed about 15m to the north-east, in the bed and banks of a small creek). The visible length of the fence is constructed of at least 40 roundwood posts, typically spaced at intervals of 30–40cm. These posts measure 5–8cm in diameter and survive to depths of 30cm. Some are set vertically, while others slope slightly towards the west.

There is evidence for repair or reconstruction. The main post-and-wattle fence diverges into two separate post-and-wattle features at a point 3.4m north-east of the 'eye' or apex of the structure. The latter two fences measure 4.5m (northern fence) and 4m (southern fence) in length. The southern fence is more closely aligned with the overall structure and is therefore probably the older one. The posts are narrower nearer the estuary channel, where they measure 4–6cm in diameter. They are also more tightly spaced, set at intervals of 0.15–0.2m, with horizontal wattles woven between them.

The second post-and-wattle fence (the lower or 'flood' fence) runs along the foreshore at a slight angle to the low-water mark. It measures 4.5m in length and is oriented north-west/south-east. It comprises at least thirteen vertical roundwood posts, 3–6cm in diameter and typically spaced at intervals of 4–5cm, but more densely clustered near the eye. The posts are either vertically set or slope down the shore, towards the south-west. There is a pronounced gap in this structure, about 2m north-west of the eye.

The eye or trap of the fishing structure may have been situated at the convergence of the two main post-and-wattle fences. It appears to be defined by a concentration of

Early historic and medieval fishtraps

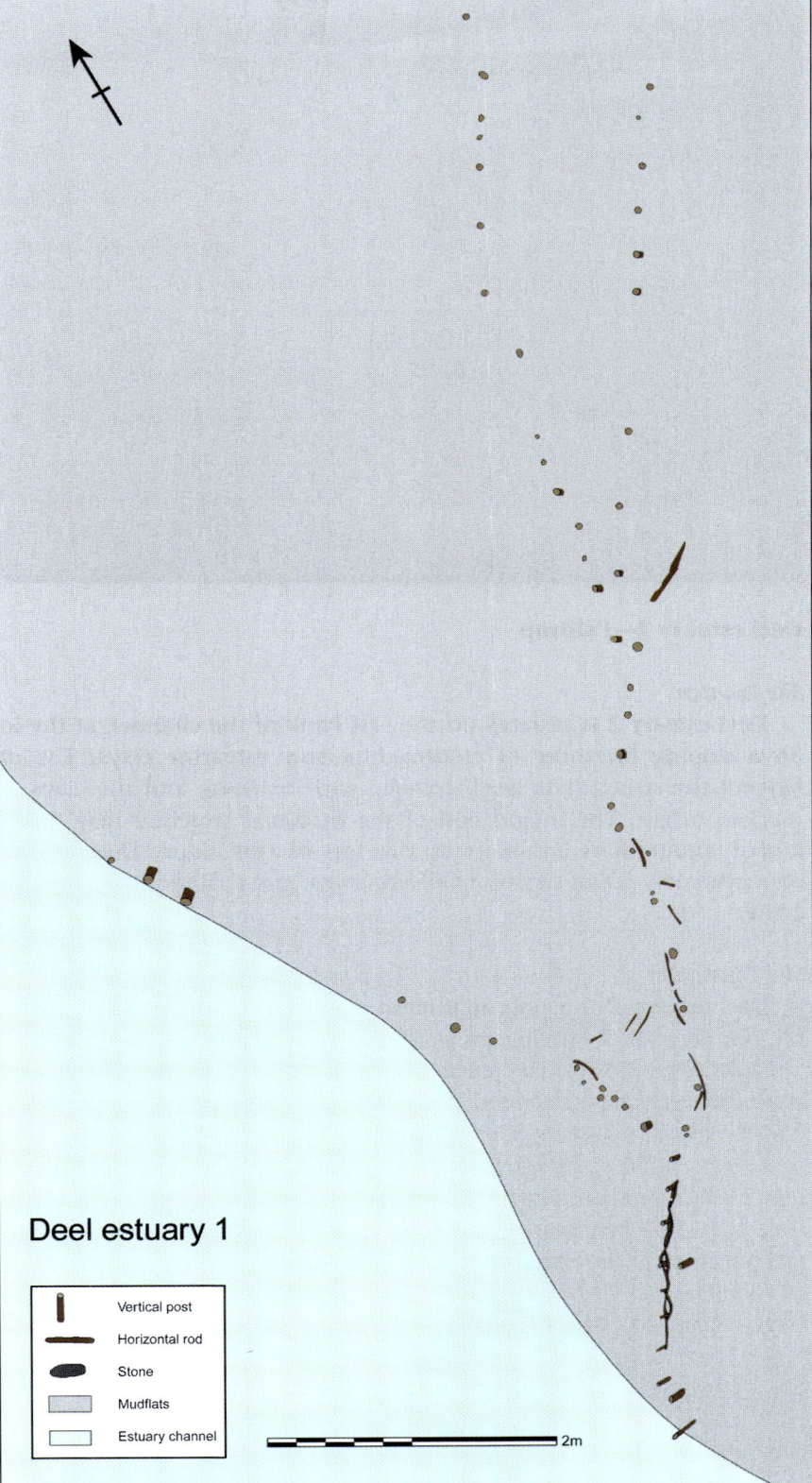

Fig. 57—*Plan of medieval fishtrap fence, Deel estuary 1.*

roundwood posts in the flood fence, and by a few rods running across the eye. The posts are tightly clustered in this area, perhaps representing an attempt to make the structure 'fishtight' down near the low-water mark. However, it is obvious that the shore fence definitely runs down the foreshore past this point, so it is possible that another trap mechanism lies submerged underwater, only visible at the lowest tides of the year.

Pl. 43—*Medieval fishtrap fence, Deel estuary 2.*

Deel estuary 2—fishtrap

Site location

Deel estuary 2 is situated on the east bank of the channel, at the low-water mark, on a sloping foreshore of eroding blue-grey estuarine clays. The upper foreshore beyond the structure is level, covered with seaweed, and the clays are evidently of modern origin. The inland end of the medieval structure may therefore be largely buried under these mudflats at the top of this slope. Deel estuary 2 is located approximately 500m north of Goleen Creek, and *c.* 50m upstream of the Deel estuary 1 site.

Site description

Deel estuary 2 is a post alignment erected on a north-east/south-west orientation (Pl. 43; Fig. 58). A single post produced a radiocarbon date of 740 ± 15 BP (cal. AD 1262–92; GrN-20975). The fence measures at least 5.6m in length. It consists of at least nineteen vertical roundwood posts, typically now surviving to only about 20cm in length and measuring 5–8cm in diameter. The posts are irregularly spaced, at intervals of 4–6cm. At the middle of the structure there is a cluster of five small posts, possibly related to a trap mechanism. The worked ends of the posts are starting to be exposed near the low-water mark, with tool-marks and even the actual tips of posts visible. Otherwise only the short stumps of the posts remain. This clearly indicates that most of this structure has been eroded away and that it was originally set in mudflats that were at least 20–30cm higher than the modern level.

Deel estuary 3—fishtrap

Site location

Deel estuary 3 is situated at the low-water mark, eroding out of a foreshore of level blue-grey clays, approximately 300m north of Goleen Creek. It was recorded during a flooding tide, so it is likely that other features lie hidden in the clays and channel.

Site description

Deel estuary 3 is a single post alignment, erected on a east/west orientation. A single post produced a radiocarbon date of 640 ± 20 BP (cal. AD 1297–1392; GrN-21931). The post alignment consists of at least 5–6 vertical roundwood posts, typically 15–20cm in

Early historic and medieval fishtraps

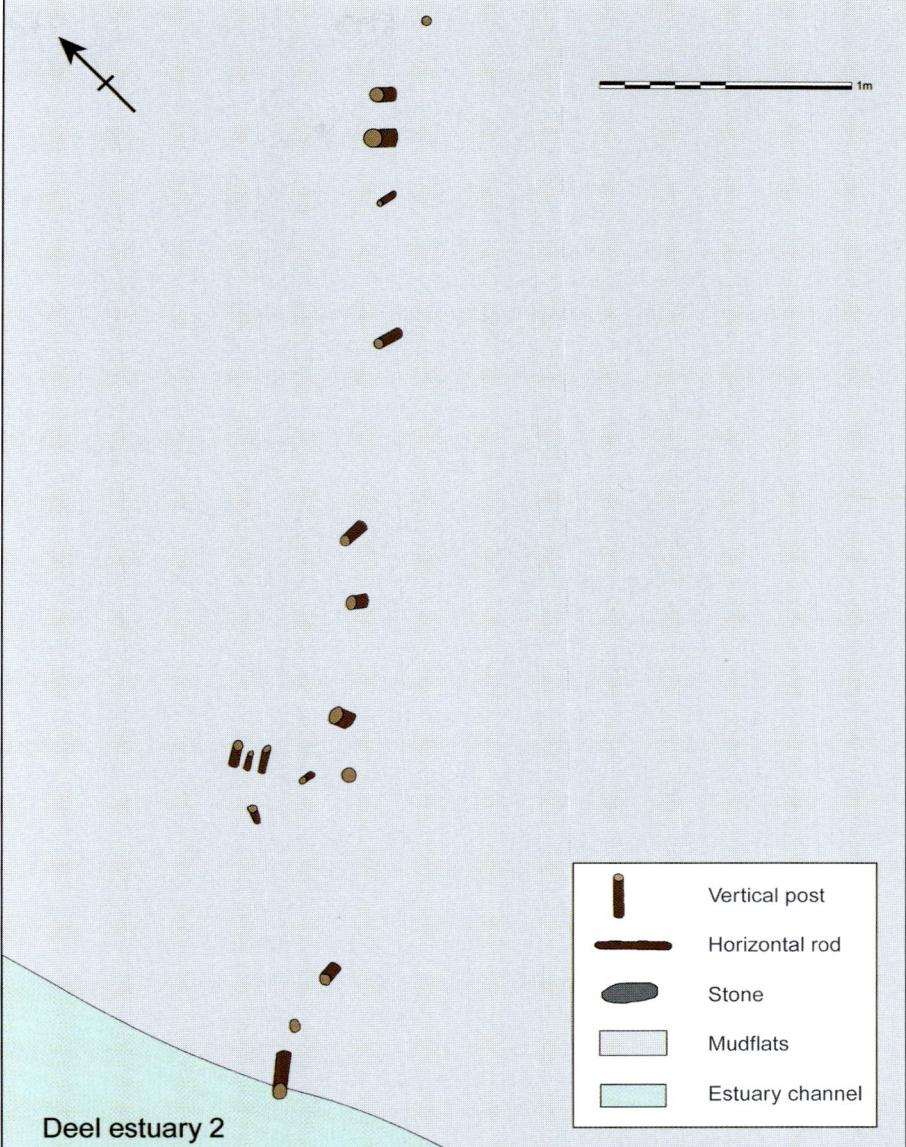

Fig. 58—*Plan of Deel estuary 2 medieval fishtrap fence.*

length and 5–8cm in diameter. The posts were irregularly spaced, at intervals of 50–60cm. The entire structure measures no more than 4m in length, but it is probable that most of it has been eroded away.

Deel estuary 4—single post

Site location

Deel estuary 4 is a single worked wooden post, situated at the top of the sloping eroding terrace of clays, 8m from the low-water mark. It was found *in situ* on the foreshore between Deel estuary 1 and Deel estuary 2, about 20m north of the latter.

Site description

Deel estuary 4 was a single waterlogged roundwood post, 9cm in diameter and 15cm in length. Only the worked end survived. It was sharpened to a pencil point using a narrow iron blade. It may be the single remaining post of a completely eroded-out fence, probably associated with the other medieval fishing structures in the vicinity.

Foragers, farmers and fishers

Discussion
There is some evidence for medieval settlement in the immediate vicinity of the Deel estuary, contemporary with the fishtraps (Fig. 56). The earliest fishtrap (Deel estuary 1), dated to between the mid-eleventh and the early thirteenth centuries, may pre-date the Anglo-Norman invasion and may have been constructed at a time (i.e. *c.* 1050–1150) from which we have little good archaeological evidence for rural settlement in Ireland. There are ringforts (e.g. at Tomdeely North) and enclosures along the Deel estuary that may have been occupied during this period. Alternatively, unenclosed or nucleated settlements may have been located along the estuary's banks. By the thirteenth and fourteenth centuries, sites of possible medieval castles or tower-houses at Courtbrown and at Ballynash (situated only 400m to the east at the high-water mark) may have become the centres of more intensive settlement. The Ballynash site, of which there is now no archaeological trace, may have been a focus for local settlement and it is probable that its inhabitants were responsible for the construction and use of the fisheries.

There is also a significant medieval settlement to the south-west of the Deel estuary, at Tomdeely North, where there is an early thirteenth-century hall-house (repaired at a later stage), a series of earthworks and a late medieval parish church and graveyard (Sweetman 1999, 89–91, fig. 69). In addition, proximity to the significant Anglo-Norman borough of Askeaton (located 3km to the south), with its harbour, friaries and castles, would have been a major influence on the local economy in the thirteenth and fourteenth centuries. The Deel estuary fishtraps may have been used to catch fish for the local communities inhabiting the settlements along the river, although it is also possible that they produced fish to be sold to, and by, the urban fishmongers of Askeaton.

The Deel estuary 1–4 fishtraps provide evidence for the use, repair and management of local fishtraps between the eleventh and fourteenth centuries. The Deel estuary 1 structure is the best preserved and most complete, and can be used to reconstruct the type of fishtrap used locally. It was a V-shaped structure, oriented as a flood weir to catch migratory salmon moving upstream along the River Deel. The main shore fence provided a barrier to fish moving upstream along the edge of the channel, forcing them into a basket or net where the shore fence joined the flood fence. The use of a flood weir probably meant that local fishermen had to wait in boats until the slack tide to empty the traps, although it may have been possible to lift the basket or net out of the water. The Deel estuary 2–3 structures are poorly preserved, representing only the last remnants of the medieval traps.

Our archaeological evidence shows that fishtraps were being used on the Deel estuary between the eleventh and fourteenth centuries. Historical sources suggest that they continued to be erected and maintained on the Deel from the fifteenth century onwards. Interestingly, there may have been shifts in location and variations in intensity of exploitation throughout the late medieval period. The clearest historical evidence deals with the fisheries around the medieval town of Askeaton. Thus we know that the rent of the 'farmers of Askeaton' in 1452 included the sum of 16s. 8d. for the *gurgitibes* or fisheries (Went 1960b, 143). A century later, an inquisition of 20 May 1584 mentions that the mill of Inniskesty was worth 30s., while its weir was worth 16s. Despite the difference in scale and industry between the mill and the weir, it is evident that the fish-weir was of considerable value (Westropp 1903b, 157).

There were quite a number of fishtraps on the Deel in the sixteenth century. A survey of 1586 refers to the fish-weirs within the manor of Askeaton. 'The fishing of the Dyle' (i.e. Deel) was called the 'cole ffysshinge . . . as well as the fishing of Lyn Assa around the castle walls and island. The various portions of the fishery were called Lyn-en-assa, Lyn-en-monea, Lyn-en-allorte and En-pool-ne-cally. The weirs were called Corre-en-Earl whynred; the Earl's weir at the salmon leap under the bridge, Corrennumrare or the friar's weir and Corre-edy-oge-Lacy, the weir of Edmond oge Lacy next the Shannon' (Westropp 1904, 127–8). The fish-weir known as Corre-edy-

Early historic and medieval fishtraps

oge-Lacy, located 'next the Shannon', may well have been situated somewhere near the Deel estuary 1–4 fishtraps. By the time of the Civil Survey in 1654–6, the emphasis in the region seems to have shifted north-eastwards onto the Shannon estuary, where fish-weirs were in use at Ballycanauna, Ballinvoher and Beagh, Co. Limerick (Went 1960b). By the mid-nineteenth century the Deel fish-weirs at Askeaton had been completely abandoned.

Medieval fishtraps, Bunratty, Shannon estuary

Introduction

Medieval fishtraps were also recorded on the Shannon estuary mudflats adjacent to the townland of Bunratty West, Co. Clare (Fig. 59). The upper Shannon estuary is quite broad in this area, with extensive mudflats, rock outcrops and islands on both banks. The Owenagarney River (also known locally as the Ratty River) flows into the estuary on the north bank, curving to the east around Little Quay Island before emptying into the Shannon estuary between Quay Island (also known locally as Cain's Island) and Green Island. There are several former islands, Illaunmore ('big island'), Illaunbeg ('little island') and Tradree Point, that are now hills in the reclaimed corcass. The medieval fishtraps are located in two specific areas. Bunratty 1–4 are located in a cluster on the east bank of the River Owenagarney, immediately to the north-east of Little Quay Island (Fig. 60). A submerged peat shelf (Bunratty 5) of probable prehistoric date is also located here. Bunratty 6 is located out on the mudflats in the bed of a large creek that drains the wide foreshore between Quay Island and Illaunbeg Point.

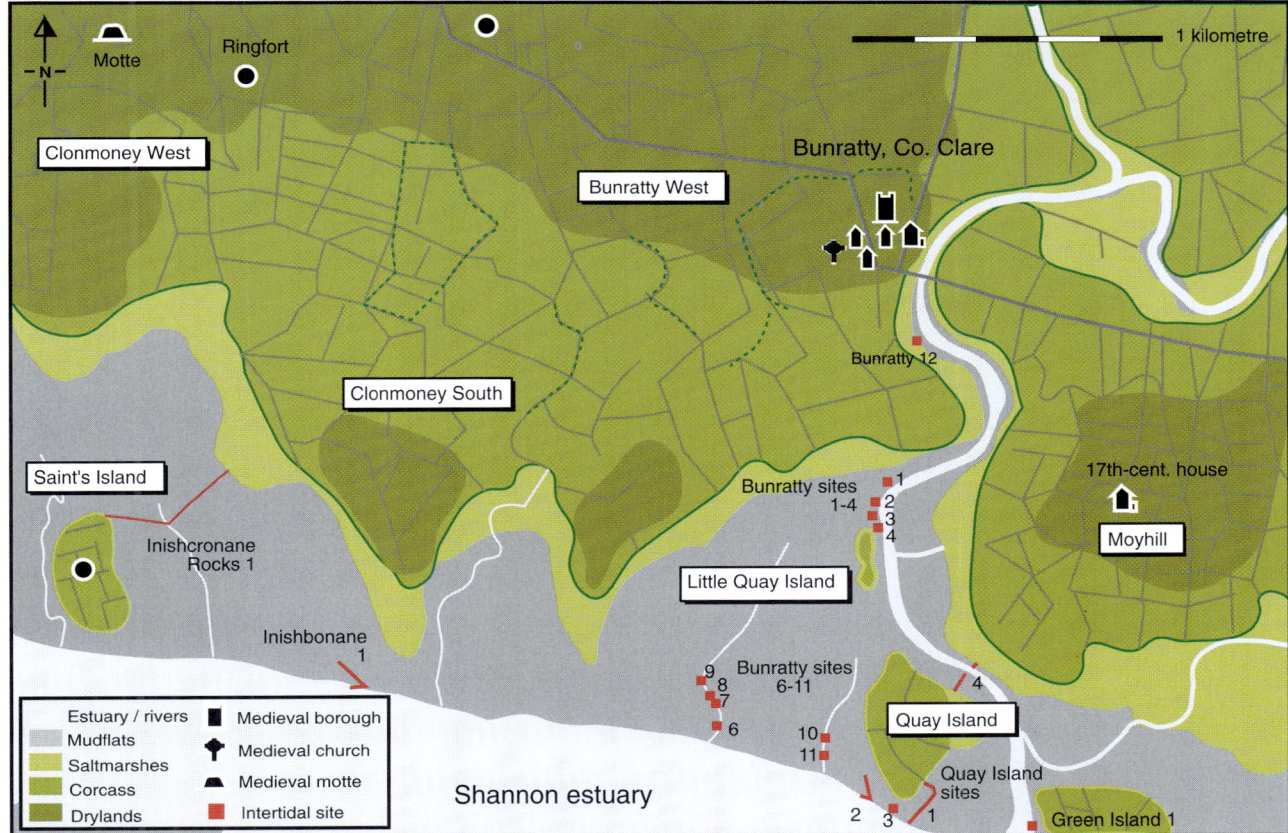

Fig. 59—*Map of Bunratty, Co. Clare, showing location of medieval fishtraps, Bunratty 1–6, in relation to the Anglo-Norman borough and other medieval settlement sites on the drylands.*

Foragers, farmers and fishers

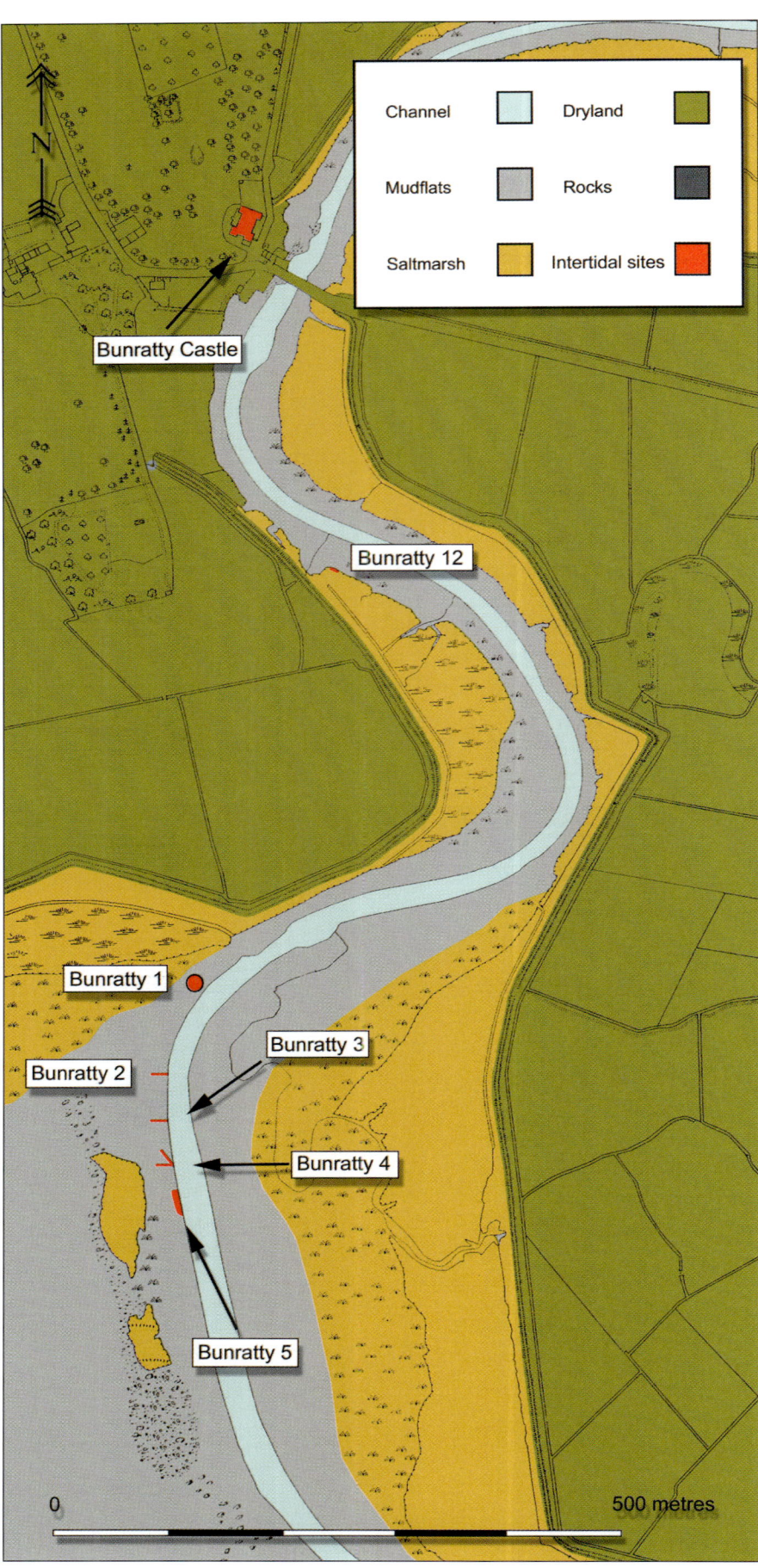

Fig. 60—*Detailed map of Bunratty foreshore at Little Quay Island, showing location of Bunratty 1–5 sites.*

Bunratty 4 and 6 were recorded during the intertidal survey in autumn 1995, when they were also sampled for radiocarbon dating. In February 1997 more detailed archaeological survey and excavation were carried out on these fishtraps. A team of five archaeologists travelled by boat to the sites each day (over a four-day period). The structures were cleaned of silts, drawn at a scale of 1:20 and photographed using both SLR cameras and video cameras. Wood samples were taken for species identifications, tree-ring counts and radiocarbon dating. During these investigations, the tides fell to some of the lowest levels ever encountered during the Shannon estuary survey, so that the structures were probably at their most visible. In March 1998, a brief revisitation of Bunratty 6 revealed that its post-and-wattle fence was more extensive than previously believed, and this new information has been incorporated in the following discussion.

Bunratty 1—post-and-wattle fences

Site location
Bunratty 1 is located on the west bank of the River Owenagarney channel, approximately 160m north-north-east of Little Quay Island, immediately to the south of the modern saltmarsh. The site consists of several individual features exposed during extremely low tides on a narrow, steeply sloping foreshore of blue-grey estuarine clays, over an area 14m in length by 1m in width (Fig. 61). They include a vertical post-and-wattle fence (Bunratty 1.1), a horizontal post-and-wattle panel (Bunratty 1.2), and several other vertical posts and horizontal pieces of roundwood further to the south-east.

Site description
Bunratty 1.1 is a vertical post-and-wattle fence, 1.3m in length, oriented north-north-east/south-south-west. A single large post inserted at an oblique angle into the clay beside it appears to be the structural support for the smaller vertical post-and-wattle panel. The post measures 5cm in diameter and stands to a height of 41cm. There are several narrow vertical stakes with interwoven rods both to the north and to the south of this single large post. These measure 2–3cm in diameter and are barely exposed above the clays. The horizontal rods are 1–2cm in diameter.

Bunratty 1.2 is a horizontal post-and-wattle panel exposed in the clays, 9m to the south-east (Pl. 44). It measures 1.3m in length and 30cm in exposed width, and is composed of five individual roundwood sails spaced at intervals of 22–25cm. The sails were knotty and of varying sizes, ranging in diameter from 3cm to 6cm. At least ten rods were woven tightly around these sails, typically 3–4cm apart. The rods also varied in size, ranging in diameter from 1cm to 3cm. This post-and-wattle panel was clearly rather crudely made, with thick, knotty branches used for the individual sails and rods that were clearly taken from topwood, branchwood and twigs. The evidence for woodworking indicated the use of flat iron axes. Bunratty 1.2 is probably the remains of a collapsed vertical post-and-wattle fence.

There are at least five vertical roundwood posts spaced at irregular intervals along the mudflats in the vicinity. There are also four horizontal pieces of roundwood. There are no indications that these posts and roundwood are part of another post-and-wattle structure, but given their context, location and size, they are almost certainly related to the Bunratty 1.1 and Bunratty 1.2 post-and-wattle features.

Site interpretation
The Bunratty 1.1 and 1.2 post-and-wattle features may represent two converging fences of a small V-shaped trap. The trapping mechanism would probably have been 10–15m further to the south-east, out under the modern course of the river channel. The structure is undated, but its form, location and preservation suggest strongly that this is an early historic or medieval structure.

Foragers, farmers and fishers

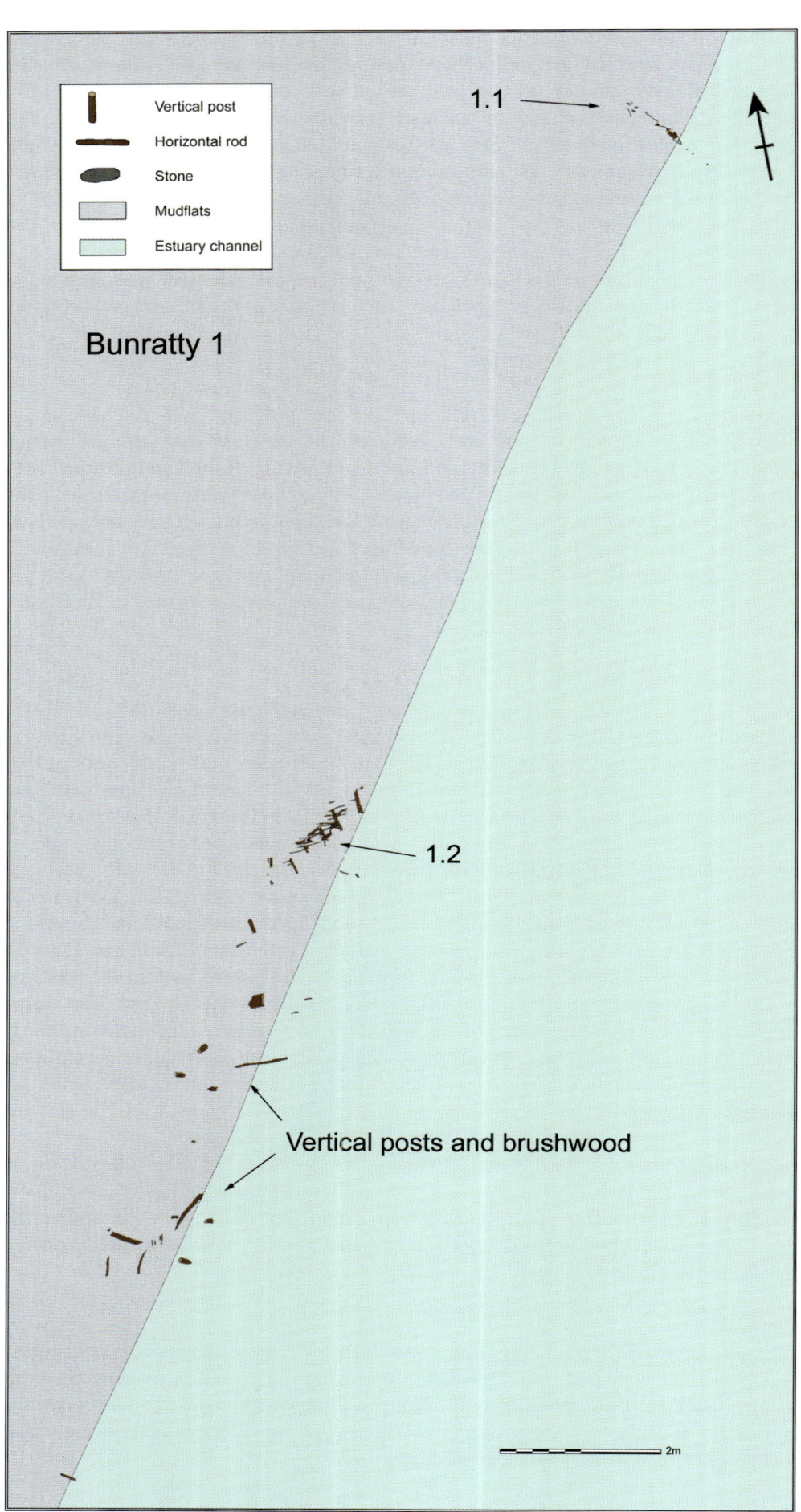

Fig. 61—*Plan of Bunratty 1 post-and-wattle features.*

Early historic and medieval fishtraps

Pl. 44—*Detail of Bunratty 1.2 horizontal post-and-wattle panel from north-east.*

Bunratty 2—fishtrap

Site location
　　Bunratty 2 is situated in blue-grey estuarine clays on the west bank of the Owenagarney River, 18m south of a small creek and about 80m north-north-east of Little Quay Island. The Bunratty 3 fishtrap site is located immediately to the south.

Site description
　　Bunratty 2 is a single post-and-wattle fence, oriented east-north-east/west-south-west, at a 90° angle to the modern channel (Pl. 45; Fig. 62). It measures 4m in exposed length. The roundwood posts were driven vertically into the clays, and are spaced at intervals of 30–40cm. The posts measured 3–6cm in diameter. Horizontal rods and branches, 2–3cm in diameter, were interwoven between these posts. However, there are no interwoven branches on the lower part of the foreshore, where intertidal and channel erosion has exposed several of these posts right down to their sharpened tips. This probably indicates that the structure was formerly used on a foreshore that was slightly higher and more level than that of today. The wood was taken from knotty topwood and branches, and the woodworking evidence indicated the use of flat iron axes.

Foragers, farmers and fishers

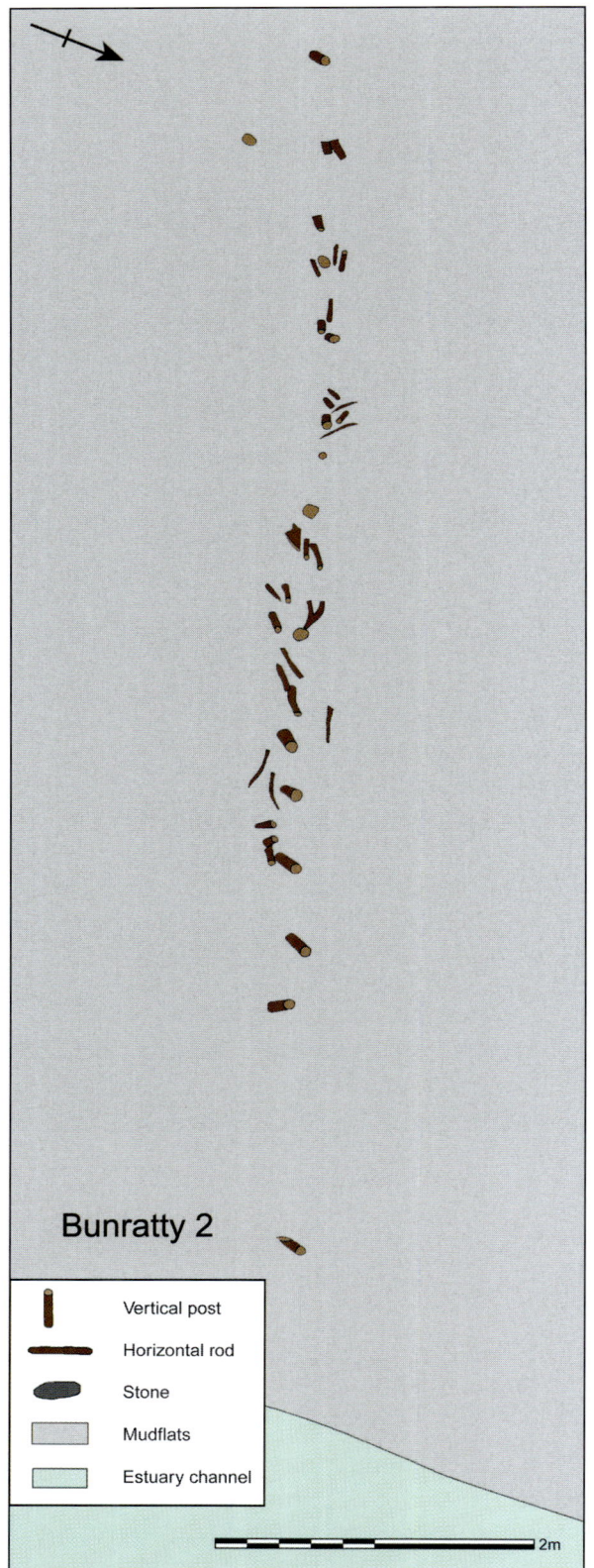

Fig. 62—*Plan of Bunratty 2.*

Site interpretation
Bunratty 2 appears to be a single post-and-wattle fishtrap fence, possibly with a basket situated at its end. It may also have held netting, working as a net weir rather than a head weir. It probably dates from the late medieval period, although the density and state of preservation of the wood might suggest that it is late medieval or post-medieval in date.

Early historic and medieval fishtraps

Pl. 45—*Bunratty 2 post-and-wattle fence, general view from north (the Bunratty 3 fence and woven baskets and then the Bunratty 4 medieval fishtrap with its multiphase fences are in the background).*

Pl. 46—*Detailed view of Bunratty 3A basket at low-water mark. This basket is only exposed to view for a few hours each year, during the lowest possible tides.*

Bunratty 3—fishtraps (post alignment and baskets)

Site location

Bunratty 3 is a post alignment and two baskets located on the west bank of the River Owenagarney, about 60m north-north-east of Little Quay Island, in blue-grey estuarine clays on a steeply sloping foreshore (Fig. 63). A rock outcrop or ballast dump lies immediately to the south-west. The two baskets are on the extreme lower foreshore, below the mean low-water mark, and are only visible during extremely low tides. The site consists of a single post alignment (Bunratty 3.1) and two horizontal baskets (Bunratty 3A and 3B) buried in the clays at the eastern end of the fence.

157

Foragers, farmers and fishers

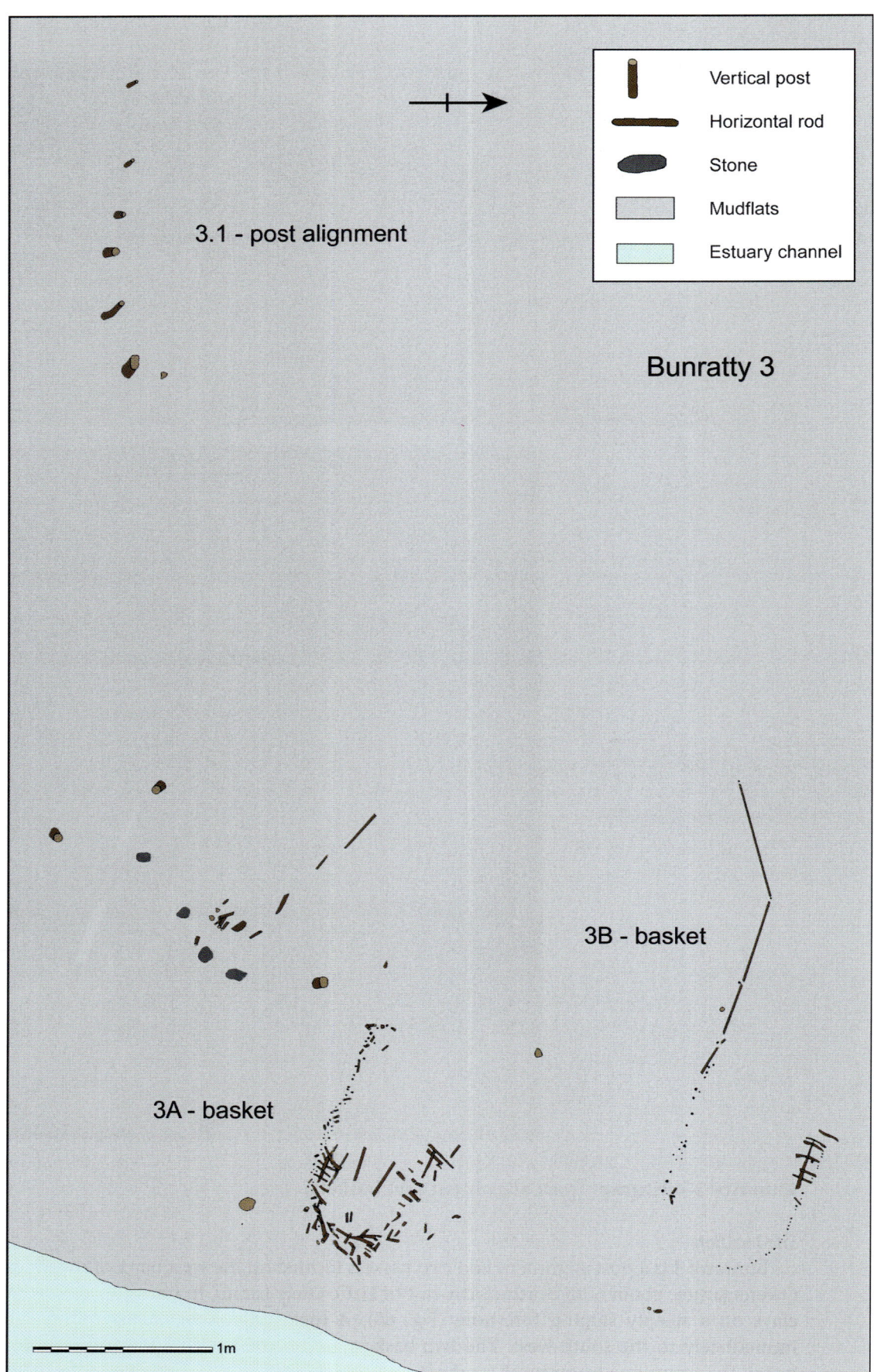

Fig. 63—*Plan of Bunratty 3, showing fences and baskets.*

The post alignment

The post alignment (Bunratty 3.1) is oriented east/west and is constructed of fifteen vertical roundwood posts, separated at intervals of 15–25cm. The posts measure 4–10cm in diameter and protrude above the clays to a height of 15cm. The structure measures 5.6m in length, although there is a gap 2.2m wide between the posts near the eastern end. At the eastern end, five vertical posts and a few horizontal rods may indicate the presence of a buried post-and-wattle panel.

Bunratty 3A—basket

A small basket (Bunratty 3A) is located at the north-east end of the post alignment, lying horizontally in the clays (Pl. 46). It appears to be U-shaped in plan, with straight sides and a gently rounded end. It is oriented west-north-west/east-south-east, with its mouth facing up the foreshore. It measures at least 1.2m in length and 80cm in width at the mouth, narrowing to 30cm in width at the opposite end. The basket was woven with a simple weave, using single long stakes (3–4 visible) of roundwood around which the narrower rods or weavers (at least 52 visible) were tightly woven. The stakes measured 2–3cm in diameter, the rods 1–3cm in diameter. There were three vertical roundwood posts (8–10cm in diameter) beside the basket, two to the south-west and one to the north-north-east. These may have been used to hold the basket at the end of the vertical fence.

Bunratty 3B—basket

The second woven basket is located 1.2m further to the north, 2.8m from the eastern end of the post alignment. It also lies buried in the clay, with its mouth facing west-north-west. It may have been funnel-shaped, with a wide splaying mouth leading to a narrower body. It is also gently curved at the end. It measures at least 2.8m in length, possibly narrowing from a diameter of 1.4m at the mouth to 0.6m at the narrow end. It may have had a more open weave. There were 5–6 stakes exposed, each measuring 2–3cm in diameter, and 47 rods, 1–2cm in diameter. Two vertical posts were situated at the south-east end of the basket, possibly to pin it in position.

Site interpretation

The Bunratty 3 site could be interpreted as a fishtrap composed of a single vertical fence leading down to horizontal baskets. The baskets may have been simply anchored in place in a creek bed or pinned down with a few posts, such as those found beside basket 3A. The baskets would have been portable traps that could be left in creeks, streams and even artificial mill-streams to catch eels. It is also possible that they were removed from a larger V-shaped fishtrap, such as the Bunratty 4 structure only a few metres to the south, after they were too rotten or damaged to use. The site is undated, but is very likely to be medieval.

Bunratty 4—fishtraps (complex of post-and-wattle fences)

Site location

Bunratty 4 is located on the west bank of the Owenagarney River, about 40m north-east of Little Quay Island, 15m to the south of the Bunratty 3 site. It is a complex, multiphase site consisting of a sequence of post-and-wattle fences, post alignments and brushwood (Pls 47 and 48; Fig. 64). The structures are mostly situated in blue-grey estuarine clays on a steeply sloping foreshore, but also run down the foreshore across a band of grey-brown silty peats. A hazel rod from one of these post-and-wattle fences (Bunratty 4.3) has been radiocarbon-dated to 960 ± 20 BP (cal. AD 1018–1159; GrN-21933).

Site description

The Bunratty 4 site has evidence for a sequence of V-shaped or U-shaped fishtraps

Foragers, farmers and fishers

Pl. 47—*Bunratty 4 medieval fishtrap from north, looking along post-and-wattle fence 4.2.*

Pl. 48—*Detail of upper fences at Bunratty 4 medieval fishtrap, showing evidence for several phases of repair and reconstruction.*

of converging post-and-wattle fences, some of which have a narrow opening for a basket at the apex. There is clear evidence for repair and reconstruction, making it a difficult site to interpret in terms of its construction, use and chronology. The site consists of at least four separate post-and-wattle fences (Bunratty 4.1, 4.3, 4.4 and 4.5) running down the foreshore, closely spaced and parallel to each other. They are all oriented east-north-east/west-south-west, measure about 9.5m in length and are spread over an area 1.4m wide. At the mid-point of these combined fences, a fourth, shorter post-and-wattle fence (Bunratty 4.6) comes in from the north, before turning sharply left to run down the foreshore. There is also a fifth fence, Bunratty 4.2, at the bottom of the foreshore, constructed of post-and-wattle, brushwood, branches and twigs. Other posts, pieces of brushwood and possible wattle panels are lying in the clays, particularly on the lower foreshore. These are grouped together and described here as Bunratty 4.7 and Bunratty 4.8.

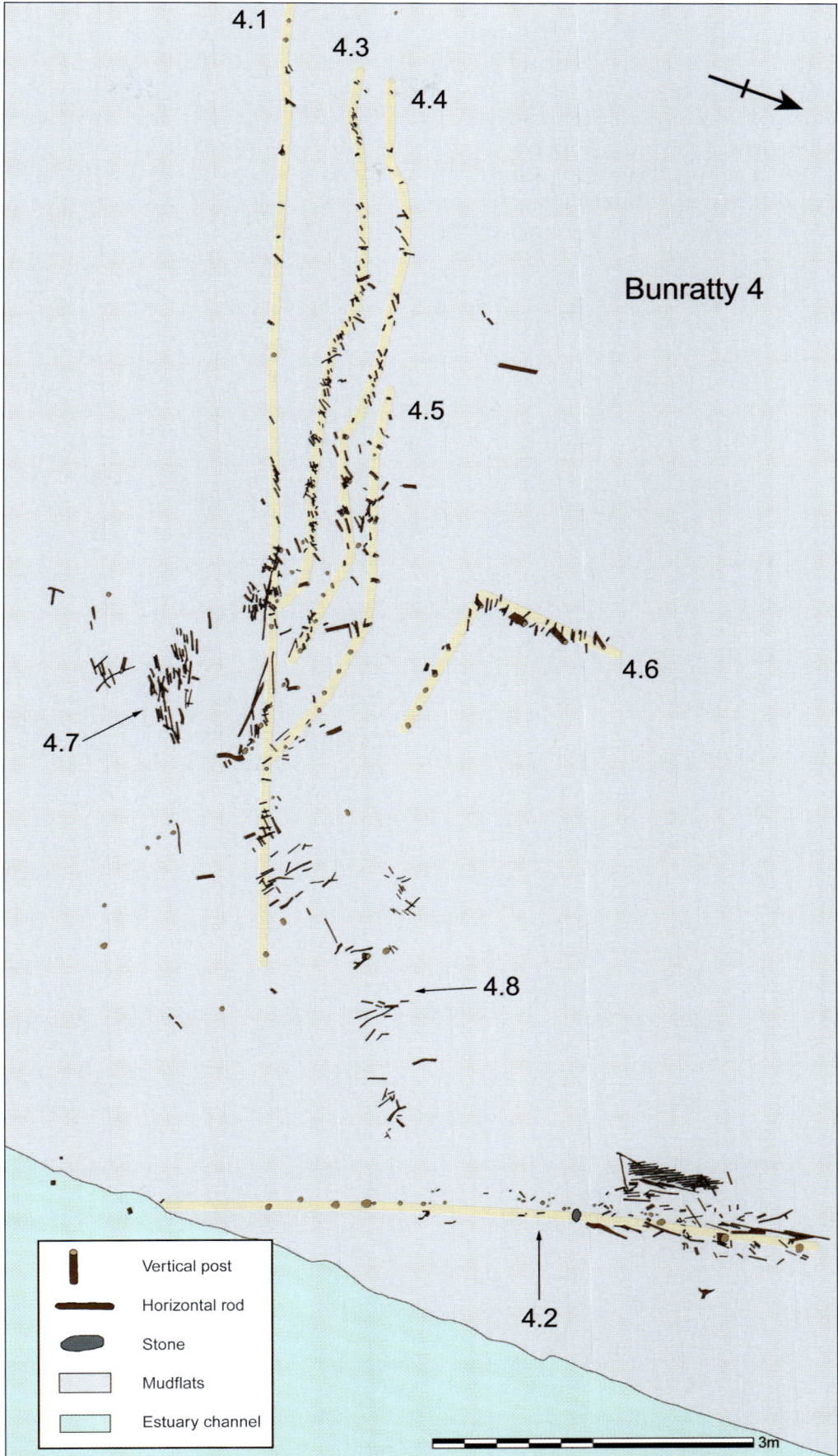

Fig. 64—*Plan of medieval fishtrap at Bunratty 4.*

Foragers, farmers and fishers

A hypothetical phased model for the chronological sequence of activity at Bunratty 4 is proposed (Fig. 65). In this model, the southernmost (4.1) and easternmost (4.2) post-and-wattle fences represent the earliest shore and flood fences respectively of the earliest trap on the site (Phase A). The need to repair the fences and the introduction of a new style of V-shaped fishtrap using horizontal baskets may have required the movement of the shore fence northwards in two phases (Phases B and C). In the final phase of activity (Phase D), the largest and most prominent post-and-wattle fences (4.5 and 4.6) represented the last reconstruction and repair of the trap. Thereafter the site was abandoned and no further attempt was made to repair it.

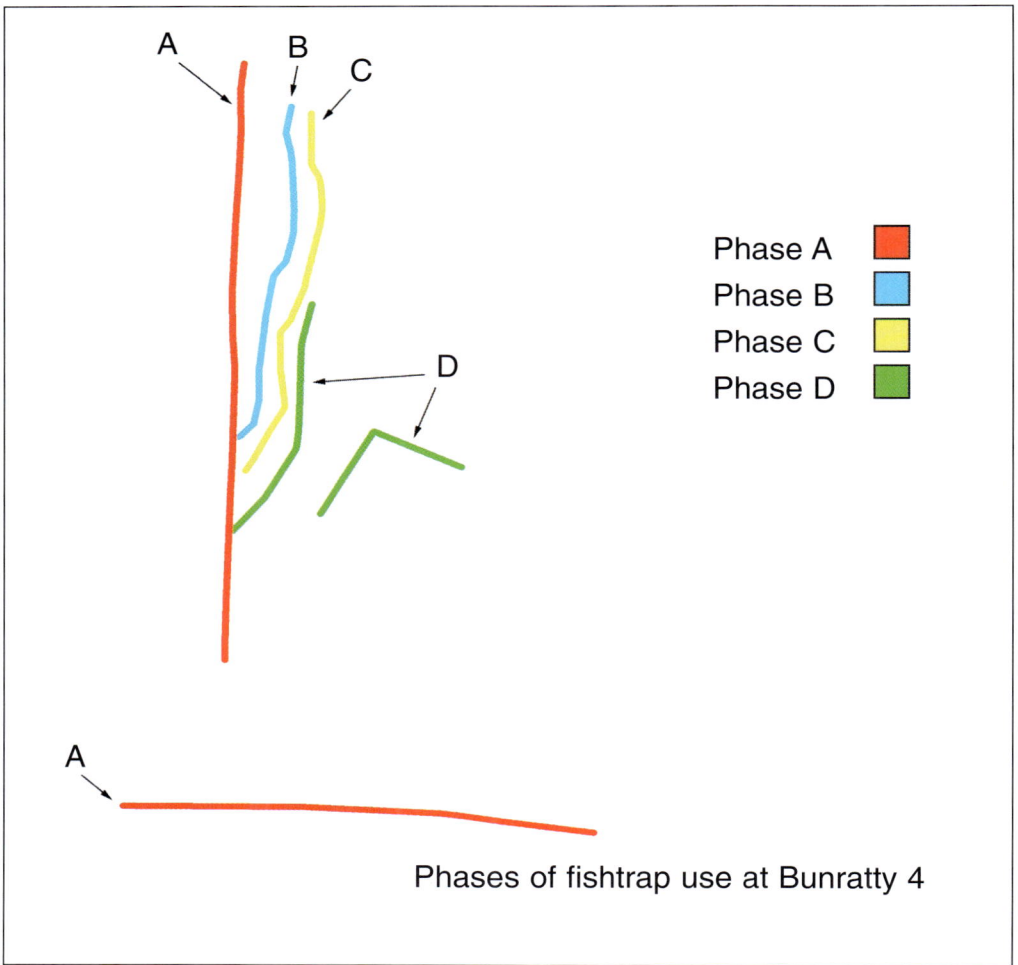

Fig. 65—*Schematic plan indicating possible phases of activity at medieval fishtrap at Bunratty 4.*

Phase A

The earliest fishtrap appears to have been a simple V-shaped structure of two converging fences of vertical posts, wattle, brushwood and twigs, represented by the southern and eastern fences, Bunratty 4.1 and 4.2. This fishtrap was probably oriented towards the north-west.

Bunratty 4.1, the possible southern or shore fence of this fishtrap, is a vertical post alignment, oriented east-north-east/west-south-west, running directly down the modern foreshore. It is constructed of at least sixteen vertical narrow roundwood posts, 2–4cm in diameter, spaced at intervals of 50cm. Some rods are interwoven around these posts. The fence is at least 5m long, but possibly runs for up to 12m down the foreshore to the southern end of a second fence, B4.2.

Bunratty 4.2, the flood fence of this early fishtrap, is located at the eastern edge of the site. It runs diagonally down the foreshore and is oriented north-north-west/south-south-east. It is constructed of at least 27 vertical roundwood posts and measures at least 7m in length. The posts vary in size, with the larger posts towards the northern end of the fence measuring 4–6cm in diameter. Most of the posts, however, measure 2–3cm in diameter. The large posts are spaced at 55–65cm intervals, the smaller posts at 25cm intervals. Horizontal rods are woven around these vertical posts. Brushwood rods, branches and twigs lie against the western side of the structure, forming a 'mat' about 1.5m long by 50cm wide which may have been a trackway designed to provide a stable walking surface beside the vertical fence. Its posts have been eroded down to their sharpened tips, suggesting that the mudflats contemporary with the structure were originally 10–20cm higher than the modern level.

Phase B

Phase B, the second phase of fishtrap construction, is possibly represented by Bunratty 4.3, a vertical post-and-wattle fence 50cm north of Bunratty 4.1. It is oriented east-north-east/west-south-west and measures 5.6m in length before it merges with Bunratty 4.1. The largest vertical posts are 3–4cm in diameter and are widely spaced at intervals of about 50cm. However, between these larger vertical posts there are smaller vertical stakes (2–3cm in diameter) and horizontal rods (1–3cm in diameter), making the entire structure dense and tightly woven. The Bunratty 4.3 fence meanders slightly as it descends the foreshore, and it is possible that it also turns towards the south-east, where there is a dense cluster of posts and brushwood.

Phase C

Phase C, the third phase of fishtrap construction, may be represented by Bunratty 4.4, a vertical post-and-wattle fence in the middle of the complex. It is situated 20cm north of Bunratty 4.3 and runs parallel with it. It is oriented east-north-east/west-south-west before turning slightly to the right, from which point it is oriented east-south-east/west-north-west. It is only a short (3.5m) length of post-and-wattle, constructed of vertical roundwood posts, 6.5–8.5cm in diameter, spaced at 20–30cm intervals. Between these vertical posts, stout rods (4–5cm in diameter) were diagonally interwoven using an unusual post-and-wattle technique. The resulting fence was of quite dense construction.

Phase D

Phase D, the fourth or final phase of fishtrap construction, may be represented by two individual features, Bunratty 4.5 and 4.6. Bunratty 4.5, possibly the shore fence, is a vertical post-and-wattle fence 20–30cm to the north of Bunratty 4.4. It runs parallel to this feature and is initially oriented east-north-east/west-south-west before turning down the foreshore to an east-south-east/west-south-west orientation. It measures 7m in length and is constructed of at least sixteen vertical roundwood posts (5–7cm in diameter), spaced at intervals of 3–4cm. Numerous smaller rods (2–3cm in diameter) were woven diagonally down between these vertical posts, creating a tightly woven post-and-wattle fence. There are several vertical posts at the eastern end of the fence, although these are not associated with any brushwood or rods.

Bunratty 4.6 may be the flood fence of this final fishtrap and is situated 1m to the north. It is a small, unusual, L-shaped feature. Its northern end is a stoutly built post-and-wattle fence, oriented roughly north/south, 1.3m in length. It is constructed of four vertical posts, 6–8cm in diameter, spaced at intervals of 50cm. It turns sharply to the east at its southern end, where it becomes a vertical post alignment running down the foreshore, oriented roughly east/west, composed of six vertical roundwood posts (6–8cm in diameter). Between them, Bunratty 4.5 and 4.6 create a small, narrow, V-shaped structure leading to a regular rectangular space on the lower foreshore which may have been the location of a woven basket.

Other brushwood features

Other enigmatic features are located on the site. Bunratty 4.7 is a small area (2m by

Foragers, farmers and fishers

Pl. 49—*Aerial photograph of creek flowing through mudflats to the south of Bunratty. The medieval fishtrap at Bunratty 6 is located on the right of the large curve in the creek in the middle foreground, near the main Shannon estuary channel (photo: Shannon Estuary Ports).*

1.5m) of horizontal post-and-wattle, brushwood and twigs to the south-east of Bunratty 4.3. It may have been a trackway or brushwood structure for fishermen to walk on. Bunratty 4.8 is a linear scatter of brushwood (4.5m by 1m), oriented north-east/south-west, located south-east of Bunratty 4.5 and 4.6 and running towards Bunratty 4.2. It may have been designed to prevent the tides from scouring out the clays behind the trap, or it could have been for fishermen to walk on when they were removing fish from the baskets.

Site interpretation

Bunratty 4 was clearly reconstructed and repaired on several occasions. The interpretation offered here proposes that there were at least four phases of activity at the site, representing two different styles of fishtrap. The earliest fishtrap (Phase A) may have been a simple, basic V-shaped structure. The second (Phase B), third (Phase C) and fourth (Phase D) phases of activity involved the use of slightly more complex, although still small, V-shaped fishtraps. Phase D gives the best impression of the appearance of the fishtrap towards the end of its life. It was a small, V-shaped structure of two converging post-and-wattle fences, with a rectangular space defined at the apex by two parallel rows of vertical posts. A basket or net may have been placed within this area. Indeed, the layout and dimensions of this space (4.6m in length by 80cm in width) compare closely with the actual dimensions (4.2m in length by 70cm in width) of the surviving Bunratty 6 basket (see below). There are also two baskets to the north (Bunratty 3A and 3B) that may have been used in this structure.

Bunratty 6—fishtrap (post-and-wattle fence and basket)

Site location

Bunratty 6 is located on the north bank of the Shannon estuary, in a creek on the mudflats more or less midway between Quay Island and Illaunbeg Point (Fig. 59; Pl. 49), *c.* 80–100m north of the LWM of the Shannon estuary channel. The site is being exposed by erosion of the sides of a modern creek that flows in a generally south-eastern direction across the mudflats. Bunratty 6 lies on the east bank of this creek, just where it meanders towards the south. The site is a spectacularly well-preserved medieval fishtrap, with a post-and-wattle fence leading to a large woven horizontal basket. A hazel 'stake' from the basket was radiocarbon-dated to 820 ± 35 BP (cal. AD

1164–1279; GrN-21934).

Repeated visits to the site have revealed various details of its construction. In September 1995 the basket appeared to measure 2.5m in length, and only a 5m length of the post-and-wattle fence was exposed to the north. In February 1997 considerably more detail about the fence was recorded, and the basket (now seen to be 4.1m in length) was excavated, with two narrow (1m by 0.3m) trenches dug across it. In March 1999 a brief visit to the site revealed that the post-and-wattle fence was longer, more substantial and more complex than had previously been realised.

The site in its original environment

Bunratty 6 is situated today on a low, level shelf of blue-grey estuarine clays on the east bank of the modern creek. The orientation of the structure directly towards the sloping sides of the creek indicated that it could never have functioned as a fishtrap in modern times. The stratigraphical and lithological evidence of finely laminated, downward-tilting sediments in the 'cliff' at the western edge of the clay shelf also suggests that the structure originally functioned in the bed of a now-buried palaeochannel. The modern creek is cutting across and exposing this ancient, silted-up palaeochannel (a previous channel of the River Owenagarney?), which probably flowed in a north-east/south-west direction. The Bunratty 6 fishtrap was originally constructed in the bed of that large creek.

Site description

The Bunratty 6 site (Pl. 50; Fig. 66) comprises a vertical post-and-wattle fence (6.1) leading to a large, woven, horizontal basket (6.2). Three obliquely set posts (6.3) in the clays to the west of the fence may be the remains of diagonal braces for the vertical structure. A horizontal post-and-wattle panel (6.4) lies immediately beside the fence at its southern end, beside the basket. The basket lies deeply buried in the clays and is itself surrounded by vertical posts (6.5). There is also a small cluster of vertical wooden posts at the end of the basket (6.6).

Pl. 50—*Medieval fishtrap at Bunratty 6, showing basket and posts of wooden supporting framework in foreground.*

Foragers, farmers and fishers

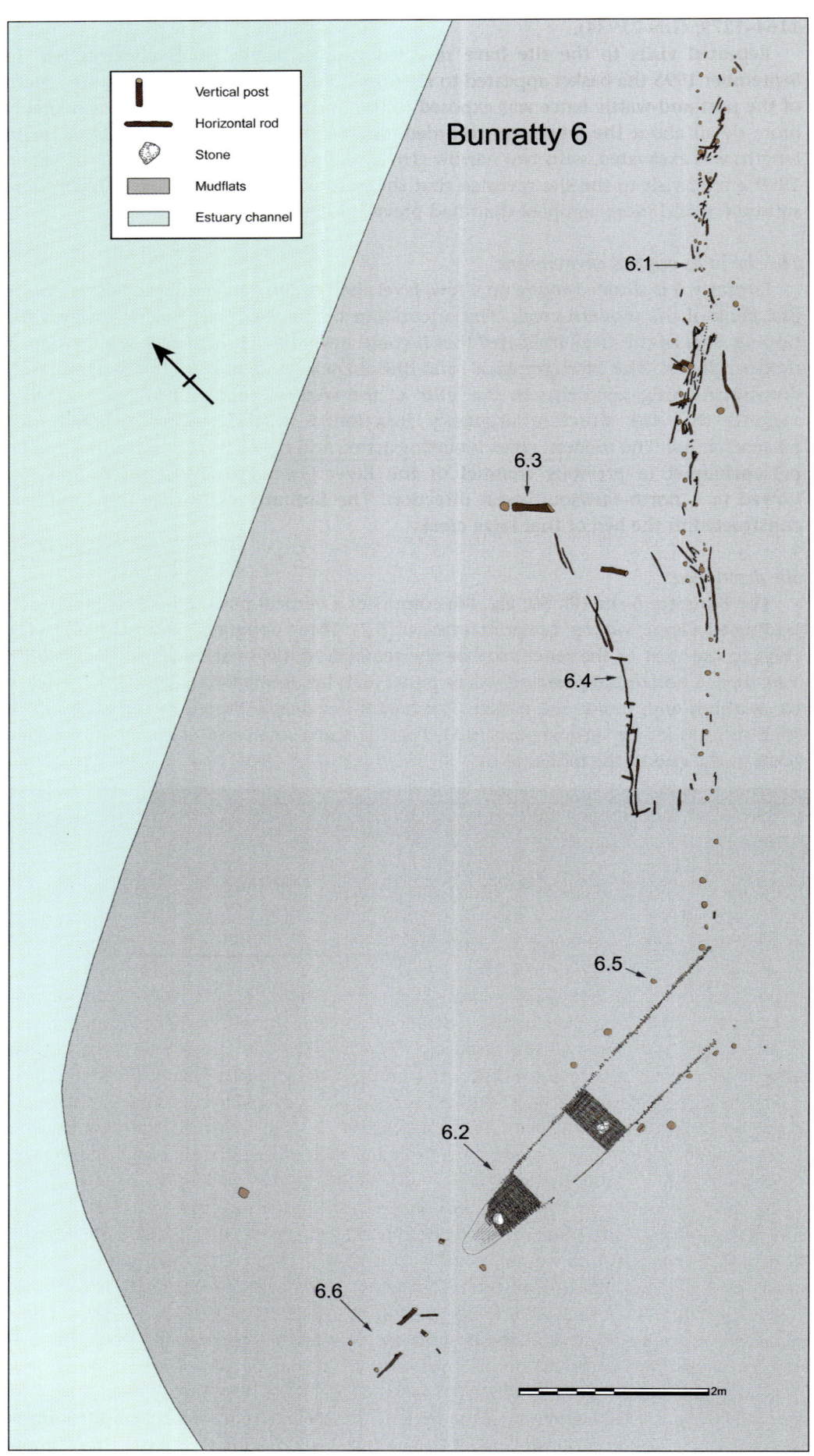

Fig. 66—*Plan of Bunratty 6 medieval fishtrap.*

Early historic and medieval fishtraps

Pl. 51—Medieval fishtrap at Bunratty 6 from north-east, showing post-and-wattle fence.

The vertical fence—post-and-wattle and posts

The vertical fence (6.1) is oriented north/south and measures at least 10m in exposed length (although the presence of three vertical posts 11m further to the north suggests that it actually measures up to 22m in length). It is set at an angle of 45° to the basket and is *c.* 50cm wide. It is constructed of at least 69 vertical posts, with horizontal rods, brushwood and post-and-wattle panels. The vertical posts vary in spacing, height and diameter, but appear to form a double row of posts and stakes. Numerous stout brushwood rods lie beside and in the space between these two vertical post-and-wattle structures (Pl. 51).

The main post alignment was constructed of 33 posts, 6–8cm in diameter, spaced at intervals of 20–30cm. The posts protrude above the clays to a height of 20cm, although one survived to a height of 50cm. In places, two posts are set beside each other, probably to strengthen or repair the fence. The post alignment bellies out to the west at a point 3m north of the basket, perhaps as a result of repair or sagging. An oblique roundwood post set against the fence at this point may have been intended as a supporting brace (see 6.3 below). Horizontal rods, 2–4cm in diameter, are woven around some of these vertical posts.

A second post-and-wattle fence of slighter construction appears to be located immediately to the east, running parallel with this post alignment. It was constructed of at least 28 narrower, vertical roundwood stakes, 3–4cm in diameter, spaced at 20cm intervals. These stakes have a dense layer of horizontal rods, 2.5–3.5cm in diameter, interwoven between them. This second post-and-wattle fence is at its most substantial at the curved-out area of the structure.

A separate post-and-wattle panel, 1m in width, may have been placed against the main vertical fence at a point 6.2m north of the basket. This panel, represented by 20–30 narrow rods pointing out of the clays, appears to have been placed up on its end in the clays, with its long axis pointing upwards. It may have been laid against the

Foragers, farmers and fishers

Pl. 52—*Detail of medieval fishtrap fence, showing repair in mid-length, the horizontal post-and-wattle panel in the clays, and the obliquely set supporting timber in the background.*

fence and pinned in position.

There are also stout, vertical roundwood posts 'in front of', or to the east of, the two parallel vertical post-and-wattle structures. They are located 20cm east of the main fences, measure 6–7cm in diameter and survive to heights of 10cm. These posts, typically located towards the middle and north-eastern ends of the fence, may have served to support the entire structure against the force of the incoming or flooding tide.

The vertical fence—its obliquely set braces

Three obliquely set posts (6.3) are located to the west of the vertical structure. Two are set at 10cm and 20cm intervals respectively from the fence, while the third is set tightly against it. These oblique posts are all of roundwood, 6–8cm in diameter, surviving to lengths of 60cm. They are set at an angle of 20–30° from the horizontal, with their upper ends pointing towards the east. Their size and orientation suggest that their original upper ends would have been jammed against the post-and-wattle fence, 1–2m above its base. They are located at the middle of the fence, where it may have been sagging or collapsing, and can be interpreted as roundwood poles deliberately shoved or braced against the vertical post-and-wattle fence on its downstream side, to support it against the force of the ebbing tide (Pl. 52).

The vertical fence—the horizontal post-and-wattle

A post-and-wattle panel (6.4) lies horizontally in the clays, west of the vertical fence and immediately north of the basket. It measures 1.6m in length by 60cm in width and is constructed of five vertical sails, 3–4cm in diameter, spaced at 35–40cm intervals. Between these sails were woven at least nine horizontal rods, 1.8–2.8cm in diameter. The post-and-wattle panel is of stout construction, with thick, knotty sails and rods used in the weave. These sails and rods may have been taken from topwood branches

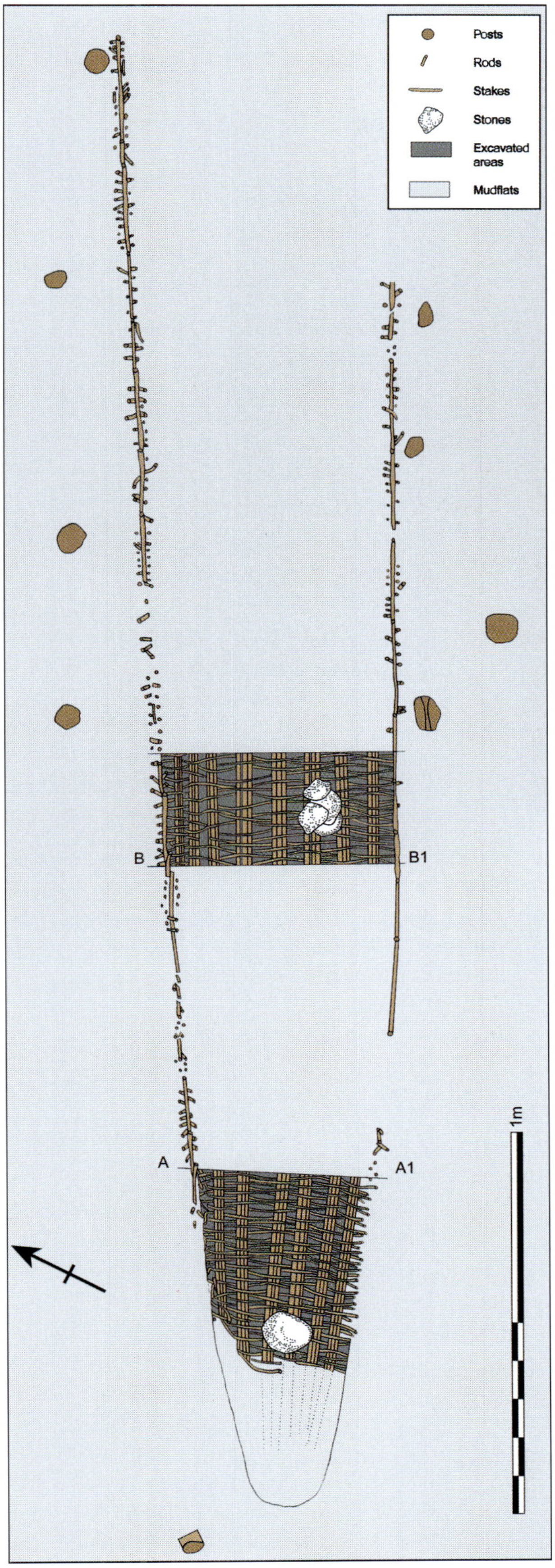

Early historic and medieval fishtraps

Pl. 53—*Detail of basket at Bunratty 6, from south-west, showing vertical posts along sides and at end.*

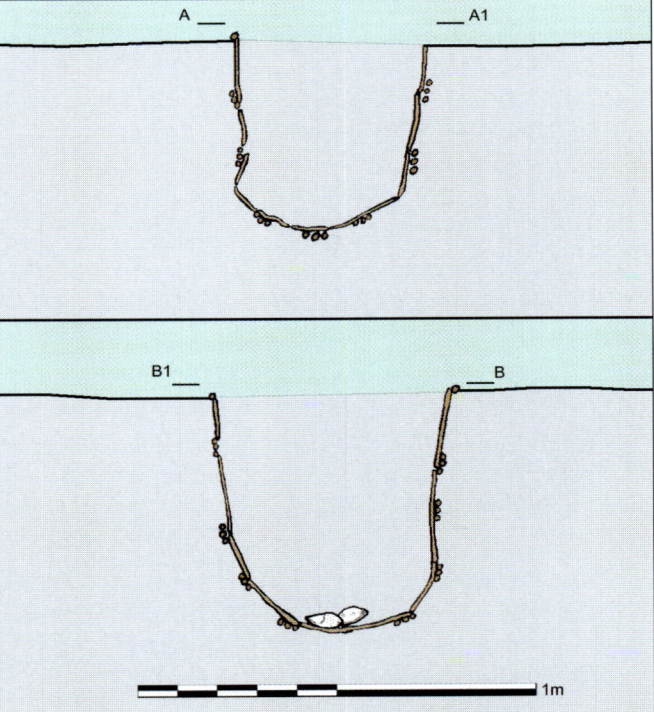

Fig. 67—*Plan (above) and cross-sections (above right) of basket at Bunratty 6.*

Foragers, farmers and fishers

Pl. 54—*Detail of weave inside end of Bunratty 6 basket.*

rather than well-managed coppice woodland, as they are thick and irregular. This post-and-wattle panel, lying recumbent in the clays just beside the vertical posts of the fence, may have fallen away from that structure.

The basket

A large basket (6.2) is situated at the south end of the vertical post-and-wattle fences (Pl. 53; Fig. 67). It was buried deep in the clays but was investigated in detail; two narrow trenches were excavated to examine its internal surfaces, revealing that the sides and base of the basket were remarkably well preserved. Although compression may have altered its shape, it survives basically intact in the clay, with only a section of its upper surface removed by erosion. The basket has a long, narrow shape, with parallel sides that narrow only slowly from the mouth, which is oriented north-east/south-west. It measures at least 4.1m in length and 70cm in maximum width (at the mouth). It is considerably narrower at the south-west end, about 20cm in width. The sides curve down to a depth of at least 0.65m, forming a broad U shape in cross-section.

The basket was made of *c.* 100–150 stakes, around which were woven hundreds of rods (known in basket-making as 'weavers'). The longitudinal 'warp' elements of the basket consisted of three hazel rods, 1.4–2cm in diameter, tightly packed together to form a single composite 'stake', 4–5cm in overall width. These stakes were spaced at 5–8cm intervals. The 'weft' was of narrow hazel rods, 0.5–1.8cm in diameter, woven around these stakes in a simple in-and-out manner. The weave of the basket was quite tight, especially towards the end of the basket (Pl. 54). The rods were also 'tucked in' behind the stakes to make a neat internal weave for the trap.

There were at least four small limestone pebbles (8–10cm in length) lying in the base of the basket near the middle. A single larger stone (10–13cm long) lay in the basket near its narrow end. It is likely that similar stones were located elsewhere in the basket, presumably to give it some extra weight and stability in the water. A large ball of moss and wood fragments (*c.* 10cm in diameter) recovered from the narrow end of the basket may have been a 'bung' used to close up the end.

The basket—its supporting vertical posts

Eight vertical roundwood posts (6.5) are situated on either side of the horizontal basket (three on its south side, five on its north side) (Pl. 53). These posts measure 5–7cm in diameter, are spaced at intervals of 0.5–1m, and are typically located *c.* 25cm

Early historic and medieval fishtraps

Fig. 68—*Reconstruction of medieval fishtrap at Bunratty 6 in its original setting, with vertical post-and-wattle fences, a basket on a framework and local fishermen using and repairing the structure from boats (painting by Simon Dick).*

from the sides of the basket. They survive to depths of 1m in the clays (it proved impossible during the excavation to obtain a sharpened end from them). They form a trapezoidal structure, 3.6m long, 1m wide at the north-eastern end and 50cm wide at the south-western end. This may have been a wooden framework or platform upon which the basket was originally laid or hung, to prevent it drifting away in the channel and from filling up with silts. The heaviest part of the basket (i.e. the body and mouth) appears to have lain within the strongest part of the structure, where it would have required most support.

The basket—the vertical posts at its end

There was also a cluster of vertical roundwood posts, 5–6cm in diameter, at the south-west end of the basket. These were situated 1.4cm from the basket and may originally have supported a 'weel' (a smaller, portable basket) at the end of the larger basket. This smaller basket could then have been taken off and emptied of fish at low tide. Alternatively, the posts may have had a supporting function in relation to the large basket.

Site interpretation

The Bunratty 6 fishtrap was probably V-shaped, with two converging fences, perhaps up to 20m in length, leading towards a woven basket on a platform. It was an ebb weir, designed to catch eels and other fish on an ebbing tide. The single exposed fence was at least 10m long (although the presence of other posts suggests that this is a minimum measurement) and was constructed of two rows of vertical roundwood posts, against which were placed several post-and-wattle panels. Brushwood and interwoven rods may also have been laid in the gap between the inner and outer rows of posts (Fig. 68).

The post-and-wattle fence probably stood to a height of at least 1.5–2m. Posts driven into the clays immediately upstream of the fence also helped to keep it upright in the tides. The post-and-wattle fence was probably repaired at the middle, where there is a dense concentration of vertical posts, a post-and-wattle panel placed on its end and some oblique or bracing posts. The basket measured at least 4.1m in length and 70cm in diameter and was supported by a wooden framework (Pl. 55). It may have had a second, portable basket placed at its end. The site is remarkably well preserved and may have been abandoned after a sudden flood event, when the entire structure was buried under a heavy burden of clays and silts.

Pl. 55—*Replica of Bunratty 6 basket on display at King John's Castle, Limerick, in summer 1999, illustrating its striking original size and appearance.*

Bunratty wood studies
AIDAN O'SULLIVAN AND MARY B. DEEVY

Wood species identifications and tree-ring counts were carried out on 121 samples taken from the Bunratty 2, Bunratty 4 and Bunratty 6 fishtraps. The samples were taken from several different features within these structures, including vertical posts, horizontal rods and woven baskets. The wood was in good condition.

Bunratty 2

Ten samples of wood were retained for analysis. Two native Irish tree species were identified in this post alignment, including seven pieces of hazel (*Corylus* sp.) and three pieces of willow (*Salix* sp.). In terms of tree-ring ages, the posts were relatively immature, ranging in age from 7 to 12 years, with an average age of 10 years. The sampled posts ranged in diameter from 2cm to 4.5cm, with an average of 3.2cm.

Bunratty 4

Thirty samples of wood were retained for analysis, including nine vertical posts and 21 horizontal rods (Fig. 69). Six native Irish species of wood were identified. Hazel dominated the assemblage (17 samples), followed by smaller amounts of alder (6), oak (4), birch (1), ash (1) and willow (1). In terms of species selection, the posts were mostly of alder, with single posts of hazel, oak and willow. The posts ranged in age from 7 to 26 years, with an average of 14.9 years, and measured 2.5–5cm in diameter. The rods were overwhelmingly of hazel (16), with a few oak rods (3) and single examples of ash and willow. They ranged in age from 3 to 20 years, with an average age of 7 years. They ranged in diameter from 1.3cm to 2.3cm.

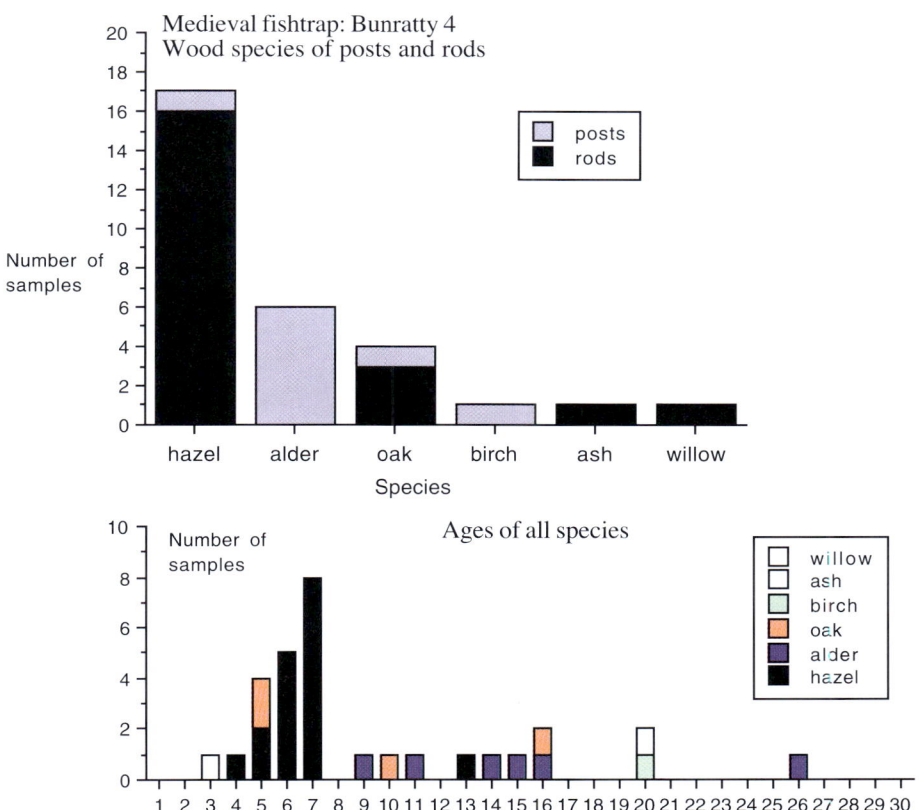
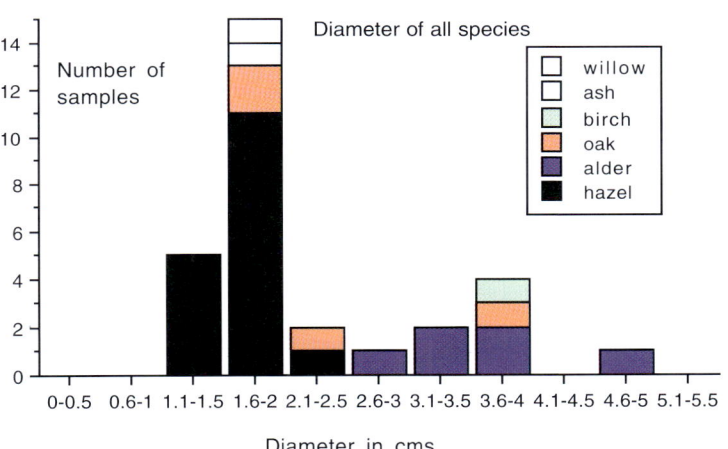

Fig. 69—*Wood species identifications from Bunratty 4.*

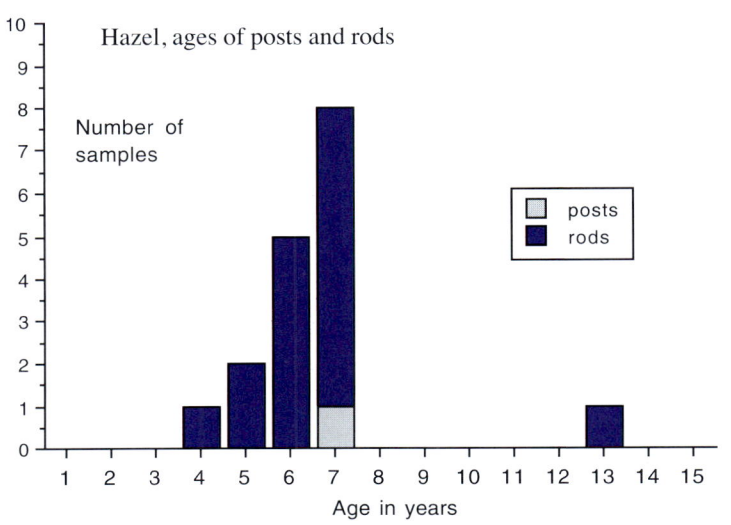

Foragers, farmers and fishers

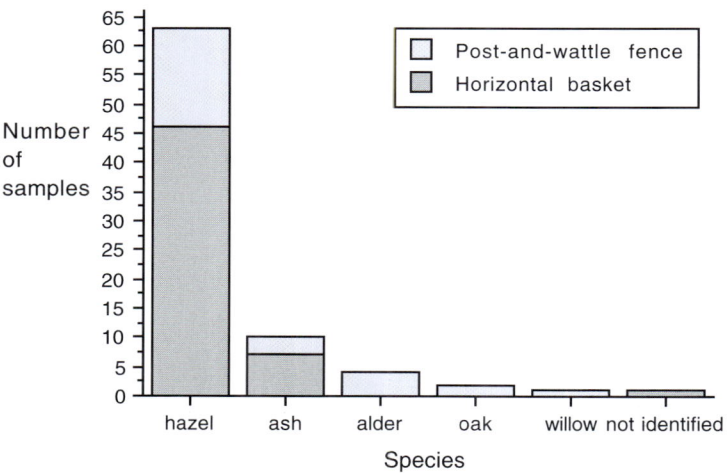

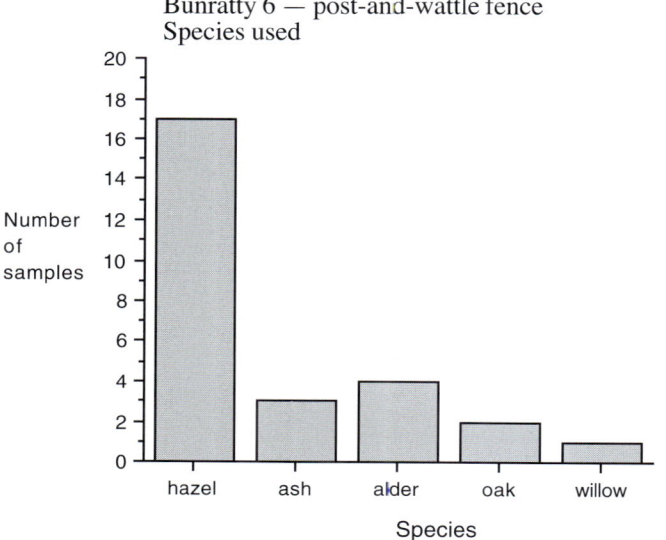

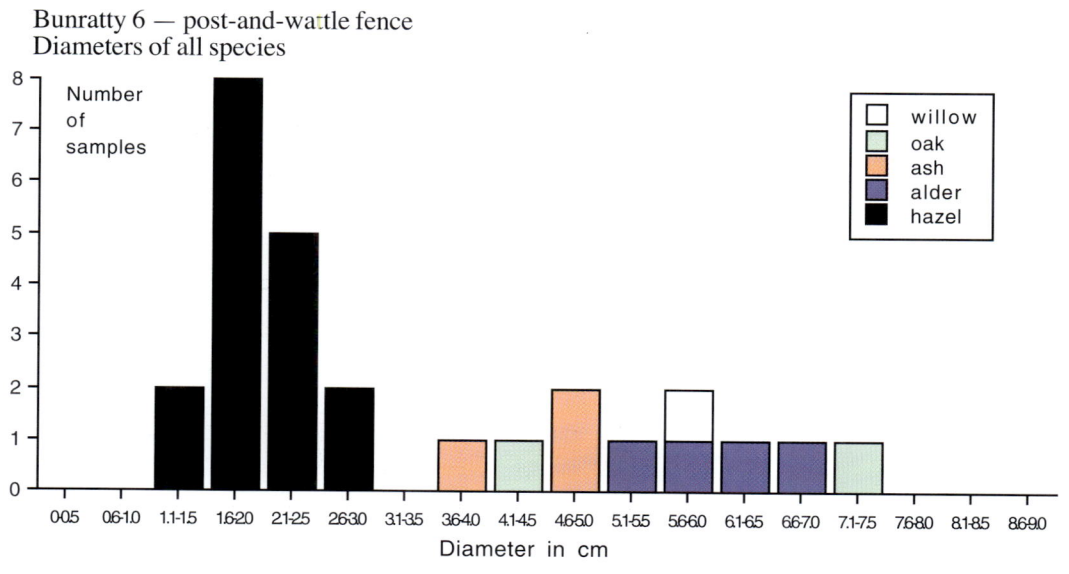

Fig. 70 *(left and opposite)—Wood species identifications from Bunratty 6.*

Early historic and medieval fishtraps

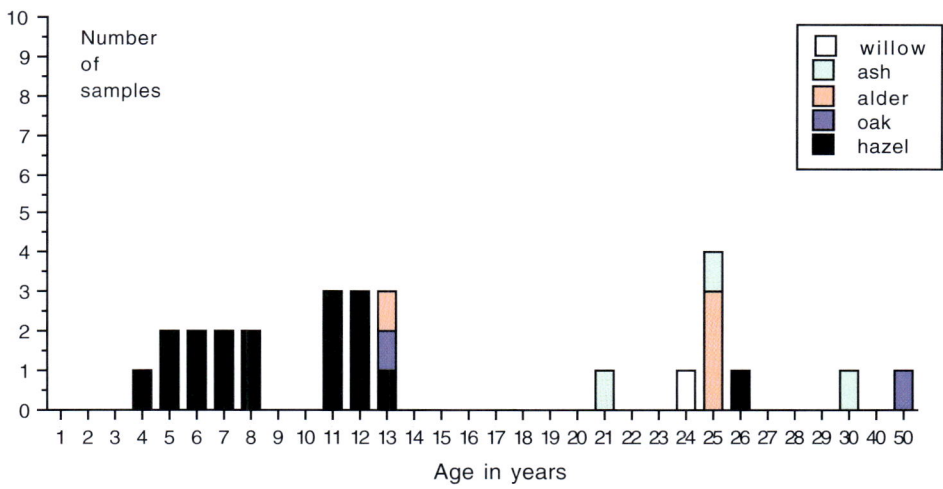

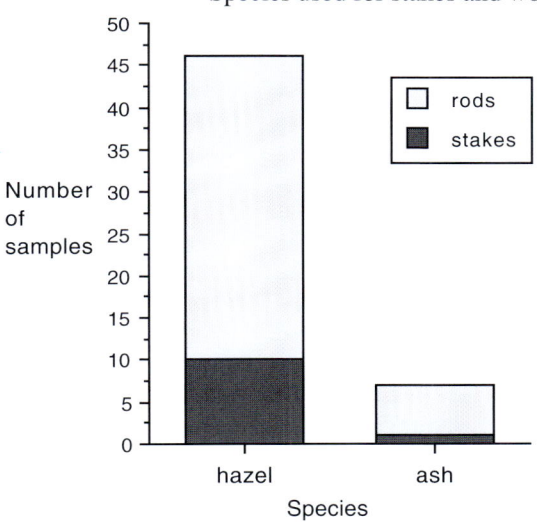

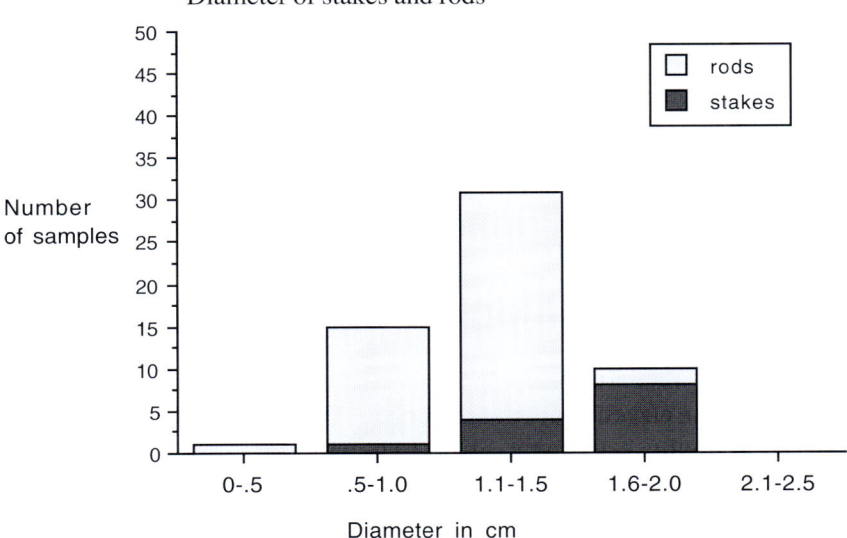

175

There was some evidence for woodland management in the hazel rods. Although they ranged in age from 4 to 13 years, with an average age of 6.6 years, most were aged 6–7 years. This is a typical age for coppiced woodland cropping. The alder posts and rods ranged more widely in age from 9 to 26 years, with an average of 15 years. It is likely that a combination of wetland woodland and some dryland woodland was used for Bunratty 4. The hazel woodland may have been managed, although the sample is too small to ascertain this.

Bunratty 6

The Bunratty 6 fishtrap was extensively sampled for wood species identification and tree-ring studies. Eighty-one samples of wood were examined, 54 from the basket and 27 from the post-and-wattle fence (Fig. 70). Five native Irish tree species were identified. Hazel (*Corylus avellana*) dominated the assemblage with 63 samples, followed by ten pieces of ash (*Fraxinus excelsior*), four pieces of alder (*Alnus* sp.), two of oak (*Quercus* sp.) and one of willow/poplar (*Salix/Populus*). A single sample could not be identified because of its poor condition.

The vertical post-and-wattle fence was constructed mostly of hazel (17), with smaller amounts of alder (4), ash (3), oak (2) and a post of either willow or poplar. The samples from the fence were aged from 4 to 50 years, with an average age of 15.4 years. They ranged in diameter from 1.3cm to 7.5cm, with an average of 3.4cm. The hazel posts tended to be the youngest, ranging in age from 4 to 26 years, with an average age of 9.6 years. The alder posts ranged in age from 13 to 25 years. The ash posts were typically more mature, ranging in age from 21 to 30 years.

The horizontal basket was made almost entirely of hazel. Of the 54 samples of wood examined (including 11 stakes and 43 rods) 46 were of hazel, with a small but significant amount of ash (7). The longitudinal stakes of the basket were almost exclusively of hazel (10 samples), with only a single stake of ash. These hazel stakes ranged in age from 3 to 6 years, with an average age of 4.7 years. They measured between 1.4cm and 2cm in diameter, with an average of 1.7cm. The rods were also mostly of hazel (36 samples), with 6 rods of ash. They ranged in diameter from 0.5cm to 1.8cm, with an average of 1.2cm. In terms of tree-ring ages, the hazel rods were aged between 2 and 6 years, with an average age of 4.5 years. The hazel wood used was tightly restricted in age profile, typically 4–5 years. It seems likely that the Bunratty 6 basket was made from rods harvested from a managed, coppiced woodland of hazel and ash. Only such high-quality woodland would have produced the fine, regular rods needed for this intricate task.

Discussion

The Bunratty fishtraps are located on the mudflats immediately south of one of the most significant medieval nucleated settlements on the Shannon estuary. Bunratty, Co. Clare, as attested by historical evidence, was probably a focus of settlement from at least the tenth century to the seventeenth century (J. Bradley 1988b; J. Bradley and King 1991; J. O'Brien 1999; Ryan 1981). In particular, it was an important Anglo-Norman borough between the mid-thirteenth and early fourteenth centuries. However, although there are obviously late medieval fortifications like Bunratty Castle itself (Pl. 56) and a late medieval parish church, there are few archaeological traces of pre-fifteenth-century settlement activity (J. Bradley and King 1991). Indeed, it might be argued that the eleventh- to thirteenth-century fishtraps of Bunratty 4 and Bunratty 6 are the first *archaeological* evidence for earlier medieval settlement in the vicinity.

The Bunratty 4 fishtrap has been radiocarbon-dated to 1018–1159, well before any Anglo-Norman activity at this location. This may indicate that there was some settlement at Bunratty in the eleventh or twelfth century, but whether this was a native Irish dwelling or an outlying settlement associated with Hiberno-Norse Limerick remains unknown. There is a possible early historic ringfort at Clonmoney West and there are other settlement enclosures in the vicinity, such as at Saint's Island in the

Early historic and medieval fishtraps

Pl. 56—*Aerial photograph of the late medieval castle at Bunratty, probably located on the site of the Anglo-Norman borough (CUCAP AJW 03).*

estuary. The historical sources, while ambiguous, suggest that there may have been a Viking settlement at Bunratty in the tenth century. The twelfth-century *Cogadh Gaedhael re Gallaibh* states that they established a fortress in Tratraighe (Tradree) *c.* 960 (*CGG*, 61), possibly at Bunratty (J. Bradley 1988b, 20).

The earliest evidence for Anglo-Norman settlement at Bunratty may be represented by a motte-and-bailey at Clonmoney West (Fig. 59), possibly relating to the granting of territories at Traddery to Arnold Keating in 1199. The motte-and-bailey overlooks the Shannon estuary and consists of a circular, flat-topped mound with an adjoining triangular bailey (Ryan 1981; J. O'Brien 1999). However, the Anglo-Norman manor of Bunratty was first established in earnest in 1248, with the granting of the cantred of Traderry to Robert de Muscegros. By 1251 a possible castle or ringwork was under construction, and by 1253 de Muscegros was allowed to have a 'vill', with a weekly market and yearly fair, in his land at 'Bunraty'. In 1277 Bunratty passed to Thomas de Clare, who built a stone castle (Murphy 1980) and, according to the fourteenth-century *Caithréim Thoirdhealbhaigh*, populated it with English tenants (O'Grady 1929, 7–8).

By this stage, Bunratty had acquired borough status (Fig. 59). There is no charter for the borough, but on de Clare's death in 1287 an extent of the manor of Bunratty was drawn up which indicates that it had a substantial population, with 226 burgages (implying a population of about 1000) paying £131. 6s. in annual rent. The extent also notes that the borough had a seigneurial castle, a hundred court, a shambles (market) worth 3s. yearly, fairs worth half a mark yearly, a watermill, a fish-pool and a rabbit warren (J. Bradley 1988b, 20–1). The 'fishery of a pool' provided an income of 20s. a year. This was probably a fish-pond, as in 1289 a grant was given to the lord to enlarge the fish-pool (Murphy 1980, 19). In 1321 Thomas de Clare filli Ricardi had fish-weirs and rabbit warrens worth 20s. a year at Bunratty (Went 1981). These fishtraps were probably in use on the River Owenagarney and on the Shannon estuary. The Bunratty 6 fishtrap, dated to 1164–1279, was probably one of them.

Bunratty was for about 70 years (1248–1318) an important and intense focus of Anglo-Norman settlement in south-east Clare. The borough may have been surrounded by an earthen bank and ditch, a feature that is described in the *Caithreim Thoirdhealbhaigh* as 'broad-based, high-crested ramparts, running from the stream to the sea'. Westropp (1913–15) described the presence of earthen ramparts around

Bunratty, but recent excavations have cast doubt upon their early date (J. Bradley and King 1991). It is possible that these earthen banks are the remains of seventeenth-century reclamation features. Similar reclamation banks and ditches can be seen elsewhere in the corcass, particularly in the form of an unusual rectilinear enclosure at Clonmoney West, to the south-west of Bunratty (J. O'Brien 1999). There were also arable lands and meadows at various locations around the manor, including three islands in the estuary.

Bunratty was a significant medieval port or harbour, situated as it was on a low ridge overlooking a crossing-point of the river, near the mouth of the *Bun Ráite* river (the Owenagarney River), with extensive views to the south over the Shannon estuary. The fourteenth-century *Caithreim Thoirdhealbhaigh* refers to 'Bunratty of the wide roads, oared galleys and safe harbour' (O'Grady 1929, vol. ii, 122). There may also have been a plank bridge (*claidroichead*) across the river. There was one during Toirdhealbhach Ó Briain's siege of Bunratty, when *Caithreim Thoirdhealbhaigh* refers to a plank bridge that spanned the sea-channel to the opposite shore (*ibid.*, 31), preventing ships from gaining access to the castle. Throughout the late thirteenth and fourteenth centuries, Bunratty was exposed to such attacks from the Gaelic Irish. After the defeat of the Anglo-Normans at the Battle of Dysart O'Dea in 1318 the castle and town were burnt, and thereafter the borough was largely deserted. Bunratty Castle remained a significant fortification throughout the late Middle Ages, being in Irish hands throughout the fifteenth century (J. Bradley 1988b, 24).

In summary, the Bunratty 1–6 medieval fishtraps provide interesting new insights into this medieval landscape, in terms of woodland management, the consumption of fish by the local population and the economic exploitation of the estuary itself. Indeed, it is likely that the medieval fisheries on the Shannon estuary mudflats would have been an important source of revenue, providing salmon, eels and trout for the borough's markets and households.

Possible medieval fishtrap, Bush Island, Shannon estuary

Bush Island 3—basket

Site location

Bush Island 3 is located on the north bank, on the foreshore adjacent to Moyhill townland, Co. Clare, *c.* 450m west of Bush Island and *c.* 80m north-east of the estuary LWM. It is situated on the east side of a creek on the lower foreshore, in firm, shell-rich, dark grey estuarine clays that are being exposed by erosion from underneath the modern silts. These clays are very similar to the context of the medieval fishtrap at Bunratty 6.

Site description

The basket is buried in the clay, with only parts of its sides exposed (Pl. 57). It is clear that it was unusually large. It is presently subrectangular in plan, although its present shape may be due to collapse in the muds. It is difficult to assess the original form of the basket, but the convergence of stakes (i.e. the 'warp' or longitudinal elements) towards the south-south-east end may indicate that it was narrowing in that direction and therefore that its end or 'nose' was situated there, with the mouth at the opposite end.

The basket may originally have been broadly U-shaped, oriented with its mouth facing north-north-east. It measures 3.9m (east-south-east/west-north-west) in exposed width (i.e. across the mouth) by 3.6m in exposed length (north-north-east/south-south-west). The longitudinal 'warp' elements or 'stakes' of the basket were made of

Early historic and medieval fishtraps

Pl. 57—*Undated woven basket buried in dark grey clays by creek at Bush Island 3, possibly of medieval date.*

three closely spaced rods (2.2–2.5cm in diameter) set at 15cm intervals. The weft of the basket was of narrow rods (1.2–1.5cm in diameter) woven around the stakes as single, double and occasionally treble weaves. The basket was quite tightly woven. An area of narrow rods in the clays within the basket (oriented west-north-west/east-south-east, over an area 70cm by 30cm) may be fallen rods from the body of the basket.

Five roundwood posts, 6–10cm in diameter, are set in the clays at the north-east end of the basket, between it and the creek. A single post was driven vertically into the clay. The other four posts lie horizontally, with exposed sharpened points on three posts. A crude post-and-wattle panel measuring 50cm (east/west) by 40cm (north/south) lies at the north-east corner of the basket. This was woven of at least five sails (3–4cm in diameter) and five rods (2–3cm in diameter). A few small pebbles lay in the clays around the basket.

Site interpretation

The Bush Island 3 basket was first identified and rapidly recorded after the intertidal survey was completed, at a low spring tide on 4 July 2000, when it was exposed to view for about one hour. Further archaeological excavation is intended to establish its date and function. However, the similarities of context, size, method of manufacture and general appearance with the medieval baskets at Bunratty 6 (also found in clays at the side of a creek) and Bunratty 4 strongly suggest that Bush Island 3 also dates from the medieval period. It may have been pinned onto the clays of a creek, like the putts used on the Severn estuary (Godbold and Turner 1994). On the other hand, large baskets of this form were used to transport peat and fish in the eighteenth century, so further discussion will have to await future investigations.

Interpreting early historic and medieval fishtraps on the Shannon estuary

Ownership and use of the medieval fishtraps

In the Middle Ages, fishing was an important source of income, livelihood and food in coastal and maritime areas, and the ownership, regulation and use of fisheries was a key aspect of the organisation of local society and economy. Fish and shellfish were of great importance in the medieval diet (as the church forbade meat consumption on two days a week, as well as on holy days and during the six weeks of Lent). Both sea fish and freshwater fish were caught for local consumption or were preserved and transported to settlements inland, occasionally across large distances. By and large, in the early Middle Ages fishing would have been a largely rural subsistence activity, carried out by small operators, working for themselves or more frequently on behalf of local lords or monastic houses. By the later Middle Ages, the development of urban markets, improved methods of preservation and the development of Atlantic sea fisheries would have made fishing a significant source of wealth and power (Hutchinson 1994, 129–45; Aston 1988; T. O'Neill 1987). The historical and archaeological evidence presented here (and discussed in Chapter 1) suggests that fishing (using both boats and wooden fishtraps) was a significant aspect of daily life and landscape on the Shannon estuary in the early historic, Viking and medieval periods.

The early historic fishtrap at Fergus estuary east 2, dated to between the fifth and seventh centuries, certainly indicates the exploitation of fisheries at this period. Early Irish laws, hagiographies and other historical sources (although they refer to islandwide patterns) and the siting of ringforts, churches and monastic settlements along the estuary suggest that estuarine resources were certainly of some importance. At least two fishtraps (Deel estuary 1 and Bunratty 4) date from between the early eleventh century and the mid-twelfth century, a period of significant social change in Ireland. Some historians have suggested that by this stage Irish society was changing from one of clientship to one based on labour services to a lord, with the emergence of nucleated settlement forms and lordships that were semi-feudal in character (e.g. Doherty 1998, 312–29; O'Keeffe 2000, 26). Such nucleated settlements may have already been present at places like Bunratty and on the Deel estuary, and fish may have been one of the sources of food and income for their populations. It is also likely that Hiberno-Norse Limerick had an impact on the local and regional economy, providing a growing urban market for fish a few miles upstream. In any case, it is clear that a fishing industry was thriving on the Shannon estuary by the early twelfth century. For example, the Annals of Inisfallen record that in 1105 'there was caught by fishermen in the sea of Luimnech (i.e. the Shannon estuary) a fish of unheard-of size, which measured fifteen feet, and two ingots' weight were obtained for it'. The size of the fish probably indicates the use of boats and nets. More importantly, the reference to the price obtained for the fish suggests that professional fishermen were working on the estuary for a cash income.

We should envisage the fisheries of the upper Shannon estuary as a significant economic operation, in which all levels of local society were involved. The practical operation of a fishtrap requires its users to live near by, as it would need to be checked twice a day during the season. It is possible that specialist or full-time fishermen, who may occasionally have worked as free or unfree tenants on local estates and manors, were using the fishtraps. However, while the upper echelons of society may not have been directly involved with daily fishing, they would have received considerable income from the levies imposed on fishermen. It is apparent that some fisheries were owned by the local nobility and were often donated to a monastery or church. For example, the charter bequeathed to Clare Abbey by Donal Mór O'Brien in 1189 granted various fisheries and fishing rights to the Canons Regular of St Augustine (MacMahon 1993, 22).

By the Anglo-Norman period, significant social and economic changes were in train on the upper estuary, as elsewhere. Anglo-Norman manors, ecclesiastical houses, boroughs and towns were all developing, with an intensive manorial economy based on tillage, pastoralism and haymaking on the meadows and corcass. It is possible that fishing was also of importance. Certainly, there are several fishtraps that date from the Anglo-Norman period, between the late twelfth and fourteenth centuries (Bunratty 6, Deel estuary 2 and 3). It is likely that by this stage most fisheries on the upper estuary would have been taken into the hands of monastic houses, bishops and manorial lords.

Interestingly, despite significant socio-political change at Bunratty, there is little evidence for any changes in the style of fishtraps used across time (i.e. before and after the Anglo-Norman colonisation). This is unsurprising as it is likely that there was significant social and cultural continuity at Bunratty anyway, with the Gaelic Irish perhaps working as free tenants or betaghs on the Anglo-Norman manor of Bunratty in the thirteenth and fourteenth centuries. While English burgesses and peasant farmers may well have been introduced into Bunratty (as claimed in the fourteenth-century *Caithréim Thoirdhealbhaigh*), the archaeological evidence suggests that local Gaelic Irish fishermen continued to use and tend the fishtraps on the mudflats, employing fishing techniques similar to those used by their forefathers for generations.

Some fisheries would have supplied salmon, eels, trout and flounder directly to local households, while other fish may have been sold in local urban markets. It is also possible that fish were smoked, salted or dried at processing centres in places like Askeaton, Bunratty or Limerick and thereafter transported over larger distances inland. However, the small size of the fishtraps at the Deel estuary and Bunratty may indicate that they were primarily designed to catch fish for local communities living in the immediate vicinity. But even if the fishtraps were primarily for local production in the thirteenth and fourteenth centuries, it is still likely that their construction and use were closely regulated and their annual catch used to provide a valuable rental income for their Anglo-Norman or Gaelic lords. Indeed, historical sources attest to a variety of grants, leasings and court cases concerning the fisheries of the Shannon estuary in the medieval period. For example, the fisheries of Limerick town are first mentioned in 1200, when William de Braose received the honour of Limerick 'with all its appurtenances in . . . water and mills and fish-ponds and ponds and fisheries and ponds' (Lenihan 1866, 48–9). Indeed, the name *Lex Were* or *Lax Weir* is mentioned for the first time in a charter of Henry V which granted the salmon fishery on the River Shannon to the north of Limerick to the citizens of the city in 1414 (Herbert 1946–7, 53).

It is likely that the fifteenth-century tower-houses prominently sited on the estuary at places like Ballysteen, Courtbrown and Beagh, Co. Limerick, and at Cratloemoyle, Cratloekeel and Castledonnell, Co. Clare, were all sited with the estuary's navigation and fisheries in mind. The sea fisheries on the lower Shannon estuary had also become important, with cod, hake and herring being caught there by boat. Indeed, it has been suggested that the herring fisheries in particular brought increased income to the Shannon estuary, partly funding the renewed building of monasteries, churches and tower-houses from the late fifteenth century onwards (T. O'Neill 1987, 34–8). In an era when 100 days of the year were designated as days of abstinence from meat, salmon in particular was in constant demand, especially in wealthy households. Thus salmon, like any valuable commodity, attracted criminal interest, such as that indicated by the fourteenth-century case in which Robert, son of John de Burgo, was charged with robbing Theobald Troye's fishermen of salmon and preventing them from carrying their catch to Limerick (*Cal. Justic. Rolls Ire.* 1311, 215), while near Killmallock Richard Carragh was hanged for attacking Thomas, son of Geoffrey, and Peter le White and taking two loads of fish worth a mark (*Cal. Justic. Rolls Ire.* 1311, 215). In the Middle Ages, then, the Shannon estuary fisheries should be interpreted in terms of the organisation of contemporary society, with various social classes (free and unfree tenants, peasant farmers, burgesses, lords, abbots and bishops) all potentially contesting and negotiating for this valuable resource.

Site distribution and location

It is clear that local medieval fishermen had a detailed practical knowledge of the movements of fish according to seasons, tides and so on. The siting of the medieval fishtraps probably reflects a traditional knowledge of the best locations for the construction of weirs and baskets. A certain amount of their 'lore' and knowledge of this landscape can be recovered through the study of the location, form, size and orientation of the traps. There are some interesting variations in terms of style of construction, orientation, use, repair and abandonment. The early historic and medieval fishtraps are located as far apart as the upper Fergus estuary, the Deel estuary, the River Owenagarney (Bunratty 1–4) and the main channel of the Shannon estuary (Bunratty 6). It is likely, then, that many other examples remain to be found. It is interesting, however, that some were found in clusters. The Bunratty 1–4 and Deel estuary 1–3 fishtraps obviously represent an intense or continuous tradition of fishing at those locations.

Siting in relation to riverbanks and nearby settlements

The Bunratty 1–4 and Deel estuary 1–3 fishtraps are situated quite close to medieval settlements on the dryland (the Anglo-Norman borough of Bunratty, Co. Clare, and a possible medieval settlement at Ballynash, Co. Limerick). The Fergus estuary fishtrap, although it is not too far from dry ground (the slopes along the north bank of the River Rine), is actually quite isolated in terms of contemporary settlements. The nearest ringfort is some 1.5km to the west. The most isolated fishtrap is Bunratty 6, which today is hundreds of metres from dryland. In the medieval period, the predominance of saltmarshes in place of the modern corcass would have made it even more isolated. However, these distances are relative; all of the medieval fishtraps could have been reached with ease using a small boat, and this is undoubtedly how it would have been managed.

Siting on estuary channels, mudflat creeks and river mouths

The fishtraps are found in a range of specific locations. Some (Deel estuary 1–3, Fergus estuary east 2) are found immediately adjacent to the main estuary channel, while others are located on smaller rivers (Bunratty 1–4) or creeks (Bunratty 6) entering it. The fishtraps tend to be found close to the outlets of small creeks flowing into the estuary. Thus the Deel estuary 1–3 fishtraps are situated immediately downstream of Goleen Creek, and the Fergus estuary east 2 site is located immediately downstream of the River Rine. It is possible that these were better fishing-grounds because of the greater amounts of food and nutrients in the water near these smaller rivers.

Siting in relation to low water and tidal cycle

The medieval fishtraps are typically found at locations close to the low-water mark. Indeed, Bunratty 3 is located today below the MLWM and is now visible for about an hour during the lowest tides of the year. It is likely, then, that the fishtraps were usually only exposed for one or two hours at low tide, just as the last surge of water was draining out of the creeks. Fish could have been caught moving down these creeks in the last hour or two of the ebb tide. These fishtraps could have caught fish through much of the monthly tidal cycle, using both nightly and daily tides.

Size, form and orientation

The medieval fishtraps on the Shannon estuary are typically small V-shaped structures built of converging post-and-wattle fences leading to wicker baskets. The small size of the Shannon estuary fishtraps can be usefully contrasted with, for example, the massive tidal traps of Strangford Lough or the Blackwater estuary on the Essex coast (see below). However, fishtraps of comparable small size have also been recorded on the Severn estuary (see below).

Length of post-and-wattle fences

The vertical post-and-wattle fences typically measure only about 10–20m in length. The Fergus estuary post-and-wattle fence was 8m long. The Deel estuary 1 post-and-wattle fences were at least 20m long, while the Bunratty 6 post-and-wattle fence may have measured up to 22m in length. It is apparent that this small size is largely related to local foreshore topography. The Shannon estuary medieval fishtraps were well suited to the particular conditions of the mudflats, with its numerous little creeks and narrow channels flowing through wide expanses of treacherous muds. However, despite their small size, the steep banks of these creeks meant that they carried most of the water of the ebbing tide, so that only a small fishtrap (20–30m) spanning the width of the creek was needed to trap fish.

Height of fences

It is more difficult to assess the height of the fences. The vertical posts in the fences survive to depths of 30cm at Deel estuary 1, while the posts of Bunratty 6 may lie as deep as 1m in the clay. The height of the fence would have depended on the depth of water. On the Shannon estuary this could have been 3–4m at high tide. Post-and-wattle fences in fishtraps typically measure 1.5–2.5m in height. It is likely, given the tidal range, the depth of water, the steep banks of the creeks and the force of the tides, that the Shannon estuary fishtraps had fences measuring between 1.5m and 3m in height.

Enclosed angles

The enclosed angles within the converging fences vary from narrow to wide. The Deel estuary 1 structure is quite narrow, enclosing an angle of about 45°. The Bunratty 4 structure encloses an angle of 90°, while the Bunratty 6 structure may enclose an angle of up to 120°. However, given the short length of the fences, only a small area of the foreshore is enclosed.

Orientation

The fishtraps were constructed both as ebb weirs and as flood weirs. Most of the Shannon estuary traps are oriented with their 'eyes' pointing downstream and the open mouth of the fence oriented upstream. These, then, are ebb weirs, designed to catch fish coming down with the ebbing tide. The single possible exception is the Deel estuary 1 fishtrap, which appears to have its mouth oriented downstream. It may be a flood weir, designed to catch salmon moving upstream towards the headwaters in the spring.

The use of wood in the fishtraps

The Shannon estuary medieval fishtraps would have been small but sturdy structures, and would have required some considerable labour to procure the hundreds of poles and rods needed, to transport this raw material out to the estuary mudflats, and finally to erect the various wooden structures in the few hours available between tides. All the wood and tools—especially the baskets, which were large, unwieldy items—would have had to be transported out by boat and manhandled onto the foreshore. Thereafter the fishtraps would have been managed, repaired and reconstructed over the years of their use.

Wood species selection and woodland environments

A wide range of species were used for constructing the fences, including hazel (*Corylus* sp.), alder (*Alnus* sp.), ash (*Fraxinus excelsior*), willow (*Salix* sp.), oak (*Quercus* sp.) and birch (*Betula* sp.). These suggest the harvesting of a range of woodland habitats. Hazel could have been found in local wetlands, but it prefers well-lit, open conditions and was most probably found on the drier, transitional zone at the edge of the nearby dryland slopes. Birch prefers moist, peaty soils, but was probably growing in mixed association with the other species listed above. There is a range of types of willow species native to Ireland; most prefer wetland soils, but all are tolerant of a range of conditions. The main native willows, grey willow (*Salix cinerea*), goat willow (*Salix caprea*) and eared willow (*Salix aurita*), would probably have been found on marsh edges, riverbanks, field ditches and damp scrub woodland. Alder usually grows on constantly or seasonally waterlogged soils, as long as the water is not stagnant. It can often be found growing in amorphous soils of an organic ooze in which there is a permanently high water-table. Wet alder woodland ('carr') often contains smaller numbers of other species, such as hazel, downy birch (*Betula pubescens*) and grey willow (*Salix cinerea*). It would have grown on the estuarine alluvium, kept wet by freshwater springs and drainage at low tide and inundated by brackish estuary water at high tide.

The wood used in the fishtraps was nearly always left in the round; only rarely were cleft posts or split rods used. Bark was left on the poles and branches, no attempt being made to remove it. The woodworking carried out was usually of an elementary nature: the posts were simply sharpened by cutting pencil points and wedge ends, and the rods were trimmed to chisel ends with a few blows of a sharp iron axe. There were no hints of any joinery or complex carpentry. In terms of age and tree-ring patterns, there is evidence for use of both natural coastal woodlands and coppiced woods. In the early historic fishtrap fence at Fergus estuary east 2, hazel, willow and alder, typically aged up to nine years, were used. These were probably simply cropped from hedgerow trees or taken from the dense carr woodlands that would have been growing along the Fergus estuary.

In contrast, in the medieval Bunratty 6 fishtrap, much more mature hazel, alder, ash and oak poles, aged up to 30–40 years, were used in the fences, while the wood used for the basket was much more restricted in species and age. Hazel dominated the assemblage, and this was wood taken from very young rods, aged only 3–6 years. These were of uniform size, smooth, with few side branches. Quite simply, it would be difficult to obtain such high-quality underwood from natural woodland. It is likely that the wood from the basket in particular was taken from coppiced hazel woodland, growing on the islands, around Bunratty or even in the famous medieval Cratloe Woods to the east.

Building the wooden fences

The fishtraps were built using a range of techniques, but the predominant form involved the use of two converging post-and-wattle fences leading to a trap mechanism. The fences were built in one of two ways: post-and-wattle panels were supported by posts driven into the riverbed, or wattle was woven around vertical posts already in place. In the Fergus estuary east 2, Bunratty 4 and Deel estuary 1 structures, wattles were simply woven around *in situ* roundwood posts that had been sharpened and driven vertically into the muds. An unusual technique may have been used at Bunratty 4, where it appears that rods were woven diagonally down through the posts rather than horizontally around them.

At Bunratty 6 a different technique was used, involving the placing of post-and-wattle hurdles and horizontal brushwood up against a sturdier fence of vertical poles. These posts may also have had wattles woven around them. A single wattle panel was inserted against the fence so that its main axis was vertical rather than horizontal, perhaps because the fence was sagging or damaged in this area. It is possible that diagonal braces were inserted into the clays downstream of the fence, to prevent them from collapsing during the great rush of water in the last hour or so of the ebbing tide. This feature was known as a 'gellog' (from the Irish, meaning 'forked prop') in recent times on the Munster Blackwater fishtraps (Went 1961, pl. 4).

The use of wicker baskets

There are three well-preserved baskets associated with the medieval fishtraps, one at Bunratty 6 and two at Bunratty 3. It is also likely that Bunratty 4 employed a similar basket. The nature of the trap mechanisms used on the Fergus estuary east 2 and Deel estuary 1 structures is unclear. The Bunratty 6 basket is a remarkable artefact in terms of both its technology and its state of preservation, indicating clearly both the skills of contemporary basket-makers and the techniques used by local fishermen.

Similar baskets have commonly been found with Anglo-Saxon and Norman fishtraps in England and Wales, particularly in conditions that ensured good preservation. Anglo-Saxon and Norman baskets are known from the mudflats of the

Early historic and medieval fishtraps

Fig. 71—*Woven portable eel-trap, 'kiddle' or 'weel' in use in an English mill-stream in an illustration in the fourteenth-century Luttrell Psalter (British Library: Luttrell Psalter, additional MS 42130: f. 181).*

Severn estuary (Godbold and Turner 1994). These are remarkably similar to those used in recent times on that estuary, where large conical baskets made of three separate components were supported in rectangular frameworks. Long, small-meshed baskets in the shape of an 'eel wheel' were fitted over the ends of the larger cone-shaped basket (Jenkins 1974a; 1974b; Salisbury 1991, 80). Small baskets were also used as individual fishtraps. Medieval book illuminations occasionally illustrate the use of such portable wicker traps or 'weels' for catching eels. The best-known example is the conical basket shown in the fourteenth-century Luttrell Psalter being used in the leat of a mill-race (Fig. 71). There are also medieval historical references to the use of woven baskets and wicker traps in Ireland. In 1225 the people of Cúl Cearnadha were attacked by Aodh mac Cathail Chrobhdheirg and a band of Normans. Many of the people fleeing the scene were drowned, and the grisly detail was recorded that the baskets of the weir were found to be full of drowned children (*a llan intib do lenbaib arna mbaduth*) (*AFM*).

Use, repair and abandonment

The Shannon estuary fishtraps provide a wide range of evidence for medieval fishing techniques, including the use of tidal V-shaped structures with basket traps, post alignments and possibly small, portable baskets. These Bunratty fishtraps would have caught fish during the last few hours of the ebbing tide. Fish would have congregated within the creeks and drifted down the main estuary channels. At the ebb tide, the fishtrap fences would have diverted fish firstly to the mouth of the basket and then on into the body of the basket itself. However, as there was no exit at the narrow end, with the bung in position, the fish would have remained in the basket. As the water drained away, the fish would have been stranded out of water and 'drowned'. The local fishermen would have moved down the foreshore, removing the dead fish from each trap by means of gaffs or by simply reaching into the basket at its narrow end. In contrast, the Deel estuary fishtraps may have caught fish on the flooding tide.

The early historic and medieval post-and-wattle fences and the baskets on the Shannon estuary would have had to be constantly repaired and reconstructed before they were finally abandoned. Fishtraps used in freshwater rivers have a useful life of about 30 years; the vertical posts last about ten years before they collapse, while the wattle panels have to be replaced after five years. In coastal waters and estuaries, the exposure to high winds, onrushing tide and wave action and the constant wetting and drying across the tidal cycle would have meant that the individual elements in the fishtraps would have deteriorated much faster. There is clear evidence for repair and reconstruction in the traps, with extra posts driven in beside vertical fences (Bunratty 6), or even entire post-and-wattle fences replaced (as at Deel estuary 1 and Bunratty 4). Some traps may have had to be abandoned very suddenly, owing to damage after floods or burial under silts. The quality of preservation of the basket at Bunratty 6 may suggest that it had been suddenly buried in silts and that the local fishermen, instead of digging it out, cut their losses and constructed a new fishtrap elsewhere.

The archaeology of early historic and medieval fishtraps in Britain and Ireland

Introduction

In recent years, significant discoveries of medieval fishtraps have been made at several locations around the coasts of Britain and Ireland. It is interesting that regional variations in style and method of construction can now be discerned. Obviously, in some cases this variation is simply due to the character of the local foreshore and tides; in other cases it is possible that cultural factors were important. The early historic and medieval fishtraps from the Shannon estuary can usefully be compared with these other fisheries, revealing that the Shannon estuary sites can be seen as a local, regional expression of a social and economic tradition that was widespread on the estuaries of medieval north-west Europe.

Early historic and medieval fishtraps, Strangford Lough, Northern Ireland

The Shannon estuary fishtraps can be contrasted with similarly dated structures from Strangford Lough, Northern Ireland. These are mostly located in Grey Abbey Bay and around Chapel Island in the north-eastern part of the lough. At least fifteen wooden and stone-built fishtraps have been recorded, and the wooden traps have been radiocarbon-dated to between the eighth and thirteenth centuries AD (Tom McErlean and Rosemary McConkey, pers. comm.; Williams 1996; O'Sullivan *et al.* 1996; 1997). Strangford Lough would have had a large potential fish population, including salmon, sea trout, plaice, flounder, mackerel, cod, grey mullet and skate, with large numbers of eels in the abundant kelp growth. The Strangford Lough fishtraps were ebb weirs, intended to catch fish drifting down with the falling tide. They usually have two long stone walls or wooden fences which converged in a V shape to a point on the lower foreshore, so that at every low tide they were exposed for about two to three hours, enclosing a large area of foreshore yet leaving sufficient time to remove the fish or repair the structures.

The Strangford Lough wooden fishtraps have fences measuring between 40m and 200m in length and are more or less V-shaped in plan. The fences were made both of single lines of posts and of complex arrangements of paired posts, thus creating an inner and outer fence. Post-and-wattle panels could have been carried out to the traps, slotted between these paired uprights and pinned in position using bracing props and horizontal pegs. Wooden fishtraps at Cunningburn and Gregstown, near Newtownards, also had stone walls along the base of the fences to protect them from erosion and undercutting. At the eye of the converging fences, baskets or nets were probably hung on rectangular structures. The wooden fences would have deteriorated quickly and needed periodic repair. It is obvious that a significant amount of labour was required for their construction. Thousands of hazel, ash and oak poles and rods would have been felled, trimmed and hauled out from the neighbouring woodlands.

At Chapel Island a large wooden fishtrap has provided a radiocarbon date of AD 711–889. It has a lower flood fence, 147m long, running parallel to the shore, and a second, shorter fence running up towards the island. Archaeological excavations suggest that it was the subject of frequent repairs or that there was an attempt to make the fences 'fishtight' through the use of hundreds of closely spaced posts. Interestingly,

Early historic and medieval fishtraps

Pl. 58—*Aerial photograph of stone fishtrap at Chapel Island, Co. Down, Northern Ireland. Recent intertidal surveys on Strangford Lough by the EHS Coastal Research Unit have led to the identification of numerous intertidal archaeological sites there (photo: Gail Pollock, Environment and Heritage Service, Northern Ireland).*

there is archaeological evidence on the island for settlement, including a structure within a promontory enclosure defined by a substantial bank and ditch. Traces of stone field walls can also be seen on the nearby slopes. The Chapel Island fishtraps may have been linked to the significant early historic monastic site of Nendrum, on the opposite side of the lough.

In Grey Abbey Bay, 1.5km to the east, three wooden traps and four stone traps have been recorded. At South Island a large, V-shaped wooden trap crosses a tidal channel. This structure measures over 100m in length, was constructed of at least 500 posts, and has a rectangular structure and possible basket at the eye. It has provided two separate radiocarbon dates of 1023–1161 and 1250–73. Similar V-shaped wooden traps found elsewhere in the bay have produced radiocarbon dates of 1037–1188 and 1046–1218. The traps may have used nets, baskets or rectangular pounds (post-and-wattle enclosures, inside which the fish remained until removed). The Strangford Lough fishtraps were clearly in use in the bay during the early historic and medieval periods. Some of the large wooden and stone fishtraps may have been the property of the Cistercian community of Grey Abbey, founded in 1193. It is known that the early Cistercian communities were determinedly self-sufficient, and the use of fisheries in the bay probably intensified after their arrival.

The Strangford Lough stone-built fishtraps are broadly similar in size, form and orientation (Pl. 58). They typically measure between 50m and 300m in length, 1.1m in width and probably between 0.5m and 1m in height. Fish could have swum over them on a flooding tide but would be trapped behind the wall during the last hours of the ebbing tide. The stone fishtraps are variously V-shaped, sickle-shaped and tick-shaped in plan, mainly depending on the nature of the local foreshore. Large numbers of heavy beach boulders would have been collected from the foreshore for their construction. They would have needed repair after winter storms—no doubt a difficult task, with barnacles on the rocks and only several hours available for work. Although the Strangford Lough fishtraps are broadly similar to the Shannon estuary structures, their larger scale and their form indicate a particular local response to the broad, sandy beaches of the lough.

Anglo-Saxon fishtraps, Blackwater estuary, Essex, England

Perhaps the most impressive Anglo-Saxon fishtraps known from the English coast are those from the Blackwater estuary in Essex (Clarke 1993; Crump and Wallis 1992; Gilman 1998; Strachan 1997; 1998a; 1998b). These fishtraps, dated to between 650 and 883, are distributed along the lower Blackwater estuary, with particularly important sites at Collins Creek, Bradwell Creek, Sales Point and Mersea Flats. They are typically situated right at the MLW so that they are only visible for a few days a year, making them especially difficult to record. There are at least eight known fishtraps on the Blackwater estuary, ranging in length from *c.* 170m (West Mersea) to over 1660m (Collins Creek). The Collins Creek complex of fishtraps measured 2250m in total length, and yielded radiocarbon dates of cal. AD 650–797, 654–858 and 662–883.

Two basic styles of Anglo-Saxon fishtrap were used on the Blackwater estuary. V-shaped traps were typically located on a wide stretch of foreshore or at the end of a tidal channel. Long fences also run parallel to the MLW, with shorter fences running out from them at angles to make a V-shape. The vertical fences were constructed of parallel rows of upright oak and alder posts, between which there may have been laid bundles of hazel roundwood and post-and-wattle panels. Diagonal braces may also have been used to support the fences against the weight of the ebbing tide. Horizontal post-and-wattle panels were laid on the mudflats running along beside the fences to prevent the fishermen's feet from churning up the clay. Wooden structures or pounds found at the apex of fences were used to trap the fish, while intact baskets were also found within these pounds, indicating the use of large conical baskets (Fig. 72). The wattle panels and the baskets were typically made of hazel. At a ninth- to tenth-century fishtrap at Sales Point there was evidence that fish were actually gutted on site, presumably to reduce the weight of the fish to be hauled back to the dryland. This fish bone deposit found in the clay measured 6m by 4m and up to 15cm in depth. It is not known to whom the Blackwater estuary fishtraps belonged, but there are references to them in the Domesday Book and it is suspected that they were owned by monastic houses at some distance from the coast.

Anglo-Saxon and Norman fishtraps, Severn estuary, Wales

In recent years, intertidal survey and excavation at a number of locations on the Severn estuary have produced a range of Anglo-Saxon and medieval wooden fishtraps, baskets and post-and-wattle fences. In particular, two large-scale archaeological projects have been carried out on the intertidal zone of the Severn estuary, including excavations at Sudbrook Point (Godbold and Turner 1993; 1994) and at Magor Pill (Nayling 1997). One of the most fascinating things about these Severn estuary fishtraps is how they enable intriguingly long continuities (over 1000 years) with modern forms and locations of fisheries on the estuary to be traced (Godbold and Turner 1993; 1994).

On the Severn estuary in the Anglo-Saxon and Norman periods fishtraps typically consisted of rows of large, conical wicker baskets, known as putts, placed at the end of V-shaped arrangements of vertical post-and-wattle panels (Pl. 59). At Sudbrook, baskets, post-and-wattle fences and post settings produced radiocarbon dates of between 900 and 1080. Small V-shaped structures designed to hold baskets were also dated to the late thirteenth and fourteenth centuries. These fishtraps could be identified in documentary sources, which note the granting of weirs to the bishops of Llandaff (Godbold and Turner 1994, 48). Similar fishtraps have been recorded elsewhere along the Severn estuary. At Magor Pill 1, at least nine V-shaped groups of

Early historic and medieval fishtraps

Fig. 72—*Reconstruction of Anglo-Saxon fishtrap in use at Collins Creek, on the Blackwater estuary, Essex (painting by Nick Nethercoat, reproduced by permission of Essex County Council Planning Division).*

posts were laid out along a line at least 60m in length. These posts, dendrochronologically dated to the thirteenth century, probably held basket traps and would have caught fish on the falling tide. A larger V-shaped structure at Magor Pill 2 was dated to 1120, with evidence of repair in 1149, almost 30 years later (Nayling 1997). These putts were still being used on the Severn estuary up until recent years.

Anglo-Saxon and Norman fishtraps on the River Trent, northern England

Anglo-Saxon and medieval fishtraps have been excavated and recorded in great detail in a series of gravel quarries at Colwick, Castle Donnington and Hemington, along the ancient course of the River Trent, in northern England (Salisbury 1988; 1991; 1992; 1996; Brown 1997). These fisheries are amongst the most intensively documented and researched in these islands. Although they are riverine fishtraps, they provide many similarities with the Shannon estuary early historic and medieval fisheries.

At Colwick, on the River Trent near Nottingham, Anglo-Saxon and Norman fish-weirs consisted of rows of posts extending in a V shape from the riverine shallows, with wattle hurdles between the posts (Losco-Bradley and Salisbury 1988; Salisbury 1991). The Anglo-Saxon fish-weir produced a calibrated radiocarbon date of 810–80. Its fence, which measured 35m in length, was made of a double row of oak, hawthorn and holly posts. Between the rows of posts were inserted wattle panels made of hazel, ash, holly and willow. The fence had collapsed over onto some stone rubble, and it was believed that these stones were used to support the braces which held up the fence. A Norman fish-weir, dated to 1070–1200, was also excavated at Colwick, 1km downstream of the Anglo-Saxon site. This weir was buried under 4–5m of floodplain deposit, the posts having been driven into a gently sloping, ancient cobbled riverbed. The V-shaped weir had its mouth oriented upstream, with one wing 30.8m in length and the other wing approximately 100m in length. It was built of a double row of oak posts that supported post-and-wattle panels. Bound bundles of twigs were placed at the foot of the hurdling

Pl. 59—Eleventh- to twelfth-century fish basket excavated at the former outfall of the River Nedern/Troggy, at Sudbrook, near Caldicot on the Welsh shore of the Severn estuary (photo: Steve Godbold and Rick Turner, Cadw, Wales).

to make the fence 'fishtight'. As at Bunratty 4, the remains of earlier weirs were found behind the fence, represented by lines of posts. There were also vertical posts at the eye of the trap, presumably used for holding baskets or nets, or for supporting a framework from which the fishermen worked. It is likely that this weir was used for catching eels.

In recent years, archaeological research has been concentrated in the River Trent gravel quarries at Hemington Fields, Leicestershire (Salisbury 1996). Forty-four fishtraps have been investigated, situated at various points along the braiding channels of the river and ranging in date from the eighth century to the thirteenth century. The Hemington fishtraps were generally constructed of single or double rows of posts, with occasional surviving fragments of wattle and brushwood. An Anglo-Saxon structure (No. 52), radiocarbon-dated to between the mid-seventh and tenth centuries, was in such good condition that it was possible to record its full dimensions. A post alignment of oak supported hazel wattle panels. The two fences or 'wings' measured 16m and 32m in length, enclosing an angle of 139°, with the mouth of the broad V shape oriented upstream, suggesting that it was used for catching eels (coming down the river during the autumn). Other fish-weirs, including post rows and post-and-wattle structures, have been dated to between the eleventh and thirteenth centuries. Fisheries are mentioned for every parish bordering the River Trent in the Domesday records, and the majority of these were of the fish-weir type. The impression is of a river teeming with fish-weirs, mills and other riverine structures (Salisbury 1991, 87).

Medieval fishtraps in Britain and Ireland—emerging regional traditions

It is interesting that broad similarities are apparent between Anglo-Saxon and Norman fishtraps in England and Wales and the early historic and medieval fishtraps on Strangford Lough and the Shannon estuary in Ireland. These were coastal ebb weirs, typically V-shaped wooden structures, with post-and-wattle fences, brushwood trackways, oblique braces and baskets of varying size and construction. However, it is also clear that there are significant differences in size, location, building materials and actual form. For example, the trap mechanisms (basket 'putts' supported on post settings) of the Severn estuary differ from those found on the Shannon estuary (baskets at the end of post-and-wattle fences), the Blackwater estuary ('kiddles', using nets and baskets) and Strangford Lough (rectangular pounds, nets, fishtight fences?). There are other differences too, particularly as regards size. The Blackwater estuary and Strangford Lough fishtraps were massively built (with fences often measuring

300m–1.6km in length), contrasting with the small Shannon estuary and Severn estuary traps (30–40m in length).

There are also interesting chronological patterns. In general terms, it seems that the use of fishtraps in Britain and Ireland peaked at various periods, at about the eighth century and perhaps also between the twelfth and fourteenth centuries. Thereafter they may have declined in the face of an increasingly commercial sea-fishing industry. The fishtraps also provide evidence for regional traditions and styles around Britain and Ireland. Local fishing lore, the particular topography of the foreshore and the range of building materials available probably influenced these regional variations. However, cultural traditions and local social factors must have been of even greater importance. For example, fishtraps associated with monastic sites and religious houses (Blackwater estuary; Strangford Lough) were much larger than those associated with secular settlements (Shannon estuary; Severn estuary), indicating much more intensive coastal exploitation by the former, whether by reason of their large populations or because of their involvement in a market economy. It is also fascinating that post-medieval fishing traditions in all these separate regions show strong continuities with the early Middle Ages, reflecting the conservatism and strength of tradition amongst coastal communities.

Conclusions

In conclusion, the Shannon estuary intertidal fishtraps provide new, unique and occasionally spectacularly well-preserved evidence for the existence of a local fishing industry between at least the eleventh and thirteenth centuries, an industry that was, however, largely operated by local people and was small-scale in character, serving the needs of rural settlements and boroughs along the estuary. It is also likely that some fishing was done for the populations of the medieval towns of Limerick and Askeaton, while boat fisheries for herring would have been important on the lower estuary. This local industry probably continued in conjunction with Limerick's sea fisheries in the North Atlantic in the fourteenth and fifteenth centuries.

6. POST-MEDIEVAL AND MODERN FISHTRAPS

AIDAN O'SULLIVAN AND JAMES LYTTLETON

Introduction

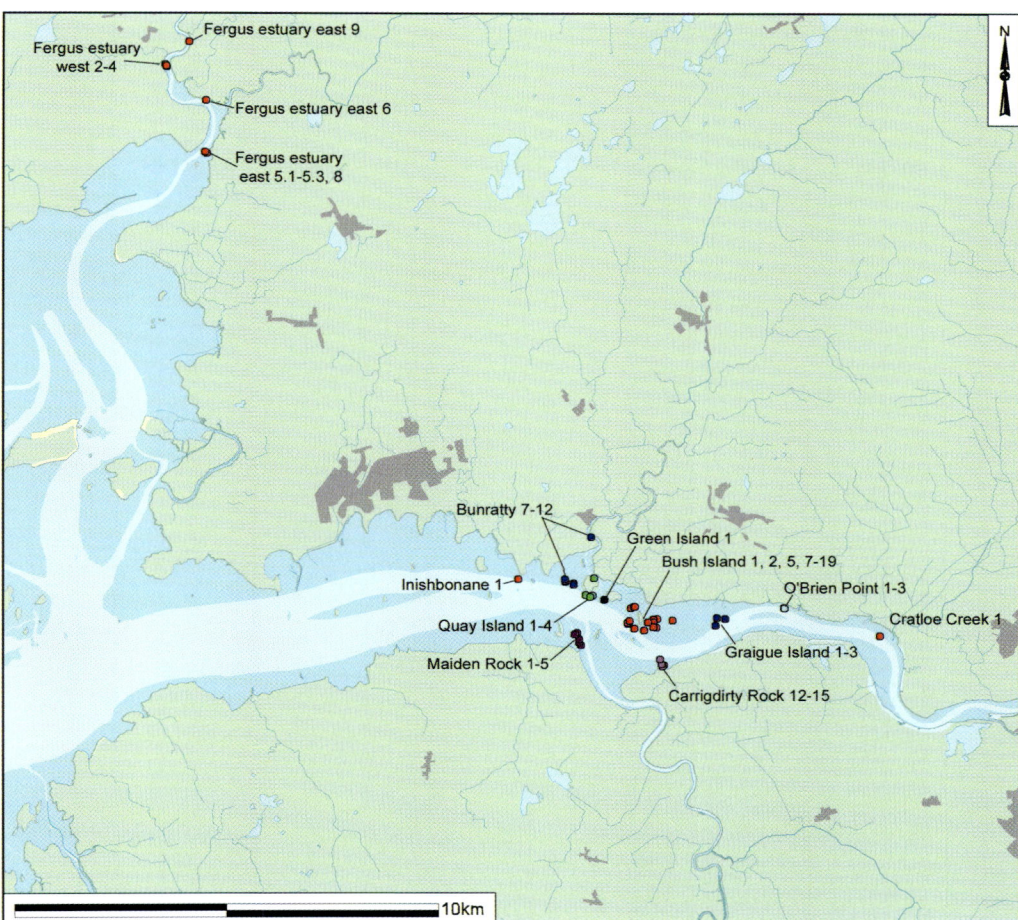

Fig. 73—*Map of upper Shannon estuary, showing location of post-medieval fishtraps and other structures.*

Post-medieval (1534–1700) and modern (1700–1900) sites recorded on the upper Shannon estuary consisted almost entirely of wooden fishtraps and post-and-wattle trackways, although a small number of stone and wooden slipways, quays and jetties were also identified (Fig. 73). The post-medieval fishtraps are easily the most visible features today on the modern intertidal zone, owing to their large size, location and excellent preservation. Until recently, Irish archaeologists have tended to ignore most archaeological evidence of post-medieval or modern date, but this approach would be nonsensical on the Shannon estuary, where these sites are clearly significant elements in the long-term history of human activity in this landscape. In particular, the post-medieval and more recent fishtraps on the Shannon estuary indicate the continuity of fishing practices in this region since the medieval period, a tradition that had largely disappeared by the twentieth century.

Traditional fishing practices involving the use of tidal or coastal fishtraps are now largely fading out in Ireland, and only a few are still used in Irish waters (e.g. in Waterford Harbour). However, we do have good sources of information on the use of

193

fishtraps in the various ethnological or folklife studies of the vanishing tradition of 'fixed engine' fisheries (i.e. fishing structures of a permanent nature, as opposed to the temporary use of nets, rods or spears). In particular, the extensive historical sources detailed by A. E. J. Went reveal a tradition of fisheries on Irish rivers and coastal waters in the post-medieval period. Mitchel's (1965) review of the River Bann fisheries also usefully details the various components and terminologies used in wooden fishtraps. Similar work by Jenkins (1974a; 1974b), Momber (1991), Jones (1983) and Bannerman and Jones (1999) on the modern Welsh coastal fisheries also provides valuable insights into the nature, durability, and daily and seasonal management of both stone and wooden fishtraps.

Fishtraps were extremely common up until recent times on most Irish rivers, notably the Bann, Erne, Corrib, Boyne, Blackwater, Suir and Shannon. These types of weirs, partially or entirely spanning the width of a river, varied in form, though the principle would have remained the same: fish were captured in suitably positioned nets or concentrated within a confined space, from which they could be removed at leisure with a spear, gaff or net (Went 1946, 176). Riverine weirs were typically formed of complex post-and-wattle barriers or stone-built walls with several box-shaped enclosures or 'cribs' situated along their lengths (Went 1964, 213). Depending on the type of weir, salmon and other fish were caught on their way upstream and eels were trapped while migrating downstream in autumn. The eel-weirs at Toome, Co. Antrim, were particularly famous and were strategically placed to catch mature silver eels moving down the River Bann from Lough Neagh. They consisted of a series of V-shaped wattle lanes or 'skeaghs' which guided the eels into heavy 'coghill' nets, enabling catches of up to 150 tons a year (Mitchel 1965).

Historical sources also indicate that riverine salmon-weirs were used at a number of places in the Shannon estuary region, such as the Lax Weir on the Shannon at Limerick City, at Ennis on the River Fergus, at Askeaton on the River Deel, and at Adare on the River Maigue. The Limerick Lax Weir has a particularly rich documented history from the turn of the thirteenth century to 1927, when operations ceased there (Herbert 1946–7). There are a number of sixteenth- and seventeenth-century references to the use of other riverine weirs on the freshwater tributaries of the Shannon estuary, such as on the River Fergus in the vicinity of Ennis (*Fiants* 1569, 190; *Thomond Papers: Spaight 1681*, ff 38, 54; *ibid.: Manor Courts Clonrond and Innish*, 11 April 1676).

Head weirs

In places like the Shannon estuary and other tidal waters, fishtraps were usually constructed as 'head weirs', of two post-and-wattle fences which converged to an apex (the 'eye') in a V-shape, an L-shape, a 'tick'-shape (i.e. with two fences of unequal length) or a C-shape. The fence nearest the land is termed the 'shore fence'; that at the low water is termed the 'flood fence'. The mouth or widest opening of these traps often faced upstream or inland, working as 'ebb weirs' to funnel fish coming down on the ebbing tide into the 'eye'. 'Flood weirs', in contrast, would be oriented to catch fish moving up the channel with the incoming or flooding tide (Pl. 60). In post-medieval and modern times, fish were usually trapped in a 'coghill' net that was suspended from a raised platform at the eye of the weir. These nets were usually conical or tubular in shape, being long, composite mesh bags kept open by means of attachments to the uprights of the wooden platform. More primitive forms of tidal head weir (and possibly of early origin) were the stone-built 'fish-pounds' or 'salmon walls' found in Doonbeg Bay, Co. Clare, and Lough Swilly, Co. Donegal (Went 1946; 1964). Head weirs were typically in use in Irish tidal waters until the mid-nineteenth century, after which virtually all of them were banned, although no doubt many would still have been used in defiance of government legislation. At least some of the small fishtraps (particularly the hidden creek traps) discussed here must have been built and used in recent decades.

Post-medieval and modern fishtraps

Pl. 60—*Modern wooden tidal head weir in Waterford Harbour, Co. Kilkenny, oriented to catch fish moving upstream or with the flooding tide. A long shore fence runs diagonally down from the shore to meet a shorter flood fence, with a raised platform situated at the eye of the trap. The Shannon estuary post-medieval and modern fishtraps were broadly similar (photo: Aidan O'Sullivan).*

Stake-net weirs

In the early nineteenth century, a different form of 'fixed engine' began to be used on the Shannon estuary in competition with the earlier head weirs (Went 1946; 1964). These were known as stake-net weirs or Scotch nets because they entailed the use of straight walls of netting anchored to the shore by long stakes or poles. They were much more ruthless and efficient than head weirs and quickly replaced them in Irish estuaries. They were reputedly both a hazard to navigation and such a threat to fish stocks that successive legislative attempts were made to restrict their use. All head weirs and stake nets, other than those used at Buttermilk Castle, Co. Wexford, Castlebellingham, Co. Louth, and Bunratty, Co. Clare, were abolished by government legislation after 1863 (Went 1964).

In this chapter, the Shannon estuary post-medieval fishtraps will be described and analysed as individual sites or complexes in terms of their location (i.e. Bush Island, Quay Island, etc.). In this study, a distinction is made between head weirs (large V-shaped, tick-shaped or C-shaped structures on the channel) and creek traps (simple post alignments crossing small creeks and runnels). The fishtraps will then be discussed in terms of form, siting, use, repair and abandonment. The available historical evidence for their ownership and use on the upper Shannon estuary and Fergus estuary will also be presented. Finally, brief ethnological case-studies of some Irish post-medieval and modern fishtraps will be presented to provide comparisons with the Shannon estuary fisheries.

Post-medieval fishtrap, Inishbonane, Co. Clare (Inishbonane 1)

Site location

The post-medieval fishtrap at Inishbonane 1 is located on the north bank of the Shannon estuary, adjacent to the townland of Clonmoney South, Co. Clare (Fig. 74; Pl. 61). Inishbonane (also known as Tradree Point) is the prominent headland which runs down as a rock outcrop to the LWM, to the south-west of Bunratty. It is located in estuarine clays on the channel, *c.* 50m west of the rocky outcrop, and is only fully exposed during spring low tides.

Foragers, farmers and fishers

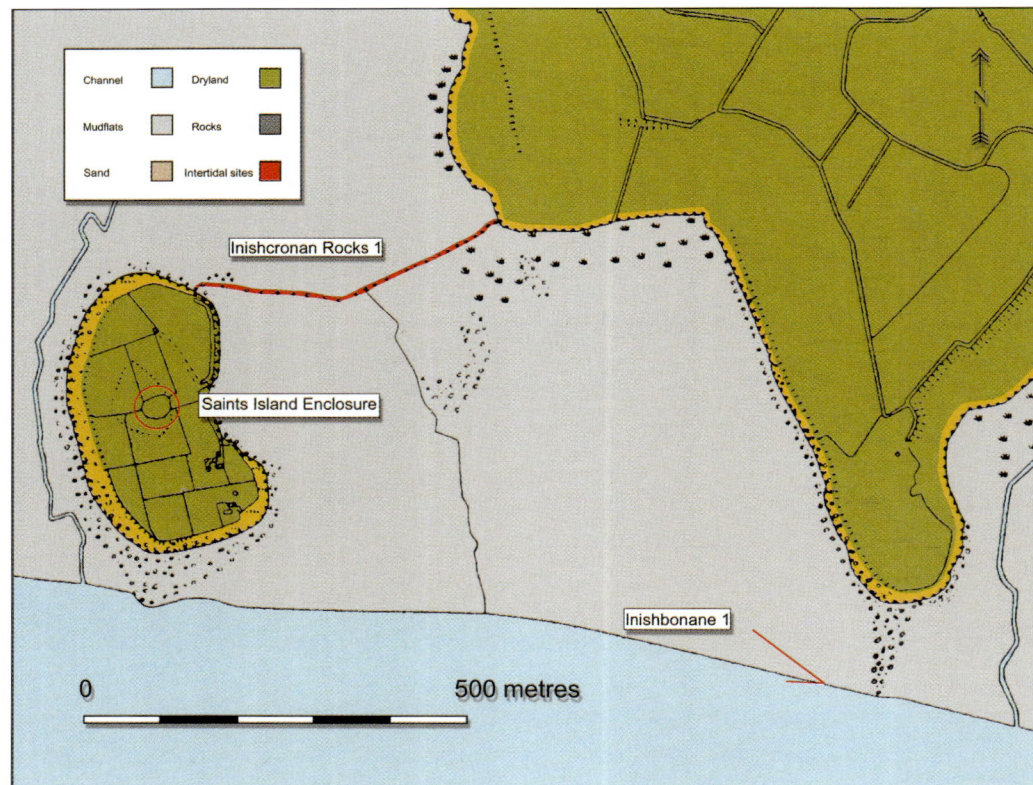

Fig. 74—*Location of Inishbonane 1 post-medieval fishtrap.*

Pl. 61—*Inishbonane 1 post-medieval fishtrap from east.*

Site description

Inishbonane 1 is a large tick-shaped wooden structure of two converging vertical fences which enclose an angle of 25–30°. The flood fence measures *c.* 23m in length, is oriented east/west and runs diagonally across the LWM. The shore fence, oriented north-west/south-east, is much larger, measuring *c.* 63m in exposed length, and weaves irregularly up the foreshore before its posts disappear under the deeper clays of the upper foreshore (this fence probably measures at least 80m in length). The wooden fences were constructed of hundreds of vertical roundwood posts, 10cm in diameter, spaced at 20–30cm intervals, surviving to a height of 40cm, with stone slabs thrown down at the base of the posts near the eye. It is likely that the fences were reconstructed on several occasions, as they survive today as a broad band (1.2m north/south) of posts.

Site interpretation
Inishbonane 1 is a large head weir, oriented with its mouth facing downstream, probably to catch salmon and other fish moving up the channel or with the flooding tide. It is possible that a wooden platform or 'perch' was used at the eye for hanging a net. The site's excellent state of preservation suggests an eighteenth- or nineteenth-century date, but it may be based on an earlier site referred to in 1703, when Thomas Moland's survey indicates that there was a salmon-weir at *Clunmunny farm* (possibly Clonmoney South) worth £10 per annum (Ainsworth 1961, 102). The present site is not mentioned in historical sources or depicted on maps, suggesting that it was abandoned by the mid-nineteenth century.

Post-medieval fishtrap, Quay Island, Shannon estuary (Quay Island 2)

Site location
The post-medieval fishtrap at Quay Island 2 is located on the north bank of the Shannon estuary, adjacent to Quay Island, Co. Clare (Fig. 74). Quay Island (also known as Cain's Island) is a large island situated immediately to the west of the outlet of the River Owenagarney. There are a number of post-medieval intertidal features around this island, including this large wooden fishtrap (Quay Island 2), two wooden jetties or piers (Quay Island 1, Quay Island 3), and a stone-built causeway (Quay Island 4) leading to Moyhill and the drylands to the north of the island. The fishtrap is located on the narrow, gently sloping foreshore to the south-west of Quay Island, between its rocky foreshore and the channel.

Site description
Quay Island 2 is a large, U-shaped wooden fishtrap of unusual construction, with a narrow internal enclosed space and a rounded end. It is constructed of two converging fences, each consisting of a double row of vertical wooden posts, some of which incline inwards. The shore fence is oriented north-west/south-east and is at least 45m long. The flood fence is oriented west-north-west/east-south-east and measures *c*. 30m in length (but disappears under the upper foreshore muds, so it may be substantially longer). The posts are quite stout, being of roundwood and cleft trunks, 10–14cm in diameter, and are typically closely spaced at 30–50cm intervals. A low mound or ridge (10m north/south by 2m east/west) of limestone slabs is located inside the flood fence, 8m west of the eye. This may have been intended to prevent the fence from being undercut by erosion.

Site interpretation
Quay Island 2 is probably a head weir, oriented to catch salmon and other fish on the flooding tide. As it is located below the mean low-water mark, it is likely that its trap would always have been in shallow water. The trap may have been a net or basket suspended from vertical poles at the eye. The present structure probably dates from the early to mid-nineteenth century.

Post-medieval creek traps, Bunratty, Co. Clare

Introduction
The post-medieval creek traps at Bunratty are located on the north bank of the Shannon estuary, adjacent to the townlands of Bunratty West, Co. Clare (Fig. 51). The fishtraps are situated in the mudflat creek that flows south-eastwards across the

Foragers, farmers and fishers

mudflats, midway between Illaunbeg Point and Quay Island. A medieval fishtrap (Bunratty 6; see Chapter 5) was found in the same creek *c.* 100m to the south-east.

Bunratty 7—creek trap

Bunratty 7 is a single post alignment of four roundwood posts crossing the creek. Three posts are clustered together to the south and one is located to the north of the water-channel. The post alignment is oriented north-east/south-west, and measures 5m in length. The three posts measure 6–8cm in diameter, are spaced at 20cm intervals and survive to a height of 10–20cm above the soft, creekbed silts.

Bunratty 8—creek trap

Bunratty 8 is located *c.* 10m north of Bunratty 7, crossing the creek and running up its northern bank. It is a single post alignment, oriented north-east/south-west, measuring 8m in length. It is constructed of at least seventeen roundwood posts, 8–9cm in diameter, spaced at intervals of 40–50cm. These posts typically survive to a height of 30cm, but the posts in the north-east bank are more substantial. The posts at the north-east end form a double row.

Bunratty 9—creek trap

Bunratty 9 is located in the creek *c.* 60m north-west of Bunratty 8. It is a double post alignment, oriented north-east/south-west and measuring *c.* 9m in length, and is mostly set in the base of the creek. The main structure was of at least eleven roundwood posts, 5–7cm in diameter, spaced at 60–70cm intervals. Immediately downstream (1m to the south) of this main post alignment were three obliquely set, stout (9–10cm in diameter) roundwood posts serving as braces for the main vertical structure.

Discussion

The Bunratty 7–9 wooden structures are all of similar design, construction and condition, and were probably small creek traps designed to catch fish in the waters draining out of the mudflats at low tide. Similar creek traps (Bunratty 10–11) were also observed in the mudflat creek to the east, but were not recorded in detail during a flooding tide. Bunratty 9 probably held a woven net across the creek, the structure being supported against the rush of the ebbing tide by the wooden braces downstream. Bunratty 7 and 8 (especially the latter) may have been stouter post-and-wattle or brushwood structures, behind which fish were caught by simply stranding them in the creek. These traps are probably modern in date and may even be the remains of recent illegal poacher's creek traps, as they would not have been visible from the Shannon estuary's navigable channel.

Post-medieval fishtrap, Green Island, Co. Clare (Green Island 1)

Introduction

The post-medieval fishtrap at Green Island 1 is located on the east bank of the River Owenagarney, adjacent to Green Island, Co. Clare (Fig. 75; Pl. 62). Green Island is a small, formerly inhabited island on the north bank of the Shannon estuary mudflats. A hard was situated at the south-west end of the island, providing access for boats to the lower foreshore.

Site description

Green Island 1 is a single post alignment, situated on the sloping foreshore of firm, gray estuarine clays to the south-west of Green Island. It runs diagonally down the foreshore from a low stone cairn or ballast dump to the north-east. It is oriented north-

Post-medieval and modern fishtraps

Pl. 62—*Green Island 1 fishtrap fence, either a stake-net weir (with vertical poles holding nets) or a partly submerged head weir with the flood fence underwater.*

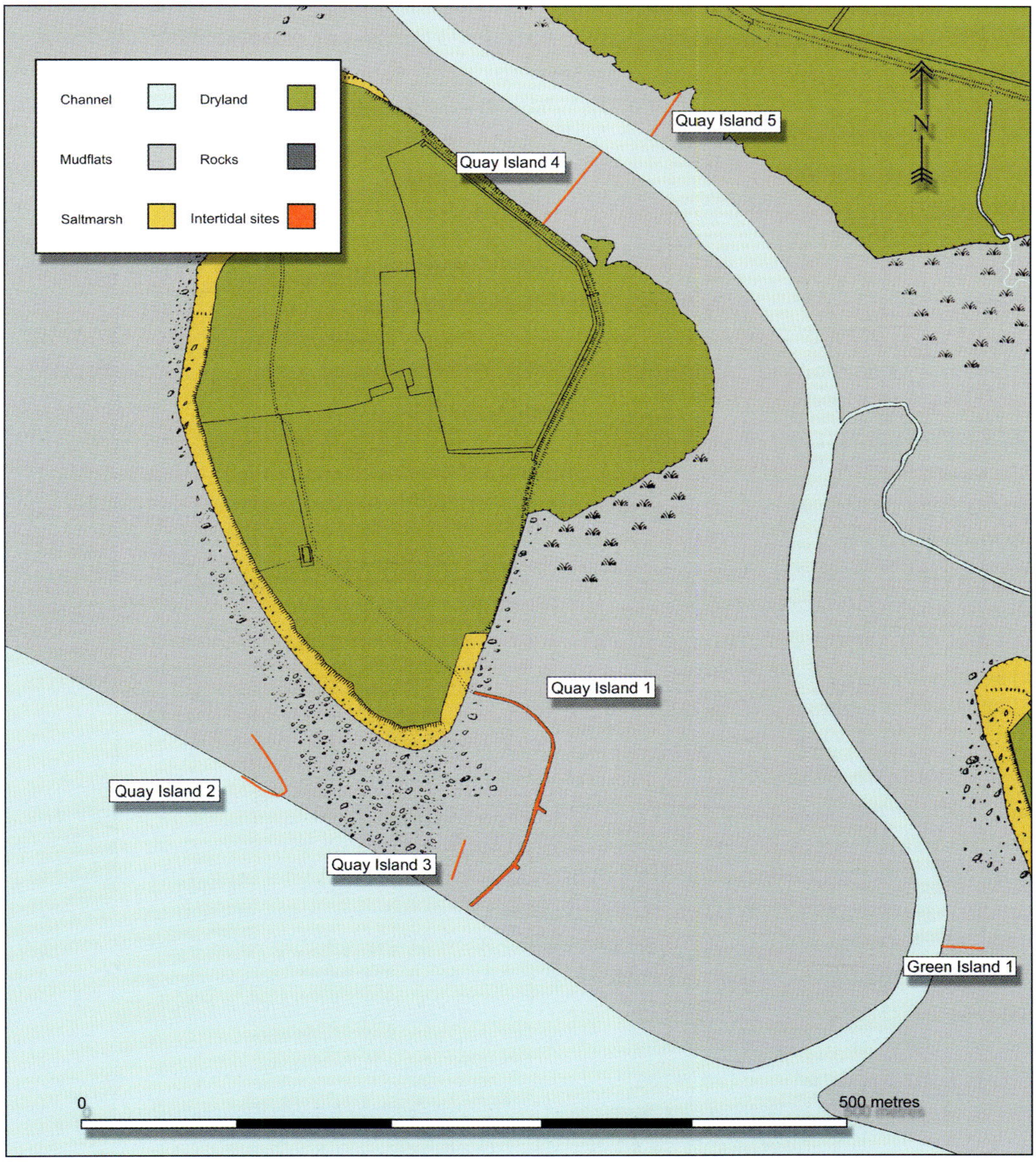

Fig. 75—*Location of Quay Island 2 post-medieval fishtrap, situated on the south-west shore of Quay Island. There are also post-medieval wooden jetties off the south-east shore.*

199

east/south-west, measures *c.* 17m in length and is constructed of at least 36 vertical roundwood posts, 9–12cm in diameter, regularly spaced at intervals of 50–60cm. The posts survive to heights of 15–20cm. There is evidence for stone packing at the upper end of the fence, against its northern side.

Site interpretation

Green Island 1 is either the remains of a post-and-wattle flood fence of a small head weir or the poles of a small stake-net weir. It probably dates from the post-medieval or modern period.

Post-medieval fishtraps, Bush Island, Co. Clare

Introduction

The post-medieval fishtraps at Bush Island are the most prominent structures recorded on the upper Shannon estuary. They are located off both the western and eastern shores of the island, all on the north bank of the Shannon estuary, adjacent to the townlands of Moyhill (west shore) and Ballymorris (east shore), Co. Clare (Fig. 76). Bush Island itself is a small, low, grassy island, surrounded by extensive mudflats dissected by two main creeks. On the west and north-west shore a particularly large creek hooks around the island and flows into the estuary between Bush Island and Green Island. On the east shore a wide, shallow creek appears during the ebbing tide, flowing down from the north-east.

Bush Island is surrounded by at least eighteen wooden fishtraps, of varying size and complexity. The largest are the tick-shaped traps at Bush Island 2 (south-west of the island), but there are also smaller post-alignment creek traps to the north-west (Bush Island 3–11), and several large C-shaped and L-shaped fishtraps in the wide creek to the east of the island (Bush Island 12–19). Despite their spectacularly large size, some (e.g. Bush Island 2) only appear at the extreme low-water mark, and are exposed to view for only 1–2 hours during spring tides. The Bush Island sites were rapidly surveyed in spring tides on 3–4 July 2000, but much more detailed historical research and intertidal and instrument survey will be needed to clarify their ownership, chronology, form and variation. The fishtraps may have been used by the families living on Green Island or in the small hamlet or clachan at Moyhill, where there is also a seventeenth-century house.

The Bush Island sites are discussed in terms of their location, from the fishtraps on the Shannon estuary channel (Bush Island 1–2) and the traps in the western creek (Bush Island 4–11) to the dense cluster of traps in the eastern creek (Bush Island 12–18). A single isolated basket of possible medieval date at Bush Island 3 has already been discussed in Chapter 5.

Location of Bush Island 1–2

Bush Island 1–2 are located on the Shannon estuary channel to the south and south-west of the island (Fig. 76). Bush Island 1 is 50m south-west of the island, running down its foreshore to the LWM, across a narrow channel of water, and up onto a muddy shoal in the middle of the channel. The Bush Island 2 complex consists of four separate wooden structures (2A–2D), representing at least four phases of use of large, tick-shaped wooden fishtraps. These structures are located *c.* 300m west of Bush Island at the LWM.

Bush Island 1—post alignments

Bush Island 1 is an unusual structure of four parallel post alignments, oriented north/south, set at right angles to the channel (Pl. 63). The main post alignment is

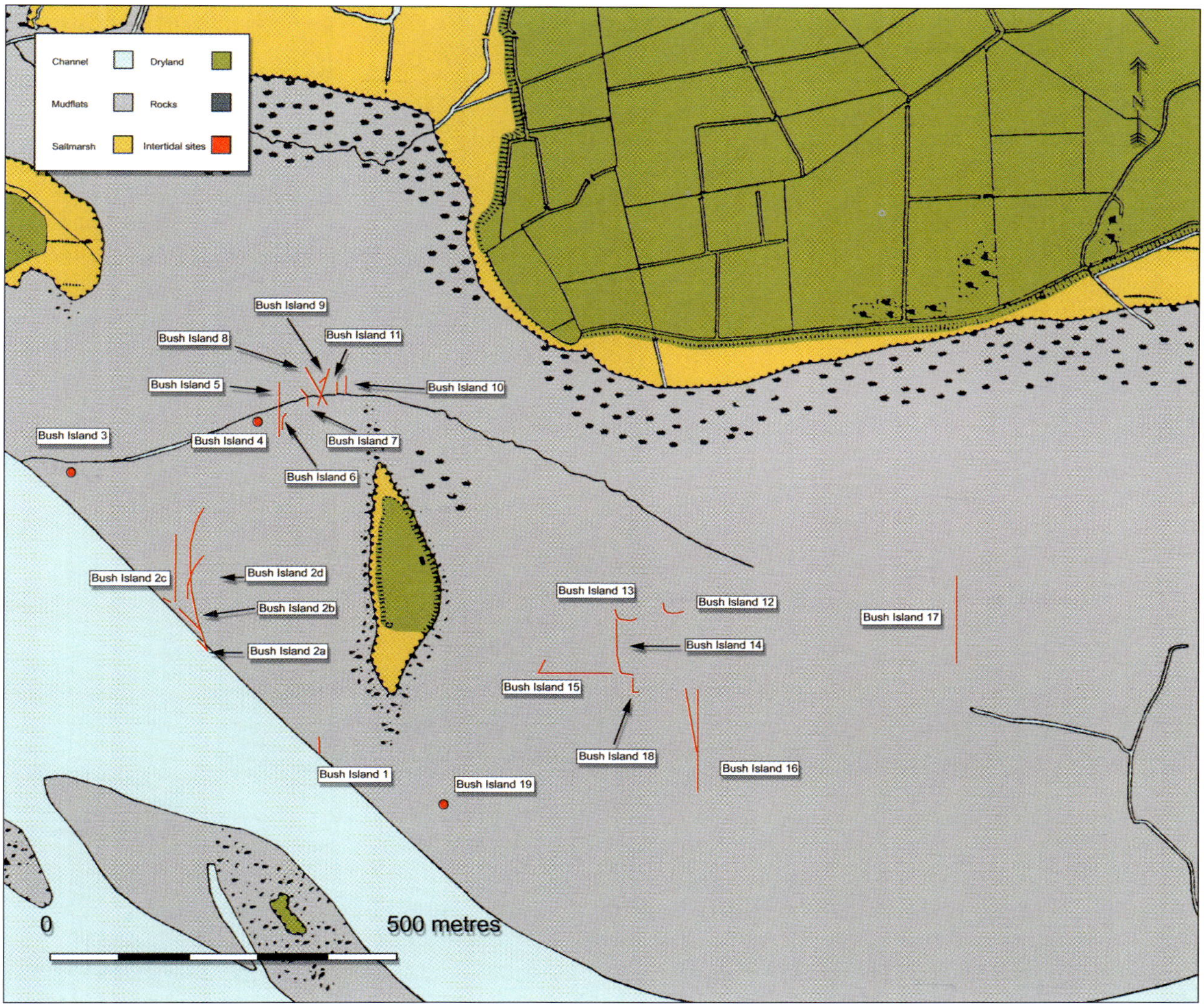

Post-medieval and modern fishtraps

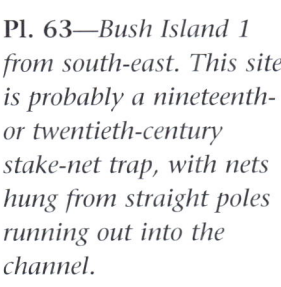

Fig. 76—*Location of post-medieval fishtraps at Bush Island 1–17.*

Pl. 63—*Bush Island 1 from south-east. This site is probably a nineteenth- or twentieth-century stake-net trap, with nets hung from straight poles running out into the channel.*

Foragers, farmers and fishers

Pl. 64—*Bush Island 2B, a massive nineteenth- or twentieth-century (?) flood weir off the south-west shore of the island, with an upper shore fence measuring over 300m in length and a shorter flood fence 47m in length.*

constructed of *c.* 20 vertical elements (each of 5–6 closely packed posts, 10–12cm in diameter, 50cm in height), spaced at 1.2m intervals. A second post alignment is situated 3m to the east. It is constructed of six widely spaced posts, 10–12cm in diameter, set at 6m intervals and all angled towards the east. A third post alignment 4m to the west is constructed of five vertical posts, spaced at 7–8m intervals, each post angled towards the west. The four rows of posts cover a total area of 35m north/south by 15m east/west. At the south end of the main post alignment a fifth post alignment runs away to the south, oriented east/west, 8m in length. Bush Island 1 is probably the remains of several phases of a nineteenth-century stake-net weir.

Bush Island 2A—fishtrap

Bush Island 2A is a large tick-shaped fishtrap, with a long curving shore fence and a short, straight flood fence. The flood fence is oriented north-west/south-east (parallel to the channel) and measures 8m in length. It is a double row (60cm apart) of vertical posts, 8–10cm in diameter, 50cm in height, spaced at 60cm intervals. The shore fence is generally oriented north/south (it curves up the shore) and measures *c.* 370m in length. It was also constructed of a double row of posts (the downstream or western posts being more substantial), 8–9cm in diameter and set at 60cm intervals. The two fences converge to an eye measuring 1m in width, with an enclosed angle of *c.* 30°. This fishtrap is probably an eighteenth- or nineteenth-century flood weir.

Bush Island 2B—fishtrap

Bush Island 2B is a large tick-shaped wooden fishtrap situated 50m north of Bush Island 2A, and using the same shore fence as that structure (Pl. 64). The flood fence is oriented north-west/south-east, measures 47m in length and 60cm in width, and was constructed of a double row of vertical posts, 7–10cm in diameter, set at 60cm intervals. The shore fence measures 320m in length. The two fences converge to an eye 50m north of the LWM, with a total enclosed angle of *c.* 40°. The fishtrap is probably an eighteenth- or nineteenth-century flood weir.

Bush Island 2C—fishtrap

Bush Island 2C is a large tick-shaped wooden fishtrap 30m west of Bush Island 2B. The flood fence is oriented north-west/south-east and measures 10m in length. The shore fence is oriented north/south and is 120m long. The upper (north) end of the shore fence was constructed of a single row of posts, 12–13cm in diameter, 30cm in height, set at regular 80cm intervals, with bracing timbers on its east side, 12cm in diameter and 80cm apart. The lower end of the fence is much more strongly built, with a line of vertical posts (12–13cm in diameter) braced on both the eastern and western sides by two to three rows of obliquely set roundwood posts (15cm in diameter, set at 1.9m intervals). The flood fence is a single line of posts, 12cm in diameter, set at 80cm intervals. It has obliquely set braces (15cm in diameter, at 1.9m intervals) at its south side. The two fences converge to an eye with an enclosed angle of *c.* 60°. The fishtrap is probably an eighteenth- or nineteenth-century flood weir.

Bush Island 2D—post-and-wattle fence

Bush Island 2D is a single post-and-wattle fence curving slightly down the foreshore, intersecting with the shore fence of Bush Island 2A–2B. It is oriented north-north-east/south-south-west, measures 159m in length and is constructed of small vertical roundwood posts, 5–7cm in diameter, 30cm in height, closely spaced at 10–15cm intervals. There are oblique braces set in clays on the east (upstream) side. This fence is probably the remains of a robbed-out eighteenth- or nineteenth-century fishtrap, possibly taken apart when Bush Island 2A–2B were being built.

Discussion

The Bush Island 2 structures are the most impressive and largest fishtraps recorded on the Shannon estuary. They were all massive tick-shaped fishtraps, oriented as flood weirs, with lengthy (120–370m) post-and-wattle fences converging at narrow eyes, where baskets or nets were probably hung. They would have dominated the north bank of the estuary, enclosing huge areas of muddy foreshore and even a substantial part of the water-channel. Indeed, they would clearly have provided difficulties for navigation in the shallow channel. Some of the vertical timbers in Bush Island 2A were sawn across at the top, presumably at the time of their destruction in the late nineteenth century.

In terms of phasing, Bush Island 2D is probably the earliest structure, its single post-and-wattle fence being all that remains of a robbed-out fishtrap. Bush Island 2C may then have been constructed to the west, and after its abandonment Bush Island 2A and 2B were built and used as contemporary fishtraps, using the same massive shore fence.

Location of Bush Island 4–11

The Bush Island 4–11 fishtraps are located in the narrow tidal creek on the upper foreshore, *c.* 120m north-west of Bush Island. These post alignments run down the east bank of the creek, across its bed and up onto the opposite north bank. They are densely clustered at a meander in the creek and indicate several phases of reconstruction and repair. The sites were numbered 4–11, moving north-eastwards up the creek.

Bush Island 4—U-shaped fishtrap

Bush Island 4 is a small, U-shaped post structure on the east bank of the creek (Pl. 65). It is oriented north/south and measures 3.6m in length, 1.8m in width at the north end and 80cm in width at the south end. The vertical roundwood posts are 6–8cm in diameter, 50cm in height, and are spaced at 35–60cm intervals. Stout rods and branches (3–5cm in diameter) were woven between these posts. A vertical post-and-wattle fence, 2m in length, leads to this structure from the north-west. On the east side the post-and-wattle fence disappears into the bank. This structure is quite similar to the Bunratty 4 medieval fishtrap (see Chapter 5) and may also be of medieval date.

Foragers, farmers and fishers

Pl. 65—*Bush Island 4, a small undated fishtrap, perhaps constructed to hold a conical or tubular basket at the side of a creek. Although sited near some obvious post-medieval structures, it is similar in form and size to the radiocarbon-dated eleventh- to twelfth-century fishtrap at Bunratty 4, and perhaps is also of medieval date.*

Pl. 66—*Bush Island 5, a large, straight post alignment spanning the creek. These post-medieval creek traps may have simply used post-and-wattle to prevent the egress of fish from the mudflats.*

Bush Island 5—creek trap

Bush Island 5 is a single post alignment crossing the creek (Pls 65 and 66). It is oriented north-north-east/south-south-west and measures 84m in length. The vertical posts are well preserved and measure 12–15cm in diameter and 1.2m in height, spaced at 60cm intervals. Smaller roundwood posts were set as braces at the downstream (south-western) side. The posts are exposed at their sharpened, worked points, suggesting that the structure was originally set in much higher clays. A substantial post-and-wattle fence (Bush Island 6), oriented north/south and 6m in length, is embedded in the creek bank clays immediately to the north-east and may be part of this post alignment. This structure was probably a nineteenth-century stake weir.

Bush Island 7—V-shaped fishtrap

Bush Island 7 is a V-shaped post-and-wattle fence in the creek. It is oriented north-north-east/south-south-west and measures 30m in length. The posts are 5–6cm in diameter, 20cm in height, and are set at 34cm intervals. This is an unusual structure, possibly indicating the use of a flood weir in the creek to catch fish moving up towards the land.

Bush Island 8—creek trap

Bush Island 8 is a post alignment crossing the creek, oriented north/south and measuring 80m in length, of posts 5–6cm in diameter, 12cm in height and set at 20cm intervals. There are two lines of oblique bracing to the west, on the downstream side. This structure was probably a nineteenth-century stake weir.

Bush Island 9—creek trap

Bush Island 9 is a narrow V-shaped structure of two closely spaced post alignments. The double post alignments are oriented north-north-east/south-south-west and measure 80m in length. The posts are 10cm in diameter and 35cm in height. This is probably a structure of multiphase construction, dating from the nineteenth century.

Bush Island 10—creek trap

Bush Island 10 is a post alignment crossing the creek, oriented north/south, 40m in length, braced on the western side. The posts measured 8cm in diameter and 20–40cm in height. This structure was probably a nineteenth-century stake-net weir.

Bush Island 11—creek trap

Bush Island 11 is a post alignment (double post row) on the north bank of the creek; it is oriented north/south and is 20m in length. The posts were 5–10cm in diameter and were spaced at 20cm intervals. This structure was probably a nineteenth-century stake-net weir.

Discussion

Bush Island 4–11 are a remarkable concentration of at least seven creek traps in a very tightly confined area, no doubt indicating the excellent fishing in that sheltered creek (and perhaps also its hiddenness from the watchful eyes of bailiffs?). These fishtraps could not all have been in use at the same time, and probably represent several phases of activity, perhaps over generations. It is significant that they are actually depicted on the OS first edition six-inch maps (surveyed in 1841, published in 1844). They are not depicted on subsequent editions. This suggests that they were in use in the early to mid-nineteenth century. In contrast, Bush Island 4 may actually be of medieval origin.

Location of Bush Island 12–18

The Bush Island 12–18 fishtraps are situated to the east and north-east of Bush Island, mostly on the north side of a broad, shallow mudflat creek that appears on the upper foreshore during the ebbing tide (Fig. 76). They are widely scattered along the length of this creek, typically being found on the upper to mid-foreshore, and they vary in size, form and construction.

Bush Island 12—C-shaped fishtrap

Bush Island 12 is a C-shaped fishtrap on the west bank of the creek, oriented east/west, measuring 36m in length and 25cm in width (Pl. 67). It is constructed of vertical post-and-wattle, with a double row of posts 8–9cm in diameter. The posts are in pairs, set 25cm apart (north/south), with each pair spaced at 1m intervals along the length of the fence. Obliquely set bracing timbers, 12cm in diameter and 28cm in height, were driven into the clay 60cm to the south (downstream) of the fence, at 0.8–1m intervals. This was an ebb weir, using only a post-and-wattle barrier to strand fish on the mudflats during an ebbing tide.

Foragers, farmers and fishers

Pl. 67—*Bush Island 12, a post-medieval fishtrap in a creek to the east of the island, constructed of a C-shaped post-and-wattle fence, 36m in length.*

Pl. 68—*Bush Island 14, a large L-shaped fishtrap, with a long shore fence (104m in length) running across a creek to meet a short (26m) flood fence near the channel. Like other post-medieval fishtraps, its fence was secured against the rush of the ebbing tide by braces and hefty vertical posts.*

Bush Island 13—C-shaped fishtrap

Bush Island 13 is a C-shaped fishtrap on the west bank of the creek, located 50m to the south-west of Bush Island 12. It is oriented east/west, measures 47m in length, and is constructed of a double row of posts 5–9cm in diameter, 30cm in height and spaced at 30–40cm intervals. The horizontal wattles are 2–3cm in diameter. Obliquely set bracing timbers, 9cm in diameter, 30cm in height and set at intervals of 1.4m, were driven into the clays 30–50cm to the south of the fence. There was also a horizontal post-and-wattle panel (2m east/west, 1m north/south) in the clays 7m to the south-east of the fence. Post-and-wattle panels may have been simply slotted between the uprights. This was an ebb weir, using only a post-and-wattle barrier to strand fish during an ebbing tide.

Bush Island 14—L-shaped fishtrap

Bush Island 14 is a large L-shaped fishtrap with a double post-and-wattle fence, large vertical posts and downstream braces (Pl. 68), located immediately south-west of Bush Island 13. It is oriented north/south and measures 129m in total length, with a flood fence 24m long and a shore fence 105m long. The double post-and-wattle fences were densely constructed, with vertical posts 5–6cm in diameter, 25cm in height and set 25cm apart. The horizontal wattles are 3–4cm in diameter. Large vertical posts (serving as structural supports), 8–9cm in diameter, are located 12cm south-west (downstream) of these fences. Obliquely set bracing timbers, 8cm in diameter and 70cm apart, were driven at an angle of 70° into the clays 40cm to the south of the vertical posts. This was a very large ebb weir, designed to cut off the entire channel at mid-tide. There is no evidence for a trapping mechanism and it may have operated as a simple barrier.

Bush Island 15—L-shaped fishtrap

Bush Island 15 is a large L-shaped fishtrap 13m to the south-east of Bush Island. It is oriented north-east/south-west, with a flood fence 32m in length and a shore fence 125m in length, enclosing an angle of 90°. It was constructed of a double line of posts, 6–7cm in diameter and 20cm in height, set at 25cm intervals. The vertical posts were supported by oblique braces, 6cm in diameter, set 80cm apart. This was a large ebb weir crossing the creek near its outlet into the main estuary channel.

Bush Island 16—two post alignments

Bush Island 16 is a pair of post alignments on the north bank of the creek. One post alignment (16A) is oriented north/south and measures 182m in length. A second post-and-wattle fence, oriented north-north-west/south-south-east and 40m in length (16B), converges with it from the north-west, 69m from its southern end. The vertical posts measure 7–8cm in diameter and 35cm in height, and are spaced at intervals of 65cm. There are braces on the downstream side, 7cm in diameter, spaced at 1.5m intervals. These two structures may represent two phases of fishtrap construction.

Bush Island 17—post alignment

Bush Island 17 is a substantial post alignment crossing two creeks, *c*. 360m east of Bush Island 12. It is oriented north/south and measures 100m in length. It is built of vertical posts 9–10cm in diameter and 75cm in height, spaced at 60cm intervals. It is braced on both the eastern (upstream) and western (downstream) sides (against the flooding and ebbing tide). The bracing timbers on the east were 7cm in diameter, spaced at 5m intervals and angled at 70° into the clays. Heavier timbers were used as braces on the downstream side (against the force of the ebbing tide). Bush Island 17 was probably a nineteenth-century stake-net weir.

Bush Island 18—L-shaped fishtrap

Bush Island 18 is an L-shaped post-and-wattle fishtrap, oriented north-north-east/south-south-west and 19m in total length, 6m to the south of Bush Island 14. The flood fence, oriented east-north-east/west-south-west, was 3m long. The shore fence, oriented north-west/south-east, was 16m long, with a slight 'kink' along its length. The enclosed angle of the two fences was *c*. 90°. The structure was built of post-and-wattle, braced on either side with obliquely set roundwood posts 5cm in diameter, spaced at 80cm intervals. This was an ebb weir at the south side of the more substantial Bush Island 14 structure.

Discussion

The Bush Island 12–18 structures represent several different types of fishtrap. There are medium-sized C-shaped traps (Bush Island 12–13) as well as substantial L-shaped traps (Bush island 14–15, 18). These were all head weirs fishing on the ebbing tide. These fishtraps were unusual in that, rather than using nets or baskets, they caught fish merely by stranding them on the muds after the ebb tide. The fences were 'fishtight' and allowed no fish to pass through them. There are also two straight post alignments (Bush Island 16–17). These may have been stake weirs that held nets. Significantly, the largest structure, Bush Island 14, is depicted in the creek on the OS first edition six-inch maps (surveyed in 1841). None of these fishtraps are depicted on subsequent editions. These head weirs and the stake weirs are probably mostly eighteenth- to nineteenth-century in date, and may have been owned and maintained by the landlords, labourers and tenants of Ballymorris House, situated on the drylands to the north.

Post-medieval fishtraps, Graigue Island, Co. Clare

Site locations

The post-medieval fishtraps at Graigue Island are located on the north bank of the Shannon estuary, adjacent to the townland of Garrynacurra, Co. Clare. Graigue Island is a small, low, grassy island that rises steeply to a flat-topped crest, from where there are good views across the mudflats. There are at least three wooden fishtraps (Graigue Island 1–3) immediately adjacent to the island. The Graigue Island post alignments are probably creek traps or stake-net weirs of post-medieval date, possibly of nineteenth- to twentieth-century origins.

Graigue Island 1—post alignment

Graigue Island 1 is located in firm, grey estuarine clays on a level area of foreshore at extreme low water, *c.* 250m east-north-east of Graigue Island. It is a single post alignment, running diagonally down the foreshore, oriented north/south and *c.* 8m long. Its roundwood posts measure 5–8cm in diameter and are spaced at 30–40cm intervals. This may have been a small head weir or stake-net weir.

Graigue Island 2—post alignment

Graigue Island 2 is located in estuarine clays on a level area of foreshore at extreme low water, south-south-east of the island itself, between its rocky foreshore and the water. It is a single post alignment running directly down the foreshore to the channel, oriented north-west/south-east and *c.* 26m in length. Its posts measure 6–10cm in diameter and are spaced at 50–60cm intervals. This may have been a small head weir or stake-net weir.

Graigue Island 3—post-and-wattle

Graigue Island 3 is located in soft, estuarine silts, *c.* 100m north-north-east of the island. It is a scatter of narrow vertical posts with interwoven rods, stretching over an area of foreshore measuring 5m by 8m. The posts appear to form an alignment running east/west, possibly crossing a small tidal creek that runs to the east of Graigue Island.

Post-medieval fishtraps, O'Brien's Point, Co. Clare

Site location

The post-medieval fishtraps at O'Brien's Point are located on the north bank of the Shannon estuary, adjacent to the townland of Portdrine, Co. Clare (Fig. 77). They are situated on a gently sloping foreshore of very firm grey, sandy, estuarine silts, *c.* 200m west of O'Brien's Point Rock. This is a complex site, with at least seven post alignments closely spaced on the foreshore. The sites are described here in terms of three main concentrations, the two post alignments at O'Brien's Point 1 and 2 (at the west end of the site) and the multiple post alignment complex at O'Brien's Point 3 (at the east end of the site).

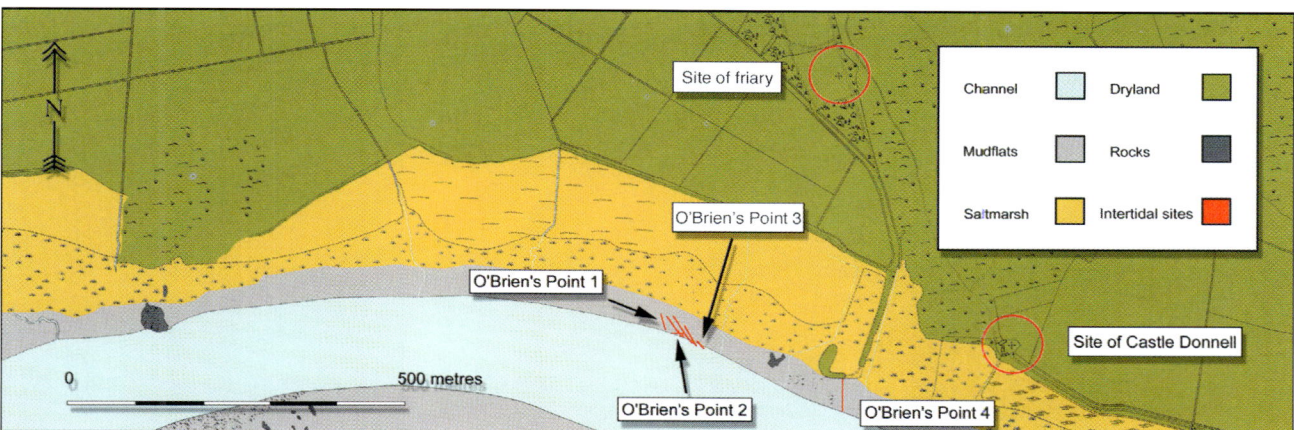

Fig. 77—*Location of O'Brien's Point post-medieval fishtraps.*

O'Brien's Point 1—post alignment

O'Brien's Point 1 is a post alignment running down the foreshore from the saltmarsh, oriented north-west/south-east and 85m in length. Its posts measure 8–10cm in diameter and up to 10–15cm in height above the mudflats, and are spaced at intervals of 30–40cm. There are also at least two fences converging towards its lower end from the west, measuring 8m and 14m in length.

O'Brien's Point 2—post alignment

O'Brien's Point 2 is a post alignment, oriented north-east/south-west (in an opposite direction to the other alignments on this shore). It is exposed at the LWM, measuring at least 35m in length, with posts 8–10cm in diameter spaced at intervals of 10–20cm, with interwoven branches and wattle. This alignment may converge with O'Brien's Point 1 below the LWM, thus creating a broad V-shaped structure to fish the ebbing tide.

O'Brien's Point 3—complex of multiple post alignments

O'Brien's Point 3 is composed of at least five closely spaced parallel rows of vertical post alignments, all oriented north-west/south-east. The post alignments measure between 80m and 100m in length and are spread over an area 43m wide (Pl. 69). The posts vary in diameter, but most measure 6–10cm; they are spaced at 10–20cm intervals and stand to heights of up to 30cm. The largest post alignments have interwoven wattle, branches and poles laid between them. There is also evidence for the use of heavy diagonal braces to the east and west, typically angled in at 30° towards the central line of posts. Stone packing was used on the lower foreshore to prevent erosion. They may have been used as shore fences in large head weirs or stake weirs.

Discussion

The O'Brien's Point complex of structures appears to represent several multiple phases of fishtrap reconstruction and repair. Most of the post alignments (apart from O'Brien's Point 3) are oriented north-west/south-east, running diagonally down the foreshore to below the LWM. These may be the shore fences of head weirs (similar to those at Quay Island 2, Inishbonane 1 and Bush Island 2A) fishing the flooding tide. It is also possible that some of the post-and-wattle structures were nineteenth-century stake weirs. There are several archaeological sites on the neighbouring drylands, including a tower-house and bawn (Castledonnell, SMR 62:14), a friary (Clare SMR 62:13) and a large eighteenth-century house (Cratloe Woods). It is likely, therefore, that fishtraps were being used at this site between the sixteenth and nineteenth centuries. Further archaeological survey and excavation will be needed to clarify the date and construction of these fishtraps.

Foragers, farmers and fishers

Pl. 69—*O'Brien's Point 3 post-medieval fishtrap fences. The parallel rows of posts clearly represent several phases of fishtrap construction in recent times, but the presence of late medieval castles and friaries on the nearby shore might suggest late medieval fishing activity here too.*

Post-medieval fishtrap, Cratloe Creek, Co. Clare (Cratloe Creek 1)

Site location
The post-medieval fishtrap at Cratloe Creek 1 is located on the north bank of the Shannon estuary, adjacent to the townland of Meelick, Co. Clare (Fig. 22; Pl. 70). Cratloe Creek 1 is situated in very firm, grey, sandy, estuarine silts on a narrow, gently sloping foreshore, midway between Meelick Rocks and Cratloe Creek, with saltmarsh cliffs immediately to the north.

Site description
Cratloe Creek 1 is a single post alignment oriented north-north-west/south-south-east, running diagonally down the foreshore, constructed of at least 121 vertical roundwood posts. It measures 48m in length (although it disappears into both the upper foreshore muds and the low water). The vertical posts are 4–6cm in diameter, were driven to depths of at least 50cm into the clays, and are spaced at intervals of 20–30cm. There is no evidence for any interwoven wattles.

Wood studies

AIDAN O'SULLIVAN AND MARY B. DEEVY

Nine pieces of roundwood were sampled from the south-south-east end of the structure: four posts of alder (*Alnus* sp.), two of birch (*Betula* sp.), one each of oak (*Quercus* sp.) and willow (*Salix* sp.), and one that could only be identified as either alder or birch. The wood used for the structure was of a fairly restricted age and diameter. The posts ranged in age between 11 and 17 years, with an average age of 13.8 years. The samples measured between 3.8cm and 6cm in diameter, with an average of 4.7cm. The wood was quite firm and dense, with an odour of rot upon snapping, both being typical features of wood of post-medieval date.

Site interpretation

The Cratloe Creek 1 fishtrap is probably the shore fence of a tick-shaped head weir, designed to catch fish on the flooding tide. The flood fence is probably submerged underwater. The structure is poorly preserved, with the vertical posts eroded down to stumps, although the wood is firm and dense. The site may be late medieval to post-medieval in date. Interestingly, there is documentary evidence for the existence of a weir at Cratloe in 1692 that provided one Laurence Chroe with £4 (Ainsworth 1961, 102). This structure may actually be a seventeenth-century fishtrap.

Pl. 70—*General view of Cratloe Creek 1 fishtrap, an eroded structure of late medieval or more probably post-medieval date.*

Post-medieval fishtraps and post-and-wattle trackways, Carrigdirty Rock, Co. Limerick

Introduction

The Carrigdirty Rock post-medieval fishtraps and trackways are located on the south bank of the Shannon estuary, adjacent to the townland of Newtown, Co. Limerick (Fig. 25). Neolithic and Bronze Age archaeological and environmental deposits are located on the other side of the island (see Chapters 3 and 4) to the east. On the west shore there are two post-medieval wooden fishtraps (Carrigdirty Rock 14–15) and two possible post-medieval post-and-wattle trackways (Carrigdirty Rock 12–13), all found on the broad, level mudflats off Carrigdirty Rock.

Carrigdirty Rock 12—post-and-wattle trackway

Site location

Carrigdirty Rock 12 is a post-and-wattle panel *c.* 80m south-west of Carrigdirty Rock, on the broad, level expanse of mudflats immediately north of a creek. A sample of hazel rod provided a post-medieval radiocarbon date of 220 ± 20 BP (cal. AD 1646–1943; GrN-20977).

Site description

This is a horizontal post-and-wattle panel exposed over a total area of 4m (Pl. 71; Fig. 78). It is oriented east/west and measures 2.2m in length and 1m in width. There are at least three sails or posts visible, measuring 3–5cm in diameter; the rods are 2–3cm in diameter. Roundwood sails and rods were also exposed in the clays to the east, suggesting that the structure is of greater length.

Site interpretation

This may have been a trackway to provide access across the broad mudflats to the south of Carrigdirty Rock. There seems to have been no attempt to fasten the structure to the mud, so it is also possible that this post-and-wattle was washed out of a vertical fishtrap fence. However, the presence of other horizontal roundwood buried in the clays further to the east, on the same alignment, suggests that this was indeed a trackway crossing the mud on an east/west orientation (from Carrigclogher to Carrigdirty Rock).

Carrigdirty Rock 13—post-and-wattle trackway

Site location

Carrigdirty Rock 13 is a post-and-wattle panel located in soft, grey estuarine clays, beside a saltmarsh cliff, to the south of the mudflat creek. There are other wooden roundwood poles in the soft muds in the vicinity.

Site description

This is a post-and-wattle panel, oriented north-east/south-west (towards Carrigdirty Rock island), measuring 2.5m in length and 60cm in width (Pl. 72). It was constructed of at least 4–5 posts or sails, spaced at 60cm intervals, measuring about 4–5cm in diameter. There are also several exposed horizontal rods, which vary in diameter. The stouter rods measured 5–6cm in diameter, but most were 2–3cm. Most of the post-and-wattle is buried in the clays, and the presence of other wooden branches to the north-east suggests a greater size.

Site interpretation

Carrigdirty Rock 13 is probably post-medieval in date. It was a trackway or platform

Post-medieval and modern fishtraps

Pl. 71—*Carrigdirty Rock 12 post-and-wattle panel buried in clays, which could be interpreted as a trackway or as a wattle panel washed out from a fishtrap fence in the vicinity. It was radiocarbon-dated to the post-medieval period.*

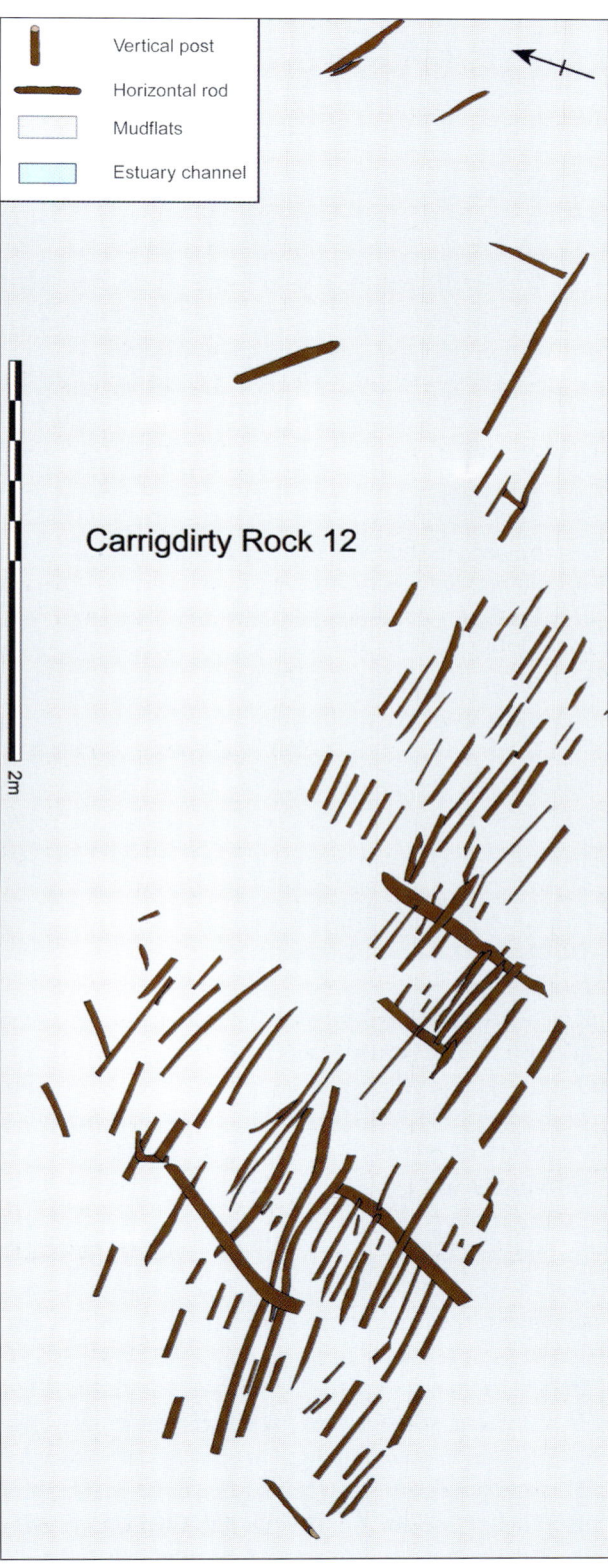

Fig. 78—*Plan of Carrigdirty Rock 12 post-medieval post-and-wattle panel.*

213

Foragers, farmers and fishers

Pl. 72—*Carrigdirty Rock 13 post-and-wattle panel at base of saltmarsh cliff leading towards creek, possibly a trackway.*

to provide access for local fishermen moving down the saltmarsh to get to the fishtraps situated to the north (Carrigdirty Rock 14, 15).

Carrigdirty Rock 14—post-and-wattle fence

Site location
   Carrigdirty Rock 14 is located on the broad, level, upper foreshore near Carrigclogher Rocks (the nearby rock outcrop at the saltmarsh edge), *c.* 160m south-west of Carrigdirty Rock. It is situated in firm, grey estuarine clays and runs down the foreshore from near the saltmarsh edge, across the sides of a mudflat creek (Pl. 73).

Site description
   This is a substantial post-and-wattle fence, constructed of at least 150 vertical roundwood posts. It is oriented north-east/south-west and measures *c.* 60m in length (it is partly buried). The posts typically measure 5–9cm in diameter and are spaced at intervals of 25–30cm, with horizontal rods at the south-west end and narrow bracing timbers set at oblique angles against the structure on its east side. There are also several limestone slabs beside the post alignment near its north-east end, where there is also a cluster of 8–10 posts.

Site interpretation
   Carrigdirty Rock 14 may be the remains of a stake weir, designed to catch fish moving upstream or downstream between the island and the marshes. It was braced on its eastern side with oblique posts, against the flooding tide and prevailing winds. The cluster of posts at the north-east end may have supported a net.

Post-medieval and modern fishtraps

Pl. 73—*Carrigdirty Rock 14 post-medieval post-and-wattle fence. There are seventeenth-century references to fisheries in this location.*

Carrigdirty Rock 15—post-and-wattle fence

Site location

Carrigdirty Rock 15 is located on the main Shannon estuary channel, in estuarine clays at the low-water mark, *c.* 160m west of Carrigdirty Rock.

Site description

This is a vertical post-and-wattle fence, oriented north-north-east/south-south-west, running diagonally down the foreshore to below the LWM (Pl. 74) and measuring *c.* 16m in length (it disappears into the upper foreshore clays). It is constructed of 40–50 vertical roundwood posts, 5–8cm in diameter, which protrude only slightly above the mud. The posts are spaced at 25–35cm intervals. The vertical posts have stout wattle rods and branches, 3–5cm in diameter, interwoven around them. There are also posts set against the structure on its western side, serving as braces against the ebbing tide.

Site interpretation

Carrigdirty Rock 15 appears to be a post-and-wattle shore fence of a tidal head weir, designed to catch fish on the flooding tide. Its date is unknown, but its small size, poor state of preservation and location may suggest a late medieval or post-medieval date.

Discussion

Carrigdirty Rock 12–15 appear to represent a complex of post-medieval fishtraps on the western shore of the island. A post-and-wattle head weir on the estuary channel (Carrigdirty Rock 15) may have been replaced by a stake weir constructed further up the foreshore (Carrigdirty Rock 14). Two post-and-wattle trackways, one situated at the base of the saltmarsh cliff (Carrigdirty Rock 13) and the other on the level mudflats (Carrigdirty Rock 12), may have been used to gain access to these fisheries.

Foragers, farmers and fishers

Pl. 74—*Carrigdirty Rock 15 post-medieval fishtrap at LWM, possibly the remains of a small post-and-wattle fence leading towards a trap that is submerged underwater.*

Post-medieval fishtraps and post-and-wattle, Maiden Rock, Co. Limerick

Introduction
The post-medieval fishtraps and post-and-wattle at Maiden Rock are located on the south bank of the Shannon estuary, adjacent to the townland of Mellon, Co. Limerick (Fig. 73). The sites are on the west bank of the River Maigue, directly north of Rinekirk Point. There are at least five wooden structures. Maiden Rock 1–2 are both substantial post alignments running down towards the River Maigue channel, Maiden Rock 3 is a post-and-wattle panel at the LWM, while Maiden Rock 4–5 are two small post alignments at the rock itself.

Maiden Rock 1—post alignment
Maiden Rock 1 is located on the estuarine foreshore immediately north of Rinekirk Point, running down from the saltmarsh towards the main channel of the River Maigue to the north-east. It is a single post alignment, oriented north-east/south-west. It measures *c.* 80m in length and is constructed of *c.* 40 roundwood posts driven vertically into the clays. The posts measure 6–9cm in diameter and are typically widely spaced at 2m intervals. They are even more widely spaced to the north-east, nearer the low-water mark of the River Maigue channel. Several small angular stones are also scattered along its length. The posts typically protrude above the clays to a height of 10cm. This is probably a nineteenth-century stake-net weir. The wide intervals between the posts and the presence of stones along the fence line suggest that a net was hung from this fence and weighted down with small stones against the force of the tides.

Maiden Rock 2—post alignment
Maiden Rock 2 is located *c.* 60m north-west of Maiden Rock 1, also on a broad, level foreshore, in firm grey estuarine clays. It is a single post alignment, oriented north-east/south-west, measuring *c.* 30m in length. It is constructed of fifteen roundwood posts, 5–10cm in diameter, spaced at 0.5–1.8m intervals. This is probably also a stake-net weir, possibly earlier in date than Maiden Rock 1.

Maiden Rock 3—post-and-wattle panel

Maiden Rock 3 is located on level, blue-grey estuarine clays just above the LWM on the channel of the River Maigue, immediately to the north-west of Maiden Rock 2. It is a horizontal post-and-wattle panel, exposed over an area measuring 5m by 2m. The panel is constructed of stout posts around which a few roundwood rods were woven. The posts lie in a north-west/south-east direction and measure 4–5cm in diameter. The interwoven rods are 2–3cm in diameter. This post-and-wattle panel could be a trackway laid down to provide easier footing near the end of the fishtraps, or it could simply be a post-and-wattle panel that has drifted away from its original vertical structure.

Maiden Rock 4–5

There were also two post alignments to the west of Maiden Rock 1–3, measuring 10–15m in length. They were situated to the south of the rocks, oriented north-west/south-east. These were clearly of modern date, with very well-preserved wooden posts. They appear to be small creek traps.

Discussion

The Maiden Rock 1–2 sites are substantial, well-constructed post-medieval fishtraps. The widely spaced posts and the presence of small stones suggest that Maiden Rock 1 was a nineteenth-century stake-net weir, oriented to catch fish coming down the River Maigue with the ebbing tide. Maiden Rock 2 is probably of similar date and function. The fisheries were perhaps owned by the occupants of Mellon House, on the adjacent drylands.

Post-medieval fishtraps and post-and-wattle, Fergus estuary, Co. Clare

Introduction

Post-medieval sites recorded on the Fergus estuary include a possible fishtrap (Fergus estuary east 9), a post-and-wattle trackway or panel (Fergus estuary west 2) and two wooden post alignments (Fergus estuary west 3–4). These sites were recorded on the narrow sloping foreshore of the upper estuary at Carrownanelly, and several hundred metres downstream at Lissan West. Other post-medieval features noted in the vicinity include substantial wooden piles driven into the muds to protect the sea walls at various locations and a number of cairns of stone on the foreshore (e.g. at Fergus estuary west 3–4). These may be either ballast dumps from boats sailing up to Clarecastle or mounds of stone left on the foreshore for the construction of the nineteenth-century sea walls. Other post-medieval features related to marsh and mudflat reclamation are the various wooden features and post alignments at Fergus estuary east 5.2, between the saltmarsh and Crow Island (see O'Sullivan 1993).

Fergus estuary east 9—post alignment

Site location

Fergus estuary east 9 is located on the east bank of the estuary, adjacent to the townland of Carrownanelly, Co. Clare (Figs 73 and 79; Pl. 75). It is situated on the lower foreshore, eroding out of gently sloping estuarine clays, and is overlooked by dryland slopes to the east.

Site description

This post alignment is oriented north-west/south-east and measures 8m in length. It is composed of at least 20 roundwood posts, 4–8cm in diameter, set at intervals of 20cm. A cluster of roundwood posts submerged in shallow water at the north-west end

Foragers, farmers and fishers

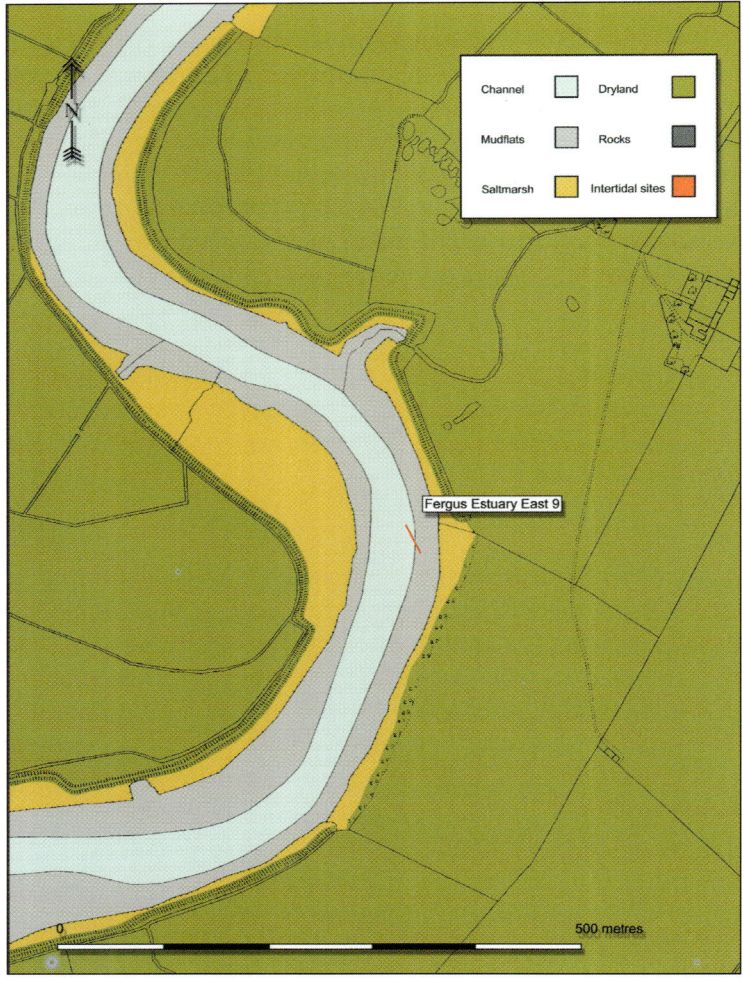

Fig. 79—*Location of Fergus estuary east 9 post alignment, adjacent to Carrownanelly townland, Co. Clare.*

of the structure may be a possible support for a trap. These posts measure 3–8cm in diameter and are spaced at 10–15cm intervals.

Site interpretation

This may be a small fishtrap (either a stake weir or a head weir), oriented to catch fish on the flooding tide. It is of unknown date.

Fergus estuary west 2—post-and-wattle trackway

Site location

Fergus estuary west 2 is located on the west bank, adjacent to the townland of Lissan West, Co. Clare (Fig. 73; Pl. 76). It is buried under 10–15cm of compact grey estuarine clays at the LWM. There is a small mudflat creek 10m to the south. Probing in the upper foreshore clays indicates that the structure has only been partly exposed. A sample of roundwood produced a post-medieval radiocarbon date of 160 ± 15 BP (cal. AD 1669–1942; GrN-21927).

Site description

This is a horizontal post-and-wattle panel, oriented north/south and measuring at least 1.4m in exposed length by 70cm in width. It had at least eight roundwood sails, 4–5cm in diameter, spaced at intervals of 25–35cm. These were sharpened with a metal axe to wedge ends and chisel points at their lower ends. There were also at least fourteen horizontal interwoven rods, each measuring 2–3cm in diameter. More of the structure lies buried in the clays 2m to the south.

Pl. 75—*Fergus estuary east 9 post alignment, possibly a post-medieval or modern fishtrap on the narrow Fergus estuary channel.*

Site interpretation

This may have been a post-and-wattle trackway designed to enable people to cross or approach the creek on the east bank of the estuary. A possible fishtrap (Fergus estuary west 3) is located to the south, and the trackway may have approached it from the north. It is also possible that the post-and-wattle derives from the vertical fence of one of those fishtraps.

Fergus estuary west 3—post alignment

Fergus estuary west 3 lies approximately 100m to the south of Fergus estuary west 2, also on the west bank, adjacent to the townland of Lissan West, Co. Clare (Fig. 73; Pl. 77). It is situated on a sloping foreshore of clays, at the LWM and a cairn of stone.

This is an unusual wooden post alignment. It is oriented north-east/south-west, measures *c*. 8m in length, and is constructed of at least 20 posts of varying diameter and height. The largest posts are 10–12cm in diameter and are spaced at intervals of 0.8–1m. They survive to a height of 30cm. Between these heavier posts are several closely spaced, narrower (6–9cm in diameter) roundwood poles and branches, also driven down into the clays. Both the large posts and the narrower branches incline at an angle to the north-west, against the force of the ebbing tide. Immediately (40–50cm) downstream of this main post alignment are three heavy diagonal or bracing posts, set 2m apart.

Fergus estuary west 4—post alignment

Fergus estuary west 4 is located 7m to the north-west (Pl. 77). It is a short, discontinuous post alignment, 6m long and oriented north-east/south-west. It is constructed of at least nine vertical posts, irregularly spaced at intervals of between 40cm and 1m. These posts typically measure 8–10cm in diameter.

Site interpretations

Fergus estuary west 3–4 may be post-medieval fishtraps, designed to catch fish on an ebbing tide, possibly post-dating the cairn of stones beside them, which was itself probably dumped here in the mid-nineteenth century during reclamation works. The Fergus estuary west 4 structure may be a stake weir, designed to catch fish on the ebbing tide. It may have been taken apart to facilitate the larger structure downstream, thus accounting for its irregular construction.

Pl. 76—*Fergus estuary west 2 post-and-wattle trackway buried under clay on the lower foreshore, radiocarbon-dated to the post-medieval period.*

The ownership, use and abandonment of post-medieval fishtraps on the Shannon and Fergus estuaries

Introduction

The post-medieval fishtraps of the Shannon estuary and Fergus estuary vary in size, form and orientation. They include large tick-shaped flood weirs (e.g. Inishbonane 1, Quay Island 2, Bush Island 2A–2C), L-shaped ebb weirs (Bush Island 14–15) and C-shaped ebb weirs (Bush Island 12–13), as well as numerous straight post alignments that are either partially buried or submerged head weirs (e.g. Carrigdirty Rock 15, Cratloe Creek 1, Green Island 1) or were the poles used for hanging nets in stake weirs or Scotch nets (e.g. Carrigdirty Rock 14, Maiden Rock 1–2). There are also numerous small post alignments across creeks that are here termed creek traps—simple barriers across steeply shelving creeks and runnels in the mudflats (e.g. Bunratty 7–9, Bush Island 5–11). These various types provide a range of information on the use, repair and abandonment of fishtraps along the upper Shannon estuary over the last few hundred years.

Ownership of fisheries on the Shannon estuary, from the sixteenth to the late nineteenth century

Who owned and used the post-medieval fishtraps recorded on the Shannon estuary mudflats? The simple answer is that many people did. The ownership of fishtraps was

Post-medieval and modern fishtraps

Pl. 77—*Fergus estuary west 3 and 4 (in background) structures, both probably post-medieval fishtraps.*

a complex, tortuous subject, and fishing rights in both rivers and estuaries were jealously guarded. Fisheries were often the subject of legal disputes and controversies over control, ownership and access, ultimately leading to unemployment amongst local people, social unrest and even, occasionally, violence. The Shannon estuary fishtraps must have been bought out, confiscated or otherwise appropriated at various stages throughout the post-medieval period, but typically ownership resided in the hands of local landlords, magnates, corporations, bishops, etc. The people who actually worked the traps, the local communities of the islands and local villages or farms, would usually have done so after paying rent in money or fish to these various owners.

However, there must also have been fishtraps erected by local men and women on their own initiative, essentially poaching structures from which no rent was forthcoming, providing nutritious food and vitamins for a hungry people or profits that were quietly pocketed. Indeed, Spellissy (1998, 186) notes that in early May in 1790 poorer people on the river and estuary built temporary causeways several yards out into the water and fished with nets for eel fry, catching so many that 'each individual filled a couple of washing tubs with them at every tide'. Such fishtraps would leave absolutely no historical trace, but might remain as the many simple post alignments that we have identified at the low-water mark. In other words, as in earlier periods, the ownership of the fishtraps would have been fluid, contested and varying according to location. Although the larger head weirs would have been visible to bailiffs and police, the many hidden creeks and channels could have been quietly fished by local people. It is difficult to track down specific details about the ownership of individual fishtraps on the upper Shannon estuary and the Fergus estuary (although local historians could probably do so by careful detective work), but the following general review of historical sources will give a flavour of the complexity and contestation of ownership rights.

Sources of information

There are various published and unpublished documentary sources that provide a range of information on fishing, land reclamation, seaweed-gathering, navigation, agriculture, trade and military issues on the Shannon estuary. Official documents such as the Calendar of State Papers and the Calendar of Patent Rolls give details on trade, fisheries and transport. Estate papers include such sources as deeds, leases, returns, maps and even manor court rolls, and give an insight into the management of the various resources along the Shannon estuary, its corcass and islands. These sources are listed in Richard Hayes's 'Manuscript sources for the history of Irish civilisation', a catalogue of periodicals and manuscripts relating to the histories of various places and subjects, held in the National Library of Ireland. By the mid-nineteenth century there is also a deluge of government reports, pamphlets, periodicals, correspondence, company records and documents available relating to the use of fisheries on the Shannon estuary.

Other sources of information are available in the National Archives, which holds papers from various government departments, including material from the various fishery authorities over the last 150 years (now under the name of the Department of the Marine). These include correspondence relating to the legality and certification of particular fishtraps. There are also various queries relating to different fishing methods and their legal standing under the various government acts. The Quit Rent Office, which was responsible for Crown property, has significant documentary material relating to the foreshores of the Shannon estuary (because the mudflats between the low- and high-water mark belonged to the Crown unless proven otherwise by an earlier grant), mostly dealing with titles to particular stretches of mudflats, reclamation schemes and the value of the land reclaimed. Cartographic sources include the Ordnance Survey's fair plans of their six-inch maps, which were essentially pre-publication proof copies of the maps. Some contain additional information not included in the final production, and some illustrate stake-net weirs with their leaders and heads along certain lengths of the Shannon estuary. Finally, Arthur Went (1960b; 1981) published two significant articles on the fisheries of the tributaries of the Shannon estuary and of the Shannon estuary itself.

Ownership and disputes in the sixteenth and seventeenth centuries

During the course of the sixteenth century the fishing of salmon remained of considerable importance in the Shannon estuary, for both the home and export markets. In the aftermath of the dissolution of the monasteries in the mid-sixteenth century, the granting of monastic fisheries to secular interests was a common occurrence (Went 1960b, 141; 1981, 107). Legal documents indicate the inclusion of fisheries in leases and deeds, such as the set of articles between Mora Ny Brian and Dermot McEdmond O'Dea, dated 13 September 1587, which allowed Richarde Goldinge a part of the fishing at the weir of Balycanie (Ainsworth 1961, 906).

The 1609 charter granted by James I to the city of Limerick conferred an exclusive admiralty jurisdiction over the Shannon estuary, bestowing on the mayor the responsibility to uphold the legislation governing the fisheries (Herbert 1946–7, 55; Lenihan 1866, 134). The great riverine salmon-weir at the Lax Weir just upstream from the city of Limerick attracted various royal grants during the course of the sixteenth and seventeenth centuries (Lenihan 1866, 201–2). Both Irish and English merchants exported large quantities of salmon to England (T. O'Neill 1987, 38) in the post-medieval period, and the fishing stocks were over-fished to the extent that during the reign of Charles I legislation was enacted in the Irish parliament to restrict the use of weirs (*Rep. Select Comm. Fish. 1849*, 405–6, 1613). This perception of a danger to fish stocks is at variance with the testimony of the local Franciscan friar, Fr Anthony MacBrody, who appeared to be either unaware of or unconcerned about the depletion of fish stocks, writing in 1669 that the Shannon and Fergus estuaries 'abound in almost every kind of fish, especially salmon, eels, trout etc.' (Ó Dálaigh 1998, 41). No doubt this difference of opinion between an Irish Catholic friar and government sources confirms that the control of fisheries was a political act.

Various land rentals and grants of property illustrate the importance of the Shannon's fisheries. For example, Sir George Preston was granted by the Crown 'the pike and salmon fish, eel weirs and mills on the Shannon' on 29 March 1661 (*CSPI*,

1660–62, 282). This was confirmed by Section 157 of the 1662 Act of Settlement: 'provided always, That this Act or any thing therein contained shall not extend to prejudice his Majesties grant under the great seal unto Sir George Preston, knight, and his heirs of the forfeited mills, wares and fishings upon the river of Shannon . . .' (Irish, 14 and 15 Chas. II, cap. 2; Anon. 1995). According to an abbreviated covenant dated 1 August 1678, one Thomas Power, as part of his lease of lands from the earl of Thomond's estates in the barony of Bunratty, was to pay 'one Runlett' of salmon every year to be sent to England (*Thomond Papers: Spaight 1681*, f. 18). One wonders if this 'runlett' refers to the catch of one of our creek traps, structures that merely crossed creeks and runlets rather than large channels?

In the vicinity of Ennis, along the River Fergus, 'fishings and fishing weirs' were leased to John Ellis and John Gore in the late seventeenth century (*Thomond Papers: Spaight 1681*, ff 38, 54). Further downstream along the Fergus were 'weares' operated by James Aylmer and George Stamer at Clarecastle and Islandavanna that would have been situated in tidal waters (*Thomond Papers: Spaight 1681*, ff 39, 43). There is no sign of these fishtraps today. Presumably they were destroyed during marshland reclamations in the nineteenth century. As stated above, on the Shannon estuary itself, Laurence Chroe set a weir at Cratloe in 1692 for over £4 (Ainsworth 1961, 102), possibly referring to our fishtraps at O'Brien's Point or at Cratloe Creek 1. Interestingly, it was also possible for two closely adjacent fishtraps to be owned by two different individuals. For example, the Civil Survey records that in August 1655 there were two 'fishinge weares upon the sd River of Shanon' at Coonagh, Co. Limerick (today this foreshore is buried under silt), just downstream of the city. The 'moytie' (i.e. rent) of one belonged to 'Barnebie, Earle of Thomond', while the other belonged to 'Sr Nichollas Comyne of Limike', an 'Irish Papist' (Simington 1938, 451).

Disputes over fishing rights were not a rare occurrence, with instances of people taking the law into their own hands. In the late seventeenth century a man named Lillis was recorded as having 'committed a trespass on ye River of Furgus' in pulling down fishing weirs (*Thomond Papers: Manor Courts, Clonroad and Innish*, 11 April 1676). In 1699 the Grand Jury complained of a weir at Limerick being a nuisance to both the fisheries and navigation, especially 'by adding seaven cribbs more to it lately on the Earle of Thomd. land' (Ainsworth 1961, 156). The sheriff was duly instructed to have the weir removed so that the counties further upstream would be able to benefit from access to adequate fish stocks, indicating the growing interest in the conservation of fish stocks in the closing years of the seventeenth century.

The Bunratty fisheries were a closely guarded resource at the turn of the seventeenth century. Henry, the 8th earl of Thomond, leased 'Bunratty Castle' for 99 years to Robert Amory on 4 October 1709. Subsequently, a lease 'for ever' was made by the earl to Thomas Amory on 26 May of the 'Castle, farm and lands of Bunratty . . . with free liberty to hunt and hawke, fish and fowl upon the premises'. In 1725 the Amory family sold their interest to the Studderts, who possessed Bunratty until at least 1915 (MacNamara 1915, 312). The fishings that the Studderts held included a tidal head weir.

Ownership and disputes in the eighteenth and nineteenth centuries

The question of ownership and control of the fisheries in the Shannon estuary in the eighteenth and nineteenth centuries was to lead to tensions between social classes. During the mid-nineteenth century, salmon in the Dublin markets was selling for three shillings a pound (while just across the Irish Sea in Carlisle the same fish would fetch only 15d. or 16d. a pound). In other words, the profits to be derived from new effective forms of fishtraps, such as stake nets, were too attractive an option to be ignored. In the eighteenth and nineteenth centuries, landlords whose properties adjoined the mudflats of the lower Shannon estuary in particular had stake-net weirs erected at various locations (Went 1960b; 1964).

The number of stake nets increased substantially after the enactment of legislation to regulate the Irish fisheries in 1842. Landowners along the estuary interpreted this act as giving them freedom to erect stake nets on the foreshores adjoining their properties. The advent of the railways and steamboats and the building of ice-houses now greatly facilitated the export of freshwater fish in good condition to markets where the industry was able to charge high prices (*Rep. Select Comm. Fish. 1849*, 1965–9; Went 1969a, 60). William Ffennell, a commissioner of the Irish Fisheries, compared the stake-net weirs in Clonderalaw Bay, Co. Clare, to a 'grove of trees', there were so many of them (*Rep. Select Comm. Fish. 1849*, 451).

According to a Mr Alton, a clerk in the Limerick Board of Conservators in 1855, where the estuary narrowed at Clonderalaw Bay and Cratloe, Co. Clare, the fisheries and navigation were greatly interfered with by the substantial numbers of stake-net weirs (Lysaght, n.d.). This might suggest that the prominent fishtraps at O'Brien's Point (off Cratloe) were in use in 1855. Vessels, such as lighters carrying turf and market produce, were obstructed in their passage along the estuary (*Rep. Select Comm. Fish. 1849*, 4540–4), and small open fishing-boats operated by local fishermen were being forced further out into the estuary's waters, where the tides and winds could be dangerously strong (*ibid.*, 1362). Even today the fishtraps at Bush Island 1–2 offer a barrier to navigation (although this channel is very shallow anyway). In the nineteenth century Royal Irish Constabulary constables and fishermen attempted to rescue a boat of eight to ten tons which was caught on a stake-net weir owned by the Knight of Glin while on its way to Querin (on the lower estuary). According to eyewitness accounts, there was great difficulty in releasing the vessel from the clutches of the stakes, despite men using saws and hatchets (Lysaght, n.d., 16–17).

While the owners of the stake-net weirs enjoyed huge catches of fishes, both the gentry and the peasantry along the upper Shannon estuary were concerned about the falling numbers of fish being caught along their banks. The restrictive fisheries legislation of the 1840s, however, had created antipathy amongst the people whose best interests lay in the conservation of the fisheries (Lysaght, n.d., 13). Protective associations had been a feature of the Shannon in the eighteenth century, but by the nineteenth century interest had been whittled down to such an extent that very little finance could be found amongst the interested parties to fund proper policing of the waters or the pursuance of cases through the courts (*ibid.*, 12). The exploitation by individuals of the loopholes in legislation had greatly diminished the amount of fish going upstream to spawn. In one week during April 1862 over 20 tons of fish caught in the lower Shannon were exported to London, while the total amount during the same week on the upper Shannon estuary (including the great Lax Weir) was merely 7.5cwt (*ibid.*, 6).

By May 1862 there were 35 stake weirs and nineteen fly nets on the Shannon estuary (*ibid.*). In 1863 there was an investigation into the legality of these existing fixed fishtraps. Many owners (by and large the local gentry whose properties bordered the foreshores) were not sure of their legal standing and therefore gave up the exploitation of the traps until the necessary certificates of legality were issued by the authorities (Went 1981, 111). By 1892 there were certificates for 51 stake nets, one fly net and one head weir, mostly on the lower Shannon estuary (Conner 1892, appendix E).

Stake-net weirs extending beyond the low-water mark interrupted the activities of the draft-net fishermen working from boats, who couldn't draw their nets across the same areas of water. The stake-net weirs were also causing collateral damage to the fishing of other fish as well as the salmonid species (*Rep. Select Comm. Fish 1849*, 4525–7). Furthermore, they did not require the same amount of manpower as boat fishing, leading to an increase in unemployment, and this at a time of agrarian unrest and poverty. The contestation of who had access to, and therefore the responsibility for protecting, the fisheries was played out against the social inequalities and unrest of the late nineteenth century.

Post-medieval bag nets, draft nets, snap nets

It is worth emphasising that various other fishing methods were used on the

Shannon estuary throughout the post-medieval period. Most importantly, there are cartographic depictions of fishermen using draft nets from boats (for a detailed description of the form and use of these nets see Went 1964) on the Shannon estuary in the seventeenth and eighteenth centuries. Draft nets continue to be used by local fishermen on the Shannon estuary and Fergus estuary today, and snap nets were formerly in use around the River Maigue and at its mouth (Went 1981). Snap-net fishermen are still active on the River Suir, Co. Waterford (see Wilkins 1998 for a thorough discussion of the lives and work of snap-net fishermen). Bag nets were placed out in the open water of the channel, kept in place by a combination of buoys and anchors. It has been suggested that bag nets were introduced into Ireland in the 1830s (Went 1964, 212; 1981, 111). They would leave little archaeological trace. In other words, boat fishing has also been an important source of income and employment for local communities throughout the post-medieval period.

Origins and chronology of the post-medieval fishtraps

The chronology of the fishtraps, post-and-wattle structures and post alignments described in this chapter must remain, then, for the moment unresolved. Clearly, the post-medieval fishtraps have their origins in an earlier tradition, and, taken in conjunction with the early historic and medieval fishtraps discussed in Chapter 5, they show the importance of fishing to local communities since the Middle Ages. However, we have little sense of whether there was a continuity of practice (or whether fishing waxed and waned). Fishtraps have been assigned to the post-medieval or modern periods in this chapter largely on the basis of their excellent state of preservation (i.e. the height of their individual posts and the density or non-waterlogged nature of the wood). Radiocarbon dating in the post-medieval period is too imprecise for this task. For example, while the Carrigdirty Rock 12 and Fergus estuary west 2 post-and-wattle trackways are definitely confirmed as post-medieval in date, their radiocarbon determinations can only be calibrated to a vague (and useless) date lying somewhere between 1650 and 1940 (see Appendix 1). On the other hand, it is possible that some sites included in this chapter (in particular Bush Island 4, Cratloe Creek 1 and Carrigdirty Rock 15) are actually medieval or late medieval structures.

Seventeenth-century head weirs

At least some of the post-medieval fishtraps must date from the seventeenth century. The Civil Survey of Limerick indicates that there were at least 35 head weirs (not including the Limerick Lax Weir) either being used or 'unsett and out of repayre' (e.g. Simington 1938, 346) on the Limerick shore of the upper Shannon estuary, or on its tidal tributaries, in August 1655. It is interesting, too, how many fishtraps were out of repair in these years, presumably owing to the unsettled nature of the times. Although the Deel estuary possessed eel-weirs and salmon-weirs only at the town of Askeaton, the Shannon estuary head weirs were located at several named places, such as 'Ballycannanena' (Ballycanauna Point, at the mouth of the Deel), 'Ballynvohr' (the modern townland of Ballinvoher), 'Beahy' (Beagh Castle), 'Islandmore' (Bushy Island?) and 'Pallas' (off Pallaskenry?). There were also several weirs upstream on the River Maigue estuary, with a concentration at 'Mullane' (Mellon townland), 'Ballynacarriga' (Ballynacarriga) and 'Ballycullane' (Ballyculhane).

There were also 'two salmon weares' at a place named Carrigclohir (possibly Carrigcloher Point, near Carrigdirty Rock), and a 'salmon weare' and a 'fishing weare' at 'Corkagsmowtane' and 'Ballinoe' respectively (both places in the immediate vicinity of Carrigdirty Rock). In other words, the Carrigdirty 14–15 fishtraps could actually occupy the sites of those referred to (Simington 1938, 392, 388, 39; Went 1960b; 1981). It is also possible that the large fishtraps at Inishbonane 1, Quay Island 2, Bush Island 2A–2C and Cratloe Creek 1 were all constructed on sites used on and off since the seventeenth century. Inishbonane 1 (off Clonmoney South townland, Co. Clare) may be on the site of a fishtrap referred to in Thomas Moland's Survey of 1703, which states that 'Clunmunny farm' was 'bounded on the south by the river Shannon on which is a salmon weir worth £10 per annum' (Ó Dálaigh 1998, 80). In 1692 there was a weir at Cratloe that provided one Laurence Chroe with £4 (Ainsworth 1961, 102). This may be the site of the fishtraps either at O'Brien's Point 1 or Cratloe Creek 1.

Eighteenth- to nineteenth-century head weirs

Some of the fishtraps are clearly of eighteenth- or nineteenth-century date. Indeed, Bush Island 5–11 and 12–18 are depicted in a general way on the first edition of the OS six-inch maps, surveyed in 1841 and published in 1844. There is also potential historical evidence for when the fishtraps went out of use. The massive and highly visible tick-shaped head weirs at Inishbonane 1, Quay Island 2 and Bush Island 2A–2C are not mentioned in the *Second Report of the Commissioners of Inquiry into the State of the Irish Fisheries* (Went 1981, 109), suggesting either that they were out of use by this date (1836) or that they had yet to be built (this is less likely). In any case, after 1864 virtually all fishtraps (both head weirs and stake nets) were prohibited on the Shannon estuary because of concern about the destruction of fish stocks (Went 1981, 111). Thus 1863 may be the latest date for the construction and use of particularly large structures. Nevertheless, it is undoubtedly true that local people would have defiantly continued to build fishtraps up until recent times, at hidden locations in creeks and behind rocky islands. On the other hand, there are also clear and definitive accounts of weirs in the nineteenth century that have now disappeared. A wooden head weir was illustrated in an 1841 Ordnance Survey fair plan (Ordnance Survey 105, B373) at Bunratty, and in 1867 a certificate was issued by the authorities to regularise its use under legislation (Certificate for fixed engine, no. 25, Department of the Marine). The site may have been situated immediately upstream of Bunratty Castle, but there is little visible trace of it today.

Nineteenth-century stake-net weirs

By the 1800s stake-net weirs or Scotch nets had been introduced into the Shannon estuary (Went 1960b, 148). Some may have been built on the sites of older head weirs. Went (1964, 211) suggests that the first stake-net weirs were made of post-and-wattle, with nets replacing the wattles after a short period of time. Certainly many of the post alignments around Bush Island were simply constructed of vertical posts with interwoven wattles. Others, such as Maiden Rock 1, with their widely spaced posts were probably used to support vertical nets. These stake-net weirs fished automatically during the tidal cycle without requiring the immediate presence of a fisherman, and did not need much labour to keep them in good working order (Went 1964, 208). Their use increased dramatically after the enactment of the 1842 Fisheries Act that laid down conditions for the use of stake-net weirs and other fixed engines. This act in effect legalised the use of stake-net weirs in Ireland for the first time since the Irish parliament in the reign of Charles I had abolished their use (*Rep. Select Comm. Fish. 1849*, 405–6, 1613).

The Ordnance Survey fair plans and maps of the early 1840s and the certificates issued by the Fishery Commissioners under the 1863 amendment Act illustrate the location and form of some of these stake nets. They were mostly situated on the lower Shannon estuary, between Beal Point (near the mouth of the Shannon estuary) and Durnish Point, at Foynes, Co. Limerick. There were particularly large numbers in Clonderalaw Bay, Co. Clare. An undated pamphlet by William Lysaght with a map of these stake nets indicates that there was only one site on the upper Shannon estuary in 1862, at Cratloe, Co. Clare (Went 1981, fig. 32). This may have been one of the sites at O'Brien's Point 1–3. The reason for this lack of recorded stake-net weirs on the upper Shannon estuary is unclear, but it is possible that the success of the lower estuary fisheries led to the abandonment of both stake nets and head weirs on the upper estuary.

Post-medieval and modern fishtraps

Size, form and orientation

Head weirs

The large tick-shaped head weirs (Inishbonane 1, Quay Island 2, Bush Island 2A–2C) were constructed of two converging post-and-wattle fences that met at or just below the low-water mark (Fig. 80). Typically, a long shore fence (between 80m and 320m in length) ran down the foreshore to meet a shorter flood fence (between 10m and 45m in length). The two fences usually enclosed fairly acute angles of about 30°, although wider angles (40–60°) were also found. The fences were constructed of hundreds of closely set wooden posts, sometimes with vertical post-and-wattle, and sometimes with double rows of posts with wattle placed between them. These fences, perhaps standing up to 3–4m in height, would have been subject to wind, wave and tidal forces and would have needed constant strengthening and repair. Indeed, at both Inishbonane 1 and Quay Island 2, stones were laid at the base of the fences to protect them. Otherwise the use of obliquely set braces was common, especially in the Bush Island structures, where diagonal posts were wedged against the uprights to support them against the rush of water at the ebb tide.

The large tick-shaped head weirs on the main estuary channel (Inishbonane 1, Quay Island 2, Bush Island 2A–2C, Cratloe Creek 1) were oriented as flood weirs and may have been emptied of their catch by boat at high tide. They were probably largely intended to catch salmon coming up the estuary in the spring and early summer towards their freshwater spawning-grounds, but they would also have caught a range of other fishes, such as trout, sprats, codling, plaice, flounders, whiting, herrings, mackerel, coalfish, mullet, soles, dabs and bass. Each of these species would have been either prized or despised, depending on its market value. The C-shaped and L-shaped head weirs at Bush Island 12–14 were used as ebb weirs, to catch the same fish, or perhaps eels coming down with the tides in October–November.

Creek traps

There are several post alignments that merely cross small creeks (e.g. Bunratty 7–9, Bush Island 4–11). It is obvious that these small 'creek traps', many probably unlicensed or illegal, were well suited to the particular conditions of the Shannon estuary mudflats. Each of the numerous little creeks and narrow channels flowing through the wide expanses of treacherous muds would have provided excellent

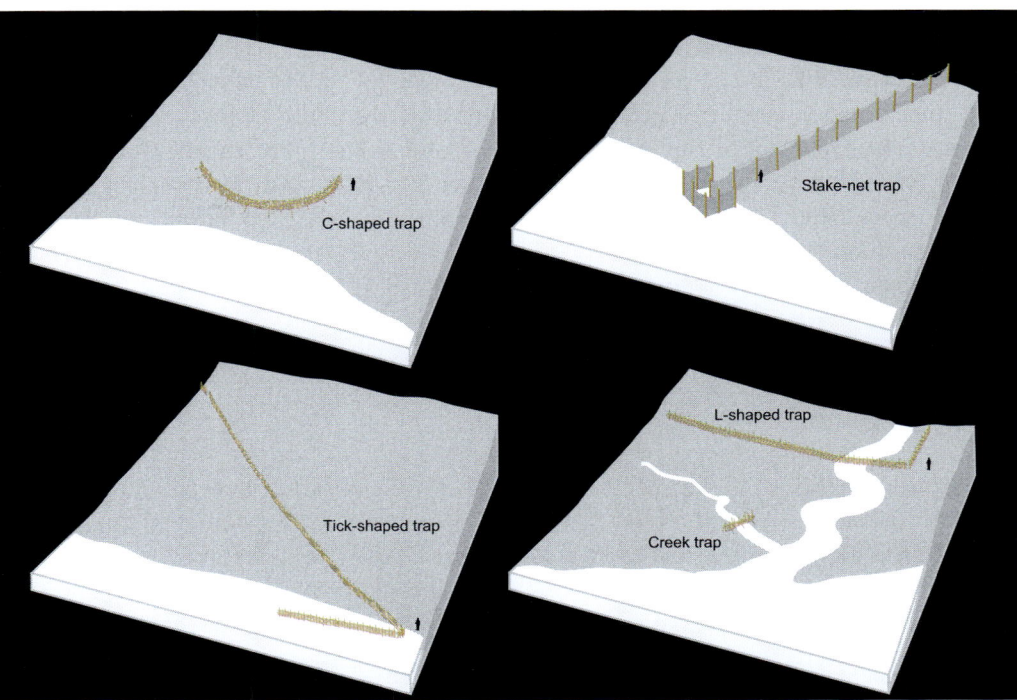

Fig. 80—*Schematic drawings showing types of post-medieval fishtraps used on the Shannon estuary.*

fishing. These narrow creeks, 10–15m in width, typically have steep banks, and during the last few hours of the ebbing tide they carry virtually all of the water out from the marshes. A barrier spanning these narrow creeks need only be about 10m in length to trap most of the fish in it at low water, although these post alignments occasionally measured up to 80m in length. The creek traps are occasionally braced downstream and may have used either nets or brushwood to trap fish.

Stake-net weirs

There are a few possible stake-net weirs on the upper Shannon estuary, perhaps constructed of widely spaced posts that held a wall of netting (Carrigdirty Rock 14, Maiden Rock 1) stretching out from the shore, perhaps with some form of netting pound or 'puzzle trap' situated near the end. Fish ascending or descending the estuary would have found their way barred by these nets. They would then have made their way down the foreshore, beside the leader, moving into the opening in the trap, and would eventually have been concentrated into a small space. They were then removed with a gaff or net or were simply picked up from the foreshore. Two post-medieval post-and-wattle trackways are associated with these fisheries at Carrigdirty Rock 14, perhaps intended to facilitate access onto and across the mudflats.

Site distribution and location

In terms of their distribution, the post-medieval fishtraps on the upper Shannon estuary are typically found in clusters along the north and south banks, at Quay Island, Inishbonane, Green Island, Bush Island (especially), Graigue Island, O'Brien's Point and Cratloe Creek, Co. Clare, and at Carrigdirty Rock and Maiden Rock, Co. Limerick. There were also post-medieval structures on the upper Fergus estuary, Co. Clare. These dense concentrations indicate both continuity in fishing practices and the location of ideal fishing-pools.

Siting by estuary channels, islands and river mouths

In terms of the local siting of the fishtraps there are some interesting patterns. The large tick-shaped head weirs on the main estuary channel (Inishbonane 1, Quay Island 2, Bush Island 2A–2C, and perhaps O'Brien's Point 1–2) were situated right at the low-water mark, immediately downstream of rocky outcrops or islands and near outlets of large creeks or river channels. These locations were probably ideal because of the shallowness of the water, the ease of access to the structures from the islands, and the increased amount of food and nutrients in the water near the rivers and headlands. Post-medieval fishermen, no less than their medieval predecessors, would also have had an extensive store of knowledge about the movement of fish along the upper estuary. The situation of the traps on the channel at the LWM meant that they were only visible during spring low tides, but their low-lying positions on the mudflats would have been ideal as they could have caught fish throughout much of the monthly tidal cycle, using both night and day tides. It is possible that their trapping mechanisms would have been emptied at the high tide (i.e. during a flooding tide) by the local fishermen in boats.

It is also interesting that the smaller creek traps are often found near these larger structures (e.g. at Bush Island). Both the head weirs and the creek traps may have been used by the same people, according to the appropriate season (i.e. the head weirs for salmon in the spring and summer, the creek traps for eels in October). It is also probable that the smaller creek traps were used well after the larger head weirs were banned in the mid-nineteenth century. The possible nineteenth-century stake-net weirs at Maiden Rock 1–2 and Carrigdirty Rock 14 exhibit a strong continuity with the earlier head weirs in the locality. This is unsurprising, given that local landowners and fishermen would have shifted over to the use of these structures as soon as it became apparent how effective the stake-net weirs were.

Siting in relation to riverbanks and nearby settlements

The post-medieval fishtraps may have been located close to the settlements of the local fishermen and landowners. The Maiden Rock, Bush Island, O'Brien's Point and Cratloe Creek fishtraps are all near the drylands, while Inishbonane 1 (near Saint's Island) and Quay Island 2 (by Quay Island) are also located off historically inhabited islands. Lewis's (1837) *Topographical dictionary of Ireland* (in his entry on Bunratty) states that both Quay Island and Saint's Island were inhabited in the early nineteenth century, Quay Island being the home of one family, Saint's Island being a 'richly soiled island of 50 acres' with two families. These local families were probably responsible for the construction and maintenance of the fisheries. The O'Brien's Point fishtraps and Maiden Rock fishtraps are both situated beside large landlord houses (Cratloe Woods and Mellon House) and their estates, and these again were probably the homes of the main owners of these traps.

Folklife and historical studies of some post-medieval fishtraps in Ireland

Introduction

The Shannon estuary fishtraps can be usefully compared with fisheries from elsewhere in Ireland as a result of the indefatigable work of Arthur Went in recording Irish fishing traditions. It is thanks to his astonishing range of papers that we still have access to knowledge of the construction, management and use of fishtraps in Irish coastal, estuarine and riverine waters (Went 1945; 1946; 1948; 1950; 1953; 1956; 1958; 1959; 1960a; 1960b; 1961; 1964; 1969a; 1969b; 1976; 1981). Unfortunately, the upper Shannon estuary fishtraps had been largely abandoned by the time Went was writing, but his work on similar structures at Castlebellingham, Co. Louth, and in Waterford Harbour provides useful clues as to how the Shannon estuary fishtraps would have been used. The stone fish-weirs at Doonbeg Bay, Co. Clare, on the Atlantic coast to the north of the Shannon estuary mouth, also provide revealing insights into potentially early fishing traditions in the region.

Waterford Harbour ebb weirs and flood weirs

The Shannon estuary head weirs are very similar to those used in Waterford Harbour, where fishtraps have been used since at least the thirteenth century (Went 1946, 177; 1959, 91). Historical references indicate their use through the sixteenth century on the River Barrow and the River Suir. For example, in 1514 Richard Elward of ffylyn (Faithleg, Co. Waterford) assigned to Gerald fitzThomas, earl of Kildare, and his heirs 'one of the weirs called Cottok in Dovlokt in Waterford Harbour' (Went 1946, 179). The Cistercian abbey of Dunbrody, Co. Wexford, also held a number of fish-weirs in Waterford Harbour. These 'weares for taking of salmon' are mentioned in historical records through the sixteenth and seventeenth centuries. An inquisition of 1541 named three weirs in its possession—'Scarre Ware', 'Goddiswere' and 'le Ebbe Weare'. They varied in productivity. The 'Scarre Ware' had an annual value of 66s. 8d, giving a yearly return of 40s. to the owner, while the 'Goddiswere', with a broadly similar annual value of 60s., only returned an income of 3s. 4d. The 'le Ebbe Weare' was worth only 5s. a year (Went 1946, 178–9).

The 'Scarre Ware' may have been located at Nook, Co. Wexford, downstream of Dunbrody Abbey (Pl. 78). A late medieval tower-house known as Buttermilk Castle on the steep slopes beside the fishtrap may have been built to defend it (Moore 1996, 177). When head weirs were prohibited in Waterford Harbour, as elsewhere, in 1863 (with the result that 44 head weirs were demolished there in the latter half of the nineteenth century), the ebb weir at Buttermilk Castle was not deemed a nuisance to navigation and was granted a certificate authorising its use on 4 December 1865. This weir is still fished today by Mr Jim Doherty of Cheekpoint, Co. Waterford, and at least four other

Pl. 78—*W.F. Wakeman's depiction in 1840 of the wooden head weir at Buttermilk Castle, Nook townland, Co. Wexford, downstream of Dunbrody on the east bank of Waterford Harbour. This site has been used as a fishtrap since at least the mid-sixteenth century (National Library of Ireland: 1975 TX Frazier Sketch Books).*

head weirs are still in use elsewhere on Waterford Harbour. Recent underwater archaeological surveys on the Buttermilk Castle ebb weir have revealed the presence of thousands of stumps of posts around it in the riverbed, indicating its repair and reconstruction since the late medieval period (Colin Breen, pers. comm.).

The Waterford Harbour fishtraps were either ebb weirs or flood weirs and, like the Shannon estuary head weirs, were 'tick'-shaped in plan, with a long shore fence converging with a shorter flood fence. The Waterford Harbour head weirs are quite similar in form to the wooden fishtraps at Inisbonane 1, Quay Island 2 and Bush Island 2A–2C, and presumably give a good idea of their original appearance (Pl. 60). The fences were constructed of upright poles, with other poles attached across them to create a 'noisy' obstruction for fish as the water gurgled against them. Netting or mesh was also hung on the fences. The trapping mechanism was situated on a platform on four posts at the eye, where a net was hung down into the water. Fish were removed from this net by taking its end into a boat and taking out the fish. The Shannon estuary head weirs were presumably managed in the same way. The traps stand in fairly deep water, at least 2–3m even at low tide, and a considerable current flows through them. The Waterford Harbour fishtraps typically take sole, flats, codling (from about 4lb weight down) and can be rigged for salmon and trout (Seán Doherty, pers. comm.).

Went (1959, 91) stated that the sprat-weirs of Waterford Harbour were not suitable for catching adult salmon. However, salmon fry would be caught if the sprat-weirs were operated during the smolt run to the sea. A local tradition dictated that sprat-weirs, and probably the other head weirs too, were not to be utilised for two months following 20 April, hence preserving salmon stocks for future fishing. Fish taken by these weirs also included sprats, codling, plaice, flounders, whiting, herrings, mackerel, coalfish, mullet, soles, dabs, bass and a few other species (Went 1959, 93).

Castlebellingham head weir, Co. Louth

In Dundalk Bay, north of Annagassan, Co. Louth, on the Irish Sea coast, a large head weir was used up until the late 1940s. It was situated on the sandy flats of the bay, and consisted of two converging fences of unequal length, of stakes and wattles. The weir was unusual in that it possessed a 'fish gate', constructed of post-and-wattle and hinged so that it could move freely with the tide, the flood tide opening it and the ebb tide closing it (thus allowing fish to come upstream). The fish were caught inside a purse or conical net, the mouth of which was attached to an iron hoop about 1.4m in diameter

Pl. 79—*Stone fish-pounds on the Atlantic Ocean at Doonbeg Bay, Co. Clare, exposed during low tide. Although Went records this structure as being used in the early twentieth century, the siting of late medieval tower-houses overlooking the fishtraps raises the possibility that the pounds could be of late medieval date.*

were stabilised by unusual cylindrical baskets called hurls, within which large rocks were placed to give strength to the portion of the wing that needed it the most. At the flood tide fish would make their way through the fish gate, or around or over the fences. With the ebb tide, which had already caused the fish gate to close, fish would have dropped down the shore and were caught between the two wings of the weir inside a purse or net. Flounders and other fish as well as salmon were caught in the Castlebellingham weir (Went 1946, 192–4).

Doonbeg Bay 'fish-pounds', Co. Clare

Stone fishtraps are a common feature of the coasts of Britain and Ireland, although they are not found on the upper Shannon estuary owing to the soft nature of the mudflats. However, they are known at Doonbeg, Co. Clare, on the Atlantic coast to the north of the Shannon estuary, where a series of low stone walls were constructed to trap fish on both Doonmore and Doonbeg Strands (Pl. 79). The two weirs consisted of loose stone walls, up to 1.6m in height. The walls follow the contours of the beach, so they run irregularly across the shore, with various indentations to create pools behind them (Went 1946, 190). When the tidal flood covered the strands and weirs, the fish moved upstream. If freshwater conditions were suitable upstream, the fish moved into the river system. However, if the river was low owing to lack of rain, the fish came back downstream with the ebb of the tide. The ebbing tidal waters flowed through the loose stone walls and through eyes or gratings placed along the lengths of the walls, but the fish were trapped behind the walls. At low tide a small haul or draft net was used to take the fish out of the small pools (Went 1946, 190–2).

Stone was used in the construction of these weirs probably because natural rock beds were quite close to the surface of the strand, preventing the use of stakes. It is interesting that the Doonmore Strand weir could be used in all tidal stages, though the Doonbeg Strand weir, being on a lower contour than its western neighbour, could not be fished at certain neap tides. Other species of fish besides salmon were captured here, particularly flounder (Went 1946, 190–2). The Doonbeg Bay weirs are similar to the Welsh *goradau* stone head weirs found on mudflats in places like the Menai Straits in Gwynedd, north Wales (Jones 1983), in Strangford Lough, Northern Ireland (O'Sullivan *et al.* 1997), and at various locations in Scotland (Bathgate 1949) and England (Fulford *et al.* 1997).

Conclusions

In conclusion, the post-medieval fishtraps of the upper Shannon estuary, easily the most common archaeological site encountered on the intertidal zone, vary widely in location, size, type and preservation. Although most are undated, it is likely that between the seventeenth and the late nineteenth century massive wooden flood weirs were constructed at the low-water mark to trap salmon and other fishes moving upstream, while smaller C-shaped, L-shaped and linear post structures were erected in creeks to trap eels and other fishes on the ebbing tide (with some used in recent decades). These wooden fishtraps provided employment and a source of cash income to a range of social classes and food for local urban populations. Although now largely abandoned, they were once a key social and economic feature of the Shannon estuary.

7. POST-MEDIEVAL SHIPWRECKS, HARBOURS AND LIGHTHOUSES

COLIN BREEN AND CLAIRE CALLAGHAN

Introduction

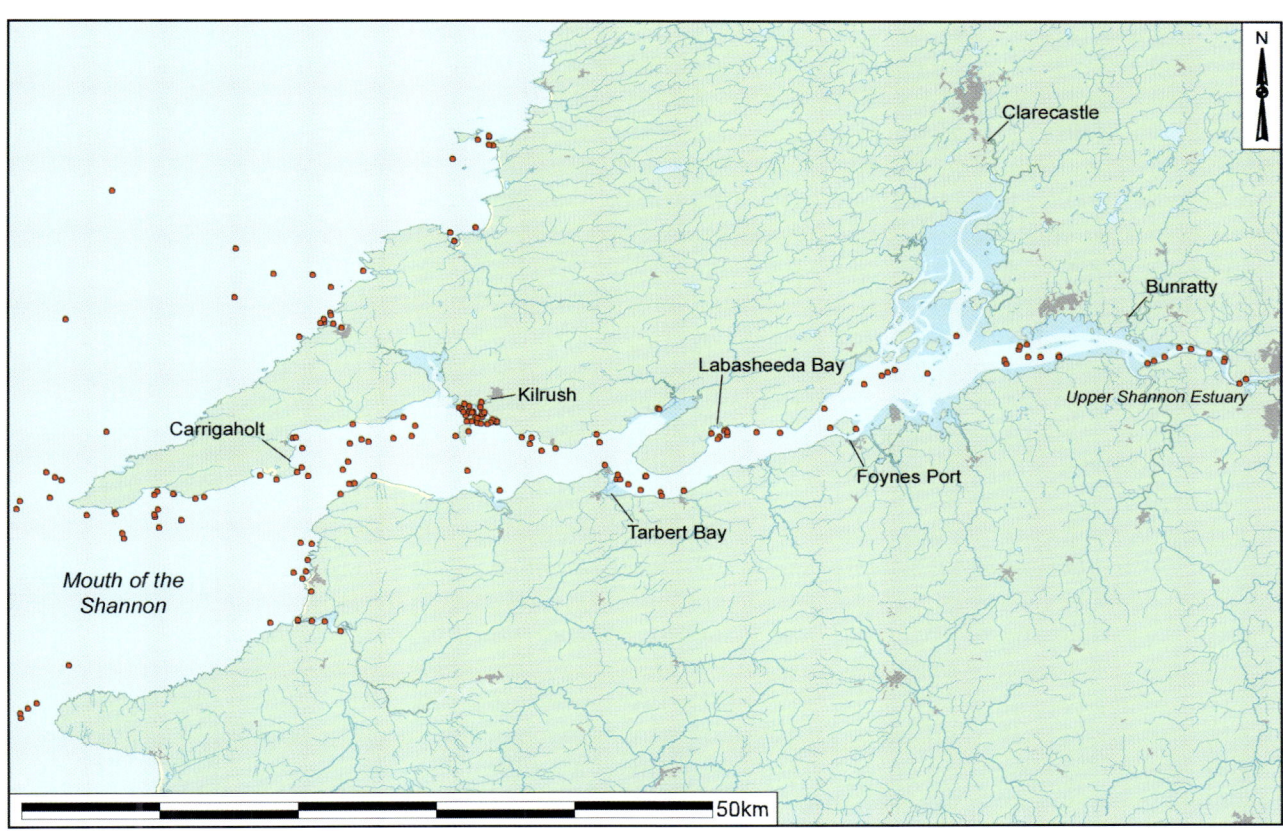

Fig. 81—*Distribution of shipwrecks on the Shannon estuary (Maritime SMR: Dúchas The Heritage Service).*

The Shannon estuary, the largest inlet on the Irish coast and the main water artery into the heart of the country, has been a significant harbour and nautical routeway since prehistoric times. However, as Irish archaeology has been slow to grasp the importance of maritime archaeology, our knowledge of early boats and ships is sadly lacking. This chapter provides a brief study of the historical and archaeological evidence for the use of boats on, and the presence of shipwrecks in, the Shannon estuary (Fig. 81). It is largely derived from the work of the National Maritime Archaeological Survey, based within *Dúchas* The Heritage Service. This survey was established in February 1997 to carry out a desk-based assessment of the nature and extent of the underwater archaeological resource contained within Ireland's territorial waters. Information on sites such as wrecks, old harbours, landing-places and submerged landscapes was taken from a variety of documentary and cartographic sources, including medieval texts, seventeenth-, eighteenth- and nineteenth-century government reports, and British Admiralty survey data. To date, in excess of 10,000 incidents of wreck records have been documented, while records of other site types continue to increase. All of these data have been incorporated into a Geographical

Foragers, farmers and fishers

Information System and are proving to be a valuable management and research tool for baseline research into Ireland's maritime heritage. This survey is essentially a continuation of the existing Archaeological Survey of Ireland, which has been ongoing since the 1960s, and extends this extensive work into the intertidal and subtidal environments that surround this island. Ongoing and future underwater survey can only further enhance our knowledge of this valuable resource. The following account will discuss wrecks along the full extent of the Shannon estuary, as well as within the study areas investigated by the Discovery Programme's intertidal survey.

Prehistoric, early historic and Viking Age boats

In a watery environment like the Shannon estuary, boats would always have been one of the primary means of communication and transport (McGrail 1987). While we have a good general knowledge of the nature of ships and boats in the medieval and later periods, much of our image of earlier water-based activity remains theoretical and speculative. Prehistoric and early medieval communities who inhabited the fringes of the upper Shannon estuary and Fergus estuary must have made extensive use of dug-out boats and other craft. Dug-out boats have been found in recent years on the Cashen estuary, Co. Kerry (Kelly 1981), and on the Fergus estuary, Co. Clare (Kelly 1987). It is also possible that plank-built boats, perhaps similar to those found in recent years on the Severn estuary, the Humber estuary and at Dover (e.g. Wright 1990; McGrail 1997), were in use on the Shannon estuary during the Bronze Age, and it is likely that further intertidal surveys will lead to their discovery. Wood may not have been the only local boat-building material, and it is possible that local communities made use of the Shannon estuary's extensive reed-beds. Wakeman (1873, 76) refers to the use of reeds as a boat-building material in the early nineteenth century, and this material was undoubtedly used in earlier times. This reed craft was in use near Ely Lodge, near Lough Erne. It was built using wreaths of bulrushes which were tied onto a frame or a raft made of rough branches of trees, producing a composite wood and reed craft, with the bulrushes providing buoyancy and a water sealant for the craft. Other examples of this type of craft are known from around the country for use in fishing and ferrying.

The use of skin-covered boats is well documented in the early Irish texts. These boats, with a light timber hull covered with skins, such as oxhides, are one of the most widespread and durable boat types throughout north-west Europe. The curraghs and naomhógs of the western Irish seaboard represent modern survivors of this boat type, which was certainly used in Britain and Ireland in late prehistoric times. Caesar, writing in the last century BC about one of his campaigns in Spain in his *War commentaries*, describes encountering difficulties in crossing a river. He directed his troops to 'build a number of boats, modelled on some that I have once seen in Britain. The keels and ribs were made of light timber; the rest of the hull was of wickerwork covered with hides' (Hope 1990, 11).

Documentary evidence for the use of skin-covered boats in Ireland is contained in the sixth-century voyage tales of Brendan the Navigator (O'Meara 1991). Brendan's first voyage was undertaken in a light vessel with wickerwork sides and ribs which were covered with cowhide, tanned in oak bark, and tarred at the joints. Butter was carried on board to dress the hides for repair. Many of Brendan's activities were based around the north Kerry coast, immediately to the south of the Shannon estuary. The descriptions contained in the voyage tales must represent a common boat type of the region, one that has survived to the present day in the form of the curragh. The physical location and identification of such boats from this period may prove elusive, but it is important to realise that their character and form survive in contemporary boat traditions (particularly in the naomhóg). Their survival represents the continuity of maritime traditions and shows how human adaptation to coastal environments changes little over the centuries.

The coming of the Vikings to Ireland in the last decade of the eighth century introduced radical new boat-building traditions and forms. The slender, clinker-built, double-ended dragon ships of the Vikings represented something that was both special and terrifying to the boatmen of the western seaboard. The Shannon estuary would have been attractive to these newcomers, given its strategic and economic importance. A Viking fleet and stronghold were established on these waters by the early part of the ninth century, and became a raiding base for much of the inland waterways of the country. Throughout the next 200 years Viking fleets were active in raiding and conflicts all along the adjacent coast and waterways, particularly on the River Shannon. Native Irish fleets also appear to have been active on the River Shannon. The *Annals of the Four Masters* refer to the fleets of Cormac and Flaithbheartach on the Shannon in 902 (*AFM*), while the *Annals of Innisfallen* refer to Donnchad, son of Brian, with the crew of one ship, coming upon a fleet of fourteen galleys on the Shannon in 1035 (*AI*).

Medieval boats and ships

The arrival of the Normans in 1169 led to profound economic and social changes in the country. Mercantile activity greatly increased and the urban centres became successful ports, entertaining ships from all over Europe. The protection of the ports and the safe passage of shipping were essential, and special vessels called galleys were built to provide this security. Galleys were wooden clinker-built, double-ended boats which were powered by oars. They appear to have come in a number of different sizes and were very versatile and manoeuvrable craft. In 1205 King John had a fleet of five galleys based in Ireland, while in 1222 Henry III mandated the men of Limerick, Dublin, Waterford, Drogheda and the other ports of Ireland to build galleys in each of their ports for the defence of the king's realm in Ireland (Sweetman 1875, 161, entry 1049; McGrail 1993, 87). In 1234 six galleys were ordered to be built in Irish ports, two with 60 oars and four with 40 oars. Seven years later the men of Drogheda were ordered to build a second galley to accompany their existing one, while Waterford was to build two and Cork and Limerick one each (Sweetman 1875, 377, entry 2532; T. O'Neill 1987, 112). Bunratty, which appears to have acted as an outport for Limerick, was also home to a number of galleys and, as noted in Chapter 5, was described in the fourteenth century as 'Bunratty of the wide roads, oared galleys and safe harbour' (O'Grady 1929, II, 122; J. Bradley 1988b).

The increase in mercantile activity led directly to a need for vessels with larger cargo-carrying capacities. A ship type known as the cog emerged to cater for these needs, and it must have been a common sight on the Shannon estuary during the fourteenth and fifteenth centuries. These ships had a flat, flush-laid bottom with a sharp bilge turn and were clinker-built, with iron spike fastenings attaching the planking to the frame. Straight raked stem and stern posts were the most distinctive feature of this new type of craft, with the rounded ends of the older Scandinavian type of vessel being discarded. Cogs were fitted with one central mast with a large square sail. Large after castles were built on the vessels in recognition of the security required for the cargo carried in an open space in the centre of the hull, forward of the castle. The far larger carrying capacity of these cargo ships did not go unnoticed by the enterprising Irish merchants and mariners of the ports of the Shannon estuary, and in 1338 Maurice, son of the earl of Desmond, hired the cog *La Rode cogge* that was based at Limerick for a journey to Gascony (T. O'Neill 1987, 111–12).

Late medieval and post-medieval ships on the estuary

Profound changes in ship construction began to take place in early fifteenth-century Europe (Gardiner 1994). Carvel construction, or the end-to-end joining of ship planking, became the more common construction technique on larger craft, but the clinker or overlapping technique continued to be used on smaller, more localised boats. The introduction of the carvel vessels meant that shipwrights could build larger vessels which were more structurally sound and more economical, requiring less timber and manual labour in their construction. Larger superstructures could also be accommodated on top of carvel hulls, which was particularly useful for military vessels. Carvel hulls could accommodate gunports, which were particularly important as naval tactics increasingly came to depend on firepower. Two or three masts began to be added, and fore and aft castles were merged into the hull of the vessel—the aft castle in particular becoming much larger and playing a more central role in the internal layout of the ship. By the middle of the sixteenth century hulls had become more rounded to increase stability and increase carrying space.

With the development of new ship-building technology, Irish ports began to witness many new vessel types. The carrack, more than any other ship type, epitomised this change. Although originally developed early in the fourteenth century in the Mediterranean, it quickly evolved and was adopted throughout north-west Europe. Carracks were big, heavy ships with large fore and aft castle structures. Initially they were rigged on the fore and main masts with single square sails, but later they essentially became three-masted ships. Evolutionary trends continued with the emergence of the galleon in the early part of the sixteenth century. Galleons differed from carracks in that they had high, narrow sterns with a lower forecastle and a low beakhead. This distinctive feature protruding from the hull below the bowsprit, a large spar extending from the stem of sailing vessels and used as a rigging support, was used for ramming and later provided a platform for handling headsails. Galleons also had a strongly braced hull adopted for almost continuous use in the strong Atlantic seas. There were many variants of this ship type throughout Europe, with different regions displaying characteristics adapted to suit local needs. Although primarily associated with a military or naval function, galleons were also frequently used for mercantile and fishing purposes. Much of the surviving evidence for these medieval ship types in Irish waters comes from the most famous naval episode in medieval European maritime history, when a formidable Spanish naval armada tried to defeat the English navy and to support an attempted invasion of England in 1588.

The Shannon estuary was witness to the events of 1588. The Armada was far from successful; after a humiliating defeat in the English Channel the Spanish vessels retreated homeward, choosing the route around Scotland, down the western seaboard of Ireland and thence to Spain (Martin 1978; Martin and Parker 1988). This retreat coincided with some of the worst sea storms on record, and 26 Spanish ships, already badly damaged during the Channel engagement, were wrecked on the north and west Irish coasts. One vessel, the *Annunciada*, a 700-ton merchantman carrying 24 guns and 275 crew, was burnt near Scattery Island and Kilrush on the lower Shannon estuary. Nicholas Cahan, an official of the sheriff's office at Liscannor, reported at the time that seven Armada ships had anchored off Carrigaholt (Whiting 1988, 200) at the mouth of the estuary. Two 1000-ton ships, two 400-ton ships and three barques had sent a boat ashore to try and bring on supplies, but were refused. The Spanish offered the *Annunciada* as payment for any goods but this was also refused (Stenuit 1972, 108). Weather conditions improved, allowing the Spanish to leave after they had burnt the much-damaged merchantman, leaving Cahan to comment: 'God be praised, those seven ships are gone, but one ship they have burned' (Whiting 1988, 200). A document listed in the footnotes of the *Annals of the Four Masters* and located in the State Papers Office in London details the following: 'Ships and men sunk, drowned or killed, and taken upon the coast of Ireland in the month of September, 1588, as followeth . . . in Shannan, one burnt, none lost, because the men were likewise embarked in other ships, signed Geff. Fenton' (*AFM*).

Despite such brief historical moments of excitement, the Shannon estuary continued to be a focus of more mundane maritime economic activity. Attempts by the Planters to improve transportation in the region utilising the estuary can, for example, be seen in correspondence between the lord deputy of Ireland, Sir Arthur Chichester, and the New English gentry of Askeaton in 1605, when the new ferry service across the

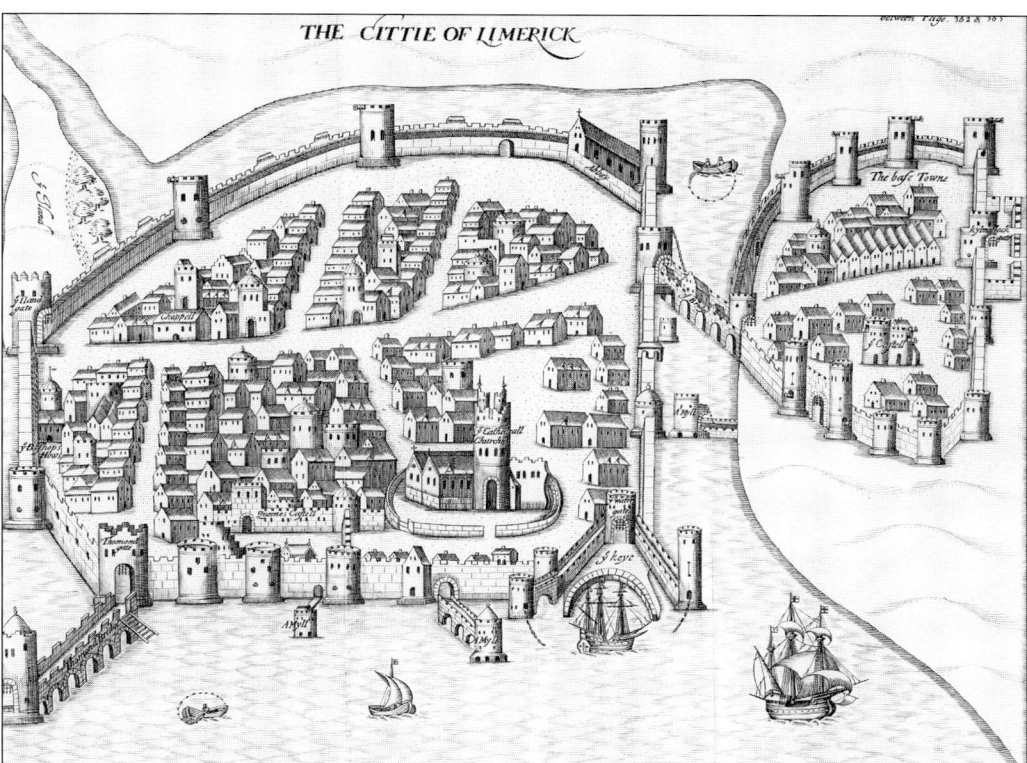

Fig. 82—*The 'Cittie of Limerick' as depicted in* Pacata Hibernia *c. 1633, showing ocean-going ships docked at the Great Quay, constructed c. 1500. Other, smaller river craft and fishing-boats (with the fishermen using nets in the way they still do today) are also shown (National Library of Ireland: Ir 91405s2).*

upper Shannon estuary between Beagh and Rineanna was being proposed (Russell and Prendergast 1872, 352–3; Feheney 1998, 141). Richard Stanihurst in the late sixteenth century had also noted the advantages for shipping on the Shannon estuary, which allowed seagoing ships (Fig. 82) with a burden of 200 tons to dock over 60 miles from the sea (Spellissy 1998, 44), a factor which also permitted Bunratty, home of the earls of Thomond, to be involved with overseas trade (Appleby 1992, 199, 212, 239). An idea of the volume of shipping plying the Shannon estuary can be gained by the fact that customs duties in 1633 came to £1619.07, which allowed Limerick to possess an imposing custom-house from an early period (Spellissy 1998, 199).

An interesting account of a typical incident of this shipping comes from the records of a court case in 1631 in the archives of the Admiralty High Court (Appleby 1992, 199). Paul Philips, a 26-year-old mariner from Redriff, recounts in his deposition before the court that the ship *Pilgrim* of London, under John Correll, arrived at Bunratty on 11 April 1630 in order to load a cargo bound for London. Tristram Mogridge, the merchant who freighted the ship, arrived after two days and ordered the vessel to be made ready for loading. The crew offloaded their ballast and readied the ship, but were to remain at Bunratty for a further five weeks owing to the delay in receiving and loading the cargo. Eventually the *Pilgrim* left Bunratty with the first convenient wind for London, arrived in the River Thames on 7 June, and delivered all the goods laden aboard in Ireland. Edward Rochford, an employee of Mogridge's from Limerick, later testified that the ship's cargo included 1000 dressed sheepskins (*ibid.*, 246).

In separate depositions, a second maritime incident is described before the court in 1632 and 1633. Robert Zachary, master of the 80-ton ship *John* of Dover, leased his ship to the merchant Bernard Mitchell in order to load a cargo of corn in Ireland and transport it to Lisbon. The lease was for a period of four months, at a cost of £25 per month, with the possibility of an extension of another four months if the voyage could not be completed in the time allocated. While on passage to Limerick the ship was chased by two men-of-war off the south-west coast and was forced into Ballinskelligs Bay, 60 miles south of Limerick. It remained there for a number of days before sailing safely on to Limerick. Hundreds of barrels of corn were loaded at Limerick quays, where a dispute arose between the captain and the merchant over the exact quantity loaded

Foragers, farmers and fishers

Fig. 83—*The town of Askeaton on the River Deel, c. 1799, with large sailing-boats and other small craft at the quayside (National Library of Ireland: 1408 TA).*

before the vessel sailed to Bunratty. Here the *John* sent boats up into the country to fetch corn to load the ship, while corn was also 'brought out of the country on horse's backs, and some on men's backs, and brought aboard the ship' (Appleby 1992, 210–12). The whole process took three months, during which time the ship's carpenter and master's mate Edward Whiting stole two sacks of corn and traded them with the locals for salmon. Zachary also lost money gambling and had to sell a cannon from the vessel to meet his debts. Finally the ship left and sailed to Lisbon, where it offloaded the corn and took on a cargo of salt bound for Weymouth.

Eighteenth- and nineteenth-century ships and boats on the Shannon estuary

The eighteenth and nineteenth centuries were to see an intensification of maritime activity around the Shannon estuary. There was a general increase in shipping and a proliferation of coastal industries which required waterfront facilities and vessels to transport their goods. Much of this increase in activity was due to individual entrepreneurs and landowners taking advantage of a more open economic system. By the mid-eighteenth century, ships from Limerick port were involved in the large-scale exportation of its hinterland's agricultural surplus to Europe and the wider world. The scale of this can be seen by the fact that customs duties on shipping in 1775 amounted to £51,000, with 67 customs officers based at Limerick, Scattery Island, Kilrush and

Tarbert (Spellissy 1998, 199). Lloyd's *Tour of Clare*, published in 1780 (*ibid.*), mentions that vessels from overseas were daily transporting goods down the Shannon estuary, while local cargo boats also brought agricultural produce to neighbouring markets at Askeaton, Ennis and Tralee (Fig. 83). There were also at least 70 large vessels transporting turf to Limerick and various other villages along the estuary (Henry 1996, 174–6).

The quantity of shipping on the estuary led to the Limerick Chamber of Commerce's being entitled by Royal Charter in 1815 to protect the port's trade and control the pilotage of the estuary (*ibid.*, 174–6). By 1857 the Limerick Harbour Commissioners had built the Wet Dock at Limerick, and its increased handling capacity of 6000–8000 tons of shipping indicated the volume of traffic expected on the channel (Spellissy 1998, 236). Other harbours developed in the nineteenth century included Foynes, Glin, Tarbert and Kilrush (Henry 1996, 141), while Killadysert, Clarecastle and Barrington piers were utilised for the unloading of supplies (*ibid.*, 176). It is from this later period that most of the following information relating to wrecks and other maritime facilities is taken.

The history and archaeology of shipwrecks on the Shannon estuary

Sources of information

Historical research has shown that at least 127 vessels are recorded as having been wrecked in the Shannon estuary from the sixteenth to the early twentieth century (Fig. 81; see Appendix 3). Documentary evidence for wreck is heavily biased towards the post-medieval period, but this is related to the nature of the inventory sources rather than the actual physical evidence. Recording of ship loss was only initiated in the 1740s, by Lloyd's, the insurance and shipping company in London, when the extent of wrecking began to have a detrimental effect on the British economy, which was heavily dependent on maritime trade and communications. Systematic recording only began in the middle of the nineteenth century, reflecting an increasing concern about the loss of life at sea. However, the negative impact of shipping loss on the economy remained the overriding concern. This is reflected in the fact that it was the British Board of Trade who published the annual lists of shipping loss after 1850, rather than a life-saving organisation like the Lifeboat Society. These annual lists published by the House of Commons, coupled with the accounts of shipping loss published in *Lloyd's List*, the biweekly newsletter produced by Lloyd's, form the basis of the documentary record for shipwreck in Ireland. These sources were usually only concerned with larger vessels and rarely mention the loss of smaller local craft, engaged in fishing or used for leisure purposes. Local and national newspaper accounts are valuable sources for these vessels, and tend to give a more accurate and localised version of the loss than was produced and recorded by civil servants in London acting on second-hand information.

Accounts of incidents of shipwreck from the period prior to 1740 are more difficult to find. There was no systematic recording of ship loss in the medieval period, and researchers are dependent on a number of passing references to wrecking in the known medieval texts. Most of the few recorded losses in these texts refer to major political events such as the ill-fated Spanish Armada of 1588 or to the loss of large merchant vessels. There are also a number of references to instances of litigation in relation to the ownership of wreck material that had been salvaged or washed up on the coast. For the earlier period, the annals provide some information on the use and loss of a number of Viking and native Irish fleets and boats, but these may be exaggerated accounts and are unreliable. The wreck inventory presented here must therefore be treated with caution, given its inherent bias towards the later period and its other limitations. Many other vessels were undoubtedly lost around the Shannon estuary region. Shipping and boat loss was not simply a product of the post-medieval period but has occurred since the earliest occupation of the region, and continues to the present day; 127 vessels lost since 1588 is a large number of wrecks, but a truer figure may be closer to 500 lost since prehistoric times.

Problems in wreck archaeology

Analysis of the data on wrecks on the Shannon estuary is still valuable, albeit selective and incomplete. It can be used as an indicator of the overall nature of the wreck resource in the estuary and as a tool for the interpretation and management of the sites. It can also be useful in providing a predictive model for wreck distribution and as an aid towards site location. The actual positioning of a wreck site is probably the largest problem facing maritime archaeologists. The inventory and documentary sources will often provide the name and location of a wreck site, but this is rarely accurately positioned. The name of a topographic feature such as a rock or a bay will usually be the extent of the locational information provided. The wreck, however, may be partially or totally buried in the sediment at that location, depending on the nature of the underwater environment, or may be scattered over a wide area of the seabed. Wrecks can be discovered in widely varying states of preservation, ranging from upright complete hulls to a number of ferrous objects such as concreted cannon. Underwater site formation processes complicate the issue, ensuring that no two sites will develop in the same way on the seabed. Underwater sites are, for the most part, absent from the visible landscape and can only be located through the use of sophisticated marine survey equipment and through intensive underwater survey.

Type of vessel and date of loss

The types of vessel lost on the Shannon estuary include barques, brigs, brigantines, cruisers, ferry boats, frigates, iron lighters, motor vessels, row-boats, 'sailing-boats', schooners, fishing-smacks, steamers and turf-boats (Fig. 84; Pl. 80). Most vessels were under sail, with schooners and brigs commonly lost. In terms of date of loss, of the 127 wrecks recorded in the Shannon estuary over 90% were lost in the nineteenth century and 8% were lost in the eighteenth century, with the remainder being 'cast away' in the fifteenth, sixteenth and twentieth centuries (Fig. 84). The earliest historical recorded loss is the Spanish Armada vessel the *Annunciada*, burnt near Scattery Roads in 1588. The last vessel included in the inventory is the motor vessel (the *E.D.J.*) wrecked near Kilrush in 1941. The cut-off date for the inventory has been set at 1945 to include the many important World War I and II losses. Interestingly, though, the 1941 wreck is the only wartime loss recorded for the Shannon estuary. This contrasts sharply with the large number of vessels lost in the Irish Sea and the North Channel, two strategically and economically important marine areas during these periods of conflict.

The number of wrecks on the estuary peaked in the 1840s. This reflects the volume of traffic, weather conditions and the types of ships in use. The vast majority of the vessels lost in the Shannon estuary were wooden vessels from the age of sail, dependent solely on the power of wind for their propulsion. A radical change in ship technology occurred in the middle of the nineteenth century, when ships increasingly began to be built of iron and were dependent on steam and engines for propulsion. This led to much-improved safety records and shipping loss began to decrease rapidly, with the obvious exception of losses due to war.

Reasons for loss

There are many reasons why a vessel is lost at sea (Fig. 84b). Ships can be driven ashore, founder, strike rocks, capsize, collide with other craft, or be burnt or lost through human error or the use of poor equipment. However, weather frequently underpins all of these reasons. Over 80% of the vessels wrecked in the Shannon estuary

Post-medieval shipwrecks, harbours and lighthouses

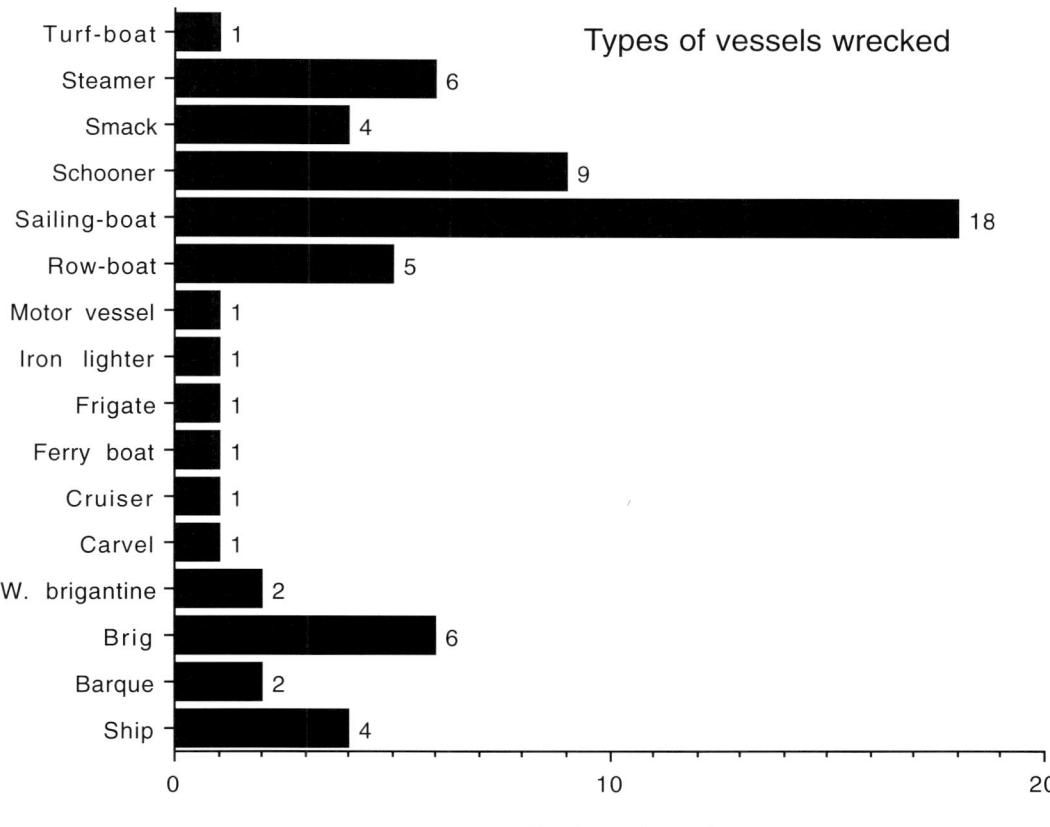

Fig. 84a—*Types of vessel and dates of loss (Colin Breen).*

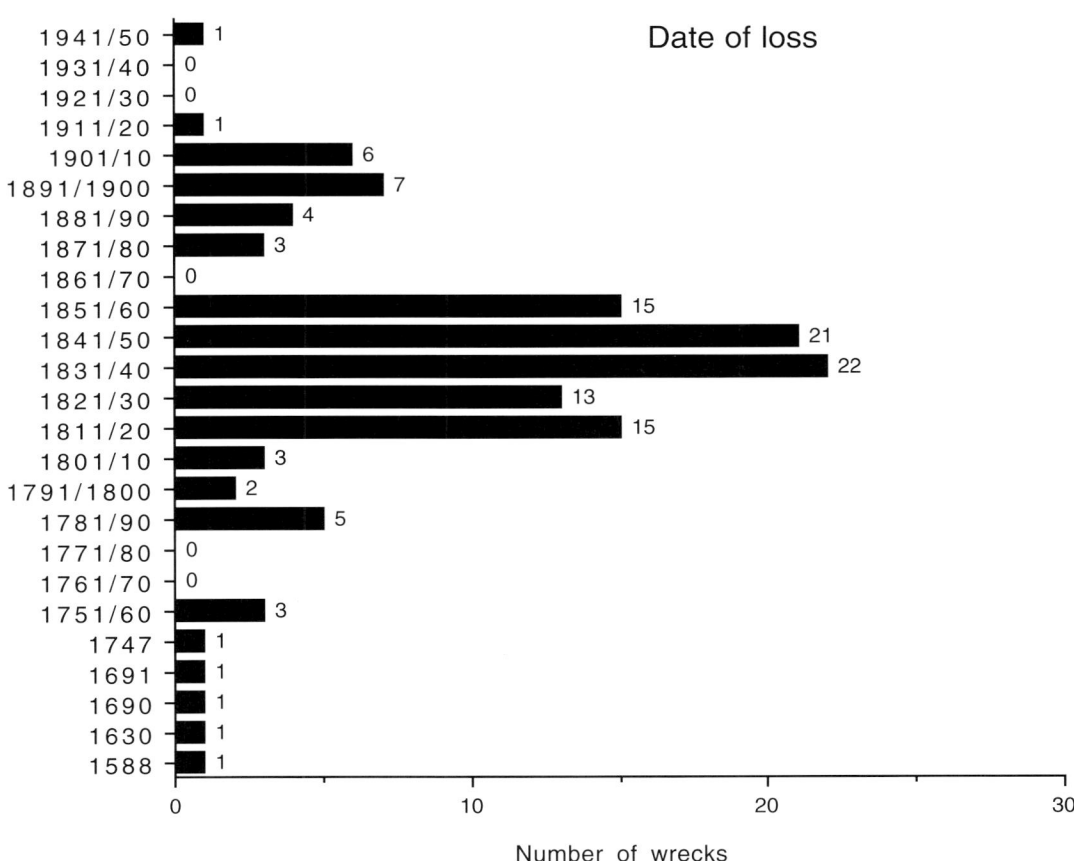

Foragers, farmers and fishers

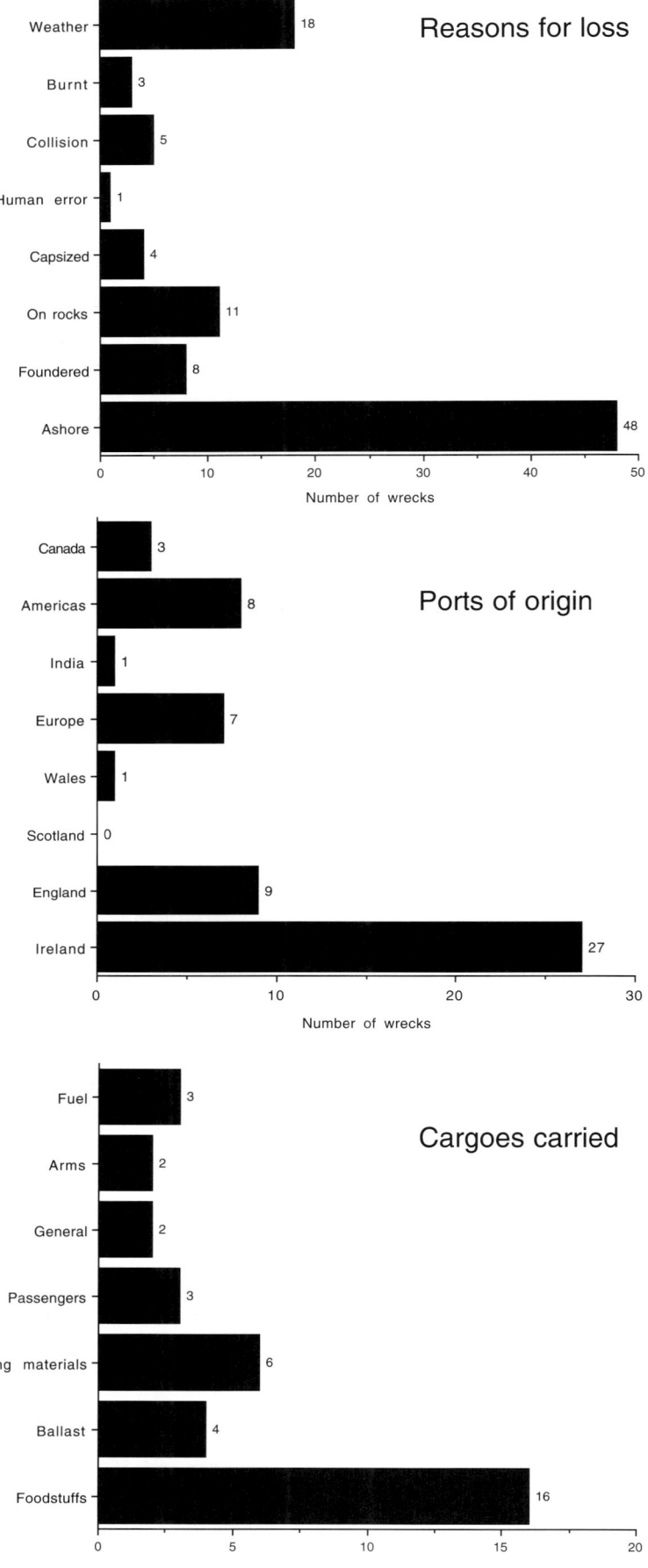

Fig. 84b—*Reasons for loss, ports of origin and types of cargo (Colin Breen).*

Pl. 80—*Foynes Harbour, Co. Limerick, c. 1890–1910, with masted ships and small craft and gandalows in the harbour (National Library of Ireland: Laurence Collection R9707).*

were lost as a direct or indirect result of bad weather conditions, and more specifically high winds with gales resulting in rough seas. In a relatively enclosed area like the Shannon estuary, sailing-vessels are at the mercy of the wind and seas once the weather turns bad. In open water ships will normally be able to run with the seas and weather out a storm, but in estuaries and enclosed bays there is usually nowhere to run. It is unsurprising, then, that 48 of the vessels listed as lost are described as having 'run ashore'. This type of loss has implications for the preservation of wrecks on the foreshore. Being stranded, they would have been subject to immediate salvage attempts by their crew and by local people. In the event that the boat could not be refloated it would have been stripped and possibly burnt to the waterline to prevent it from being a hazard to navigation. The remains of many of these hulks around the Shannon estuary would manifest themselves as little more than the lowermost portion of hull planking, possibly encased in stone ballast mounds.

At least eighteen vessels were lost as a direct result of the weather, but it is not clear in a number of cases whether these were lost in open water or on the coast. One of the interesting things to emerge from the wreck data is that there appears to be a direct correlation between loss and intense episodes of bad weather. This information can then be used as an indicator of climatic events and can be used to support other sources of climatic data in researching past weather patterns and specific events. There are a number of marked peaks in the Shannon estuary wreck data centred around the years 1836–7 and the early to middle 1840s. Interestingly, these appear to coincide with the period of the Famine and a number of the episodes that are commonly referred to in folklore as the nights of the 'big winds'.

Location of losses

The distribution map (Fig. 81) of historical wrecks reveals some interesting patterns relating to channels, shoals, prevalent winds and so on. The mouth of the Shannon has obviously long been a treacherous location, with numerous wrecks off Carrigaholt, Co. Clare. The densest concentration of wrecks, however, is off Kilrush, Co. Clare, where there are frequent references to south-westerly winds driving ships onto the coast. In the mid-estuary, wrecks were also common off Tarbert Bay, Co. Kerry, and in

Labasheeda Bay, Co. Clare. On the upper Shannon estuary, a combination of south-westerly winds and the tidal conditions at the confluence with the Fergus must have made this location dangerous. There were also several wrecks on the upper Shannon estuary, particularly on the rocks and shoals at 'The Middle Ground' and near Hog's Head Rock.

Many wrecks were driven ashore onto rocks and mudflats. Some of these may survive today. For example, a sailing-ship known as the *Sabrina*, laden with grain, was apparently wrecked at Quirk Rock, north of Beeves Lighthouse, in 1897. A local fisherman managed to obtain the salvage rights, removed the grain and towed the ship to Courtbrowne. Feheney (1998, 123) has recently stated that this wreck can still be seen submerged in the mud off Courtbrown Point, Co. Limerick. Other wrecks undoubtedly lie waiting to be discovered. Eight vessels are listed as foundering in the open water within the main body of the Shannon estuary. These sites are likely to be more structurally intact than foreshore examples. The bottom mud of the Shannon estuary can be many metres deep, and a vessel deposited into this environment would quickly become sealed, ensuring good preservation. However, the identification of the physical location of these sites is extremely difficult and is for the most part dependent on chance finds by local fishermen, finds made during dredging work, or through the deployment of marine geophysical survey equipment in targeted survey areas.

Ports of origins, cargoes and loads

Further analysis of the wreck data provides valuable information on the nature of the local maritime economy. Although the recorded wrecks are only a tiny percentage of the overall amount of shipping in the Shannon estuary, they are nevertheless a representative sample. An examination of the ports of origin of the lost vessels reveals, unsurprisingly, that 50% of the boats originated in Irish ports, indicating the extent of local coastal trade in the post-medieval period. The eighteenth and nineteenth centuries in particular saw an upsurge in this coastal trading, resulting in an increase in localised industries and individual entrepreneurial activity. A total of 16% of the vessels originated in English ports, while 2% originated in Wales. No vessels are recorded as having originated in Scottish ports, pointing to the prevalence of trade with England and to a lesser extent with Wales. These data could then be used to point to the existence of a maritime region based along to the south-western and eastern seaboard of Ireland, similar to the Irish Sea region and north coast of Ireland and south-west Scotland region. Vessels originating in Europe and the Americas are well

Pl. 81—*Limerick City, with passenger steamboat pulling away from quay wall at the Wet Dock, c. 1900. These steamers conveyed people down the estuary to towns and villages and served to link the region together (National Library of Ireland: Laurence Collection R5297).*

Post-medieval shipwrecks, harbours and lighthouses

represented, demonstrating the international nature of maritime activity and the lack of discrimination of the sea as regards wrecking.

Foodstuffs dominate the known cargoes of the wrecked craft (Fig. 84b), indicating that food production and carriage dominated the local economy. Fish, corn and cattle were all transported by sea to markets around the Irish coastline and further afield to Britain and continental Europe. Other common cargoes included 'ballast', building materials, passengers, armaments and fuel. Indeed, there is a range of historical evidence for the movement of turf-boats around the Shannon estuary during earlier centuries. The loss of crew and passengers on wrecks also reminds one of the human losses and grief endured by local populations and by foreign travellers on the estuary over the centuries (Pl. 81).

The history and archaeology of harbours and landing-places

Introduction

Boat and ship remains are only one component of the potential maritime cultural landscape of the Shannon estuary. Harbours, small local piers and landing-places are dotted around the estuary. These sites were selected because they were safe and suitable places to bring boats ashore, offering shelter from the winds and prevailing weather conditions. They provided access to coastal settlement and defensive sites, and to the estuary's hinterland. It is probable that they have been in use for many centuries, given that a suitable landing-place would have been repeatedly used. It follows, then, that a pier, while it may look modern, could be located on a site that has been in continuous use for a long time and might actually contain an earlier core within its modern form. It is this continuity of usage and repeated upgrading that has led many researchers to ignore their importance as cultural monuments. Yet for centuries they were the key interface points between the extensive hinterland and the foreland of the estuary and the western seaboard of Ireland as a whole. They provided a focus for fishing and industrial activities, and their location often attracted and governed settlement patterns.

Quays and landing-places on the upper Shannon estuary

Interestingly, the intertidal survey identified few quays and landing-places on the upper Shannon estuary, presumably because boats there would have been drawn up onto the mudflats and marshes. Even today, local fishermen working off Carrigdirty Rock draw their 'gandolas' up to the edge of the marshes, tying them up in small inlets in the saltmarsh cliffs. However, some small stone quays and slipways were recorded on the north bank at O'Brien's Point 4, off Portdrine (the location of a medieval friary and tower-house), and quays can also be seen on the south bank at Ringmoylan Quay and Beagh Castle, Co. Limerick (the latter presumably based on a late medieval quay and used by the inhabitants of the local nineteenth-century fishing-village). There are also stone quays at Bunratty, Co. Clare. Wooden quays were recorded at Quay Island 1 and Quay Island 3 (see Appendix 2). These survive today as large wooden pile structures running down the foreshore. Quay Island 1 is depicted on both Admiralty charts and Ordnance Survey maps, and is obviously related to the use of this island as a pilotage for Limerick City in the nineteenth and twentieth centuries. In contrast, on the Deel estuary there are at least nine stone quays depicted on Ordnance Survey maps. These were most probably built by local farmers in the eighteenth and nineteenth centuries, when the Deel was an important trade route, with grain, fish and seaweed being landed at Askeaton while farm produce and timber were exported from local farms (Henry 1996, 141). 'Farm quays' were probably used on the Deel estuary because

245

Foragers, farmers and fishers

conditions were slightly rockier there. Further studies will undoubtedly locate many more quays of this form.

The port of Limerick

The Shannon estuary region is dominated by the port of Limerick, founded by the Vikings but consolidated as a mercantile port by the Anglo-Normans. Pococke's 1758 *Tour of Limerick* states that the port has 'a good mole for shipping to lye in' (McVeagh 1995, 97). By the late eighteenth century Limerick's prosperity as a port was growing, and vessels of 500 tons could sail up the Shannon and lie at its quays (Maxwell 1949, 228). This prosperity was reflected in the changing form of the waterfront, with large warehouses being built by local entrepreneurs to facilitate the corn and provisions trade. Merchants like the Roches, who owned a number of ships and were involved in the West Indian trade, built a number of waterfront structures, while other buildings on the waterfront included the premises of the Limerick Lock Mills. By the early nineteenth century the waterfront had continued to expand and many of the premises had access to their own landing facilities. The Mining Company of Ireland owned land and a landing-quay on the waterfront in 1828, and was only one of several companies which availed of such facilities (National Archives file OPW 8/- 235/1). While the port continued to prosper, facilities for the ever-increasing amount of shipping visiting the port were not adequate.

An inquiry into the state of British and Irish harbours in the mid-1840s reported:

> 'Limerick, at the head of the estuary of the Shannon, by the energy of the Board of Public Works rendered navigable almost throughout its whole length, offers great facility for navigation and commercial enterprise. Here there is a magnificent bridge, built across the harbour at a cost of 85,000*l.*; yet, although the same Act under which it was erected expressly gives powers for the construction of floating docks, the harbour still remains without a dock or place of shelter, and vessels at low water lie on the rocky bottom, and exposed to damage; while its income of 4000*l.* a-year, levied upon shipping, is mortgaged to pay the interest of money chiefly expended in building the bridge. It is also stated in evidence that while more than half a million of money has been laid out in improving the Upper Shannon (i.e. the River Shannon), the estuary of that river, from Limerick to the sea, has been denied even a few hundred pounds to buoy and beacon the dangerous shoals which, although easily removed, are allowed to remain, and obstruct the navigation of the port' (CSP 1846, vol. 18).

Following this report, a decision was quickly made to facilitate the construction of a wet dock, and work on the project had started before the Commissioners' report was published. Work on the structure, built of ashlar blocks, limestone and wood, progressed well, and it was estimated that it would open for commercial trade in the spring of 1853 (National Archives files OPW 8/- 235/2, OPW 8/- 235/3, Piers and Harbours; CSP 1852–3, vol. 41, 47–51). By 1857 the wet dock had a handling capacity of 6000–8000 tons of shipping (Spellissy 1998, 236).

The ancient port of Bunratty

For a period Bunratty was the second port in the Shannon estuary and was an integral component of the maritime infrastructure of the region. A port and quayage were built here in medieval times to facilitate shipping to its castle and manor. Siltation was a continual problem, though, and with the increasing dominance of Limerick the port ceased to be of major significance in the eighteenth century. The remains of a post-medieval stone quay are visible running under the foundations of the old stone bridge which crosses the River Owenagarney. It was built of large flat stones laid horizontally, and stands to a height of over 1m in places. This structure may constitute part of the medieval waterfront or may represent a later structure that follows the line

Post-medieval shipwrecks, harbours and lighthouses

Pl. 82—*Bunratty Castle, Co. Clare, with men sitting in Shannon estuary 'gandalow' in channel of River Owenagarney with a stone quay on the opposite shore, c. 1880. Bunratty was a significant outport for Limerick through the late Middle Ages, until siltation hampered its use (National Library of Ireland: Spec. Collection SP 1858).*

of an earlier quay. A post-medieval slipway was also situated on the mudflats to the south, of flat angular stones running down to the low-water mark. This must have been used to haul small boats above the high-water mark and ashore. In the eighteenth and nineteenth centuries, small-scale fishing and some transportation operated out of Bunratty, aided by the construction of a 'new Quay' in the middle of the nineteenth century (Pl. 82).

Other ports, piers and harbours

The Commissioners of Fisheries or the Irish Fisheries Board were appointed in 1819 in an attempt to organise the fishing industry. They were primarily responsible for the administration of funds for pier- and boat-building, while their engineers, including Alexander Nimmo, undertook coastal surveys and small-scale building projects (McDowell 1964, 202). The Office of Public Works was established in 1831 by an Act of Parliament and took over much of the work of the Commissioners in finishing uncompleted piers and the repair of existing piers. They also became involved in navigation and were responsible for the erection of beacons and lights. A number of years previously, in 1827, the Commissioners had spent £29,845 on pier construction and repairs, including work on the piers at Carrigaholt and Dunbeg, while an application for the construction of a pier at Querrin in County Clare was also being considered (Brabazon 1848, 102). Querrin, four miles from Carrigaholt, had been actively engaged in the fishing industry in the eighteenth and nineteenth centuries but lacked formal landing facilities. The Inspector of Fisheries appeared hostile to the improvement of facilities here in the late 1820s (National Archives file OPW 8/- 297, Piers and Harbours), yet both the agents of the landlords and the local fishermen had volunteered contributions (Anon. 1836, 224). Twenty-five fishing-boats of between seven and twelve tons, fourteen trading-boats of 40–45 tons, and about 50 small boats called 'canoes' operated out of the town, and the owners of the boats each vouched to bring two loads of stone to assist in making a pier or quay in 1836 (*ibid.*, 225).

Carrigaholt

There had been landing facilities at Carrigaholt since medieval times but they had

Foragers, farmers and fishers

lessened in value by the eighteenth century. A total of £477 had been granted by the Fisheries Board and by various committees to redevelop the harbour in 1822 and to rebuild the old harbour, which was in poor shape. Alexander Nimmo visited the site on the estate of Mr William Westby in 1824–5 and reported on the repairs being carried out (National Archives file OPW 8/65, Piers and Harbours). The Commissioners of Fisheries reported in 1836 that it was a useful pier for both fisheries and trade, with six hookers of seven tons each, and that 'upwards of 500 canoes or corachs [sic], (small cots, some covered with horse-hides, others with canvass laid over with composition,) give employment to about 400 persons in fishing, and to farmers occasionally' (Anon. 1836, 123). Turf, one of the primary local commodities, was also shipped from the pier. The harbour at the town consisted of a pier 150 feet in length, and a quay wall extending inland, 290 feet in length, which had an excavated channel to admit craft. In 1879 the harbour was reported as being in good order, but by 1881 there were again calls to enhance its facilities to accommodate the fishery steamers exploiting the mackerel at the mouth of the Shannon (Anon. 1880, 9; Anon. 1882). The suggestion for improvement was taken on board; £12,160 was granted to upgrade the facilities, and the work was expected to be finished by November 1886 (Anon. 1885, 10).

Kilrush

The pier at Kilrush on the northern shore of the estuary was originally built late in the eighteenth century but was handed over to the Commissioners of Fisheries, who grant-aided its repair. In June 1825 the Board granted £1367 1s. 8d. for this work from the fund acquired under the Act of 5th Geo. IV. cap. 64, with the landowner of the estate, the Right Honourable John Ormsby Vandeleur, undertaking to contribute £456 13s. 10d., or one fourth of the estimated expense (Anon. 1836, 114–15). James Peterson from Kilrush must have been one of the primary local movers behind the pier reconstruction as he is listed in 1828 as repaying £17 to the Commissioners (Anon. 1829, appendix no. 7). The port appears to have been the focus of the fishing industry in the estuary at this time, and the same report lists two decked vessels, 163 half-decked vessels, twelve open sail-boats and 425 row-boats operating out of the harbour. Over 2400 fishermen and tradesmen were employed in the industry at the port, while it was estimated that nearly 5000 women may have been engaged in activities such as net-making and repair and the curing of fish (De Courcy Ireland 1981, 54–5).

By 1836 the town was benefiting greatly from its trade in fish and corn, but the pier was not yet deep enough to allow vessels to lie alongside at all states of the tide. Boats could not gain access to the landing facilities at low water, but had to lie at anchor and

Pl. 83—*Kilrush Harbour, Co. Clare, in the late nineteenth century, with masted ships, steamboats and smaller craft at Cappagh Pier (National Library of Ireland: Laurence Collection R4252).*

wait for the flooding tide to bring them to the quay. The Fisheries Board therefore decided to extend the Revenue Quay into 2m of water below low spring tides, by adding 165 feet to its length. The government provided a grant of £1340, while Vandeleur also contributed towards the cost. Twenty small hookers are listed as being engaged in fishing and dredging for oysters at the port in this year, affording employment to 200 people, while a small steam vessel operated between Kilrush and Limerick (CSP 1836, 123). The proprietor of the soil, Mr Vandeleur, laid claim to the rights of the pier and charged a small toll, producing about £35 a year, which was put towards the protection and repair of the pier and harbour. This toll was not levied on fishing-boats. Documents in the National Archives show that by 1848 the quay wall had been extended to a custom-house that was built on the site, and that the pier sustained damage in the early 1840s (National Archives file OPW 8/- 211). These documents go on to show that the piers at Kilrush, Querrin, Killadysert, Clarecastle, Saleen, Foynes and Kilterry passed out of local hands into the care of local authorities later in the century (National Archives file OPW 43211/83) (Pl. 83).

Killard and Labasheeda

A whole network of other, smaller landing-places were in operation for use by the local fishermen along the Clare coastline. The sheltered sandy beach at Killard was frequently used, while Pullen was merely an 'opening in the cliffs, of about 500 feet long, and forty broad, but it is not possible for any other craft than canoes to enter this fishing place' (Anon. 1836, 224). Labasheeda was also used as a landing-place, but a pier was not built here until late in the nineteenth century (National Archives file OPW 5672/95, Piers and Harbours).

Foynes Port

Foynes Port in County Limerick was the main fishing and transit port on the southern shore of the estuary (Pl. 80). Work began on redeveloping the port in the 1840s, and dredging work and new foundations enabled the largest trading-vessels in the estuary to use the wharf at the site (National Archives file OPW 8/- 147, Piers and Harbours; CSP 1852–3, vol. 41, 47–51). Further improvements took place in the 1880s, in line with the upsurge of the mackerel industry. A new jetty was constructed and further dredging works undertaken in 1915, paving the way for its future development as a centre for flying planes. Work on the construction of a suitable harbour at Glin, further to the west of Foynes, began in 1873 and was completed by 1875 (Anon. 1874; Anon. 1876, 9).

Tarbert

Tarbert was the main County Kerry port in the estuary throughout the post-medieval period. Landing facilities had been developed here on an *ad hoc* basis for a number of years before the City of Dublin Steam Packet Co. leased a section of the shore and set about building a stone pier and wharf in the nineteenth century (National Archives file OPW 8/- 347, Piers and Harbours). With these new facilities the harbour consolidated its position as the main ferry point across the estuary, taking advantage of the relative narrowness of the water at this point. By 1880 there were two piers here; one was the property of the Steam Packet Company, while the second belonged to the Shannon Commissioners. The piers were not in a good condition and siltation of the harbour was a growing problem (Anon. 1880, 10).

The development of the fishing industry continued to be of prime importance to the government throughout the nineteenth century. In 1846 the Fisheries (Ireland) Act was introduced to further the development of a deep-water fishing industry. Finance under this act was used to part-fund the development and construction of piers and harbours which would be useful in this enterprise (Lohan 1994, 10). The Sea Fisheries (Ireland) Act 1883 allowed for full grant-aid to be given for pier construction and established the Fishery Piers and Harbours Commission. In 1891 the Congested

Foragers, farmers and fishers

Districts Board was set up with the primary aims of alleviating poverty and further developing the infrastructure and agricultural industry of the congested areas of Ireland, which were for the most part located along the western seaboard. A number of these areas were located around the estuary, but there does not appear to have been a pier- or harbour-building project which was specific to this programme in the region.

History and archaeology of lighthouses on the Shannon estuary

The importance of the safety of ships entering the estuary was recognised in the seventeenth century when a lighthouse was built at Loop Head around 1665. This lighthouse was unlike the towers that we are familiar with around the coast today, and was actually a small, heavily built cottage with battered walls and a barrel-vaulted roof. The remains of this building can still be seen within the compound of the later nineteenth-century lighthouse (Hague and Christie 1975, 86). The interior contained a number of small rooms that accommodated the keeper and his family, while a stone stairway, since lost, led to the platform on the roof where a coal-fuelled brazier burned. It did not remain in operation for long and had fallen out of use by the end of the century.

In 1717 the merchants and aldermen of Limerick City petitioned the Irish parliament to replace the light, and a lighthouse was re-established here in 1720. Over 80 years later, Thomas Rogers built a new tower in 1802. This new structure was 277 feet high and contained four rooms and a lantern fuelled with oil (BPP 1834, 142). The lantern was twelve feet in diameter and contained twelve lamps, each with a concave parabolic reflector. The light passed through a convex lens of solid glass, 22 inches in diameter, and the fixed bright light could be seen up to 22 nautical miles away. In 1825 the number of lights and reflectors was increased to fifteen.

In 1836 the Chamber of Commerce of Limerick commented that the light was poor and recommended that the tower be rebuilt. An inspector reported that the light was as good as any other, but in 1843 he suggested that a new optic and tower should be provided. In 1844 Mr William Burgess of Limerick was contracted to build a new tower, which was subsequently designed by George Halpin and located 30 feet east-north-east of the 1802 tower (BPP 1845, 605). On 1 May 1854 this new tower took over. The old tower was demolished so that it would not affect the light from the new tower. An 'explosive fog signal' was put in place in 1898, while the light was further improved in 1912 (Robinson 1988).

Several other lighthouses were built in the nineteenth century to protect and warn mariners on the estuary, notable examples being those at Tarbert, Kilcredaun, Scattery Island (built in 1872) and Beeves Rock (McCarthy 1997). A white tower, 26 feet high and located 107 feet above sea level, was built at Kilcredaun Point in 1824 (BPP 1834, 142, 144). It had one fixed light with twelve burners showing a deep red light to the sea and a bright light to the river. It showed from east seaward to west by north, and was visible up to sixteen nautical miles away in good weather (BPP 1845, 605). Ten years later, on 31 March 1834, a light came into operation on Tarbert Rock. Its tower was 67 feet high, the base submerged at high water, and had one fixed light with nineteen burners which showed from west 1/2 south seaward to south-east 1/2 east (BPP 1834, 142, 144; BPP 1845, 582, 605).

An unlit tower was also first built in 1816 at Beeves Rock, at the junction of the Shannon and Fergus estuaries. This unusual lighthouse and its buildings appear almost like a ship at high tide, as the rock on which it is situated is awash. Two keepers and their families lived on the buildings beside the tower until they moved to shore dwellings near Askeaton in 1908. River pilots living on the Fergus estuary islands would row across to Beeves Rock to meet and then guide ships coming up the estuary to

Limerick (McCarthy 1997, 82). Numerous towers, beacons and buoys were also placed on the channel. One highly visible and distinctive tower is situated on the mid-channel at The Scarlets, on the upper estuary, built on a treacherous sheet of bedrock that is exposed to view at low water. These lighthouses and towers are another important aspect of the maritime heritage, as they enabled ships and boats to sail to and from Limerick on an estuary that flows for 60 miles down to the ocean.

Conclusions

The Shannon estuary intertidal survey has successfully identified a range of prehistoric, medieval and post-medieval sites on the mudflats along the upper Shannon estuary and the Fergus estuary. However, it is clear that a comprehensive underwater and maritime archaeological survey is now also required, to further enhance our knowledge of the estuary's cultural heritage. This should comprise an intensive geophysical survey of the estuary channels, coupled with environmental and oceanographic modelling and physical examination by divers. This type of survey should be seen as the natural second stage to the compilation of the wreck inventory. Much of this survey will be reconnaissance mapping, so more intensive site survey and landscape research projects need to be undertaken by the various institutions associated with the region in order to develop a comprehensive understanding of the maritime past of the Shannon estuary.

8. PEOPLE, PLACE AND TIME ON THE SHANNON ESTUARY

Introduction

The Shannon estuary intertidal survey has produced a remarkable and diverse assemblage of archaeological sites and palaeoenvironmental evidence, ranging in date from the Neolithic to the post-medieval period. In this concluding chapter, the various strands of this evidence will be drawn together to present some overall interpretations of the archaeology and environment of the Shannon estuary. I will also attempt to approach an understanding of how people would have experienced this estuary landscape, according to their own background and their sense of place and time. Finally, the Shannon estuary survey has to be seen as only the first attempt to explore estuarine archaeology in Ireland, so I conclude with some proposals for future archaeological, historical and palaeoenvironmental investigations.

Archaeology and environment on the Shannon estuary

Neolithic foragers and farmers in a wetland landscape

By the Neolithic (4000–2500 BC), the upper Shannon estuary probably had several broad channels flowing through much more extensive mudflats and saltmarshes, fens, reed-swamps, carr woodlands and other estuarine wetlands. The islands on the modern mudflats would have been places of dry ground densely covered with hazel, ash and blackthorn scrub, while in the wetlands between them stretched alder, birch and willow carr woodlands. Scots pine, oak, elm and hazel woodland would have grown on the surrounding hills, and these may have remained largely uncleared until the Late Neolithic. Neolithic submerged forests, recorded at several different locations on both the lower and upper Shannon estuary, will provide good palaeoenvironmental evidence for future landscape reconstruction and sea-level change studies on the estuary. At Meelick Rocks, Co. Limerick (Pl. 84), the trunks and root systems of a probable oak–alder woodland in peats on the upper foreshore have been dated to the Late Neolithic, 4160 ± 20 BP (2875–2634 BC; GrN-21930), while submerged roots in peats at the lower part of this foreshore have been dated to the Mesolithic at 6240 ± 25 BP (5299–5078 cal. BC; GrN-21929). Submerged Scots pine forests have also been recorded at Rinevalla Bay, Bunaclugga Bay and Poulnasharry Bay, Co. Clare, all on the lower Shannon estuary. The forest at Poulnasharry Bay produced radiocarbon dates of 4960 ± 35 BP (3892–3655 cal. BC; GrN-20145) before it was covered by peats and thereafter by estuarine clays in the late Iron Age at 1640 ± 40 BP (cal. AD 262–534; GrN-21928). Neolithic animal bone has been found in estuarine clays, with red deer bone recorded on the upper Fergus estuary, Co. Clare, and dated to 4245 ± 40 BP (2919–2689 cal. BC; GrN-20140).

The early prehistoric estuarine landscape would have teemed with eels, salmon and other fish, and the woods would have been the haunt of wild pig and red deer, while wildfowl such as geese, ducks and swans would have inhabited the marshes. It would have been a highly attractive landscape to local early prehistoric communities, who perhaps combined cattle-herding and arable farming with a broad-spectrum foraging

Pl. 84—*Aerial view of site of Neolithic submerged forest stone axe findspot at Meelick Rocks, Co. Limerick. Neolithic communities probably settled the nearby hills, and hunted, fished and herded cattle along the estuary marshes (photo: Shannon Estuary Ports).*

and fishing economy. Although the archaeological evidence for Early Neolithic settlement along the estuary is scanty (mostly consisting of stray finds of stone axes and some Late Neolithic wedge tombs or megalithic tombs), we could presume from settlement evidence elsewhere in the south-west region that there are indeed houses, field systems and other activity sites located on the drylands and hills overlooking the estuary. Significantly, a possible Neolithic wetland occupation site has now been identified at Carrigdirty Rock 5, on the upper Shannon estuary. This site has produced, from organic-rich, minerogenic clays on the lower foreshore, basketry dated to 3702–3386 cal. BC (4820 ± 50 BP; Beta-102087 and GrA-6520) and a single fragment of human skull (as well as a human clavicle) from an adult aged at least 25–35, dated to the Early Neolithic at 3634–3370 cal. BC (4710 ± 60 BP; Beta-102086). Other finds from the site include a miniature stone axe, two deliberately struck chert chips, a possible hammerstone and deposits of swan and cattle bone, as well as worked and charred wood, charcoal and fragments of hazelnuts and bone emerging from the clays.

The site is interpreted as a short-stay camp of local foragers and farmers who would have moved through this coastal wetland landscape, perhaps grazing cattle on the marshes while foraging for wild plant foods (e.g. hazelnuts), hunting wildfowl, pig or deer, and fishing the channels. It is also possible that this was some kind of place for human burial, although the practical and the symbolic would not have been separate in early prehistoric people's lives and a complex perception of this estuary landscape would have easily allowed for economic subsistence and symbolic activities at the same place.

Bronze Age farmers and sacred places in the marshlands

By the Bronze Age, a period of marine regression (perhaps caused by changes in sea level or local alterations on the estuary channel) may have led to fens, carr woodlands and reed-swamps colonising the estuarine mudflats at places that are now submerged in the intertidal zone (e.g. at Carrigdirty Rock and Meelick Rocks). Bronze Age settlement evidence along the hills fringing the upper Shannon estuary and Fergus estuary includes stone enclosures, standing stones, *fulachta fiadh* and the occasional metalwork find (Pl. 85). Bronze Age evidence from the mudflats suggests that these local communities made use of the estuary's resources by means of a mixed farming strategy, with cattle and sheep being herded on the coastal marshes for the spring and summer pastures and perhaps livestock and crops being tended on the dryland terraces and hills, while no doubt fishing and hunting were also important. The estuarine wetlands may also have been seen as a sacred space, within which there were particular places where otherworldly spirits and entities could have been encountered and contacted.

At Carrigdirty Rock 1, a circular wooden structure recorded on a shelf of submerged organic peats, constructed of light poles carefully sharpened so that they could be driven down into the peat, produced a single piece of immature calf bone and a radiocarbon date of 1681–1529 cal. BC (3330 ± 25 BP; GrN-20976), in the Middle Bronze Age. This and other possible features in the vicinity were probably constructed in a fen or carr woodland at some distance back from the estuary channel, although the sites may have been occasionally influenced by brackish conditions introduced by high spring tides. The Carrigdirty Rock structure could be interpreted as the remains of a small roundhouse, perhaps 4.6–6m in diameter, constructed with posts holding up a roof thatched with reeds or turf. It could have provided substantial shelter for herders living with the cattle, hunting or fishing on the marshes during the summer months. Other undated features from the Carrigdirty Rock intertidal peats include post features and two very large cleft oak planks, laid horizontally and at irregular orientations in the peat. These planks may have served as trackways or creek bridges in the wetlands. At Carrigdirty Rock 3, a shallow oval pit amongst the trunks and roots of a fen-carr woodland produced disarticulated red deer bone and pink-footed goose bone, while chopped pig bone and mature deer antler were recovered from the nearby peat surface. These various features may indicate other later prehistoric activities in these environments.

A Late Bronze Age wooden structure at Fergus estuary west 1, near Islandmagrath, Co. Clare, was built of two parallel rows of post-and-wattle fences, hurdle panels, brushwood and branches. A sample of narrow hazel rod provided a radiocarbon date of 2540 ± 20 BP (797–551 BC; GrN-20974). The structure, possibly laid down on intertidal estuarine clays with reed-swamps in the vicinity, could be interpreted as either an unusual fishtrap, a 'hard' or complex wooden jetty for beaching and unloading boats, or more likely as a well-built trackway providing access across the mudflats and reed-swamp. It may well have been an important routeway for people and animals crossing the upper Fergus estuary, moving between islands and drylands.

Pl. 85—*View from Carrigogunnel hill, Co. Limerick, across the huge area of reclaimed corcass and estuarine alluvium out towards the Neolithic and Bronze Age occupation sites at Carrigdirty Rock. Bronze Age settlement sites,* fulachta fiadh, *standing stones and an important hoard of bronze horns are known from these hills.*

Foragers, farmers and fishers

Certainly the landscape to the east is now known to have been intensively settled at about 900–850 BC, when Mooghaun hillfort, hilltop enclosures and smaller farmsteads were occupied by a wealthy, socially stratified and regionally powerful community. By the Late Bronze Age especially, these local communities were depositing gold dress-fasteners, bracelets and gorgets, bronze axes and weapons into the estuary's marshes, creeks and bogs, as can be seen from the Late Bronze Age Carrigogunnel hoard, the Shannongrove gorget, and finds of a Late Bronze Age gold bracelet and a gold dress-fastener on the upper Fergus estuary, Co. Clare. Again, these are hints that the sacred and the secular were intertwined in these coastal wetlands.

Early historic and medieval fishing and economy

By the early historic and medieval periods, the upper Shannon estuary was probably somewhat similar to its present appearance. Sea levels had probably neared present-day levels, the estuary channel flowed through mostly saltmarshes and mudflats, and the islands of the estuary would have been largely cut off at low tide. However, in the absence of reclamation banks, there would have been extensive areas of waterlogged marshes and corcass. Historical sources suggest that these corcass lands were used in the Middle Ages for grazing cattle, sheep and horses. There is little doubt that the estuary would have been teeming with craft of various forms—small dug-outs, coracles and fishing-boats, as well as the large ships plying back and forth between the port of Limerick and its subsidiary ports on the river at Bunratty, Askeaton and Ennis.

We have good evidence for settlement in the Middle Ages on the lands fringing the estuary, including early historic ringforts, churches and monastic sites on the dryland and islands, while by the tenth and eleventh centuries Hiberno-Norse Limerick was one of the most significant ports in Ireland. By the thirteenth and fourteenth centuries Anglo-Norman and Gaelic Irish hall-houses, castles and fortresses were being built along the banks of the estuary, while medieval churches (at Newtown, Kilconry, etc.), friaries (Cratloewoods) and abbeys (Canon Island) were also established. Limerick too was a thriving medieval port. By the fifteenth century, tower-houses occupied by the Desmond lords and the O'Briens and MacNamaras of Thomond were located along the upper Shannon estuary, at places like Beagh and Carrigogunnel, Co. Limerick, and at Castledonnell, Cratloekeel and Cratloemoyle, Co. Clare. These tower-houses were sited so as to be visible statements of power and wealth on a significant regional routeway, and their landing-places would have been used for boats and ships, with their fisheries a closely guarded resource. Indeed, the fisheries of the Shannon estuary, traditionally owned by the citizens of Limerick, were of great importance throughout the Middle Ages.

We now have spectacular and unique archaeological evidence that local communities settled along the estuary were constructing and using wooden fishtraps to provide food for the table and fish for local and urban markets. These structures on the Fergus estuary, the Deel estuary and especially at Bunratty on the Shannon estuary provide us with some of our best insights yet into fishing practices and fishing technology in medieval Ireland. The fishtraps were both ebb weirs and flood weirs on creeks and channels, with post-and-wattle fences designed to guide fish moving with the tides into woven baskets. Our earliest evidence for these fishtraps is an early historic post-and-wattle fence on the upper Fergus estuary, Co. Clare, dated to 1495 ± 35 BP (cal. AD 442–644; GrN-20139), possibly contemporary with early historic ringforts on the drylands. Medieval fishtraps have been located on the mudflats of the Deel estuary, where there is evidence that the structures were repaired and replaced between the eleventh and thirteenth centuries. Deel estuary 1, dated to 900 ± 20 BP (cal. AD 1041–1208; GrN-21932), is a V-shaped fishtrap, oriented to catch fish on the flooding tide, with two converging post-and-wattle fences perhaps measuring over 30m in length. Deel estuary 2, of apparently similar construction and orientation, has been radiocarbon-dated to 740 ± 15 BP (cal. AD 1262–92; GrN-20975). A third, similar wooden fence (Deel 3) is situated yet further to the south and has been dated to 640 ±

Pl. 86—*Medieval fishtrap at Bunratty 6. Other medieval fisheries must be located along the mudflats of the upper Shannon estuary.*

20 BP (cal. AD 1297–1392; GrN-21931). Medieval settlements contemporary with the fishtraps include a thirteenth-century hall-house at Tomdeely North, as well as earthworks, churches and sites of castles at Ballynash, Courtbrown and Ballysteen. The nearby medieval town of Askeaton would have provided a ready market for fish caught in these traps.

At Bunratty, Co. Clare, medieval landscape, settlement and coastal wetland exploitation can be explored across the estuary from the drylands down to the mudflats. The Anglo-Norman borough of Bunratty was one of the most important medieval settlements and ports in the region. By 1287 it is known to have had a substantial town population, a harbour, a seigneurial castle, a parish church, markets, a watermill, a fish-pond and a rabbit warren. The Anglo-Norman manor probably encompassed arable fields closer to the town and cattle pasture on the corcass down towards the estuary. It is now also clear that local fishermen were using complex wooden fishtraps on the estuary, and they would have moved along the foreshore in small craft, removing salmon, eels, trout, flat-fish and other fishes. It is also apparent that repair and reconstruction were part of the daily work of local fishermen. Bunratty 4 had several separate rows of post-and-wattle running down the foreshore, indicating at least three phases of use of the site, with the fences repaired every few years. Bunratty 4 has been radiocarbon-dated to 960 ± 20 BP (cal. AD 1018–1159; GrN-21933), possibly indicating the presence of a Gaelic Irish settlement at Bunratty prior to the Anglo-Norman invasion. Bunratty 6 is easily the best-preserved and most complete fishtrap yet known from medieval Ireland (Pl. 86), with the spectacular remains of post-and-wattle fences and a unique woven basket, 4.2m long, dated to 820 ± 35 BP (cal. AD 1164–1279; GrN-21934). It is interesting that fishtraps of broadly similar design were

Foragers, farmers and fishers

Pl. 87—*Probable post-medieval C-shaped fishtrap and post-and-wattle panel in clays at Bush Island 13. Further historical and folklife research could aim to establish the ownership and use of these fisheries.*

being constructed between the eleventh and thirteenth centuries. Local Gaelic Irish lords and their tenants were apparently exploiting the fisheries prior to the Anglo-Norman colonisation, perhaps supplying local settlements as well as the urban markets of the Hiberno-Norse town of Limerick. These local, native fishermen probably continued to work the traps as free tenants or betaghs on the Anglo-Norman manors and estates in the thirteenth and fourteenth centuries, when the estuary's fisheries would have been a closely guarded resource.

Post-medieval fisheries, shipwreck and landscape reclamation

During the post-medieval period, the Shannon estuary's fisheries, seaweed, oysters, reed-beds, saltmarshes and other resources were all being exploited in an increasingly entrepreneurial fashion. Our own investigations have focused on the archaeology of the upper Shannon estuary and Fergus estuary mudflats, and have shown that in the seventeenth, eighteenth and nineteenth centuries fishtraps of increasingly ambitious design and size were being constructed and used at such places as Inishbonane, Quay Island, Bush Island, O'Brien's Point and Cratloe Creek on the Clare foreshore, and at Carrigdirty Rock and Maiden Rock on the Limerick foreshore (Pl. 87). These fishtraps probably range in date; some may date from the seventeenth century (when the Civil Survey describes 'salmon weares' as being 'unsett' or out of use at various locations on the upper Shannon estuary), while others must be of eighteenth- or early nineteenth-century origin. In the nineteenth century, massive head weirs and stake-net weirs were constructed at various locations along the estuary, before they were prohibited in the mid-nineteenth century by acts of parliament as a menace to navigation and fish stocks. These fishtraps would have been largely controlled by local landlords, but their ownership, management and income were undoubtedly contested and they were certainly a source of local friction and class divisions in the nineteenth century. It is also true that several of the smaller creek traps would have been erected by local people for catching eels until recent times. In other words, the post-medieval fishtraps testify both to long continuities in fishing on the estuary and to the involvement of various social classes in this industry.

Historical and archaeological evidence suggests that by the seventeenth century the Shannon estuary landscape was beginning to be transformed by wetland reclamation projects. Although the history of this reclamation remains to be written, it was certainly ongoing in the sixteenth and seventeenth centuries on the upper estuary. However, the main reclamation schemes were probably carried out in the eighteenth and nineteenth centuries, supported by government funding and local entrepreneurial ventures. Over the centuries, sequences of earthen and stone sea-banks gradually pushed towards the estuary, and drainage ditches and field systems were built to retain and drain the corcass, creating the huge areas of low-lying alluvial levels that can be seen on both the Clare and Limerick coastlines today. The Shannon estuary has been profoundly transformed by these post-medieval sea-banks, as large areas were drained for the growing of wheat, barley, oats, coleseed and hay, as well as for cattle pasture.

During the post-medieval period, the Shannon estuary continued to serve as a major nautical routeway and provided access to the growing port and town of Limerick, while other ports at Askeaton and elsewhere on the lower Shannon estuary were engaged in mercantile trade. Throughout the late medieval and post-medieval periods, over 100 ships and boats came to grief on the estuary, ranging in size from small fishing-boats and turf-boats to large ocean-going ships. The cargoes and ports of origin of these ships testify to trade and contacts between Limerick and Europe and the wider world. Concern over losses was also to lead to various attempts to prevent wreck, including the construction of lighthouses and beacons on shoals and shallows.

The people of the estuary

Introduction

People have lived on the Shannon estuary since at least the fourth millennium BC, so over the centuries hundreds of generations have lived, worked and died in this landscape. Obviously, across this great span of time there have been significant social and ethnic changes amongst the peoples of the Shannon estuary. In recent years archaeologists have come to realise that the landscapes of the past have to be understood in terms of social ranking, age and gender, examining the complex social relationships between different members of the community. While as archaeologists we emphasise the material remains of the past, it is important to remember that the archaeology of the Shannon estuary is in the end about people, their societies, identities, choices and actions in these wetland environments.

Ethnicity and identity

However, it is worth pointing out that there has never really been such a phenomenon as 'the people of the Shannon estuary'. Although across time local communities might have had a common sense of place and knowledge of the estuary, they were in every other sense diverse. The Shannon estuary as a nautical routeway out to the wider world has long facilitated the movement into this area of many different ethnic groups. Throughout the prehistoric period, Mesolithic hunter-gatherers, Neolithic farming communities, and Bronze Age and Iron Age (e.g. the *Gangani* and *Auteini* of Ptolemy's 'map' of Ireland) tribal groups may have moved into the region (e.g. Grogan 1995). We have suggested that local communities on the estuary in the

Foragers, farmers and fishers

Early Neolithic might have seen themselves as distinct from neighbouring farming communities elsewhere in north Munster (e.g. on the Burren or at Lough Gur, Co. Limerick), in terms of their familial descent, kinship and cosmology. It is possible that the people of the upper Shannon estuary in the mid-fourth millennium BC saw the world differently than did people in other places, such as the passage tomb landscape of the Boyne Valley or the Neolithic farmlands of Céide Fields in north Mayo. Indeed, this is hardly surprising, as archaeologists are recognising that different localities and regions throughout Ireland developed their own identities through the Neolithic period (Cooney 1997; 2000a; 2000b). It is also true that in the Middle and Late Bronze Age regionally distinctive social groups may have emerged in the north Munster region, although their identity would have been shaped less by ethnic differences than by identification with particular places or chiefdoms.

At the beginning of the historic period, historians can trace the emergence of various tribal dynastic groups, of both local and wider regional origins, along the estuary (Byrne 1973; Bhreathnach 1999), while there is certainly historical evidence for the movement of some Scandinavian peoples into the region. Limerick probably had a distinctive mixed Irish and Hiberno-Norse population by the tenth and eleventh centuries AD. In the Middle Ages, Anglo-Norman lords, their peasant farmers and tenants, and merchants from the Severn estuary region would have colonised areas like Tradree and Limerick county, while new English and Dutch settlers were introduced during the sixteenth- and seventeenth-century plantations. German Palatines immigrated into Limerick in the early eighteenth century, some residing at Beagh, on the south bank. The port town of Limerick has also had a tradition of diverse ethnic communities since at least the Middle Ages (including Jews, Flemings, Huguenots, etc.) because of its extensive trading contacts with France, Spain and other north-west European countries.

The Shannon estuary as a nautical routeway must have had a major influence on the ethnically heterogeneous character of the region, but it was also at times the centre of a landscape contested by different ethnic groups. For some of the 'people of the Shannon estuary' the introduction of new settlers, whether in the Anglo-Norman period or in the post-medieval period, would have led to dispossession and alienation, the confiscation and colonisation of their lands along the estuary, the appropriation of their fishing rights by outsiders, the displacement of their own native rulers, and the banning of their legal practices and religious beliefs. The settlers would have felt mistrust and fear of the natives, with their peculiar habits, names and social and economic organisation, and mistrust too, perhaps, of the wild, watery places of the estuary. Indeed, cartographic and historical evidence suggests that the major transformation of the estuary landscape, the reclamation and taming of the marshes by the construction of sea-banks, was initiated by new English settlers in the sixteenth and seventeenth centuries.

Yet there must also have been accommodation and close cultural and economic relationships. Interestingly, in the medieval period there are hints of ethnic continuity in the face of local social and political changes. It is likely that the people managing the fishtraps were specialists, well versed in the local migratory routes and movement of salmon, trout and eels and the most appropriate fishing techniques for this particular landscape. It is interesting, then, that on the Deel estuary and at Bunratty essentially the same types of traps appear to have been used before and after the late twelfth century, despite profound social and cultural changes in the local landscape (e.g. the Anglo-Norman invasion and colonisation of Tradree and Limerick). At Bunratty, it is probable that the eleventh-century fishtraps were first managed by Irish tenants on the O'Briens' estates, and the twelfth- to thirteenth-century fishtraps by Irish betaghs or tenants on the Anglo-Norman manor of Bunratty. In other words, despite these cultural and ethnic changes and a shift in power at the top end of the social scale, the same ethnic group (i.e. the native Gaelic Irish) may have continued to maintain the fisheries out on the estuary.

Social class and gender

In social terms, it also seems likely that the archaeology of the Shannon estuary mudflats directly reflects the daily work of ordinary men and women, the people 'outside history', usually ignored by the traditional focus of archaeologists on the major dwellings and fortified residences of the upper classes and the powerful. Indeed, we have suggested that although some post-medieval fishtraps may have been owned and controlled by local landlords, there must also have been many traps in use that were constructed by the local poor, labourers or cottiers, in spite of bailiffs and police. However, while the estuary archaeology reflects in a sense a landscape built from the bottom up, we have emphasised in this study that all levels of society were involved in the exploitation of its resources—not only different social classes, but also different members of the community in terms of kinship, gender and age.

If the Carrigdirty Rock 5 site is evidence for a Neolithic short-stay cattle-grazing camp, perhaps also associated with hunting and fishing in late summer or early autumn, then we can imagine it as having been occupied by a group of people who stayed no longer than a few days, lit a fire, worked stone, and perhaps cooked and consumed some meat or plant foods. This might have been a group of men or women, or a small family group. Both men and women would have gathered plant foods, hunted for small animals, trapped fish, and knapped chert. The small size of the stone axe found at the site might indicate its use in small-scale food preparation activities rather than woodworking. In other words, there is no social, economic or physical reason why men, women and children could not all have been present in this landscape. Indeed, Pollard (1996) has suggested that the coastal foreshore was *primarily* a place for women and children, who played an active role not only in shellfish-gathering (as in the traditional model of women as food-collectors) but also in the active manufacture of fishing equipment, preparation of bait, management of fishtraps, processing, butchery, etc.

The Bronze Age houses and trackway in coastal wetlands on the Shannon and Fergus estuaries are interpreted here as evidence for the herding of cattle or sheep on the saltmarshes by local farming communities. Although the Carrigdirty Rock site may not have been particularly far from its local settlement, saltmarshes and fens are difficult landscapes to traverse on foot, and people may have preferred to stay down there for weeks or months in the warm summer or early autumn. It is possible that a family could have come down to live in the marshes, as quite substantial wetland dwellings are known from Bronze Age Ireland (e.g. O'Sullivan 1998, 69–96). However, by and large, given the intensive character of Bronze Age settlement, landscape exploitation and farming and the fact that society was probably quite hierarchically structured, it seems more likely that certain members of the community would have had responsibility for certain tasks. It seems likely that these herders would have been either, or both, young men and women, perhaps even children.

Traditionally, fishing has been seen as a male activity. In some historical and ethnological contexts, men fix their own nets, tend their boats and avoid women on the way to sea. A woman's presence at the launching of a boat or on a boat was traditionally seen as bad luck. The sea was seen as feminine, as was the boat, but men worked the sea. The strong continuities and conservative traditions in maritime culture suggest that it is likely that throughout the medieval period fishing was also divided into gender roles. Men would have fished the estuary in boats, made the fences and baskets, and managed the traps out on the foreshore. In historic times, women worked largely at gutting and processing the fish on the pier or harbour (a task rarely done by men). Indeed, in the nineteenth century large groups of women worked as migrant labourers and moved around the Irish Sea region to work in the herring industry. At Kilrush, on the lower Shannon estuary, huge numbers of local women were involved in net-making and repair and the curing of fish. In other words, while during the medieval and post-medieval periods work on the construction, repair and management of the fishtraps through the season would probably have been done by men and boys,

Foragers, farmers and fishers

Pl. 88—*Early nineteenth-century fishing-boats and people on the foreshore below Wellesley Bridge (now Sarsfield Bridge), Limerick City, from Bartlett's* Scenery and antiquities of Ireland, *published in 1842 (National Library of Ireland: 1442 TA).*

the processing, curing and salting of the catch might have been carried out by women and girls back at the landing-place (Pl. 88). Therefore entire families (and even communities, such as in the nineteenth-century fishing-village at Beagh and elsewhere) could have been engaged in the fisheries of the Shannon estuary.

Landscape, space and place on the estuary

Introduction

In emphasising the importance of people in interpreting the archaeology of the Shannon estuary, we can also explore how people would have experienced its places and landscapes. In particular, we can see that the Shannon estuary would have been a 'landscape of knowledge' built up by daily work and practice along its channel, mudflats and marshes. Although this study, like most wetland archaeological projects, has taken a strongly environmental and economic perspective, it is important to remember that economic strategies are only part of the human experience, and the way people perceived and moved through the world around them, while dependent on their own gender, age, social background, and ideological and religious beliefs, would have been important in the creation of this unusual archaeological record.

From space to place in a watery landscape

In recent years, archaeologists have started to explore how people in the past would have experienced space and place and how this might impact on the archaeological record (Austin and Thomas 1990; Bender 1993; 1996; R. Bradley 1993; Fleming 1996; Hirsch 1995; Rossignol and Wandsnider 1992; Schama 1995; Tilley 1994). For example, some archaeologists are using the sociological theories of Pierre Bourdieu (the concept of *habitus*—the influence of everyday encounters with the world on people's perception of their place in society), the philosophical theories of Martin Heidigger (*being-in-the-world*—how people experience the world), and the theories of phenomenological geographers such as Yi-Fu Tuan (1977), who has developed ideas about how space becomes known to people as a series of interconnected places. It is recognised that our modern view of *landscape* derives from the western artistic tradition of landscape painting, so that we think of landscapes as being views of beautiful spaces (Bender 1993). In contrast, small-scale societies are more interested in *land-forms* or particular places, such as rocks, mountain-tops, rivers, estuaries and so on.

These theories help us to recognise that local foragers, farmers, fishermen and mariners on the estuary would have had a profound sense of place in this watery landscape. For the people of the Shannon estuary, particular creeks, islands, rocks, pools and tidal races and currents would have been identified through placenames, stories, songs and the performance of work at these locations. In particular, some places would have been identified in terms of memory and imagination with people, events, or disasters such as drownings, shipwreck, bad fishing years, etc. Indeed, it is precisely this personal experience of the landscape that makes what is merely *empty space* to one person a *place* to another. The entire landscape would have been a tapestry of such places to local communities, and this is what is meant by a local 'sense of place', where people were at home in the world around them (Pl. 89).

For example, on the Shannon estuary a particularly good fishing-pool would have been known, exploited and named for a person or event. This can be seen on the River Shannon at Limerick, where the local 'abbey fishermen' divided the river from Doonass to Barrington's Pier into *enuires* (possibly from the Middle English or Anglo-French term *en cure*, meaning 'in use' or 'practice'; Herbert 1946–7; Spellissy 1998, 123–6). Each *enuire* was allotted to every fisherman's team of four, who fished from two cots with nets, and an old fisherman in 1946 recounted that the names on the river below Limerick included such places as *Shaungower*, *Traghgower*, *Teannainnaluinge* and *Leenthawn*. Presumably similar names were in use on the upper estuary too. Yet at the same time the communities of the surrounding drylands, who would have been otherwise engaged in farming or other work only a mile or two away, would have been entirely ignorant of the location, character and importance of these places. Most of the estuary's named places would really only have been known to the people who moved along its waters, yet only English names were recorded by maritime surveyors for use in Admiralty charts by post-medieval merchants and mariners. Similarly, numerous lost placenames are recorded in the marshlands in the seventeenth-century Civil Survey, such as '*Corkagsmowtane*' near Newtown, Co. Limerick. The very earliest Gaelic Irish names of rocks, islands, creeks and headlands are now probably largely gone, but at least some of the names recorded (e.g. Carrigclogher, Shawn-a-garra) may well go back into the late Middle Ages, while Battle Island, Dead Woman's Hand Rock, Kippen Rock and Horril's Rock may testify to later people or events.

Pathways and journeys in a landscape of movement

People experience the landscape by moving through it. The Shannon estuary's physical landscape is also one of perpetual movement, with the river and its tidal tributaries constantly flowing westwards out to the sea, opposing the south-westerly prevailing winds and flooding tides. Since earliest times, local communities have moved through this watery world along pathways and routes to fish, hunt, wildfowl, gather resources, herd animals or transport goods along the waterways.

Foragers, farmers and fishers

Pl. 89—*Modern Shannon 'gandalow' drawn up on the bank at Clonmacken, Co. Limerick, with alder trees and reed-beds at the fringes of the saltmarshes of the upper Shannon estuary.*

Pl. 90—*Steamer loading cargo at the quay at Clarecastle, on the upper Fergus estuary, Co. Clare, c. 1900. The estuaries have long served as significant routeways and means of communication through the region (National Library of Ireland: Lawrence Collection NS 3032).*

The movement of livestock onto the estuary wetlands is one important aspect of this landscape of travel. Since at least the Early Neolithic, local farmers on the Shannon estuary have been driving their cattle and sheep down onto the corcass and the saltmarshes. In the Bronze Age, trackways such as that at Fergus estuary west 1 may have been constructed to enable both people and animals to cross particularly dangerous creeks and mudflats. All along the estuary, the predominant line of communications is east–west, along the dryland ridges or inland of them. However, here and there are pathways, lanes and roads running down into the corcass. These were undoubtedly droveways for cattle or for gaining access to tillage and crops on the corcass. There are also roads leading down towards quays and jetties on the estuary, such as at Ringmoylan Quay and at Beagh Castle, Co. Limerick. At Newtown, Co. Limerick, a long straight road runs down from Carrigogunnel, past a possible medieval church and settlement and on down to the mudflats at Newtown Point. On the opposite bank there is a quay at O'Brien's Point, so it is possible that this was a medieval routeway to a ferry point or landing-place.

The second important aspect of movement was that of people moving through the marshes in search of estuarine resources and raw materials, whether these were fish, waterfowl, reeds for basketry, plant foods, or willow, alder and hazel wood for making the spectacular fishtraps and baskets recorded during the intertidal survey. At Carrigdirty Rock 3, an undated pit may contain evidence for both hunting and wildfowling (red deer and pink-footed goose, and perhaps also wild pig). We could speculate that both early and later prehistoric communities trapped fish on the Shannon estuary, although direct archaeological evidence for this is lacking. However, fishing was certainly of prime importance throughout the historic period, as indicated by discoveries of early historic and medieval fishtraps at Bunratty, the Deel estuary and the Fergus estuary. Again, we have to envisage local fishermen moving back and forth from their traps, transporting building materials, checking nets and baskets, and bringing their catch back to fishing-villages or upstream to Limerick.

The third important aspect of movement was in terms of people using ships and boats to travel up and down the Shannon estuary. Since the Middle Ages, we have historical evidence for Irish and Viking war-fleets on the estuary, for medieval galleys operating out of Limerick, and for cogs, hulcs and caravels plying its waters on their way to northern European ports. In the post-medieval period the Shannon estuary was a routeway for literally hundreds of ships and boats, ferrying passengers, turf, agricultural produce, stone and other materials between Limerick and other ports such as Clarecastle, Foynes, Bunratty, Kilrush and Askeaton. Over the centuries there have been numerous losses on shoals, rocks and foreshores, and pilots were stationed on islands to guide ships up to Limerick, while lighthouses, beacons and towers were constructed to safeguard passage for shipping. The historical shipwreck inventory alone testifies to the importance of the estuary as a routeway, while the quays and jetties identified at various locations on the Shannon estuary indicate more local travel and communications (Pl. 90).

Life, work and beliefs in a watery landscape 'at the edge'
In general terms, somewhere like the Shannon estuary would be seen by most archaeologists as a place at the edge, marginal, peripheral and unimportant in comparison with more visibly settled spaces. This is in keeping with the modern perception of wetlands as marginal landscapes—bleak, exposed and undifferentiated wilderness spaces. This viewpoint can also be seen in the writings of eighteenth- and nineteenth-century travellers on the Shannon estuary, who praised wetland *reclamation* and *drainage* schemes, ignoring other activities of local people in the wetlands. In contrast, the Shannon estuary archaeology illustrates that for many people across time the mudflats, saltmarshes and islands would have been places at the centre, beneficial places, places of easy movement and interconnections, and places to belong to. For medieval and post-medieval fishermen, for example, the estuary's wetlands were the significant centre of their daily lives. It is even possible that the people who worked down on the estuary would have been led by their experience to think of their role in society in certain ways. Fishermen working out on the estuary or farmers living on its islands would have spent much of their time in the often hidden places of woodland, marsh and creek, and their everyday encounters with these places and their own specialised knowledge and experience of the estuary might have encouraged a sense of identity different from that of neighbouring townspeople or villagers.

There are also hints that the estuary was simultaneously seen as a place at the edge. People have long been fascinated with waters and the beings that live in them. In the medieval period (and in modern folklore), seas, lakes and rivers were still believed to be populated with beings that could alternate between this world and what lies beyond, beings of allurement, danger and power (Smyth 1996). Folklore and ethnology, by collating modern beliefs and legends and investigating them in detail in their time and place, also provide insights into the relationship between people and watery environments, particularly at an ideational level (Lysaght *et al.* 1999). Water was seen as an important liminal space, where different worlds came into contact, one of darkness, cold and damp, the other of light, warmth and dryness. The Shannon estuary, situated simultaneously at the centre and the edge of people's worlds, may have been a place of danger and potential, a place between worlds, where water spirits, otherworldly beings and ancestors resided.

Perhaps, at the Neolithic site at Carrigdirty Rock 5, human bone was placed at a particularly evocative sacred place in the wetlands (a place that was perhaps also good for fishing or hunting). In the Late Bronze Age, metalwork, such as gold ornaments, bronze horns and tools, may have been deliberately put in creeks and saltmarshes, much as other hoards were put in lakes and rivers. Although the early historic monastic islands and medieval abbeys of the Shannon and Fergus estuaries were not the subject of detailed study in this work, we could also interpret some of the islands (e.g. Canon Island, Scattery Island, Saint's Island) as being sacred places within a continuum on the estuary. Obviously there are other day-to-day rituals to be considered also, in terms of the 'superstitions' and beliefs of local fishermen and sailors, who would certainly have told legends and tales of the beings that they expected to encounter at sea or in the estuary. Indeed, the folklore and beliefs of local fishermen in the early part of the last century would be an interesting avenue of future scholarly enquiry.

Time, tides and traditions on the estuary

Introduction

The approach taken in this study was broadly chronological, moving from traditionally defined period to period. It is also possible to interpret the archaeology of the Shannon estuary in terms of different scales or rhythms of time. In particular, the approaches of the French *Annales* school of historical studies to time are useful, whereby settlement and landscape are interpreted according to varying geographical and temporal scales, such as long-term, medium-term and historical time (Bintcliff 1991; 1996; Gosden 1994; Barrett 1989). A long-term, structural perspective can be used to identify the deep, underlying and essential structures of life in this particular landscape. A medium-term perspective helps us towards an understanding of the way of life in the landscape as it is lived by an individual person or community, and their perception or mental view of the world. The landscape can also be explored in terms of the short-term events of military or political history, or even in terms of sudden environmental changes.

Irish historical geographers in the past, such as Emyr Estyn Evans (1973), F.H.A. Aalen (1978) and Frank Mitchell (1986), were all influenced by this scholarship in their regional approaches to Irish cultural landscapes, while Henry Glassie's (1982) ethnological work on the rural communities of Ballymenone, Co. Fermanagh, can also be seen within this structuralist tradition. For Evans (1973, 16), landscape, environment, place and memory played key roles in shaping Irish culture and identity. He felt that Irish historians had turned their back on the land and had concentrated on the histories of great men, political movements and events. While *Annales* scholarship is not without its problems (especially the favouring of environmental forces over human agency), some of these ideas help to explore the potential human experience of time in the Shannon estuary's landscapes.

The 'timelessness' of the Shannon estuary

A long-term view of the Shannon estuary archaeology reveals several interesting things in relation to continuities in human activity in these places. Fernand Braudel (1972) in his influential historical study of the Mediterranean region in the sixteenth century recognised a repeated underlying structure or pattern in the use of the landscape by the people of the region. Transhumance was a vital aspect of the use of this dry, parched land across time, with people constantly driving animals up into the hills in summer. On the Shannon estuary we can see that these patterns of seasonal movement are reversed: people went down towards the water, and clearly they did it repeatedly, generation after generation. Evans (1973, 83) suggested that movement down into lowlands was the earliest form of transhumance in Ireland, with people moving from settlements in the hills down into the lowland woodlands and marshy areas in the summer. However, it is important to remember that on the Shannon estuary this was not transhumance in the classic sense, more a seasonal movement of cattle onto local summer pastures, a localised activity, part of the complex use of the entire landscape, from the hillslopes to the wetlands.

Indeed, the tradition of driving cattle down onto the summer marshes on the Shannon estuary may have its origins in early prehistory. In the Neolithic, foragers and fishers may have moved through the coastal wetlands, perhaps wildfowling, hunting and fishing, but perhaps also herding cattle through the largely open (unlike the probably wooded uplands) landscape of the estuary. In the Bronze Age, cattle and sheep may also have been driven down from the surrounding farmlands into the marshes and out to the islands for the summer grazing, leading to the construction of trackways and shelters. Cattle and sheep both have little difficulty in grazing and inhabiting wetland environments; only goats suffer from foot-rot in these places. The herding of cattle, sheep and horses on the corcass and islands clearly continued in the medieval period, with cattle being rustled from the marshes at Corkanree and horses captured on the corcass during the siege of Bunratty in 1641. Indeed, around the tower-houses (Cratloekeel, Castledonnell, Beagh) of the upper Shannon estuary, seasonal grazing was available within sight of the dwellings. In the early nineteenth century, local men were employed to herd cattle on the estuary islands, being paid with access to land for their own animals and for tillage. Finally, now, at the beginning of the twenty-first century, the corcass of the Fergus estuary and Shannon estuary is still considered (as I was told by a farmer at Inch, Co. Clare) the 'best grazing land in Ireland', especially during the summer months, being rich in lime, nutrients and abundant grasses. Haymaking and tillage may also have been of importance throughout the post-medieval period.

There are other threads of long-term continuity and activity on the estuary. During the fishing season in the early historic and medieval periods, it is probable that local people spent large parts of their day down on the estuary, building, repairing and using fishtraps, catching salmon and eels and other fish. Indeed, we could suggest that the people who used the fishtraps of the Middle Ages, the seventeenth century or the nineteenth century, or indeed the modern draft-net fishermen working from their flat-bottomed boats or gandolas, can all be seen to be part of a thousand-year-old tradition of fishing on the Shannon estuary. Similarly, the estuary has been used as a significant nautical routeway since at least the Iron Age, and local knowledge of safe channels, anchorages and tidal currents probably goes back into the Middle Ages at least (Pl. 90).

How people experienced environmental change and the passing of time

How did people perceive environmental change?

The Shannon estuary landscape has developed slowly over thousands of years, with people and environment, continuity and change, growth and decline some constant themes of its archaeological record. In contrast, the actual archaeological sites on the mudflats reflect, at most, brief snapshots of activity over days, months or years. The Neolithic and Middle Bronze Age wetland occupation sites at Carrigdirty Rock may have been respectively occupied for only a few days in the early autumn or two or three months during the summer. The early historic, medieval and post-medieval fishtraps on the Shannon estuary would have been used for a brief period before being replaced. In other words, these sites represent mere moments of time in the millennia through which the Shannon estuary has flowed constantly out to sea. Yet during this time the estuary has undergone significant landscape and environmental changes.

However, despite environmental changes, there are some striking continuities of settlement and economic activities at particular places. This is especially striking at Carrigdirty Rock. It is likely that this particular location has witnessed several transitions, from Neolithic brackish reed-swamps, saltmarsh creeks and mudflats to Bronze Age freshwater fens, carr woodland or raised bog, to historic period and modern estuarine mudflats. Nevertheless people have come back, time and time again, to this particular place, in the Early Neolithic, in the Middle Bronze Age and in the post-medieval period, to forage and hunt, to graze cattle and to catch fish. Realistically, there is no link at all between these different phases of human activity, literally separated as they are by metres of peats, clays and other environmental deposits. But why did people come to this particular place time after time?

It is possible that Carrigdirty Rock as a place was important to different communities across time. The reasons for this probably lie in a continuum of settlement on the terraces and slopes overlooking the estuary at Carrigdirty Rock, where different farmsteads and dwellings may have been inhabited over thousands of years. The islands of the upper estuary, its marshes, creeks and mudflats were a constant attraction to people living in these places, and Carrigdirty Rock must have been situated on a routeway down into the wetlands, making it a focus of attention

Pl. 91—*Aerial view of Quay Island, looking westwards towards the Bunratty and Inishbonane mudflats. Archaeological and historical evidence suggests that there have been fisheries at this location since the Middle Ages (photo: Shannon Estuary Ports).*

over long periods. Often people would have been fairly oblivious to long-term environmental changes. On the other hand, there must have been times (through a generation or a person's life) when local communities would have been aware that the estuary's environments were changing, as bogs were replaced by saltmarshes and as mudflats were colonised by reed-beds. Indeed, in historic times, sudden flood events would have been major catastrophes along the estuary, causing loss of life, property and livestock.

The passing of the years

The passing of the years could certainly be seen by local people in the ever-changing location of the channels, the erosion of saltmarshes and mudflats, and the gradual erosion or disappearance under mud of man-made structures. An individual fishtrap would have been constructed and used for, say, 15–20 years. During that time it would have been constantly repaired and reconstructed, but eventually a decision to abandon it entirely and erect a new trap would have been made. Despite these changes, knowledge endured. The Shannon estuary fishermen would have been aware of the appearance and location of ancient, abandoned traps (they would have been visible for decades), and the lore of best fishing-grounds would have been passed down from father to son over generations. Indeed, this knowledge clearly survives today. Between Inishbonane and Quay Island, we have shown that there is archaeological and historical evidence for the use of wooden fishtraps at various times from the eleventh century, the thirteenth century, the seventeenth century and the late nineteenth century. During a boat trip down the estuary in 1998, I was looking through binoculars at one of these, the medieval fishtrap at Bunratty 6, when the local harbour pilot standing behind me nodded over in its general direction and said that the channel off Quay Island is still considered the best salmon fishing-grounds on the upper Shannon estuary. In fact, an older fisherman apparently once told him that 'if you can't catch a salmon there, you might as well feck off home'. In that pithy phrase one gets a sense of the understanding that has been passed down (or continually rediscovered) through generations of human experience (Pl. 91).

Foragers, farmers and fishers

The seasons through the year

The change of the seasons would also have been signalled to the people of the estuary. The departure and return of migratory birds, the appearance of salmon and eels in summer and early autumn, even the yellowing of the reed-beds or the falling of leaves from the carr woodlands in autumn would have heralded the beginning of winter, the bleakest and coldest time down on the mudflats. In recent times, coastal dwellers believed the spring tide nearest the festival of St Brigid's Day (1 February), known as *Rabharta Féile Bríde*, to be the greatest spring tide of the year. It was considered a good time to cut and gather seaweed to fertilise crops and to collect shellfish and other shore produce. In May the first spring tide was known as *Rabharta Mór na n-Éan*, 'the great spring tide of the birds', as it was believed that birds observed the tides to ensure that their nests in the marshes were built above high-water level. Spring and early summer would have been a good time to cut reeds along the estuary, for thatching and basket-making. Even today, freshly cut bushels of reeds can be seen stacked at collection points along the estuary coast in the early summer months. The salmon runs up the estuary during May and October and the eel runs down the creeks, rivers and channels during the dark moonlit nights of November would also have provided another marker of time passing as the year progressed. Life on the estuary would have been measured by these seasonal rhythms.

Time and tides, or everyday experiences

Time and tides would also have governed some aspects of day-to-day work on the Shannon estuary. The twice-daily ebb and flow of the tides would have been a clock of sorts, and most people that lived along the estuary would have been very familiar with the patterns of the tides. Local people would also have known that the tides were not constant but varied in timing through a cycle of 24 hours (or whatever time division was used), and that they varied in height from springs to neaps. It might have been known that these tidal changes were related to the lunar cycle, to the waxing and waning of the moon. Indeed, through much of the summer and autumn, the rhythms of the tides would have governed a medieval fisherman's daily life, with trips made down to the mudflats at very low tide. For fishermen, daily life itself was measured by the tides.

The future of the past on the Shannon estuary

Introduction

The Shannon estuary intertidal survey has been highly successful in many ways. However, it is also clear that our discoveries are only the first hints of the unrecorded archaeological sites and palaeoenvironmental deposits on the estuary. In this concluding section, I propose some further multidisciplinary studies that should now be undertaken on the Shannon estuary, focusing on a number of themes and locations.

Archaeological survey and excavation

While the Discovery Programme's Shannon estuary intertidal survey is finished, the archaeological investigation of this type of environment in Ireland has only just begun. Even on the Shannon estuary, the survey should only be seen as a first attempt in a long-term programme of research. The tide, wave and channel erosion going on every day exposes new sites, while channel deposition hides others under soft, deep silts. On the Humber estuary, in north-east England, intertidal survey has been carried out on a relatively short foreshore (1–2km) since the Second World War, and new discoveries are still being made (E.V. Wright, pers. comm.). Clearly, intertidal survey has to be seen as a long-term activity. I am confident that if the Shannon estuary survey were to be done again tomorrow, entirely new prehistoric and medieval sites would be recorded in the study areas that we have already walked across. It is also clear that some previously identified sites should now be the subject of much more detailed archaeological and palaeoenvironmental investigations.

Intertidal survey and excavation of eroding sites

Many of the archaeological sites described here were only made available for recording through their exposure by tidal erosion. Some sites, such as Carrigdirty Rock 5, Bunratty 1–6, Deel estuary 1–4 and all the Fergus estuary sites, are still subject to this erosion, including both the gradual, daily erosion caused by each passing tide and the occasional catastrophic destruction during a storm (although the shelter of the upper estuary reduces this impact) or mud-slump. It is not yet possible to predict either the rate or the extent of this destruction. The Essex coast intertidal survey noted that newly discovered Iron Age wooden trackways in minerogenic clays were often destroyed within three years of their first exposure (Wilkinson and Murphy 1995). On the Severn estuary, houses and trackways in peats are similarly subject to rapid and completely destructive erosion (Bell *et al.* 2000, 319). The archaeological sites on the Shannon estuary appear to be subject to similar, if slower (owing to their sheltered locations and the narrow channels), patterns of erosion. The Bunratty 6 medieval fishtrap site, for example, although exposed to a much greater degree in 1998 than it was in 1995, is not yet being drastically eroded. However, all the prehistoric and medieval sites are under threat and should certainly be monitored over the next 5–10 years, with excavations carried out if necessary.

Intertidal survey and excavation at Carrigdirty Rock

Ironically enough, as some sites are destroyed by erosion, other, entirely new sites will be revealed for the first time from underneath the muds. The Neolithic and Bronze Age submerged landscapes at Carrigdirty Rock (Carrigdirty Rock 1–8 and 20–1) are particularly important, and there is both ongoing erosion and deposition of muds on this foreshore. At the Neolithic site at Carrigdirty Rock 5, I would certainly expect that further artefacts, bone and human remains will emerge from the clays. In contrast, the possible Bronze Age sites at Carrigdirty Rock 1–4 and 20–1 are now being buried under a mantle of modern, mobile sediments. However, at some point in the near future, the erosion and deposition patterns may shift course again, whisking away the soup of modern muds that hide this foreshore. There are potentially amazing sites hidden in the peats at Carrigdirty Rock, and a strategy to locate and investigate them is now needed.

Intertidal surveys on the lower Shannon estuary

At the same time, there are huge areas on the lower Shannon estuary that received little or no attention during this project. For example, Scattery Island, at the mouth of the Shannon estuary, and the bays and inlets around Ballylongford and Tarbert, Co. Kerry, Glin, Co. Limerick, and Labasheeda, Co. Clare, all hold great potential for exciting survey work. The islands of the lower Fergus estuary (Canon Island, Deer Island, Feenish Island, etc.) are also places of very high archaeological potential, as the historic ecclesiastical and secular settlements of these small islands would have required a wide range of intertidal structures (fisheries, landing-places and causeways). Indeed, the Fergus estuary islands would be an ideal location for a landscape archaeological project. On the upper Shannon estuary there are also areas that were insufficiently surveyed, such as the Deel estuary, the Maigue estuary and Saint's Island. In all these locations, local scholars will hopefully be responsible for future discoveries.

Underwater and geophysical surveys

An underwater geophysical and archaeological survey is now required along the channels and mouth of the estuary, to build on the historical research presented by Colin Breen and Claire Callaghan in Chapter 7. There are undoubtedly medieval and post-medieval ships and boats preserved in the silts and sands on the channel and along the mudflats of the lower estuary in particular. These ships came to grief on journeys along the estuary and they have much to tell us about the maritime cultures and traditions of the region.

Future thematic studies

Our understanding of the prehistoric, medieval and post-medieval settlement and exploitation of the Shannon estuary's landscapes is still very basic. At this point in time, there is a need for a series of small-scale, local and more intensive investigations of particular landscapes, for certain chronological periods, or across time. Future studies should also certainly take a much broader landscape perspective, integrating more fully the history and archaeology of the drylands with those of the estuary (rather than just concentrating on the intertidal zone and the corcass). Some chronological and subject-based themes, incompletely covered in this monograph, that could be studied are listed here.

(1) Mesolithic/Neolithic transition in coastal wetlands, exploring the local and regional character and identity of early prehistoric societies, their settlement, economy and funerary activities along the estuary.

(2) Bronze Age and Iron Age landscape, settlement and environment along the estuary marshes and its hinterland (to explore the relevance of the North Munster Project's settlement model away from the Mooghaun study area, e.g. the hilltop enclosures, enclosures, *fulachta fiadh* and findspots around Carrigdirty Rock).

(3) Early historic and Viking Age (*c.* AD 400–1100) settlement, marshland exploitation, fishing industries, maritime trade and transport, and the political, social and economic relationships between secular and ecclesiastical rural settlements.

(4) Anglo-Norman and Gaelic Irish landscape, settlement and economy, looking at the different cultural and socio-economic approaches to the estuary between different ethnic communities and the impact of medieval towns on the rural landscape.

(5) Post-medieval (1650–1850) historical geography of coastal wetland reclamation along the Shannon estuary (sequence and chronology of sea-bank construction), combined with local historical and folklife studies of nineteenth- and early twentieth-century fishing, farming and maritime traditions (harbours, landing-places, ships and boats, local boat styles, etc.).

Palaeoenvironmental investigations

It is clear that any future archaeological studies should be carried out within a long-term, multidisciplinary programme of investigations. Ideally, future work on the Shannon estuary should be driven by a palaeoenvironmental research programme, as this is the area which most needs detailed investigation in the short term. Andrew Wheeler and Michael Healey have outlined some of the issues that need to be addressed in Chapter 2. Future studies of sea-level and environmental changes on the estuary could be carried out by a multidisciplinary team of coastal geographers and palaeoecologists, and could aim firstly to establish the essential Holocene stratigraphic and chronological framework for the various phases of saltmarsh, reed-swamps, fens, woodlands and raised bogs of the Shannon and Fergus estuaries. Indeed, most of the archaeological sites recorded here still need to be investigated in terms of their precise environmental contexts and chronology. A concerted radiocarbon-dating programme is now definitely needed.

Our understanding of the chronology and sequence of coastal and sea-level change in the Shannon estuary is also completely lacking. The prehistoric submerged forests at Meelick Rocks, Carrigdirty Rock, Rinevalla Bay, Poulnasharry Bay and Bunaclugga Bay hold key information on calibrating environmental and sea-level change in the region. The intercalated organic peats and minerogenic clays at Carrigdirty Rock, Meelick Rocks and Islandmagrath also preserve the pollen, diatoms, Foraminifera, macrofossils, beetles, plant remains and perhaps even dendrochronological evidence that could be used to establish the relative chronology of marine regression and transgression phases along the Shannon estuary, but particularly on the upper estuary. These palaeoenvironmental investigations could include stratigraphical coring, pollen analysis, radiocarbon dating of peats, peat/clay contact zones and submerged woodland trunks, and a programme of diatom studies, potentially in association with archaeological excavations. The ideal location for the next phase of work would be Carrigdirty Rock, Co. Limerick, with its intercalated Neolithic and Bronze Age minerogenic clays, peats and archaeological sites.

Multidisciplinary projects on the Shannon estuary's landscapes

Multidisciplinary projects could rapidly build on the results of this survey. In fact, a Shannon estuary research group could now be established, involving coastal and historical geographers, palaeoecologists, marine geophysicists, archaeologists, underwater archaeologists, historians, local scholars, folklore and placename experts, as well as a range of other specialists. The Shannon estuary region has a great potential for such long-term multidisciplinary, landscape research projects, and, with its large and interested local rural and urban populations, there is obviously an audience there for the stories that have still to be told. Indeed, given the increasing awareness of environmental issues in the region, allied to the likely future detrimental impacts of predicted global sea-level rise on low-lying coastal areas on the Shannon estuary, there is no time to be lost. The model for such a research group could be the Severn Estuary Levels Research Committee, which has in ten years accomplished an enormous amount in south Wales and on the English coast. Ideally, future studies should be carried out as much as possible by local academics, historians and students, people who live and work in this Shannon estuary landscape today.

Towards an understanding of coastal foreshore archaeology in Ireland

Finally, the Shannon estuary survey should be seen as only the first attempt to investigate coastal wetland and foreshore archaeology in the Republic of Ireland. While the highly successful Strangford Lough project in Northern Ireland is now being followed up by surveys elsewhere, there are few plans as yet in the Republic to begin to explore and record this marvellous archaeological resource. The various institutions involved in the organisation of Irish archaeology have recently started to recognise that maritime and coastal archaeology has become one of the most exciting fields of scholarship, as *Dúchas* The Heritage Service, the Heritage Council, the Discovery Programme, and Departments of Archaeology in the various universities all move in various ways towards tackling this unexplored topic. These institutions should certainly now move to fund, equip and carry out intertidal and coastal landscape projects on other Irish estuaries, such as Dundalk Bay, the Boyne estuary, the north Dublin estuaries, Wexford Harbour, Waterford Harbour, the Blackwater estuary, Cork Harbour, Sligo Bay and other western inlets and estuaries. This work should also be seen as an ongoing programme of targeted research in regional study areas, against the backdrop of the Maritime Archaeological Survey of Ireland, which has already broken major new ground in establishing a wreck inventory for the Irish coast. Hopefully, in a few years the Shannon estuary survey will be seen to be what I consider it—the tip of the iceberg (Pl. 92).

Foragers, farmers and fishers

Pl. 92—*The Fergus estuary saltmarshes, reed-beds and mudflats in December 1995. Although the coastal foreshore has previously been ignored by Irish archaeologists, the Shannon and Fergus estuary intertidal survey indicates the potential of coastal foreshore archaeology in Ireland.*

Conclusions

On the Shannon estuary the tide ebbs away as I write, a huge body of water sliding out to sea. The brackish water drains back through the saltmarshes and reed-beds, and small creeks gather together before they gurgle down across the mudflats to the grey, murky channel. The water slips away, exposing things to view on the modern foreshore, things that have not been seen in millennia—submerged landscapes, animal bones, stone and organic artefacts, wooden fishtraps—and the past is thus revealed to sight. Some of this archaeology is exposed and gradually eroded with every tide, but even more lies buried deep, deep under the glistening muds. Much more remains to be discovered than has been found. This book has attempted to draw together what we did find, to begin to tell the stories of the people of the Shannon estuary since earliest times. Prehistoric foragers and farmers, medieval and post-medieval fishermen, mariners, farmers, landlords, tenants and labourers have all left their traces on the estuary mudflats. All told, it is a long story of human endeavour and daily work in these ever-changing coastal wetlands. But this book does not tell the whole story, and as more is gradually revealed by the tides and investigated by others in the years ahead, so will our understanding improve. Under the mudflats of the Shannon estuary there were certain things, and in this book these things have now become words. But hopefully they will not be the last words.

REFERENCES

Aalen, F.H.A. 1978 *Man and the landscape in Ireland*. London.

Adovasio, J.M. 1977 *Basketry technology*. Chicago.

AFM = J. O'Donovan (ed.), *The Annals of the Kingdom of Ireland by the Four Masters* (7 vols) (Dublin, 1848–51).

AI = S. MacAirt (ed.), *The Annals of Inisfallen* (Dublin, 1951).

Ainsworth, J. (ed.) 1961 *The Inchiquin Manuscripts*. Dublin.

Aldhouse-Green, S.H.R., Whittle, A.W.R., Allen, J.R.L. *et al.* 1993 Prehistoric human footprints from the Severn estuary at Uskmouth and Magor Pill, Gwent, Wales. *Archaeologia Cambrensis* **41**, 14–55.

Allen, J.R.L. 1996 Three later Bronze Age occupations at Rumney Great Wharf on the Wentlooge Level, Gwent. *Archaeology in the Severn Estuary 1995* **6**, 9–12.

Allen, T., Gill, H. and Miles, D. 1997 A line of time: approaches to archaeology in the upper and middle Thames valley, England. *World Archaeology* **29** (1), 114–29.

Andersen, S. 1987 Mesolithic dug-outs and paddles from Tybrind Vig, Denmark. *Acta Archaeologica* **57**, 87–106.

Andersen, S.H. 1994 New finds of Mesolithic logboats in Denmark. In C. Westerdahl (ed.), *Crossroads in ancient shipbuilding*, 1–10. Oxford.

Andrews, J.H. 1997 *Shapes of Ireland*. Dublin.

An Foras Talúntais 1966 *Soils of County Limerick*. Dublin.

Anon. 1829 *Tenth report of the Commissioners for Irish Fisheries*. British Parliamentary Paper. London.

Anon. 1836 *First report of the commissioners of inquiry into the state of the Irish fisheries; with the minutes of evidence, and appendix*. Dublin. HMSO.

Anon. 1860 *Explanation to accompany sheets 131 and 132 of the maps of the Geological Survey of Ireland illustrating a portion of the County of Clare*. Geological Survey of Ireland, Dublin.

Anon. 1862 *Explanation to accompany sheet 133 of the map of the Geological Survey of Ireland illustrating a portion of the County of Clare*. Geological Survey of Ireland, Dublin.

Anon. 1864 [In] *The Dublin Builder* **6** (110) (15 July 1864), 135.

Anon. 1874 *Report of the Inspectors of Irish Fisheries on the sea and inland fisheries of Ireland for 1873*. Dublin. HMSO.

Anon. 1876 *Report of the Inspectors of Irish Fisheries on the sea and inland fisheries of Ireland for 1875*. Dublin. HMSO.

Anon. 1880 *Report of the Inspectors of Irish Fisheries on the sea and inland fisheries of Ireland for 1879*. Dublin. HMSO.

Anon. 1882 Report of the Inspectors of Irish Fisheries on the sea and inland fisheries of Ireland for 1881. Dublin. The Queen's Printing Office.

Anon. 1885 *Report of the Inspectors of Irish Fisheries on the sea and inland fisheries of Ireland for 1884*. Dublin. The Queen's Printing Office.

Anon. 1979 Estuarine embankments on the Shannon. *Oibre* **7**, 19–20.

Anon. 1995 *The Irish Statutes, revised edition, 3 Edward II to the Union. AD 1310–1800*. Blackrock and Portland.

Appleby, J.C. (ed.) 1992 *A calendar of material relating to Ireland from the High Court of Admiralty Examinations 1536–1641*. Dublin.

Ashbee, P., Bell, M.A. and Proudfoot, E.V. 1989 *Wilsford Shaft: Excavations 1960–62*. English Heritage Archaeological Report 11. London.

Aston, M. (ed.) 1988 *Medieval fish, fisheries and fishponds in England*. British Archaeological Reports, British Series 182. Oxford.

Atkinson, E.G. (ed.) 1899 *Calendar of the State Papers relating to Ireland of the reign of Elizabeth, 1599, April–1600, February*. London.

Atkinson, E.G. (ed.) 1974 *Calendar of the State Papers relating to Ireland of the reign of Elizabeth, 1600, March–October*. Nendeln, Liechtenstein.

AU = W.M. Hennessy and B. McCarthy (eds), *The Annals of Ulster* (4 vols) (Dublin, 1887–1901).

Austin, D. and Thomas, J. 1990 The 'proper study' of medieval archaeology: case study. In D. Austin and L. Alcock (eds), *From the Baltic to the Black Sea: studies in medieval archaeology*, 43–78. London and New York.

Baily, W.H. 1859 Notice of Upper Silurian fossils from Ballycar South, one and a half miles west of the village of Trough. *Journal of the Geological Society of Dublin* **8**, 109–10.

Bannerman, N. and Jones, C. 1999 Fish-trap types: a component of the maritime cultural landscape. *International Journal of Nautical Archaeology* **28** (1), 70–84.

Barber, E.J.W. 1992 *Prehistoric textiles*. New Jersey.

Barr, C. 1998 Wetland archaeological sites in Aotearoa (New Zealand) prehistory. In K. Bernick (ed.), *Hidden dimensions: the cultural significance of wetland archaeology*, 47–55. Vancouver.

Barrett, J.C. 1989 Time and tradition: the rituals of everyday life. In H. Nordström and A. Knape (eds), *Bronze Age studies: Transactions of the British–Scandinavian colloquium in Stockholm, May 10–11, 1985*, 113–36. Stockholm.

Barry, D. 1977 Local placenames. *The Other Clare* **1**, 16.

Bathgate, T.D. 1949 Ancient fishtraps or yairs in Scotland. *Proceedings of the Society of Antiquaries of Scotland* **87** (7th Series), **11**, 98–102.

Bell, M. 1992a The Goldcliff project. *NewsWARP* **11**, 8.

Bell, M. 1992b Goldcliff excavation 1991. *Severn Estuary Levels Research Committee: Annual Report 1991*, 13–19.

Bell, M. 1992c Field survey and excavation at Goldcliff 1992. *Severn Estuary Levels Research Committee: Annual Report 1992*, 15–29.

Bell, M. 1993a Intertidal archaeology at Goldcliff in the Severn estuary. In J. Coles, V. Fenwick and G. Hutchinson (eds), *A spirit of enquiry. Essays for Ted Wright*, 9–13. Exeter.

Bell, M. 1993b Field survey and excavation at Goldcliff, Gwent 1993. *Archaeology in the Severn Estuary 1993*, 81–101.

Bell, M. 1995 Archaeology and nature conservation in the Severn estuary, England and Wales. In M. Cox, V. Straker and D. Taylor (eds), *Wetlands archaeology and nature conservation*, 49–61. London.

Bell, M. 1999 Prehistoric settlements and activities in the Welsh Severn Estuary. In B. Coles, J. Coles and M.S. Jørgensen (eds), *Bog bodies, sacred sites and wetland archaeology*, 17–25. Exeter.

Bell, M. and Neumann, H. 1996 Intertidal survey in the Welsh Severn estuary. *Archaeology in the Severn Estuary 1995* **6**, 29–33.

Bell, M. and Neumann, H. 1997 Prehistoric intertidal archaeology and environments in the Severn estuary, Wales. *World Archaeology* **29** (1), 95–113.

Bell, M. and Neumann, H. 1998 Intertidal survey in the Welsh Severn estuary. *Archaeology in the Severn Estuary 1997* **8**, 13–28.

Bell, M., Caseldine, A. and Neumann, H. 2000 *Prehistoric intertidal archaeology in the Welsh Severn estuary*. CBA Research Report 120. York.

Bender, B. 1993 Landscape—meaning and action. In B. Bender (ed.), *Landscape, politics and perspectives*, 1–17. Oxford.

Bender, B. 1996 Landscape and anthropology. In F.H.A. Aalen (ed.), *Landscape study and management*, 93–102. Dublin.

Bengsston, H. and Bergh, S. 1984 The hut sites on Knocknarea Mountain. In G. Burenhult (ed.), *The archaeology of Carrowmore: environmental archaeology and the megalithic tradition at Carrowmore, Co. Sligo, Ireland*, 216–318. Stockholm.

Bergh, S. 2000 Transforming Knocknarea—the archaeology of a mountain. *Archaeology Ireland* **14**, 14–18.

Berrow, S.D., Holmes, B. and Kiely, O.R. 1996 Distribution and abundance of bottle-nosed dolphins *Tursiops truncatus* (Montagu) in the Shannon Estuary. *Biology and Environment: Proceedings of the Royal Irish Academy* **96B**, 1–9.

Betts, R.C. 1998 The Montana Creek fishtrap 1: archaeological investigations in southeast Alaska. In K. Bernick (ed.), *Hidden dimensions: the cultural significance of wetland archaeology*, 239–51. Vancouver.

Bhreathnach, E. 1999 Part 4. The construction of the stone fort at Cahercommaun: a historical hypothesis. *Discovery Programme Reports* **5**, 83–91.

Bintcliff, J. 1991 The contribution of an Annaliste/structural history approach to archaeology. In J. Bintcliff (ed.), *The Annales school and archaeology*, 1–33. London and New York.

Bintcliff, J. 1996 Interactions of theory, methodology and practice. *Archaeological Dialogues* **3** (2), 248–55.

Blythe, C. 1996 Diatom analysis of sample associated with Late Bronze Age structure, Islandmagrath, Fergus estuary, Co. Clare. An unpublished report for the Discovery Programme, Dublin. Coastal Resources Centre, University College Cork.

Blythe, C., Dominey-Howes, D. and Wells, J.M. 1996a Stratigraphy and microfossil analyses from sediments associated with a late Bronze Age structure at Islandmagrath, Fergus Estuary, Co. Clare. An unpublished report for the Discovery Programme, Dublin. Coastal Resources Centre, University College Cork.

Blythe, C., Sinnott, A. and Dominey-Howes, D. 1996b Stratigraphy and palaeoenvironmental investigations of sediments associated with Bronze Age finds, Carrigdirty, Co. Limerick. An unpublished report for the Discovery Programme, Dublin. Coastal Resources Centre, University College Cork.

Bourke, E.J. 1994 *Shipwrecks of the Irish coast* (2 vols). Dublin.

Bourke, E.J. 1998 *Shipwrecks of the Irish coast: 932–1997*, vol. 2. Dublin.

BPP 1834 = British Parliamentary Papers, *Report from the Select Committee on Lighthouses, with the Minutes of Evidence*, 136–69. London.

BPP 1845 = British Parliamentary Papers, *Report from the Select Committee on Lighthouses, with the Minutes of Evidence*, 582–609. London.

Brabazon, W. 1848 *The deep sea coast and fisheries of Ireland*. Dublin.

Bradley, J. 1988a The interpretation of Scandinavian settlement in Ireland. In J. Bradley (ed.), *Settlement and society in medieval Ireland*, 49–78. Kilkenny.

Bradley, J. 1988b The medieval borough of Bunratty. *North Munster Antiquarian Journal* **30**, 19–25.

Bradley, J. 1997 Excavations at Moynagh Lough, Co. Meath, 1995–96. *Ríocht na Mídhe* **9**, 50–61.

Bradley, J. 1999 Excavations at Moynagh Lough, Co. Meath, 1997–98. *Ríocht na Mídhe* **10**, 1–17.

Bradley, J. and King, H.A. 1991 Archaeological trial excavations at Bunratty, Co. Clare. *North Munster Antiquarian Journal* **33**, 16–21.

Bradley, R. 1990 *The passage of arms. An archaeological analysis of prehistoric hoards and votive deposits*. Cambridge.

Bradley, R. 1993 *Altering the earth*. Edinburgh.

Bradley, R. and Gordon, K. 1988 Human skulls from the River Thames. *Antiquity* **62**, 501–9.

Bradley, R. and Hooper, B. 1973 Recent discoveries from Portsmouth and Langstone harbours; Mesolithic to Iron Age. *Proceedings of the Hampshire Field Club and Archaeological Society* **30**, 17–27.

Bradshaw, B. 1975 Fr. Wolfe's description of Limerick City, 1574. *North Munster Antiquarian Journal* **17**, 47–53.

Brampton, A.H. 1992 Engineering significance of British salt-marshes. In J.R.L. Allen and K. Pye (eds), *Salt-marshes: morphodynamics, conservation and engineering significance*, 115–22. Cambridge.

Braudel, F. 1972 *The Mediterranean and the Mediterranean world in the age of Philip II.* London.

Brewer, J.S. and Bullen, W. (eds) 1867 *Calendar of the Carew Manuscripts 1515–1574.* London.

Brewer, J.S. and Bullen, W. (eds) 1868 *Calendar of the Carew Manuscripts 1575–1588.* London.

Bridge, J.S., Van Veen, P.M. and Matten, L.C. 1980 Apects of the sedimentology, palynology and paleobotany of the Upper Devonian of southern Kerry Head, Co. Kerry, Ireland. *Geological Journal* **15**, 143–70.

Brindley, A.L. and Lanting, J.N. 1996 Irish logboats and their European context. *Journal of Irish Archaeology* **7**, 85–95.

Brindley, A.L., Lanting, J.N. and Mook, W.G. 1989–90 Radiocarbon dates from Irish fulacht fiadh and other burnt mounds. *Journal of Irish Archaeology* **5**, 25–33.

Brown, A.G. 1997 *Alluvial geoarchaeology. Floodsplain archaeology and environmental change.* Cambridge, Melbourne and New York.

Brunning, R. and O'Sullivan, A. 1997 Bronze Age wood species selection and woodworking techniques. In N. Nayling and A. Caseldine (eds), *Excavations at Caldicot, Gwent: Bronze Age palaeochannels in the Lower Nedern Valley*, 163–87. CBA Research Report 108. York.

Bryam, S. 1998 Fishing weirs in Oregon coast estuaries. In K. Bernick (ed.), *Hidden dimensions: the cultural significance of wetland archaeology*, 199–219. Vancouver.

Buckland, P.C., Beal, C.J. and Heal, S.V.E. 1990 Recent work on the archaeological and palaeoenvironmental context of the Ferriby boats. In S. Ellis and D.R. Crowther (eds), *Humber perspectives: a region through the ages*, 131–46. Hull.

Buckley, V.M. (ed.) 1990 *Burnt offerings: international contributions to burnt mound archaeology.* Dublin.

Byrne, F.J. 1973 *Irish kings and high-kings.* London.

Byrne, F.J. 1984 Ptolemy's Map of Ireland. In T.W. Moody, F.X. Martin and F.J. Byrne (eds), *A new history of Ireland, vol. 9. Maps, genealogies and lists*, 16. Oxford.

Byrne, F.J. 1993 The trembling sod: Ireland in 1169. In A. Cosgrove (ed.), *A new history of Ireland, vol. II. Medieval Ireland, 1169–1534*, 1–42. Oxford.

Cahill, M. 1998 A gold dress-fastener from Clohernagh, Co. Tipperary, and a catalogue of related material. In M. Ryan (ed.), *Irish antiquities*, 27–78. Bray.

Cal. Justic. Rolls Ire. = H. Wood, A.E. Langman and M.C. Griffith (eds), *Calendar of Justiciary Rolls, Ireland, 1308–14* (Dublin, no date, but post-1922).

Carter, R.G.W. 1982 Sea-level changes in Northern Ireland. *Proceedings of the Geological Association* **93**, 7–23.

Carter, R.G.W. 1988 *Coastal environments: an introduction to the physical, ecological and cultural systems of coastlines.* London.

Carter, R.W.G. 1991 *The impact on Ireland of changes in mean sea-level.* Report no. 2. Programme of expert studies on climate change, Department of the Environment, Dublin.

Carter, R.W.G. and Woodroffe, C.D. (eds) 1994 *Coastal evolution: Late Quaternary shoreline morphodynamics.* Cambridge.

Carter, R.W.G., Devoy, R.J.N. and Shaw, J. 1989 Late Holocene sea-levels in Ireland. *Journal of Quaternary Science* **4** (1), 7–24.

Cartwright, C.R. 1984 Field survey of Chicester harbour 1982. *Sussex Archaeology Collection* **122**, 23–7.

Casparie, W.A., Mook-Kamps, B., Palfenier-Vegter, R.M., Struijk, P.C. and Van Zeist, W. 1977 The paleobotany of Swifterbank. *Helinium* **17**, 28–55.

Caulfield S. 1978 Neolithic fields: the Irish evidence. In H.C. Bowen and P.J. Fowler (eds), *Early land allotment in the British Isles: a survey of recent work*, 137–43. British Archaeological Reports, British Series 48. Oxford.

Caulfield, S. 1983 The Neolithic settlement of north Connaught. In T. Reeves-Smyth and F. Hamond (eds), *Landscape archaeology in Ireland*, 195–215. British

Archaeological Reports, British Series 116. Oxford.

Caulfield, S. 1988 *Ceide Fields and Belderrig. A guide to two prehistoric farms in north Mayo*. Killala.

CDI = H.S. Sweetman (ed.), *Calendar of documents relating to Ireland, 1171–1307* (5 vols) (London, 1875–86).

CEC 1995 *The impacts of climate and relative sea-level rise on the environmental resources of the European coasts*. Commission of the European Communities, Research Contract Publication, Contract No. EV5V-CT93-0258, Brussels.

CGG = J.H. Todd (ed.), *Cogadh Gaedhel re Gallaib* (London, 1867).

Chaney, G. 1998 The Montana Creek fishtrap II: stratigraphic interpretation in the context of southeastern Alaska geomorphology. In K. Bernick (ed.), *Hidden dimensions: the cultural significance of wetland archaeology*, 252–66. Vancouver.

Chapman, V.J. 1977 *Ecosystems of the world 1: wet coastal ecosystems*. Amsterdam.

Christensen, C. 1990 Stone dug-out boats in Denmark: occurrence, age, form and reconstruction. In D.E. Robinson (ed.), *Experimentation and reconstruction in environmental archaeology*, 119–41. Oxford.

Clarke, C.P. 1993 Archaeology in Essex 1992. *Essex Archaeology and History* **24**, 209.

Clayton, G., Johnstone, I.S., Sevastopulo, G.D. and Smith, D.G. 1980 The micropalaeontology of a Courceyan (Carboniferous) borehole section from Ballyvergin, Co. Clare, Ireland. *Journal of Earth Sciences of the Royal Dublin Society* **3**, 81–100.

Cleary, R.M. 1995 Later Bronze Age settlement and prehistoric burials, Lough Gur, Co. Limerick. *Proceedings of the Royal Irish Academy* **95C**, 1–92.

Coles, B. and Coles, J. 1986 *Sweet track to Glastonbury: the Somerset Levels in prehistory*. London.

Coles, B.J. and Coles, J.M. 1989 *People of the wetlands: bogs, bodies and lake-dwellers*. London.

Collins, A.E.P. and Seaby, W.A. 1960 Structures and small finds discovered at Lough Eskragh, Co. Tyrone. *Ulster Journal of Archaeology* **23**, 25–37.

Condit, T. and Connolly, M. 1998 Ritual enclosures in the Lee Valley, Co. Kerry. *Archaeology Ireland* **12** (4), 8–12.

Condit, T. and O'Sullivan, A. 1999 Landscapes of movement and control: interpreting prehistoric hillforts and fording-places on the River Shannon. *Discovery Programme Reports* **5**, 25–39.

Conner, H.D. 1892 *The Fisheries (Ireland) Acts 1842 to 1891*. Dublin.

Connolly, M. 1999 *Discovering the Neolithic in County Kerry: a passage tomb at Ballycarty*. Bray.

Connors, P. 1999 Embankments, habitation, peat layer and sea-level. *The Other Clare* **23**, 22–3.

Cooney, G. 1997 Images of settlement and the landscape in the Neolithic. In P. Topping (ed.), *Neolithic landscapes*, 23–31. Oxbow Monograph 86. Oxford.

Cooney, G. 2000a *Landscapes of Neolithic Ireland*. London.

Cooney, G. 2000b Recognising regionality in the Irish Neolithic. In A. Desmond, J. Johnson, M. MacCarthy, J. Sheehan and E. Shee Twohig (eds), *New agendas in Irish prehistory: papers in commemoration of Liz Anderson*, 49–65. Bray.

Cooney, G. and Grogan, E. 1994 *Irish prehistory, a social perspective*. Bray.

Cooney, G. and Mandal, S. 1998 *The Irish Stone Axe Project: monograph 1*. Bray.

Cooney, G., Feehan, J., Grogan, E. and Stillman, C. 1990 Stone axes in County Tipperary. *Tipperary Historical Journal* **2**, 197–203.

Crowfoot, E. 1954 Textiles, basketry, and mats. In C. Singer, E.J. Holmyard and A.R. Hall (eds), *A history of technology*, vol. 1, 37–53. Oxford.

Crowther, D.R. 1987 Sediments and archaeology of the Humber foreshore. In S. Ellis (ed.), *East Yorkshire Field Guide*, 99–105. Cambridge.

Crump, B. and Wallis, S. 1992 Kiddles and the Foulness fishing industry. *Essex Journal* **27** (2), 38–42.

CSP = Commons Sessional Papers.
CSP 1836 Mr Donnell's report on the fishery harbours, appendix, vol. XVIII.
CSPI = Calendar of State Papers for Ireland.
Culleton, E.B. and Gardiner, M.J. 1985 Soil formation. In K.J. Edwards and W.P. Warren (eds), *The Quaternary history of Ireland*, 133–53. London.
Danaher, K. 1985 *Irish country households*. Cork and Dublin.
Darvill, T. 1987 *Ancient monuments in the countryside: an archaeological management review*. London.
Decima, E.B. and Dincauze, D.F. 1998 The Boston Back Bay fish weirs. In K. Bernick (ed.), *Hidden dimensions: the cultural significance of wetland archaeology*, 157–72. Vancouver.
De Courcy Ireland, J. 1981 *Ireland's sea fisheries: a history*. Dublin.
Devoy, R. 1991 *Sea level changes and Ireland*. ENFO briefing sheet 27. Dublin.
Diemer, J.A., Bridge, J.S. and Sanderson, D.J. 1987 Revised geology of Kerry Head, County Kerry. *Irish Journal of Earth Sciences* **8**, 113–38.
Dillon, M. (ed.) 1962 *Lebor na Cert: the Book of Rights*. London.
Dinan, B. 1987 *Clare and its people. A concise history*. Cork and Dublin.
Dincauze, D.F. 1988 Sticks in the mud. *NewsWARP* **4**, 8–10.
Doherty, C. 1998 The Vikings in Ireland: a review. In H.B. Clarke, M. Ní Mhaonaigh and R. Ó Floinn (eds), *Ireland and Scandinavia in the early Viking Age*, 288–330. Dublin.
Dolan, J.M. 1984 A structural cross-section through the Carboniferous of north-west Kerry. *Irish Journal of Earth Sciences* **6**, 95–108.
Doody, M. 1987 Late Bronze Age huts at Curraghatoor, Co. Tipperary. In R.M. Cleary, M.F. Hurley and E.A. Twohig (eds), *Archaeological excavations on the Cork–Dublin gas pipeline (1981–82)*, 36–42. Cork.
Doody, M.G. 1997 Bronze Age settlements in Co. Tipperary: fifteen years of research. *Tipperary Historical Journal* (1997), 94–106.
Dortch, C.E. 1997 New perceptions of the chronology and development of Aboriginal fishing in south-western Australia. *World Archaeology* **29** (1), 15–35.
Dunne, L. and Kiely, J. 1999 Archaeologists discover Neolithic settlement in Tralee. *Archaeology Ireland* **13** (1), 14.
Edwards, K.J. and Warren, W.P. (eds) 1985 *The Quaternary history of Ireland*. London.
Edwards, N. 1990 *The archaeology of early medieval Ireland*. London.
Ellis, S. and Crowther, D. (eds) 1990 *Humber perspectives: a region through the ages*. Hull.
Enright, F. 1981 The pre-Famine worker in the Shannon/Newmarket area. *The Other Clare* **5**, 7–9.
Eogan, G. 1965 *Catalogue of Irish bronze swords*. Dublin.
Eogan, G. 1974 Regionale Gruppierungen in der Spätbronzezeit Irlands. *Archäologisches Korrespondenzblatt* **4**, 319–27.
Eogan, G. 1983 *Hoards of the Irish Later Bronze Age*. Dublin.
Eogan, G. 1993 The Late Bronze Age: customs, crafts and cults. In E.S. Twohig and M. Ronayne (eds), *Past perceptions. The prehistoric archaeology of south-west Ireland*, 121–33. Cork.
Eogan, G. 1994 *The accomplished art: gold and goldworking in Britain and Ireland during the Bronze Age (c. 2300–650 BC)*. Oxford.
Eogan, G. 2000 *The socketed bronze axes of Ireland*. Prähistorische Bronzefunde Abteilung IX, Band 22. Stuttgart.
Evans, C. 1987 Nomads in 'Waterland'? Prehistoric transhumance and fenland archaeology. *Proceedings of the Cambridge Antiquarian Society* **76**, 27–39.
Evans, E.E. 1951 Ancient fish weirs on the Co. Down coast. *Ulster Journal of Archaeology* **14**, 57.
Evans, E.E. 1957 *Irish folk ways*. London.
Evans, E.E. 1973 *The personality of Ireland*. Belfast.
Expugnatio = A.B. Scott and F.X. Martin (eds), *Expugnatio Hibernica: The Conquest of Ireland by Giraldus Cambrensis* (Dublin, 1978).

Feheney, J.M. 1998 *Ballysteen, the people and the place*. Cork.

Fiants = E. Burke (ed.), *The Irish fiants of the Tudor sovereigns* (4 vols) (Blackrock, Co. Dublin, 1994).

Finch, T.F. 1971 *Soils of County Clare*. Dublin.

Finch, T.F. and Ryan, P. 1966 *Soils of County Limerick*. Dublin.

Fleming, A. 1996 Total landscape archaeology: dream or necessity? In F.H.A. Aalen (ed.), *Landscape study and management*, 81–91. Dublin.

Fletcher, W., Chapman, H., Head, R., Fenwick, H., Van de Noort, R. and Lillie, M. 1999 The archaeological survey of the Humber estuary. In R. Van de Noort and S. Ellis (eds), *Wetland heritage of the Vale of York: an archaeological survey*, 205–41. Hull.

Flood, J. 1995 *Archaeology of the dreamtime*. Sydney.

Forbes, R.J. 1964 *Studies in ancient technology*, vol. IV. Leiden.

Frost, J. 1893 *The history and topography of the county of Clare*. Dublin.

Fry, M.F. 2000 *Coití: logboats from Northern Ireland*. Northern Ireland Archaeological Monographs 4. Belfast.

Fulford, M., Champion, T. and Long, A. 1997 *England's coastal heritage: a survey for English Heritage and the RCHME*. English Heritage Archaeological Report 15. London.

Furlong, N. 1996 The history of land reclamation in Wexford Harbour. In D. Rowe and C.J. Wilson (eds), *An anthology of the Wexford Slobs and Harbour*, 83–90. Enniscorthy.

Gallagher, S.J. 1996 The stratigraphy and cyclicity of the late Dinantian platform carbonates in parts of southern and western Ireland. In P. Strogen, I.P. Somerville and G.L. Jones (eds), *Recent advances in Lower Carboniferous geology*, 239–62. Geological Society of London Special Publication 107. London.

Gardiner, M.J. and Radford, T. 1980 *Soil associations of Ireland*. Dublin.

Gardiner, R. (ed.) 1994 *Cogs, caravels and galleons: the sailing ship 1000–1650*. London.

Gill, W.D. 1979 *Syndepositional sliding and slumping in the west Clare Namurian basin, Ireland*. Geological Survey of Ireland Special Paper 4. Dublin.

Gilman, P.J. 1998 Essex fishtraps and fisheries: an integrated approach to survey, recording and management. In K. Bernick (ed.), *Hidden dimensions: the cultural significance of wetland archaeology*, 273–89. Vancouver.

Glassie, H. 1982 *Passing the time in Ballymenone*. Dublin.

Godbold, S. and Turner, R.C. 1993 *Second Severn crossing, archaeological response, phase 1—the intertidal zone in Wales*. Brentwood.

Godbold, S. and Turner, R.C. 1994 Medieval fishtraps in the Severn estuary. *Medieval Archaeology* **38**, 19–54.

Godwin, H. and Turner, J.S. 1933 Vegetational succession at Calthorpe Broad, Norfolk. *Journal of Ecology* **21**, 235–62.

Godwin, H., Godwin, M.E. and Clifford, M.H. 1935 Controlling factors in the formation of fen deposits as shown by peat investigations at Wood Fen, near Ely. *Journal of Ecology* **23**, 509–35.

Gosden, C. 1994 *Social being and time*. Oxford and Cambridge.

Gowen, M. 1988 *Three Irish gas pipelines—new archaeological evidence in Munster*. Dublin.

Green, S. 1989 Some recent archaeological and faunal discoveries from the Severn estuary levels. *Bulletin of the Board of Celtic Studies* (1989), 187–99.

Grogan, E. 1989 The early prehistory of the Lough Gur region: Neolithic and Bronze Age settlement patterns in north Munster south of the River Shannon. Unpublished Ph.D. thesis, National University of Ireland.

Grogan, E. 1995 Changing places: settlement patterns in prehistory. *The Other Clare* **20**, 48–52.

Grogan, E. 1996 Neolithic houses in Ireland. In T. Darvill and J. Thomas (eds), *Neolithic houses in northwest Europe and beyond*, 41–60. Oxbow Monograph 57. Oxford.

Grogan, E. 1999 *Mooghaun*. Dublin.

Grogan, E. and Condit, T. 1994 The later prehistoric landscape of south-east Clare. *The Other Clare* **18**, 8–12.

Grogan, E. and Eogan, G. 1987 Lough Gur excavations by Seán P. Ó Ríordáin: further Neolithic and Beaker habitations on Knockadoon. *Proceedings of the Royal Irish Academy* **87C**, 299–506.

Grogan, E., Condit, T., O'Carroll, F., O'Sullivan, A. and Daly, A. 1995 Preliminary assessment of the prehistoric landscape of the Mooghaun study area. *Discovery Programme Reports* **2**, 47–56.

Grogan, E., Condit, T., O'Carroll, F., O'Sullivan, A. and Daly, A. 1996 Tracing the later prehistoric landscape in north Munster. *Discovery Programme Reports* **4**, 26–46.

Grogan, E., O'Sullivan, A., O'Carroll, F. and Daly, A. 1999 Knocknalappa, Co. Clare: a reappraisal. *Discovery Programme Reports* **5**, 111–24.

Hague, D.B. and Christie, R. 1975 *Lighthouses, their architecture, history and archaeology*. Bangor.

Hall, D. and Coles, J. 1994 *Fenland survey. An essay in landscape and persistence*. English Heritage Archaeological Report 1. London.

Hannan, K. 1981 The sandmen. *The Old Limerick Journal* **8**, 21–2.

Harbison, P. 1969a *The axes of the Earlier Bronze Age in Ireland*. Prähistorische Bronzefunde 9:1. Munich.

Harbison, P. 1969b *The daggers and halberds of the Early Bronze Age in Ireland*. Prähistorische Bronzefunde 6:1. Munich.

Harbison, P. 1988 *Pre-Christian Ireland*. London.

Harbison, P. 1999 The boy with the squirrel—Henry Pelham (1749–1806). *Ireland of the Welcomes* **48**, 18–25.

Harper, J.C. 1939 The Lower Palaeozoic rocks of Slieve Bernagh and the Cratloe Hills, Co. Clare. *Proceedings of the Geologist's Association* **50**, 302–4.

Haughey, F. 1999 The archaeology of the Thames: prehistory within a dynamic landscape. *London Archaeologist* **9** (1), 17–21.

Hayes, R. (n.d.) Manuscript sources for the history of Irish civilisation. National Library of Ireland.

Healy, M.G. 1995a The lithostratigraphy and biostratigraphy of a Holocene coastal sediment sequence in Marazion Marsh, west Cornwall, UK, with reference to sea-level movements. *Marine Geology* **124**, 237–52.

Healy, M.G. 1995b An introduction. In M.G. Healy and J.P. Doody (eds), *Directions in European coastal management*, 1–6. Tresaith, Cardigan.

Henry, M. 1996 *The River Shannon*. Dublin.

Herbert, R. 1946–7 The Lax Weir and Fishers Stent of Limerick. *North Munster Antiquarian Journal* **5** (2 and 3), 49–61.

Hill, J. 1997 *The building of Limerick*. Cork and Dublin.

Hillam, J. 1976 The dating of Cullyhanna hunting lodge. *Irish Archaeological Research Forum* **3** (1), 17–20.

Hind, W. 1905 Notes on the homotaxial equivalent of the beds which immediately succeed the Carboniferous Limestone in the west of Ireland. *Proceedings of the Royal Irish Academy* **25B**, 93–116.

Hirsch, E. 1995 Landscape: between place and space. In E. Hirsch and M. Hanlon (eds), *The anthropology of landscape: perspectives on place and space*, 1–30. Oxford.

Hodges, H.W.M. 1958 A hunting camp at Cullyhanna Lough near Newtown Hamilton, Co. Armagh. *Ulster Journal of Archaeology* **21**, 7–13.

Hodson, F. 1954a The beds above the Carboniferous Limestone in north-west County Clare, Ireland. *Quarterly Journal of the Geological Society of London* **109**, 259–83.

Hodson, F. 1954b The Carboniferous rocks of Foynes Island, County Limerick. *Geological Magazine* **91**, 153–60.

Hodson, F. and Lewarne, G.C. 1961 A mid-Carboniferous (Namurian) basin in parts of the counties of Limerick and Clare, Ireland. *Quarterly Journal of the Geological Society of London* **107**, 307–33.

Holland, C.H., Feehan, J. and Williams, E.M. 1988 The Wenlock rocks of the Cratloe Hills, County Clare. *Irish Journal of Earth Sciences* **9**, 61–9.

References

Hope, R. 1990 *A new history of British shipping*. London.

Hudson, R.G.S. and Sevastopulo, G.D. 1966 A borehole section through the Lower Tournaisian and Upper Old Red Sandstone, Ballyvergin, County Clare. *Scientific Proceedings of the Royal Dublin Society* **A2**, 287–96.

Hutchinson, G. 1994 *Medieval ships and shipping*. London.

Hutton, A.W. (ed.) 1970 *Arthur Young, a tour in Ireland; with general observations on the present state of that kingdom; made in the years 1776, 1777, and 1778* (4th edn) (2 vols). Shannon.

Innes, J., Tooley, M., Daniels, R. and Tann, G. 1991 Excavation of the intertidal 'submerged forests' at Hartlepool Bay, Cleveland, north-east England. *NewsWARP* **10**, 14–17.

Jeffrey, D.W., Wilson, J.G., Harris, C.R. and Tomlinson, D.L. 1985 The application of two simple indices to Irish estuary pollution status. In J.G. Wilson and W. Halcrow (eds), *Estuarine management and quality assessment*, 147–61. London.

Jenkins, J.G. 1974a *Nets and coracles*. Newton Abbot, North Pomfret and Vancouver.

Jenkins, J.G. 1974b Fish weirs and traps. *Folk Life, a Journal of Ethnological Studies* **12**, 5–19.

Jones, C. 1983 Walls in the sea—the *goradau* of Menai, some marine antiquities of the Menai Straits. *International Journal of Nautical Archaeology and Underwater Exploration* **12** (1), 27–40.

Joyce, P.W. 1913 *The origin and history of Irish names of places* (3 vols). Dublin. [Reprinted 1995.]

Kelleher, C.E. 1998 The maritime archaeological landscape of Baltimore, Co. Cork. Unpublished MA thesis, University College Cork.

Kelly, E.P. 1974 Aughinish Island. In T.G. Delaney (ed.), *Excavations 1974*, 20–1. Belfast.

Kelly, E.P. 1981 A log boat from Derryco. *Journal of the Kerry Archaeological and Historical Society* **14**, 10–13.

Kelly, E.P. 1987 A log boat from Clenagh, Co. Clare. *North Munster Antiquarian Journal* **29**, 93–4.

Kelly, E.P. and O'Donovan, E. 1998 A Viking longphort near Athlunkard, Co. Clare. *Archaeology Ireland* **12** (4), 13–16.

Kelly, F. 1997 *A guide to early Irish law*. Dublin.

Kemmy, J. (ed.) 1996 *The Limerick anthology*. Dublin.

Kemmy, J. (ed.) 1997 *The Limerick compendium*. Dublin.

Khan, M.F.H. 1955 The Old Red Sandstone of the Kerry Head Anticline, County Kerry. *Proceedings of the Royal Irish Academy* **57B**, 71–8.

Lamplugh, G.W., Wilkinson, S.B., Kilroe, J.R., McHenry, A., Seymour, H.J. and Wright, W.B. (eds) 1907 *The geology of the county around Limerick*. Memoirs of the Geological Survey of Ireland. Dublin.

La Tène Maps 1999 *Irish Aquaculture Directory & Guide* (4th edn). La Tène Maps, Dublin.

Lee, A. and Miller, J. 1995 Waulsortian banks. *Special publication of the International Association of Sedimentologists* **23**, 191–271.

Lee, D. (ed.) 1997 *Remembering Limerick*. Limerick.

Lees, A. 1964 The structure and origin of the Waulsortian (Lower Carboniferous) 'reefs' of west-central Ireland. *Philosophical Transactions of the Royal Society of London* **B247**, 483–531.

Lenihan, M. 1866 *Limerick; its history and antiquities, ecclesiastical, civil and military, from the earliest ages*. Dublin.

Lewis, S. 1837 *A topographical dictionary of Ireland* (2 vols). London.

Loader, R., Westmore, I. and Tomalin, D. 1997 *Time and tide, an archaeological survey of the Wootton-Quarr coast*. Isle of Wight.

Lohan, R. 1994 *Guide to the Archives of the Office of Public Works*. Dublin.

Long, A.J. and Shennan, I. 1994 Sea-level change in Washington and Oregon and the

'Earthquake Deformation Cycle'. *Journal of Coastal Research* **10**, 825–38.

Losco-Bradley, P.M. and Salisbury, C.R. 1988 A Saxon and a Norman fish weir at Colwick, Nottinghamshire. In M. Aston (ed.), *Medieval fish, fisheries and fishponds in England*, 329–51. British Archaeological Reports, British Series 182. Oxford.

Louwe Kooijmans, L.P. 1985 *Sporen in Hetland: De Nederlandse Delta in de Prehistorie*. Amsterdam.

Louwe Kooijmans, L.P. 1987 Neolithic settlement and subsistence in the wetlands of the Rhine/Meuse Delta of the Netherlands. In J.M. Coles and A.J. Lawson (eds), *European wetlands in prehistory*, 227–51. Oxford.

Louwe Kooijmans, L.P. 1993a The Mesolithic/Neolithic transformation in the lower Rhine basin. In P. Bogucki (ed.), *Case studies in European prehistory*, 95–145. Boca Raton.

Louwe Kooijmans, L.P. 1993b Wetland exploitation and upland relations of prehistoric communities in the Netherlands. In J. Gardiner (ed.), *Flatlands and wetlands: current themes in East Anglian archaeology*, 71–116. East Anglian Archaeology Report No. 50. Norwich.

Lucas, A.T. 1960 National Museum of Ireland: archaeological acquisitions for the year 1958. *Journal of the Royal Society of Antiquaries of Ireland* **90**, 1–40.

Lucas, A.T. 1989 *Cattle in ancient Ireland*. Kilkenny.

Lynch, A. and Ó Donnabháin, B. 1994 Poulnabrone portal tomb. *The Other Clare* **18**, 5–7.

Lysaght, P., Ó Catháin, S. and Ó hÓgáin, D. (eds) 1999 *Islanders and water-dwellers. Proceedings of the Celtic–Nordic–Baltic folklore symposium, Dublin 1996*. Blackrock.

Lysaght, W. (n.d.) *Some remarks upon Mr MacMahon's Bill*. London.

McCabe, A.M. 1985 Glacial geomorphology. In K.J. Edwards and W.P. Warren (eds), *The Quaternary history of Ireland*, 67–93. London.

McCarthy, K.M. 1997 *Lighthouses of Ireland*. Sarasota.

McCarthy, M. 1998 Archaeozoological studies and early medieval Munster. In M.A. Monk and J. Sheehan (eds), *Early medieval Munster: archaeology, history and society*, 59–75. Cork.

McCarthy, M. 2000 Hunting, fishing and fowling in late prehistoric Ireland: the scarcity of the bone record. In A. Desmond, J. Johnson, M. McCarthy, J. Sheehan and E. Shee Twohig (eds), *New agendas in Irish prehistory: papers in commemoration of Liz Anderson*, 107–17. Bray.

MacCurtain, M. 1988 A lost landscape: the Geraldine castles and tower-houses of the Shannon estuary. In J. Bradley (ed.), *Settlement and society in medieval Ireland*, 429–44. Kilkenny.

McDonnell, R. 1993 Preliminary archaeological assessment in Bridgwater Bay: Gore Sand and Stert Flats. *Archaeology in the Severn Estuary 1993*, 41–6.

McDowell, R.B. 1964 *The Irish administration 1801–1914*. London.

McErlean, T., McConkey, R., McCooey, P. and Williams, B. 1998 A review of the archaeological resources of the Northern Ireland coastline. Unpublished report for EHS, Belfast.

McGrail, S. 1981 *The Brigg 'raft' and her prehistoric environment*. British Archaeological Reports, British Series 89. Oxford.

McGrail, S. 1983 Interpretation of material from two maritime sites. In P. Annis (ed.), *Sea studies*, 41–3. Greenwich.

McGrail, S. 1987 *Ancient boats in north-west Europe*. London.

McGrail, S. 1993 *Medieval boat and ship timbers from Dublin*. Dublin.

McGrail, S. 1997 The boat timbers. In M.F. Hurley and O.M.B. Scully (eds), *Late Viking Age and medieval Waterford: excavations 1986–1992*, 636–42. Waterford.

McInerney, B. 1978 Cratloe. *The Other Clare* **2**, 12.

MacMahon, M. 1993 The charter of Clare Abbey and the Augustinian 'province' in Co. Clare. *The Other Clare* **17**, 21–7.

McNally, A. 1990 Dendrochronology of subfossil pine as evidence for environmental change. In G. Doyle (ed.), *Ecology and preservation of Irish peatlands*, 15–22. Dublin.

MacNamara, G.U. 1915 Bunratty, Co. Clare. *Journal of the North Munster Archaeological Society* **3** (4), 220–313.

McVeagh, J. 1995 *Richard Pococke's Irish tours*. Dublin.

Mahr, A. 1937 New aspects and problems in Irish prehistory. *Proceedings of the Prehistoric Society* **3**, 262–436.

Mallory, J.P. and McNeill, T.E. 1991 *The archaeology of Ulster from colonization to plantation*. Belfast.

Malone, E. 1996 Reconstruction of the palaeoenvironment of a saltmarsh associated with a Late Bronze Age intertidal site, Islandmagrath, Co. Clare. Unpublished BA (Hons.) dissertation, Dept. of Geography, University College Cork.

Mandal, S. 1996 The petrology of the Irish stone axe. Unpublished Ph.D. thesis, Trinity College, Dublin.

Mandal, S. 1997 Striking the balance: the roles of petrography and geochemistry in stone axe studies in Ireland. *Archaeometry* **39** (2), 289–308.

Martin, C. 1978 *Full fathom five: wrecks of the Spanish Armada*. London.

Martin, C. and Parker, P. 1988 *The Spanish Armada*. London.

Maxwell, C. 1949 *Country and town in Ireland under the Georges*. Dundalk.

Meddens, F.M. 1996 Sites from the Thames estuary wetlands, England, and their Bronze Age use. *Antiquity* **70** (268), 325–34.

Merne, O.J. 1985 The infauna of the Shannon and Fergus estuarine mudflats as a food resource for shorebirds. Unpublished M.Sc. thesis, Environmental Studies Unit, Trinity College, Dublin.

Milne, G., Bates, M. and Webber, M.D. 1997 Problems, potential and partial solutions: an archaeological study of the tidal Thames, England. *World Archaeology* **29** (1), 130–46.

Mitchel, N.C. 1965 The Lower Bann fisheries. *Ulster Folklife* **11**, 1–32.

Mitchell, G.F. 1986 *Reading the Irish landscape*. Dublin.

Mitchell, G.F. 1989 *Man and environment in Valencia Island*. Dublin.

Mitchell, G.F. 1990 *The way that I followed*. Dublin.

Molloy, K. 1997 Prehistoric farming at Mooghaun—a new pollen diagram from Mooghaun Lough. *Archaeology Ireland* **11** (3), 22–6.

Molloy, K. (forthcoming) Holocene vegetation and land-use history at Mooghaun, S.E. Clare, with particular reference to the Bronze Age. In E. Grogan, *The later prehistoric landscape of south-east Clare*. Discovery Programme Monographs. Dublin.

Momber, G. 1991 Gorad Beuno: investigation of an ancient fish-trap in Caernarfon Bay, N. Wales. *International Journal of Nautical Archaeology* **20** (2), 95–109.

Monk, M. 1993 People and environment. In search of the farmers. In E. Shee Twohig and M. Ronayne (eds), *Past perceptions. The prehistoric archaeology of south-west Ireland*, 35–52. Cork.

Monk, M. 2000 Seeds and soils of discontent: an environmental archaeological contribution to the nature of the early Neolithic. In A. Desmond, J. Johnson, M. McCarthy, J. Sheehan and E. Shee Twohig (eds), *New agendas in Irish prehistory: papers in commemoration of Liz Anderson*, 67–87. Bray.

Moore, M. 1996 *Archaeological Inventory of County Wexford*. Dublin.

Moore, P.D. and Bellamy, D.J. 1974 *Peatlands*. London.

Mordant, D. and Mordant, C. 1992 Noyen-sur-Seine: a Mesolithic waterside settlement. In B.J. Coles (ed.), *The wetland revolution in prehistory*, 55–64. Exeter.

Moroney, M. 1998 The mapping of Ireland. *Cara Magazine* **31** (6), 12–16.

Moss, M.L. and Erlandson, J.M. 1998 A comparative chronology of Northwest coast fishing features. In K. Bernick (ed.), *Hidden dimensions: the cultural significance of wetland archaeology*, 180–98. Vancouver.

Mount, C. 1994 Aspects of ritual deposition in the Late Neolithic and Beaker periods at Newgrange, Co. Meath. *Proceeedings of the Prehistoric Society* **60**, 433–43.

Murphy, C. 1980 The Norman manor of Bunratty. *The Other Clare* **4**, 19.

Murphy, P. and Wilkinson, T.J. 1991 Survey and excavation on the tidal foreshore. In

J.M. Coles and D. Goodburn (eds), *Wet site excavation and survey*, 10–12. WARP, Exeter.

Nairn, R., Smith, J., Moore, J. and Elliott, R. 1997 Shannon estuary oil spill sensitivity maps and clean-up guidelines. A limited circulation report to Shannon estuary anti-pollution team from CORDAH/OPRU, Neyland, Pembrokeshire. Report No. OPRU/40/97.

Nayling, N. 1993 Tales from the riverbank: Bronze Age palaeochannels in the alluviated Nedern Valley at Caldicot Castle Lake, Gwent. In J. Coles, V. Fenwick and G. Hutchinson (eds), *A spirit of enquiry. Essays for Ted Wright*, 72–6. Exeter.

Nayling, N. 1996 The excavation, recovery and provisional analysis of a medieval wreck from Magor Pill, Gwent Levels. *Archaeology in the Severn Estuary 1995* **6**, 85–95.

Nayling, N. 1997 Further fieldwork and post-excavation: Magor Pill, Gwent Levels intertidal zone. *Archaeology in the Severn Estuary 1996* **7**, 85–93.

Nayling, N. 1998 *The Magor Pill medieval wreck*. CBA Research Report 115. York.

Nayling, N. and Caseldine, A. 1997 *Excavations at Caldicot, Gwent: Bronze Age palaeochannels in the lower Nedern valley*. CBA Research Report 108. York.

Needham, S. and Longley, D. 1980 Runnymede Bridge, Egham, a Late Bronze Age riverside settlement. In J. Barrett and R. Bradley (eds), *The British Later Bronze Age*, 397–436. British Archaeological Reports, British Series 83 (ii). Oxford.

O'Brien, B. 1995 Ross Island and the origins of Irish–British metallurgy. In J. Waddell and E.S. Twohig (eds), *Ireland in the Bronze Age*, 38–48. Dublin.

O'Brien, B. 1999 *Sacred ground: megalithic tombs in coastal south-west Ireland*. Galway.

O'Brien, J. 1977 Towerhouses of south Clare. *The Other Clare* **1**, 19–23.

O'Brien, J. 1978 The siege of Bunratty. *The Other Clare* **2**, 15–18.

O'Brien, J. 1999 An outline of the history of the civil parishes of Bunratty and Drumline c. 1200–1700. *The Other Clare* **23**, 34–43.

O'Carroll, C. 1978 Shannon/Tradaree historical background. *The Other Clare* **2**, 31–5.

O'Carroll, C. 1980 Rural crafts, Shannon (Rineanna) area. *The Other Clare* **4**, 47–8.

O'Connell, M. 1988 Streamstown Bay—partially submerged peat as evidence for later post-glacial sea-level change. In M. O'Connell and W.P. Warren (eds), *Connemara: IQUA Field Guide* **11**, 44–9. Galway.

O'Connor, P.J. 1987 *Exploring Limerick's past, an historical geography of urban development in county and city*. Newcastlewest.

Ó Dálaigh, B. (ed.) 1998 *The stranger's gaze, travels in County Clare 1534–1950*. Ennis.

Ó Danachair, C. 1971 The Shannon in military history. *North Munster Antiquarian Journal* **14**, 53–64.

Ó Danachair, C. 1983–4 Summer pasture in Ireland. *Folk Life, a Journal of Ethnological Studies* **22**, 36–41.

O'Farrell, P. 1983 *Shannon through her literature*. Cork and Dublin.

Ó Floinn, R. 1992 A Neolithic cave burial in Limerick. *Archaeology Ireland* **6** (2), 19–21.

Ó Floinn, R. 1998 The archaeology of the early Viking Age in Ireland. In H.B. Clarke, M. Ní Mhaonaigh and R. Ó Floinn (eds), *Ireland and Scandinavia in the early Viking Age*, 131–65. Dublin and Portland.

O'Grady, S. (ed.) 1929 *Caithréim Thoirdealbhaigh* (2 vols). London.

O'Keeffe, T. 2000 *Medieval Ireland: an archaeology*. Stroud.

O'Kelly, M.J. 1951 An Early Bronze Age ringfort at Carrigillihy, Co. Cork. *Journal of the Cork Historical and Archaeological Society* **56**, 69–86.

O'Kelly, M.J. 1954 Excavations and experiments in ancient Irish cooking-places. *Journal of the Royal Society of Antiquaries of Ireland* **84**, 105–15.

O'Kelly, M.J. 1989 *Early Ireland*. Cambridge.

O'Loughlin, T. 2000 Giraldus Cambrensis' view of Europe. *History Ireland* **8** (2), 16–21.

Ó Maolfabhail, A. 1990 *Logainmneacha na hÉireann. Contae Luimnigh* (iml. 1). Baile Átha Cliath.

O'Meara, J.J. 1991 *The Voyage of St Brendan*. Buckinghamshire.

Ó Murchadha, C. 1984 Seventeenth century Clare, a brief survey. *The Other Clare* **7**, 32–4.

Ó Murchadha, C. 1991 In search of James MacNemara, merchant of Ennis. *The Other Clare* **15**, 33–4.

O'Neill, J. 2000 A summary of investigations by the Lisheen Archaeological Project. *Tipperary Historical Journal* (2000), 173–90.

O'Neill, T. 1987 *Merchants and mariners in medieval Ireland*. Blackrock, Co. Dublin.

O'Rahilly, C. 1995 Medieval Limerick: the growth of two towns. In H.B. Clarke (ed.), *Irish cities*, 163–76. Cork and Dublin.

Ordnance Survey of Ireland 1974 *Shannon Estuary, Sheet 17, 1:26,720 Series*. Dublin.

Orme, B.J. 1982 Prehistoric woodlands and woodworking in the Somerset Levels. In S. McGrail (ed.), *Woodworking techniques before A.D. 1500*, 79–93. British Archaeological Reports, International Series 129. Oxford.

Orme, B.J. and Coles, J.M. 1983 Prehistoric woodworking from the Somerset Levels: 1. Timber. *Somerset Levels Papers* **9**, 19–43.

Orme, B.J. and Coles, J.M. 1985 Prehistoric woodworking from the Somerset Levels: 2. Species selection and prehistoric woodlands. *Somerset Levels Papers* **11**, 7–24.

Orpen, G.H. 1894 Ptolemy's Map of Ireland. *Journal of the Royal Society of Antiquaries of Ireland* **24**, 115–28.

O'Sullivan, A. 1993 Intertidal survey on the Fergus Estuary and the Shannon Estuary. *Discovery Programme Reports* **1**, 61–8.

O'Sullivan, A. 1993–4 An Early Historic period fish weir on the upper Fergus estuary, Co. Clare. *North Munster Antiquarian Journal* **35**, 52–61.

O'Sullivan, A. 1994 Harvesting the waters. *Archaeology Ireland* **27**, 10–12.

O'Sullivan, A. 1995a Marshlanders. *Archaeology Ireland* **31**, 8–11.

O'Sullivan, A. 1995b Medieval fish weirs on the Deel estuary, Co. Limerick. *Archaeology Ireland* **32**, 15–17.

O'Sullivan, A. 1995c Intertidal archaeological surveys in the estuarine wetlands of north Munster. *International Journal of Nautical Archaeology* **24** (1), 71–3.

O'Sullivan, A. 1995d Medieval fish weirs and coastal settlement in north Munster. *Group for the Study of Irish Historic Settlement Newsletter* **4**, 3–5.

O'Sullivan, A. 1996a Exploring ancient woodlands. *Archaeology Ireland* **36**, 14–15.

O'Sullivan, A. 1996b Later Bronze Age intertidal discoveries on north Munster estuaries. *Discovery Programme Reports* **4**, 63–72.

O'Sullivan, A. 1996c Neolithic, Bronze Age and Iron Age woodworking techniques. In B. Raftery, *Trackway excavations in the Mount Dillon Bogs, Co. Longford, 1985–1991*, 291–342. Irish Archaeological Wetland Unit Transactions 3. Dublin.

O'Sullivan, A. 1997a Medieval fishtraps at Bunratty, Co. Clare. *The Other Clare* **21**, 40–2.

O'Sullivan, A. 1997b Last foragers or first farmers? *Archaeology Ireland* **40**, 16–18.

O'Sullivan, A. 1998 *The archaeology of lake settlement in Ireland*. Discovery Programme Monograph 4. Dublin.

O'Sullivan, A. and Condit, T. 1995 Late Bronze Age settlement and agriculture by the marshlands of the upper Fergus estuary, Co. Clare. *The Other Clare* **19**, 5–9.

O'Sullivan, A. and Daly, A. 1999 Prehistoric and medieval coastal settlement and wetland activities on the Shannon estuary. In B.J. Coles, J. Coles and M.S. Jørgensen (eds), *Bog bodies, sacred sites and wetlands archaeology*, 177–84. Exeter.

O'Sullivan, A. and Sheehan, J. 1997 *The Iveragh peninsula. An archaeological survey of south Kerry*. Cork.

O'Sullivan, A., McConkey, R., McErlean, T. and McCooey, P. 1996 Coastal foreshore archaeology in Strangford Lough, Co. Down: survey and excavation 1995–6. Unpublished report for EHS, Belfast.

O'Sullivan, A., McErlean, T., McConkey, R. and McCooey, P. 1997 Medieval fishtraps in Strangford Lough, Co. Down. *Archaeology Ireland* **39**, 36–8.

O'Sullivan, G. 1983 The intertidal fauna of Aughinish Island, Shannon, Co. Limerick. *Irish Naturalists' Journal* **21**, 62–9.

Parfitt, K. and Fenwick, V. 1993 The rescue of Dover's Bronze Age boat. In J. Coles, V. Fenwick and G. Hutchinson (eds), *A spirit of enquiry. Essays for Ted Wright*, 77–9. Exeter.

Parry, S. and McGrail, S. 1991 A sewn plank boat and a hard from Caldicot Lake, Gwent, Wales. *NewsWARP* **10**, 9–10.

Patterson, W.H. 1892 On a newly discovered site for worked flints in the county of Down. *Journal of the Royal Society of Antiquaries of Ireland* **22**, 154–5.

Pedersen, L. 1995 7000 years of fishing: stationary fishing structures in the Mesolithic and afterwards. In A. Fischer (ed.), *Man and sea in the Mesolithic, coastal settlement above and below present sea level*, 75–86. Oxbow Monograph 53. Oxford.

Pedersen, L. 1997 They put fences in the sea. In L. Pedersen, A. Fischer and B. Aaby (eds), *The Danish Storebælt since the Ice Age—man, sea and forest*, 124–43. Copenhagen.

Penn, G. 1833 *Memorials of the life and times of Sir William Penn, 1644–70* (2 vols). London.

Plummer, C. 1922 *Bethada Náem nÉrann: Lives of Irish saints* (2 vols). Oxford.

Pollard, T. 1996 Time and tide: coastal environments, cosmology and ritual practice in early prehistoric Scotland. In T. Pollard and A. Morrison (eds), *The early prehistory of Scotland*, 198–212. Edinburgh.

Pollock, A.J. and Waterman, D.M. 1964 A Bronze Age habitation site at Downpatrick. *Ulster Journal of Archaeology* **27**, 31–58.

Powell, T.G.E. 1974 The Sintra Collar and the Shannongrove gorget: aspects of Late Bronze Age goldwork in the west of Europe. *North Munster Antiquarian Journal* **16**, 3–13.

Power, D. 1991 The archaeology of the Munster plantation. In M. Ryan (ed.), *The illustrated archaeology of Ireland*, 198–201. Dublin.

Power, J. 1986 Terry Alt and Lady Clare. *The Other Clare* **10**, 15–18.

Pryor, F. 1999 *Farmers in prehistoric Britain*. Stroud.

Raftery, B. 1990 *Trackways through time: archaeological investigations on Irish bog roads, 1985–1989*. Rush.

Raftery, B. 1994 *Pagan Celtic Ireland*. London.

Raftery, B. 1996 *Trackway excavations in the Mountdillon Bogs, Co. Longford, 1985–1991*. Irish Archaeological Wetland Unit Transactions 3. Dublin.

Raftery, J. 1970 Prehistoric coiled basketry bags. *Journal of the Royal Society of Antiquaries of Ireland* **100**, 167–8.

Ratcliffe, J. and Straker, V. 1996 *The early environment of Scilly*. Truro.

Reeves-Smyth, T.J.C. 1983 Landscapes in paper: cartographic sources for Irish archaeology. In T. Reeves-Smyth and F. Hamond (eds), *Landscape archaeology in Ireland*, 119–77. British Archaeological Reports, British Series 116. Oxford.

Rep. Select Comm. Fish. 1849 = *Report from the Select Committee on Fisheries (Ireland); together with the proceedings of the Committee. Minutes of evidence and appendix* (London, 1849).

Rider, M.H. 1974 The Namurian of west County Clare. *Proceedings of the Royal Irish Academy* **77B**, 125–42.

Rippon, S. 1995a Human–environment relations in the Gwent Levels: ecology and the historic landscape in a coastal wetland. In M. Cox, V. Straker and D. Taylor (eds), *Wetland archaeology and nature conservation*, 62–74. London.

Rippon, S. 1995b The evolution of a historic wetland landscape: the Gwent Levels historic landscape study. *Archaeology in the Severn Estuary 1994*, 7–19.

Rippon, S. 1996 *Gwent Levels: the evolution of a wetland landscape*. CBA Research Report 105. York.

Rippon, S. 1997 *The Severn estuary*. London and Washington.

Robinson, D. 1988 The Loop Head lighthouse. *North Munster Antiquarian Journal* **30**, 55–7.

Rohan, P.K. 1986 *The climate of Ireland*. Dublin.

Rossignol, J. and Wandsnider, L. (eds) 1992 *Space, time and archaeological landscapes*. New York.

Rowe, D. and Wilson, C.J. (eds) 1996 *High skies—low lands, an anthology of the Wexford slobs and harbour*. Enniscorthy.

Rowe, V. 1988 Offshore from paradise. *Ireland of the Welcomes* **37**, 36–9.

Russell, C.W. and Prendergast, J.P. (eds) 1872 *Calendar of the State Papers relating to Ireland of the reign of James I, 1603–06*. London.

Ryan, G. 1981 Fresh evidence of Norman occupation in the Bunratty area. *The Other Clare* **5**, 12–13.

Ryan, G. 1985 Pre-reformation church and monastic sites in the barony of Bunratty lower, *c*. 500 AD–1550 AD. *The Other Clare* **9**, 44–50.

Ryan, S. 1998 *The wild red deer of Killarney*. Dingle.

Salisbury, C.R. 1988 A Saxon and Norman fish weir at Colwick, Nottinghamshire. In M. Aston (ed.), *Medieval fish, fisheries and fishponds in England*, 329–51. British Archaeological Reports, British Series 182. Oxford.

Salisbury, C.R. 1991 Primitive British fish-weirs. In G.L. Good, R.H. Jones and M.W. Ponsford (eds), *Waterfront archaeology*, 76–87. CBA Research Report 74. London.

Salisbury, C.R. 1992 The archaeological evidence for palaeochannels in the Trent valley. In S. Needham and M.G. Macklin (eds), *Alluvial archaeology in Britain*, 155–62. Oxbow Monograph 27. Oxford.

Salisbury, C.R. 1996 Hemington Fields—a medieval landscape (Leicestershire SK 459302). *NewsWARP* **19**, 24–32.

Schama, S. 1995 *Landscapes and memory*. London.

Schofield, A.J. 1989 Recent finds from Rainbow Bar and some thoughts on site formation. *Lithics* **10**, 9–15.

Schultz, R.W. and Sevastopulo, G.D. 1965 Lower Carboniferous volcanic rocks near Tulla, Co. Clare, Ireland. *Scientific Proceedings of the Royal Dublin Society* **A2**, 153–62.

Schweingruber, F.H. 1990 *Microscopic wood anatomy* (3rd edn). Birmensdorf.

Scott, G. 1906 Some unrecorded finds of gold ornaments, from the counties of Limerick, Clare and Tipperary. *Journal of the Limerick Field Club* **3** (10), 27–37.

Sevastopulo, G.D. 1981 Upper Carboniferous. In C.H. Holland (ed.), *A geology of Ireland*, 173–87. Edinburgh.

Shackley, M. 1978 The behaviour of artefacts as sedimentary particles in a fluviatile environment. *Archaeometry* **20**, 55–61.

Share, B. 1995 *Bunratty, rebirth of a castle*. Dingle.

Shennan, I. 1986 Flandrian sea-level changes in the Fenland I: the geographical setting and evidence of sea-level change. *Journal of Quaternary Science* **1**, 119–54.

Shennan, I. 1994 Clastic sedimentary environments. In M.P. Waller (ed.), *The Fenland Project, number 9: Flandrian environmental change in Fenland*, 36–8. East Anglian Archaeology Report No. 70. Cambridgeshire County Council.

Shepard-Thorn, E.R. 1963 The Carboniferous Limestone Succession in north-west County Limerick, Ireland. *Proceedings of the Royal Irish Academy* **62B**, 267–94.

Sheppard, R. 1993 *Ireland's wetland wealth*. Dublin.

Silvester, R.J. 1991 *The Fenland Project, number 4: the Wissey Embayment and the Fen Causeway, Norfolk*. East Anglian Archaeology Report No. 52. Norfolk Archaeology Unit, Dereham, Norfolk.

Simington, R.C. (ed.) 1938 *The Civil Survey A.D. 1654–1656, County of Limerick* (vol. 4). Dublin.

Sleeman, A.G. and Pracht, M. 1999 *Geology of the Shannon Estuary: a geological description of the Shannon Estuary region including parts of Clare, Limerick and Kerry, to accompany the bedrock geology 1:100,000 scale map series, sheet 17, Shannon Estuary*. Dublin.

Smyth, M. 1996 *Understanding the universe in seventh-century Ireland*. Woodbridge.

Somerville, I.D. and Jones, G.L. 1985 The Courceyan stratigraphy of Pallaskenry Borehole, Co. Limerick, Ireland. *Geological Journal* **20**, 377–400.

Somerville, I.D. and Strogen, P. 1992 Ramp sedimentation in the Dinantian limestones of the Shannon Trough, Co. Limerick, Ireland. *Sedimentary Geology* **79**, 59–75.

Somerville, I.D., Strogen, P. and Jones, G.L. 1992 Biostratigraphy of Dinantian limestones and associated volcanic rocks in the Limerick syncline, Ireland. *Geological Journal* **27**, 201–20.

Spellissy, S. 1998 *The history of Limerick city*. Limerick.

Stenuit, R. 1972 *Treasures of the Armada*. Newtown Abbot.

Stewart, H. 1977 *Indian fishing: early methods on the north-west coast*. Seattle.

Stout, G. and Stout, M. 1997 Early landscapes: from prehistory to plantation. In F.H.A. Aalen, K. Whelan and M. Stout (eds), *Atlas of the Irish rural landscape*, 31–63. Cork.

Stout, M. 1997 *The Irish ringfort*. Dublin.

Strachan, D. 1997 *Blackwater Estuary Management Plan (BEMP): C14 dating of some intertidal fish-weirs in Essex: dates and discussion*. Area Archaeological Project: Report No. 1, Archaeological Advisory Group, Planning Department, Essex County Council.

Strachan, D. 1998a *Essex from the air: archaeology and history from aerial photographs*. Chelmsford.

Strachan, D. 1998b Inter-tidal stationary fishing structures in Essex, some C14 dates. *Essex Archaeology and History* **29**, 274–82.

Strogen, P. 1988 The Carboniferous lithostratigraphy of southeast County Limerick, Ireland, and the origin of the Shannon Trough. *Geological Journal* **23**, 121–37.

Stuiver, M. and Reimer, P.J. 1993 Extended 14C database and revised CALIB radiocarbon calibration programme. *Radiocarbon* **35**, 215–30.

Stuiver, M., Reimer, P.J., Bard, E. *et al*. 1998 INTCAL98 Radiocarbon age calibration 24,000–0 cal BP. *Radiocarbon* **40**, 1041–83.

Sweetman, H.S. (ed.) 1875 *Calendar of documents relating to Ireland preserved in Her Majesty's Public Record Office, London, 1171–1251*. London.

Sweetman, P.D. 1999 *The medieval castles of Ireland*. Cork.

Swift, M. 1999 *Historical maps of Ireland*. London.

Synge, F.M. 1966 *Soils of County Limerick*. Soil Survey Bulletin No. 16. An Foras Talúntais, Dublin.

Synge, F.M. 1969 The Würm ice limit in the west of Ireland. In *Quaternary geology and climate*, 89–92. Publication 1701. National Academy of Sciences, Washington, D.C.

Synge, F.M. 1985 Coastal evolution. In K.J. Edwards and W.A. Warren (eds), *The Quaternary history of Ireland*, 221–33. London.

Taylor, R.B., Carter, R.W.G., Forbes, D.L. and Orford, J.D. 1986 Beach sedimentation in Ireland: contrasts and similarities with Atlantic Canada. *Current Research, Canadian Geological Survey* **1986A**, 55–64.

Therkorn, L., Brandt, R.W., Pals, J.P. and Taylor, M. 1984 An early Iron Age farmstead: Site Q of the Assendelver Polders Project. *Proceedings of the Prehistoric Society* **50**, 351–73.

Thomas, C. 1985 *Exploration of a drowned landscape: archaeology and history of the Isles of Scilly*. London.

Thomas, J. 1991 *Rethinking the Neolithic*. Cambridge.

Thomond Papers: Manor Courts Clonrond and Innish = Rolls and books recording proceedings at various manor courts held on the estates of the earl of Thomond. (In the Petworth Collection.)

Thomond Papers: Spaight 1681 = An abstract of such rents and revenues as doe belong to the Right Hon[ble] Henry Earl of Thomond ... Taken 1681, by Thomas Spaight. (In the Petworth Collection.)

Tilley, C. 1994 *A phenomenology of landscape: places, paths and monuments*. Oxford.

Tooley, M.J. 1978 The history of Hartlepool Bay. *International Journal of Nautical Archaeology and Underwater Exploration* **7**, 71–5.

Tooley, M.J. 1980 Theories of coastal change in north-west England. In F.H. Thompson (ed.), *Archaeology and coastal change*, 74–86. London.

Topographia Hibernica = J.J. O'Meara (ed.), *Topographia Hibernica: The History and Topography of Ireland by Gerald of Wales* (Harmondsworth, 1982).

Tuan, Y.-F. 1977 *Space and place*. Minneapolis.

Ussher, R.J. 1903 The crannog at Ardmore, County Waterford. *Journal of the Royal Society of Antiquaries of Ireland* **33**, 387–8.

Ussher, R.J. and Kinahan, G.H. 1879 On a submarine crannog discovered by R.J. Ussher at Ardmore, Co. Waterford. *Proceedings of the Royal Irish Academy* **16**, 61–5.

Van de Noort, R. and Ellis, S. (eds) 1995 *Wetland heritage of Holderness. An archaeological survey*. Hull.

Van de Noort, R. and Ellis, S. (eds) 1999 *Wetland heritage of the Vale of York. An archaeological survey*. Hull.

van Wijngaarden-Bakker, L.H. 1989 Faunal remains and the Irish Mesolithic. In C. Bonsall (ed.), *The Mesolithic in Europe*, 125–33. Edinburgh.

Waddell, J. 1998 *The prehistoric archaeology of Ireland*. Galway.

Wakeman, W.F. 1873 Curach note. *Journal of the Royal Society of Antiquaries of Ireland* (4th series) **2**, 74–6.

Walker, D. 1970 Direction and rate in some British post-glacial hydroseres. In D. Walker and R.G. West (eds), *Studies in the vegetational history of the British Isles: essays in honour of Harry Godwin*, 70–82. Cambridge.

Wallace, P.F. 1992 The archaeological identity of the Hiberno-Norse town. *Journal of the Royal Society of Antiquaries of Ireland* **122**, 35–66.

Waller, M. 1994 *The Fenland Project, number 9: Flandrian environmental change in Fenland*. East Anglian Archaeology Report No. 70. Cambridgeshire County Council.

Walsh, A. 1998 A summary classification of Viking Age swords in Ireland. In H.B. Clarke, M. Ní Mhaonaigh and R. Ó Floinn (eds), *Ireland and Scandinavia in the early Viking Age*, 222–38. Dublin and Portland.

Walsh, P.T. 1968 The Old Red Sandstone west of Killarney, Co. Kerry, Ireland. *Proceedings of the Royal Irish Academy* **66B**, 9–26.

Warren, S.H., Piggott, H.S., Clark, J.G.D., Burkitt, M.C., Godwin, H. and Godwin, M.E. 1936 Archaeology of the submerged landsurface of the Essex coast. *Proceedings of the Prehistoric Society* **2**, 178–210.

Weir, J.A. 1962 Geology of the Lower Palaeozoic inliers of Slieve Bernagh and the Cratloe Hills, Co. Clare. *Scientific Proceedings of the Royal Dublin Society* **A1**, 233–63.

Weir, J.A. 1975 Palaeogeographical implications of two Silurian shelly faunas from the Arra Mountains and Cratloe Hills, Ireland. *Journal of Earth Sciences of the Royal Dublin Society* **2**, 61–3.

Went, A.E.J. 1945 Fishing weirs of the River Erne. *Journal of the Royal Society of Antiquaries of Ireland* **75**, 215–23.

Went, A.E.J. 1946 Irish fishing weirs I: notes on some ancient examples fished in tidal waters. *Journal of the Royal Society of Antiquaries of Ireland* **76**, 176–94.

Went, A.E.J. 1948 Irish fishery weirs II: the Duncannon weir. *Journal of the Royal Society of Antiquaries of Ireland* **78**, 1–4.

Went, A.E.J. 1950 Eel fishing at Athlone—past and present. *Journal of the Royal Society of Antiquaries of Ireland* **80**, 146–54.

Went, A.E.J. 1953 Fisheries of the River Liffey. *Journal of the Royal Society of Antiquaries of Ireland* **83**, 163–73.

Went, A.E.J. 1956 Historical notes on the fisheries of the River Suir. *Journal of the Royal Society of Antiquaries of Ireland* **86**, 192–202.

Went, A.E.J. 1958 The salmon fishery of Carrick-A-Rede and Larry Bane, Co. Antrim. *Journal of the Royal Society of Antiquaries of Ireland* **88**, 57–65.

Went, A.E.J. 1959 Sprat or white-fish weirs in Waterford Harbour. *Journal of the Royal Society of Antiquaries of Ireland* **89**, 91–3.

Went, A.E.J. 1960a Fisheries of the Munster Blackwater. *Journal of the Royal Society of Antiquaries of Ireland* **90**, 97–115.

Went, A.E.J. 1960b Historical notes on the fisheries of some tidal tributaries of the River Shannon. *North Munster Antiquarian Journal* **8** (3), 138–55.

Went, A.E.J. 1961 Fisheries of the Munster Blackwater. *Journal of the Royal Society of Antiquaries of Ireland* **91**, 19–41.

Went, A.E.J. 1964 The pursuit of salmon in Ireland. *Proceedings of the Royal Irish Academy* **63C**, 191–243.

Went, A.E.J. 1966 Historical notes on the fisheries of Lough Swilly and its tributaries. *Journal of the Royal Society of Antiquaries of Ireland* **96**, 121–32.

Went, A.E.J. 1969a Historical notes on the fisheries of the two County Sligo rivers. *Journal of the Royal Society of Antiquaries of Ireland* **99**, 55–61.

Went, A.E.J. 1969b The ancient 'sprat' fishing weirs in the south of Ireland. *Industrial Archaeology* **6**, 254–60.

Went, A.E.J. 1976 Fishing gear in the Enniscorthy and Wexford museums. *Journal of the Royal Society of Antiquaries of Ireland* **106**, 127–8.

Went, A.E.J. 1981 Historical notes on the fisheries of the estuary of the River Shannon. *Journal of the Royal Society of Antiquaries of Ireland* **111**, 107–18.

Westropp, T.J. 1903a Notes on Askeaton, County Limerick: part I—the history, AD 900 to 1579. *Journal of the Royal Society of Antiquaries of Ireland* **33**, 25–40.

Westropp, T.J. 1903b Notes on Askeaton, County Limerick: part II—the history after 1579. *Journal of the Royal Society of Antiquaries of Ireland* **33**, 153–74.

Westropp, T.J. 1904 Notes on Askeaton, County Limerick: part IV—the churches and the castle. *Journal of the Royal Society of Antiquaries of Ireland* **34**, 111–32.

Westropp, T.J. 1907 The principal ancient castles of the County Limerick. *Journal of the Royal Society of Antiquaries of Ireland* **36**, 24–40.

Westropp, T.J. 1908 Carrigogunnel Castle and the O'Briens of Pubblebrian, in the county of Limerick, part II—the ruins and the later families. *Journal of the Royal Society of Antiquaries of Ireland* **38**, 141–59.

Westropp, T.J. 1913 Early Italian maps of Ireland from 1300 to 1600, with notes on foreign settlers and trade. *Proceedings of the Royal Irish Academy* **30C**, 361–428.

Westropp, T.J. 1913–15 The earthworks and castle of Bunratty, Co. Clare. *North Munster Antiquarian Journal* **3**, 314–27.

Wheeler, A.J. 1995 Saltmarsh development from fen: analysis of late Holocene deposits from north-central Fenland, UK. *Quaternary International* **26**, 139–45.

Whiting, R. 1988 *The enterprise of England: the Spanish Armada*. London.

Whittle, A.W. 1989 Two later Bronze Age occupations and an Iron Age channel on the Gwent foreshore. *Bulletin of the Board of Celtic Studies* (1989), 200–23.

Whittle, A. 1996 *Europe in the Neolithic: the creation of new worlds*. Cambridge.

Wignall, S. 1982 *In search of Spanish treasure*. London.

Wilkins, N.P. 1989 *Ponds, passes and parcs, aquaculture in Victorian Ireland*. Sandycove, Co. Dublin.

Wilkins, N.P. 1998 *Men, tides and salmon. Snap-netting on the Barrow, Nore and Suir*. Clonmel.

Wilkinson, T.J. 1986 Estuarine wetlands of Essex, England. *NewsWARP* **1**, 15–16.

Wilkinson, T.J. 1989 The archaeological survey of coastal estuarine wetlands. In J.M. Coles and B.J. Coles (eds), *The archaeology of rural wetlands in England*, 23–6. Exeter.

Wilkinson, T.J. and Murphy, P. 1986 Archaeological survey of an inter-tidal zone: the submerged landscape of the Essex coast, England. *Journal of Field Archaeology* **13** (2), 177–94.

Wilkinson, T.J. and Murphy, P. 1988 Wetland development and human activity in Essex estuaries during the Holocene transgression. In P. Murphy and C. French (eds), *The exploitation of wetlands*, 213–38. British Archaeological Reports, British Series 186. Oxford.

Wilkinson, T. and Murphy, P. 1995 *The archaeology of the Essex coast: the Hullbridge Survey*. Norwich.

Williams, B.B. 1978 Excavations at Lough Eskragh, Co. Tyrone. *Ulster Journal of Archaeology* **41**, 37–48.

Williams, B.B. 1996 Intertidal archaeology in Strangford Lough. *Archaeology Ireland* **10** (3), 12–15.

Wilson, J.G., Brennan, M. and Brennan, B. 1993 Horizontal and vertical gradients in sediment nutrients on mudflats in the Shannon Estuary, Ireland. *Netherlands Journal of Aquatic Ecology* **27**, 173–80.

Wood, E., Hoagland-Grey, H. and Smith, E. 1996 *The west coast of Ireland: an environmental appraisal*. Texaco, Enterprise Oil PLC, Kerr–McGee Oil (UK) PLC and Statoil (UK) Ltd. London.

Woodman, P.C. 1977 Recent excavations at Newferry, Co. Antrim. *Proceedings of the Prehistoric Society* **43**, 155–99.

Woodman, P.C. and Johnston, G. 1991–2 A petrological examination of some Mesolithic stone artefacts. *Ulster Journal of Archaeology* **54–5**, 134–7.

Woodman, P.C. and O'Brien, M. 1993 Excavations at Ferriter's Cove, Co. Kerry: an interim statement. In E. Shee-Twohig and M. Ronayne (eds), *Past perceptions: the prehistoric archaeology of south-west Ireland*, 25–34. Cork.

Woodman, P.C., Anderson, E. and Finlay, N. 1999 *Excavations at Ferriter's Cove, 1983–95: last foragers and first farmers in the Dingle Peninsula*. Bray.

Woodman, P.C., Duggan, M.A. and McCarthy, A. 1984 Excavations at Ferriter's Cove. *Journal of the Kerry Archaeological and Historical Society* **17**, 5–9.

Wood-Martin, W.G. 1886 *The lake-dwellings of Ireland or ancient lacustrine habitations of Erin commonly called crannogs*. Dublin.

Wright, E.V. 1976 *The North Ferriby boats*. Maritime Monographs and Reports 23. Basildon.

Wright, E.V. 1990 *The Ferriby boats*. London and New York.

APPENDIX 1: RADIOCARBON DATES

Site name	Lab. no.	Sample	Date BP	Cal. BC/AD
Meelick Rocks 1	GrN-21930	Submerged trunk (upper shore)	4160 ±20	2875–2634 BC
Meelick Rocks 2	GrN-21929	Submerged tree bark (lower shore)	6240 ± 25	5299–5078 BC
Poulnasharry Bay 1	GrN-20145	Submerged forest trunk (saltmarsh)	4960 ± 35	3892–3655 BC
Poulnasharry Bay 1.2	GrN-21928	Peat/clay contact (saltmarsh)	1640 ± 40	AD 262–534
Fergus estuary east 3	GrN-20140	Red deer bone	4245 ± 40	2919–2689 BC
Carrigdirty Rock 8	GrN-21936	Wooden plank	5820 ± 40	4779–4551 BC
Carrigdirty Rock 5	Beta-102087	Alder basket	4820 ± 50	3702–3386 BC
Carrigdirty Rock 5	GrA-6520	Alder basket	4820 ± 50	3702–3386 BC
Carrigdirty Rock 5	Beta-102086	Human skull	4710 ± 60	3634–3370 BC
Carrigdirty Rock 1	GrN-20976	House site (sharpened post)	3330 ± 25	1681–1529 BC
Coonagh Point 1	GrN-21926	Worked wood	3240 ±20	1598–1441 BC
Fergus estuary west 1	GrN-20974	Post-and-wattle structure (rod)	2540 ± 20	797–551 BC
Fergus estuary east 2	GrN-20139	Fishtrap	1495 ± 35	AD 442–644
Bunratty 4	GrN-21933	Fishtrap	960 ± 20	AD 1018–1159
Bunratty 6	GrN-21934	Fishtrap basket	820 ± 35	AD 1164–1279
Deel estuary 1	GrN-21932	Fishtrap	900 ± 20	AD 1041–1208
Deel estuary 2	GrN-20975	Fishtrap	740 ± 15	AD 1262–92
Deel estuary 3	GrN-21931	Fishtrap	640 ± 20	AD 1297–1392
Carrigdirty Rock 12	GrN-20977	Post-and-wattle trackway	220 ± 20	AD 1646–1943
Fergus estuary east 5.2	GrN-20141	Reclamation fence	155 ± 30	AD 1665–1946
Fergus estuary east 5.3	GrN-20142	Reclamation fence wattle	215 ± 25	AD 1645–1947
Fergus estuary west 2	GrN-21927	Post-and-wattle panel	160 ± 15	AD 1669–1942
Clonderalaw Bay 3	GrN-20144	Fishtrap	250 ± 30	AD 1522–1941
Clonderalaw Bay 1.4	GrN-20143	Post-and-wattle	135 ± 30	AD 1675–1946
Poulnasharry Bay 2	GrN-20146	Boat wreck	245 ± 30	AD 1524–1943

APPENDIX 2: SUMMARY INVENTORY OF INTERTIDAL ARCHAEOLOGICAL SITES RECORDED ON THE SHANNON ESTUARY AND FERGUS ESTUARY

A summary inventory of recorded intertidal archaeological sites on the Fergus estuary, upper Shannon estuary and lower Shannon estuary is provided here for rapid reference. Sites are given in alphabetical order, with entries as to site name, date or period, site type, adjacent townland, Ordnance Survey map (sheet, plan, trace) and National Grid Reference (estimated by reference to various topographical features). Precise NGR and Ordnance Datum heights are available for some of the Carrigdirty Rock sites, as these were plotted using a survey instrument. A summary site description is included, with radiocarbon dates (if available) and month and year of the last site visit.

FERGUS ESTUARY, CO. CLARE

Fergus estuary east 2
Early historic
Fishtrap
Ballygirreen, Co. Clare
OS 42:9:5   NGR 136287, 170334
Post-and-wattle fence in estuarine clays at LWM, oriented ENE–WSW, 8.2m long, of 25 vertical roundwood stakes (2–3cm in diameter) with narrow interwoven rods (1.7–1.9cm). Post-and-wattle panels lie in muds at the WSW end. Radiocarbon-dated to 1495 ± 35 BP (cal. AD 442–644; GrN-20139). Planned July 1992; revisited May 1995.

Fergus estuary east 3
Neolithic
Red deer bone
Ballygirreen, Co. Clare
OS 42:13:2   NGR 136047, 169938
Red deer bone, articulated and from single animal, in estuarine clays 2m SE of LWM. Radiocarbon-dated to 4245 ± 40 BP (2919–2689 BC; GrN-20140). May 1994.

Fergus estuary east 5.1–5.3
Post-medieval
Post alignments (reclamation features)
Ballygirreen, Co. Clare
OS 42:13:2   NGR 136135, 169951
Post alignment (FEE5.1), spread of roundwood branches (FEE5.2) and a horizontal wattle panel (FEE.3) on level, soft estuarine clays between saltmarsh and Crow Island. FEE5.2 was dated to 155 ± 30 BP (AD 1665–1946; GrN-20141). FEE 5.3 was radiocarbon-dated to 215 ± 25 BP (AD 1645–1947; GrN-201412; O'Sullivan 1993). May 1994.

Fergus estuary east 6
Post-medieval?
Stone jetty
Manusmore, Co. Clare
OS 42:9:2   NGR 136105, 171240
Stone-built jetty at the saltmarsh edge, oriented NE–SW, 16m long, 2m wide, 50cm high. Located c. 100m NW of Latoon Creek. Built of irregular limestone slabs laid as a double kerb with a rubble infill. May 1995.

Fergus estuary east 7
Neolithic?
Red deer bone
Carrownanelly, Co. Clare
OS 42:5:4   NGR 135322, 171881
Red deer bone, articulated from single animal, 2m E of LWM in steeply sloping foreshore of estuarine clays. September 1995.

Fergus estuary east 8
Post-medieval?
Sheep skull
Ballygirreen, Co. Clare
OS 42:13:2   NGR 136081, 169982
Sheep skull (*Ovis aries* L.) recovered from an unstratified position on estuarine clays at LWM, 10m N of Fergus estuary east 3. May 1994.

Fergus estuary east 9
Post-medieval
Post alignment
Carrownanelly, Co. Clare
OS 42:5:1   NGR 135711, 172685
Post alignment (possible fishtrap) in estuarine clays at LWM, oriented NW–SE, *c.* 8m long. Other posts are submerged underwater. November 1995.

Fergus estuary west 1
Late Bronze Age
Post-and-wattle structures
Islandmagrath, Co. Clare
OS 42:9:1   NGR 135457, 171173
Post-and-wattle structures running diagonally down foreshore of estuarine clays, oriented WNW–ESE, *c.* 35m long, *c.* 2m wide. Two vertical or obliquely set post-and-wattle fences have horizontal wattle panels and brushwood laid between them. A withy tie was found at the WNW end. A rod was radiocarbon-dated to 2540 ± 20 BP (797–551 cal. BC; GrN-20974). August 1994; last visited November 1995.

Fergus estuary west 2
Post-medieval
Post-and-wattle panel
Lissan West, Co. Clare
OS 41:8:6   NGR 135144, 172124
Post-and-wattle panel buried in estuarine clays at LWM with a creek to the S, oriented N–S, *c.* 1.4m in exposed length by 70cm in width. Radiocarbon-dated to 160 ± 15 BP (cal. AD 1669–1942; GrN-21927). September 1995.

Fergus estuary west 3
Post-medieval
Fishtrap
Lissan West, Co. Clare
OS 41:8:6   NGR 135181, 172070
Post alignment at LWM, beside possible ballast dump, oriented NE–SW, *c.* 8m long. Constructed of both large and narrow roundwood posts, with obliquely set braces at downstream side. September 1995.

Foragers, farmers and fishers

Fergus estuary west 4
Post-medieval
Fishtrap
Lissan West, Co. Clare
OS 41:8:6   NGR 135170, 172089
Post alignment at LWM, oriented NE–SW, *c.* 6m long. September 1995.

Clenagh 1
Prehistoric/medieval?
Dug-out boat
Clenagh, Co. Clare
OS 51:13:2   NGR 136405, 163328
Dug-out boat of oak in a saltmarsh creek, surviving as the incomplete prow section of a medium-sized vessel, which thickens towards the prow. It is oriented E–W. Length 2.88m, max. width 0.85m, thickness 0.05–0.3m (Kelly 1987). July 1992.

UPPER SHANNON ESTUARY, CO. CLARE

Bunratty 1
Medieval?
Post-and-wattle fences
Bunratty West, Co. Clare
OS 62:5:1   NGR 145095, 160178
Post-and-wattle fence (Bunratty 1.1), horizontal post-and-wattle panel (Bunratty 1.2) and vertical posts and horizontal branches in estuarine clays exposed below the mean LWM over an area measuring 10m (NE–SW) by 1m. February 1997.

Bunratty 2
Medieval/post-medieval?
Fishtrap
Bunratty West, Co. Clare
OS 62:5:1   NGR 145046, 160089
Post-and-wattle fence, oriented ENE–WSW, 4m long, on the sloping estuarine clays at LWM. February 1997.

Bunratty 3
Medieval?
Fishtrap with woven baskets
Bunratty West, Co. Clare
OS 62:5:1   NGR 145048, 160044
Post alignment (Bunratty 3.1) and two woven baskets (Bunratty 3A and 3B) in sloping estuarine clays at LWM. The post alignment is oriented E–W, *c.* 5.6m long, and leads to the baskets. Bunratty 3A is U-shaped, oriented WNW, and 1.2m long. Bunratty 3B is funnel-shaped, oriented WNW, and 2.8m long. February 1997.

Bunratty 4
Medieval
Fishtraps
Bunratty West, Co. Clare
OS 62:5:1   NGR 145053, 160017
Post-and-wattle fences and brushwood structures representing at least four phases of reuse and reconstruction of V-shaped fishtraps on the steeply sloping estuarine clays. Rod radiocarbon-dated to 960 ± 20 BP (cal. AD 1018–1159; GrN-21933). February 1997.

Appendix 2

Bunratty 5
Prehistoric?
Submerged forest and peats
Bunratty West, Co. Clare
OS 62:5:1   NGR 145058, 159977
Submerged peats (brown, silty, poorly humified) at LWM, parallel to channel, over 30m (N–S) by 5m (E–W) to the east of Little Quay Island. Large, recumbent oak trunks and stumps (20cm in diameter, 4–5m long) visible in peat. February 1997.

Bunratty 6
Medieval
Fishtrap with woven basket
Bunratty West, Co. Clare
OS 62:8:6   NGR 144566, 159384
Post-and-wattle fences (Bunratty 6.1) and basket (Bunratty 6.2) of V-shaped fishtrap. Fence oriented N–S, 10–22m long, constructed of rows of vertical posts, laid brushwood, post-and-wattle panels and oblique braces. Basket 4.1m long, 88cm wide at mouth and 35cm at end. Hazel rod radiocarbon-dated to 820 ± 35 BP (AD 1164–1279; GrN-21934). Excavated February 1997; revisited March 1999. Site location estimated.

Bunratty 7
Post-medieval
Fishtrap
Bunratty West, Co. Clare
OS 62:8:6   NGR 144604, 159460
Post alignment (creek trap), oriented N–S, 8m long, crossing modern mudflat creek, to the NW of Bunratty 6. February 1997.

Bunratty 8
Post-medieval
Fishtrap
Bunratty West, Co. Clare
OS 62:8:6   NGR 144600, 159485
Post alignment (creek trap), oriented NE–SW, 8m long, crossing modern mudflat creek, 10m N of Bunratty 7. February 1997.

Bunratty 9
Post-medieval
Fishtrap
Bunratty West, Co. Clare
OS 62:8:3   NGR 144587, 159534
Post alignments (creek trap with obliquely set braces), oriented NE–SW, 9m long, c. 60m NW of Bunratty 8. February 1997.

Bunratty 10
Post-medieval
Fishtrap
Bunratty West, Co. Clare
OS 61:8:6   NGR 144798, 159426
Post alignment, oriented E–W, 4–5m long, in narrow modern mudflat creek to the west of Quay Island. February 1997.

Foragers, farmers and fishers

Bunratty 11
Post-medieval
Fishtrap
Bunratty West, Co. Clare
OS 61:8:6   NGR 144794, 159397
Post alignment, oriented E–W, 4–5m long, in narrow mudflat creek to the west of Quay Island. February 1997.

Bunratty 12
Post-medieval?
Wooden jetty or pier
Bunratty West, Co. Clare
OS 62:1:4   NGR 145212, 160577
Wooden structure in estuarine clays at saltmarsh, on west bank of the River Owenagarney near drainage sluice. Composed of five roundwood trunks (20cm in diameter) of pine, laid across a longitudinal roundwood substructure. Trunks are jointed (lap joints and mortises) and crudely cut across at ends. February 1997.

Bush Island 1
Post-medieval
Fishtraps
Moyhill, Co. Clare
OS 62:9:2   NGR 146222, 158324
Multiple post alignments on muddy shoal in channel, 50m to S of island, at LWM. Largest post alignment (of multiple, closely spaced posts), set at right angles to channel, is oriented N–S and measures 35m in length. A single parallel alignment of posts to E and two parallel post alignments to W make overall structure 15m wide (E–W). A fifth post alignment runs E–W at S end of main post alignment. Probable nineteenth-century stake weirs. July 2000.

Bush Island 2A
Post-medieval
Fishtrap
Moyhill, Co. Clare
OS 62:9:2   NGR 146081, 158444
Large tick-shaped wooden fishtrap in estuarine clays at LWM, *c.* 300m SW of Bush Island. Flood fence oriented NW–SE, 8m long. Shore fence oriented N–S, 370m long. The enclosed angle is *c.* 30°. July 2000.

Bush Island 2B
Post-medieval
Fishtrap
Moyhill, Co. Clare
OS 62:9:2   NGR 146088, 158458
Large tick-shaped wooden fishtrap in estuarine clays at LWM, 50m N of Bush Island 2A, constructed to use the same shore fence. Flood fence oriented NW–SE, 47m long. Shore fence oriented N–S, 320m long. The enclosed angle is *c.* 40°. July 2000.

Bush Island 2C
Post-medieval
Fishtrap
Moyhill, Co. Clare
OS 62:9:2   NGR 146060, 158465
Large tick-shaped wooden fishtrap in estuarine clays at LWM, 30m W of Bush Island 2B. Flood fence oriented NW–SE, 10m long; shore fence oriented N–S, 120m long. The

Appendix 2

enclosed angle is *c.* 60°. July 2000.

Bush Island 2D
Post-medieval
Fishtrap (post-and-wattle fence)
Moyhill, Co. Clare
OS 62:9:2   NGR 146116, 158507
Post-and-wattle fence curving down foreshore to LWM, intersecting with shore fence of Bush Island 2A–2B. Oriented NNE–SSW, 159m long. Probable fence from robbed-out fishtrap. July 2000.

Bush Island 3
Medieval?
Woven basket (fishtrap)
Moyhill, Co. Clare
OS 62:5:5   NGR 145876, 158732
Basket buried in ancient estuarine clays exposed in E side of creek on lower foreshore, *c.* 450m W of Bush Island, *c.* 80m NE of Shannon estuary channel LWM. Basket is of a broad U-shape, oriented NNE–SSW, 3.9m in exposed width and 3.6m in exposed length. A post-and-wattle panel and four large roundwood posts are buried in clays at NNE end of basket. July 2000.

Bush Island 4
Medieval?
Fishtrap
Moyhill, Co. Clare
OS 62:5:5   NGR 146128, 158822
U-shaped post structure in bank of creek on upper foreshore, NW of Bush Island, oriented N–S, 3.6m long, 1.8m wide (at mouth), 80cm wide at S end. A vertical post-and-wattle fence, 2m long, leads to this structure from NW. Possible medieval fishtrap, similar in form to Bunratty 4. July 2000.

Bush Island 5
Post-medieval
Fishtrap
Moyhill, Co. Clare
OS 62:5:5   NGR 146149, 158822
Post alignment crossing creek on upper foreshore, NW of Bush Island, oriented NNE–SSW, 84m long. A post-and-wattle fence (Bush Island 6), oriented N–S, 6m long, is embedded in clays immediately to NE of post alignment and may be part of this structure. July 2000.

Bush Island 7
Post-medieval
Fishtrap
Moyhill, Co. Clare
OS 62:5:5   NGR 146219, 158849
V-shaped post-and-wattle fence in creek on upper foreshore, NW of Bush Island, oriented NNE–SSW to catch fish on flooding tide, 30m long. July 2000.

Bush Island 8
Post-medieval
Fishtrap
Moyhill, Co. Clare
OS 62:5:5   NGR 146224, 158849

Post alignment with two lines of obliquely set bracing, crossing creek on upper foreshore (intersecting with Bush Island 9), NW of Bush Island, oriented N–S, 80m long. July 2000.

Bush Island 9
Post-medieval
Fishtrap
Moyhill, Co. Clare
OS 62:5:5   NGR 146235, 158860
Post alignments (double row) on N bank of creek on upper foreshore, NW of Bush Island, oriented NNE–SSW, 80m long. July 2000.

Bush Island 10
Post-medieval
Fishtrap
Moyhill, Co. Clare
OS 62:5:5   NGR 146240, 158860
Post alignment crossing creek on upper foreshore, NW of Bush Island, oriented N–S, 40m long, braced on W side. July 2000.

Bush Island 11
Post-medieval
Fishtrap
Moyhill, Co. Clare
OS 62:5:5   NGR 146235, 158860
Post alignment (double post row) on N bank of creek on upper foreshore NW of Bush Island, oriented N–S, 20m long. July 2000.

Bush Island 12
Post-medieval
Fishtrap
Ballymorris, Co. Clare
OS 62:9:3   NGR 146759, 158558
C-shaped post-and-wattle fence on W bank of creek, on upper foreshore, to W of Bush Island. Oriented E–W, 36m long; mouth faces upstream to catch fish on ebbing tide. July 2000.

Bush Island 13
Post-medieval
Fishtrap
Ballymorris, Co. Clare
OS 62:9:3   NGR 146673, 158547
C-shaped post-and-wattle fence (double row of posts with downstream braces) on W bank of creek on upper foreshore, 50m to SW of Bush Island 12. Oriented E–W, 47m long; mouth faces upstream to catch fish on ebbing tide. A horizontal post-and-wattle panel (2m E–W, 1m N–S) is buried in clays 6m to E of fence. July 2000.

Bush Island 14
Post-medieval
Fishtrap
Ballymorris, Co. Clare
OS 62:9:3   NGR 146668, 158477
Large L-shaped structure (of post-and-wattle fence, vertical posts and downstream braces) immediately SW of Bush Island 13. Oriented N–S; flood fence 24m long, shore fence 105m long. Mouth faces upstream as ebb weir. July 2000.

Bush Island 15
Post-medieval
Fishtrap
Ballymorris, Co. Clare
OS 62:9:3 NGR 146540, 158477
Large L-shaped post alignment immediately SW of Bush Island 13 (mostly buried in clays). Oriented NE–SW; flood fence 32m long, shore fence 125m long. Mouth faces upstream as ebb weir. July 2000.

Bush Island 16
Post-medieval
Fishtraps
Ballymorris, Co. Clare
OS 62:9:3 NGR 146737, 158349
Post alignment (16a) on N side of creek on upper foreshore, oriented N–S, 182m long. A second post alignment (16b) with braces converges with this structure from NW, oriented NNW–SSE, 40m long. July 2000.

Bush Island 17
Post-medieval
Fishtrap
Ballymorris, Co. Clare
OS 62:9:3 NGR 147128, 158520
Post alignment with obliquely set braces on both sides (heavier timbers used on downstream side), crossing two creeks on upper foreshore. Oriented N–S, 100m long. July 2000.

Bush Island 18
Post-medieval
Fishtrap
Ballymorris, Co. Clare
OS 62:9:3 NGR 146673, 158365
L-shaped post-and-wattle fence, oriented NNE–SSW, 19m in total length, located 6m S of Bush Island 14. Flood fence oriented ENE–WSW, 3m long. Shore fence oriented NW–SE, 16m long. Enclosed angle *c.* 90°. July 2000.

Bush Island 19
Post-medieval
Ship's timber
Ballymorris, Co. Clare
OS 62:9:3 NGR 146449, 158285
Ship's timber (futtock or floor timber) in estuarine clays at LWM. Sawn from oak, with treenail holes. Length 1m, width 15cm, thickness 11cm. Identified on flooding tide, not subsequently relocated. A nineteenth-century ship, the *William Ash,* was lost in 1851 at Hog's Head Rock in the channel to S. The timber may derive from this wreck. July 1994.

Cratloe Creek 1
Post-medieval (or medieval?)
Fishtrap
Meelick, Co. Clare
OS 62:11:3 NGR 152022, 158130
Post alignment (widely spaced posts), oriented NNW–SSE, 48m long, situated in firm, gently sloping estuarine clays on N bank of estuary. July 1996.

Graigue Island 1
Post-medieval?
Fishtrap
Garryncurra, Co. Clare
OS 62:10:2   NGR 148376, 158559
Post alignment, oriented N–S, 8m long, on level estuarine clays at low water, *c.* 250m ENE of Graigue Island. July 1994.

Graigue Island 2
Post-medieval?
Fishtrap
Garryncurra, Co. Clare
OS 62:10:2   NGR 148143, 158393
Post alignment, oriented NW–SE, 26m long, on level estuarine clays to SSE of island. July 1994.

Graigue Island 3
Post-medieval?
Post-and-wattle structures
Garryncurra, Co. Clare
OS 62:10:2   NGR 148177, 158578
Posts with interwoven rods, *c.* 100m to the NNE of Graigue Island. Possible alignment oriented E–W, 8m long, crossing a small tidal creek. July 1994.

Green Island 1
Post-medieval?
Fishtrap?
Green Island, Co. Clare
OS 62:5:4   NGR 145516, 159031
Post alignment, oriented NE–SW, 16m long, in estuarine clays at LWM, SW of Green Island. February 1997.

Inishbonane 1
Post-medieval
Fishtrap
Clonmoney South, Co: Clare
OS 61:8:2   NGR 143477, 159531
Large V-shaped wooden fishtrap in estuarine clays at LWM, W of Inishbonane or Tradree Point. Flood fence oriented E–W, 23m long; shore fence oriented NW–SE, 63m long. February 1997.

Inishcronan Rocks 1
Unknown date
Stone causeway/intertidal wall
Saint's Island, Co. Clare
OS 61:8:1   NGR 142850, 160057
Large V-shaped stone wall or causeway, *c.* 370m long, buried under silts between Inishcronan Point and Saint's Island. The feature is depicted on the OS 6" second edition map Clare No. 61 (it is not marked on first edition) and Admiralty charts of the Shannon estuary (No. 1540). Function unknown; may be causeway to island, failed mudflat reclamation feature, fishtrap or tidal watermill. Observed from saltmarsh after completion of survey, March 1999.

Appendix 2

O'Brien's Point 1
Post-medieval (medieval?)
Fishtrap
Portdrine, Co. Clare
OS 62:7:4   NGR 149754, 158819
Post alignment, oriented NW–SE, 85m long, in firm, sandy estuarine clays at LWM. March 1999.

O'Brien's Point 2
Post-medieval (medieval?)
Fishtrap
Portdrine, Co. Clare
OS 62:7:4   NGR 149763, 158808
Post alignment, oriented NE–SW, 35m long, appears to converge with the SE end of O'Brien's Point 1 below LWM. March 1999.

O'Brien's Point 3
Post-medieval
Fishtraps
Portdrine, Co. Clare
OS 62:7:4   NGR 149768, 158808
Multiple post alignments (at least five rows) running down the foreshore, all oriented NW–SE, 80–100m long, 35m wide. The strongest posts were situated at the downstream side, with heavy branches and poles used as wattle, stones laid beside fences and rows of diagonal braces to the E and W. March 1999.

O'Brien's Point 4
Medieval?
Stone slipway
Portdrine, Co. Clare
OS 62:7:4   NGR 150024, 158673
Stone-built slipway or jetty running down foreshore from rock outcrop across foreshore to channel, oriented NW–SE, 32m long, 0.5–1m high, 3m wide. Located *c.* 30m W of creek which flows out to the S of Portdrine. Built of regular limestone slabs laid as a double kerb with a rubble infill, possibly robbed out for construction of later sea wall. March 1999.

Quay Island 1
Post-medieval
Wooden jetty
Quay Island, Co. Clare
OS 62:5:4   NGR 145247, 159127
Wooden jetty on estuarine clays on E shore of Quay Island, of double row of vertical timbers, oriented N–S (curves in towards island on mid-foreshore), *c.* 180m long, *c.* 2m wide, with timbers surviving to heights of 3–4m. Depicted on OS maps and Admiralty charts as pier used for island's harbour pilots. August 1995.

Quay Island 2
Post-medieval
Fishtrap
Quay Island, Co. Clare
OS 62:5:4   NGR 145078, 159138
Large V-shaped or U-shaped fishtrap in estuarine clays at LWM, to SW of Quay Island. Flood fence oriented WNW–ESE, 45m in exposed length; shore fence oriented NW–SE, 30m in exposed length. February 1997.

Quay Island 3
Post-medieval
Wooden jetty
Quay Island, Co. Clare
OS 62:5:4   NGR 145185, 159100
Wooden jetty in estuarine clays S of Quay Island. Two rows of vertical posts, c. 26m in exposed length, possibly curves around to E below low water. Vertical posts, 15–25cm in diameter, spaced at intervals of 1.5–2m. February 1997.

Quay Island 4
Post-medieval
Stone jetty/hard
Quay Island, Co. Clare
OS 62:5:1   NGR 145271, 159550
Stone-built causeways, on both S and N banks of River Owenagarney, running down foreshore to channel. Linear structures of stone slabs, c. 100m in overall length and c. 2–3m wide. Depicted on OS 6" sheet 62 and Admiralty chart (1054) as 'quay' and 'hard'. February 1997.

UPPER SHANNON ESTUARY, CO. LIMERICK

Carrigdirty Rock 1
Bronze Age
House site
Newtown, Co. Limerick
OS 4:10:3   NGR 147343, 157573   OD –0.465m
Wooden oval structure, 4.8m (E–W) by 4.6m (N–S), defined by inner ring of posts with possible ring of smaller stakes outside, c. 6m in diameter. There are at least 23 sharpened vertical roundwood posts and stakes, 4–12cm in diameter, driven into a reedy, woody fen peat. A few stone slabs lie on the peat to the NE of the structure. A single calf mandible was recovered at the S side. A vertical post was radiocarbon-dated to 3330 ± 25 BP (1681–1529 cal. BC; GrN-20976). July 1994.

Carrigdirty Rock 2
Bronze Age?
Hut structure? (wooden posts, stone slabs and animal bone)
Newtown, Co. Limerick
OS 4:10:3   NGR 147294, 157577   OD –0.622m
Wooden posts (with metal tool-marks), limestone slabs and cattle bone in fen peats, on sloping foreshore WNW of Carrigdirty Rock 1. Posts (8–10cm in diameter, 30cm long) set in an arc c. 5m long; posts and stone located in peats over an area 8m (N–S) by 5m (E–W). July 1994.

Carrigdirty Rock 3
Bronze Age/Iron Age?
Pit with animal bone
Newtown, Co. Limerick
OS 4:10:3   NGR n/a
Shallow pit in fen peat, rich in woody fragments and reeds, on level foreshore 15m N of saltmarsh cliff, to SE of Carrigdirty Rock 4. Oval in plan, 90cm long (NW–SE), 50cm wide and 15cm in surviving depth. Erosion has removed its upper surface. Filled with a gritty, shell-rich, grey clay deposit and disarticulated bones of red deer and pink-footed goose. Pig bone and deer antler (Carrigdirty Rock 9) also found on adjacent foreshore. December 1995.

Appendix 2

Carrigdirty Rock 4
Neolithic/Bronze Age?
Post feature
Newtown, Co. Limerick
OS 4:10:3   NGR 147096, 157519   OD –1.141m
Two roundwood posts and one cleft post in fen peats on the sloping E bank of modern mudflat creek, S of Carrigdirty Rock. Two posts lay horizontally in peat and a single post was driven at an angle into peats. This post was cleft on four surfaces to a sharpened point. July 1996.

Carrigdirty Rock 5
Neolithic
Occupation site
Newtown, Co. Limerick
OS 4:10:3   NGR 147830, 157693   OD –1.591m
Possible Neolithic wetland occupation site represented by a scatter of both stratified and unstratified finds on the lower foreshore. The finds are emerging from organic-rich, reedy, grey estuarine clays over an area 30m (E–W) by 2m (N–S). They include worked and charred roundwood, charcoal, fragments of basketry, a portion of human skull and clavicle, cattle and swan bone, a stone axe, chert flakes, a possible hammerstone and a few fragments of charred bone and hazelnuts. The human skull has been radiocarbon-dated to 4710 ± 60 BP (3634–3370 cal. BC; Beta-102086). The basket has provided two similar radiocarbon dates of 4820 ± 50 BP (3702–3386 cal. BC; GrA-6520) and 4820 ± 50 BP (3702–3386 cal. BC; Beta-102087). September 1998.

Carrigdirty Rock 7
Neolithic?
Carved wood fragment
Newtown, Co. Limerick
OS 4:10:3   NGR n/a
A fragment of worked wood, recovered as a stray find from grey estuarine clays on the mid-foreshore, *c.* 100m E of Carrigdirty Rock 5–8. Possibly a fragment of the end of a carved wooden vessel, trough or dish. Possible tool-marks on the thickest surface. July 1994.

Carrigdirty Rock 8
Late Mesolithic
Wooden plank
Newtown, Co. Limerick
OS 4:10:3   NGR 147830, 157699   OD –2.375m
Wooden plank in clays at LWM, oriented NNE–SSW, 4.3m long, 37cm in max. width, 7cm in 'depth'; side edges and base 1–2.5cm thick. U-shaped in cross-section, curved at intact end (buried under the clays). Bark and sapwood possibly adhering to undersurface. Possibly of natural origin. Radiocarbon-dated to 5820 ± 40 BP (4779–4551 cal. BC; GrN-21936).

Carrigdirty Rock 9
Bronze Age?
Red deer antler
Newtown, Co. Limerick
OS 4:10:3   NGR n/a
Red deer antler from mature animal found unstratified on peats, 10m SE of Carrigdirty Rock 3. Antler broken away from skull. May 1996.

307

Carrigdirty Rock 10
Bronze Age?
Red deer and pig bone
Newtown, Co. Limerick
OS 4:10:3   NGR n/a
Two animal bones unstratified on the peat surface, 10–15m N of Carrigdirty Rock 3. Bones are lower jaw from red deer (*Cervus elaphus* L.) and rib from pig (*Sus domesticus erxl.*). May 1996.

Carrigdirty Rock 11
Mesolithic/Neolithic?
Brushwood feature
Newtown, Co. Limerick
OS 4:10:3   NGR 147799, 157690
Brushwood feature at LWM, oriented N–S, exposed in clays over 2m stretch, 30–40cm into the clays, composed of tightly packed narrow (1–2cm in diameter) rods and woody stems in clays. May be natural in origin. July 1994.

Carrigdirty Rock 12
Post-medieval
Post-and-wattle panel
Newtown, Co. Limerick
OS 4:10:5   NGR 146927, 157428
Post-and-wattle structure, oriented E–W, 2.2m long, 1m wide, horizontal in estuarine clays to SW of Carrigdirty Rock. Radiocarbon-dated to 220 ± 20 BP (1646–1943 cal. AD; GrN-20977). August 1994.

Carrigdirty Rock 13
Post-medieval
Post-and-wattle panel
Newtown, Co. Limerick
OS 4:10:5   NGR 146889, 157390
Post-and-wattle structure in clays near saltmarsh cliff, south of mudflat creek, oriented NE–SW, 2.5m long and 60cm wide. August 1994.

Carrigdirty Rock 14
Post-medieval
Fishtrap
Newtown, Co. Limerick
OS 4:10:5   NGR 146860, 157443
Post alignment, oriented NE–SW, 60m long, in estuarine clays on upper foreshore. Roundwood branches woven around vertical posts at SW end and limestone slabs laid at NE end. August 1994.

Carrigdirty Rock 15
Post-medieval?
Fishtrap
Newtown, Co. Limerick
OS 4:10:2   NGR 146833, 157575
Post-and-wattle fence, oriented NE–SW, 25m long, in estuarine clays at low water. August 1994.

Carrigdirty Rock 16
Neolithic/Bronze Age?
Submerged forest

Newtown, Co. Limerick
OS 4:10:3　　　　　NGR 147101, 157552
Submerged fen peats and carr woodland trunks to SE of Carrigdirty Rock, exposed on mid-foreshore and in E bank of mudflat creek, over an area 200m (N–S) by 100m (E–W), with closely spaced roots, branches and horizontal trunks of immature shrubby trees, 8–10cm in diameter. August 1994.

Carrigdirty Rock 20
Bronze Age?
Oak plank
Newtown, Co. Limerick
OS 4:10:3　　　　　NGR 147844, 157683　　　　　OD –0.405m
Large, tangentially cleft oak plank, oriented N–S, 3.4m long, 46–54cm wide, in peats on mid-foreshore. Edges of plank irregular, with notches and protrusions. July 1996.

Carrigdirty Rock 21
Bronze Age?
Oak plank
Newtown, Co. Limerick
OS 4:10:3　　　　　NGR 147777, 157660　　　　　OD –0.425m
Large, cleft oak plank, oriented E–W, 5.6m long, 76cm wide, 5.5cm thick. Set in fen peats, 2m S of the edge of the intertidal peat shelf. Tangentially cleft from a massive, knotty oak trunk. The plank was worked to a blunt oblique point at its W end, cut directly across at its E end. Side edges quite thin and 'feather-edged', owing to splitting of trunk. July 1996.

Coonagh Point 1
Bronze Age
Worked wood in submerged forest peats
Coonagh West, Co. Limerick
OS 5:13:2　　　　　NGR 154226, 156545
Oak trunks, roots and branches exposed in section in peats in saltmarsh cliff, over an area 30–40m long. Cleft oak stake and two pieces of worked roundwood recovered from the peats at the base of a saltmarsh cliff (1.5m below surface of saltmarsh). Cleft oak stake radiocarbon-dated to 3240 ± 20 BP (1598–1441 cal. BC; GrN-21926). July 1995.

Cooperhill 1
Viking Age
Sword findspot and wooden causeway
Cooperhill, Co. Limerick
OS 4:12:5　　　　　NGR 15179, 15689
An iron Viking Age sword was found on the S bank in 1958, at a depth of 16ft, on a substantial causeway of 'oak trunks all laid flat in one direction' beside a creek. The brief description of the findspot and the depth at which it was found suggests that this was a wooden trackway or boat-hard in a saltmarsh creek. (NMI files.) Not visited.

Deel estuary 1
Medieval
Fishtrap
Ballynash, Co. Limerick
OS 10:8:3　　　　　NGR 132748, 153133
V-shaped wooden fishtrap in estuarine clays, constructed of two converging post-and-wattle fences, oriented as flood weir, with shore and flood fences measuring 26m and 4.5m in length. Radiocarbon-dated to 900 ± 20 BP (cal. AD 1041–1208; GrN-21932). July 1994.

Deel estuary 2
Medieval
Fishtrap
Ballynash, Co. Limerick
OS 10:8:3　　　　　NGR 132752, 153035
Post alignment, oriented NE–SW, 5.6m long, in estuarine clays at LWM. Posts survive only as short eroded stumps, with worked points exposed. Radiocarbon-dated to 740 ± 15 BP (cal. AD 1262–92; GrN-20975). July 1994.

Deel estuary 3
Medieval
Fishtrap
Ballynash, Co. Limerick
OS 10:8:3　　　　　NGR 132801, 152957
Post alignment, oriented E–W, 4m long, in estuarine clays at LWM, to S of Deel estuary 2. Fence submerged underwater. Radiocarbon-dated to 640 ± 20 BP (cal. AD 1297–1392; GrN-21931). July 1994.

Deel estuary 4
Medieval
Roundwood post
Ballynash, Co. Limerick
OS 10:8:3　　　　　NGR 132748, 153051
Single post in estuarine clays 8m E of LWM, on sloping eroding terrace of clays. Post 9cm in diameter, 15cm long. Worked end exposed. Probably from eroded-out medieval fishtrap fence. May 1993.

Maiden Rock 1
Post-medieval
Fishtrap
Mellon, Co. Limerick
OS 4:9:3　　　　　NGR 144973, 157925
Post alignment, oriented NE–SW, 80m long, in soft estuarine clays on W bank of River Maigue. The posts, 5–9cm in diameter, are typically spaced at 2m intervals. Several small angular stones are scattered along length of structure. August 1994.

Maiden Rock 2
Post-medieval
Fishtrap
Mellon, Co. Limerick
OS 4:9:3　　　　　NGR 144918, 158002
Post alignment, oriented NE–SW, *c.* 30m long, in estuarine clays on W bank of River Maigue, *c.* 60m NW of Maiden Rock 2. Constructed of fifteen roundwood posts, 5–10cm in diameter, spaced at 0.5–1.8m intervals. August 1994.

Maiden Rock 3
Post-medieval
Post-and-wattle panel
Mellon, Co. Limerick
OS 4:9:3　　　　　NGR 144918, 158078
Post-and-wattle, oriented NW–SE, in estuarine clays on W bank of River Maigue, immediately NW of Maiden Rock 2. Composed of large poles (4cm in diameter) with interwoven wattle rods (2cm in diameter) exposed over an area measuring 5m by 2m. August 1994.

Appendix 2

Maiden Rock 4
Post-medieval
Fishtrap
Mellon, Co. Limerick
OS 4:9:3   NGR 144879, 158223
Post alignment oriented NW–SE, 10–15m long, in estuarine clays to S of Maiden Rock. August 1994.

Maiden Rock 5
Post-medieval
Fishtrap
Mellon, Co. Limerick
OS 4:9:3   NGR 144815, 158196
Post alignment, oriented N–S, 5–6m long, in estuarine clays of creek to S of Maiden Rock. August 1994.

Meelick Rocks 1
Neolithic
Submerged forest
Coonagh East, Co. Limerick
OS 4:12:3   NGR 152367, 157947
Submerged peats and forest, with extensive root systems and branches of oak and alder, on upper foreshore, exposed over an area measuring 150m (NW–SE) by 50m (NE–SW). A single sample of an oak root from one buttress on the mid-foreshore was radiocarbon-dated to 4160 ± 20 BP (2875–2634 cal. BC; GrN-21930). September 1995.

Meelick Rocks 2
Neolithic
Stone axe and animal bone findspot
Coonagh East, Co. Limerick
OS 4:12:3   NGR 152303, 157918
Findspot of stone axe, recovered from gravels on a peat and clay ridge at the LWM, 48m due SE of the modern navigation beacon. Cattle, pig and dog bone recovered from the peat in the immediate vicinity of the findspot, with recumbent tree trunks and bark located 1m to the SW. Radiocarbon sample from tree bark in peat 1m E of the findspot dated to 6240 ± 25 BP (5299–5078 cal. BC; GrN-21929). September 1995.

LOWER SHANNON ESTUARY, CO. CLARE

Clonderalaw Bay 1.1–1.4
Post-medieval
Fishtraps (stake weirs?)
Ballygeery West, Co. Clare
OS 68:4:4   NGR R113549, 154812
Post alignments and isolated posts on mudflats in estuarine clays on S bank of Cloon River at its outlet into the bay. CWB 1.1 was four vertical oak posts, 10–15cm in diameter, forming trapezoidal structure *c.* 3m long and 1.5m wide. CWB 1.2 was a horizontal roundwood trunk, associated with four vertical posts. CWB 1.3 was a single isolated vertical roundwood post, 8cm in diameter. CWB 1.4 was a post-and-wattle fence oriented NW–SE towards CWB 1.1. CWB 1.4 was radiocarbon-dated to 135 ± 30 BP (cal. AD 1675–1946; GrN-20143). July 1992.

Foragers, farmers and fishers

Clonderalaw Bay 2
Post-medieval
Fishtrap
Ballina, Co. Clare
OS 68:7:2   NGR 111926, 154247
Tick-shaped head weir of roundwood posts and split stakes in estuarine clays at the LWM on channel in middle of bay. Shore fence, *c.* 18–20m long, oriented ENE–WSW, is composed of 100 posts, 9–12cm in diameter, spaced at 50cm intervals and standing to a height of 50cm. Flood fence submerged. A wooden framework stands at eye. Probably a nineteenth-century ebb weir. Local informants state that all of the Clonderalaw Bay fishtraps were out of use 'before the war'. (O'Sullivan 1993.) July 1992.

Clonderalaw Bay 3
Post-medieval
Fishtrap
Ballina, Co. Clare
OS 68:7:2   NGR 11809, 154193
Tick-shaped head weir at LWM in estuarine clays on S bank of channel in middle of Clonderalaw Bay. Two converging fences of vertical roundwood posts and split stakes. Shore fence oriented NE–SW, 20m long, with posts and stakes 8–13cm in diameter, spaced at 30–50cm intervals and standing to heights of 40cm. Flood fence 10m long. Radiocarbon-dated to 250 ± 30 BP (cal. AD 1522–1941; GrN-20144; O'Sullivan 1993). July 1992.

Clonderalaw Bay 4
Post-medieval
Watermill paddle
Carrowbane, Co. Clare
OS 68:7:2   NGR 11956, 154320
Wooden paddle from watermill, found on N bank of Cloon River channel. Long square-sectioned shaft with trapezoidal head that narrows towards top and has rounded and crushed sides. The head is convex on the damaged undersurface and has a flat upper surface. The shoulders above shaft are steeply cut. Length 0.355m, width 0.075m, thickness 41cm. Probably used as 'priest' for killing fish (O'Sullivan 1993). July 1992.

Poulnasharry Bay 1
Neolithic
Submerged forest
Moyasta, Co. Clare
OS 56:12:6   NGR 954160, 158001
Submerged forest and peats in saltmarsh cliff and on foreshore over area 200m long. Scots pine (*Pinus sylvestris* L.) root buttresses survive to heights of 1.5m, measure 35–80cm in diameter and lie at depths of 1.5m below saltmarsh, based on brown peaty clays and overlain by a thick discontinuous band of charcoal. This pine and charcoal layer is overlain by up to 1m of peat. The lower part of the peat is rich in *Phragmites* rhizomes; the upper layers are of *Sphagnum* peat. The peats are sealed by 30cm of estuarine clays. A submerged forest trunk was radiocarbon-dated to 4960 ± 35 BP (3892–3655 cal. BC; GrN-20145). A sample from the peat/clay contact was dated to 1640 ± 40 BP (cal. AD 262–534; GrN-21928). July 1992.

Poulnasharry Bay 2
Post-medieval
Plank-boat
Moyasta, Co. Clare
OS 56:12:6   NGR 095595, 158181
Boat hulk on mudflats, survives as planks, floor timbers and ballast to 5m in length,

2–3m in width, 50cm in height. Sawn oak floor timbers taken from 'crucked' branches were attached to the planks and the keel with wooden pegs. Other large worked timbers in vicinity. Limestone ballast in position. Floor timber radiocarbon-dated to 245 ± 30 BP (cal. AD 1524–1943; GrN-20146). July 1992.

Poulnasharry Bay 3
Neolithic
Submerged forest
Termon West, Co. Clare
OS 56:11:6   NGR 931380, 158048
Submerged forest trunks in saltmarsh creeks and cliffs at NW of bay, near Blackweir bridge. July 1992.

Rinevalla Bay 1
Neolithic
Submerged forest
Rahona East and West, Co. Clare
OS 72:3:3   NGR 083392, 149600
Submerged forest of Scots pine and oak in peat shelf on upper foreshore, which disappears under the cobbles of a storm beach inland which is low-lying and marshy. July 1992.

Rinevalla Bay 2
Post-medieval?
Cultivation ridges in submerged peats
Rahona West, Co. Clare
OS 72:3:3   NGR 083185, 149653
Cultivation ridges in intertidal peats on E side of bay, on upper foreshore, running N–S down the peats. They are located over an area of 50m and measure 1.2m in width and 0.2m in depth. Probable traces of late medieval/post-medieval lazy-bed cultivation. July 1992.

LOWER SHANNON ESTUARY, CO. KERRY

Bunaclugga Bay 1
Neolithic/Bronze Age?
Submerged forest
Carrigane, Co. Kerry
OS 2:10:2   NGR 094165, 147592
Submerged peat deposits on upper foreshore, exposed over an area 300m long and c. 40m wide. The peats contain oak and pine trunks and roots and fen wood. There are also stone alignments in the peat, most probably the remains of ancient field systems or drainage ditches. Further inland, behind the storm beach, are low-lying marshy fields. May 1993.

Bunaclugga Bay 2
Post-medieval
Fishtrap
Carrigane, Co. Kerry
OS 2:10:2   NGR 094445, 147685
V-shaped arrangement of stone on upper foreshore, depicted on OS maps and in nineteenth-century Admiralty charts as a 'herring weir'. Maps indicate that this was an ebb weir, with arms c. 180m long. Site visit indicates that it is now eroded out and consists merely of a scatter of stone across the foreshore. May 1993.

Appendix 3: Inventory of historic shipwrecks on the Shannon estuary

This inventory of historic wrecks is taken from the Wreck Inventory of the National Maritime Archaeological Survey, and is provided courtesy of *Dúchas* The Heritage Service. Entries consist of site name (ship or boat name), date of loss and place of loss. Names and placenames are spelled as they appeared in the original source. (*L.L.* = *Lloyd's List*.)

COUNTY CLARE

Site name *Agenoria*
Date of loss 28 January 1847
Place of loss Kilrush
This 117-ton sailing-vessel was on the shore.
(CSP 1851, vol. LII, 6)

Site name *Albion*
Date of loss 6 January 1839
Place of loss Labasheeda Bay
This vessel ran ashore.
(Bourke 1994, 172)

Site name *Alice*
Date of loss 30 March 1814
Place of loss In the Shannon
This vessel was *en route* from Limerick to Liverpool, under Captain McPherson, when she foundered during a gale. The crew was rescued by the pilot.
(*L.L.* April 1814; Bourke 1998, 131)

Site name *Alice & James*
Date of loss 10 December 1826
Place of loss Scarlet Rocks, River Shannon
This vessel was *en route* from Limerick to Liverpool when she was lost.
(*L.L.* December 1826; Bourke 1998, 128)

Site name *Anna Belle*
Date of loss 21 November 1881
Place of loss Boland Bay, Kilrush
This 19-year-old wooden brigantine of Bristol weighed 153 tons. The owner was W. McGillard of Carnlough, Co. Antrim, and the master was R. Emerson. She was *en route* from Limerick to Penarth (CSP) or Penrith (Bourke) for orders with a cargo of oats and five crew. She was stranded in a SSW force 10 gale and became a total wreck. The crew survived.
(CSP 1883, vol. LXIII, 113)

Site name *Anne*
Date of loss 27 January 1847
Place of loss Kilrush
This 161-ton sailing-vessel was on the shore.

Appendix 3

(CSP 1851, vol. LII, 6)

Site name *Annunciada*
Date of loss 1588
Place of loss Scattery Island/Carngholt

This 700-ton Ragusan Armada ship was converted from a merchantman and carried 275 men and 24 guns. The vessel was burned and sank, but the crew and supplies were taken off by the accompanying Spanish ships.
(*AFM*, 1588; Wignall 1982, 43; Whiting 1988, 200)

Site name *Atlanta*
Date of loss 17 March 1836
Place of loss Dunaha

This vessel was a brig.
(Bourke 1994, 173)

Site name *Bridgewater*
Date of loss 6 January 1818
Place of loss Mouth of the Shannon

This vessel was *en route* from Sligo to London when she was wrecked.
(*L.L.* January 1818; Bourke 1994, 176)

Site name *Calpe*
Date of loss 13 November 1847
Place of loss Kilrush

This 104-ton sailing-vessel ran aground.
(CSP 1851, vol. LII, 35)

Site name *Carolinea*
Date of loss 27 January 1847
Place of loss Kilrush

This sailing-vessel was on the shore.
(CSP 1851, vol. LII, 6)

Site name *Catherine*
Date of loss 4 November 1849
Place of loss In the Shannon

This Isle of Man vessel was *en route* to Liverpool when she was lost. The crew survived.
(CSP 1852–3, vol. XCVIII, 3)

Site name *Charity*
Date of loss 6 January 1839
Place of loss Labasheeda Bay

This vessel ran ashore.
(Bourke 1994, 172)

Site name *Cicero*
Date of loss 1833
Place of loss On River Shannon

This vessel of Newcastle weighed 434 tons. She was 57 years old when she was wrecked.
(CSP 1836, vol. XVII, appendix 8, 359; Bourke 1998, 130)

Site name *Ciro*
Date of loss 27 January 1847
Place of loss Kilrush

315

Foragers, farmers and fishers

This sailing-vessel was on the shore.
(CSP 1851, vol. LII, 6)

Site name   *Commerce*
Date of loss   5 April 1791
Place of loss   Entrance to Limerick River
This vessel was *en route* from Philadelphia to Dublin, under Hooper, when she was totally lost. The crew survived.
(*L.L.* no. 2287, 5 April 1791)

Site name   *Daniel O'Connell*
Date of loss   6 January 1839
Place of loss   Near Limerick
This large sail-boat was lost.
(Bourke 1994, 173)

Site name   *Defiance*
Date of loss   1835
Place of loss   In the Shannon
This 35-ton vessel of Limerick was lost.
(Bourke 1998, 131)

Site name   *Ed*
Date of loss   28 January 1847
Place of loss   Kilrush
This 142-ton sailing-vessel was on the shore.
(CSP 1851, vol. LII, 6)

Site name   *E. D. J.*
Date of loss   1940 or 1941
Place of loss   Islevaroo, near Kilrush
This motor vessel had a succession of owners. She was originally owned by Glynn's of Kilrush, who sold her to Mr P. O'Keefe. She was used for dredging aggregate in Bantry before being sold to O'Sullivan's of Ballylongford. She was on her usual route from Kilrush to Limerick, with turf, when she was driven onto the rocks. The hull was repaired to some extent, but she only made it as far as Tarbert, where she was sold for scrap.
(Bourke 1994, 173)

Site name   *Eleanor*
Date of loss   29 December 1823
Place of loss   Labasheda
This vessel was *en route* from Limerick to Liverpool, under Captain Wallace, when she went ashore and was on her beam-ends.
(*L.L.* no. 5870, 6 January 1824)

Site name   *Eliza*
Date of loss   20 January 1821
Place of loss   Kilrush
This vessel was *en route* from Trinidad to Cork when she broke from her cables and went ashore.
(*L.L.* January 1821; Bourke 1998, 129)

Site name   *Eliza*
Date of loss   8 February 1822

Appendix 3

Place of loss   Near Kilrush

This vessel was *en route* from Limerick to Swansea, under Captain Potts, when she went ashore.
(*L.L.* February 1822; Bourke 1998, 128)

Site name   *Eliza*
Date of loss   24 December 1852
Place of loss   Rocks in Scattery Roads (Clare?)

This 59-ton schooner of Port Madoc was *en route* from Sligo to London with meal and four crew. She encountered a SW wind with hazy conditions and was driven from her cables and totally wrecked. The estimated loss on the vessel was £300, and £400 on the cargo.
(CSP 1852–3, vol. LXI, 210–11; vol. XCVIII, 7)

Site name   *Eliza and Ann*
Date of loss   27 January 1847
Place of loss   Kilrush

This sailing-vessel went ashore.
(CSP 1851, vol. LII, 6)

Site name   *Elizabeth*
Date of loss   27 January 1847
Place of loss   Kilrush

This sailing-vessel was on the shore.
(CSP 1851, vol. LII, 6)

Site name   *Elizabeth and Mary*
Date of loss   13 January 1843
Place of loss   In the Shannon

This vessel was *en route* from Limerick to Liverpool, under the master Goodill, when she went on shore. She was got off with a small amount of damage and put back.
(CSP 1843, vol. IX, appendix no. 7, 56)

Site name   *Esther*
Date of loss   18 March 1854
Place of loss   At sea—put into Kilrush

This vessel of Bristol was *en route* from Newport to New York with a cargo of iron. She became leaky whilst at sea owing to stress of weather and put into Kilrush. She had to discharge for repairs.
(CSP 1854–5, vol. XXXIV, copy 'of the Admiralty Register of Wrecks', 44–5)

Site name   *Flora*
Date of loss   16 January 1818
Place of loss   Mouth of the Shannon

This vessel was *en route* from Quebec to London under Captain Caldwell. She was driven ashore but the crew survived.
(*L.L.* no. 5246, 16 January 1818)

Site name   *Fowey*
Date of loss   1 August 1813
Place of loss   Kilbaha

This vessel was *en route* from Limerick to Plymouth, under Captain McDonnell, with 200 barrels of pork. She was captured by an American brig privateer with 18 guns, was set on fire and came ashore at Kilbaha.
(*L.L.* August 1813; Bourke 1998, 130)

Foragers, farmers and fishers

Site name	*Friendship*
Date of loss	27 January 1847
Place of loss	Kilrush

This 94-ton sailing-vessel was on the shore.
(CSP 1851, vol. LII, 6)

Site name	*Garryone*
Date of loss	6 January 1839
Place of loss	Beach at Kilrush

This steamer ran aground but was not badly damaged. It was hoped to refloat the vessel.
(Bourke 1994, 172)

Site name	*Georgina*
Date of loss	9 May 1884
Place of loss	On the Shannon

This schooner was owned by McMorland of Greenock. She had just left Limerick for Greenock when she collided with the SS *Vale* of Calder, which was *en route* to Liverpool. The *Georgina* was hit amidships and sank instantly. Captain Montgomery, his wife and the five crewmen survived.
(Bourke 1994, 175)

Site name	*Glencoe*
Date of loss	27 January 1847
Place of loss	Kilrush

This 155-ton sailing-vessel lost her mainmast and ran ashore.
(CSP 1851, vol. LII, 6)

Site name	*Grecian*
Date of loss	6 January 1839
Place of loss	Kilrush

This vessel of Hull was caught in the 'Big Wind' and was driven onshore on her beam. Three boys held onto the rigging and were saved the next day. The rest of the crew were lost.
(Bourke 1994, 172)

Site name	*Hamilton*
Date of loss	6 January 1839?
Place of loss	Kilrush

This revenue cruiser ran ashore and lost her copper bottom.
(Bourke 1994, 172)

Site name	*Helen*
Date of loss	28 December 1894
Place of loss	Scattery Island

This iron barque was *en route* from Limerick to San Francisco with a cargo of grain when she ran ashore. It was hoped to get her off with tugs.
(Bourke 1994, 173)

Site name	*Henry and Anne*
Date of loss	c. 20 November 1850
Place of loss	Island opposite Kilrush

This vessel was washed ashore during a gale.
(Bourke 1994, 170)

Appendix 3

Site name *Hepzibah*
Date of loss 1 October 1912
Place of loss Kilcredane, Carrigaholt
This 90-ton Gloucester schooner was *en route* from Kilrush to Aran, in ballast, when she was wrecked.
(Bourke 1994, 175)

Site name *Hope*
Date of loss 20 January 1821
Place of loss Kilrush or Loop Head
This vessel was *en route* from London to Limerick, under Captain Ferris, when she parted her cables and went ashore.
(Bourke 1998, 129)

Site name *Isabella*
Date of loss 6 January 1839?
Place of loss Labasheeda Bay
This vessel ran ashore.
(Bourke 1994, 172)

Site name *John*
Date of loss 1 December 1825
Place of loss Mouth of the Shannon
This vessel was *en route* from Dublin to Limerick when she went to pieces and was totally lost.
(*L.L.* December 1825; Bourke 1998, 130)

Site name *Lamb*
Date of loss 12 April 1751
Place of loss Kilrush
This vessel was *en route* to Limerick, under Captain Lewis, when she was lost.
(*L.L.* April 1751; Bourke 1998, 129)

Site name *Lark*
Date of loss 28 January 1803
Place of loss In the Shannon
This vessel was *en route* from Limerick, under Captain Perry, to go fishing. The vessel was lost but the crew survived.
(*L.L.* January 1803; Bourke 1998, 130)

Site name *Maas*
Date of loss 27 January 1847
Place of loss Kilrush
This sailing-vessel was on the shore, full of water.
(CSP 1851, vol. LII, 6)

Site name *Margaret*
Date of loss 6 January 1818
Place of loss Mouth of the Shannon
This vessel was *en route* from Liverpool to Limerick when she was lost.
(CSP 1836, vol. XVII, appendix no. 7, 291)

Site name *Mary*
Date of loss 24 December 1811

Foragers, farmers and fishers

Place of loss In the Shannon

This vessel was *en route* from Limerick to London, under Captain Hammond. She parted from her anchors and went ashore.
(*L.L.* December 1811; Bourke 1998, 130)

Site name Mary
Date of loss 13 November 1908
Place of loss 'Supposed off Querrin'

This unregistered wood and canvas canoe weighed 2 tons. She was 2 years old and worked out of Kilrush. She set out from Kilrush to go fishing with three crew aboard. She was in ballast when she is thought to have capsized. There were no survivors but the vessel was recovered later.
(CSP 1910, vol. LXXXI, app. C, table 2, 125)

Site name Mary Ann
Date of loss 5 December 1817
Place of loss Kilrush

This vessel of Limerick was *en route* from Limerick to Galway, under Collins, when she was lost. The crew survived.
(*L.L.* no. 5238, 16 December 1817)

Site name Mary Collins
Date of loss 8 December 1817
Place of loss Cappa, near Kilrush

This vessel was *en route* to Galway with a cargo of Luagh stone when she sank. The crew survived.
(*L.L.* December 1817; Bourke 1994, 176)

Site name Mary of Milford
Date of loss 1875
Place of loss Boland Rocks, Kilrush

This 75-ton schooner was wrecked.
(Bourke 1994, 176)

Site name Myrtle
Date of loss 1828
Place of loss In the Shannon

This vessel of Greenock weighed 100 tons. She was 13 years old and classed as E1 when she was wrecked.
(CSP 1836, vol. XVII, app. no. 8, 343; Bourke 1998, 131)

Site name Perseverance
Date of loss 3 December 1820
Place of loss Kilrush

This vessel was *en route* from Pernambuco to Liverpool, under Vanghan, when she was totally wrecked. The master and cook were lost.
(*L.L.* no. 12, December 1820)

Site name Prudence
Date of loss 31 March 1818
Place of loss Into the Shannon

This Portuguese schooner was *en route* from St Ubes to Limerick when she was driven into the Shannon. The revenue cruiser tried to tow her but she sank. Two men took to the masts and survived.
(*L.L.* April 1818; Bourke 1998, 128)

Appendix 3

Site name   *Rebecca*
Date of loss   9 April 1853
Place of loss   Kilrush
This vessel of Cork was *en route* from Newport to New York with iron. She became leaky at sea and put into Kilrush in a damaged state. She had to discharge for repairs.
(CSP 1854, vol. XLII, 28–9)

Site name   *Spilling Rock*
Date of loss   7 October 1889
Place of loss   Shannon region
This vessel was driven ashore during a SW gale.
(Bourke 1994, 175)

Site name   *Treenaglass*
Date of loss   1 August 1833
Place of loss   Bridges Bank, near Palaskenry, Shannon estuary
This 1513-ton steamer was built in 1882 by Edwin Hain & Sons and was valued at £50,000. She was working under the command of Captain Giles and carried maize to Mr S. Paiget of Limerick. She ran aground and, when the tide ebbed, broke amidships. She became a total loss.
(Bourke 1994, 175)

Site name   *Triumph*
Date of loss   1 August 1851
Place of loss   Off Hog Is., Kilrush
This vessel was *en route* from America to Limerick. She was grounded off the island when running into Limerick but was expected to get off after discharging.
(CSP 1852, vol. XLIX, 180–1; 1852–3, vol. XCVIII, 5)

Site name   *Union*
Date of loss   15 January 1819
Place of loss   Labashheda
This vessel was *en route* from Limerick to London when she went ashore. The ship was lost but the cargo was saved.
(*L.L.* January 1819; Bourke 1998, 130)

Site name   *United Kingdom*
Date of loss   24 January 1834
Place of loss   Kilrush
This vessel was *en route* from Galway to London when she was wrecked.
(Bourke 1994, 177)

Site name   *Venus*
Date of loss   12 December 1818
Place of loss   Labasheeda
This vessel was *en route* from Limerick to London when she went ashore. The vessel was condemned but the cargo was saved.
(*L.L.* December 1818; Bourke 1998, 128)

Site name   *Venus*
Date of loss   22 May 1890
Place of loss   Near Beeves Rock LH, R. Shannon
This unregistered wooden smack weighed around 60 tons. The master and owner was M. Hayes of Kilrush. She was *en route* from Kilrush to Limerick with three crew and a

Foragers, farmers and fishers

cargo of turf. She foundered in squally conditions with the loss of three lives.
(CSP 1890–1, vol. LXXVI, appendix C, 158)

Site name	*Victoria*
Date of loss	4 November 1853
Place of loss	In the Shannon

This 100-ton schooner of Liverpool was *en route* from Limerick to London with six crew and a cargo of oats. She encountered an ESE force 2 wind with hazy conditions. She became wrecked on a rock around 600 yards from Kilcradare Lighthouse. It was thought to have occurred owing to negligence. She went to pieces on 10 November.
(CSP 1854, vol. XLII, 64–5)

Site name	*Vietury*
Date of loss	18 January 1805
Place of loss	Kilrush

This vessel was *en route* from Limerick to London, under Captain Wheatly, when she went ashore.
(*L.L.* January 1805; Bourke 1998, 128)

Site name	*Welcome*
Date of loss	6 January 1839
Place of loss	Labasheeda Bay

This vessel ran ashore.
(Bourke 1994, 172)

Site name	*Wentworth Beaumont/Wentworth*
Date of loss	30 September 1873
Place of loss	Carrigaholt, one mile west of Kilcreadane Lighthouse

This 254-ton brig of North Shields or Beaumont was *en route* from Limerick to Shields in ballast. She became stranded and was totally wrecked. One of the eight crew was lost. A stowaway also survived.
(CSP 1875, vol. LXX, 43, 61)

Site name	*William Ash*
Date of loss	17 November 1851
Place of loss	Hog's Head Rock, Shannon

This London vessel was under the command of Ash when she struck the rock while coming up the river. She was still there in 1852.
(CSP 1852, vol. XLIX, 256–7)

Site name	Unknown
Date of loss	14 November 1690
Place of loss	Mouth of the Shannon

This French frigate was carrying arms and ammunition for the Jacobite army when she was swept away at the mouth of the river. The crew of the ship were lost, along with 28 army officers. Two cannon found in the Shannon are housed in the National Museum.
(Bourke 1994, 178)

Site name	Unknown
Date of loss	4 November 1691
Place of loss	River Shannon

This French longboat capsized while transferring men to another ship. Twenty-two officers were lost. Money belonging to King James and money and a plate belonging to

Appendix 3

Count Lausun were lost. The French paymaster's chest was also lost. In total £50,000–90,000 is thought to have been lost. This event occurred after the siege of Limerick, during the Williamite wars.
(Bourke 1994, 178)

Site name Unknown
Date of loss 12 August 1788
Place of loss Near Foynes Island
This sailing-boat, carrying three men from Limerick, overturned in a squall. Two of the men drowned.
(*Dublin Chronicle*, 16–19 August 1788)

Site name Unknown
Date of loss 20 November 1816
Place of loss Whelp Rock, River Shannon
This was a large sail-boat.
(*L.L.* November 1816; Bourke 1994, 178)

Site name Unknown
Date of loss February 1826
Place of loss Kilbaha Bay
Three letters to Robert Keane on 19, 21 and 24 February report that more than 400 'pieces' of timber were washed up on the coast around Kilbaha Bay.
(Official Papers, National Archives of Ireland, ref. OP 906/2)

Site name Unknown
Date of loss 18 February 1826
Place of loss Kilbaha, Loop Head
This large ship was lost.
(*L.L.* February 1826; Bourke 1998, 128)

Site name Unknown
Date of loss *c.* 20 November 1850
Place of loss Between Kilrush and Tarbert
This ferry boat, operating between Kilrush and Tarbert, was caught in a gale and sank. The nineteen 'cattle jobbers' on board were lost.
(Bourke 1994, 170)

Site name Unknown
Date of loss 6 January 1839
Place of loss Near Limerick
Thirty vessels carrying turf or oats were presumed lost.
(Bourke 1994, 173)

Site name Unknown
Date of loss 1 January 1871
Place of loss Carrigaholt
(Bourke 1994, 178)

Site name Unknown
Date of loss February 1903
Place of loss Near Carrigaholt
This 'canoe' was washed off the beach and was totally destroyed.
(CSP, Report on the Sea and Inland Fisheries of Ireland for 1903, xix)

Foragers, farmers and fishers

COUNTY LIMERICK

Site name	*Adeona*
Date of loss	18 January 1825
Place of loss	Hogshead Rocks, R. Shannon

This vessel of Dumfries was *en route* from Limerick to Liverpool, under Captain Whitehead. She struck the rocks and fell over but the crew survived.
(*L.L.* January 1825; Bourke 1998, 128)

Site name	*Aid*
Date of loss	24 December 1852
Place of loss	Tarbert Road, Shannon

This vessel of Sunderland encountered a force 10 wind and was stranded. She was got off and taken to Limerick for repairs.
(CSP 1852–3, vol. LXI, 210–11)

Site name	*Astrea*
Date of loss	June 1834
Place of loss	Limerick?

The *Limerick Star* newspaper received the names of the 220 crew, passengers and children lost on the *Astrea*.
(*Freemans Journal,* June 1834, Dublin)

Site name	*Briget Cafey*
Date of loss	5 April 1788
Place of loss	Unknown
Location	48 25N, 48 50W

This Cork-based ship was *en route* from New York to Newport Prat with flax-seed, staves and provisions. On the 5th (April), when lying at the above coordinates, she encountered a sea which carried away her two boats, tackling, the companion, binnacle, cabuse, compasses, quarter rails, quarter and main deck staunches, hen-coops, water casks, a quantity of spare yards, topmasts, spars and windlass. It broke the tiller, shook the rudder and gunwale, started all the bolts and trunnions above the water, and stove in the dead lights. Some of the crew were lost. She managed to get into Limerick in distress.
(*Dublin Chronicle,* 8–10 April 1788)

Site name	*British Queen*
Date of loss	2 February 1847
Place of loss	Limerick

This sailing-vessel was on the shore.
(CSP 1851, vol. LII, 7)

Site name	*Cassandra*
Date of loss	7 January 1794
Place of loss	20 leagues from Limerick River

This vessel was *en route* from St Ubes to Limerick when she became stranded.
(*L.L.* no. 2575, 7 January 1794)

Site name	*Castleragget*
Date of loss	October 1833
Place of loss	Foynes Island

This turf-boat was *en route* from Limerick to Ballylongford with passengers. She was hit by a brig near Foynes Island, Co. Limerick. Nine lives were lost.
(*Freemans Journal,* 16 October 1833, Dublin)

Appendix 3

Site name *Columbus*
Date of loss 4/5 December 1851
Place of loss Harold Rock

This Sunderland vessel was *en route* from Odessa to Limerick when she hit the rock. The deck bilged, distorting her shape. The masts were cut away and the cargo was completely saturated. The crew survived.
(CSP 1852, vol. XLIX, 272–3; 1852–3, vol. XCVIII, 5)

Site name *Dorothy*
Date of loss 20 November 1851
Place of loss Limerick

This Plymouth schooner was *en route* from Limerick to London, under master Carlisle, with a cargo of oats. She strained at the quays, was damaged and had to discharge.
(CSP 1852, vol. XLIX, 258–9)

Site name *Edgecumbe*
Date of loss 21 December 1854
Place of loss Beal Bay, River Shannon

This 108-ton brig was *en route* from St John's, N.B., to Limerick with a cargo of deals &c. She was wrecked at 8 a.m., during a NNW force 11 wind with hail. The coastguard rescued the crew. The estimated loss on the vessel was £1000 but it was only insured for £500.
(CSP 1854–5, vol. XXXIV, copy 'of the Admiralty Register of Wrecks', 104–5)

Site name *Elanor*
Date of loss December 1832
Place of loss Limerick

This 400-ton vessel, under Captain Reed of Limerick, was lost.
(*Freemans Journal,* December 1832, column—'Melancholy Shipwrecks and loss of lives')

Site name *Elentheria*
Date of loss 6 February 1847
Place of loss Limerick

This sailing-vessel had been on the shore.
(CSP 1851, vol. LII, 7)

Site name *Eliza*
Date of loss December 1759
Place of loss Limerick Haven

This vessel was *en route* from London to Limerick, under Dunn, when she was driven from her anchors and was totally lost.
(*L.L.* no. 2501, 1 January 1760)

Site name *Flora*
Date of loss September 1802
Place of loss Near Limerick

This vessel of Greenock went ashore while under the command of Kerr. The vessel and cargo were expected to be lost.
(*L.L.* no. 4288, 7 September 1802)

Site name *Hannah*
Date of loss 22 January 1747
Place of loss Near Limerick

This vessel was *en route* from Newfoundland to Limerick, under Captain Cotton, when she was lost.

Foragers, farmers and fishers

(*L.L.* February 1747; Bourke 1998, 129)

Site name	*Helena and Mary Hegarty*
Date of loss	December 1785
Place of loss	Cratsoe

This vessel from Jamaica ran onto a reef of rocks near Cratsoe. The cargo was saved.
(*Freemans Journal*, 1 January 1785–31 December 1785)

Site name	*Heroine*
Date of loss	24 December 1852
Place of loss	Limerick

This 374-ton barque of Shields was 17 years old. The master was Atkinson. The vessel was wrecked in a gale but was insured in Shields.
(CSP 1852–3, vol. LXI, 210–11)

Site name	*Jessy*
Date of loss	10 November 1851
Place of loss	Meelick

This vessel was *en route* from Quebec to Limerick, under Mr Gorman, when she went aground and was considerably strained.
(CSP 1852, vol. XLIX, 250–1)

Site name	*Liverpool*
Date of loss	8 November 1825
Place of loss	Between Tarbert and Glynn

This vessel of Liverpool went onto the rocks. She filled with water but the spars and rigging were saved. The *Brittannia* was lost at the same time and place.
(*L.L.* November 1825; Bourke 1998, 128)

Site name	*Louis Eleonie*
Date of loss	24 April 1852
Place of loss	Limerick

This schooner was *en route* from Tampico to Harve. She left Bristol on 19 April but was making large amounts of water and so put back. She had to discharge.
(CSP 1852–3, vol. LXI, 70–1)

Site name	*Maid of the Mist*
Date of loss	10 March 1847
Place of loss	Limerick

This sailing-vessel was on the shore.
(CSP 1851, vol. LII, 12)

Site name	*Medusa*
Date of loss	19 November 1850
Place of loss	Limerick Harbour

This 67-year-old brig weighed 310 tons. She was carrying wheat when she was stranded in a northerly force 12 wind and became a partial wreck. One of the eleven aboard was lost.
(CSP 1861, vol. LXIII, 38)

Site name	*Minerva*
Date of loss	17 December 1829
Place of loss	Shannon River

The 86-ton schooner was *en route* to Greenock, under McArthur of Greenock, with oats and butter. She struck part of the Wellesley Bridge works, at the point of Shannon

Appendix 3

Quay.
(*Freemans Journal* 1829, column—'Shipwreck in the Shannon')

Site name   *Osprey*
Date of loss   8 September 1851
Place of loss   Between Tarbert and Glin

This vessel was *en route* from Swansea, under Cock, when she went onshore.
(CSP 1852, vol. XLIX, 190–1)

Site name   *Peggy*
Date of loss   December 1790
Place of loss   Limerick River

This vessel was *en route* from Limerick to Greenock, under Campbell, when she was lost.
(*L.L.* no. 2260, 31 December 1790)

Site name   *Premier*
Date of loss   26 November 1898
Place of loss   Between Kilcredane Light and Beal Bar Buoy, River Shannon estuary

This steel steamship of Glasgow weighed 196 tons. She was 4 years old and classed by Lloyd's as '100 A1'. The date of her last survey was March 1898. The master was D. Murray and the owner was J. Simpson of Glasgow. The vessel was *en route* from Hamburg to Limerick with eleven crew and a cargo of sugar. She collided with the steamship *Mermaid* of Waterford in a NNE force 4 and became a total loss.
(CSP 1900, vol. LXXVII, Shipping Casualties (1898–9), 154)

Site name   *Solidade*
Date of loss   28 December 1781
Place of loss   Limerick River

This vessel was *en route* from Lisbon to Waterford, under Santos, when she went ashore. She was seriously damaged and most of the cargo was lost.
(*L.L.* no. 1326, 11 January 1782)

Site name   *Thrasher*
Date of loss   16 August 1892
Place of loss   River Shannon

This unregistered wooden smack was 20 years old and weighed 40 tons. The master was T. Scanlan and the owner was P. Roughan, Carrigaholt, Co. Clare. She was loading a general cargo at Limerick, with two crew aboard, when she went on fire and burnt. The two aboard were killed. There was a westerly force 1 at the time.
(CSP 1894, vol. LXXVI, Shipping Casualties (1892–3), 158)

Site name   *Topaz*
Date of loss   28 December 1900
Place of loss   1 mile below Glin Pier

This wooden brigantine of Swansea weighed 196 tons and was 30 years old. The master and owner was J. Furlong of Arklow. She was *en route* from Foynes to Garstone with five crew and a cargo of wood. She became stranded in a NW force 10 wind and was a total loss.
(CSP 1902, vol. XCII, Shipping Casualties (1900–1), 131)

Site name   *Venus*
Date of loss   1890
Place of loss   River Shannon

Foragers, farmers and fishers

This smack was in a derelict state when she was noted by the lightkeeper of Beeves Rock. She sank in the river but was not considered a danger to navigation. A notice was issued and the wreck was buoyed.
(CSP 1894, vol. LXXVI, Floating Derelicts, appendix C, no. 3, 85)

Site name	*Witte Leeuw*
Date of loss	10 January 1849
Place of loss	Off Limerick

This vessel was *en route* from Rotterdam when she was lost. The crew survived.
(CSP 1852–3, vol. XCVIII, 2)

Site name	*York*
Date of loss	November 1758
Place of loss	Near Limerick

This vessel was *en route* from Bombay, under Lassells, when she was lost. The crew survived.
(*L.L.* no. 2384, 14 November 1758)

Site name	Unknown
Date of loss	December 1630
Place of loss	Limerick/R. Shannon?

This Spanish carvel, laden with fish and salt, was captured by Captain Henry Hastings of the *Dove* while off the coast of Barbary. She was brought into Limerick and was seized as pirates' goods by the mayor of Limerick. A pilot boarded to bring her into the harbour but she went onto the rocks and bilged. Some cargo was lost but the remainder was taken from Hastings by the mayor.
(Appleby 1992, 198–9, 857)

Site name	Unknown
Date of loss	June 1832
Place of loss	Between Monsells Creek and Ballincurra Creek

This open sail-boat was lost on the river. Three people were lost but four survived.
(*Freemans Journal*, Dublin, 16 June 1832, column—'Fatal accident')

Site name	Unknown
Date of loss	February 1833
Place of loss	Kerry Head, River Shannon

This large brig, with a cargo of salt, was dashed to pieces with the loss of all aboard.
(*Freemans Journal*, Dublin, 8 February 1833, column—'Ship News')

Site name	Unknown
Date of loss	November 1850
Place of loss	The river, Limerick

This smack was lost.
(CSP 1852–3, vol. XCVIII, 4)

Site name	Unknown
Date of loss	November 1850
Place of loss	The river, Limerick

This vessel was a smack.
(CSP 1852–3, vol. XCVIII, 4)

Site name	Unknown
Date of loss	25 December 1852
Place of loss	Limerick

This brig of Shoreham was carrying a cargo of oats when she went adrift in a gale. She had to discharge.
(CSP 1852–3, vol. LXI, 212–13)

Site name	Unknown
Date of loss	6 August 1905
Place of loss	Muckinish Strait

This unregistered wooden pleasure-boat (sailing) weighed 2 tons and was 2 years old. The master was T. Fahy and the owner was F. Sampson of Finavarra, Co. Clare. She was *en route* from Ballyvaughan to Finavarra, in ballast, with three crew aboard. She sank in a WNW force 4 wind but was later recovered. One life was lost.
(CSP 1907, vol. LXXV, 144, 1284)

COUNTY KERRY

Site name	*Brittania*
Date of loss	8 November 1825
Place of loss	Between Tarbert and Glynn

This vessel of Rothsay went onto the rock. She filled with water but the spars and the rigging were saved.
(*L.L.* November 1825; Bourke 1998, 128)

Site name	*Diana*
Date of loss	6 February 1820
Place of loss	A rock near Tarbert

This vessel was *en route* from London to Limerick when she was lost.
(*L.L.* February 1820; Bourke 1998, 123)

Site name	*Llanthewy/Llanthenry*
Date of loss	27 December 1902
Place of loss	Beale Bar, Shannon estuary

This iron steamship of Newport, Mon., weighed 148 tons. She was 18 years old and classed by Lloyd's as '100 A1'. The date of her last survey was February 1902. The master was T. A. Prewett or Captain Brooks and the owner was W. Brooks, Newport, Mon. The vessel was *en route* from Garston to Limerick with ten crew and a cargo of coal. She became stranded in a SW force 8 wind and was a total loss.
(CSP 1904, vol. LXXXVI, 130)

Site name	*Margaret*
Date of loss	6 January 1818
Place of loss	Mouth of River Shannon

This vessel was *en route* from Liverpool to Limerick when she was lost.
(*L.L.* January 1818; Bourke 1998, 123)

Site name	*Premier*
Date of loss	26 October/November 1898
Place of loss	Between Beale Bar buoy and Kilcreadine light
Position	52 35 00 N, 009 38 00 W

This 537-ton steel steamer was built by J. Shearer at Glasgow in 1894 and was owned by Simpsons. She was *en route* from Hamburg to Cleeves, of Limerick, with a cargo of sugar. She collided with the *Mermaid*, a Waterford paddle steamer, and sank within 20

minutes. All those aboard survived. The wreck was located during a sonar survey and is known locally as the Sugar wreck.
(Admiralty data 1996)

Site name Quereda
Date of loss 27 January 1834
Place of loss Off Carrig Island, River Shannon

This Sunderland vessel was *en route* from Limerick to London when she struck the Beale Bar. She drifted two miles up the river before she sank.
(Bourke 1994, 176)

Site name Thetis
Date of loss 30 November 1834
Place of loss Beale Bar, Shannon estuary, off townland of Corcas and Sandhills

This vessel was *en route* to Limerick when she became stranded on the bar.
(This wreck site is marked on the 1921 edition OS 6" map, Sheet 1, SMR No. 001)

Site name Unknown
Date of loss November 1839
Place of loss The Beeves, near Tarbert
(Bourke 1994, 165)

Site name Unknown
Date of loss 15 August 1893
Place of loss Off Tarbert

This 18-foot rowing-vessel of Tarbert was owned by Maurice Murphy. She was *en route* from Tarbert Island to Kilrush, with a party going to Kilkee. That evening the boat left Kilkee but never reached its destination, Saleen Pier. She sank a short distance off the Kerry coast. Although the cries of those on board were heard, it was too dark to render assistance. All seventeen aboard were drowned.
(Schools' Folklore Collection, Imleabhar 401, 195, 399, 400; Imleabhar 403, 69–70; Imleabhar 404, 21)

Site name Unknown
Date of loss 10 September 1903
Place of loss Beale Point

This 'canoe' was running for shelter when she struck the point and broke up.
(*Report on the Sea and Inland Fisheries of Ireland for 1903*, xix)

Site name Unknown
Date of loss 9 February 1904
Place of loss Tarbert Roads

This unregistered iron lighter weighed 12 tons. The master was J. O'Dea and the owner was the Waterford S.S. Company, Waterford. The vessel was moored at Tarbert with a general cargo. There was no one aboard when she foundered in a SW force 1 and became a total loss.
(CSP 1905, vol. LXXI, 113, 617)

Appendix 4: NMI reg. nos of artefacts found in the Shannon estuary survey

NMI no.	Site	Period	Object	Material	Context	Year of find
95E0228:1	Carrigdirty 5	Neolithic	Basket	Alder	Stratified, clay	1994
95E0228:2	Carrigdirty 7	Undated	Carved fragment	Wood	Stratified, clay	1994
95E0228:3	Meelick Rocks 2	Neolithic	Stone axe	Schist	Unstratified, peats	1995
95E0228:4	Carrigdirty 8	Mesolithic	Plank?	Wood	Stratified, clay	1995
95E0228:5	Carrigdirty 5	Neolithic	Flake 1	Chert	Stratified, clay	1996
95E0228:6	Carrigdirty 5	Neolithic	Flake 2	Chert	Stratified, clay	1996
95E0228:7	Carrigdirty 5	Neolithic	Pebble 1	Limestone	Unstratified	1996
95E0228:8	Carrigdirty 5	Neolithic	Pebble 2	Quartz clasts	Unstratified	1997
95E0228:9	Carrigdirty 5	Neolithic	Pebble 3	Green dolerite	Unstratified	1997
95E0228:10	Carrigdirty 5	Neolithic	Pebble 4	Granite	Unstratified	1997
95E0228:11	Carrigdirty 5	Neolithic	Worked wood 1	Hazel	Stratified, clays	1997
95E0228:12	Carrigdirty 5	Neolithic	Charred wood 2	Hazel	Stratified, clays	1997
95E0228:13	Carrigdirty 5	Neolithic	Charred wood 3	Pomoideae	Stratified, clays	1997
95E0228:14	Carrigdirty 5	Neolithic	Charred wood 4	Hazel	Stratified, clays	1997
95E0228:15	Carrigdirty 5	Neolithic	Stone axe	Slate	Unstratified, clays	1998

INDEX

References to figures have the suffix 'f' and those to photographs 'pl'.
Site numbers are enclosed in parentheses, for example Bunratty (3), to avoid confusion with page numbers.

Aalen, F.H.A. 267
abbeys 8, 180, 187, 256
   see also monastic sites, friaries
Adeona 324
Admiralty High Court 237
Agenoria 314
Aghintemple 81
agriculture 1, 90
Aid 324
Albion 314
alder (*Alnus*) 37, 51, 56, 141, 184
   fishtraps 172, 176, 183, 265
   Neolithic baskets 79, 295, 331
   post-and-wattle fences 141
Alice 314
Alice & James 314
alluvium 24, 52, 184
An Foras Talúntais 46
Anchcolme River 120
Anglo-Norman and Gaelic Irish settlements and maritime trade 8–9
Anglo-Saxon fishtraps 23, 24, 188
animal bone 63–4, 85, 100, 253, 306, 311
Anna Belle 314
Annagh, Co. Limerick 3, 87, 91
Annaghbeg, Co. Longford 72
Annals of the Four Masters 235, 236
Annals of Inisfallen 180, 235
Anne 314
Annunciada 236, 240, 315
apple trees 37
Archaeological Survey of Ireland 234
Ardglass, intertidal survey 25
Ardmore Harbour, Co. Waterford 25
Arklow 327
artefacts, bronze 4
artefacts found, NMI reg. nos. 331
Arterial Drainage Act (1945) 54
Arthur, Nicholas Thomas 9
ash 37, 172, 176, 183
Askeaton 14, 18, 144, 181, 236, 238f, 239, 250, 256
   Deel estuary fishtraps and 150, 191, 257
   Franciscan friary 8
   limestone 13
   sea trade 245, 259, 266
Assendelver Polders, Netherlands 129
Athlunkard, Co. Clare 7
Atlanta 315
Audacht Morainn 144
Aughinish, Co. Limerick 13, 15, 45, 121, 125, 144
Auteini tribe 4, 16, 259
axes 62–3, 119
   bronze 256
   flat iron 155
   stone 254, 307, 311, 331

Ballina, Co. Clare 312
Ballinacarriga, Co. Limerick 89
Ballinaphunta, Co. Clare 64, 89
Ballinclough 54
Ballincurra Creek 328
Ballinskelligs Bay 237
Ballinvoher 15, 151
Ballycahane Lower, Co. Limerick 3
Ballycanauna 151
Ballycar South 64
Ballycarty, Co. Kerry 3, 87
Ballycasey, Co. Clare 15
Ballyconneelly 127, 141, 143
Ballycotton, Co. Cork 57
Ballygeery West, Co. Clare 311
Ballygirreen townland, Co. Clare 65, 135, 138, 296, 297
Ballyhoura Hills Project 27
Ballykilty 127
Ballylongford, Co. Kerry 18, 271, 316, 325
Ballymenone, Co. Fermanagh 267
Ballymorris, Co. Clare 15, 302, 303
Ballynacarriga townland 85, 123, 124
Ballynacragga, Co. Clare 127
Ballynash townland, Co. Limerick 15, 18, 144, 150, 257, 309, 310
Ballyneety 8
Ballysteen 181, 257
Ballyvaughan, Co. Clare 329
Ballyvourney, Co. Cork 98
Baltimore Harbour, Co. Cork 25
barques 240, 318, 326
Barrington pier 14, 239, 263
Barrow River 32
baskets 70, 78–82, 85, 164, 181, 185, 186, 190, 265, 307
   Bunratty (2) 156
   Bunratty (3) 157–9
   Bunratty (6) 299
   Carrigdirty (5) 331
   horizontal 157, 159, 165, 176
   Neolithic 95
   vertical posts 170–1
   wicker 182, 184–5
   woven 84, 135, 172, 298, 301
Battle Island 263
Beagh Castle, Co. Limerick 14, 21, 28, 245, 265
Beagh, Co. Limerick 236, 260, 262, 268
   tower-house 10, 181, 256
   weirs 151
Beal Bar, Shannon estuary 327, 329, 330
Beal Bay, River Shannon 325
Beal Point 10, 330
beetle studies 24, 129
Beeves, near Tarbert 244, 250, 321, 328, 330
Beginish Island, Co. Kerry 143
Belderrig, Co. Mayo 122
birch (*Betula*) 37, 141, 172, 183, 184
birds 3, 77, 270

333

Foragers, farmers and fishers

Blackwater estuary, Cork Harbour 273
Blackwater estuary, Essex, England 23, 182, 188, 190
Blackweir bridge 313
boats 3, 13, 120, 131, 180, 234–5
    dug-out 72, 141, 256, 298
    ferry 240
    fishing 259
    flat-bottomed 268
    prehistoric 131
    radiocarbon dates 295
    survey 31pl, 35
Boazio, Baptista 17, 18–19
Body, William 10
bogs 1, 4, 93, 121, 268, 272
Boland Bay, Kilrush 314
Boland Rocks, Kilrush 320
bones 76, 77, 84, 255, 307
    animal 100–1
    cattle 97, 100
Bordieu, Pierre 263
Boyne 25, 32, 260, 273
bracelets, gold 256
Bradwell Creek 188
Brendan the Navigator 234
Brickhill, Co. Clare 64, 89
bridges, Bronze Age 133
Bridges Bank, near Palaskenry, Shannon estuary 321
Bridgewater 315
brigantines 240, 327
Brigdall, Hugh 53
Briget Cafey 324
brigs 240, 315, 329
Bristol 316, 326
Britain
    early historic and medieval fishtraps 186–91
    Late Bronze Age and Iron Age houses and trackways 128–33
British Admiralty survey data 233
British Board of Trade 239
British Queen 324
Brittania 326, 329
Bronze Age
    cattle- and sheep-herding 267
    circular houses 121
    estuarine archaeology 133
    farmers and sacred places 254–6
    houses and trackways 261
    post alignments 24
    settlement and economy in Ireland 121–2
    settlement and society 4
    sewn plank boats 105
    trackways 72, 265
    tribal groups 259
Brooks, W. 329
Brosna River 40
Brue Valley, Somerset Levels 127
brushwood 70, 107, 159, 190, 308
    Bunratty (4) 160, 164, 298
Bunaclugga Bay, Co. Kerry 29, 35, 55, 56–7, 253, 273, 313
Bunratty 18, 19, 47, 181, 235, 256, 266
    ancient port 246–7
    creek traps 197–8
    fishtraps 27, 32, 34, 35, 135, 151–78, 176, 260, 265
    flood protection 54
    mudflats 29
    overseas trade 237
    settlements 177, 257
    stone axes 89
    stone quays 245
    tower-house 10
    wood studies 172–6
Bunratty (1) 151, 153–4, 155pl, 178, 182, 271, 298, 299
Bunratty (2) 155–6, 157pl, 178, 182, 298
    erosion 271
    fishtraps 37
    location of 151
    wood studies 172
Bunratty (3) 155, 157–9, 178, 182, 271, 298
    baskets 184
    location of 151, 155
Bunratty (4) 153, 159–64, 176, 183, 186, 190, 301
    baskets 179
    erosion 271
    fishtraps 37, 178, 257, 298
    location of 151, 182
    radiocarbon dates 295
    wood studies 172, 173f
    wooden fences 184
Bunratty (5) 57, 151, 178, 271, 299
Bunratty (6) 34pl, 153, 164–71, 165, 177, 180, 183, 269
    baskets 172pl, 179
    erosion 271
    fishtraps 178, 257, 299
    location of 151, 182
    radiocarbon dates 295
    wood studies 172, 174f, 176
    wooden fences 184
Bunratty (7–9) 198, 299
Bunratty (10) 299
Bunratty (11–12) 300
Bunratty Castle 11, 12, 52, 177pl, 247pl
Bunratty Court 21
Bunratty East 63
Bunratty West townland, Co. Clare 151, 298, 299, 300
Burgess, William 250
burial sites 82
Burren, Co. Clare 89, 90, 260
Bush Island 29, 85, 105, 178–9, 200, 258
    fishtraps 27, 178–9, 201f
Bush Island (1) 200, 201pl, 300
Bush Island (2) 200, 202-3, 300-1
Bush Island (3) 135, 178–9, 301
Bush Island (4) 135, 203, 204pl, 301
Bush Island (5) 203, 204, 301
Bush Island (7) 203, 204, 301
Bush Island (8) 203, 205, 301
Bush Island (9) 203, 205, 302
Bush Island (10) 203, 205, 302
Bush Island (11) 203, 205, 302
Bush Island (12) 205, 206pl, 302
Bush Island (13) 205, 206, 258pl, 302
Bush Island (14) 205, 206, 302
Bush Island (15) 205, 207, 303
Bush Island (16) 205, 207, 303
Bush Island (17) 205, 207, 303
Bush Island (18) 205, 207, 303
Bush Island (19) 303

Cadw intertidal archaeological project 26
Cahan, Nicholas 236
Cahercalla 127

334

Index

Cain's Island 151
Caird, James 54
Caithréim Thoirdhealbhaigh 177, 178, 181
Caldicot, South Wales 24, 26, 105, 113, 120, 131
Cambrensis, Giraldus 8, 16–17
Canon Island 6, 8, 256, 266, 271
Cappa, near Kilrush 320
Carhan, Cahersiveen, Co. Kerry 68
Carlisle 325
Carngholt 315
Carnlough, Co. Antrim 314
Carolinea 315
carr woodlands 1, 64, 93, 184, 255, 268, 270
Carragh, Richard 181
Carrig Island 13, 14, 18, 330
Carrigafoyle Castle, Co. Kerry 10, 11
Carrigaholt, Co. Clare 236, 243, 247–8, 322, 323, 327
Carrigane, Co. Kerry 313
Carrigdirty 46, 51
Carrigdirty Rock 20, 27, 29, 35, 36, 70, 93, 123, 212, 254
    Bronze Age settlement and environment 94–106
    fishermen 212, 245
    fishtraps 258
    house 122
    intertidal peats 37
    intertidal survey and excavation 271
    Mesolithic and Neolithic sites 69–70
    Middle Bronze Age settlements 124
    Neolithic forager-farmers 89–91
    occupation sites 28, 35, 36, 268
    organic and lithic artefacts and bone 73
    pit 106, 125, 255, 265, 306
    prehistoric submerged forests 273
    submerged peats 94–6
    trackways 212
Carrigdirty Rock (1) 33, 65, 93, 122, 123f, 306
    house site 94–9, 121, 133, 134, 255
    radiocarbon dates 295
    structural posts 129
Carrigdirty Rock (2) 33, 65, 94, 99, 134, 306
Carrigdirty Rock (3) 33, 65, 94, 100–1, 134
Carrigdirty Rock (4) 33, 94, 101–3, 134, 307
Carrigdirty Rock (5) 82f, 83pl, 84–6, 87, 89, 105, 261, 271
    artefacts and bone 73–6
    coiled basketry 80f, 81
    human bone 91, 266
    location of 90f
    Neolithic basket 79pl, 95, 331
    occupation site 31, 55, 70, 254, 307
    radiocarbon dates 295
    stone axes 63, 83f
    wood species identification 78pl
Carrigdirty Rock (7) 75, 307, 331
Carrigdirty Rock (8) 55, 70, 71–2, 75f, 295, 307, 331
Carrigdirty Rock (9) 306, 307
Carrigdirty Rock (10) 308
Carrigdirty Rock (11) 70, 73, 308
Carrigdirty Rock (12) 212, 213f, 213pl, 295, 308
Carrigdirty Rock (13) 212, 214pl, 308
Carrigdirty Rock (14) 214, 215pl, 308
Carrigdirty Rock (15) 215, 216pl, 308
Carrigdirty Rock (16) 36, 56, 95, 308
Carrigdirty Rock (20) 103, 131, 134, 309
Carrigdirty Rock (21) 103, 104, 131, 134, 309

Carrigillihy, Co. Cork 122
Carrigogunnel, Co. Limerick 8, 123, 124, 128, 255pl, 256, 265
Carrowbane, Co. Clare 312
Carrownanelly, Co. Clare 67, 120, 127, 297
carvels 235, 236, 265
Cashen estuary, Co. Kerry 4, 6, 234
Cassandra 324
Castle Blath 9
Castle Donnington 189
Castlebellingham head weir, Co. Louth 230–1
Castledonnell, Co. Clare 10, 18, 181, 256, 268
Castlemungret 123
Castleragget 325
castles 256
Castletown 14
Catalan portolan charts 17, 18f, 22
Catherine 315
cattle 90, 245, 259, 265, 267, 268
    bone 77, 84, 97, 99, 100, 254, 307
    grazing 85, 261, 268
    herding 3, 255, 268
causeways 304, 309
Céide Fields, north Mayo 88, 260
cereal-growing 88
Cervus elaphus (red deer) 65, 67, 68, 101, 308
Chancellorsland, Co. Tipperary 98–9, 122
Chapel Island 186, 187
Chapeltump, Gwent 24, 99, 128
charcoal 84, 307
cherry trees 37
chert 82f, 84, 85, 254, 261, 307, 331
Chichester, Arthur, Sir 236
Chichester Harbour, Sussex, intertidal surveys 24
churches 9, 180, 256
    late medieval parish 150
    sites 5, 6
Ciarraige Luachra 6
Cicero 315
Ciro 315
Civil Survey (1650s) 11, 151
Clare Abbey 180
Clare, Co.
    historic shipwrecks 314–23
    south-east 87, 141
Clarecastle 14, 29, 40, 47, 53, 54, 266
    Anglo-Norman castle 8
    pier 239, 249, 265pl
Clarina 47
clays 44, 45, 331
    estuarine 155, 157, 159, 165, 178
    stratigraphy 138
Cleeves 329
Clenagh, Co. Clare 29, 298
climate 46
    sea-level and 49–50
clinkers 235
Cloghers, Lee Valley, Co. Kerry 3, 87
Clonbony, Co. Longford 101
Clonderalaw Bay, Co. Clare 27, 29, 295, 311, 312
Clonmacken, Co. Limerick 15, 264pl
Clonmoney 15
Clonmoney South, Co. Clare 304
Clonmoney West 8, 176, 177, 178
Cloon River 311
Cloonconeen Pool 48

335

coastal environments, change in 50
coastal reed-swamps 51
coastal wetlands 52
   activities in 133
   archaeology of 2
   Bronze Age houses and trackway 93–134
   Mesolithic/Neolithic 272
Cogadh Gaedhael re Gallaibh 7, 177
cogs 235, 265
Cold Harbour, Gwent 26, 99, 130
coleseed 12, 53, 259
Collins Creek 188, 189f
Collister Pill, Severn estuary 99, 128, 129, 133
Colmanswell, Co. Limerick 7
Columbus 324
Colwick 189
Commerce 316
Commissioners of Fisheries 247, 248
Commissioners for the Improvement of the River Shannon 13
Commissioners of Public Works 54
Coney Island, lower Fergus estuary 6
Confederate rebellion (1641) 20
Congested Districts Board 249
Conigar, Co. Limerick 15, 123
Coonagh 54
Coonagh East townland, Co. Limerick 5, 7, 59, 89, 311
Coonagh Point 1, Co. Limerick 93, 95, 106, 107f, 295, 309
Cooperhill, Co. Limerick 7, 27, 46, 309
copper artefacts 4
coracles 141, 256
corcass 9, 12, 52, 53, 178, 265, 330
   drainage 259
   farming 11
Corcovaskin 8
Corcu Baiscinn 6
Cork 235, 316, 321
Corkanree, near Limerick 15, 268
Corlea, Co. Longford 89, 101, 119, 120
Correl, John 237
court tombs 3, 87
Courtbrown, Co. Limerick 15, 150, 181, 244, 257
crannog sites, early historic 143
Crataegus sp. 37
Cratloe, Co. Clare 8, 18
Cratloe Creek, Co. Clare 37, 210, 258, 303
Cratloe Hills, Co. Clare 64, 89
Cratloe Woods, Co. Clare 8, 12, 184, 256
Cratloekeel 10, 181, 256, 268
Cratloemoyle, Co. Clare 10, 181, 256
Cratsoe 326
creeks 51, 159, 182
   bridges 255
   tidal 93
   traps 197, 227f, 228, 259, 299
Creggaun 18
Crininish 29, 127
Crompaun River 59
crop cultivation 3
Crouch 23
Crouch Site 1, Late Bronze Age wooden platform 131
Crow Island 65, 296
Crowfoot's Type 1 basket 79
Cúl Cearnadha 185
Culleenamore, Co. Sligo 88

Cullen, Bog of, Co. Tipperary 4, 121
Cullyhanna, Co. Armagh 98, 122
Cunningburn 186
Curraghatoor, Co. Tipperary 98
curraghs 234
customs duties 237, 238

Dál Cais dynasty 8
Daniel O'Connell 316
de Braose, William 181
de Burgo, John 181
de Burgo, Robert 181
de Clare filli Ricardi, Thomas 177
de Clare, Thomas 177
de Muscegros, Robert 177
de Turre, Petrus 16
de Wit, F. 20
Dead Woman's Hand rock 263
Deel estuary 28, 52, 180, 256, 265, 271
   fishtraps 27, 35, 135, 144–51, 181, 182, 185
   stone quays 245
   trade route 14
Deel estuary (1) 145–7, 148, 149, 186
   erosion 271
   fences 183
   fishtraps 184, 309
   location 144, 182
   radiocarbon dates 256, 295
Deel estuary (2) 148, 149, 180
   erosion 271
   fishtraps 150, 310
   location 144, 182
   radiocarbon dates 256, 295
Deel estuary (3) 148–9, 180
   erosion 271
   fishtraps 150, 310
   location 144, 182
   radiocarbon dates 256, 295
Deel estuary (4) 149–51, 182, 310
   erosion 271
   location 144
Deel River 11, 18, 45, 144, 150
Deer Island 6, 271
Defiance 316
Denmark, Mesolithic and Neolithic fishtraps 136
Derg, Lough 40
Derryoghil trackways, Co. Longford 119, 120
Diana 329
diatom studies 24, 36
Discovery Programme 2, 26, 27, 234, 270, 273
dolphins, bottle-nosed 48
Doon, cliffs of 10
Doonass 8, 263
Doonbeg Bay, Co. Clare 25, 231
Dorothy 325
Dove 328
Dover 105, 234
Down coast, Co. 24
Down Survey (1654–6) 20, 22
Drogheda 235
Dromoland 141
Duane 123
Dublin 235, 273, 316, 319
Dúchas The Heritage Service 36, 233, 273, 314
Dulcert, Angelino 17
Dumfries 324

Dunaha 13, 315
Dunbeg 247
Dundalk Bay 273
Dundrum Bay, Co. Down 25
Dysert O'Dea, battle of 8

early historic
   boats 234–5
   fishtraps 36
   settlements and maritime communications 5–7
Early Neolithic, wetland occupation site 55, 70
earthworks 150
ebb weirs 183, 190, 312, 313
   Bunratty (6) 171
   Strangford Lough 186
   Waterford Harbour 229–30
Ed 316
Edgecumbe 325
E.D.J. 240, 316
eels 13, 159, 178, 181, 253, 259, 270
Elanor 325
Eleanor 316
Elentheria 325
Eliza 316, 317, 325
Eliza and Ann 317
Elizabeth 317
Elizabeth I, Queen 10, 11
Elizabeth and Mary 317
Ely Lodge, near Lough Erne 234
Emerson, R. 314
Enagh, Lough, Co. Derry 89
enclosures 6, 87, 124, 254
England
   settlers from 260
   trade with 244
Ennis, Co. Clare 10, 12, 13, 47, 53, 239, 256
environmental changes 268–70, 272
Eriophorum 58
Erne River 16
erosion, tidal 271
Eskragh, Lough, Co. Tyrone 122
Essex coast, England 23, 128, 131, 137, 271
Esther 317
Europe 136, 244, 245
Evans, E. Estyn 25, 267

Fahamore, Co. Kerry 25, 57
Fahy, T. 329
farmers 266
farming, mixed 255
Feale River, Co. Kerry 11
Feenish Island 271
fences 97, 183, 184, 295
Fenn Creek, England 133
fens 1, 64, 268, 272
Fergus estuary 6, 8, 28, 53, 217–20, 256, 274pl, 296–306
   dug-out boats 234
   erosion 271
   fishtraps 138–44, 265
   geology 41–2
   mudflats 69
   palaeoenvironment of 50–2
   post-and-wattles 107–20, 182
   trackways 35, 131
Fergus estuary east (2) 135, 180, 295, 296
   location 182
   post-and-wattles 138–41
   wood in 184
   wood species identifications 142f
Fergus estuary east (3) 65–6, 67pl, 295, 296
Fergus estuary east (5) 295, 296
Fergus estuary east (6) 296
Fergus estuary east (7) 65, 67–9, 297
Fergus estuary east (8) 297
Fergus estuary east (9) 217, 218f, 219pl, 297
Fergus estuary west (1) 33, 93, 117pl, 131, 134, 255, 295, 297
   post-and-wattles 107–15, 119, 120, 125
   site recording 33
   trackways 127
Fergus estuary west (2) 218, 220pl, 295, 297
Fergus estuary west (3) 219, 221pl, 297
Fergus estuary west (4) 219, 221pl, 298
Fergus River 11, 12, 40, 54, 127
Ferriter's Cove, Co. Kerry 3, 87
Finavarra, Co. Clare 329
fish 143, 179, 181, 245, 253, 265
   consumption of 178
   curing of 261
   importance of 144
Fisheries (Ireland) Act (1846) 249
fishermen 266, 268
Fishery Piers and Harbours Commission 249
fishing 3, 85, 130, 255, 261, 267, 268
   early historic and medieval 256–8
   industry 191
   manufacture of equipment 261
   post-medieval 225
fishing structures, post-medieval and modern 2
fishing-boats 256, 259
fishing-smacks 240
fishtraps 9, 11, 35, 37, 120, 133, 265
   11th-century 260
   Anglo-Saxon and Norman 137, 184, 188, 189
   Bunratty 151
   Bush Island 301
   Deel estuary 144–51, 185
   early historic 2, 135–91, 296
   Fergus estuary 138–44, 265, 298
   Graigue Island 304
   Inishbonane 304
   location of 181–2, 228
   lower Shannon estuary 311–13
   medieval 2, 27, 31, 34, 37, 135–91, 190, 298, 309, 310
   orientation of 183
   post-medieval and modern 193–232
   radiocarbon dates 295
   regional traditions in Britain and Ireland of medieval 190
   size of 182–3
   stone 25, 137, 186, 187
   tick-shaped wooden 227f, 300
   upper Shannon estuary 298–311
   use of 143, 185–6, 268
   wicker 185
   wooden 25, 135, 180, 183–6, 256, 257, 269, 304, 309
   woven baskets 298, 299
flood fences 300, 305, 309, 312
flood weirs 150, 183, 229, 256, 309
Flora 317, 325

folklore, of local fishermen 266
Foraminifera studies 36
forests
    submerged 2, 273, 295, 308, 311, 312, 313
        submerged peats and 299
        submerged Scots pine 253
fortresses 256
Fowey 317
Foynes 8, 13, 17, 41, 47, 239, 243pl, 327
    overseas trade 14
    port 249, 266
Foynes Island, Co. Limerick 13, 18, 323, 325
France, Mesolithic and Neolithic fishtraps 136
Fraxinus excelsior (ash) 37, 172, 176, 183
friaries 256
    see also abbeys, monastic sites
Friendship 318
fruitwood, pomaceous 78
fulachta fiadh 121, 122, 123, 124, 254
Funen, Scandinavia 81
Furlong, J. 327

Gallowshill, Co. Clare 63, 89
Galway 320, 321
Gangani tribe 4, 16, 259
Garrynamone, Co. Clare 15
Garryncurra, Co. Clare 304
Garryone 318
Garston 329
gender, social class and 261, 261–2
geophysical surveys, underwater and 271–2
Georgina 318
glacial deposits 44–5
Glasgow 327, 329
Glassie, Henry 267
Glencloy, Co. Antrim 88
Glencoe 318
Glin, Co. Limerick 14, 19, 239, 249, 271, 327
Glynn 326, 329
Goghes, John 17
gold 4
    dress-fasteners 127, 128pl, 256
    ornaments 266
Goldcliff, Wales 34, 99, 105, 130, 131
Goldcliff West 129, 133
Goleen Creek 144, 145, 148
gorgets 128, 256
Graigue Island, Co. Clare 27, 85, 105, 208, 304
granite 331
graveyard, late medieval parish church and 150
Great Famine (1840s) 14
Grecian 318
green dolerite 331
Green Island, Co. Clare 32, 151, 198, 199pl, 304
Greenish Island 144
Greenock 318, 320, 325, 326, 327
Gregstown 186
Grey Abbey Bay 186, 187
Gribble, William 11
Grogan, Eoin 26
Gur, Lough, Co. Limerick 3, 88, 90, 98, 121, 260
    Neolithic settlements 87, 89
    schist axes 63
Gwent Levels 131

Hain, Edwin 321

hall-houses 150, 256
Halpin, George 250
Hamburg 327, 329
Hamilton 318
hammerstone 82f, 83, 84, 85, 254, 307
Hannah 325
harbours, post-medieval 233–51
Harold Rock 324
Hartlepool Bay, Cleveland, England 24
Hastings, Henry 328
Haughey's Ford, Co. Armagh 119
hawthorn 37
Hayes, M. 321
hazel (*Corylus*) 3, 37, 78, 141, 172, 176, 183, 184, 265, 331
    fishtraps 183, 184
    wood studies 141, 172, 176
hazelnuts 77, 84, 254, 307
head weirs 13, 136, 156, 194, 195pl, 227, 258
    17th century 225
    18th to 19th century 226
    tick-shaped 312
    tidal 11
Heidigger, Martin 263
Helen 318
Helena and Mary Hegarty 326
Hemington Fields, Leicestershire 189, 190
Henry and Anne 318
Henry III, King 235
Henry V, King 11, 181
Henry VI, King 9, 11
Hepzibah 319
Heritage Council 273
Heroine 326
herring 13, 313
hillforts 4, 121, 126
hilltop enclosures 4, 126, 127, 256
Hog Island, Kilrush 321
Hogs Head Rock, Shannon 303, 322, 324
Holocene 49, 50, 54, 272
    deposits 29
    peats 23
    stratigraphy 37
Hope 319
horns, bronze 266
Horril's Rock 263
house sites 295, 306
Hull 318
Hullbridge Basin survey, Essex coast 23
human
    activities 52
    bone 76, 84
    skulls 133, 295, 307
Humber estuary, England 23, 126, 128, 131, 234, 279
hunting 85, 125, 255, 265, 267, 268
hurdles 130, 131, 132pl, 133, 255
Hurler's Cross 47
huts, circular wooden 128

Ilex (holly) 37
Illaunbeg 151, 164
Illaunmore 151
In Deis Tuaiscirt 6
Inch 29
Ingoldesby, Henry 53
Iniscathy *see* Scattery Island

Index

Inishbonane, Co. Clare 32, 195, 196pl, 258, 269, 304
Inishcronan Point 304
Inniskesty, mill 150
Inny River 40
intertidal
    deposits 25, 49
    sandflats 51
    wall 304
    zones 24
intertidal archaeology 29
    in Britain 23–4
    in Ireland 24–6
    surveys 30–3, 137
Iraghticonnor, north Kerry 8
Ireland
    coastal archaeology 273
    fishtraps in Britain and 186–91
    Neolithic farmers and foragers 88–9
Irish Fisheries Board 25, 247
Irish Life of Brendan 6
Irish Life of Ciaran of Clonmacnoise 7
Irish names of places, P.W. Joyce 14
iron 321
    axes 184
    fishing spears 143
    lighters 240, 330
Iron Age 37
    estuarine archaeology in Britain and Ireland 133
    houses 34, 128, 129
    maritime communities 4–5
    rectangular buildings 129
    trackways 128, 271
    tribal groups 259
Isabella 319
Island MacHugh, Co. Tyrone 89
Island Point 14
Islandavanna, Co. Clare 15, 21, 29, 65, 120, 126, 127
    reclamation 54
    stratigraphy 46
Islandmagrath, Co. Clare 15, 28, 53, 107, 120, 126, 127
    Fergus estuary west (1) 255, 297
    palaeoenvironmental investigations 273, 297
    reclamation 54
    stratigraphy 46
Isle of Man 315
Isles of Scilly, intertidal surveys 24
Islevaroo, near Kilrush 316
Iveagh archaeological survey 25

James I, King 11
James II, King 12, 322
Jessy 326
jettys 296, 300, 305, 306
John 237, 319
John, King 235
Joyce, P.W. 14

Keane, Robert 323
Keating, Arnold 177
Kerry, Co.
    historic shipwrecks 329–30
    north 87
Kerry Head, River Shannon 328
Kilbaha 13, 317, 323
Kilconry, Co. Clare 8, 10, 256
Kilcradare Lighthouse 322

Kilcreadane Lighthouse 322, 327, 329
Kilcredane, Carrigaholt 319
Kilcredaun Point 250
Kildine 54
Kildysart, Co. Clare 40
Kilfentinane 53
Kilkee 330
Kilkerin 13
Killadysert 14, 239, 249
Killala Bay, Co. Mayo 25
Killaloe, Co. Clare 3, 63, 87
Killard 249
Killimer 14
Killmallock 181
Kilnasullagh 53
Kilrush, Co. Clare 13, 14, 236, 238, 248–9, 261, 266
    harbour 239
    historic shipwrecks 240, 243, 314–16, 318–23, 330
Kilterry 249
King John's Island 7
Kippen Rock 263
Knackyboy, Scilly Isles 81
Knockanimana 141
Knockaunaglanshy, Co. Kerry 57
Knocknalappa, Co. Clare 121, 127
Knocknarea, Co. Sligo 88, 89

Labasheeda Bay, Co. Clare 243, 314, 315, 319, 322
Labasheeda, Co. Clare 40, 249, 271, 316, 321
Lagore 143
Lahardaun bog 126
Lamb 319
Land Commission 54
land use 46, 47
landscapes 262, 272
    reclamation 258
Langough 127
Lark 319
Larrybane, Co. Antrim 143
Late Bronze Age 123, 126
    gold bracelets 127
    gold dress-fasteners 127, 128pl
    horns 123, 128
    houses and trackways 128
    landscape and settlement on upper Fergus estuary 125–7
    metalwork 266
    post alignments 133
    post-and-wattle 107–20, 134
    sacred places 127–8
    stone enclosures 125
    trackways 35, 119, 121, 130–3
    wooden structures 255
Late Mesolithic wooden plank 55, 70
    and brushwood 71–3
Late Neolithic Grooved Ware 23
late and post-medieval
    boats and ships 235
    settlements 9–12
Latoon 53, 127, 296
le White, Peter 181
Lewis, Samuel 13
Lifeboat Society 239
lighthouses 233–51, 266
Limerick 10, 18, 28, 191, 235, 237, 249
    bridge commissioners 14

339

Chamber of Commerce 239, 250
customs officers 238
east 87
ethnic communities 260
Hiberno-Norse 176, 180, 256, 258, 260
historic shipwrecks 314, 316–22
Lax Weir 7, 11, 13, 14, 181
Lock Mills 246
Merchant's Quay 10
port 12pl, 246, 256, 259, 266
turf trade 13
Wet Dock 14, 239, 244pl, 246
Limerick City 4, 9pl, 18, 40, 47, 48, 89, 245, 262pl
fisheries 11
merchants and aldermen 250
Limerick, Co. 260
glacial drift map 45
historic shipwrecks 324–9
Limerick Harbour 326
Limerick Harbour Commissioners 14, 239
Limerick Haven 325
Limerick River 324, 327
Limerick Star newspaper 324
limestone 13, 41, 43, 44, 45, 331
Lisbon 237, 238, 327
Liscannor 236
Lisheen, Co. Tipperary 126
Lissan West, Co. Clare 297, 298
Little Quay Island 151, 153, 157, 159, 299
Liverpool 314, 315, 316, 319, 320, 322, 324, 329
Liverpool 326
Lloyd, *Tour of Clare* 13, 238
Lloyd's, insurance and shipping company 239
London 315, 317, 319, 320, 321, 322
Loop Head 250, 319, 323
Loughanleagh 123
Louis Eleonie 326
lower Fergus estuary 6, 48
lower Shannon estuary 55, 271
   Co. Clare 311–13
   Co. Kerry 313
Luagh stone 320

Maas 319
MacBrody, Anthony 11
mac Cathail Chrobhdheirg, Aodh 185
macehead, Late Neolithic stone 64
McGillard, W. 314
MacKenzie, Murdoch 20f, 21
MacNamaras of Thomond 9
Magor Pill 24, 26, 34, 133, 188
Mahon, Lough, Cork Harbour 25
Maid of the Mist 326
Maiden Rock 216, 217, 258, 310, 311
Maigue estuary 27, 28, 52, 271
Maigue River 11, 17, 18, 40, 53, 54, 85, 89, 310
   Carrigdirty Rock 20, 69
   glacial deposits 45
   settlements 123
Malin Head 50
Manusmore, Co. Clare 296
maps 15–22
   location of intertidal surveys 2f, 41f
Margaret 319, 329
Maritime Archaeological Survey 36, 273
maritime surveys, 18th-century 20–1

marshes 1, 47
Mary 319, 320
Mary Ann 320
Mary Collins 320
Mary of Milford 320
Meadowlands, Co. Down 98, 122
Meare Heath 127
medieval boats 34
   and ships 235
medieval fishtraps 2, 27, 31, 34, 37, 135–91, 298, 309, 310
Medusa 326
Meelick, Co. Clare 303, 326
Meelick Rocks 27, 29, 83pl, 95, 254, 295, 311, 331
   stone axe 61–3, 64, 89
   submerged forests 36, 55, 56, 59–61, 65, 253, 254pl, 272
megalithic tombs 87, 88, 254
Mellon, Co. Limerick 310, 311
Mellon House 12
Mellon–Ringmoylan embankment 54
Melton 131, 132pl
Mercator, Gerard 17–19
Mermaid 327, 329
Mersea Flats 188
Mesolithic
   artefacts 331
   hunter-gatherers 3, 87, 259
   and Neolithic sites 69–70
   and Neolithic submerged forests 56–61
metalwork find 255
midden, early historic coastal shell 143
Middle Bronze Age 126
   boats 23
   house sites 94, 105, 121
   landscape and settlement 122–5
   trackways 23
   wooden structure 95
   worked wood 106
'Middle Ground, The' 244
Mill Bog, Aghintemple td, Co. Longford 80
Millin Bay 25
Minerva 326
Mining Company of Ireland 246
Mitchell, Bernard 237
Mitchell, Frank 267
Mogridge, Tristram 237
Moland, Thomas 12, 53
Molyneaux, Edward 11
monastic sites 5, 7, 180, 256
   see also abbeys, friaries
Moneteen 123
Monsells Creek 328
Mooghaun hillfort 5pl, 27, 126, 127, 256
Mooghaun Lough, Co. Clare 4, 89, 121, 126
Morat, Lake 81
Moreena Point 144
motte-and-bailey 8, 177
Mount Gabriel, Co. Cork 4
Mount Sandel 62
Moyasta townland, Co. Clare 57, 312
Moyhill, Co. Clare 178, 300–2
Moynagh Lough, Co. Meath 83, 99, 122
Muckinish 15, 51, 329
mudflats 1, 30, 51, 52, 85, 131, 153
   creek fishtraps 182

estuarine 268
tower-houses 10
Mullaghfarna, Co. Sligo 88
Mungret, Co. Limerick 6
Murphy, Maurice 330
Murray, D. 327
Myrtle 320

naomhógs 234
National Library of Ireland 15
National Maritime Archaeological Survey 233
National Parks and Wildlife Service 48
Natural Heritage Areas 47f, 48
Naylane, James 10
Nendrum, early historic monastic site 187
Neolithic
    artefacts 331
    burial activities 91
    coastal wetland occupation site 73–86
    economy 87
    farming communities 259
    farmland 260
    fishtraps and trackways 24
    foragers and fishers 267
    funerary sites 3
    houses 88
    pottery 91
    red deer bone deposits 65–9
    settlement, society and economy 87
    skulls 87
Neolithic farmers, settlements and megalithic tombs 3–4
Neolithic farmers and foragers 253–4
    in Ireland 88–9
    in wetlands 253
Neolithic submerged forests 27, 55
    Mesolithic and 56
Neolithic woodlands, use and perception of 64
Neptune Gallery 15
Netherlands 103, 126, 129, 136
nets 14, 156, 164, 186, 261
new and exact hydrographic survey of the River Shannon from Limerick to the sea, A (1794) 21
New York 317, 321, 324
Newcastle, Co. Down 25
Newferry, Co. Antrim 62, 63
Newgrange, Co. Meath 68
Newmarket-on-Fergus 47
Newport 317, 321, 329
Newtown, Co. Limerick 18, 53, 256, 263, 265
Newtown Point, mudflats 265
Newtown townland, Co. Limerick, Carrigdirty Rock 69, 73, 94, 306–9
Newtownards 186
Nimmo, Alexander 247
Norman fishtraps 188
North Ferriby, Humber estuary 23, 105, 113, 120, 131
North Munster Project 2, 4, 23, 26, 27, 94, 121, 126
North Shields 322
Northern Ireland, intertidal surveys 25
Nottingham 189

oak (*Quercus*) 3, 37, 78, 172, 176, 183, 313
    and alder carr woodland 59
    fen woodland 51
    plank 309

scrub woodland 96
split and charred 78
Ó Briain, Toirdhealbhach 178
O'Brien, Donal Mór 180
O'Brien, kings of Thomond 8
O'Brien, Terlagh 53
O'Brien's Point, Co. Clare 208, 209, 210pl, 245, 258, 265, 305
occupation sites 31, 55, 65, 70
    Carrigdirty Rock 86, 268, 307
    Neolithic coastal wetland 73
O'Dea, J. 330
Odell-Westropp, Edward 13
O'Donnell, Red Hugh 11
Office of Public Works 247
O'Keefe, P. 316
Oketfagh, David 9
Ó Mynok, William 9
Ordnance Datum heights 33
Ordnance Survey maps 21, 245
Osprey 327
Oughtymore, Co. Derry 143
Ovis aries L. (sheep) skull 297
Owenagarney River 8, 21, 31, 151, 178, 182, 246, 306
    fishtraps 155, 157, 159, 177
    flood protection 54
    jettys 300, 306
    post-and-wattles 153
oyster beds 13, 131

Pacata Hibernia 237f
Paiget, S. 321
palaeoenvironmental investigations 24, 28, 35–7, 272–3
palaeohydrography 48
palisades, wooden 122
Pallaskenry, Co. Limerick 18, 40, 47
passage tombs 4, 68, 87, 89
Patterson, James 13
Patterson, W.H. 24
peats 151, 331
    grey-brown silty 159
    submerged 255, 299, 313
pebbles 83–4, 331
Peggy 327
Pelham, Henry 21, 22f
Pernambuco 320
Perseverance 320
Peterson, James 248
petrography 62
Petty, William 20, 22
Philips, Paul 237
Phragmites 25, 58, 96, 312
Phragmites australis 51
Piggott, Stuart 23
pigs 101
    bone 125, 255, 306, 308
    wild 3, 253
Pilgrim 237
pink-footed goose 106, 125, 255, 306
Pinus sylvestris L. 58, 59, 312
piracy 9, 11
placenames, evidence for settlement and coastal exploitation 3–37
plank-boats, post-medieval 312
planks, wooden 295, 307

Plassey 8
Plymouth 317
Pococke, *Tour of Limerick* 246
pollen 24, 36, 89, 96, 107, 273
Pomoideae 331
Populus (poplar) 37, 71, 176
Port Madoc 317
portal tombs 3, 87
Portdrine, Co. Clare 305
Portsmouth Harbour, Hampshire 24
post alignments 185, 298, 299, 305, 310, 311
    Bronze Age 24
    Bunratty (3) 157–9
    Bush Island 301
    Graigue Island 304
    L-shaped 303
    multiple 300
    post-medieval 296, 297
    single 148, 157
post-and-wattle fences 25, 27, 31, 138, 160, 190, 255
    and basket 164–71
    Bunratty (6) 296–9
    C-shaped 227f, 302
    converging 184
    Deel estuary 145–7
    early historic 135
    Graigue Island 304
    horizontal 164, 168–70
    L-shaped 227f, 302
    Late Bronze Age 93
    length of 182–3
    lower foreshore 113
    mid-foreshore double 109–11
    parallel 113
    radiocarbon dates 256, 295
    single 155, 156
    species selection 116
    U-shaped 135
    upper foreshore vertical 108–9
    V-shaped 301
    vertical 136, 153, 163, 165, 170, 176, 182, 301
    wood studies 141
    woven panels 107–8
post-and-wattle panels 168, 170, 171, 179, 184, 186
    Bush Island 301
    Carrigdirty Rock 308
    horizontal 111–13, 153, 188
    post-medieval 297
    radiocarbon dates 295
post-and-wattle trackways 36, 212, 295
post-medieval 37
    fisheries, shipwrecks and landscape reclamation 258–9
    fishtraps 27, 32, 35, 37, 195
pottery 87
Poulnabrone, Co. Clare 87
Poulnasharry, Co. Clare 13, 14, 27, 29, 35
    radiocarbon dates 295
    submerged forests 55–9, 253, 273, 312–13
    woodlands 64
prehistoric
    boats 234–5
    settlement in coastal wetlands 90
    wetland succession patterns 50
Premier 327, 329
Preston, George 11

Prewett, T.A. 329
Prudence 320
Prunus avium (cherry) 37
Ptolemy 4, 16, 259
Pullen 249
putts 188

quartz clasts 331
Quay Island, Co. Clare 151, 164, 299, 300, 305, 306
    fishtraps 197, 199f, 258, 269
    wooden quays 245
quays 245, 246
Quebec 317, 326
Quereda 330
Querin 13
Querrin, Co. Clare 247, 249
Quirk Rock 244
Quoile River 122

radiocarbon dating 33, 37, 49, 153, 295
Rahona, Co. Clare 313
Rathjordan, Co. Limerick 89
Ratty River *see* Owenagarney River
Rebecca 321
reclamation 52–4, 272, 296
red deer 101, 253
    antler 125, 255, 306, 307
red deer bone 106, 297, 306, 308
    Carrigdirty Rock 3 pit 125, 255
    Fergus estuary east (3) 67pl, 295
    Neolithic 55, 296
    upper Fergus estuary 253
Redwick 99, 129, 130
Ree, Lough 7, 40
reed-beds 14, 85, 270
reed-swamps 1, 56, 268, 272
reeds 234, 265
Reenroe, Ballinskelligs, Co. Kerry 25
Rineanna 14, 28, 48, 54, 236
Rinevalla Bay, Co. Clare 27, 29, 35, 64, 313
    submerged forests 36, 55, 56, 253, 273
ringforts 5, 141, 144, 176, 256
    Ballyconneely 143
    Deel estuary 150
    Fergus estuary 180
Ringmoylan Quay 245, 265
Ringmoylan–Foynes embankment 54
rivers 4, 182, 250
Rochford, Edward 237
Rogers, Thomas 250
rope, wooden 113
Ross Island, Co. Kerry 4
Roughan, P. 327
roundhouse 255
Rumney 24, 128

Sabrina 244
sacred places 254
safety, intertidal surveys 30
sailing-boats 240
St Brigid's Day 270
St Cummine Foda, bishop of Clonfert 6
St Ubes 320, 324
Saint's Island, Co. Clare 28, 176, 266, 271, 304
Saleen 249, 330
Sales Point 188

sally woods 14
salmon 7, 150, 178, 181, 253, 270
saltmarsh cliffs 32, 94
saltmarsh creeks 268, 309
saltmarshes 1, 9, 47, 56, 64, 93, 265, 272
   animal pasture on 126
Sampson, F. 329
Sandhills 330
sandmen 14
sandstone 41, 44, 45
Scandinavia 81, 260
Scanlan, T. 327
Scarlet Rocks, River Shannon 314
Scarlets, The 250
Scattery Island 7, 10, 11, 13, 17, 18, 236, 266, 271
   customs officers 238
   lighthouse 250
   monastic site 6
   shipwrecks 315, 318
Scattery Roads 17, 240
schist 62, 83pl, 331
Scotland, stone-built fishtraps 137
Scots pine 58, 59, 253, 312, 313
Sea Fisheries (Ireland) Act (1883) 249
sea-banks 53, 259
sea-level, changes 24, 36, 49–50, 273
seaweed 14, 25
Second Report of the Commissioners of Inquiry into the State of the Irish Fisheries 14
sedge fens 51, 93
settlements 1, 2, 121
   early historic 141, 272
   fishtraps and 182
   medieval 150
   Viking Age 272
settlers, Dutch 260
Severn estuary 133, 179, 271
   baskets 185
   fishtraps 137, 182, 188
   intertidal archaeological survey 23, 26
   Late Bronze Age and Iron Age houses and trackways 128–31
   plank-built boats 234
Severn Estuary Levels Research Committee 24, 273
Shanid, east Limerick 4
Shannon Airport 28, 47, 48, 54
Shannon Commissioners 249
Shannon estuary 52
   18th century 12–13
   19th century 13–14
   archaeology 2, 253–9, 270–2
   Bronze Age settlement, society and economy 121–8
   coastal landscapes and environmental change 39–54
   economic exploitation of 178
   environs 40–1
   evidence for settlement and coastal exploitation 3–37
   fauna and flora 47–8
   fisheries from 16th to late 19th century 221
   geology of 41–4
   glacial deposits and related features 44–6
   historic shipwrecks 314
   hydrography of 48–9
   intertidal archaeological sites summary 296–313
   landscape, space and place 262–6
   life on 266
   location map 41pl
   map of Neolithic sites 55f
   maps 15–22
   morphology of 52
   Neolithic settlement, society and economy 87–92
   palaeoenvironment 36–7, 50–2
   passing of years 269–70
   people on 253–74
   satellite image 39pl
   soils 46–7
   structures and finds 35–6
   time, tides and traditions 267–70
   work on 266
Shannon estuary intertidal survey 2, 251, 270
   aims, objectives and evolution of 26–8
   designing future 34–5
   methodology of 29–34, 31
   origins and evolution of 23–37
Shannon estuary landscapes, multidisciplinary projects 273
Shannon estuary region, Mesolithic hunter-gatherers 3
Shannon Heritage and Banquets 27
Shannon Industrial Complex 47
Shannon River 4, 11, 40, 87, 263, 326, 328, 329
Shannon wetlands 50
Shannongrove, Co. Limerick 123, 128, 256
Shannongrove House, Co. Limerick 12
Shapwick Heath 127
Sharpham 127
Shearer, J. 329
sheep 255, 267, 268, 297
shellfish 3, 14, 179, 261
shelters 267
Shields 322, 326
ships 256, 303
   late medieval and post-medieval 235–8
   ocean-going 259
ships and boats
   18th- and 19th-century 238
   medieval and post-medieval 272
shipwrecks 10, 12, 233f, 258
   history and archaeology of 239–45
   inventory of historic 314–30
Silurian shale and slate 45
Simpson, J. 327
Sinnenus 16
sites
   excavation 33–4
   intertidal survey and excavation of eroding 271
   sampling 35
Sixmilebridge 21
Skinner's Wood 127
slate 82f, 83pl, 331
Slieve Barnagh 8
Sligo 315, 317
Sligo Bay 273
slipways, stone 305
soils, Shannon estuary 46–7
Solent estuary 133, 137
Solidade 327
Somerset Levels, England 103, 117
Sorbus sp. 37
South Island 187
Spanish Armada 236, 239, 240, 315
Special Protection Area 48
species identifications 153

Speed, John, 'The kingdome of Irland' (1612) 19
Sphagnum peat 58, 312
Spilling Rock 321
stake weirs 300, 311
stake-net weirs 14, 195, 226, 227f, 228, 258
standing stones 123, 124, 254
Stanihurst, Richard 236
Steam Packet Company, City of Dublin 249
stone axes 64, 82–3, 84, 85, 89, 91
    distribution of 87
    Meelick Rocks 61–3
    Neolithic 3
stone chisels 83
stone slabs 99
Stoneyisland Bog, Co. Galway 91
Stour estuary 23
Strafford Survey 20
Strangford Lough, N. Ireland 138, 273
    archaeology of 25
    fishtraps 186–8, 190
    tidal traps 182
Strokestown 143
submerged landscapes, archaeological and environmental deposits identification 29–30
Suck River 40
Sudbrook 24, 26, 188, 190pl
superstitions 266
Sus domesticus 101, 308
swans 253
    bone 84, 254, 307
Swansea 327
Swifterbank, Netherlands 103
sword, iron, Viking Age 7f, 309

Tankardstown, Co. Limerick 3, 87, 88
Tara Project 27
Tarbert, Co. Kerry 10, 14, 19, 40, 243, 249–50, 271, 326
    customs officers 238
    harbour 239
    shipwrecks 316, 323, 327, 329, 330
Tarbert Island 13, 48, 330
Tarbert Race 48
Tarbert Road 324, 330
Tarbert Rock 250
Termon West, Co. Clare 313
Terry Alt disturbances (1831) 13
Tervoe 123
Thackeray, William 54
Thames estuary 24, 128, 133, 137
Thames River 133, 237
Theatre of the empire of Great Britaine (1612) 19
Thetis 330
Thrasher 327
tides, changes in 270
Timoney townland, Co. Tipperary 80, 81
Tomdeely North, Co. Limerick 8, 150, 257
Tomdeely Point 144
tools 266
    bronze 4
Topaz 327
tower-houses 10, 256, 268
towers 266
Townleyhall, Co. Meath 89
trackways 2, 117, 131, 133, 255, 267
    brushwood 190
    estuary marshland 120
    Late Bronze Age 130
    Neolithic 89
    prehistoric plank 105
    wooden 131, 309
Traderry 8, 177
Tradraige 8
Tradree 177, 260
Tradree Point 304
Tralee, Co. Kerry 13, 239
transhumance 105, 267
tree-ring studies 36, 116, 153, 172, 176
Treenaglass 321
Trent River, northern England 137, 189–90
Triumph 321
trout 178, 181
Troye, Henry 9
Troye, Theobald 181
Tuan, Yi-fu 263
Tullyglass Point, Co. Clare 63, 89
turf 13, 239, 248, 322, 323
turf-boats 240, 245, 259, 325
Twyford, Co. Westmeath 80, 81
Tybrind Vig, Scandinavia 81
    geology 41
    hydrography 48
    location of Bronze Age sites 93f, 124f
    location of fishtraps 135f, 193f
    modern settlements 47
    palaeoenvironment of 50
    quays and landing-places 245
    tower-houses 256

Uí Fidgeinti 6
Union 321
United Kingdom 321
Upper Carboniferous (Namurian) sediments 41
upper Fergus estuary, map 53f
upper Fergus estuary, Co. Clare 27, 36, 55, 65, 67, 107, 121, 135, 141, 182, 253, 256
upper Shannon estuary 28, 53, 55, 63, 89, 93
    Co. Clare 298
    Co. Limerick 306
Upton, Derek 23, 26
Uskmouth 24

Vale 318
Vandeleur, John Ormsby 248, 249
Venus 321, 327
vertical fences 167–70
vessels, lost at sea 241f, 242f, 244–5
Victoria 322
Vietury 322
Viking Age
    boats 234–5
    settlements and fleets 7–8
    sword and wooden causeway 309
votive offerings 91

Wales 23, 117, 131, 244
walk-over surveys 35
Waller, John Thomas 14
Warren, Hazzeldine 23
Waterford 235, 327
Waterford Harbour 2, 25, 32, 195pl, 229, 230pl
Waterford S.S. Company 330
waterfowl 133, 265

Index

watermill paddle, post-medieval 312
wattles 24, 97, 160
weapons 4, 256
weather, loss of vessels and 240
wedge tombs 4, 64, 87, 89, 254
weels 185
weir hide 144
weirs 7, 25, 141, 156, 177, 181, 229, 313
   Beagh, Co. Limerick 151
   see also ebb, flood, head, stake and stake-net weirs
Welcome 322
Wellesley Bridge works 327
Went, Arthur E.J. 25
Westby, William 248
Western Stone Forts Project 27
wetlands 1
   occupation site 55
Wexford Harbour 273
Weymouth 238
Whelp Rock, River Shannon 323
Whiting, Edward 238
Whittle, L. 21
wildfowl 48, 85, 126, 253, 265, 267
William Ash 303, 322
William of Gloucester 9
Williamite wars (1690) 53
willow (*Salix*) 37, 184, 265
   Bunratty 6 fishtrap 176
   carr woodland 56
   post alignment 172
   post-and-wattle fences 141, 183
Wilsford, Wiltshire 113
Witte Leeuw 328
Wolfe, David 10
wood 153, 331
   carved fragments 73pl, 307
   charred 77–8, 84, 254, 331
   species identification 36, 108, 116, 172, 176
   species selection 183–4
   worked 77–8, 84–5, 118f, 254, 295, 331
wood studies 33, 36–7, 116–19, 141, 172–6
woodland, fen-carr 255
woodlands 1, 3, 56, 64, 255, 272
   environments 183–4
   management 178
   marshy carr 56
   riverine 56
Woods, Joseph 54
Wootton-Quarr, Isle of Wight 24, 133, 136–7
wreck archaeology, problems in 240
wreck inventory 273
Wreck Inventory of the National Maritime Archaeological Survey 314
Wright, Edward V. 23

York 328
Youghal, Co. Cork 24
Young, Arthur 12, 54

Zachary, Robert 237, 238